Fourth International Conference on Dependency Linguistics (Depling 2017)

Pisa, Italy
18 – 20 September 2017

Editors:

Simonetta Montemagni
Joakim Nivre

ISBN: 978-1-5108-4862-7

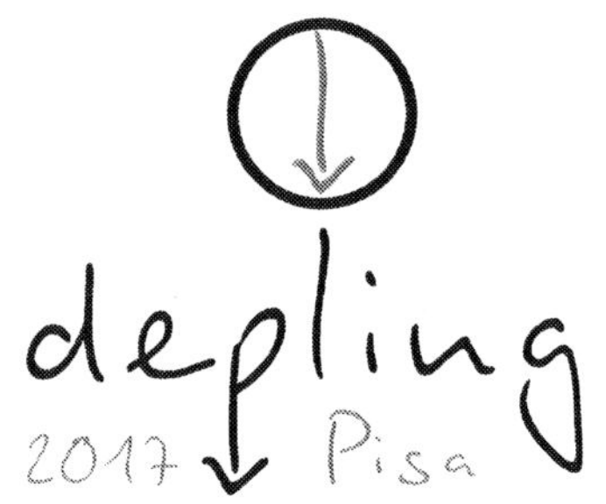

International Conference on Dependency Linguistics

Proceedings of the Conference

September 18-20, 2017

Università di Pisa

Istituto di Linguistica Computazionale "A. Zampolli", CNR Pisa

UNIVERSITÀ DI PISA

Istituto di Linguistica
Computazionale "A. Zampolli"
Consiglio Nazionale delle ricerche

Edited by Simonetta Montemagni and Joakim Nivre

Cover design Chiara Mannari

Preface

The Depling 2017 conference in Pisa is the fourth meeting in the recently established series of international conferences on Dependency Linguistics which started in Barcelona in 2011 and continued in Prague and Uppsala in 2013 and 2015, respectively. The initiative to organize special meetings devoted to Dependency Linguistics, which is currently at the forefront of both theoretical and computational linguistics, has received great support from the community. We do hope that the present conference will manage to keep up the high standards set by the previous meetings.

This year we received 41 submissions by 93 authors from 27 countries, one of which was withdrawn before reviewing. Of the remaining 40 submissions (each reviewed by 3 members of the Program Committee), 30 were accepted, resulting in an acceptance rate of 75%. All in all, the proceedings contain a wide range of contributions to Dependency Linguistics, ranging from papers advancing new theoretical models, through empirical studies of one or more languages, as well as experimental investigations of computational systems of dependency parsing and linguistic knowledge extraction, to the design and construction of dependency-based linguistic resources (both treebanks and lexicons) for a wide range of languages.

New to Depling 2017 edition is the fact that the conference is held in conjunction with the biennial meeting of SIGPARSE, namely the International Conference on Parsing Technologies (IWPT 2017), organized by the Special Interest Group on "Natural Language Parsing" of the Association for Computational Linguistics (ACL). IWPT 2017 will take place immediately after Depling 2017, from the 20th to 22nd of September 2017. The two conferences have an overlapping event, held on September 20th and focusing on different aspects of dependency parsing, in which the results of a shared task jointly organized by Depling and IWPT are presented and discussed from different and complementary perspectives.

The shared task, named "Extrinsic Parser Evaluation" (EPE) and playing the role of "bridge event" between the two conferences, is aimed at shedding light on the downstream utility of various dependency representations (at the available levels of accuracy for different parsers), that is, to seek to contrastively isolate the relative contributions of each type of representation (and corresponding parsing systems) to a selection of state-of-the-art systems (which use different types of text and exhibit broad domain and genre variation).

In addition to the accepted papers, the core conference program also includes the contribution of two distinguished keynote speakers, Yoav Goldberg (Bar Ilan University) and Eva Hajičová (Charles University in Prague). We are honoured that they accepted to contribute to Depling 2017 and thank them for agreeing to share their knowledge and expertise on key Dependency Linguistics topics with the conference participants.

Our sincere thanks go to the members of the Program Committee who thoroughly reviewed all the submissions to the conference and provided detailed comments and suggestions, thus ensuring the quality of the published papers. Many thanks to the members of the Local Organizing Committee who took care of all matters related to the local organization of the conference. Thanks are also due to Michela Carlino, who did a great job in putting the proceedings together, and to Chiara Mannari, for designing and constructing the Depling and IWPT+Depling conference websites and continuously updating them. Last but not least, we would like to acknowledge the support from endorsing organizations and institutions and from our sponsors, who generously provided funds and services that are crucial for the organization of this event. At the time of writing, Depling was sponsored by the newly founded "Italian Association of Computational Linguistics" (AILC) and by the University of Pisa. Special thanks are also due to the Institute for Computational Linguistics "Antonio Zampolli" of the Italian National Research Council (ILC-CNR) for the support in the organization of the event. Thanks finally to everyone who chose to submit their work to Depling 2017, without whom this volume literally would not exist.

We welcome you all to Depling 2017 in Pisa and wish you an enjoyable conference!

Simonetta Montemagni and Joakim Nivre

Program Co-Chairs, Depling 2017

Organizers

Program Co-Chairs

- Simonetta Montemagni, Istituto di Linguistica Computazionale "A. Zampolli" - CNR
- Joakim Nivre, Uppsala University

Local Organizing Committee

- Giuseppe Attardi, Università di Pisa
- Felice Dell'Orletta, Istituto di Linguistica Computazionale "A. Zampolli" - CNR
- Alessandro Lenci, Università di Pisa
- Simonetta Montemagni, Istituto di Linguistica Computazionale "A. Zampolli" - CNR
- Maria Simi, Università di Pisa

Program Committee

- Giuseppe Attardi, Università di Pisa
- Miguel Ballesteros, IBM Research Watson
- Xavier Blanco, Universitat Autònoma de Barcelona
- Igor Boguslavsky, Universidad Politecnica de Madrid and Russian Academy of Sciences
- Bernd Bohnet, Google
- Cristina Bosco, Università di Torino
- Marie Candito, Université Paris Diderot
- Jinho Choi, University of Colorado at Boulder
- Benoit Crabbé, Université Paris Diderot
- Eric De La Clergerie, INRIA
- Felice Dell'Orletta, Istituto di Linguistica Computazionale "A. Zampolli" - CNR
- Marie-Catherine de Marneffe, The Ohio State University
- Kim Gerdes, Sorbonne Nouvelle
- Filip Ginter, University of Turku
- Koldo Gojenola, University of the Basque Country UPV/EHU
- Carlos Gómez-Rodríguez, Universidade da Coruña
- Eva Hajičová, Charles University in Prague
- Richard Hudson, University College London
- Leonid Iomdin, Russian Academy of Sciences
- Sylvain Kahane, Université Paris Ouest Nanterre
- Marco Kuhlmann, Linköping University
- François Lareau, Université de Montréal
- Alessandro Lenci, Università di Pisa
- Beth Levin, Stanford University
- Haitao Liu, Zhejiang University
- Marketa Lopatkova, Charles University in Prague
- Ryan McDonald, Google

- Igor Mel'čuk, University of Montreal
- Wolfgang Menzel, Hamburg University
- Paola Merlo, Université de Genève
- Jasmina Milicevic, Dalhousie University
- Henrik Høeg Müller, Copenhagen Business School
- Alexis Nasr, Université de la Méditerranée
- Pierre Nugues, Lund University
- Kemal Oflazer, Carnegie Mellon University Qatar
- Timothy Osborne, Zhejiang University
- Jarmila Panevova, Charles University in Prague
- Alain Polguère, Université de Lorraine ATILF CNRS
- Prokopis Prokopidis, Institute for Language and Speech Processing/Athena RC, Greece
- Owen Rambow, Columbia University
- Ines Rehbein, Potsdam University
- Dipti Sharma, IIIT, Hyderabad
- Maria Simi, Università di Pisa
- Reut Tsarfaty, Open University of Israel
- Giulia Venturi, Istituto di Linguistica Computazionale "A. Zampolli" - CNR
- Leo Wanner, Pompeu Fabra University
- Daniel Zeman, Charles University in Prague
- Yue Zhang, Singapore University of Technology and Design

Supporting Institutions

- Università degli Studi di Pisa
    - Dipartimento di Filologia, Letteratura e Linguistica
    - Dipartimento di Informatica
- Istituto di Linguistica Computazionale "A. Zampolli", Consiglio Nazionale delle Ricerche

Sponsor

- Associazione Italiana di Linguistica Computazionale (AILC)

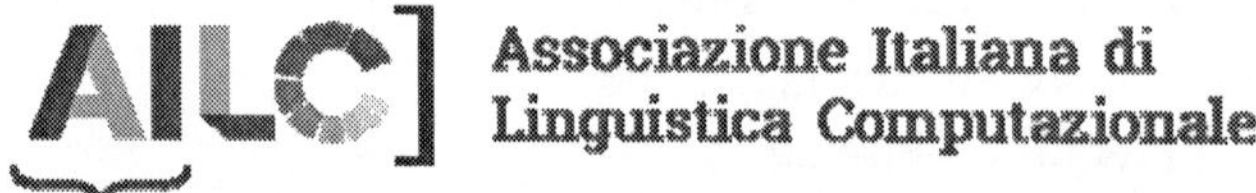

Table of Contents

Capturing Dependency Syntax with "Deep" Sequential Models

Yoav Goldberg
Bar Ilan University
Department of Computer Science
Ramat-Gan, Israel
yoav.goldberg@gmail.com

Neural network ("deep learning") models are taking over machine learning approaches for language by storm. In particular, recurrent neural networks (RNNs), which are flexible non-markovian models of sequential data, were shown to be effective for a variety of language processing tasks. Somewhat surprisingly, these seemingly purely sequential models are very capable at modeling syntactic phenomena, and using them result in very strong dependency parsers, for a variety of languages.

In this talk, I will briefly describe recurrent-networks, and present empirical evidence for their capabilities of learning the subject-verb agreement relation in naturally occuring text, from relatively indirect supervision. This part is based on my joint work with Tal Linzen and Emmanuel Dupoux. I will then describe bi-directional recurrent networks - a simple extension of recurrent networks - and show how they can be used as the basis of state-of-the-art dependency parsers. This is based on my work with Eliyahu Kipperwasser, but will also touch on work by other researchers in that space.

Proceedings of the Fourth International Conference on Dependency Linguistics (Depling 2017), page 1,
Pisa, Italy, September 18-20 2017

Syntax-Semantics Interface: A Plea for a Deep Dependency Sentence Structure

Eva Hajičová
Charles University
Faculty of Mathematics and Physics
Institute of Formal and Applied Linguistics
Prague, Czech Republic
hajicova@ufal.mff.cuni.cz

In collaboration with Václava Kettnerová, Veronika Kolářová, Markéta Lopatková, Jarmila Panevová, and Dan Zeman (and with technical support of Jiří Mírovský)

The aim of the contribution is to bring arguments for a description for natural language that (i) includes a representation (i) of a deep (underlying) sentence structure and (ii) is based on the relation of dependency. Our argumentation rests on linguistic considerations and stems from the Praguian linguistic background, both with respect to the Praguian structuralist tradition as well as to the formal framework of Functional Generative Description and to the experience with building the Prague Dependency Treebank. The arguments, of course, are not novel but we will try to gather and report on our experience when working with deep syntactic dependency relations in the description of language; the basic material will be Czech but multilingual comparative aspects will be taken into account as well.

Speaking about a "deep" sentence structure, a natural question to ask is how "deep" this linguistic structure is to be. Relevant in this respect is the differentiation between ontological content and linguistic meaning. Two relations will be discussed in some detail and illustrated on examples from Czech and English, namely the relation of synonymy and that of ambiguity (homonymy). The relation of synonymy will be specified as an identity of meaning with respect to truth conditions and it will be demonstrated how this criterion may help to test sentences and constructions for synonymy. The relation of ambiguity will be exemplified by two specific groups of examples, one concerning surface deletions and the necessity to reconstruct them in the deep structure, and the other group involving the notion of deep order of sentence elements with examples related to the phenomenon of information structure.

The necessity to distinguish surface and deep structure has led to several proposals of a multi-level description of language, both in the domain of theoretical linguistics and in the domain of annotation schemes of language corpora, such as LFG or CCG. We will describe in a nutshell the Prague Dependency Treebank, focusing on the deep (so-called tectogrammatical) level of annotation.

After some observations on the history of the dependency-based syntactic relations, attention will be focused on two basic topics, namely the issue of headedness and the notion of valency. We will outline an approach to the distinction between arguments and adjuncts and their semantic optionality/obligatoriness based on two operational criteria and we will demonstrate on the example of several Czech valency dictionaries how a dependency-based description brings together grammar and lexicon.

Among the many challenges that still await a deeper analysis, two will be briefly characterized, namely the phenomenon of projectivity and the representation of coordination.

Proceedings of the Fourth International Conference on Dependency Linguistics (Depling 2017), pages 2-3,
Pisa, Italy, September 18-20 2017

To summarize, we argue that both attributes of our approach, namely "deep" and "dependency-based" are important for a theoretical description of language if this description is supposed to help to reflect the relation between form and meaning, that is, when it is supposed to serve as a basis for language understanding. Despite undisputable recent progress in NLP which relies more on computational methods than linguistic representations or features, we believe that for true understanding, having an adequate theory is worth the effort.

This work has been supported by the LINDAT/CLARIN project of the Ministry of Education, Youth and Sports of the Czech Republic (project LM2015071) and by the project GA17-07313S of the Grant Agency of the Czech Republic.

The benefit of syntactic vs. linear n-grams for linguistic description

Melanie Andresen and **Heike Zinsmeister**
Universität Hamburg
Institute for German Language and Literature
Germany
{melanie.andresen, heike.zinsmeister}@uni-hamburg.de

Abstract

Automatic dependency annotations have been used in all kinds of language applications. However, there has been much less exploitation of dependency annotations for the linguistic description of language varieties. This paper presents an attempt to employ dependency annotations for describing style. We argue that for this purpose, linear n-grams (that follow the text's surface) alone do not appropriately represent a language like German. For this claim, we present theoretically as well as empirically founded arguments. We suggest syntactic n-grams (that follow the dependency paths) as a possible solution. To demonstrate their potential, we compare the German academic languages of linguistics and literary studies using both linear and syntactic n-grams. The results show that the approach using syntactic n-grams allows for the detection of linguistically meaningful patterns that do not emerge in a linear n-gram analysis, e. g. complex verbs and light verb constructions.

1 Introduction

Linear n-grams in the sense of adjacent strings of tokens, parts of speech, etc. are a very common and successful way of modeling language in computational linguistics. However, linguistic structures do not always work in such linear ways. From a cross-linguistic perspective, some languages are less linearly organized than others. While many (though not all) syntactic structures in English can indeed be described by linear patterns, this is much less true for languages with a more flexible word order and other syntactic properties that induce long distance relations, e. g. German.

Still, the linear n-gram approach is quite successful when used for applications in such languages. In the present paper our aim is a slightly different one. We want to employ n-grams not as a means for an application but for linguistic description itself. This requires the language modeling to be more linguistically adequate and interpretable and not just to be a means to an end. We consider the use of *syntactic n-grams* in addition to linear ones to be a possibility to achieve this aim.

In order to motivate our approach, we will first introduce the concept of syntactic n-grams (section 2) and present related work (section 3). Then we will investigate the descriptive benefit of syntactic n-grams by, firstly, looking at theoretical descriptions of non-linear German syntax (section 4.1), and secondly, by investigating empirical consequences of such structures by describing cross-linguistic differences in Universal Dependencies (UD) treebanks, with a special focus on the comparison of English and German (section 4.2).

In the main part of this paper we will present a study of stylistic comparison between different academic disciplines, namely between linguistics and literary studies in German (section 5). To capture these differences, we will compare the frequencies of n-grams between the two disciplines and contrast the results yielded by linear and syntactic n-grams in section 6.

Finally, we will summarize our results in section 7. The analyses show that syntactic n-grams capture relevant structures that would be missed in a purely linear approach, e. g. complex verbs and light verb constructions.

2 Syntactic n-grams

Linear n-gram analysis is an omnipresent method in computational linguistics and has proven to be an easy to implement and highly appropriate approximation of how language works in many ap-

Proceedings of the Fourth International Conference on Dependency Linguistics (Depling 2017), pages 4-14,
Pisa, Italy, September 18-20 2017

plications (see Jurafsky and Martin (2014, chap. 4) for an overview).

However, for the linguistic description of language this is often not satisfactory, as the underlying linguistic patterns are not always linear. One possible remedy for this issue is the approach of skip-grams (see e. g. Guthrie et al. (2006)), but they disregard linguistic structures and thus generate a lot of noise. Another approach for overcoming this problem is the use of syntactic n-grams. Instead of following the word order as it appears on the surface, they are based on dependency paths in the sentence.

A simple type of syntactic n-grams relying on unary-branching dependency structures is described by Sidorov et al. (2012):

> [...] we consider as neighbors the words (or other elements like part-of-speech tags, etc.) that follow one another in the path of the syntactic tree, and not in the text. We call such n-Grams syntactic n-Grams (sn-Grams). (Sidorov et al., 2012, 1)

A more sophisticated approach is suggested by Goldberg and Orwant (2013). Their definition augments the one by Sidorov et al. (2012) by including all kinds of n-ary branching subtrees:

> We define a syntactic-ngram to be a rooted connected dependency tree over k words, which is a subtree of a dependency tree over an entire sentence. (Goldberg and Orwant, 2013, 3)

This results in the additional inclusion of n-grams with more than one dependent per head, which is also advocated by Sidorov (2013).[1]

As a base for the more widespread use of syntactic n-grams, Goldberg and Orwant (2013) create a comprehensive database on the basis of the Google Books corpus for general use. In their representation of n-grams, they exclude functional words and include multiple layers of annotation (part of speech, dependency relation, head). In addition, they preserve the information about the word order in the text. Our analysis will be based on the simpler type of syntactic n-grams by Sidorov et al. (2012) (see section 5.2).

---

[1]Compare also to the concept of catenae presented in Osborne et al. (2012).

3 Related Work

In this section, we will briefly refer to other types of syntactically motivated features and applications they were used in. Then we will look at the use of n-grams and syntactic features in authorship attribution and stylistic analysis.

Dependency-based features have been used for various applications. For example, Snow et al. (2004) use dependency paths between nouns as one feature to extract lexical hypernymy relations. Padó and Lapata (2007) use similar dependency subtrees as a feature to create general semantic space models. Versley (2013) uses subgraphs to describe larger structures, in particular implicit discourse relations in texts.

Syntactic features have also been systematically compared to linguistically less informed features like linear n-grams or bag-of-words approaches. Lapesa and Evert (2017) evaluate the performance of dependency-based and simpler window-based models for computing semantic similarity and find the simpler model to be superior in most cases. Bott and Schulte im Walde (2015) present similar findings when employing syntactically informed features in the task of predicting compositionality of German particle verbs.

Sidorov et al. (2012) use syntactic n-grams in an authorship attribution task. Their syntactic n-grams include the syntactic relation labels only and achieve good results compared to linear n-grams. Stamatatos (2009) gives an overview of the use of other types of syntactic features in authorship attribution. These include for instance syntactic rewrite rules based on phrase structures and syntactic errors. In a more recent study, van Cranenburgh and Bod (2017) successfully quantify the literariness of novels by using, among others, fragments of syntactic constituency trees as features. They stress the fact that these features have the advantage of being more interpretable than others that are not syntactically motivated.

N-gram approaches have also been used for more interpretative analyses in the humanities. Biber et al. (1999) and others investigate academic language with the help of so-called 'lexical bundles'. In literary studies, Mahlberg (2013), among others, uses data-driven 'clusters' for describing the style of Charles Dickens' prose. Both approaches rely on token-based n-grams only and do not make use of syntactic annotation.

Most of the computational linguistics approaches have in common that they use syntactic n-grams or syntactic subtrees for some practical application. Even stylistic approaches of aim at classifying documents rather than describing them. On the other hand, studies in the humanities that aim at describing and interpreting language tend to use rather simple features that do not include syntactic information. By merging the means of the first with the aims of the second group, we will explore the potential syntactic n-grams hold for the linguistic description of languages.

4 Non-linear structures

We will at first motivate the need for syntactic n-grams by considering *non-linear structures* in the sense of structures that are expressed in a discontinuous token string. This means that they cannot be captured by regular linear n-grams. In particular, we are interested in structures which occur frequently enough for us to expect them to have an impact on n-gram creation. Section 4.1 gives a theoretical foundation by introducing non-linear syntactic structures from German. Section 4.2 discusses empirical consequences of these properties with a special focus on the comparison of English and German.

4.1 Theoretical foundation

To what extent the syntactic structure of a language is linear is a question of typology and differs widely between languages. The use of n-grams for linguistic applications and analyses is a method that favors languages with dominantly *linear structures*, i. e. structures that are expressed by continuous token strings. German is one example of a language that is rich in non-linear structures.[2]

We will first focus on non-linear structures that are projective, i. e. structures that do not cause dependency paths to overlap. These are commonly discussed under the model of Topological Fields that describes German as using so-called bracketing structures: Once the first part of the bracket is realized, the reader/hearer expects the second part to occur as well (see Kübler and Zinsmeister (2015, 73) or Becker and Frank (2002) for an English description). Three types of these structures can be distinguished:

---

[2]The non-linear characteristics of German are most prominently described and parodied by Mark Twain (1880).

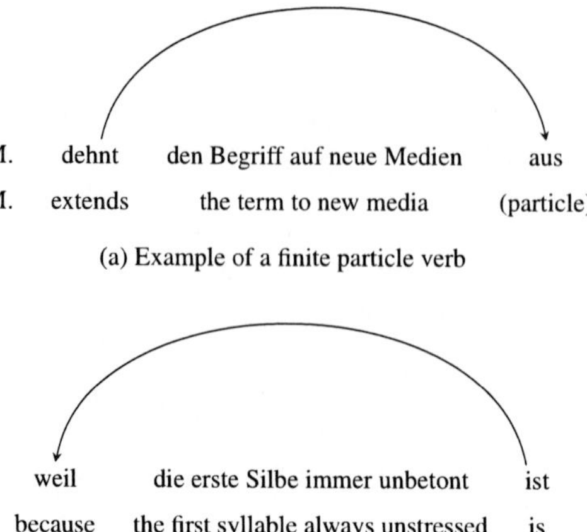

(a) Example of a finite particle verb

(b) Example of a subordinate clause with the verb in final position

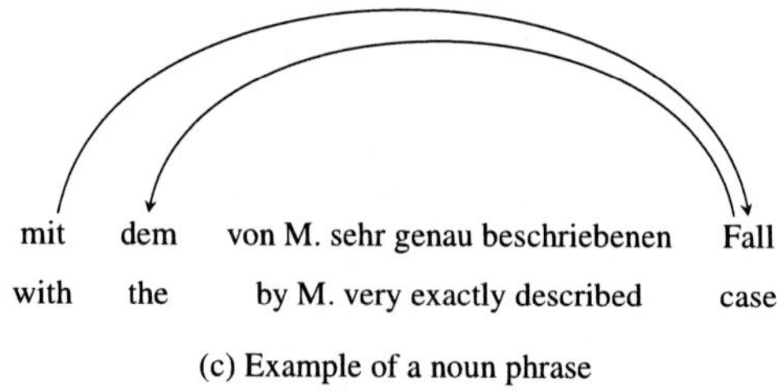

(c) Example of a noun phrase

Figure 1: Examples of non-linear structures in German

Main clauses. In main clauses, several types of complex verbal structures lead to non-linearity:

- full verbs complemented by auxiliary and/or modal verbs,
- copula verbs complemented by predicatives,
- light verb constructions,
- finite particle verbs.

In all of these verb constructions, the finite part of the verb will be in second position while the other verbal elements are in final position. The number of phrases in between, in the so-called middle field, is theoretically unlimited. Figure 1a shows an example of the particle verb *ausdehnen* ('to extend') with the finite verbal part *dehnt* in second position and the separated particle *aus* in sentence-final position.

Subordinate clauses. This bracketing structure is opened by the phrase-initial subjunction and closed by the finite and non-finite verb forms that are in sentence-final position (see example in Figure 1b).

Noun phrases. Finally, German also has non-linear structures similar to English: The noun phrase is opened by a determiner (or indirectly by a preposition) and closed by the noun itself. In between, the phrase can be extended by mainly adjective phrases. Additionally, the German noun phrase can comprise structures in pre-nominal position that would be placed post-nominally in English as shown in the example in Figure 1c.

Maier et al. (2014) present additional discontinuous structures that are characterized not only by the distance between their elements, but also by non-projective dependencies, i. e. by crossing dependencies: "extraposition, a placeholder/repeated element construction, topicalization, scrambling, local movement, parentheticals, and fronting of pronouns" (Maier et al., 2014, 1). However, these structures are much rarer than the projective non-linear ones described above and are not expected to be reflected in the frequency data of the n-gram analysis.

In the light of the example of German we have seen that there are languages with many non-linear structures that do not have an equivalent in English.

4.2 Empirical consequences

In order to empirically demonstrate and quantify the degree to which languages make use of non-linear structures and describe their nature, we focus on the distance between head and dependent in dependency annotated data in terms of surface tokens. For a cross-linguistic comparison we use the training data of Universal Dependencies 2.0 (Nivre et al., 2017). Table 1 shows the median and mean distance and standard deviation between head and dependent in several languages[3]. Punctuation and the root were excluded from the calculation. A distance of 0 means that head and dependent are directly adjacent.

First, we can see that even in English – the language most applications were primarily developed for – head and dependent are often non-adjacent. On average, 1.77 words are in between head and dependent. Second, it becomes clear that the distances vary greatly also within languages, with Arabic and Persian having a very high standard deviation of 6.78 and 5.09, respectively. Even though one should bear in mind that some differ-

	median	mean	sd
Persian	0	2.62	5.09
German	1	**2.28**	**4.02**
Arabic	0	2.14	6.78
Dutch	1	2.06	3.54
English	1	**1.77**	**3.32**
French	1	1.71	3.92
Russian	1	1.70	3.51
Swedish	1	1.70	4.79
Czech	1	1.70	3.24
Turkish	0	1.69	3.46
Italian	1	1.68	4.12

Table 1: Distance between head and dependent in UD treebanks (without punctuation and root)

ences might be due to the language-specific implementations of the Universal Dependencies, we can assume that there are in fact differences between the languages.

Figure 2 exemplary shows the distribution of the distances of the part of speech `sconj` (= subordinating conjunctions) to its head in more detail. Here, the differences between the languages are more pronounced than with other parts of speech. Turkish and Arabic do not have this part of speech. With a median of six (marked by the black line inside the box), German features the highest distance, followed by Persian, another verb-final language, and Dutch, which is similar to German in this respect.

In the remainder of this paper we will focus on German as an example of a language in which the average distance is significantly higher than in English[4] and more variable.

----
[4]t = 42.998, df = 386460, p-value < 2.2e-16

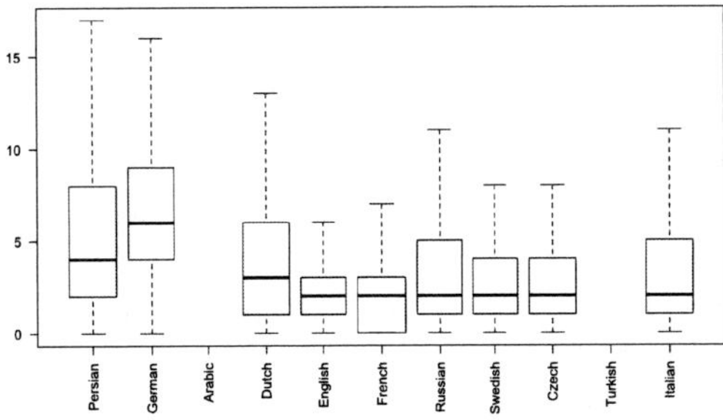

Figure 2: Distance to head of words with the part of speech `sconj` in all languages

----
[3]The sample of languages is only a subset of more than 50 languages available in UD.

Which syntactic structures are related to these differences? Figure 3a shows boxplots of the distance distributions between heads and dependents in English and German grouped by the part of speech of the dependent. The most obvious differences relate to the theoretical findings in section 4.1. German verbs and auxiliary verbs show much larger distances from their heads than their English counterparts, as can be expected because of the German bracketing structure. Subordinating conjunctions (SCONJ) show the largest difference in the two languages with the interquartile ranges of their distributions not even overlapping. This reflects the German brackets in subordinate clauses, which result in a large distance between the subjunction and the finite verb of the subordinate clause.

Another clear difference is in pronouns, which are positioned early in the sentence in German (before or immediately after the finite verb, the so-called 'Wackernagel position', Cardinaletti and Roberts (2002, 133)), while their head (usually the main verb) can be sentence-final. Also nouns and adverbs tend to be slightly further away from their head in German than in English. This can probably be attributed to the generally freer word order in German (empirically shown in Futrell et al. (2015)).

Figure 3b shows the same relation from the other direction: The same distances grouped by the part of speech of the head. Again, German verbs and auxiliary verbs prove to be further away from their dependent than the English ones. Adjectives are another notable case. According to the Universal Dependencies' guidelines, adjectives are considered the root of the sentence when they occur in predicative structures (e. g. *This is very easy.*). The copula is one of its dependents, which can again be far away from the predicative adjective in German.

Finally, all of the phenomena described above are also reflected when looking at the distances grouped by syntactic relation: Many of the high-distance relations in German refer to different types of clauses (`acl`, `advcl`, `ccomp`, `csubj`) and complex verbs (`aux`, `compound:prt` (particle verbs)), especially in combination with passives (`csubj:pass`, `nsubj:pass`, `aux:pass`). `mark` is the relation between subjunctions and finite verbs in subordinate clauses. It also features a clear difference

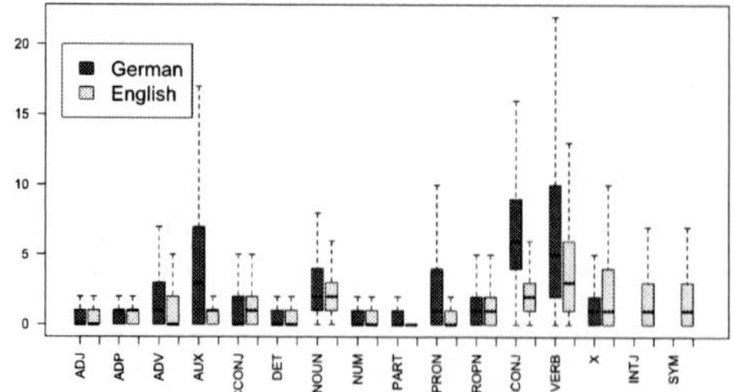

(a) Distance by pos of dependent

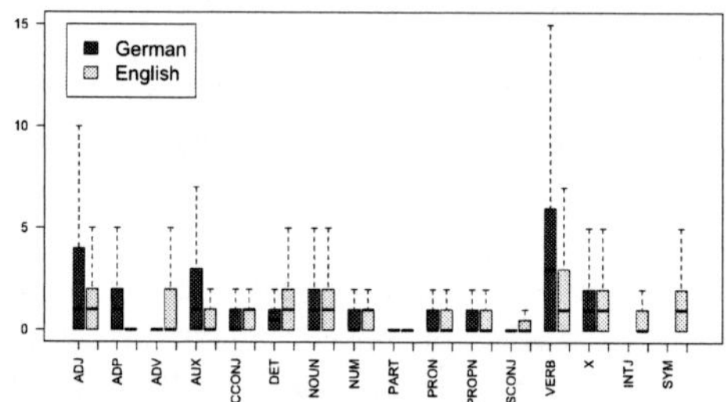

(b) Distance by pos of head

Figure 3: Distance between head and dependent in UD treebanks (without outliers)

in distance between the two languages.

This section has shown that the non-linear structures described in section 4.1 have an impact on the distance between head and dependent. It could be demonstrated that these distances are much larger in German dependency structures than in English ones. This means that the modeling of German using only linear n-grams is not fully adequate for its linguistic description. In the next section, we will compare the contribution of syntactic and linear n-grams to a stylistic analysis of German academic language.

5 Study: Disciplinary differences in academic writing style

The following study is part of a larger project on stylistic analysis of German academic texts written in the disciplines of linguistics and literary studies, respectively. This field of research is motivated by the fact that these two disciplines are often combined in one common study program such as German Studies or German Language and Literature. While this suggests that the disciplines are very closely related, writing styles differ widely (see e. g. Afros and Schryer (2009)). We present an attempt to capture these differences by an n-gram analysis based on linear and syntactic n-grams.

5.1 Data and preprocessing

The study is based on a corpus of 60 German PhD theses, 30 for each of the two disciplines linguistics and literary studies.

All texts were accessible as PDF files. In a first preprocessing step, we converted them to HTML to use the HTML markup for semi-automatically deleting irrelevant parts of the text. In particular, we deleted parts that do not belong to the targeted varieties and often interrupt the running text: tables and figures, footnotes, citations and examples. We also removed all text sequences in parentheses as most of them comprise references, especially in linguistics. Additionally, we excluded sentences with more than 40% of the words in quotes, assuming that they do not represent the target variety either. Other elements we had to exclude manually, e. g. title page, table of contents, and list of references. The resulting plain text version has a total count of 3,579,437 tokens.

We tokenized the texts using the system *Punkt* (Kiss and Strunk, 2006)[5] and annotated the sentences with an off-the-shelf version of MATE dependency parser (Bohnet, 2010) trained on the TIGER Corpus (Seeker and Kuhn, 2012). Note that in contrast to the previous chapter, we decided against using Universal Dependencies. As this part of the study deals with German only, we consider the tag set developed specifically for German more appropriate. For the purpose of evaluation, two annotators consensually created a gold standard for a random sample of 22 sentences (600 tokens) against which we compared the parser's output. The parser performance is good (UAS: 0.95, LAS: 0.93), especially given that it is applied to out-of-domain data.

5.2 N-gram generation

We extracted several data sets from the preprocessed corpus:

- **linear n-grams** of sizes 2-5 using tokens, lemmas, pos-tags and dependency relation labels,
- **syntactic n-grams** of sizes 2-5 using tokens, lemmas, pos-tags and dependency relation labels, generated by taking every word of the

sentence as a starting point and following the dependency path backwards by n steps.

The data set for the present analysis is not sufficiently large to allow for a representation of syntactic n-grams that includes as many annotations as Goldberg and Orwant (2013) used. To avoid issues of data sparsity, only one level of information at a time is included, e. g. token OR lemma OR part of speech OR the dependency relation label. In line with Sidorov et al. (2012), the analysis is restricted to unary syntactic n-grams following only one branch in the syntactic tree.

We exclude n-grams with a total frequency of less than 10 from further analysis. For all the resulting n-grams we calculate relative frequencies in all 60 texts. The difference in frequency between the two subcorpora is assessed based on the t-test as suggested by Paquot and Bestgen (2009) and Lijffijt et al. (2014). Each data set is then ranked according to the t-test's p-values.

6 Results and Discussion

In the analysis, we inspect the degree of overlap between linear and syntactic n-grams in order to assess whether the two types truly give us complementary information (section 6.1). However, our main question is whether both types contribute meaningfully to a linguistic description of the disciplinary differences between linguistics and literary studies. Section 6.2 therefore gives an exemplary interpretation of the most distinctive linear and syntactic 4-grams. On that basis, the final section 6.3 presents an attempt to quantify linguistic interpretability.

6.1 Overlap between linear and syntactic n-grams

In order to first get a general idea of the added value of syntactic n-grams independent of our research question about disciplinary differences, we quantify the overlap between linear and syntactic n-grams. To this end we investigated to what degree the syntactic n-grams correspond to linear n-grams.

We calculated for all four levels (token, lemma, part of speech and dependency relation), to what extent the 200 highest-scoring syntactic n-grams correspond to linear n-grams.[6] For each of the

---

[5]http://www.nltk.org/api/nltk.tokenize.html, 23.07.2017

[6]With increasing n, the number of n-grams passing the frequency threshold of 10 decreases quickly. Therefore, the number for syntactic token 5-grams is only based on 37 items

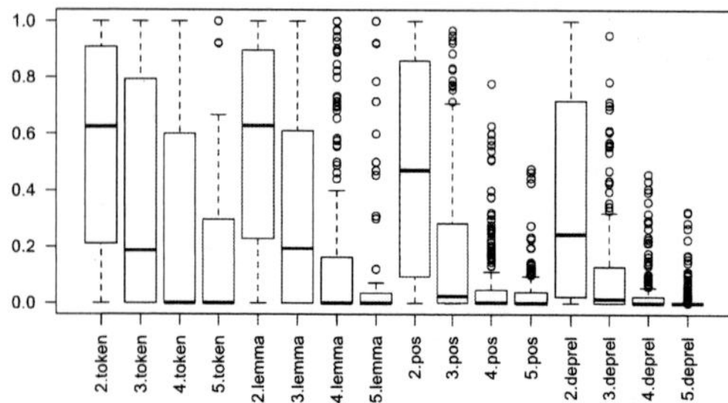

Figure 4: Proportion of syntactic n-grams that correspond to a linear n-gram (by n-gram size and level of annotation)

200 syntactic n-gram types, we checked all corresponding token instances for linearity (score 1) or non-linearity (score 0) and calculated the mean for each type. The resulting value gives us information about the overlap of linear and syntactic n-grams: A score of 1 means that all token instances of the syntactic n-gram are also linear n-grams. A score of 0 means that none of the token instances of the syntactic n-gram correspond to linear n-grams.

Figure 4 shows the resulting distribution of overlap by n-gram size and level of annotation. The proportion of linear n-grams is low, with a mean between 0.36 and 0.57 already for bigrams, depending on the level of annotation. As expected, the proportion of linear n-grams decreases as *n* increases. With every additional transition from one word to the next, the probability of at least one deviation from the linear order rises.

Additionally, there is a tendency of decreasing linearity with increasing abstractness from token to lemma to part of speech and dependency relation. One particular combination of tokens can be exclusively realized linearly but a lemma comprises several different token combinations, which will not all be realized linearly. With increasing abstractness, more heterogeneous cases are subsumed under one label, making purely linear instances less and less likely.

However, it has to be borne in mind that syntactic n-grams with more than one branch were not included. These might correspond to linear n-grams to a higher degree, resulting in a higher overlap between the two types of n-grams. In the present analysis, linear n-grams cover some structures that correspond to syntactic units, but are not captured by our narrow approach to syntactic n-grams. Consequently, the widening of our realization of syntactic n-grams is advisable in future work.

6.2 Interpretation of linear and syntactic 4-grams

We will now focus on the possibilities of interpreting linear and syntactic n-grams in order to draw conclusions about linguistic properties of the German academic languages of linguistics and literary studies. In this section, we discuss one example in detail while the next section will present possibilities of quantifying these interpretations on a larger scale. The focus will be on token n-grams as they can easily be read by humans. Especially longer part-of-speech sequences (like ART-NN-APPR-PPOSAT-NN[7]) are quite abstract and require a person with experience with the tag set and possibly a set of example instances (see Andresen and Zinsmeister (2017) for an attempt to include these).

Table 2a and Table 2b show the 15 highest-scoring 4-grams for the linear and the syntactic data set, respectively. These are the n-grams with the highest difference in frequency when comparing the disciplines. In addition to the n-gram, an approximate translation into English is provided. Given the fragmentary nature of n-grams, these translations are sometimes based on additional assumptions about the context and do therefore only represent one of several possible meanings. The row color indicates in which discipline the n-gram is more frequent: n-grams more frequent in literary studies are colored gray, those more frequent in linguistics white.

Among the linear n-grams in Table 2a, structures following a comma dominate the ranking. This can be explained by the fact that the beginning of subordinate clauses is grammatically restricted to some specific patterns. Because of the grammatical gender in German, some structures reoccur in several similar forms. Many patterns that are significantly more frequent in literary studies indicate relative clauses (rank 3, 4, 5, 7, 8 and 12). For linguistics this is only true for

---

that do not necessarily achieve low p-values in the t-test. Also, the syntactic token 4-grams and linear token 4-/5-grams are partially based on items that do not pass the level of significance (p=0.001).

[7]The tag set used here is the STTS (Schiller et al., 1999). This sequence corresponds to article – noun – preposition – possessive pronoun in attributive position – noun, e. g. *the name of his mother*.

rank	linear n-gram	literal translation	comment
1	, die bei der	, that.3SG.F/3PL at the	
2	davon aus , dass	expect that	fragment of: expect that the
3	, das in der	, that.3SG.N in the	
4	, in der er	, in which he	
5	, der sich von	, that.3SG.M it.REFL of	
6	aus , dass die	out, that the.3SG.F/3PL	fragment of: expect that the
7	, in dem sie	, in that3SG.M/N she/they	
8	, in dem sich	, in that3SG.M/N it.REFL	
9	bei der Auswahl der	in the selection of	
10	, ob es sich	, whether it it.REFL	
11	, bei denen sich	, at which it.REFL	
12	, der sich in	, that.3SG.M it.REFL in	
13	, sich in die	, it.REFL in the	
14	aus sich selbst heraus	out of it.REFL	
15	, die sich auf	, that.3SG.F/3PL it.REFL on	

(a) Linear token 4-grams

rank	syntactic n-gram	literal translation	translation
1	und>können>werden>.	and>can>be>.	and can be. (passive)
2	rückt>in>Vordergrund>den	bring>to>fore>the	bring to the fore
3	rückt>in>Nähe>die	bring>in>proximity>the	bring sth. closer to
4	ist>in>Lage>der	is>in>condition>the	is capable of
5	im>als>im>auch	in>as>in>also	in X as well as Y
6	bei>als>bei>auch	at>as>at>also	at X as well as Y
7	kann>werden>gelesen>als	can>be>read>as	can be read as
8	werden>erläutert>im >Folgenden	is>explained>in the>following	In the following, ... is explained
9	ist>in>Regel>der	ist>in>rule>the	is generally
10	war>in>Lage>der	was>in>condition>the	was capable of
11	und>kann>nicht>mehr	and>can>not>anymore	and can no longer
12	zu>Beginn>Jahrhunderts >des	at>beginning>century>the	at the beginning of the century
13	werden>vorgestellt>Im >Folgenden	is>presented>in the>following	In the following, ... is presented
14	in>Hälfte>Jahrhunderts>des	in>half>century>of the	in the ... half of the century
15	stellt>in>Mittelpunkt>den	puts>in>center>the	centers/focuses on

(b) Syntactic token 4-grams

Table 2: Highest-scoring token 4-grams for linear and syntactic n-grams (rank based on t-test; gray = n-gram is more frequent in literary studies, white = n-gram is more frequent in linguistics)

rank 1, 11 and 15. Interestingly, all of these use the pronoun *die*, which can be feminine singular, but is more likely to be plural (independent of gender). We might derive the explanatory hypothesis that literary scholars write more about individuals while linguists are rather concerned with groups of phenomena in a generic way. This is in accordance with the intuitive idea of how these disciplines work.

The results for syntactic n-grams in Table 2b are quite different. The most distinctive is a very general complex verb pattern in passive voice with the modal verb *can*, that can be combined with any main verb and is more common in linguistics. There are also some more specific complex verbs that include a main verb (rank 7, 8 and 13). Additionally, there are the light verb constructions *in den Vordergrund rücken* ('bring to the fore'), *in die Nähe rücken* ('bring sth. closer to sth. else'), *in der Lage sein* ('be able to do sth.') and *in den Mittelpunkt stellen* ('focus on sth.'). All of these structures relate to the properties of German described in section 4.1 and would not be detected in a purely linear n-gram approach. Other syntactic n-grams refer to structures that can be captured similarly by linear n-grams, e. g. the syntactic 4-gram *ist>in>Regel>der* corresponds to the linear n-gram *ist in der Regel*. This reflects the findings of section 6.1 showing overlap as well as differences between the two types of n-grams.

6.3   Quantifying linguistic interpretability

Taking these interpretations as a starting point, we made the attempt to quantify the interpretability of linear and syntactic n-grams. Thereby we hope to objectify the n-grams' potential and provide a foundation for a deepened comparison.

A sample of syntactic and linear n-grams[8] was annotated by three annotators according to the following categories:

1. This n-gram contains a (complex) lexical unit (LEX) or overlaps with one (LEX-P).

2. This n-gram contains a grammatical structure (GRAM) or overlaps with one (GRAM-P).

3. This n-gram contains a structure that is ambiguous between lexicon and grammar (LEX-P_GRAM-P).

---

[8]For the n-gram sizes 2-5, we chose the 20 highest-scoring syntactic and linear token n-grams, respectively, giving a total sample size of 160 items.

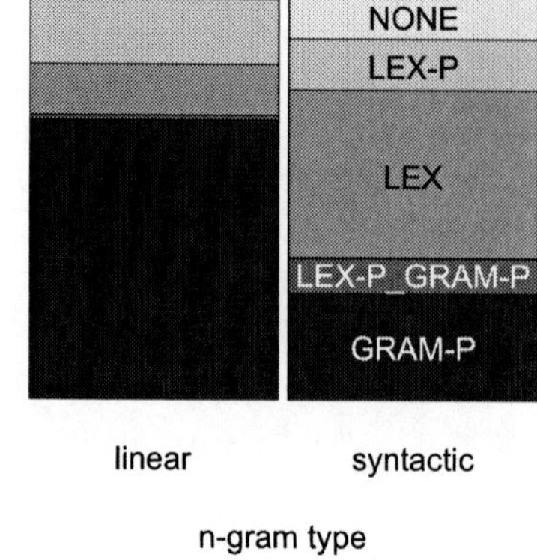

Figure 5: Annotation of information in n-grams dependent on n-gram type, n=160

4. This n-gram does not contain a (complex) lexical unit or grammatical structure (NONE).

For categories 1 to 3, the annotators were asked to additionally provide the lexical unit or grammatical structure they were thinking of.

The annotators reached an inter-annotator-agreement of Fleiss' κ 0.55 which we consider satisfying given the natural ambiguity of the task. After discussing nine elements where no agreement was reached initially, all three annotators agreed on one category for 57% of items. For the rest at least two annotators agreed on one category. The following results are based on a majority vote.

Figure 5 shows the distribution of annotation categories for the two n-gram types. For the linear n-grams, more grammatical phenomena were found, and for syntactic n-grams, more lexical phenomena (especially complete lexical items) were found. The difference is significant with p < 0.001 (Fisher's Exact Test), which shows that there are many non-linear lexical items that are detected by the syntactic n-grams only. The number of non-interpretable instances is higher in syntactic n-grams (1 vs. 10 instances). These are e. g. sequences of only one word and the following punctuation or sequences related to specific properties of the annotation scheme.

Regarding the concrete structures observed, there is a clear overlap in lexical phenomena, e. g. the sequence *in der Regel* ('as a rule') is a linear as well as a syntactic n-gram. Syntactic n-grams additionally capture light verb constructions that are non-linear (see section 4.1), e. g.

den<Vordergrund<in<rückt ('bring to the fore'), which might explain the higher proportion of lexical phenomena. In grammatical structures, on the other hand, there is hardly any overlap. While most linear n-grams (35 of 55 grammatical structures in total) capture different types of relative clauses (e. g. the trigram *, die ihm*, 'that [...] him'), among the syntactic n-grams complex verb structures (11 of 19 grammatical structures in total) and phenomena of coordination (5 of 19) dominate.

Together, linear and syntactic n-grams result in an informative comparison of the two disciplines: In literary studies we find many more relative clauses and light verb constructions, while linguistics employs more complex verb forms like passive and modal verbs. A more comprehensive interpretation of these and more data with respect to the disciplinary differences is conducted in Andresen and Zinsmeister (2017).

The annotation experiment shows that linear and syntactic n-grams capture very different phenomena and can complement each other in useful ways. At this point, it is not possible to generalize these results as they need to be verified by analyzing more data of different genres (and languages).

7 Conclusion

The research presented in this paper shows that an analysis based on syntactic n-grams, understood as n-grams following the path of dependency relations in the sentence, can give linguistically meaningful insights in the properties of a language variety. We have demonstrated theoretically and empirically that there are many non-linear structures in languages like German. These are not adequately taken into consideration in a language representation based on linear n-grams only. Through the example of comparing the German academic languages of linguistics and literary studies we showed that linear and syntactic n-grams capture very different linguistic structures. In our exemplary study, especially complex verbs and light verb constructions could not be detected by the linear n-gram analysis.[9] However, the analysis of syntactic n-grams is highly dependent on the quality of the dependency annotation. Also, some structures are frequent only because of specific properties of the annotation scheme. It re-

mains a desideratum for future research to determine the influence of the annotation scheme and the potential of Universal Dependencies to allow for a cross-linguistic comparison of this type of analysis.

For the future, it would be desirable to include syntactic n-grams that take more than one dependent per head into account. Currently, patterns such as a verb and its subject and object or a noun and two modifiers are missed by the syntactic n-grams of our study. The linear n-grams can compensate this only very partially. Also, it should be considered to systematically evaluate the potential of dependency-based annotations in comparison to other syntactic models, e. g. constituency-based models.

Acknowledgments

We would like to thank Yannick Versley and Fabian Barteld for their very helpful comments on an earlier version of the paper, Sarah Jablotschkin for contributing to the manual n-gram evaluation, and Piklu Gupta for improving our English. All remaining errors are our own.

References

Elena Afros and Catherine F. Schryer. 2009. Promotional (meta)discourse in research articles in language and literary studies. *English for Specific Purposes*, 28(1):58–68, January.

Melanie Andresen and Heike Zinsmeister. 2017. Approximating Style by n-Gram-based Annotation. In *Proceedings of the Workshop on Stylistic Variation*, Copenhagen, Denmark, September.

Markus Becker and Anette Frank. 2002. A Stochastic Topological Parser of German. In *Proceedings of COLING 2002*, pages 71–77.

Douglas Biber, Stig Johansson, Geoffrey Leech, Susan Conrad, and Edward Finegan. 1999. *Longman Grammar of Spoken and Written English*. Longman, Harlow.

Bernd Bohnet. 2010. Very High Accuracy and Fast Dependency Parsing is not a Contradiction. In *Proceedings of the 23rd International Conference on Computational Linguistics (COLING 2010)*, Beijing, China.

Stefan Bott and Sabine Schulte im Walde. 2015. Exploiting Fine-grained Syntactic Transfer Features to Predict the Compositionality of German Particle Verbs. In *Proceedings of the 11th International Conference on Computational Semantics, IWCS 2015, 15-17 April, 2015, Queen Mary University of London, London, UK*, pages 34–39.

---

[9] Our aim was to increase coverage of phenomena included in the analysis. We do not to automatically distinguish between light verb constructions and free verb-noun associations.

Anna Cardinaletti and Ian Roberts. 2002. Clause Structure and X-Second. In Guglielmo Cinque, editor, *Functional Structure in DP and IP: The Cartography of Syntactic Structures*, volume 1, pages 123–166. Oxford University Press.

Richard Futrell, Kyle Mahowald, and Edward Gibson. 2015. Quantifying Word Order Freedom in Dependency Corpora. In *Proceedings of the Third International Conference on Dependency Linguistics (Depling 2015)*, pages 91–100, Uppsala.

Yoav Goldberg and Jon Orwant. 2013. A Dataset of Syntactic-Ngrams over Time from a Very Large Corpus of English Books. In *Second Joint Conference on Lexical and Computational Semantics (*SEM), Volume 1: Proceedings of the Main Conference and the Shared Task: Semantic Textual Similarity*, pages 241–247, Atlanta, Georgia, USA, June. Association for Computational Linguistics.

David Guthrie, Ben Allison, Wei Liu, Louise Guthrie, and Yorick Wilks. 2006. A closer look at skip-gram modelling. In *Proceedings of the 5th international Conference on Language Resources and Evaluation (LREC-2006)*, pages 1–4.

Dan Jurafsky and James H Martin. 2014. *Speech and language processing*, volume 3. Pearson.

Tibor Kiss and Jan Strunk. 2006. Unsupervised Multilingual Sentence Boundary Detection. *Computational Linguistics*, 32(4):485–525, December.

Sandra Kübler and Heike Zinsmeister. 2015. *Corpus Linguistics and Linguistically Annotated Corpora*. Bloomsbury, London, New York.

Gabriella Lapesa and Stefan Evert. 2017. Large-scale evaluation of dependency-based DSMs: Are they worth the effort? In *Proceedings of the 15th Conference of the European Chapter of the Association for Computational Linguistics: Volume 2, Short Papers*, pages 394–400, Valencia, Spain, April. Association for Computational Linguistics.

Jefrey Lijffijt, Terttu Nevalainen, Tanja Säily, Panagiotis Papapetrou, Kai Puolamäki, and Heikki Mannila. 2014. Significance testing of word frequencies in corpora. *Digital Scholarship in the Humanities*, pages 1–24, December.

Michaela Mahlberg. 2013. *Corpus Stylistics and Dickens's Fiction*. Number 14 in Routledge advances in corpus linguistics. Routledge, New York.

Wolfgang Maier, Miriam Kaeshammer, Peter Baumann, and Sandra Kübler. 2014. Discosuite - A Parser Test Suite for German Discontinuous Structures. In *Proceedings of the Ninth International Conference on Language Resources and Evaluation (LREC'14)*, Reykjavik, Iceland. European Language Resources Association (ELRA).

Joakim Nivre, Željko Agić, and Lars Ahrenberg. 2017. Universal Dependencies 2.0. LINDAT/CLARIN digital library at the Institute of Formal and Applied Linguistics, Charles University.

Timothy Osborne, Michael Putnam, and Thomas Groß. 2012. Catenae: Introducing a Novel Unit of Syntactic Analysis. *Syntax*, 15(4):354–396, December.

Sebastian Padó and Mirella Lapata. 2007. Dependency-based construction of semantic space models. *Computational Linguistics*, 33(2):161–199.

Magali Paquot and Yves Bestgen. 2009. Distinctive words in academic writing: A comparison of three statistical tests for keyword extraction. In Andreas H. Jucker, Daniel Schreier, and Marianne Hundt, editors, *Corpora: Pragmatics and Discourse*, pages 247–269. Brill, January.

Anne Schiller, Simone Teufel, Christine Thielen, and Christine Stöckert. 1999. *Guidelines für das Tagging deutscher Textcorpora mit STTS (kleines und großes Tagset)*. Stuttgart, Tübingen.

Wolfgang Seeker and Jonas Kuhn. 2012. Making Ellipses Explicit in Dependency Conversion for a German Treebank. In *Proceedings of the 8th International Conference on Language Resources and Evaluation*, pages 3132–3139, Istanbul, Turkey.

Grigori Sidorov, Francisco Velasquez, Efstathios Stamatatos, Alexander Gelbukh, and Liliana Chanona-Hernández. 2012. Syntactic Dependency-Based N-grams as Classification Features. In Ildar Batyrshin and Miguel González Mendoza, editors, *Advances in Computational Intelligence*, number 7630 in Lecture Notes in Computer Science, pages 1–11. Springer, October.

Grigori Sidorov. 2013. Syntactic Dependency Based N-grams in Rule Based Automatic English as Second Language Grammar Correction. *International Journal of Computational Linguistics and Applications*, 4(2):169–188.

Rion Snow, Daniel Jurafsky, Andrew Y Ng, et al. 2004. Learning syntactic patterns for automatic hypernym discovery. In *NIPS*, volume 17, pages 1297–1304.

Efstathios Stamatatos. 2009. A survey of modern authorship attribution methods. *Journal of the American Society for Information Science and Technology*, 60(3):538–556, March.

Mark Twain. 1880. *A Tramp Abroad*. Chatto & Windus, London.

Andreas van Cranenburgh and Rens Bod. 2017. A Data-Oriented Model of Literary Language. *Proceedings of the 15th Conference of the European Chapter of the Association for Computational Linguistics: Volume 1, Long Papers*, 1:1228–1238.

Yannick Versley. 2013. A graph-based approach for implicit discourse relations. *Computational Linguistics in the Netherlands Journal*, 3:148–173.

On the Predicate-Argument Structure: Internal and Absorbing Scope

Igor Boguslavsky
Russian Academy of Sciences
Institute for Information Transmission
Problems, Russia
Universidad Politécnica de Madrid, Spain
igor.m.boguslavsky@gmail.com

Abstract

Valency filling is considered a major mechanism for constructing the semantic structure of the sentence from semantic structures of words. This approach requires a broader view of *valency* and *actant*, covering all kinds of actant-bearing words and all types of valency filling. We introduce the concept of *scope* as a generalization of *actant*: it is any fragment of a Syntactic (SyntScope) or Semantic Structure (SemScope) that fills a valency of a predicate. *Actant* is a particular case of *scope*. We discuss two classes of situations, mostly on the material of Russian, that manifest nonisomorphism between SyntScope and SemScope: (a) meaning α that fills a valency of word L constitutes only a part of the meaning of word L' (*internal scope*); (b) predicate π is an internal component of the meaning of word L; π extends its valency (distinct from valencies of L) to words different from L (*absorbing scope*).

1 Introduction

This paper is a continuation of a series of publications (Boguslavsky 1985, 1996, 1998, 2003, 2007, 2014, 2016) in which we discuss different types of valency slot filling. Several introductory remarks are in order.

First of all, instantiating valency slots, or, in a different terminology, identifying arguments of predicates, is a major step in constructing the semantic structure of the sentence, because it is the main mechanism of meaning amalgamation, a kind of semantic glue that connects meanings together. This view of valencies implies that the concepts of *valency* and *actant* (or, *argument*) should be interpreted broader than it is often done. Here we follow the tradition of the Moscow Semantic School (MSS), which in its turn, shares these notions with the Meaning – Text theory (Apresjan 1974, Mel'čuk 1974). For MSS, the starting point in defining the concept of valency of a word is the semantic analysis of the situation denoted by this word. The analytical semantic definition of a word, constructed according to certain rules (Apresjan 1995), should explicitly present all obligatory participants of the situation denoted by this word. For a word L to have a certain valency slot it is necessary, though insufficient, that a situation denoted by L should contain a corresponding participant in an intuitively obvious way. Another condition is that this participant should be expressible in a sentence along with L in a systematic way (Mel'čuk 2014). A word or a phrase that denotes such a participant is said to fill (or instantiate) the valency slot and is called an actant.

The range of valency words is not restricted to verbs and nouns. Other parts of speech, such as adjectives, adverbs, particles, conjunctions, and prepositions are equally entitled to be classed as actant-bearing words. Moreover, being non-prototypical predicates, they substantially extend our idea of the inventory of the ways which predicates use to instantiate their valencies.

The next remark is that we are going to speak about valency filling at two representation levels – at the level of the syntactic structure (SyntS) and at the level of the semantic structure (SemS). SyntS is a dependency tree, the nodes of which are lexical units (LU) – lexemes or multiword expressions that function as a whole. In SemS LUs are represented by their semantic decomposition, which is a

Proceedings of the Fourth International Conference on Dependency Linguistics (Depling 2017), pages 15-24,
Pisa, Italy, September 18-20 2017

complex composed by simpler semantic units (=semantemes) connected, in their turn, by predicate-argument relations.

Let us introduce two interrelated terms. We will call *semantic scope* of L in valency α (SemScope(L)$^\alpha$) a fragment of SemS that fills valency α of L. *Syntactic scope* of L in valency α (SyntScope(L)$^\alpha$) is a corresponding fragment of SyntS[1]. We will use the term *scope* without any specification when the difference between SyntScope and SemScope is irrelevant. Traditional terms *actant* (*argument*) have a narrower meaning and denote a particular case of *scope*.

In the prototypical case, SyntScope and SemScope are isomorphic (what it exactly means will be explained below). However, this is not always the case. In this paper, we will investigate two important classes of such situations.

The paper is structured as follows. First, we will present the prototypical situation of valency filling (Section 2). In Section 3 we introduce syntactically non-prototypical types of valency filling. Sections 4 and 5 will examine two special cases of non-isomorphism between SyntScope and SemScope – *internal scope* and *absorbing scope*. We will conclude in Section 6.

2   Prototypical Valency Slot Filling

As mentioned above, valency filling is a major mechanism of constructing SemS. According to MSS, to discover the semantic structure of a sentence, one needs, first of all, a dictionary that contains the following information for each scope-bearing word:

(a) analytical definition of its meaning; among other things, it should represent all valency slots (by means of variables);

(b) each valency slot should be assigned the information on how it can be filled; this information includes primarily the data on the syntactic position of the SyntScope in SyntS – whether it is the subject, direct or indirect object, which prepositions or conjunctions are needed to introduce it, and what lexico-grammatical form it can have. In different theoretical frameworks this information is provided by subcategorization frames, government patterns or similar data structures.

It is understandable, then, that for identifying arguments in the text, besides the dictionary, the syntactic structure of the sentence should also be available.

In the prototypical case, SyntScope and SemScope satisfy certain requirements:

(1) SyntScope:
  i. SyntScope(L) depends on L in the dependency structure;
  ii. SyntScope(L) is connected to L directly (and not through some intermediate nodes).

(2) SemScope:
  i. SemScope is isomorphic to SyntScope: if SyntScope = A, SemScope = 'A';
  ii. The word meaning is impermeable to predicate-argument relations.

Properties (i) and (ii) of SyntScope are obvious and do not seem to require explanations. Let us comment on the properties of SemScope.

The isomorphism property means that if some fragment A of SyntS is the syntactic scope of lexeme L, then the semantic argument of L will be exactly 'A' (=the meaning of A). And inversely, if a fragment 'A' of SemS fills a valency of lexeme L, then SyntScope(L) will be the fragment A of SyntS whose meaning is 'A'.

The second property states the impermeability of lexeme borders for predicate-argument relations. This property manifests itself in two ways. First, an internal (i.e. not the topmost) element of the semantic definition of L cannot be an argument of a predicate that does not belong to the same definition. The contact point for external predicates is usually the topmost component of the definition (usually, genus proximum). For example, Longman Dictionary of Contemporary English defines *bicycle* as 'a vehicle with two wheels that you ride by pushing its pedals with your feet'. The topmost component of this definition is semanteme 'vehicle'. That is why the phrase *big bicycle* is interpreted as 'big vehicle' but under no circumstances as 'big pedals' or 'big feet'.

Second, if the definition of lexeme L contains a predicate π which has its own arguments (i.e. distinct from the arguments of L), in a sentence, these arguments are fully located

---

[1] The term SemScope is denotation-wise identical to the term *semantic actant* used in the Meaning-Text Theory (Mel'čuk 2014, Ch.12). However, our SyntScope is broader than *syntactic actant*. Since we prefer to maintain the parallelism of the terms used at different levels of representation, we have opted for the pair SyntScope – SemScope.

inside the definition of *L*. They cannot include definition-external components.

As an illustration, let us consider a pair of Russian antonyms *sobljudat'* 'observe' – *narušat'* 'violate', which differ by a negation: 'observe the rules' – 'do what is allowed by the rules'; 'violate the rules' – 'do what is not allowed by the rules'. If one attaches a negation to one of then, the antonymy turns into the synonymy:

(3a) *On ne budet sobljudat' pravila priličija.*
'he will not observe the decency standards'.

(3b) *On budet narušat' pravila priličija.*
'he will violate the decency standards'.

Let us introduce an adverbial of purpose into sentences (3a) and (3b):

(4a) *On ne budet sobljudat' pravila priličija tol'ko čtoby tebe ugodit'.*
'he will not observe the decency standards only to please you'.

(4b) *On budet narušat' pravila priličija tol'ko čtoby tebe ugodit'.*
'he will violate the decency standards only to please you'

Sentence (4a) has two interpretations depending on whether or not the purpose adverbial is included in the scope of negation:

1) not [will observe the decency standards only to please you];
2) [not [will observe the decency standards]] only to please you.
Sentence (4b) has only the second interpretation.

The reason is that in (4a) the negation is expressed by a separate word, while in (4b) it makes part of the lexical meaning of *narušat'* 'violate' and therefore its scope cannot include the purpose adverbial. The rule that prohibits external material from making part of the scope of an internal predicate will be made more precise below, in section 5.2.

3   Non-Prototypical Valency Slot Filling

Linguistic phenomena rarely exist in their pure form. Most often, there is a core zone, in which the properties of the phenomenon stand out very clearly, and a periphery zone, in which these properties are weaker or undergo certain modifications. In the area of valency filling, the core zone is beyond doubt constituted by verbal constructions, in which the actants are expressed by the subject of the verb and different types of complements. In this zone, properties (1)-(2) from the previous section perfectly hold. The periphery zone is much more diverse.

As far as the syntactic aspect of valency filling is concerned, the deviation from the prototype is determined first of all by different syntactic potential of valency-bearing words. There is a wide range of syntactic positions that a SyntScope may have with respect to its predicate. From this point of view, three types of valency slot filling could be distinguished: ACTIVE, PASSIVE, and DISCONTINOUS ones (Boguslavsky 2003). If lexeme L **subordinates** its SyntScope A by means of an immediate dependency relation, we will say that such a valency filling is ACTIVE (*the boy* [A] *runs* [L], *the search* [L] *for* [A] *the solution*). This is the most typical (prototypical) case. If a lexeme **is subordinated** to its SyntScope, we will say that the filling is PASSIVE (*green* [L] *leaves* [A], *run* [A] *quickly* [L]). This kind of valency filling is characteristic of adverbials, adjectives, particles, conjunctions and prepositions. If there is **no direct syntactic link** between the lexeme and its SyntScope, we will call such valency filling DISCONTINOUS (*By habit* [L], *John* [A] *got up early*). This is a relatively infrequent type, typical of adverbials and adjectives.

In more detail, cases of violation of requirement (1), due to non-prototypical syntactic positions of SyntScope with respect to their predicates, were examined in Boguslavsky 2007. Here we will concentrate on the violation of requirement (2).

4   Internal semantic scope

When predicate-argument relations are discussed, it is usually presumed that both the predicate and its argument are lexical units – a lexeme or a multiword expression that functions as single unit.

The phenomena that we will discuss below require that lexical units be replaced by their semantic definitions, i.e. decomposed into simpler semantic units (=semantemes). We proceed from the assumption that, in the prototypical case, **if word A semantically affects word B, then the semantic definition of B should contain a meaning component for A to act upon.**

We will need not only the semantemes that make part of the lexical meaning but also those that originate in semantically relevant grammatical categories, such as tense, aspect, mood, number, etc. For example, the habitual meaning of the imperfective aspect in Russian (as in *On vstaet rano* 'He gets up early') is expressed by means of the predication 'situation P ['get up early'] takes place always or usually'. As we will see below, both lexical and grammatical semantemes can enter into predicate-argument relations with semantemes belonging to a different word, usually an adverbial or an adjective.

4.1 Temporal adverbials: *zavtra* 'tomorrow'

Let us begin with temporal adverbials such as *zavtra* 'tomorrow', *vo vtornik* 'on Tuesday', *vtorogo maya* 'on May 2', etc. All these expressions have a valency corresponding to the situation that is temporally located at the time interval specified by the adverbial. This situation is normally denoted by the verb to which the adverbial is syntactically connected. Let us look at (5):

(5) **I saw you tomorrow.*

This sentence is ungrammatical, and the reason is obvious: *tomorrow* places the seeing event in the future, while the past tense places it in the past. One can generalize this simple fact and predict that *tomorrow* cannot modify of a verb in the past. This generalization seems quite straightforward but still it is wrong. Cf. sentence (6):

(6) *Ja ždal tebja zavtra (a ty prišel segodnja).* 'I expected you tomorrow (and you came today)'.

It has the same grammatical and syntactic structure as (5), but nevertheless is quite acceptable. To explain this difference, we have to decompose the lexical meaning of *expect*. According to COBUILD, if X expects Y, X believes that Y is going to happen or arrive, because X has been told that it will. Now, it is clear that the event which *tomorrow* places in the future in (6) is not the top predication of the definition - 'X believes something', but the embedded predication 'Y is going to happen or arrive'. Hence, as opposed to (5), (6) contains no contradiction: the meanings of the past tense and of *tomorrow* apply to different events. The past tense is related to the internal state of the subject of expecting, while *tomorrow* characterizes the arrival of the object. We will call this type of valency filling INTERNAL SCOPE to convey the idea that the scope of the predicate is located inside the lexical meaning of some lexeme.

It goes without saying that this effect has nothing to do with specific properties of *tomorrow*. I have chosen this adverbial only to create a dramatic conflict between (5) and (6). As a matter of fact, the same behavior with respect to *expect* is inherent in any *when*-adverbial. On the other hand, *expect* is not the only verb that lets temporal adverbials penetrate its lexical meaning. Here are some more examples from Russian.

(7) *Ja na tebja zavtra rassčityvaju.*
 lit. 'I count on you tomorrow'
'I hope that tomorrow you will do what I am asking for'.

(8) *Ja priglašaju vas zavtra na obed.*
 lit. 'I am inviting you tomorrow for lunch'
'I am inviting you for lunch for tomorrow'.

(9) *V ponedel'nik menja vyzyvajut k dekanu.*
 'on Monday I am called to the dean'
    a) 'the call takes place on Monday'
    b) 'I have to come to the dean's office on Monday'

(10) *Poteplenie obeščali v konce nedeli.*
lit. 'warming was promised at the end of the week'
    a) 'the promise that the weather will be warmer was made at the end of the week'
    b) 'according to the promise, the weather will be warmer at the end of the week'

4.2 Temporal adverbials: *na zavtra* 'for tomorrow'

It is instructive to contrast adverbials of the type *zavtra* 'tomorrow', *vtorogo maja* 'on May 2', *v ponedel'nik* 'on Monday', etc. with the ones introduced by preposition *na* and an NP denoting localized time spans – *na zavtra* 'for tomorrow', *na vtoroe maja* 'for May 2', *na ponedel'nik* 'for Monday', etc.

(11a) *On priglasil ee na zavtra.*
'he invited her for tomorrow'

(11b) *Čto vy predlagaete na segodn'a?*
'what do you propose for today?'

(11c) *My dogovorilis' na ponedel'nik o vstreče.*

lit. 'we agreed for Monday on the meeting'
'we agreed that the meeting will take place on Monday'

(11d) *On navjazal nam na utro nikomu ne nužnuju poezdku.*
lit. 'he imposed on us for the morning a trip that nobody needed'.
'he imposed on us a trip that was to take place in the morning and that nobody needed'.

Both types of expressions (*zavtra* 'tomorrow' – *na zavtra* 'for tomorrow', etc.) seem to do the same job – they place an event in the same temporal interval but they are not perceived as synonyms and are rarely interchangeable. The difference consists in what event is being assigned a temporal characteristic. In sentences (11a-d) what is characterized temporally are not the acts of the invitation, proposal, agreement or imposition themselves, but the events that these acts imply – coming for a visit in (11a), proposed activity in (11b), a meeting in (11c) and a trip in (11d). These expressions mean the same but differ in their scope. Adverbials of the *zavtra* type usually have an external scope, and only in some cases discussed above can have an internal one. The *na zavtra* adverbials in sentences like (11a-d), on the contrary, have an internal scope and do not allow for an external one.

The range of the verbs that permit an internal scope interpretation of *na zavtra* adverbials is rather large and hardly intersect with the verbs with which *zavtra*-adverbials can have an internal scope. Some of the exceptions are *rassčityvat'* 'to count on' and *vyzyvat'* 'call'. In one of the interpretations, sentences (12a)-(12b) and (13a)-(13b) are synonymous.

(12a) <u>*Zavtra*</u> *možeš' na menya rassčityvat'.*
'you can count on me <u>tomorrow</u>'

(12b) <u>*Na zavtra*</u> *možeš' na menya rassčityvat'.*
lit. 'you can count on me <u>for tomorrow</u>'
'you can count on me tomorrow'

(13a) *On vyzval menja <u>v 3 časa</u> v ponedel'nik*
lit. 'he called me <u>at 3 o'clock</u> on Monday'
'he called me for 3 o'clock on Monday'

(13b) *On vyzval menja <u>na 3 časa</u> v ponedel'nik*
'he called me <u>for 3 o'clock</u> on Monday'.

That is why if a verb (distinct from *rassčityvat'*, *vyzyvat'* and some others) co-occurs with both types of adverbials, the phrases are not synonymous, because the adverbials have different scope; cf.:

(14a) *Čto on predložil na ponedel'nik?* 'What did he propose for Monday?' ≠

(14b) *Čto on predložil v ponedel'nik?* 'What did he propose on Monday?'

This also explains why *zavtra* and *na zavtra* adverbials are not perceived as synonyms, in spite of their semantic similarity and identical syntactic functions.

This description may raise the following objection: Do we really need to resort to such an exotic description as an internal scope? Why cannot we simply say that the verb *ždat'* 'to expect' and other verbs mentioned above have one valency more – that of the time of the internal proposition? In this case, phrases like *Ja ždal tebja zavtra* 'I expected you tomorrow' will display quite standard predicate-argument relations.

This solution could be valid, if it were only temporal adverbials that could scope over the internal proposition. But the range of such adverbials (underlined below) is much more diverse:

(15a) *My ždem ego <u>iz otpuska.</u>*
lit. 'we are expecting him <u>from vacation</u>'
'we expect him to come back from vacation'

(15b) *Kogda ždat' vas <u>k nam</u> (<u>v Moskvu</u>)?*
lit. 'when could we expect you <u>to us</u> (<u>to Moscow</u>)?'
'when could we expect you to visit us (to Moscow)?'

(15c) <u>*Nepremenno*</u> (<u>*objazatel'no*</u>) *ždem vas.*
lit. '<u>without fail</u> we are expecting you'
'we expect that you come without fail'

(15d) *Ja ždal tebja <u>s ženoj.</u>*
lit. 'I expected you <u>with your wife</u>'
'I expected that you would come with your wife'

(15e) *Ego <u>sročno</u> vyzvali k dekanu.*
lit. 'he was <u>urgently</u> called to the dean'
'he was called to the dean and must come urgently'

(15f) *Ego vyzvali v školu <u>s roditeljami.</u>*
lit. 'he was called to school <u>with his parents</u>'
'he was called to school and must go there with his parents'.

Obviously, all these adverbials cannot open separate valency slots in the verb meaning. Therefore, they can only have a circumstantial status and have an internal scope in the meaning of the verb.

We speak of an internal scope when a word semantically affects an internal component of the meaning of lexeme *L*. The capacity to have such a scope is mostly characteristic of adverbials and adjectives. Very often, this component is not difficult to find. For example, *kormit' (kogo-to)* 'to feed (somebody)' means 'to give food to somebody'. When adverbial *vkusno* 'tastily' is attached to this verb, its internal scope is obvious: 'to give tasty food'.

However, in many cases it is not that clear. As we stressed above, if word A semantically affects word B, then the meaning of B should contain a component for A to act upon. This requirement can be used in search of adequate meaning definition. Suppose we want to define the meaning of word B and see that it can be modified by A, which affects semanteme α. This is a serious argument in favour of including α in the definition of B. Let us illustrate this principle with the word *accent,* as used in sentences like (16):

(16a) *She spoke with a southern accent.*

(16b) *The man had a Spanish accent.*

(16c) *He can mimic the Georgian accent.*

We will use the definition from the Longman Dictionary of Contemporary English, which is very similar to definitions of other dictionaries:

(17) ACCENT: 'the way someone pronounces the words of a language, showing which country or which part of a country they come from'.

According to this definition, *southern accent* is interpreted as the way somebody pronounces the words of a language, showing that the speaker is from the South. This interpretation reflects the meaning of (16a) well enough. But if we try to apply this definition in other contexts, we will see that it is not sufficient. How should we interpret sentences that say something about the degree of the accent, such as (18a) or (18b)?

(18a) *He has a slight Essex accent.*

(18b) *She still speaks with a strong (heavy, pronounced) accent.*

Definition (17) does not contain any component that could justify quantifiablity of *accent*. What do we want to convey when we say that somebody has a slight Essex accent? Ob-

viously, not that the pronunciation of this person s l i g h t l y s h o w s that he/she is from Essex. Rather, we mean that, first, his/her pronunciation of English words (a) is typical for people from Essex, and second, is s l i g h t l y d i f f e r e n t from the standard. Similarly, (18b) means that the difference between the actual pronunciation and the standard is large. It is just the degree of the deviation from the standard that is characterized by degree adjectives, such as *slight* and *strong.*

Facing phrases such as *slight (strong) accent* makes us revise the definition of *accent* and introduce a component that accounts for its quantifiability. This component is the deviation from the standard. The deviation may be greater or smaller, but it is one of the semantic elements that constitute *accent.*

A definition that reflects these considerations can look like this:

(19) 'peculiarities of the pronunciation of person Y in language Z that distinguish it from the standard pronunciation of the speakers of Z and are typical for the representatives of language, group or region X'.

Examples: *French accent* (pronunciation typical for the French), *aristocratic accent* (pronunciation typical for aristocracy), *southern accent* (pronunciation typical for southerners).

4.4 *Edinstvennyj* 'the only' in the context of *syn/doč* 'son/daughter'

The standard interpretation of the phrase *edinstvennaja doč* 'the only daughter' implies that there are no other daughters, just as the phrase *edinstvennyj syn* 'the only son' means that there are no other sons. In these phrases, nouns *syn* 'son' and *doč* 'daughter' fill one of the valencies of *edinstvennyj* 'only' (Boguslavsky 2016). However, these phrases can also be used in a more general meaning – 'there are no other children'. For example, in (20a) and (20b) this is the most natural interpretation:

(20a) *K nemu prišla ženščina – vdova, – u kotoroj pogib edinstvennyj syn.*
'a woman came to him – a widow – whose only son was killed'
(20b) *Ego edinstvennaja doč i naslednitsa Varvara slyla odnoj iz samyx zavidnyx nevest Rossii.*

'his only daughter and heiress Varvara was reputed to be one of the most enviable brides in Russia'.

In the standard interpretation, the valency of the unique element is filled by the whole meaning of *son/ daughter:* 'there is nobody else that is a son/daughter (=an immediate male/female descendant)'. In (20a)-(20b) this valency is filled by only a genus proximum part of this meaning: 'an immediate descendant'.

Apparently, *syn* 'son' and *doč* 'daughter' are not the only words in which *edinstvennyj* can affect the genus proximum component alone. Cf. sentence (21a), which can be interpreted as 'there were no other pieces of seat furniture (not necessarily chairs, but also stools, arm-chairs, benches etc.)' or sentence (21b), which can mean that 'there was no more money (not necessarily roubles)'.

(21a) *On sel na edinstvennyj stul v komnate.*
'he sat on the only chair in the room'

(21b) *Ja istratil edinstvennyj rubl', kotoryj u menja ostavalsja.*
'I spent the only rouble left'.

4.5 *Tože* 'also' in the context of *po-moemu* 'in my opinion'

In Sections 4.1-4.4 we discussed cases when a valency of an adverbial or an adjective was filled by a part of the lexical meaning of a verb or a noun. Here we will deal with a case where both participants – the predicate and the word in which the predicate has an internal scope – are adverbs.

Let us begin with a two-place verb *X dumaet, čto Y* 'X thinks that Y'. There exists an adverbial – *po-moemu* 'in my opinion' – which is an adverbial realization of the predication *Ja dumaju, chto P* 'I think that P'. Due to this, sentences (22a)-(22b) may be regarded as synonymous.

(22a) *Ja dumaju, čto Real Madrid proigraet.*
'I think Real Madrid will lose'

(22b) *Po-moemu, Real Madrid proigraet.*
'in my opinion, Real Madrid will lose'

From the point of view of the argument structure, valency Y of *dumat'* is inherited by the adverbial and is expressed by means of the subordinating verb (cf. *proigraet* 'will lose' in (22b)). Valency X is incorporated in the mean-

ing of the adverbial and cannot be expressed along with it: *po-moemu, Y* = 'I think that Y'.

Now, let us take another adverbial – *tože* 'also':

(23) *Ja tože dumaju, čto Real Madrid proigraet.*
'I also think that Real Madrid will lose'.

Tože 'also' is a two-place predicate, too: *X tože P* = 'X is doing P; something or someone different from X is doing the same'. According to this definition, the meaning of (23) looks like this: 'I think that Real Madrid will lose; somebody else thinks the same'.

Now, we can introduce the key example: cf. dialogue (24a-b).

(24a) – *Po-moemy, Real Madrid proigraet.*
'in my opinion, Real Madrid will lose'.
(24b) – *Po-moemu tože, (Real Madrid proigraet).*
lit. 'in my opinion also, Real Madrid will lose'.

Let us compare (24b) with the synonymous sentence (25):

(25) *I also think that Real Madrid will lose.*

In (25), both valencies of *also* are filled (X = 'I', Y = 'think that RM will lose'). The same is true for (24b). Hence, one part of the lexical meaning of *po-moemu* ('I') fills valency X of *tože*, and another part ('think that') – valency Y.

5 Absorbing semantic scope

In this section, internal components will not act as a scope but rather as a predicate that has a scope of its own. In other words, we will be interested in the scope of the predicates that constitute only a part of the meaning of some word. From this point of view, of particular interest are meanings expressed by grammatical categories. We will speak about two such meanings: the habitual imperfective and the inchoative.

5.1 Habitual meaning

We have seen above (Section 2) that if the negation is part of the lexical meaning of word *L*, its scope cannot include circumstantials connected to *L*. However, aspectual meanings behave in a different way. For example, the habitual meaning of the imperfective aspect ('to take place always / usually') affects the whole predication formed by the verb and can easily involve its circumstantials. We can see that in (26):

(26) *Každyj den', pozavtrakav* [Perf], *Petya idet* [Imperf] *v školu.*
'every day, after having breakfast [Perf] Peter goes [Imperf] to school'.

The verb *zavtrakat'* 'have breakfast'(perf. *pozavtrakat'*) is in the perfective aspect and denotes a single event, while *idti* 'go' is in the habitual imperfective. Nevertheless, the situation that always takes place includes both events – the one expressed by the imperfective and the one expressed by the perfective.

The same is true for the negation. The verb *opazdyvat'* 'to be late' means 'to come later than is needed'. Sentence (27) with the habitual means that Peter always comes to school in time:

(27) *Petya ne opazdyvaet v školu.*
lit. 'Peter is not late for school'
'Peter is never late for school'.

Having noted this information about the habitual imperfective, we will turn to the adverb *počti* 'almost'. Let us give here a slightly simplified definition of *počti* than proposed in (Boguslavsky 1985, Wierzbicka 1987):

(28) *Počti P* = 'P does not take place; the difference between P and P′, which does take place, is very small'.

Let us compare sentences (29a) and (29b):

(29a) *Petr ne ošibsja v svoem prognoze.*
'Peter was not mistaken in his forecast'

(29b) *Petr počti ne ošibsja v svoem prognoze.*
'Peter was almost not mistaken in his forecast'.

Sentence (29a) means that Peter's forecast was correct, and (29b) – that it was almost correct, i.e. it deviated from truth very little. In other words, the SemScope of *počti* 'almost' in (29b) is 'not mistaken (=correct)'. Let us show it schematically:

(30a) not[mistaken in his forecast] = not[the forecast is not correct] = the forecast is correct

(30b) almost not [mistaken in his forecast] = almost not [the forecast is not correct] = almost [the forecast is correct]

Similarly, in (31) the SemScope of *počti* is 'was not left'.

(31) *Vremeni počti ne ostalos'.*
lit.'time almost not was-left'
'there was almost no time left'.

Now, let us put (29b) in the habitual imperfective:

(32) *Petr počti ne ošibaetsja v svoix prognozax.*
'Peter is almost not mistaken in his forecasts'.

In contrast to (29b), sentence (32) is ambiguous:

(32a) 'Peter makes very small mistakes in his forecasts, his forecasts are almost correct'
(32b) 'Peter makes mistakes (maybe quite serious) very seldom (almost never)'.

The first reading is a kind of habitual variant of (29b): 'every time Peter is making a forecast, it is either correct or almost correct'. The second interpretation is more curious. Here *počti* affects the aspectual component of the meaning ('always'): 'Peter is not always correct in his forecasts, but the deviation from "always" is very small'.

Let us summarize how the meaning of the verb is distributed among the scopes of the negation and *počti* in both interpretations of (32). In both cases, the negation affects the lexical component of *ošibit'sja* 'make-mistake', because, as mentioned above, its scope cannot include the aspectual component. As for *počti,* in (32a) it scopes over the combination of the negation with the lexical component, again, without affecting the aspectual component:

(33a) always [almost not make-mistake].

In (32b), on the contrary, its scope includes only aspectual meaning:

(33b) [almost always] [not make-mistake]

Here the aggregate meaning of the verb is "dragged apart" by the scopes of the negation and *počti*.

After distinguishing between two possible SemScopes of *počti* in (32), which account for the ambiguity of this sentence, it is easy to explain why sentence (34) is not ambiguous, although it has a verb in the habitual imperfective just as (32):

(34) *On počti ne xodit v teatr.*
lit. 'he almost does not go to the theater'
'he goes to the theater very seldom, almost never'

Theoretically, (34) can have two SemScopes, similar to (33a) and (33b):

(35a) always[almost not goes to the theater]

(35b) [almost always][not goes to the theater]

However, one of them – (35a) – is senseless: not-going to the theater cannot be quantified by 'almost'. This becomes obvious if we put (34) in the perfective aspect and thus exclude the aspectual SemScope – the sentence becomes anomalous:

(36) **On počti ne pošel v teatr.*
'he almost did not go to the theater'.

It is worth noting that *počti* can scope over the aspectual meaning only in the context of explicit negation. Sentence (37) cannot mean 'almost always makes mistakes':

(37) **Petr počti ošibaetsja v svoix prognozax.*
'Peter almost makes mistakes in his forecasts'.

Even implicit negation is not sufficient to support the 'almost never' interpretation. Sentence (38a) does have this interpretation, while (38b) does not.

(38a) *Petr počti ne sobljudaet pravila.*
'Peter almost does not observe rules'

(38b) *Petr počti narušaet pravila.*
'Peter almost breaks rules'.

5.2 Inchoative meaning

In Russian, there is a large group of verbs whose meaning contains the inchoative component. For example: *zasmejat'sja* ('begin to laugh'), *zatrepetat'* ('begin to tremble'), *zaigrat'* ('begin to play'), *zapet'* ('begin to sing'), *zasnut'* ('begin to sleep'), *zainteresovat'sja* ('begin to be interested'), etc. The meaning of inchoativity can be represented as follows:

P began =
(a) 'before moment t not-P was true';
(б) 'after t P is true'.

We showed above that an intra-word predicate cannot typically scope over the meanings expressed outside of the given word. Now we will describe some conditions in which this rule does not hold.

Let us consider sentence (39):

(39) *Zakončiv školu, Volodya vserjez zanjalsja politikoj.*
'after graduating from high school, Volodya was seriously engaged (lit. began to be engaged) in politics'.

The meaning of (39) consists of three components:
  (a) 'before moment t Volodya was not engaged in politics';
  (b) 'after t he is engaged in politics';
  (c) 'he is engaged in politics seriously'.

Component (c) has nothing to do with the scope of beginning. It is not part of the situation that did not take place before t and does take place afterwards. Now, let us move adverb *vserjez* 'seriously' to the Rheme of the sentence:

(40) *Zakončiv školu,* [*Volodya zanjalsja politikoj*]$_{Th}$ [*vserjez*]$_{Rh}$.
'after graduating from high school, [Volodya was engaged (lit. began to be engaged) in politics]$_{Th}$[seriously]$_{Rh}$'

The meaning of the sentence has changed. Now the sentence means that Volodya was engaged in politics even before t, but not seriously. The situation that did not take place before t and takes place after t is not simply 'engagement in politics' but 'serious engagement in politics'. Hence, component 'seriously', is included in the scope of 'begin'.

The situation is highly noteworthy: a rhematic component of the sentence «is absorbed» by the scope of an intraword predicate. Such a scope can be called ABSORBING.

6 Conclusion

The mechanism of valency filling (or discovering predicate-argument relations) is considered as the main instrument of combining word meanings together to obtain the meaning of the whole sentence. This approach requires that a broader class of valency-bearing words be taken into account than is usual. Predicates expressed by adverbs, adjectives and particles often fill their valencies in a different ways than verbs and nouns do. For this reason, it is expedient to generalize the concept of *actant* and introduce a broader concept that covers all types of valency filling irrespective of the way it is realized in the syntactic structure. This is the concept of *scope*.

The scope should be considered separately at the syntactic and semantic level of sentence representation, because fragments of syntactic and semantic structures filling the same valency may be non-isomorphic. We demonstrated two types of such non-isomorphism, which were called *internal* and *absorbing scope*. Of special interest is the interaction between the predicates expressed by lexical and grammatical means.

Acknowledgements

This work was supported by the RSF grant 16-18-10422, which is gratefully acknowledged. We are grateful to anonymous reviewers of the paper whose criticism helped us improve the presentation.

References

Yuri D. Apresjan. 1974. *Leksičeskaja semantika. Sinonimičeskie sredstva jazyka.* Moskva. Nauka.

Yuri D. Apresjan. 1995. *Izbrannye Trudy. Vol.* I–II. Moskva. Škola "Jazyki russkoj kultury".

Igor Boguslavsky. 1985. *Issledovanija po sintaksičeskoj semantike: sfery dejstvija logičeskix slov.* Moskva. Nauka.

Igor Boguslavsky. 1996. *Sfera dejstvija leksičeskix edinits.* Moskva. Škola "Jazyki russkoj kultury".

Igor Boguslavsky. 1998. *Sfera dejstvija načinatel'nosti I aktual'noe členenie: vtjagivanie remy.* Semiotika i informatika. Vyp. 36. Moskva.

Igor Boguslavsky. 2003. *On the Passive and Discontinuous Valency Slots.* Proceedings of the 1st International Conference on Meaning-Text Theory. Paris, Ecole Normale Supérieure, June 16–18.

Igor Boguslavsky. 2007. *Enlarging the Diversity of Valency Instantiation Patterns and Its Implications.* In: Lecture Notes In Artificial Intelligence. Logic, Language, and Computation: 7th International Tbilisi Symposium on Logic, Language, and Computation, TbiLLC 2007, Tbilisi, Georgia, October 1-5, 2007. Bosch, P; Gabelaia, D; Lang, J (Eds.) Springer-Verlag Berlin, Heidelberg, p. 206 – 220.

Igor Boguslavsky. 2014. *Argument structure of adverbial derivatives in Russian.* Proceedings of COLING 2014, the 25th International Conference on Computational Linguistics: Technical Papers, pages 1071–1080, Dublin, Ireland, August 23-29.

Igor Boguslavsky. 2016. *On the Non-canonical Valency Filling.* GramLex 2016, co-located with COLING 2016. Proceedings of the Workshop on Grammar and Lexicon: Interactions and Interfaces, pages 51–60.

Igor Mel'čuk. 1974. *Opyt teorii lingvističeskix modelej "Smysl – Tekst".* Moskva. Nauka.

Igor Mel'čuk. 2014. *Semantics. From meaning to text.* Volume 3. John Benjamins Publishing Company. Amsterdam/Philadelphia.

Anna Wierzbicka. 1987. *The Semantics of Quantitative Particles in Polish and in English.* In: Od kodu do kodu. Warszawa, s.175-189.

On the order of words in Italian: a study on genre vs complexity

Dominique Brunato and **Felice Dell'Orletta**
Consiglio Nazionale delle Ricerche
Istituto di Linguistica Computazionale "Antonio Zampolli" (ILC–CNR)
ItaliaNLP Lab
{dominique.brunato, felice.dellorletta}@ilc.cnr.it

Abstract

In this paper we present a cross-genre study on word order variation in Italian based on automatically dependency–parsed corpora. A comparative analysis focused on dependency direction and dependency distance for major constituents in the sentence is carried out in order to assess the influence of both textual genre and linguistic complexity on the distribution of phenonemena of syntactic markedeness.

1 Introduction

It is almost impossible to classify languages according to a unique, universally valid, metric of complexity. However, scholars agree on a set of properties that, at different levels of linguistic description, can be viewed as "universal" parameters of complexity across languages (McWorther, 2001; Ferguson, 1982). At syntactic level, this is the case e.g. of word order freedom, i.e. the property for which the order of elements in a sentence can vary while conveying the same meaning. According to different perspectives, free–word order languages are considered as more complex than fixed–order languages.

In linguistic and psycholinguistic literature, several explanations have been given to account for word order freedom. Information structure theory assumes that the order of words in the sentence is determined by semantic and discourse pragmatic forces (Diessel, 2005); conversely, for *performance*–related accounts unmarked structures are generally preferred by the speaker because of efficiency pressures and information structure becomes relevant only if two or more alternative orders are equally difficult to process (Hawkins, 1994; Gibson, 1998; Gibson, 2000).

Also from a Natural Language Processing (NLP) perspective, it is acknowledged that parsing free–word order languages is more challenging than parsing fixed–order languages in many respects. Based on a comparative analysis of Latin and Ancient Greek treebanks, the study of Gulordava and Merlo (2015) e.g. demonstrated that word order freedom, defined as the distance between the actual dependency length of a sentence and its optimal dependency, is a source of complexity which can be inferred both from lower parsing performance and from a trend toward more fixed word orders over time. Comparing the accuracy of dependency parsing on dative alternations in English, German and Russian, Dakota et al. (2015) showed that the larger the number of possible alternative orders to parse the more training data is needed. The effect of data sparsness on the automatic analysis of free word order language was also assessed in the study of Alicante et al. (2012) aimed at comparing the performance of constituency and dependency parsing on an Italian treebank.

In this paper we want to focus the attention on word order variation from a less–investigated perspective, aimed at assessing the influence of textual genre and linguistic complexity on the preservation of the basic (or unmarked) position of major constituents in the sentence, i.e. subject, object, adjective, adverb and subordinate clause. To this end, we carried out a corpus-based study for Italian – a Subject-Verb-Object (SVO) language – comparing the distribution of head–initial and head–final syntactic pairs across different textual genres and different language varieties, i.e. a "complex" one and a "simple" one for each genre, defined according to the expected target reader.

Differently from more traditional studies on word order variation in Italian e.g. (Fiorentino, 2009), this work relied on corpora automatically parsed up to the level of syntactic dependency annotation; this allowed us to carry out a broad comparative analysis of fine–grained features related

Proceedings of the Fourth International Conference on Dependency Linguistics (Depling 2017), pages 25-31,
Pisa, Italy, September 18-20, 2017

to word order variation according to genre and linguistic complexity, such us the average linear distance between the dependent and its head and the average depth of the syntactic tree of the dependent element, both in the canonical and non–canonical position.

2 Related Works

Syntactically annotated corpora have been promoted by several scholars as a valuable resource in the study of word order variation and related properties, especially from the perspective of language typology.

By relying on dependency direction as a typological index, Liu (2010) quantified the distribution of right- and left-branching constructions in 20 languages. Not only this study supported traditional typological classes with large quantitative data, but also provided evidence that a dominant order exists for languages left unspecified with respect to some grammatical relations (e.g. verb-object) in well-established classifications (Haspelmath et al., 2005). A similar methodology has been applied by (Liu, 2010), who conducted a comparative study based on 15 treebanks demonstrating that dependency direction is a reliable index to explain both the syntactic drift from Latin to Romance languages and to classify Romance languages as a distinct sub–group from other languages. In Futrell et al. (2015) a large cross–linguistic analysis was carried out using dependency treebanks for more than 30 languages; the comparative study allowed the authors to confirm the correlation between high order freedom and overt case–marking.

Word order variation is generally investigated together with the effect it has on dependency distance, i.e. the distance between words and their parents, typically measured in terms of intervening words. With this respect, data from dependency annotated corpora highlight that, when two or more alternative orders are possible, languages tend to prefer the order that reduces the distance between the head and its dependent (Gildea and Temperley, 2010; Futrell et al., 2015); this also holds when the examined span affects only few words, such as in the nominal domain (Gulordava et al., 2015). Such findings are thus proposed as a further demonstration that dependency length minimisation, whose effect has been widely documented in sentence processing (e.g. (Gibson,

1998; Gibson, 2000)), is a universal principle of human language.

In this paper, we want to investigate whether and to what extent word order phenomena in Italian are also influenced by textual genre. Similarly to the recent work by Liu (2017) for the English language, we focus on the two main syntactic parameters which, in a syntactic dependency paradigm, allow quantifying the effects of word order variation, i.e. dependency direction and dependency distance. The novelty of our study is that we introduce a further dimension of comparison, i.e. the level of complexity within genre, which was defined in according to the intended target reader; this was meant to assess whether some genre–specific stylistic features exist and how they affect word order properties independently from the level of complexity used in text.

In what follows, we first illustrate the corpora used in our study (Section 3) and the typology of syntactic patterns on which we focused to investigate word order variation (Section 3.1). In Section 4 we discuss the main findings of the comparative analyses carried out according to genre and linguistic complexity.

3 Data

As shown in Table 1, four genres were considered in this study: Journalism, Educational writing, Scientific prose and Narrative. For each genre, we collected two corpora, representative of a "complex" and a "simple" language variety for that genre, which were defined according to the expected readership.

The journalistic corpus is sub–divided into a corpus of general newspaper articles, *La Repubblica* (Rep), which is made of all articles published between 2000 and 2005 and a corpus of easy–to–read articles published in *Due Parole*, a monthly magazine written by linguists expert in text simplification using a controlled language for an audience of adults with a rudimentary literacy level or mild intellectual disabilities (Piemontese, 1996). The Educational corpus is articulated into two collections targeting high school (AduEdu) vs primary school (ChiEdu) students. For scientific prose, the "complex" variety is represented by a corpus of ~470,000 tokens of scientific literature covering various topics, e.g. climate change, linguistics, while the "simple" variety is represented by a corpus of Wikipedia articles of ~200,000 to-

Genre	Corpus	Tokens
Journalism	Repubblica (Rep)	232,908
	DueParole (2Par)	72,884
Educational	Educational materials for high-school (AduEdu)	47,805
	Educational materials for primary school (ChilEdu)	23,192
Scientific Prose	Scientific articles on specialized topics (ScientArt)	471,979
	Wikipedia articles "Ecology and Environment" portal (WikiArt)	204,460
Narrative	Terence&Teacher-original versions (TT orig)	27,833
	Terence&Teacher-simplified versions (TT simp)	25,634

Table 1: The corpora used in the study.

kens, extracted from the Italian Portal "Ecology and Environment". For what concerns the narrative texts, we relied on the resource described in Brunato et al. (2015), which was specifically developed for the study of automatic text simplification in Italian. The resource is made up of two sub–corpora, *Terence* and *Teacher*, representative of two different simplification strategies, the "structural" and the "intuitive" one respectively. Both *Terence* and *Teacher* contain two versions of the same text aligned at sentence-level, namely the authentic version of text and its manually simplified version targeting specific categories of readers. In particular, *Terence* comprises 32 short novels and their simplified version addressing hearing and deaf children, aged between 7–11, affected by text comprehension difficulties. *Teacher* is composed by 24 pairs of original–simplified texts, where the simplification was mostly carried out by a teacher for L2 students. To allow comparing the effect of linguistic complexity within this genre, we created a unique corpus of "complex" narrative texts (*TT orig*) containing only the authentic texts of both *Terence* and *Teacher* and a unique corpus of "simple" narrative texts (*TT simpl*), containing only the simplified versions.

3.1 Automatic Linguistic Analysis and Linguistic Features

All corpora selected for this study were automatically tagged by the part–of–speech tagger described in Dell'Orletta (2009) and dependency–parsed by the DeSR parser (Attardi et al., 2009) using Support Vector Machine as learning algorithm. DeSR is trained on the ISST–TANL treebank, which mainly includes articles from newspapers and periodical, and it achieves a performance of 83.38% and 87.71% in terms of LAS and UAS when tested on matching training data. However, it is well-known that the accuracy of parsers decreases when tested against texts of a different typology from those used in training (Gildea, 2001). Thus we can assume that the performance of DeSR will probably be worse in the analysis of texts representative of e.g. narrative and scientific writing. Despite this fact, we expect that the distributions of errors will be almost similar, at least when parsing texts of the same domain and language variety, thus allowing us to carry out a reliable internal comparison with respect to the examined syntactic patterns. In addition, the effect of genre variation on the performance of a general–purpose parser is likely to be less strong since all genres here considered contain *standard* texts, i.e. texts linguistically similar to the ones used in training.

4 Data Analysis

Based on the output of the multi–level linguistic annotation, all corpora were searched for relevant syntactic features, i.e. features related to the order and linear distance between the "dependent" element and its "head" in a syntactic dependency representation.

Specifically, we focused on the following elements: subject, object, adjective, adverb and subordinate clause. For each of them we calculated *i)* the percentage distribution in the canonical and non–canonical position (i.e. the position syntactically and/or pragmatically marked), according to the predominant SVO order in Italian, and, for each position, *ii)* the linear distance (in terms of number of tokens) between the element and the relative head.[1]

---

[1]For what concerns the subordinate clause, the linear distance is calculated as the average number of tokens between the POS of the root of the subordinate clause sub-tree and the verb of the main clause.

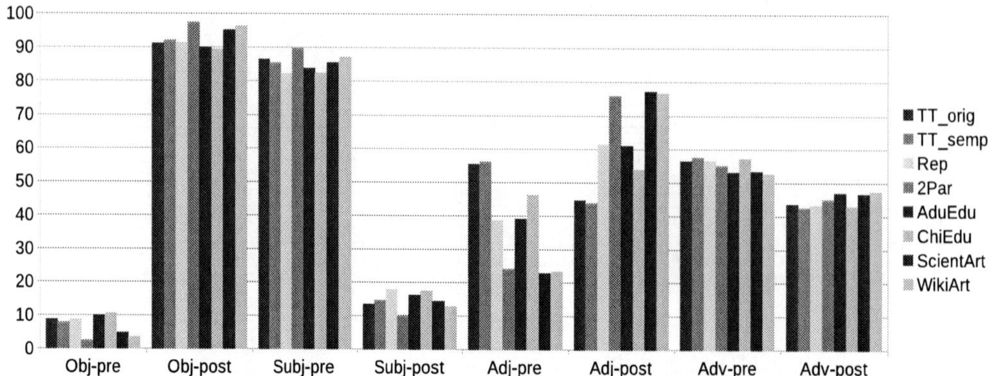

Figure 1: Percentage distribution of preverbal (Obj-pre) and postverbal objects (Obj-post), preverbal (Subj-pre) and postverbal subjects (Subj-post), prenominal (Adj-pre) and postnominal adjectives (Adj-post) and preverbal (Adv-pre) and postverbal adverbs (Adv-post) across corpora.

We also conducted a more in–depth study on subordination examining the following features: *iii)* the average length (in tokens) of the whole subordinate clause and *iv)* the average depth of the subordinate clause, calculated in terms of the longest path from the root of the subordinate sub–tree to some leaf.

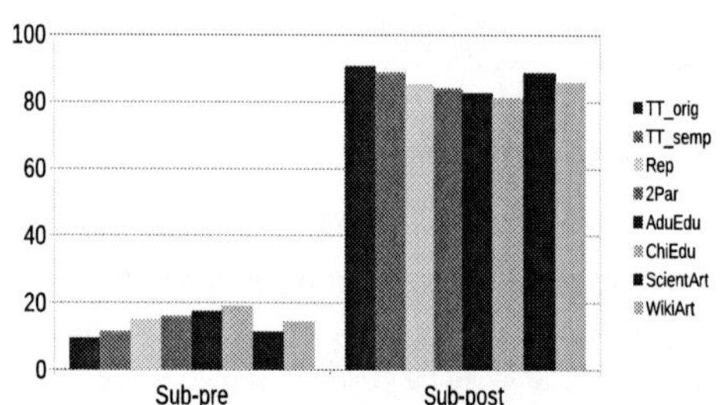

Figure 2: Percentage distribution of preverbal (Sub–pre) and postverbal subordinate clauses (Sub–post) across corpora.

Figure 1 and Figure 2 compare the percentage distribution of all the examined orders across the corpora. Let's analyse first the elements which, in all corpora, tend to occur more in their canonical position, i.e. the subject and the object.

With respect to the object, we observe that scientific texts adhere the most to the canonical order, independently from the complexity of text (ScientArt: post–verbal object: 95.14%; WikiArt: post–verbal object: 96.46%, p<0.05 [2]).; on the contrary, in narrative and especially in educational texts, the distribution of the unmarked object position decreases (AduEdu: 90%; ChiEdu: 89.33%, p<0.05). Interestingly, with the only exception of educational texts where the distribution of pre–verbal objects is almost similar in the two varieties (i.e. 9.99% vs 10.67%), all other genres show the expected positive correlation between canonical order and linguistic complexity; this is particularly evident in the journalistic genre, which reports a statistically significant difference (p<.001) of more than six percentage points with respect to the distribution of preverbal objects (*Rep*: 8.54%; *2Par*: 2.57%).

If scientific texts have a more rigid verb–object structure, they allow longer dependencies when the object follows the verb compared to all other genres (see the first two columns of Table 2). Such a finding is not influenced by the level of linguistic complexity within genre, since both the complex and the simple variety obtain almost equal values (∼ 2.70).

As in the case of the object, also with respect to the subject, the expected correlation between canonical SV order and the use of a simple language variety is particularly evident in the journalistic genre: indeed, texts belonging to *Due Parole* tend to preserve this order in almost 90% of cases, that is almost 7% more than their "com-

---

[2]Statistical significance of the difference is calculated using Mann–Whitney U test.

Corpus	Object				Subject				Adjective				Adverb			
	Pre-V		Post-V		Pre-V		Post-V		Pre-N		Post-N		Pre-V		Post-V	
	AvD	SD	AvD	SD	AvD	SD	AvD	SD	AvD	SD	AvD	SD	AvD	SD	AvD	SD
TT orig	-0.25	0.84	2.30	1.71	**-2.34**	2.24	0.57	1.67	-0.72	0.56	0.67	0.71	-1.53	2.41	0.81	1.90
TT semp	-0.21	0.8	2.25	1.58	**-2.01**	1.76	0.54	1.44	-0.73	0.58	0.63	0.66	-1.39	1.95	0.69	1.12
Rep	**-0.36**	1.43	2.56	2.22	-3.31	3.7	**0.88**	2.48	**-0.67**	0.73	0.94	0.84	-1.54	2.71	0.70	1.31
2Par	**-0.08**	0.42	2.39	1.61	-2.86	2.59	**0.51**	1.77	**-0.36**	0.61	0.96	0.60	-1.92	2.97	0.73	1.80
AduEdu	**-0.46**	1.64	**2.62**	2.20	**-3.23**	3.83	**1.09**	2.99	**-0.71**	0.65	**1.03**	1.28	-1.4	2.15	0.94	2.44
ChiEdu	**-0.26**	0.72	**2.35**	2.42	**-2.30**	2.3	**0.80**	2.17	**-0.66**	0.54	**0.91**	1.05	-1.59	2.3	0.74	1.08
ScientArt	**-0.33**	1.59	2.71	2.38	**-3.90**	4.27	**0.93**	2.86	**-0.52**	0.67	**1.12**	0.72	-0.52	0.67	0.97	2.71
WikiArt	**-0.20**	1.20	2.70	2.60	**-3.47**	3.72	**0.81**	2.67	**-0.5**	0.6	**1.1**	0.7	-1.5	2.79	0.91	2.30

Table 2: Average distance (AvD) and standard deviation (SD) of the Object, Subject, Adjective and Adverb with respect to the relative verbal (V) or nominal head (N). For values marked in bold, the difference within genre is statistically significant using Mann–Whitney U test.

plex" counterpart (*Rep*: 82,20%; *2Par*: 89,82%; p<0.01). On the contrary, both in narrative and educational texts, post–verbal subjects occur slightly more in the "simple" than in the "complex" variety, although the difference is statistically significant only for educational texts (*AduEdu*: 16.25%; *ChiEdu*: 17.61%; p<0.05).

For what concerns the narrative genre, it is worth noticing that the complex variety here examined is actually simpler than the complex variety of all the other genres; this is because the original texts of both *Terence* and *Teacher* are primarily written for a young readership. However, this finding should be more properly investigated in other corpora of the same genre because it might suggest that some marked constructions, such as post–verbal subjects, are genre–specific features allowing the writer to preserve the thematic progression in adjacent sentences and improve text cohesion. In this sense, such features are also maintained in the simplification process.

For what concerns educational materials, this is a heterogeneous genre comprising texts belonging in principle to different genres, ranging e.g. from fiction to scientific writing or reportage, thus making it difficult to detect the effect of language complexity.

Differently from the subject and the object, the order of adjectives within the nominal phrase is less rigid in Italian. Generally speaking, although the unmarked position of the adjective is post–nominal, it changes according to the semantic properties that the adjective carries with respect to the noun (Cinque, 2010). The relatively free ordering of adjective is confirmed by the empirical data obtained in this study, although the preferred

Corpus	Subordinate clause					
	Pre–verbal Subordinate Clause					
	AvD	SD	Length	SD	Depth	SD
TT orig	-1.27	(3.7)	1.17	(3.55)	0.51	(1.45)
TT semp	-1.1	(3.09)	1.01	(2.80)	0.50	(1.40)
Rep	-2.08	(5.60)	1.7	(4.51)	0.75	(1.83)
2Par	-1.85	(4.56)	1.4	(3.26)	0.71	(1.62)
AduEdu	-2.69	(5.72)	**2.34**	(4.96)	1.01	(2.07)
ChilEdu	-2.58	(5.36)	**2.05**	(4.19)	0.86	(1.73)
ScientArt	-2.64	(6.64)	2.15	(5.42)	1.00	(2.36)
WikiArt	-2.16	(5.60)	1.78	(4.69)	0.79	(1.91)
	Post–Verbal Subordinate Clause					
TT orig	3.01	(3.23)	**8.10**	(6.28)	3.91	(2.16)
TT semp	2.63	(2.56)	**7.04**	(4.88)	3.67	(2.19)
Rep	3.02	(3.91)	**10.33**	(9.89)	**4.49**	(3.12)
2Par	2.61	(2.51)	**7.26**	(6.70)	**3.73**	(2.47)
AduEdu	3.02	(3.68)	**11.11**	(11.04)	**4.57**	(3.32)
ChiEdu	2.63	(2.90)	**7.60**	(7.38)	**3.42**	(2.61)
ScientArt	**3.36**	(4.91)	**13.49**	(11.78)	**5.70**	(3.84)
WikiArt	**3.87**	(4.80)	**12.04**	(10.99)	**5.06**	(3.27)

Table 3: Average distance from the main clause (AvD), length and depth of the subordinate clause in the pre– and post–verbal position. For each parameter, standard deviation (SD) is reported. For values marked in bold, the difference within genre is statistically significant using Mann–Whitney U test.

position changes according to genres. Specifically, all but narrative genre prefer post–nominal adjectives, which is also the order that yields on average longer dependencies from the nominal head (see columns 6 and 7 in Table 2). When the internal distinction is taken into account, a stronger effect is reported by the journalistic genre, which shows a high statistically significant difference of almost 15% percentage points with respect to the distribution of post–nominal adjective (*Rep*: 61.31%; *2Par*: 75.82%; p<0.001).

Like the adjective, also the adverb has some degree of freedom in Italian since the unmarked position following the verb is quite flexible and influenced by the semantic class of the adverb (Bonvino et al., 2008). The analysis across corpora shows that the predominant position is always pre–verbal; interestingly, this order is never affected by the level of complexity within each genre.

For what concerns the subordinate clause, all genres exhibit a sharp tendency to place the subordinate clause after the main clause: in a SVO language like Italian, this is the ordering that allows the parser to recognize the constituents domains more rapidly and efficiently, as predicted by performance–based theories (Hawkins, 1994). According to this parameter, narrative texts appear as the easiest ones, since the post–verbal position of the subordinate clause reaches almost 90% both in the complex and the simple variety. On the other hand, educational texts deviate more from this order, showing a higher distribution of subordinate clauses preceding the main clause (*AduEdu*: 17.38%; *ChiEdu*: 18.89%). As expected, the greater complexity derived from placing the subordinate clause before the main clause affects the internal structure of the subordinate clause at different levels (Table 3): pre–verbal subordinate clauses tend to be structurally simpler both in terms of length (i.e. they are much shorter than post–verbal ones) and depth (i.e. pre–verbal subordinate clauses have a less–embedded structure).

5 Conclusion

We have presented a study based on automatically–dependency parsed corpora aimed at quantifying the influence of textual genre and linguistic complexity on the order of constituents in Italian. On the first side, we showed that the journalistic and scientific genre tend to preserve the basic order of constituents, differently from narrative and educational texts which exhibit a higher distribution of marked orders. On the second side, the expected correspondence between the use of a simple language and the preservation of more canonical word orders has been shown to be genre–dependent: it was mainly verified within the journalistic genre, whereas narrative and educational texts tend to preserve the non–canonical order of some constituents (e.g. post–verbal subject) also in the relative "simple" variety.

Current developments of this work go in several directions: one is to conduct a thorough analysis of the impact of errors derived by automatic linguistic annotation on the distribution of the examined linguistic parameters; another is to collect corpora distinct for genre and level of linguistic complexity in other languages in order to assess whether the effect of these variables on word order variation is also language–dependent.

References

Anita Alicante, Cristina Bosco, Anna Corazza, Alberto Lavelli. 2012. A treebank–study on the influence of Italian word order on parsing performance. In *Proceedings of LREC 2012*. Istanbul, Turkey.

Giuseppe Attardi, Felice Dell'Orletta, Maria Simi, Joseph Turian. 2009. Accurate dependency parsing with a stacked multilayer perceptron. In *Proceedings of EVALITA 2009 - Evaluation of NLP and Speech Tools for Italian 2009*, Reggio Emilia, Italy, December 2009.

Elisabetta Bonvino, Mara Frascarelli, Paola Pietrandrea. 2008. Semantica, sintassi e prosodia di alcune espressioni avverbiali nel parlato spontaneo. *La comunicazione parlata*, Massimo Pettorino, Antonella Giannini, Marianna Vallone, Renata Savy (Eds), Napoli, Liguori, 565–607.

Dominique Brunato, Felice Dell'Orletta, Giulia Venturi, Simonetta Montemagni. 2015. Design and annotation of the first Italian corpus for text simplification. In *Proceedings of LAW IX - The 9th Linguistic Annotation Workshop*. Denver, Colorado, Giugno 2015.

Guglielmo Cinque. 2010. *The syntax of adjectives: A comparative study*. In *MIT Press*.

Daniel Dakota, Timur Gilmanov, Wen Li, Christopher Kuzma, Evgeny Kim, Noor Abo Mokh and Sandra Kübler. 2015. Do free word order languages need more treebank data? Investigating dative alternation in German, English, and Russian. In *Proceedings of the 6th Workshop on Statistical Parsing of Morphologically Rich Languages (SPMRL)*, Bilbao, Spain, 14–20.

Felice Dell'Orletta. 2009. Ensemble system for part-of-speech tagging. In *Proceedings of EVALITA 2009 - Evaluation of NLP and Speech Tools for Italian 2009*, Reggio Emilia, Italy, December 2009.

Holger Diessel. 2005. Competing motivations for the ordering of main and adverbial clauses. *Linguistics*, 43 (3): 449–470.

Charles A. Ferguson. 1982. Simplified registers and linguistic theory. *Exceptional language and linguistics*, In Obler L.K. and L. Menn (eds.), New York, Academic Press, 49-68.

Giuliana Fiorentino. 2009. Complessità linguistica e variazione sintattica. In *Studi Italiani di Linguistica Teorica e Applicata (SILTA)*, (2), 281-312.

Richard Futrell, Kyle Mahowald and Edward Gibson. 2015. Quantifying word order freedom in dependency corpora. In *Proceedings of the Third International Conference on Dependency Linguistics (Depling 2015)*, 91–100.

Edward Gibson. 1998. Linguistic complexity: Locality of syntactic dependencies. *Cognition*, 68:1–76.

Edward Gibson. 2000. The dependency Locality Theory: A distance–based theory of linguistic complexity. *Image, Language and Brain*, In W.O.A. Marants and Y. Miyashita (Eds.), Cambridge, MA: MIT Press, pp. 95–126.

Daniel Gildea. 2001. Corpus variation and parser performance. *Proceedings of Empirical Methods in Natural Language Processing (EMNLP 2001)*, Pittsburgh, PA.

Daniel Gildea and David Temperley. 2010. Do Grammars Minimize Dependency Length? *Cognitive Science*, 34(2):286–310.

Kristina Gulordava and Paola Merlo. 2015. Diachronic Trends in Word Order Freedom and Dependency Length in Dependency-Annotated Corpora of Latin and Ancient Greek. In *Proceedings of the Third International Conference on Dependency Linguistics (Depling 2015)*. Uppsala, Sweden, August 24–26, pp. 121–130.

Kristina Gulordava, Paola Merlo and Benoit Crabbé. 2015. Dependency length minimisation effects in short spans: a large-scale analysis of adjective placement in complex noun phrases. In *Proceedings of the 53rd Annual Meeting of the Association for Computational Linguistics and the 7th International Joint Conference on Natural Language Processing*. Beijing, China, July 26–31, pp. 477–482.

Martin Haspelmath, Matthew S. Dryer, David Gil and Bernard Comrie (eds.). 2005. The World Atlas of Language Structures. *Oxford: Oxford University Press*.

John A. Hawkins 1994. A performance theory of order and constituency. *Cambridge studies in Linguistics*, Cambridge University Press, 73.

Haitao Liu. 2010. Dependency direction as a means of word-order typology: A method based on dependency treebanks. *Lingua*, 120(6):1567–1578.

Haitao Liu and Chunshan Xu. 2012. Quantitative typological analysis of Romance languages. *Poznań Studies in Contemporary Linguistics* 48(4), 597–625.

John H. McWorther. 2001. The world's simplest grammars are creole grammars. *Linguistic Typology*, 5, 125–166.

Maria Emanuela Piemontese. 1996. *Capire e farsi capire. Teorie e tecniche della scrittura controllata*. Napoli, Tecnodid.

Yaqin Wang and Haitao Liu. 2017. The effects of genre on dependency distance and dependency direction. *Language Sciences*, 59, 135–157.

Revising the METU-Sabancı Turkish Treebank: An Exercise in Surface-Syntactic Annotation of Agglutinative Languages

Alicia Burga, Alp Öktem
Pompeu Fabra University
Barcelona, Spain
`firstname.lastname@upf.edu`

Leo Wanner
ICREA and Pompeu Fabra University
Barcelona, Spain
`leo.wanner@upf.edu`

Abstract

In this paper, we present a revision of the training set of the METU-Sabancı Turkish syntactic dependency treebank composed of 4997 sentences in accordance with the principles of the Meaning-Text Theory (MTT). MTT reflects the multilayered nature of language by a linguistic model in which each linguistic phenomenon is treated at its corresponding level(s). Our analysis of the METU-Sabancı syntactic relation tagset reveals that it encodes deep-morphological and surface-syntactic phenomena, which should be separated according to the MTT model. We propose an alternative surface-syntactic relation annotation schema and show that this schema also allows for a sound projection of the obtained surface annotation onto a deep-syntactic annotation, as needed for the implementation of down-stream language understanding applications.

1 Introduction

Dependency treebanks are crucial for the development of statistical NLP applications, including sentence parsing and generation. To obtain good performance, well-defined and coherent treebank annotation schemas are needed. To provide an outcome that is good not only in quantitative but also in qualitative terms in the sense that it is well-suited for various down-stream applications, the annotation schemas must be equally rigorous from the linguistic viewpoint. Thus, given that different down-stream applications may start from structures of different abstraction or diferent nature, an annotation schema should strive to annotate phenomena of different nature at different layers or focus on just one layer. [1]

A conflation of different types of phenomena in one layer would make the annotation idiosyncratic and thus less appropriate for down-stream applications. In addition, in order to be appropriate for down-stream applications, an annotation schema should differentiate between different phenomena at the same layer. For instance, if a tagset uses just one label for two rather different syntactic relations (e.g., 'adjunct' for both indirect objects and preposition-governed circumstantials), it will not lead to a parse from which, e.g., a semantic role structure can be derived.

The linguistic model of the Meaning–Text Theory (MTT) (Mel'čuk, 1988) accomodates for both of the above needs: it foresees different layers of linguistic representation (each one encoding linguistic descriptions at a specific level of abstraction), and it offers a fine-grained analysis of the phenomena at each of the layers. Furthermore, it provides a theoretically sound framework for the projection of a structure at a given layer to an equivalent structure at the adjacent layer (which is very useful, again, for down-stream applications).

Nearly all available dependency treebanks annotate what in the MTT-model would be the Surface-Syntactic (SSynt) layer. However, given the multi-layer nature of a language model proposed by MTT (Sem ⇔ DSynt ⇔ SSynt ⇔ DMorph ⇔ SMorph ⇔ DPhon ⇔ SPhon), a SSynt annotation schema should accurately reflect all (surface-)syntactic phenomena of the annotated language **and** encode all information that is necessary to derive their equivalents at the DMorph and DSynt layers.

We address the task of the annotation of a Turkish corpus at the SSynt-layer in accordance with the principles of MTT. In order not to start from scratch, we draw upon already available resources.

---

[1] Note, however, that a specific phenomenon may receive different descriptions at different layers – as, e.g., *grammemes* (discussed in Section 2) are divided into semantic and syntactic grammemes (Mel'čuk, 2012a), and thus described at the semantic and (surface-)syntactic layers.

Proceedings of the Fourth International Conference on Dependency Linguistics (Depling 2017), pages 32-41,
Pisa, Italy, September 18-20 2017

For Turkish, two major treebanks are available: the METU-Sabancı treebank (Oflazer et al., 2003) ('MS' from now on), composed of 5635 sentences, and the IMST Turkish Dependency treebank (Sulubacak et al., 2016), which is an adaptation of the first one and contains the same number of sentences. In any case, until now the reference treebank for Turkish has been the MS (see, among others, (Çetinoğlu and Kuhn, 2013; Eryiğit et al., 2008; Eryiğit et al., 2011), etc.).[2]

The remainder of the paper is structured as follows. In Section 2, we discuss the separation of deep-morphological and surface-syntactic phenomena in agglutinative languages such as Turkish in general and analyze to what extent the annotation schema of the MS treebank complies with this separation. In Section 3, we present an alternative annotation schema, which respects the multilayered nature of language established by the MTT framework and allows subsequent transitions from surface to deeper layers. Section 4 outlines how this transition can be realized between the surface and deep-syntactic layers. Section 5, finally, draws some conclusions and sketches the plans for continuation of our work on MTT-based corpus annotation.

2 Annotation of agglutinative languages

As an agglutinative morphologically rich language (MRL), Turkish poses challenges to tools and annotation schemas broadly used for non-agglutinative languages with a simpler morphology. As Eryiğit et al. (2008, p. 2) point out, agglutinative languages such as Turkish raise the question about "to what extent our models and algorithms are tailored to properties of specific languages or language groups". In order to assess how and to what extent the common models and algorithms should be modified and adapted, we need to spell out the phenomena in agglutinative languages that are, in contrast to non-agglutinative languages, intertwined. In our task, these phenomena concern deep morphology and surface syntax.

2.1 Agglutination: SSynt vs. DMorph

Agglutinative languages are synthetic languages in which words consist of a base and a set of *agglu-*

tinated morphemes that modify the meaning of the base, each one separately in a predefined sense. In other words, each morpheme (whose boundaries are explicit) encodes a specific meaning, without undergoing context-dependent modifications.[3]

Thus, whereas analytical languages construct, as a rule, meaning through the grouping of words into phrases with a clear syntactic structure, agglutinative languages handle a good share of this process through the agglutination of morphemes; cf. a contrastive example in (1) and (2).[4]

(1) English (analytic):

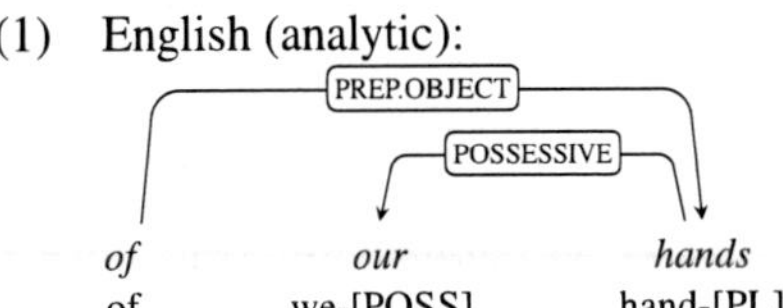

(2) Turkish (agglutinative):

> el   -ler   -imiz   -in
> hand   PL   POSS-1PL   CASE-gen
> 'of our hands'

From the viewpoint of a grammatical theory, a morpheme is the realization (or instantiation) of a specific *grammeme* or a specific *derivateme*, each as a separate element.[5] In Turkish, grammemes capture noun inflection (number, possession, case, and clause-type) and verb inflection (person, number, tense-aspect, voice, reflexivity, reciprocality/collectivity, causativity, negation, impossibility, auxiliarity); derivatemes encode noun derivation (from other nouns, adjectives or verbs), adjective derivation (from other adjectives, nouns or verbs), verb derivation (from other verbs, nouns or adjectives), and adverb derivation (from other adverbs, nouns, adjectives or verbs); see (Oflazer et al., 1994) for details. Instantiation of grammemes and derivatemes is a purely morphological procedure, which in the MTT-model is modeled at the DMorph-layer. Thus, in the syntactic structure, grammemes should be already attached to lexemes, with the information encoded by each

---

[3]Morphemes can be ambiguous in the sense that two different meanings can be encoded by the same form, but individual morphemes do not carry combined meanings.

[4]The names of the SSynt relations in the example do not belong to any SSynt tagset; we have just chosen them for the sake of the transparency of the principal characteristics of the corresponding relations.

[5]Since we deal here with syntactic and morphological phenomena only, we can define a grammeme as "an element of an inflectional category" and a derivateme "as an element that is formally expressed by the same linguistic means as a grammeme, but that is not obligatory and not necessarily regular" (Melčuk and Wanner, 2008).

---

[2]Most of the reported work has been done prior to the release of the IMST corpus. Note also that in the meantime some modifications of the original MS treebank have been made; cf. (Atalay et al., 2003). However, we use the original version.

of them stored as a feature-value pair assigned to the lexeme in question (e.g., *table* [number = PL]).

In the next subsection, we analyze the MS treebank annotation schema from the perspective of this phenomenon separation as well as from the perspective of the coverage of the individual syntactic phenomena.

2.2 Analysis of the MS tagset

Let us assess the MS tagset first with respect to its uniform treatment of morphological and syntactic phenomena and then with respect to its treatment of syntactic phenomena as such.

2.2.1 Uniform treatment of morphological and syntactic phenomena

The MS syntactic relation tagset has been designed to cover both (surface) syntax and derivational morphology, such that no separation in the spirit of an MTT model is given. To conciliate the inclusion of both derivational morphology and surface-syntactic phenomena at the same level of annotation, derivatemes are treated as independent nodes in the structure. The annotation thus contains the derivative and the base lexeme as two different nodes; consider, for illustration the codification of *davranışlı* 'behaved' in (3).

(3)   An example of the use of the relation DERIV in the MS corpus for the word *davranışlı* 'behaved':

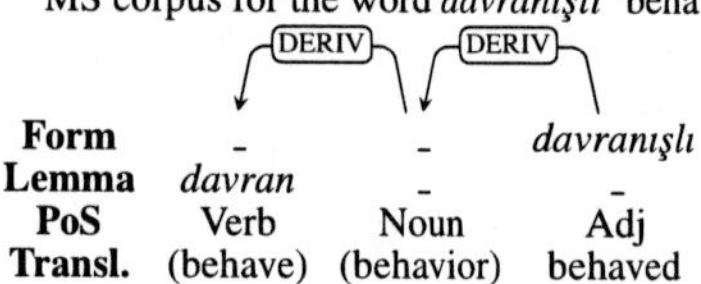

This practice leads to the appearance of extra lexical items in the annotation (the base lexemes do not materialize in the corresponding sentence(s) of the corpus), which are not present in the original corpus and which duplicate (or even multiply) specific meanings in the sentence; see also (Çetinoğlu and Kuhn, 2013). Such "artificial" lexical items that are introduced as auxiliary nodes to model a morphological phenomenon may even become the head of a syntactic relation (and thus also the root of a syntactic tree). As a consequence, the derivation of, for instance, a genuine semantic structure in the course of further analysis becomes a very tedious and unnecessarily complex task.

2.2.2 Treatment of syntactic phenomena

Apart from the problem resulting from the merge of DMorph and SSynt layers of annotation, the MS annotation reveals some issues that originate mainly from the underlying annotation guidelines and that affect directly the syntactic annotation. Let us go over these issues in what follows.

Vagueness in syntactic relation delimitation. The MS guidelines for the annotation of specific syntactic relations seem to be not sufficiently precise to ensure an unambiguous choice. Inconsistencies in the annotation are recurrent. For instance, from a total of 829 relations that take as dependent *bir* (unit that works either as an indefinite article or as a cardinal number), 738 are DETERMINER (not in all of them the unit acts, actually, as a determiner), 83 are MODIFIER, 4 are CLASSIFIER and 9 are SUBJECT (from these 96 cases, not always the unit has a cardinal number status). The remaining five cases are labeled as COORDINATION and S.MODIFIER. For illustration, compare (4) with (5).

(4) *bir* as CLASSIFIER:

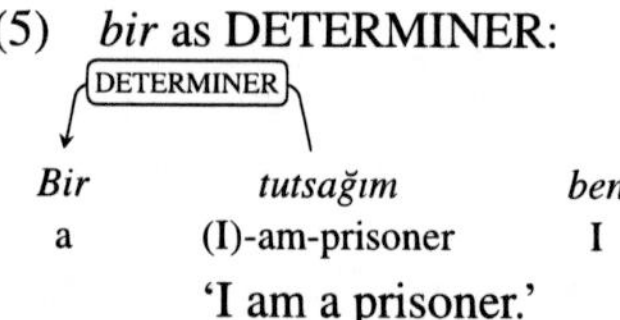

'I wanted to get away from it for a moment.'

(5) *bir* as DETERMINER:

'I am a prisoner.'

This vagueness also affects the distinction between specific relations (cf. ADJUNCT vs. OBJECT) or the overuse of some relations (cf. MODIFIER) as "default" relations. Thus, hardly any criteria are given to decide whether a verbal dependent is to be annotated as ADJUNCT (potentially further detailed by the case; cf., DATIVE.ADJUNCT) or as OBJECT. In the guidelines it is only stated that adjuncts are optional elements related to a verb,[6] and that objects are either nouns or pronouns. In cases like DATIVE.ADJUNCT, the only criterion to consider the relation to be ADJUNCT seems to be that the

---

[6] In the annotation, this condition is not always followed either: some elements related to a verb as ADJUNCT are obligatory, and in some cases, the head is a noun rather than a verb.

element must be in dative; consider, for illustration the relation between *baktı* '(he-)looked' and *bana* 'I' in (6). Obviously, the decision whether a relation is annotated as ADJUNCT or as OBJECT has important consequences for the projection of the annotated SSynt structures onto more abstract structures (such as DSynt).

(6) Object labeled as Adjunct:

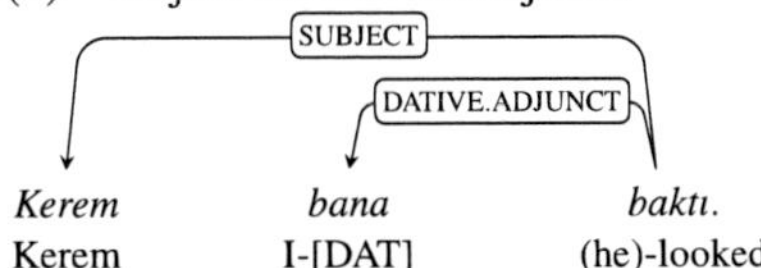

Kerem	*bana*	*baktı.*
Kerem	I-[DAT]	(he)-looked

'Kerem looked at me.'

MODIFIER is defined only with respect to the possible PoS combinations of the head and the dependent, which makes it impossible to understand or systematize the behaviour of the relation. Therefore, as mentioned above, it becomes a "default relation", overused across the corpus with very different morphosyntactic behavior among its instances, as can be observed in (7).

(7) Different MODIFIER uses:

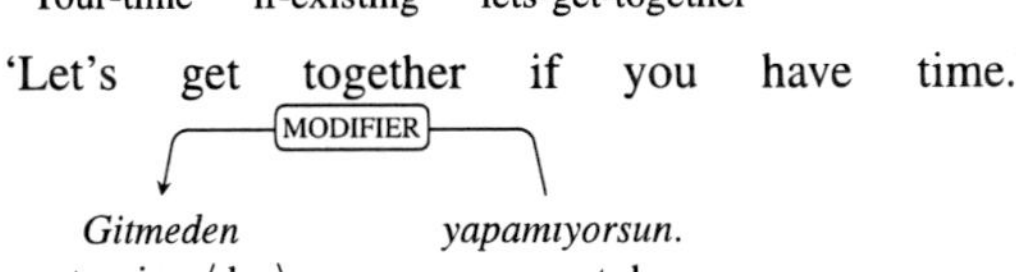

Kumral	*saçları*	*hafifçe*	*karışmıştı.*
brown	her-hair	slightly	(it)-was-messed-up

'Her brown hair was slightly messed up.'

Vaktin	*varsa*	*görüşelim.*
Your-time	if-existing	lets-get-together

'Let's get together if you have time.'

Gitmeden	*yapamıyorsun.*
not-going-⟨den⟩	you-cant-do

'You can't do without going.'

Vagueness in copulative construction annotation. To express what is known as a copulative construction of the type 'A is B', in Turkish special predicative forms of nouns and adjectives are common, in which the subject is directly linked to the predicate.[7] The predicate takes (beyond its own PoS and internal structure) verbal inflectional suffixes (person, number, tense) and becomes thus the syntactic head of the sentence; cf. (8).[8]

(8) Subject in a "copulative" (nominal predicative) sentence:

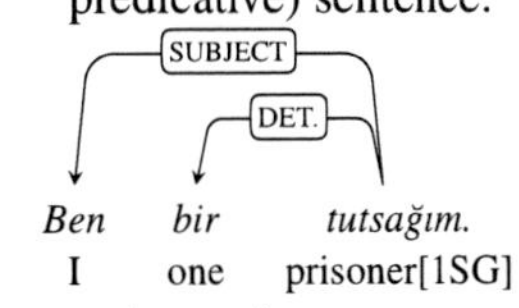

Ben	*bir*	*tutsağım.*
I	one	prisoner[1SG]

'I am a prisoner.'

However, significant syntactic differences remain between such nominal (and adjectival) predicative constructions and non-copulative constructions. Despite these differences, MS uses the same tag, SUBJECT, to mark the subjectival relation in both of them; cf. (9).

(9) Subject in a non-copulative sentence:

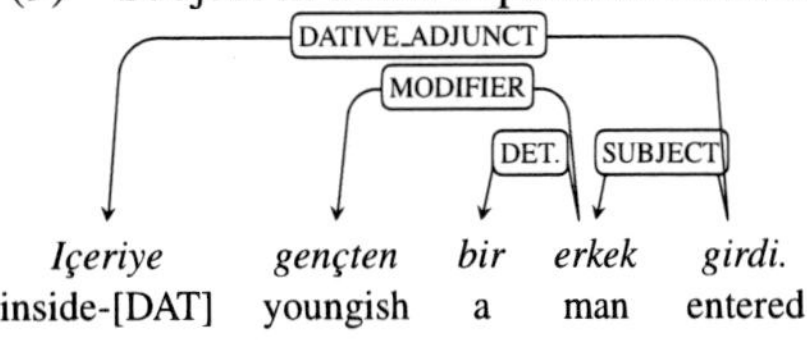

Içeriye	*gençten*	*bir*	*erkek*	*girdi.*
inside-[DAT]	youngish	a	man	entered

'A fairly young man entered inside.'

When negation comes into play (i.e., when we have a construction 'A is not B'[9]) the annotation is very inconsistent in the MS. Sometimes, the predicative element is considered head of the sentence, as in (10), and sometimes the negation element, as in (11).

(10) Negated copulative sentences:

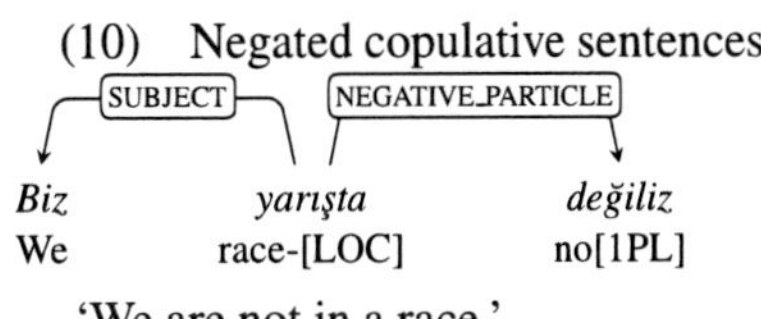

Biz	*yarışta*	*değiliz*
We	race-[LOC]	no[1PL]

'We are not in a race.'

(11) *değil* as ROOT:

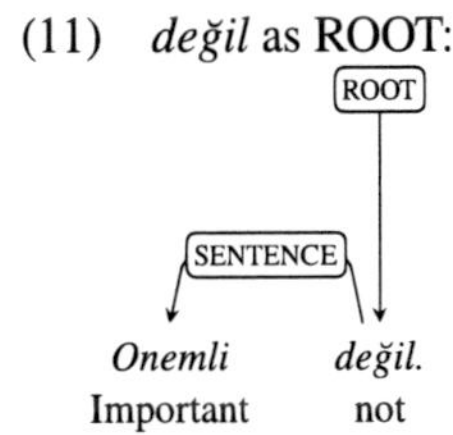

Onemli	*değil.*
Important	not

'It is not important.'

---

[7]According to the traditional grammar, the copula is expressed through the suffix *-dir*. However, the suffix is not really productive in modern Turkish.

[8]In order to keep the terminology simple, we continue to call those predicative constructions "copulative" (in quotes), although, strictly speaking, they are not copulative (Mel'čuk, 2012b).

[9]In the case of negation in a "copulative" construction, the verbal inflectional suffixes are taken by the negation element *değil*; cf. (10).

Indiscriminate annotation of _WH_-words.
Many times, just because they are included in
a question, the _WH_-words (_ne_ 'what'/ _hangi_
'which'/ _kim_ 'who'/ _kimin_ 'whose', etc.) are
linked to the verb through the relation QUES-
TION.PARTICLE, as in (12), which is the relation
used to link the verb with particles that take verbal
inflectional suffixes (when the questioned element
is the verb) and mark _yes-no_ questions. At least
two important problems arise from this annotation: (i) syntactic differences between the links
'verb–question particle' and 'verb–_wh_-words'
are ignored, given that _wh_-words can take case
suffixes (governed by the head) and question
particles cannot, and the first ones can only take
verbal inflectional suffixes in copulative sentences
(as any other noun), whereas particles take them
in any _yes–no_ question, if the questioned element
is the verb; (ii) the mapping to deeper levels
becomes truncated, given that the real syntactic function of the _wh_-words (e.g., OBJECT,
SUBJECT, etc.) is not annotated at the SSynt
layer.

(12)   _Wh_-word treated as question particle:

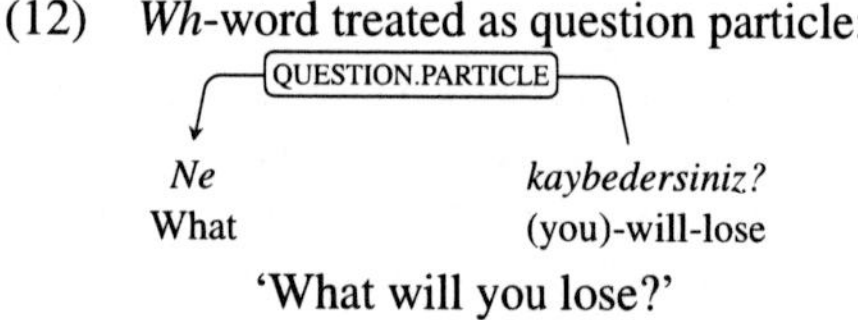

_Ne_   _kaybedersiniz?_
What   (you)-will-lose

'What will you lose?'

Inconsistent annotation of existential sentences.
Annotation of existential sentences (which are expressed in Turkish through attributive configurations with _var_ and _yok_, as in (13) and (14)) is not
unified: the attributee is linked to the existential
attributes either via the relation SUBJECT (13) or
via the relation OBJECT (14). Given that the syntactic characteristics of the relation between existential attributes and the attributee are always
the same, only one relation should be consistently
chosen. The chosen relation should depend on
whether the existing element shares its syntactic
behavior with other subjects or objects. If its syntactic characteristics are unique and exclusive, a
new relation should be created.

(13)   Existential taking SUBJECT:

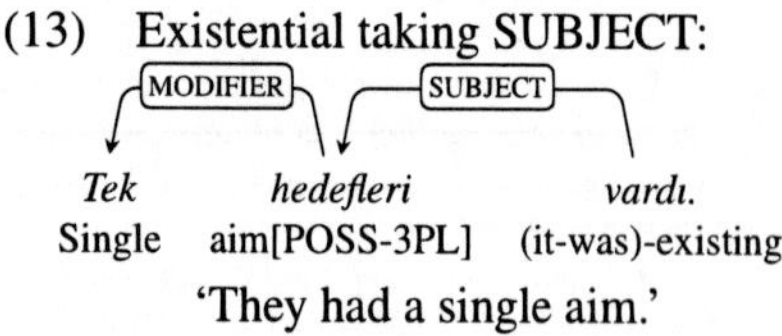

Tek   _hedefleri_   _vardı._
Single   aim[POSS-3PL]   (it-was)-existing

'They had a single aim.'

(14)   Existential taking OBJECT:

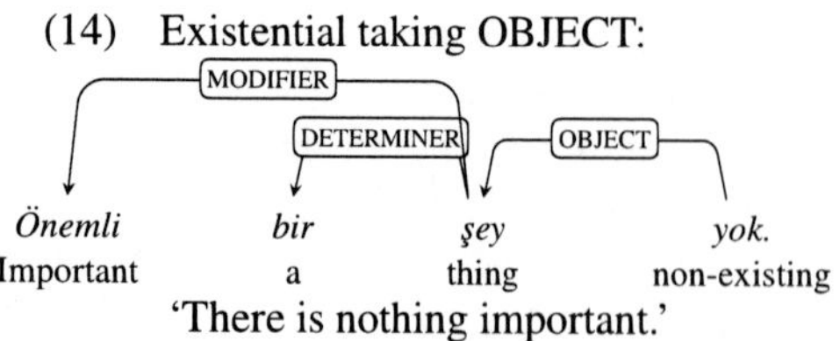

Önemli   _bir_   _şey_   _yok._
Important   a   thing   non-existing

'There is nothing important.'

3   Revising the surface-syntactic annotation of Turkish

The problems discussed in the previous section
and some others that were not touched upon due
to the lack of space made us revise the SSynt
annotation schema followed in the MS treebank,
with the MS' tagset as basis. The design of our
annotation schema follows the principles of the
MTT framework (Mel'čuk, 1988) and the methodology adopted for the elaboration of the annotation schema of the Spanish AnCora-UPF treebank
(Mille et al., 2013) and the Finnish weather corpus
(Burga et al., 2015).

The mapping of the original MS annotation into
our annotation was carried out in two stages; its
result is henceforth referred to as "UPF-METU
SSynt". In the first stage, general transformations
have been made. These transformations targeted,
first of all, the removal of the relation DERIV (encoding the corresponding morphological information in terms of morphological feature-values assigned to the corresponding nodes) and conversion of the relation SUBJECT into SUBJNOUN in
nominal and adjectival predicative ("copulative")
constructions. In the second stage, the outcome of
the transformation has been revised manually and
modifications discussed in Section 2.2.2 have been
implemented.

In parallel, a rule-based projection of the SSynt
annotation onto the deeper DSynt annotation has
been implemented. Both the original syntactic annotation of the MS treebank and the UPF-METU
SSynt annotation have been mapped onto DSynt
to validate the conversion of the MS treebank annotation into the UPF-METU annotation.

In what follows, we discuss first the initial transformation and then the modifications applied to it
in the second stage.

3.1   Removal of DMorph traces

As argued in Section 2.1, it is convinient and
cleaner from the theoretical point of view to separate the different levels of linguistic representation. Since the relation DERIV, included in the MS

SSynt tagset, relates the inflectional groups between each other and thus encodes a phenomenon that belongs to the DMorph layer (see Section 2.2), it needs to be removed from the SSynt tagset. For this purpose, the nodes related through DERIV are merged into one and the information of each node is stored in terms of feature-value pairs of the resulting node using a MATE graph transduction grammar (Bohnet and Wanner, 2010). As a consequence, an MS subtree such as shown in (15) is converted into a single node with many morphological features (as in (16)).

(15)   DERIV as SSynt relation:

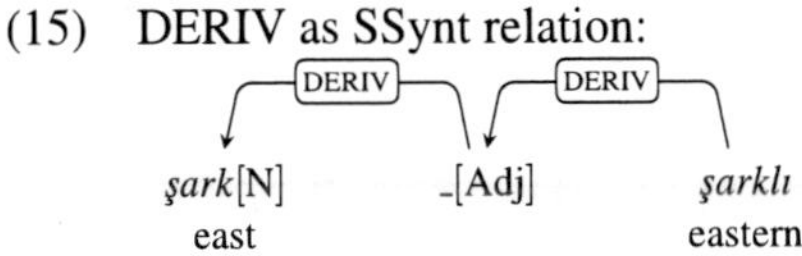

(16)   Morphological information related to DERIV:
şarklı

Attribute editor	
base	"şark"
case	"Nom"
case_deriv_2	"Nom"
deriv_step	"last"
hypernode	"yes"
id_metu	"5"
id_ssynt_upf	"3.0"
id1_orig_metu	"5"
id2_orig_metu	"4"
id3_orig_metu	"3"
lemma	"şarklı"
orig_id_metu_gov	"0"
orig_ssynt_rel	"ROOT"
own_pers_num	"A3sg"
own_pers_num_deriv_2	"A3sg"
pos	"Zero"
pos_deriv_1	"Adj"
pos_deriv_2	"Noun"
poss_pers_num	"Pnon"
poss_pers_num_deriv_2	"Pnon"
rel_noun_orig_deriv_1	"With"
slex	"şarklı"

A consequence of this transformation is that the resulting single node becomes the head of the SSyntRels that before were defined between the different nodes related through DERIV, which inevitably results in a relaxation of the head restrictions for each relation (in that relations that prototypically were headed by nouns can after the merge be headed by a lexeme with anothr PoS). In this regard, the second stage of the conversion (manual revision of relations) needs to put special attention to sentences in which automatic transformations applied, and the annotator decisions need to take into account the nature of the originally encoded derivations.

3.2   Making changes to syntactic annotations

In this subsection, we outline how the MS SSynt tagset has been revised in order to account for the issues identified in Section 2.2.2. The updated tagset contains 21 relations summarized in Table 1 at the end of this subsection.

Addressing the vagueness in syntactic relation delimitation.   According to the MTT principles, it is crucial to distinguish between adjuncts and objects in SSynt, given that each of them maps to different relations in deeper layers. Therefore, in order to distinguish between the relations ADJUNCT and OBJECT in the case of a verbal head, we consult the case suffix added to the dependent and the analysis of the meaning of the verb. In MTT, the case of objects is governed by the verbal head, while the case of adjuncts is determined by the type of information these adjunts convey. The adjuncts in Turkish can take dative,[10] locative, ablative, instrumental, or equative suffixes. Objects, on the other hand, most of the times take either accusative or nominative,[11] and they can promote (become subjects in passive sentences). Although dative, ablative or instrumental case is also possible, it is more seldom. Which case it actually is depends on lexical restrictions of each verb, which are assumed as intuitively known by native speakers of Turkish. Also, those verbs that require "nonstandard" objects cannot passivize through promotion of their objects, and do not admit adjuncts carrying the same case. Thus, our analysis of (6) would be as shown in (17).

(17)   Object with dative case:

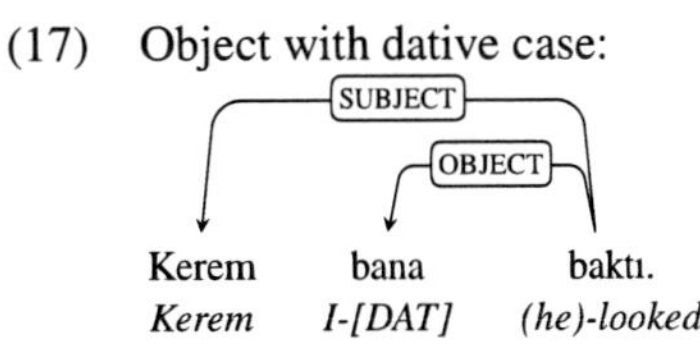

'Kerem looked at me.'

In order to sharpen the definition of MODIFIER, we draw upon the conditions established in MTT for the presence of a SSynt relation. According to these conditions a SSynt relation between two lexical items is present if (i) the position of one of the items in the sentence is established

---

[10]Even though adjuncts taking dative are uncommon – as one of the reviewers pointed out, and which is confirmed by the fact that in traditional Turkish grammar, nominal phrases in dative are always considered objects – we argue that they exist.

[11]Objects in nominative are also unusual, but they also exist, as in *Çiçek aldım*, lit. flower [nom] buy[1SG, past] 'I bought a flower.' In any case, we take the information about cases as it is included in MS. If this information is incorrect, we do not correct it.

with respect to the other item; (ii) the two lexical items have a prosodic link that connects them; or (iii) one item imposes agreement on the other item. The new relation MODIFIER that shall substitute the original MS MODIFIER has been defined as a repeatable relation, in which the dependent is not verbal, there is no agreement between the head and the dependent, the dependent always appears to the left of the head, and the head and the dependent are adjacent.[12] Thus, from the examples of MODIF in 7, the only ones that are kept as MODIFIER are those in (7a), repeated here as (18).

(18)   Restricted MODIF:

Kumral   *saçları*   *hafifçe*   *karışmıştı.*
brown   her-hair   slightly   (it)-was-messed-up
"Her brown hair was slightly messed up."

Addressing the vagueness in copulative construction annotation. Given that subjects in predicative nominal and adjectival (what we called "copulative") and non-copulative constructions have different properties regarding agreement, and agreement is one of the criteria used for differentiating SSynt relations in the MTT model, we have decided to distinguish between "typical" subjects (in which the head is a conjugated verb) from subjects in "copulative" sentences (in which the head is, strictly speaking, not a conjugated verb), we have created the relation SUBJNOUN; cf. (19) for illustration. Whereas SUBJECT implies agreement with the head in both person and number, SUBJNOUN does it obligatorily with person and optionally with number.

(19)   Treatment of subjects in nominal predicative ("copulative") constructions:

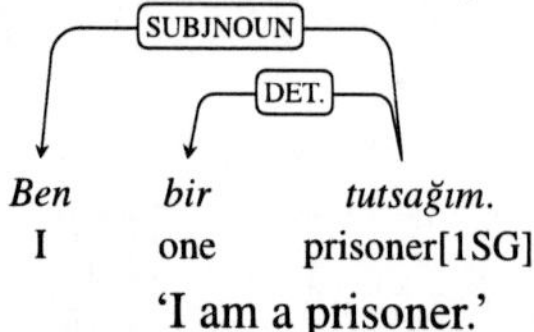

Ben   *bir*   *tutsağım.*
I   one   prisoner[1SG]
'I am a prisoner.'

"Copulative" constructions that contain negation are treated in the same way as those without negation, but the particle *değil* is linked to the negated element through the relation NEGATIVE_PARTICLE, even if, in "copulative" con-

structions, it takes the inflectional suffixes; cf. (20).[13]

(20)   "Copulative" constructions with negation:

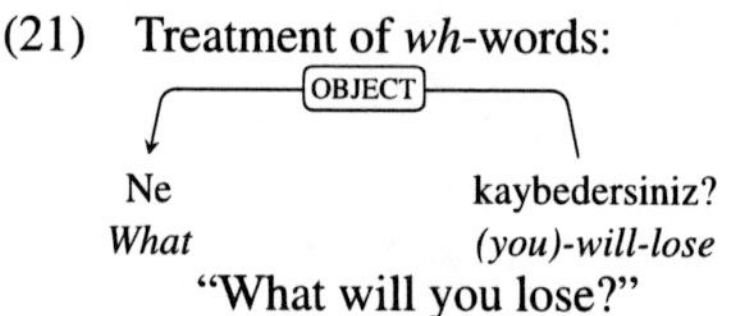

Onemli   *değil*
Important   not
'It is not important.'

Addressing the indiscriminate annotation of *WH*-words. Regarding the treatment of *wh*-words, the adapted SSynt tagset restricts the relation QUESTION.PARTICLE to those cases in which the dependent is the particle *mA*, which indicates *yes-no* questions (taking into account the prosodic link between elements involved in the relation). The governor is the element that is questioned and always appears to the right before the particle. This relation, then, always goes from left to right and its members are adjacent. If the questioned element is the verb (as the head of QUESTION.PARTICLE), the particle is conjugated. On the other hand, *wh*-words are labeled according to their syntactic similarity with other relations, without taking into account their PoS. Thus, the suggested annotation of (12) is as shown in (21).

(21)   Treatment of *wh*-words:

Ne   kaybedersiniz?
What   *(you)-will-lose*
"What will you lose?"

Addressing the inconsistent annotation of existential sentences. Existential sentences are treated as a subset of copulative sentences in which the attributive element is either the adjective *var* 'existing' or the adjective *yok* 'non-existing' Thus, the relation connecting these elements with the existing element is SUBJNOUN, as illustrated in (22).

---

[12]This adjacency is broken in those cases in which the same head governs more than one MODIFIER relation.

[13]One of the reviewers questioned the correctness of this analysis, given that Turkish is a strong head-final language. Although we have kept our initial proposal, in the near future, it will be necessary to evaluate which analysis (the one that prioritizes the head-final property, or the one in which the parallel treatment of affirmative and negative copulative sentences is followed) prevails.

(22) Existential taking SUBJNOUN:

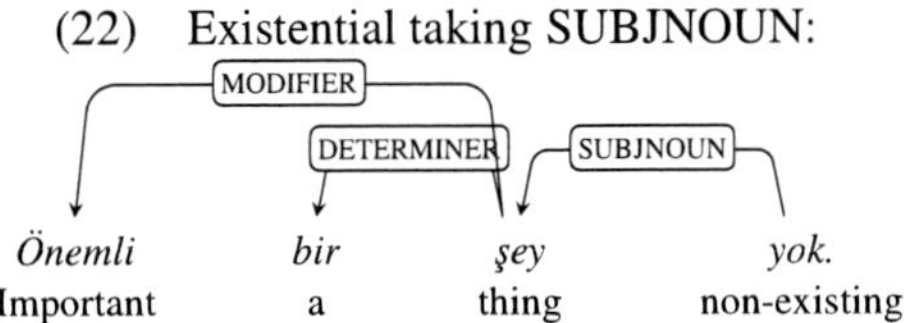

Önemli	*bir*	*şey*	*yok.*
Important	a	thing	non-existing

'There is nothing important.'

4 Projecting SSynt Structures onto Deeper Levels of Annotation

The challenge of the SSynt annotation schema design is not only to cover the syntactic phenomena of a specific language, but also to facilitate an appropriate projection to deeper levels, in our case DSynt. In contrast to the SSynt tagset, the DSynt tagset is language-independent. It is composed of the argumental relations I, II, III, IV, V, VI, and the non-argumental relations ATTR, APPEND and COORD(INATION); cf. also (Mel'čuk, 1988) An example of a DSynt tree of a sample from MS corpus is shown in 23.[14]

In total, 122 rules that map specific SSynt relations in specific configurations onto DSynt relations were created. The mapping resulted in well-formed DSynt trees, whose relations (participants as well as labels) are being manually corrected, in parallel to SSynt structures.

(23) Example of a DSynt structure:

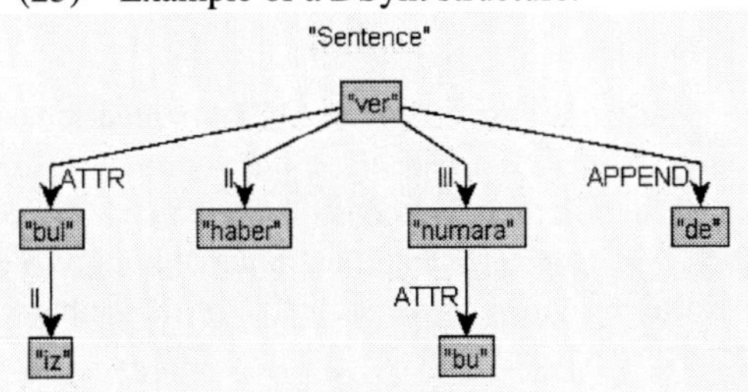

İzini	*bulursanız,*	*bu*	*numaraya*	*haber*	*verirsiniz,*	*dedi.*
iz	*bul*	*bu*	*numara*	*haber*	*ver*	*de*
his-trace	if-you-find	this	number	notice	you'd-give	he-said

'If you find his trace, you'll notify this number, he said.'

In what follows, we discuss how the issues that we identified with the original MS treebank inevitably have negative consequences for the projection of SSynt structures to DSynt structures, and how the revision offered in our proposal helps obtain a better SSynt-DSynt mapping.

First of all, the relation DERIV (that should be encoded within DMorph, as discussed in Section

---

[14]For details about the differences between SSynt and DSynt structures, see, for instance, (Burga et al., 2015).

Table 1: Dependency relations used after adaptation of the Turkish surface-syntactic layer

DepRel	Distinctive properties
adjunct	non-required element; non NOM/ACC case
apposition	for clarification; right-sided for nouns, left-sided for statements
classifier	noun modifying another noun; case NOM; left-sided relation
collocation	relates base and collocation
coordination	links coordinated elements or the 1st coordination member with the coord. Conj
coord_conj	complement of a coord Conj
determiner	non-repeatable left-side modifier of an N
intensifier	particles emphasizing the head; right-side relation
juxtaposition	for linking unrelated groups
modifier	non-required modifying element; no case taken left-sided relation
neg_particle	right-sided relation between the negated element and the particle *değil*
object	required element. It takes NOM and ACC most times, but can take DAT, ABL, INSTR
possessor	links possessed thing (in genitive case) and possessor (with possessive suffix)
punc	for punctuation signs
quasi_subj	relates object and subject of an ommited verb
ques_particle	links questioned element and question particle *mI*
relativizer	links a verb-based element to the subordinating elements *de/da* and *ki*
s_modifier	acts as a sentential adjunct; left-sided relation
subject	unrepeatable verbal dependent that controls number and person; takes NOM case
subjnoun	subjects in copulative sentences; agreement only in person
vocative	element marking the addressee; always in NOM; at the beginning or end of sentence

3.1) would lead to spurious nodes in the DSynt structure, which have absolutely no theoretical or practical justification. Obviously, auxiliary measures during the projection can be implemented in order to avoid the introduction of such spurious nodes, but this would mean a cumbersome and unnecessarily complex projection. Second, even if it is not always possible to map a SSynt relation to just one DSynt relation, the SSynt tagset should at least drastically limit the mapping options. This is why the lack of syntactic criteria when defining a tagset also generates problems for the projection of a SSynt structure to a DSynt structure.

The inconsistency in annotation, as well as the use of the same relation for pairs that behave syntactically different (see below), decreases the quality of DSynt structures (e.g., the above-discussed argument–adjunct confusion). In this sense, our attempt to restrict the syntactic characteristics of each SSyntRel serves not only the SSynt layer itself, but also to the corresponding DSynt layer.

As far as the structures of nominal / adjectival predicative (what we called "copulative") and noncopulative sentences are concerned, at the DSynt layer, their structures become homogenized since both receive a verbal root; in the case of the "copulative" construction, the subject is the first argument of the root and the predicative element its second; see (24) for illustration.

(24) DSynt tree of a adjectival predicative ("copulative") construction:

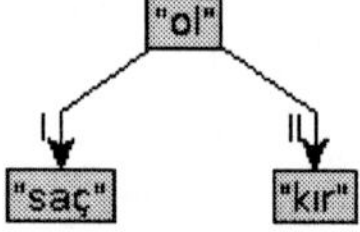

Saçları   kır.
saç   ol   kır.
hair   be   gray
"Her hair is gray."

Given that Turkish is a pro-drop language, the mapping of SSynt structures to DSynt structures introduces a subject node when it is absent in SSynt (acting as the first argument of the verbal root). This node contains the morphological features that allow agreement.

5 Summary and Future Work

In this paper, we first briefly analyzed the manifestation of morphological and (surface) syntactic phenomena in agglunitative languages such as Turkish, arguing (in accordance with the Meaning–Text Theory) that both should be described separately at different layers of the linguistic model, namely at the D(eep)Morp(logical) and S(urface)Synt(actic) layers. With the MTT model in mind, we studied the annotation schema of the MS Turkish treebank, which does not make this separation, and identified some issues that result from the uniform treatment of morphological and syntactic phenomena or from the MS-specific treatment of some syntactic phenomena. Then, we presented an MTT-based schema annotation for the SSynt of Turkish. This schema has been followed to convert the original MS annotation of the training set of the MS treebank (4997 sentences) into an MTT-affine annotation. The conversion has been carried out in two stages. In the first stage, a number of regular transformations was applied via graph transducer rules (Bohnet and Wanner, 2010). In the second stage, the automatically obtained annotation in the first stage was revised manually. Tests show that the MTT-affine annotation allows us not only to get higher quality SSynt structures, but also to derive from these SSynt structures an additional more abstract level of annotation, namely that of DSynt. As a result, downstream NLP applications that must rely upon more semantically-oriented linguistic representations can use different levels of the same annotated treebank.

The goal is to offer the MTT-oriented annotation of the MS treebank to the community. Depending on the legal constraints, which still need to be clarified, we count on being able to provide it shortly either on the webpage of the authors of the original MS treebank (`https://web.itu.edu.tr/gulsenc/treebanks.html`) or on our webpage `https://www.upf.edu/web/taln/resources`.

In the future, we plan to carry out an evaluation of parser performance when trained on the original MS-annotated treebank and on the revised treebank. Even if the size of the training treebanks is small, we expect to see clear differences. We also plan to explore how the morphological information that corresponds to the eliminated relation DERIV and the nodal feature values that specify the type of derivation should be structured, stored in DMorph structures and exploited in sentence analysis and generation tasks. In this context, it is to be noted that morphological analysis in Turkish is a real challenge due to the ambiguity of derivational suffixes themselves and also due to the ambiguity of their combination. Thus, for instance, the morphological analysis of *yarının* using the TRMorph (Çöltekin, 2010) gives us 40 possibilities of analysis, the first three having different roots (25):[15]

   (25)   Morphological analysis of *yarının*:
        yarı<Adj><0><N><gen> 'of the half'
        yarın<N><gen> 'of tomorrow'
        yar<N><p3s><gen> 'his lover's'

According to one of the reviewers, in the original MS treebank the morphological disambiguation has been done manually.

Acknowledgements

The presented work has been funded by the European Commission as part of the H2020 Programme, under the contract numbers 645012–RIA and 700024-RIA. Many thanks to the three anonymous reviewers for their detailed comments that helped us improve the paper considerably.

References

Nart B. Atalay, Kemal Oflazer, Bilge Say, and Informatics Inst. 2003. The Annotation Process in the Turkish Treebank. In *Proc. of the 4th Intern. Workshop on Linguistically Interpreteted Corpora (LINC)*.

B. Bohnet and L. Wanner. 2010. Open Source Graph Transducer Interpreter and Grammar Development Environment. In *Proceedings of the International Conference on Linguistic Resources and Evaluation (LREC)*.

Alicia Burga, Simon Mille, Anton Granvik, and Leo Wanner. 2015. Towards a multi-layered dependency annotation of Finnish. In *Proceedings of the Third International Conference on Dependency Linguistics (Depling 2015)*, pages 48–57, August.

Özlem Çetinoğlu and Jonas Kuhn. 2013. Towards Joint Morphological Analysis and Dependency Parsing of Turkish. In *Proceedings of the Second International Conference on Dependency Linguistics (DepLing 2013)*, pages 23–32, August.

Çağrı Çöltekin. 2010. A Freely Available Morphological Analyzer for Turkish. In *Proceedings of the 7th International Conference on Language Resources and Evaluation (LREC 2010)*, pages 820–827.

Gülşen Eryiğit, Joakim Nivre, and Kemal Oflazer. 2008. Dependency parsing of Turkish. *Computational Linguistics*, 34(3):357–389.

Gülşen Eryiğit, Tugay İlbay, and Ozan Arkan Can. 2011. Multiword expressions in statistical dependency parsing. In *Proceedings of the Second Workshop on Statistical Parsing of Morphologically Rich Languages*, SPMRL '11, pages 45–55, Stroudsburg, PA, USA. Association for Computational Linguistics.

Igor Melčuk and Leo Wanner. 2008. Morphological mismatches in machine translation. *Machine translation*, 22(3):101–152.

Igor Mel'čuk. 1988. *Dependency Syntax: Theory and Practice*. State University of New York Press, Albany.

Igor Mel'čuk. 2012a. *Semantics, Volume 1*. John Benjamins Publishing Company, Amsterdam.

Igor Mel'čuk. 2012b. Syntax. Bi-nominative sentences in Russian. In V. Makarova, editor, *Russian Language Studies in North America: New Perspectives from Theoretical and Applied Linguistics*, pages 86–105. Anthem Press, London.

Simon Mille, Alicia Burga, and Leo Wanner. 2013. AnCora-UPF: A multi-level annotation of Spanish. In *Proceedings of DepLing*, Prague, Czech Republic.

Kemal Oflazer, Elvan Gmen, and Cem Bozsahin. 1994. An Outline of Turkish Morphology.

Kemal Oflazer, Bilge Say, Dilek Zeynep Hakkani-Tür, and Gökhan Tür. 2003. Building a Turkish treebank. In *Treebanks: Building and Using Parsed Corpora*, pages 261–277. Springer.

Umut Sulubacak, Tuğba Pamay, and Gülşen Eryiğit. 2016. IMST: A Revisited Turkish Dependency Treebank. In *TurCLing 2016, The First International Conference on Turkic Computational Linguistics at CICLING 2016*, pages 1–6.

---

[15]Each morphological analysis is composed by the base lexeme, its PoS, and the associated grammemes and derivatemes; as soon as a derivateme appears (as <0> in the first line), a new PoS is assigned (<N> in the mentioned example).

Enhanced UD Dependencies with Neutralized Diathesis Alternation

Marie Candito
Univ. Paris Diderot, CNRS
Laboratoire de Linguistique Formelle
France
`marie.candito@linguist.univ-paris-diderot.fr`

Bruno Guillaume
Inria Nancy Grand-Est, Loria
France
`bruno.guillaume@loria.fr`

Guy Perrier
Univ. de Lorraine, Loria, UMR 7503
France
`guy.perrier@loria.fr`

Djamé Seddah
Univ. Paris-Sorbonne, Inria
France
`djame.seddah@paris-sorbonne.fr`

Abstract

The 2.0 release of the Universal Dependency treebanks demonstrates the effectiveness of the UD scheme to cope with very diverse languages. The next step would be to get more of syntactic analysis, and the "enhanced dependencies" sketched in the UD 2.0 guidelines is a promising attempt in that direction. In this work we propose to go further and enrich the enhanced dependency scheme along two axis: extending the cases of recovered arguments of non-finite verbs, and neutralizing syntactic alternations. Doing so leads to both richer and more uniform structures, while remaining at the syntactic level, and thus rather neutral with respect to the type of semantic representation that can be further obtained. We implemented this proposal in two UD treebanks of French, using deterministic graph-rewriting rules. Evaluation on a 200 sentence gold standard shows that deep syntactic graphs can be obtained from surface syntax annotations with a high accuracy. Among all arguments of verbs in the gold standard, 13.91% are impacted by syntactic alternation normalization, and 18.93% are additional deep edges.

1 Introduction

The Universal Dependencies initiative (UD, (Nivre et al., 2016)) is one of the major achievements of the last few years in the NLP field. Originating from the need of a better interopability in cross-language settings for downstream tasks (Petrov et al., 2011; McDonald et al., 2013), it has gathered dozens of international teams who released annotated versions of their treebanks, following the UD annotation scheme.

Although UD has raised criticisms, both on the suitability of the scheme to meet linguistic typology (Croft et al., 2017) and on the current implementation of the UD treebanks (Gerdes and Kahane, 2016), the existence of many treebanks with same syntactic scheme does however ease cross-language linguistic analysis and enables parsers to generalize across languages at training time, as demonstrated by Ammar et al. (2016).

The UD scheme favors dependencies between content words, in order to maximize parallelism between languages. Although this results in dependencies that are more semantic-oriented, the UD scheme lies at the surface syntax level and thus necessarily lacks abstraction over syntactic variation and does not fit all downstream applications' needs (Schuster and Manning, 2016).

This is partly why de Marneffe and Manning (2008) proposed a decade ago, in the Stanford Dependencies framework, several schemes with various semantic-oriented modifications of syntactic structures. Its graph-based, so-called *collapsed*, representation layer[1] has recently started to be extended and implemented as "Enhanced Dependencies" in the UD scheme family (Schuster and Manning, 2016). Current UD specifications leave open the possibility to include phenomena (cf. section 2) that make explicit additional predicate-argument dependencies. In practice, most current UD treebanks contain either very few or no enhanced dependencies at all[2].

---

[1] Among the various Stanford schemes, the collapsed scheme is the furthest away from the plain dependency tree.

[2] Notable exceptions in the UD 2.0 release are the SyntagRus and Finish treebanks. For English, a converter including enhanced dependencies is available within the Stanford parser (https://nlp.stanford.edu/software/stanford-dependencies.shtml).

Proceedings of the Fourth International Conference on Dependency Linguistics (Depling 2017), pages 42-53,
Pisa, Italy, September 18-20 2017

Of course, as noted by Kuhlmann and Oepen (2016), competing proposals for deep syntactic graphs already exist and are implemented through diverse and, in some few cases, multilingual *graphbanks*. More clearly semantic schemes seem to depend on the needs of the downstream application or impose their own constraints on the syntactic layer it is either built upon or plugged in. See for example the differences between abstract meaning representations (Knight et al., 2014), designed with Machine Translation in sight, and the UDEPLAMBDA's logical structures, very recently proposed by Reddy et al. (2017) and evaluated on a question-answering over a knowledge base task.

In this paper, we build on the work of (Candito et al., 2014; Perrier et al., 2014) to propose an extension to the current *enhanced* dependency framework of Schuster and Manning (2016). First, we extend the types of argumental dependencies made explicit (taking into account participles, control nouns and adjectives, non-finite verbs and more cases of infinitive verbs). Second, we neutralize syntactic alternations, in order to make linking patterns more regular for a given verb form. We believe that making explicit and normalize the predicate-argument structures, still remaining at the syntactic level, can make downstream semantic analysis more straightforward (as shown for instance in (Michalon et al., 2016)), while remaining neutral with respect to what exact semantic representation can be further derived.

The originality of our approach is to neutralize syntactic alternations using *canonical* grammatical functions, which render linking patterns of verbs more regular but are still syntactic in nature, unlike what can be found for example in the tectogrammatical layer of the Prague Dependency bank (Hajic et al., 2006).

This proposal is currently being implemented for French, and tested on two UD treebanks (Candito et al., 2014; Nivre et al., 2016) by the means of a rule-based deterministic process. We evaluated the deep syntactic graphs automatically converted from gold UD trees and obtained a 94% F-measure on a two-hundred sentences gold standard, similar to what reported Candito et al. (2014) on a similar task. Both treebanks and building rules are made available[3] to foster further work in other languages and to gather the opinion and criticisms of the community regarding the level of

abstraction we should reach when it comes to deep syntax representation.

In the following, we first briefly introduce the current Enhanced UD scheme, we detail extensions concerning arguments of non-finite verbs in section 3 and syntactic alternations for French in section 4. We present and evaluate a system to obtain enhanced graphs for French in section 5. We then discuss related work and conclude.

2 Enhanced UD representation

The current version of universal dependencies guidelines (v2.0) includes an enhanced dependencies section[4], leaving the possibility for UD treebanks to include all or only some of the following phenomena:

1. Additional subject relations for control and raising constructions
2. Propagation of conjuncts
3. Antecedent of relative pronouns in noun-modifying relative clauses
4. Modifier labels that contain the preposition or other case-marking information
5. Null nodes for elided predicates

In our implementation for French, we cope with the two first phenomena. Phenomena 3 and 4 are quite systematic and may be handled automatically and phenomenon 5 requires manual annotation. Note that while enhanced dependencies (as were Stanford dependencies) are motivated by downstream semantically-oriented applications, they remain syntactic in nature in their current stage. This results in keeping syntactic dependents that are not semantic arguments of their syntactic head, in classic cases of syntax/semantics mismatch. So for instance, subjects of raising verbs are not removed from the enhanced UD graph, although they are not a semantic argument of the raising verb, as shown in Fig. 1.

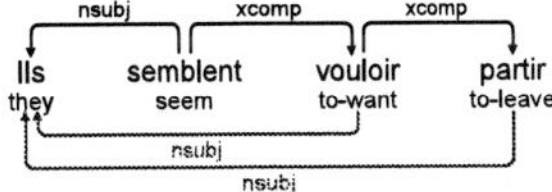

Figure 1: *Raising verb*

Following the work of Candito et al. (2014) and Perrier et al. (2014), we propose two extensions,

---

[3]`http://github.com/bguil/Depling2017`

[4]`http://universaldependencies.org/u/overview/`
`enhanced-syntax.html`

that we detail in the next two sections: the first one is to extend the cases for which arguments are added to infinitive verbs and more generally to non-finite verbs. The second one concerns the neutralisation of syntactic alternations.

3 Recovering arguments of non-finite verbs

The aim of enhancing UD dependencies is to facilitate the computation of predicate-argument relations at the semantic level. In this perspective, we propose to go beyond the explicitation of control and raising verbs subjects. We detail below other cases of obligatory syntactic control, and cases which are not as systematic but which prove feasible with rather high accuracy using heuristics.

3.1 Cases fully determined by syntax

"Control nouns" In French, some nouns take a nominal and an infinitive argument, that can be both realized within the NP or as a predicative complement (Fig. 2). In both cases, the subject of the infinitive is the nominal argument.

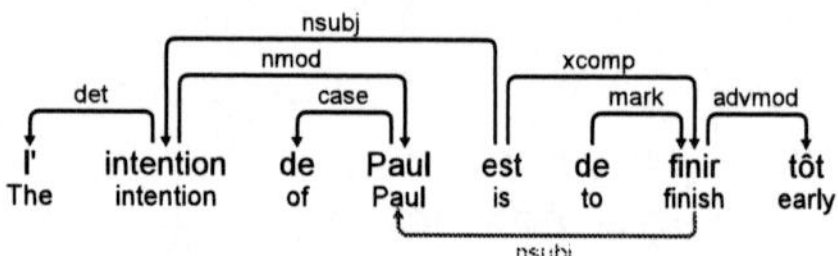

Figure 2: *Paul's intention is to finish early*

The preposition introducing the infinitival clause is determined by the control noun. It is generally *de*, more rarely *à*, as in example (1).

(1)   <u>votre</u> capacité à **conduire** un véhicule
       your capacity to drive   a vehicle

"Control adjectives" Control adjectives take an infinitive complement, whose understood subject is the noun to which the adjective applies, as shown in Fig. 3.

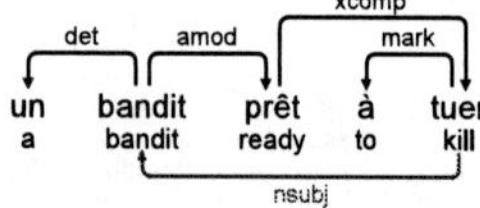

Figure 3: Control adjective

Tough movement Tough movement describes constructions in which an adjective has an infinitive as complement and the noun to which the adjective applies is the direct object of the infinitive.

The adjective can be attributive or used as a predicative adjective (Fig. 4)[5]. These cases are easy to detect using available lists of tough adjectives[6].

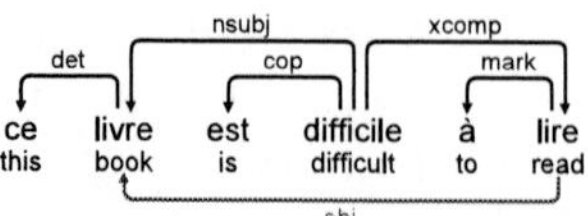

Figure 4: Tough movement

Noun-modifying participles When a past or present participle modifies a noun, the noun is the understood subject of the participle (Fig. 5).

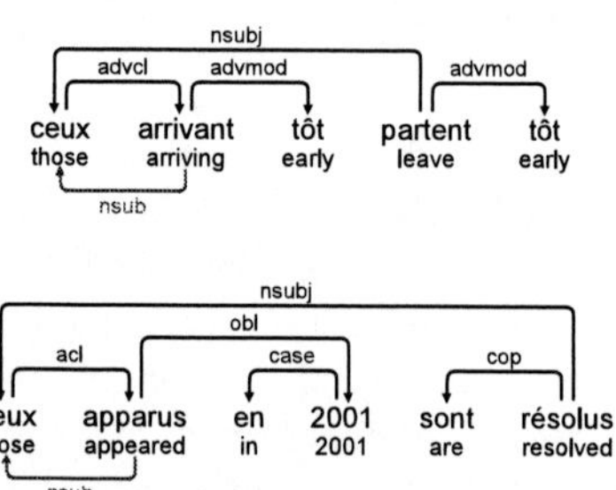

Figure 5: Noun-modifying participles

Infinitives behaving as noun modifiers In French, a transitive infinitival clause introduced with the preposition *à* can be the argument of the noun (as in example (1) in the "control nouns" section above, the noun *capacité (ability)* takes two arguments, the entity having the ability, and an infinitival clause describing what it is able of). But for any noun, an infinitival clause introduced by *à* can function as an adjunct modifying the noun, which is understood as either the object (Fig. 6) or the subject (examples (2) and (3)), depending on the transitivity of the infinitive.

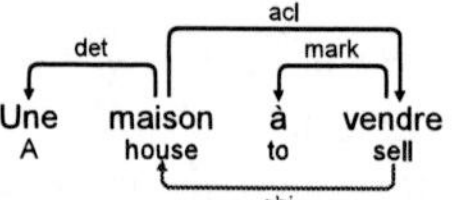

Figure 6: Infinitive modifying a noun, understood as the object of the infinitive

(2)   C'est une machine à mesurer la pression
       It's a   machine to measure the pressure

---

[5]Note in this case, the modified noun is not a semantic argument of the adjective, the dependency between *difficile (difficult)* and *livre (book)* should be dropped in a semantic representation.

[6]A few "tough nouns" exist too, as in *ce livre est un plaisir à lire (this book is a pleasure to read)*.

"It's a pressure measuring machine"

(3) Elle est la première femme à y   entrer
     She is the first   woman to in-it enter
     "she is the first woman who ever entered it"

3.2 Cases requiring semantic or world knowledge

The cases we just saw correspond to situations of *obligatory control*, in which the argument to add to the non-finite verb can be deterministically identified, given the syntactic construction, and given the specific control or raising verb, control noun or adjective. Other constructions involving an non-finite verb are ambiguous with respect to which non-local argument is understood as the argument of the verb. In some of these cases though, among all the potential positions for the non-local argument to retreive is particularly more frequent, although not strictly obligatory. For the cases detailed in this section, we performed a systematic study of the occurrences in the Sequoia corpus, and concluded that simple heuristics could be used for retreiving the non-local argument of a non-finite verb with sufficient accuracy.

Dislocated participle clauses: A participle clause modifying a noun can appear "dislocated" at the beginning or end of the sentence. In that case, its subject is most often the subject of the participle, although exceptions can be built[7].

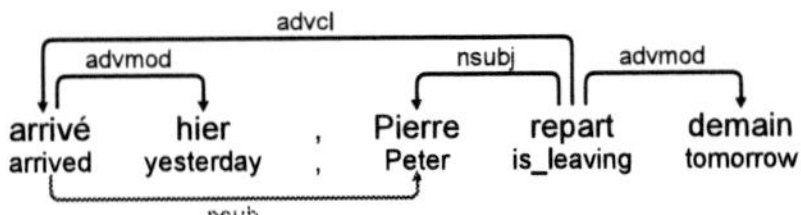

Figure 7: Dislocation

Verb-modifying infinitival and participial clauses For certain prepositions introducing infinitival clauses, the subject of the infinitive is most often the subject of the main clause, but exceptions as illustrated in ex. (4) (the subject of *terminer* is not provided in the sentence.).

(4) Cela exige beaucoup de travail pour **terminer**
     it   takes a lot   of work to   finish
     à temps
     on time

We performed an in-depth study of these cases, using the deep Sequoia corpus (Candito et al., 2014), in which all subjects of infinitive verbs present in the sentence are marked. Breaking down the 143 infinitive heads of adverbial clauses according to the voice of the main verb, we obtain the following results:

- *main verb in the active voice:* there are 114 cases and among them, the subject of the infinitive is the subject of the main verb in 95 cases; in the 16 remaining cases, the subject of the infinitive is absent of the sentence;
- *main verb in passive voice (or modal introducing a passive):* there are 29 cases; in 11 cases, the subject of the infinitive is the subject of the main verb; in the 18 remaining cases, the subject of the infinitive is a virtual agent of the passive verb, which is not present in the sentence;
- *main verb in medio-passive voice:* there are 3 cases, in which the subject of the infinitive is not present in the sentence.

A heuristic that triggers the sharing for active main verbs only will obtain a 90% recall and 83% precision only.

In a similar construction, a present participle introduced with a preposition (*en* in French and *by* in English) plays the role of a modifier for a main verb. The subject of the participle is generally the subject of the main verb but again, this does not hold if the main verb is in passive voice (or is a modal introducing a passive, as shown in ex. (5).

(5) Ce médicament doit   être pris en
     This drug   should be taken by
     mangeant
     eating
     "This drug should be taken while eating"

In Sequoia, there are 39 such constructions. For all the 30 cases in which the main verb is in active voice, the subject of the main verb is understood as the subject of the participle. For the 9 cases in which the main verb is passive, for 8 of them the subject of the participle is not present in the sentence. Therefore, an automatic procedure taking into account the voice of the main verb should produce only a very small number of errors.

Arbitrary control Arbitrary control is a construction in which the subject of an infinitive can have any position in the sentence (Baschung, 1996).

---

[7]We did not find any such exception in the Sequoia corpus. The following built up example shows one: *Exténués, on les a envoyés dormir. (Exhausted, we them have sent to-sleep) "Exhausted, they were sent to bed")*.

(6)   **Fumer** est dangereux pour la santé
     Smoking is dangerous for the health

(7)   **Fumer** est dangereux pour <u>lui</u>
     Smoking is dangerous for him

In Example (6), the subject of *fumer* is understood as generic while in Example (7), the subject is *lui*. While by definition such control cannot be easily resolved, such constructions are fortunately very rare in corpora and ignoring them produces few missing subjects of infinitives.

4 Neutralizing syntactic alternations

Syntactic alternations (like passive) are known to cause diversity in the observed linking patterns in corpora, i.e. the grammatical functions born by the semantic arguments of a verb. At least some of the existing syntactic alternations are very general and can be identified purely on syntactic grounds, without resorting to semantic disambiguation. In this work, we advocate for neutralizing such variation in an "enhanced-alt UD" representation (enhanced UD representation augmented with syntactic alternation neutralization). Following (Candito et al., 2014; Perrier et al., 2014), we propose to distinguish *canonical* versus *final* grammatical functions, and to normalize syntactically alternated verb instances by making explicit the canonical grammatical functions of their arguments. The objective is to cluster observed subcategorization frames into possibly one canonical frame, with thus one linking pattern between canonical functions and semantic arguments.

We handle the French syntactic alternations for which morpho-syntactic clues are available, namely passive, medio-passive, impersonal and causative. We detail these below, identifying for each what is feasible using morpho-syntactic and lexical clues only, and what requires semantic information.

4.1 Passive

Passive is by far the most frequent syntactic alternation, and it is fortunately rather easy to identify in a language such as French. Note that because the UD scheme uses several labels for the same argumental slot, depending on the argument's category, the basic rule of having the passive's subject being the canonical direct object has to be split. The `nsubj:pass` dependent is considered the canonical `obj`. The `csubj:pass` dependent is

the canonical `ccomp` (for full clauses), or `xcomp` (for infinitival phrases).

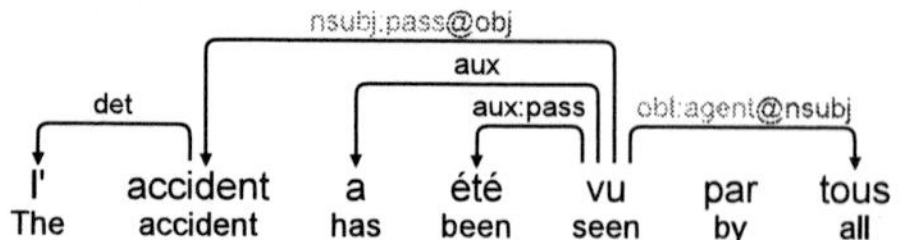

Figure 8: Passive with canonical functions made explicit.

Although passive is identified unambiguously, correctly identifying the argument that is subject in the active form (the "by-phrase" in English) is more problematic given the UD scheme. In French, it is introduced by a PP with preposition *par* (Fig. 8) or for certain verbs, with preposition *de*. But both prepositions can also introduce adjuncts, and the current French version of UD scheme uses the same label `obl` in both cases, leading to an ambiguity concerning the argumental status of the PP. In the following, we use a more specific `obl:agent` label for the *by*-phrases, as is done e.g. in the UD versions of the par-TUT parallel treebank (Sanguinetti and Bosco, 2014) (for English, French and Italian). We detail in section 5 how we can obtain this labeling for the other French UD treebanks.

4.1.1 English passive and ditransitives

Although our focus is French, we also describe here briefly how to handle passive of English ditransitives, a case that does not exist in French.

Let us first note that the current marking of passive in the UD scheme (`nsubj` versus `nsubj:pass` distinction, and `aux:pass` label for passive auxiliary) is not always directly usable to link syntactic arguments to semantic ones. First, passive forms without auxiliaries are not currently marked as such (e.g. in *the planet reached by astronauts*). Second, even for a passive form with passive auxiliary, the recommended `nsubj:pass` label is ambiguous in case of a ditransitive verb: for instance in *He was given orders* and *Orders were given to him*, the `nsubj:pass` corresponds to different semantic arguments[8]. If we choose the double object frame as canonical frame for ditransitives, then the canonical labels can be made explicit as shown in figure 9. Note that the canonical function of the

---

[8]This is already identified by Gerdes and Kahane (2016), who advocate for directly adding the semantic argument rank (1,2,3...) on top of the syntactic label.

`nsubj:pass` argument is `iobj` if the verb has a direct object (Fig. 9a) or `obj` otherwise (Fig. 9b).

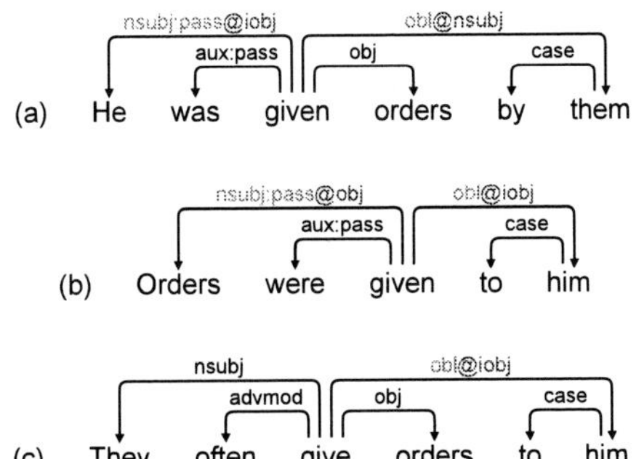

Figure 9: Syntactic alternation normalization for ditransitives.

4.2 Medio-passive

The French reflexive clitic *se* has various status. Roughly, it can mean true reflexivization (*Jean se voit (Jean SE sees) "Jean is seeing himself"*), be part of a compound verb (*s'apercevoir (to realize)*), or mark a valency alternation in which the object is promoted to subject. In the latter case, the canonical subject argument cannot be realized locally, but from the semantic point of view, an agent is either understood (Fig. 10b) or not (Fig. 10a). Disambiguating the status of a given *se* instance is a difficult task requiring semantic information. Note though the phenomenon is not massive. For instance in the Sequoia corpus (Candito et al., 2014), about 5.7% of verbs bear a *se* clitic, among which 16% correspond to a syntactic alternation.

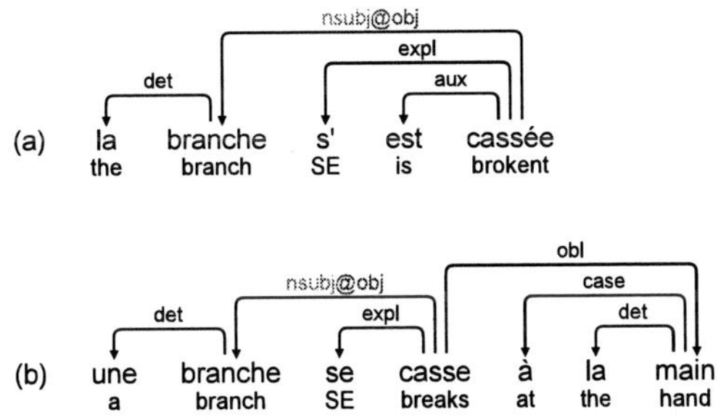

Figure 10: Medio-passive, with or without understood agent (*The branch broke* and *One can break a branch by hand*)

4.3 Impersonal

Impersonal constructions can also be viewed as syntactic alternations: in French the postverbal complement has object-like properties (in particular the pronominalization with the quantitative clitic *en (of-it)*).

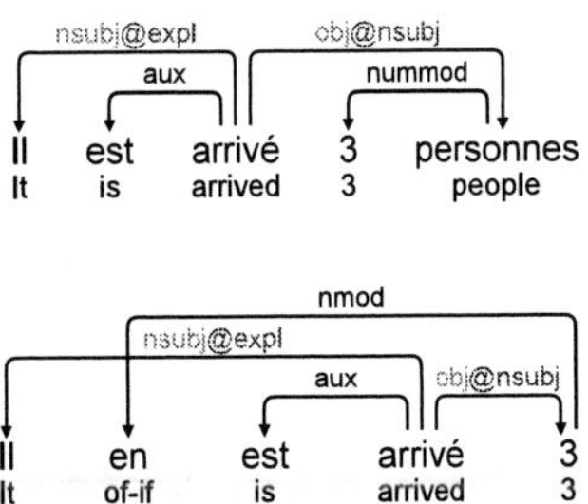

Figure 11: Impersonal construction for sentences *"There arrived 3 people"* (top) and *"Three (of them) arrived"* (bottom).

The representation of such constructions in UD is subject to debate. In the French-UD v2.0 treebank, the non-referential *il* clitic is treated as a `nsubj`, and the post-verbal argument as an object. We thus handle impersonal constructions as syntactic alternations (Fig. 11): the *il* receives an `expl` label, and the post-verbal dependent receives a canonical `nsubj` or `csubj` label (unless the verb is passive).

4.4 Causative

Causative is another construction that can be viewed as a syntactic alternation in French. It is formed syntactically with a *faire (to do)* verb followed by the infinitive of the "caused" verb. It has complex properties described in a vast litterature. For instance Abeillé et al. (1997) advocate for two competing analyses, the main one representing the *faire* + Vinf as a complex predicate, with the arguments of Vinf plus an argument for the causer, which shows as final subject (we use `nsubj:caus` as canonical function to mark it in the enhanced UD representation). The causee, which corresponds to the canonical subject of the Vinf, can show as a direct object, an oblique with preposition *à* or preposition *par*, depending on the transitivity of the Vinf, and other complex factors. So though detecting a causative construction is trivial, detecting which surface argument of the complex predicate corresponds to the causee is not. We provide in Fig.12 an example of ambiguity: *Zola* can be understood as the author that is read or the person who reads. The phenomenon is rather rare, e.g. occurring roughly once every 100 sentences in the Sequoia treebank.

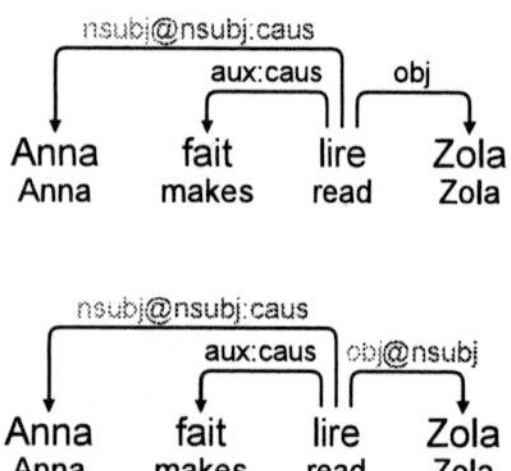

Figure 12: Ambiguous causative sentence, meaning either *"Anna makes someone read Zola"* (top) or *"Anna makes Zola read"* (bottom, *Zola* is the canonical subject).

4.5 Interaction

Syntactic alternations can interact with all the other "UD-enhanced" phenomena. For ease of reading, we provide an English example in Fig. 13, where coordination interacts with passive and a secondary predicate construction[9]. We further focus on interaction between passive and added dependents of verbs. For all the cases listed in sections 2 and 3 in which a subject is added to a nonfinite verb, the syntactic regularity concerns the *final* grammatical subject, which does or doesn't correspond to the *canonical* subject, depending on the voice of the verb. We develop below two examples: (i) noun-modifying particial phrases and (ii) control verbs.

Passive and noun-modifying participial phrases: We wrote in section 3 that a noun modified by a participle corresponds to the subject of the participle (Fig. 5). Yet, this generalization only holds if subject is intended as *final* subject. Fig. 14 shows examples of past participles, with or without auxiliaries, that modify a noun. The noun is the semantic first actant of the intransitive participle (a), but the semantic second actant of the transitive participle (b). Using the notion of final versus canonical grammatical functions, we can uniformly state that in all cases, the modified

noun is the final subject of the participle (whether past or present participle), and consider (i) all present participles as active, (ii) the intransitive participles as active, but (iii) the transitive participles as passive. For the latter, the final subject is the canonical object, as usual for passives.

Note that from a practical point of view, it is rather easy to decide whether a given nounmodifying past participle falls under case (ii) or (iii). Indeed, only a few intransitive verbs[10] can function as noun-modifying past participle phrases (case (ii)), all other instances necessarily fall under the passive case (iii).

Passive and control verbs: For control verbs we have both a syntactic constraint and a semantic (or lexical) constraint: a control verb controls which of its *semantic* argument will necessarily be the *(final) subject* of the infinitive. For instance, let's consider first the so-called "subject control verbs" (e.g. *vouloir (to want)*) or movement verbs (e.g. *venir (to come)*). The canonical subject of such verbs (*ceux (those)* in Fig. 15) is the final subject of the infinitive, but its canonical subject for active infinitives (Fig. 15a and Fig. 15c) and canonical objects for passive infinitives ((15b).

For "object control verbs", the controller (final subject of the infinitive) is their canonical object. This holds both for active (Fig. 16a) or passive object control verbs (Fig. 16b). For instance in Fig. 16b, *forcer (to force)* is passive, the controller (*ceux (those)*) is always its canonical object, but shows as its final subject.

5 Producing enhanced graphs for French UD treebanks

We have experimented the proposed enhanced scheme on two French corpora of the UD project: UD_FRENCH and UD_FRENCH-SEQUOIA. UD_FRENCH is in the UD projet since the version 1.0 (January 2015); data are taken from the Google dataset (McDonald et al., 2013) where annotations where verified by one annotator. It was later converted into a UD version which has not been manually corrected systematically. Nevertheless, the data were corrected and enriched in later versions. UD_FRENCH-SEQUOIA is part of the UD project since version 2.0 (March 2017). It was automaticaly converted from the Sequoia

---

[9]Note that for the secondary predicate construction *X demonstrates Y to be Z*, the direct object *Y* is not a semantic argument of the verb. Hence the dependency between *demonstrated* and its canonical object *charges* should be dropped in a semantic representation.

[10]These are the unaccusative verbs, which use *être (to be)* tense auxiliary instead of *avoir (to have)*.

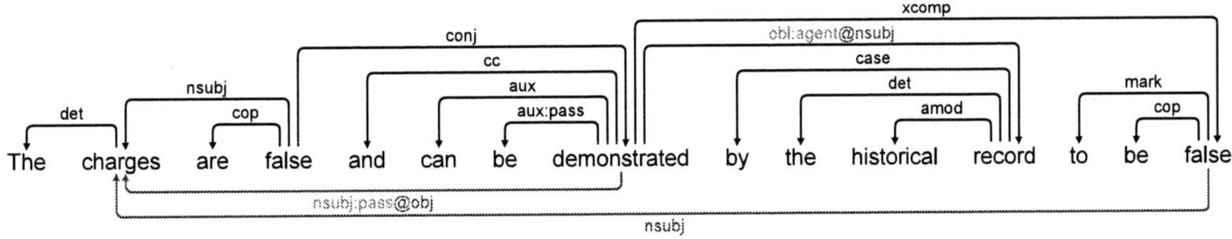

Figure 13: Enhanced UD graph, with neutralization of syntactic alternation: example with interaction of coordination, passive and predicative complement.

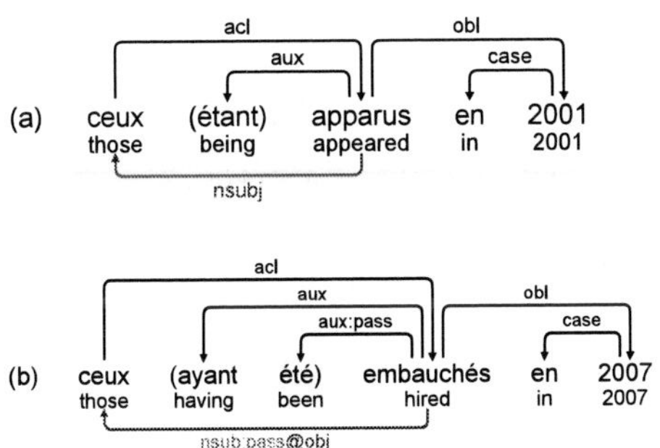

Figure 14: Noun modified by a participial phrase, with or without auxiliary

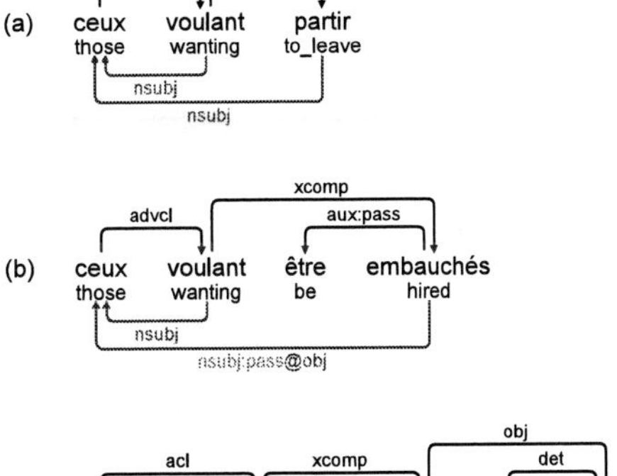

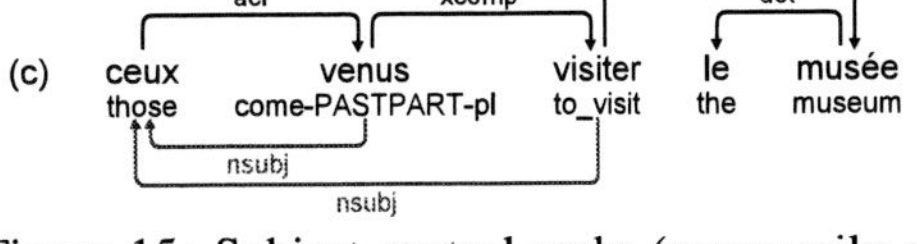

Figure 15: Subject-control verbs (necessarily active): their canonical subject is the final subject of the infinitive.

corpus[11] (Candito and Seddah, 2012) but the result was not manually corrected.

We developed two sets of rules, using two conceptually different graph rewriting systems[12], so that an adjudication of two outputs could be done.

As pointed in section 4, the full processing of syntactic alternations requires to disambiguate the argumental status of some complements: (a) which *par*-phrases are agents of passives, (b) which instances of the reflexive clitic *se* correspond to an alternation promoting object to subject, and (c) which complement of a causative complex predicate *faire*+Infinitive correspond to the subject of the infinitive.

For the Sequoia corpus, all this information is already annotated in the original corpus, and we simply had to report it on UD_FRENCH-SEQUOIA. For UD_FRENCH, we manually annotated our TEST data for the three kinds of information listed above. In the full UD_FRENCH, the number of occurences to disambiguate are: 766 for (a), 635 for (b) and 519 for (c).

5.1 Evaluation gold corpus

For evaluating the rule-based systems, we produced a reference evaluation corpus, containing 200 sentences not used for tuning the rules (half from UD_FRENCH (UD$_{test}$) and half from UD_FRENCH-SEQUOIA (SEQ$_{test}$)). The gold enhanced graphs were obtained in three steps: (1) application of the two rule-based systems on the gold UD trees, (2) manual adjudication of the two ouputs and (3) systematic check of infinitive verbs, past or present participles and coordinations.

Below, we consider two sets of edges: N is the set of new edges, mostly argument of verbs (drawn in blue and above words in our figures) and A the set of edges impacted by an alternation (namely with a canonical function different from the final grammatical function and labeled with the '@' symbol in figures). Note that these two sets are not disjoint (see for instance, Fig. 14b).

In the reference data, N represents 5.72% of the

[11]http://deep-sequoia.inria.fr
[12]The GREW system (Guillaume et al., 2012) and the OGRE system (Ribeyre et al., 2012)

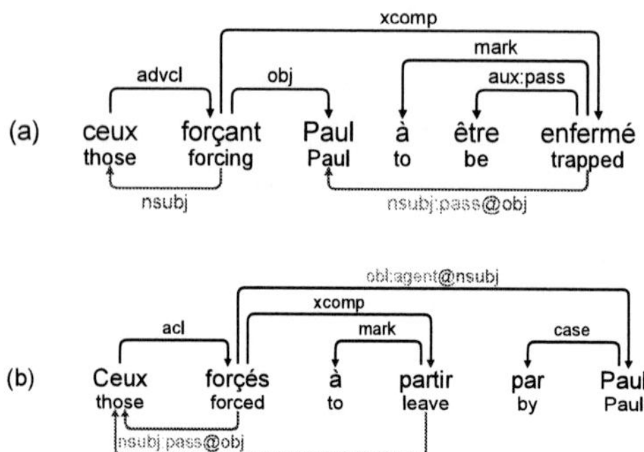

Figure 16: Object-control verb used in active and passive voice: their canonical object is the final subject of the infinitive

		PA−		PA+	
		SEQ_{test}	UD_{test}	SEQ_{test}	UD_{test}
All	OGRE	98.81	99.17	99.46	99.40
edges	GREW	99.44	99.54	99.69	99.66
$N \cup A$	OGRE	86.20	89.89	92.51	91.71
edges	GREW	93.42	94.31	95.77	95.39

Table 1: Evaluation of rule-based systems producing enhanced graphs: F-measures computed on all edges (top) or only on edges in N or A (bottom); PA− and PA+ are respectively without and with manual pre-annotation to help syntactic alternation disambiguation.

total number of edges in the 200 test sentences. If we consider arguments of verbs only (the set of core arguments of verbs and the `obl` relation), edges in N represents 18.93% of the total number of verb arguments. The edges in set A are 2.77% of the total number of edges the full test data. Again, if we consider arguments of verbs only, these edges represent 13.91% in the 200 test sentences.

5.2 Results and Error Analysis

We evaluated the production of enhanced UD graphs in two settings, depending on whether the input UD trees do (PA+) or do not (PA−) contain manual disambiguation of cases (a), (b) and (c) described above. For the PA− case, we applied basic default rules instead, known to use insufficient information. Table 1 reports the F-measures (computed considering all edges or $N \cup A$ edges only). These results confirm the validity of our approach and highlight the consistency of the resulting graphbanks. Moreover, even if manual pre-annotations are required in theory, we empirically observe that they concern a small number of cases and their effect is marginal (the difference between PA− and PA+ settings is low).

The error analysis shows that the GREW and OGRE systems have different weak points. Of the 52 errors produced by OGRE, 30 were due to a lack of distribution of the governor or dependents on the conjuncts of a coordination, while it missed 5 subjects of infinitives only. For GREW, the result is opposite. Only 4 errors out of 28 relate to the distribution of dependencies within a co-ordinated structure but 14 correspond to missing subjects of infinitives. These divergences indeed helped to improve the adjudicated gold version, and were further used to improve both rule sets.

6   Discussion and Related Works

Since the rise of large annotated corpora and given the cost of annotations of large scale project such as the PDT (Böhmová et al., 2003), methods aiming at automatically enriching syntactic trees with deeper structures have peaked a decade ago (Hockenmaier, 2003; Cahill et al., 2004; Miyao and Tsujii, 2005) but have then been subsumed by purely data-driven methods when corpora with richer annotation have been made available (Hajic et al., 2006; Oepen et al., 2014; Mille et al., 2013). Space is missing for an in-depth comparison between these different annotation scheme, we refer the reader to (Rimell et al., 2009; Ivanova et al., 2012; Candito et al., 2014; Kuhlmann and Oepen, 2016) for a more complete overview. Here, we will focus on the differences between the Meaning Text Theory (MTT, (Melčuk, 1988)), as instanced in the recent AnCora-UPF treebank (Mille et al., 2013; Ballesteros et al., 2016), and our proposal.

The MTT defines an explicit deep syntactic representation level[13], hereafter DSyntS. The AnCora-UPF Treebank follows its four layer model: morphological, surface-syntactic, deep-syntactic and semantic. The method used for annotating that corpus is similar to the procedure we used. Starting from the surface-syntactic level, the two other levels are automatically pre-annotated step by step: the annotation of a given level is rewritten to the next level using the MATE tools (Bohnet et al., 2000).

---

[13]Kahane (2003) proposed to view the deep syntactic representation as a derivation step between surface syntax and semantic representation.

The DSyntS produced by Ballesteros et al. (2016) share important properties with our extented enhanced UD graphs, in that they neutralize syntactic alternations. However, they do not contain additional arcs for argument sharing, as subjects of infinitives for instance, as they stick to tree structures. Besides the choice of representation structures, graphs in our cases, trees in the other, important differences remain: Another difference concerns the dependency labels for arguments: canonical function labels (nsubj, obj etc...) in our case versus "argument relations" for MTT, namely numbers (I, II, III etc...), ordered using a "growing obliquity" order (Iordanskaja and Melcuk, 2000). These numbers do not have a meaning per se, and are intended to be read within a lexical entry linking them to syntactic realizations. We note that using argument numbering in a deep syntactic representation, hence in the absence of word sense disambiguation, leads to the loss of plain syntactic information useful for disambiguation. For example in French: *apprendre* is ambiguous between *to learn* as in *X apprend Y de Z*, and *to teach*, as in *X apprend Y à Z*. Both senses entail different subcategorization frames *(subj, obj, obl:de)* vs *(subj, obj, obl:à)*, but bear the same argument numbers in the MTT (I, II, III), the meaning of III being too underspecified in the absence of semantic disambiguation[14].

7 Conclusion

We proposed extensions of the current enhanced universal dependencies scheme. We advocated in particular for neutralizing syntactic alternations, in order to limit the diversity of observed subcategorization frames for a given verb, while staying at the syntactic level, without resorting to word sense disambiguation. We implemented rule-based modules to obtain enhanced graphs from French UD trees. Evaluation on a 200-sentence sample shows we obtain over 90% of F-measure on the enhanced edges (edges not present in the input UD tree). Moreover, we report a 19% proportion of enhanced edges among the edges for arguments of verbs, meaning that the saturation of

predicate-argument structures for verbs concerns a non negligible amount of arguments. We hope this proposal can be tested on other languages, the most obvious ones being the Romance languages, which show very similar syntactic alternations. We position this proposal within the UD framework and remain compatible with all choices already made by the current specifications (Nivre et al., 2016; Schuster and Manning, 2016). Moreover, our de-facto adhesion to the CONLL-U representation format allows for a straight-forward use by current data-driven graph parsers. We leave this promising path of study to further work.

Acknowledgments

We warmly thank our anonymous reviewers for their insightful comments. The first and the last authors were partly funded by the ANR projects ParSiTi (ANR-16-CE33-0021), SoSweet (ANR-15-CE38-0011-01) and supported by the Program *Investissements d'avenir* managed by the Agence Nationale de la Recherche ANR-10-LABX-0083 (Labex EFL).

References

Anne Abeillé, Danielle Godard, and Philip Miller. 1997. Les causatives en français, un cas de compétition syntaxique [in french]. *Langue française*, 115(1):62–74.

Waleed Ammar, George Mulcaire, Miguel Ballesteros, Chris Dyer, and Noah A Smith. 2016. Many languages, one parser. *Transactions of the Association for Computational Linguistics*, 4:431–444.

Miguel Ballesteros, Bernd Bohnet, Simon Mille, and Leo Wanner. 2016. Data-driven deep-syntactic dependency parsing. *Natural Language Engineering*, 22(6):939–974.

Karine Baschung. 1996. Une approche lexicalisée des phénomènes de contrôle [in french]. *Langages*, 30(122):96–123.

Alena Böhmová, Jan Hajič, Eva Hajičová, and Barbora Hladká. 2003. The prague dependency treebank. In *Treebanks*, pages 103–127. Springer.

Bernd Bohnet, Andreas Langjahr, and Leo Wanner. 2000. A development environment for an mtt-based sentence generator. In *Proc. of the First International Conference on Natural Language Generation*, INLG '00, pages 260–263.

Aoife Cahill, Michael Burke, Ruth O'Donovan, Josef van Genabith, and Andy Way. 2004. Long-Distance Dependency Resolution in Automatically Acquired

---

[14]One of the anonymous reviewers pointed that because in UD some labels are distinguished according to the category of the dependent (e.g. `nsubj` vs. `csubj`), the MTT labels would still better account for linking regularities. While we do agree that the UD label distinctions multiply linking patterns maybe uselessly, we believe that on the other hand, the MTT deep labels do add ambiguity, and are thus insufficient per se.

Wide-Coverage PCFG-Based LFG Approximations. In *Proc. of ACL*, pages 320–327.

Marie Candito and Djamé Seddah. 2012. Le corpus Sequoia : annotation syntaxique et exploitation pour l'adaptation d'analyseur par pont lexical. In *Proc. of TALN*.

Marie Candito, Guy Perrier, Bruno Guillaume, Corentin Ribeyre, Karën Fort, Djamé Seddah, and Éric De La Clergerie. 2014. Deep Syntax Annotation of the Sequoia French Treebank. In *In Proc. of LREC*, Reykjavik, Islande, May.

William Croft, Dawn Nordquist, Katherine Looney, and Michael Regan. 2017. Linguistic typology meets universal dependencies. In *15th International Workshop on Treebanks and Linguistic Theories (TLT15)*, Indiana University, US.

Marie-Catherine de Marneffe and Christopher D Manning. 2008. Stanford typed dependencies manual. Technical report, Stanford University.

Kim Gerdes and Sylvain Kahane. 2016. Dependency annotation choices: Assessing theoretical and practical issues of universal dependencies. In *Proc. of the 10th Linguistic Annotation Workshop held in conjunction with ACL 2016 (LAW-X 2016)*, pages 131–140, Berlin, Germany, August.

Bruno Guillaume, Guillaume Bonfante, Paul Masson, Mathieu Morey, and Guy Perrier. 2012. Grew : un outil de réécriture de graphes pour le TAL. In *Proc. of TALN*, Grenoble, France.

Jan Hajic, Jarmila Panevová, Eva Hajicová, Petr Sgall, Petr Pajas, Jan Štepánek, Jiří Havelka, Marie Mikulová, Zdenek Zabokrtskỳ, and Magda Ševcıková Razımová. 2006. Prague dependency treebank 2.0. *CD-ROM, Linguistic Data Consortium, LDC Catalog No.: LDC2006T01, Philadelphia*, 98.

Julia Hockenmaier. 2003. *Data and models for statistical parsing with Combinatory Categorial Grammar*. Ph.D. thesis.

Lidia Iordanskaja and Igor Melcuk. 2000. The notion of surface-syntactic relation revisited (valence-controlled surface-syntactic relations in french). *Slovo v tekste i v slovare. Sbornik statej k semidesjatiletiju Ju.D. Apresjana, Moskva: Jazyki russkoj kul'tury*, pages 391–433.

Angelina Ivanova, Stephan Oepen, Lilja Øvrelid, and Dan Flickinger. 2012. Who did what to whom?: A contrastive study of syntacto-semantic dependencies. In *Proc. of the 6th Linguistic Annotation Workshop (LAW-VI 2012)*, pages 2–11.

Sylvain Kahane. 2003. On the status of deep syntactic structure. In *Proc. of the First Meaning-Text Theory conference*, Paris, France.

Kevin Knight, Lauren Baranescu, Claire Bonial, Madalina Georgescu, Kira Griffitt, Ulf Hermjakob, Daniel Marcu, Martha Palmer, and Nathan Schneifer. 2014. Abstract meaning representation (amr) annotation release 1.0. *Web download.*

Marco Kuhlmann and Stephan Oepen. 2016. Towards a catalogue of linguistic graph banks. *Computational Linguistics*, Volume 42, Issue 4, December.

Ryan T McDonald, Joakim Nivre, Yvonne Quirmbach-Brundage, Yoav Goldberg, Dipanjan Das, Kuzman Ganchev, Keith B Hall, Slav Petrov, Hao Zhang, Oscar Täckström, et al. 2013. Universal dependency annotation for multilingual parsing. In *ACL (2)*, pages 92–97.

Igor Melčuk. 1988. *Dependency syntax: theory and practice*. State University Press of New York.

Olivier Michalon, Corentin Ribeyre, Marie Candito, and Alexis Nasr. 2016. Deeper syntax for better semantic parsing. In *Proc. of COLING 2016, the 26th International Conference on Computational Linguistics: Technical Papers*, pages 409–420, Osaka, Japan, December.

Simon Mille, Alicia Burga, and Leo Wanner. 2013. AnCoraUPF: A Multi-Level Annotation of Spanish. In *Proc. of DepLing 2013*.

Yusuke Miyao and Jun'ichi Tsujii. 2005. Probabilistic disambiguation models for wide-coverage HPSG parsing. In *Proc. of ACL 2005*, pages 83–90.

Joakim Nivre, Marie-Catherine de Marneffe, Filip Ginter, Yoav Goldberg, Jan Hajic, Christopher D Manning, Ryan McDonald, Slav Petrov, Sampo Pyysalo, Natalia Silveira, et al. 2016. Universal dependencies v1: A multilingual treebank collection. In *Proc. of LREC 2016*, pages 1659–1666.

Stephan Oepen, Marco Kuhlmann, Yusuke Miyao, Daniel Zeman, Dan Flickinger, Jan Hajic, Angelina Ivanova, and Yi Zhang. 2014. Semeval 2014 task 8: Broad-coverage semantic dependency parsing. In *Proc. of the 8th International Workshop on Semantic Evaluation*, pages 63–72.

Guy Perrier, Marie Candito, Bruno Guillaume, Corentin Ribeyre, Karën Fort, and Djamé Seddah. 2014. Annotation scheme for deep dependency syntax of french (un schéma d'annotation en dépendances syntaxiques profondes pour le français) [in french]. In *Proc. of TALN 2014 (Volume 2: Short Papers)*, pages 574–579, Marseille, France, July.

Slav Petrov, Dipanjan Das, and Ryan McDonald. 2011. A universal part-of-speech tagset. *arXiv preprint arXiv:1104.2086.*

Siva Reddy, Oscar Täckström, Slav Petrov, Mark Steedman, and Mirella Lapata. 2017. Universal semantic parsing. *arXiv preprint arXiv:1702.03196.*

Corentin Ribeyre, Djamé Seddah, and Éric Ville-monte De La Clergerie. 2012. A Linguistically-motivated 2-stage Tree to Graph Transformation. In Chung-Hye Han and Giorgio Satta, editors, *Proc. of TAG+11*, Paris, France. INRIA.

Laura Rimell, Stephen Clark, and Mark Steedman. 2009. Unbounded dependency recovery for parser evaluation. In *Proc. of EMNLP*, pages 813–821.

Manuela Sanguinetti and Cristina Bosco. 2014. Part-tut: The turin university parallel treebank. In Roberto Basili, Cristina Bosco, Rodolfo Delmonte, Alessandro Moschitti, and Maria Simi, editors, *Harmonization and development of resources and tools for Italian Natural Language Processing within the PARLI project*. Springer Verlag.

Sebastian Schuster and Christopher D. Manning. 2016. Enhanced english universal dependencies: An improved representation for natural language understanding tasks. In *Proc. of LREC 2016*. Portorož, Slovenia.

Classifying Languages by Dependency Structure
Typologies of Delexicalized Universal Dependency Treebanks

Xinying Chen
School of International Studies
Xi'an Jiaotong University, China
Department of Czech Language
University of Ostrava, Czech Republic
xy@yuyanxue.net

Kim Gerdes
LPP (CNRS)
Sorbonne Nouvelle
France
kim@gerdes.fr

Abstract

This paper shows how the current Universal Dependency treebanks can be used for clustering structural global linguistic features of the treebanks to reveal a purely structural syntactic typology of languages. Different uni- and multi-dimensional data extraction methods are explored and tested in order to assess both the coherence of the underlying syntactic data and the quality of the clustering methods themselves.

1 Introduction

Language universality and language differences are a pair of questions, if not two sides of one question, that relate to most of modern linguistic research, both theoretically and empirically. This is even more true for research in language typology.

Modern language typology research (Croft 2002; Song 2001), mostly based on Greenberg (1963), focuses less on lexical similarity and relies rather on various linguistics indices for language classification, and generally puts much emphasis on the syntactic order (word order), in particular of the principal components in relation to their governing verb (Haspelmath et al. 2005).

However, just as individual constructions can display varying degrees of syntheticity and analyticality (Ledgeway 2011), different syntactic orders can also be found in the very same language. Reality seems to be messier than we would like it to be. Therefore, probabilities or quantitative approaches, which allow gradual transitions and blurred borderlines, could make some unique contributions on this matter (Liu & Xu, 2012). Moreover, empirical studies based on authentic language data can bring richer details, and then corroborate or improve our knowledge of language classification. By relying on quantitative empirical measures we do no longer expect a categorical answer of grouping languages into fixed language groups, but rather tendencies of structural proximity between languages.

Although such efforts have already been made in a few studies (Liu 2010; Liu & Xu 2012), it is not until now, with the appearance of Universal Dependencies, that we can conduct an empirical language classification study based on treebanks of different languages that share the same dependency annotation framework.

1.1 Universal Dependencies

Universal Dependencies (UD) is a project of developing a cross-linguistically consistent treebank annotation scheme for many languages, with the goal of facilitating multilingual parser development, cross-lingual learning, and parsing research from a language typology perspective. The annotation scheme is based on an evolution of (universal) Stanford dependencies (de Marneffe et al., 2014), Google universal part-of-speech tags (Petrov et al., 2012), and the Interset interlingua for morphosyntactic tagsets (Zeman, 2008). The general philosophy is to provide a universal inventory of categories and guidelines to facilitate consistent annotation of similar constructions across languages, while allowing language-specific extensions when necessary.

There are two notable advantages of using this data set for language classification studies. Firstly, it is the sheer size of the data set: It includes 70 treebanks of 50 languages, 63 of which have more than 10,000 tokens. And secondly, and most importantly, all UD treebanks use the same annotation scheme. The few previous studies of empirical language classification based on

Proceedings of the Fourth International Conference on Dependency Linguistics (Depling 2017), pages 54-63,
Pisa, Italy, September 18-20 2017

treebank data (Liu 2010; Liu & Xu 2011, 2012) still had to rely on much fewer treebanks with heterogeneous annotation schemes. Although already relatively satisfying results were obtained, the question of identifying the source of the observed language variations remains unsolved: They could be actual structural differences between languages or simply annotation schema related differences (or even genre related differences, of course – and thus being due to the underlying text). UD can, to a certain extent, reduce this problem by providing a unique framework for all languages.

However, the drawbacks of the UD 2.0 scheme are also rather obvious. The Universal Dependencies (UD) project is still at an early stage of development and many problems of UD have not been solved appropriately, the most important points being:

1. Many treebanks are a result of multiple transformations of previous phrase-structure and dependency treebanks, therefore often multiplying already existing annotation or even parse errors where no manual correction is available.
2. The UD textual data stems from very different sources and was not conceived as a parallel corpus.[1] Thus, we can never exclude that any observed difference is actually due to genre differences between the texts.
3. The current UD annotation guides are still highly underspecified resulting in low inter-annotator, and more importantly inter-corpus agreement (the authors, submitted). This is particularly true for a series of constructions (cleft, dislocations, disfluencies, …). Also, the attempt to annotate semantic non-compositionality of multi-word expressions in the (syntactic) annotation scheme without actually providing the semantic criteria, necessarily leads to incomparable annotations (Gerdes & Kahane 2016).
4. Most importantly, with the goal of possibly simplifying parsing and other NLP tasks, the basic idea underlying the UD annotation scheme is to make languages look as "similar as possible" based on semantic features, the most prominent of which being to put "content words" higher in the tree. However, the status of *content word* is a semantic distinction. This results in the infamous "Turkish" analysis of English prepositions (Chris Manning, 2016, personal communication).[2] The forced similarity of structurally different languages, like for example Turkish and English, makes the data less valuable for our study of empirical structural language classification: We cannot measure what has been suppressed.

1.2   What to measure?

In typological studies on word order, Greenberg (1963) proposed 45 linguistic universals, 28 of which are related to the order or position of grammatical units, for instance, the order of subject, object, and verb. According to Dryer's (1992) study of detailed word order correlations based on a sample of 625 languages, there are 17 correlation pairs and 5 non-correlation pairs between a verb and its object.[3] Although the importance of linear order of grammatical units has been addressed for quite a while, more recently statistical investigations of word order also play an increasingly central role in empirical studies, some of which are based on treebanks. Liu (2010) looked through the directional distributions of three pairs of grammatical units, namely, S-V/V-S, V-O/O-V, and Adj-N/N-Adj, in treebanks of 20 languages. He quantified the dependency directions by computing the percentages of positive (head-final) and negative (head-initial) dependencies, thus transforming the sentence internal dependency link into global features of the treebank. He found that these features are relatively efficient for the language classification task, thus being able to dig out human language universals from authentic data.

<hr>

[1]   With the exception of the ParTUT treebanks (Sanguinetti & Bosco 2011).

[2]   Contrary to all previous analyses of prepositions in Indo-European languages that we are aware of which see the prepositions as governors of the following noun (giving a *PP* its name), UD annotates prepositions as case markers of the noun, independently of whether it is sub-categorized by the verb (*talk to*) or semantically full (*sleep under*). This leads to a greater structural similarity between English and Turkish than typologically expected and also for example to competing annotations of complex prepositions (*on top of*) in the current treebanks (with *top* as the head of the PP or as a dependent of the embedded noun).

[3]   Examples of this type of correlations include the tendency of *O-V* languages to be postpositional, placing adpositions after their objects – while inversely *V-O* languages tend to be prepositional, placing adpositions before their objects. So the *V-O* vs *O-V* feature is correlated with the *preposition* vs. *postposition* feature.

Subsequent empirical studies of language classification have confirmed that combined measures on all dependency links, not only on the verbal and nominal arguments, provides better typological indicators than one or several specific word order measures, which may lead to conflicting conclusions (Liu & Xu 2012). In addition, macroscopic indexes, such as network parameters of dependency treebanks based on language networks, have been shown to perform even better than global measures of word order (Liu & Li 2010; Abramov & Mehler 2011; Liu & Xu 2011, 2012; Liu & Cong 2013). One way of extracting global structural language features is to fuse all equal lexical nodes, resulting in one big syntactic network where every lexical node appears only once (Ferrer-i-Cancho 2001, Chen et al. 2015). In the present work, we completely strip the treebank of the lexical nodes, taking into account only the categories as well as the frequency and directions of the dependency relations.

Although word order is clearly an important index for capturing the typological features of languages, we suspect that it is possible to refine the index by combining it with additional information or to conceive indeces that are better adapted to the classification task, such as network parameters. In the present work, we propose two means of modifying the word order (dependency direction) index for language classification task. To the quantitative measure of the dependency directions, we add the length of the syntactic relations (Liu 2008; Liu et al. 2009), i.e. we compute the *Directional Dependency Distances* (DDD) for each syntactic function with positive/negative values corresponding to the dependency direction. This DDD measure appears to be a straightforward choice of quantitative values that map directly to the dependency direction index.

Although our method follows the same 'quantitative' principle as Liu (2010) and Lu & Xu (2012), it contains different information. Instead of using the distribution percentages of the dependency directions to quantify them, we add the distance information into it and thus create a more integrated value rather than a pure direction index. The second novelty of this work is a more fine-grained dependency direction measurement: Instead of computing an overall value (the average distance or the percentage of positive relations for a whole treebank), the unified annotation scheme of UD allows us to break down the frequency, direction, and length of the links by dependency relationship. Common clustering techniques will allow analyzing and visualizing language similarities.

1.3 Outline

Following the idea of investigating the typological structural universality and diversity of languages based on authentic treebank data, the present work specifically focuses on whether and how the UD treebank set allows us to recognize language families based on purely empirical structural data. The question can be decomposed into various sections:

The following section will describe the dataset used in this study and the principal measures that we apply. In section 3 we start with a global uni-dimensional measure that imposes a natural order on the set of treebanks. We compare the measure we propose to existing work. Given the above-mentioned series of problems of the underlying treebank data, we then move on to assessing whether the current UD data is actually good enough to measure structural differences, the most evident method being whether different treebanks of the same language are actually structurally more similar to each other than to treebanks of other languages. For this, we apply our ranking to the individual treebanks as well as to the data combined by language.

We then make use of the common annotation scheme of the UD treebanks which allows us to split up the measures per syntactic functions. This multi-dimensional dataset can be used for common clustering techniques, whose results we present and discuss. We will conclude with a discussion of the results, problems, and future plans of dependency-based typology.

Our images contain very small fonts but the image resolution allows zooming in. For the PCA images, the color zones, which we describe in the text, are generally sufficient for the understanding of the clusters. Since we compute data on close to 50 languages, 70 treebanks, and 30 dependency relations, we cannot provide all numerical data in the Annex of this paper. All scripts, data, and images are freely available on https://gerdes.fr/papiers/2017/dependencyTypology/ thus allowing reproducing our results, in particular as the underlying UD treebank target is a fast moving target.

2 Methods

The main analysis includes four main steps: 1) data selection and description, 2) determination and extraction of the parameters to investigate, 3) quantitative description of the parameters, 4) clustering analysis based on measurements of step 3.

In step 1, we remove the relatively sparse languages, namely treebanks with less than 10,000 tokens, from the dataset. We also only kept *syntagmatic core relations*, removing *fixed, flat, conj*, and *root* relations from our distance measures as their direction and length are universally fixed in the annotation guide and don't indicate any interesting difference between languages.[4] Different treebanks of the same language are firstly kept separate for consistency measures and secondly combined for the main classification tasks.

In step 2, we extract dependency function distribution, direction, and distance measures from the combined treebanks. More specifically, we compute the relative frequency distributions of dependency functions and the ***Directional Dependency Distance (DDD)***, which we define as the product of the dependency distance and the direction, thus including negative values. We obtain three different central observations, as shown in Table 1, which we will also compare to other frequency measures.

Observations	Distributions (frequency)	Directional dependency distance (DDD)
1	√	×
2	×	√
3	√	√

Table 1: 3 observations based on 2 parameters

For Observation 1, we only look at the distributions of dependency functions of different languages. For the observation 2, we compute the *DDD* per syntactic function by computing the difference of the node index and the governor index for each node, adding those values up and di-

viding by the number of links[5]. The DDD of a dependency relation R is thus defined as follows:

$$DDD(R) = \frac{\sum_{r \in R} distance(r)}{frequency(R)}$$

In the third measure, we quantify this average *DDD* by means of the relative frequency of the UD functions by multiplying *DDD* with the relative frequency of the corresponding function.

At step 3, we conduct clustering analyses based on the data of the observations. We compare the results of these three observations to each other as well as to previous language classification studies to see whether they can distinguish different known language families in order to assess which observations provide the best result.

3 Unidimensional measures

To start, let us first look at the simple measures, where we get a unique numerical value per treebank or language.

We computed the DDD of all dependency relations combined. The DDD takes head-final relations as negative values and head-initial relations as positive values. Languages that have an equal number of left-spanning and right-spanning links of similar average length, will have a value close to zero.

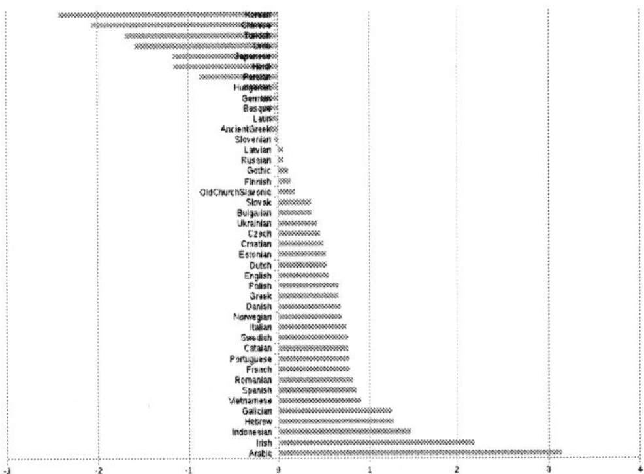

Figure 1: Languages
ordered by dependency distance

This graph gives a good idea of what kind of insights we want to gain from dependency mea-

---

[4] *Fixed* and *flat* are used for multi-word expressions, *conj* for coordinations. These three dependency relations have arbitrarily been assigned to a left-to-right bouquet structure (all subsequent tokens depend on the first token). See Gerdes & Kahane 2016 for a description and for alternatives to this choice. The *root* link is often thought of and drawn as a line straight up from the root node but it is encoded in CoNLL as a link to the zero node. Taking the root "length" into account would artificially add left-right relations to mainly head-final language (and the way around), thus lowering the average distance measures.

[5] This means that we do not take into account the variance of these links, e.g. a language that has symmetric links around each governor will have a zero distance, independently of the length of these dependency links. We also computed the standard deviation of each relation and included this value in the clustering, but this did not significantly improve the result.

sures: It comes as no surprise to find Korean at the top of the list of the most centripetal (Tesnière's term for head-final[6]) languages, and, inversely, Arabic at the bottom of the list, being the most centrifugal of the analyzed languages. The appearance of Chinese, however, between Korean and Turkish at the second place affirms how strictly head-final Chinese actually is – a fact that does not really show when classifying languages in the discrete categories of SVO, SOV etc. We see how the numerical analysis allows for new empirically-based groupings and ordering of languages that are hard to perceive on purely categorical classifications.

The Germanic language group is spread across the spectrum, starting from the negatively distanced German to the highly positively distanced Swedish. The Romance languages, however, are all very well clustered around an average distance of about 0.8.

Compare this with a measure that does not take into account the actual length of the dependencies but only the direction percentages (proposed by Liu (2010)):

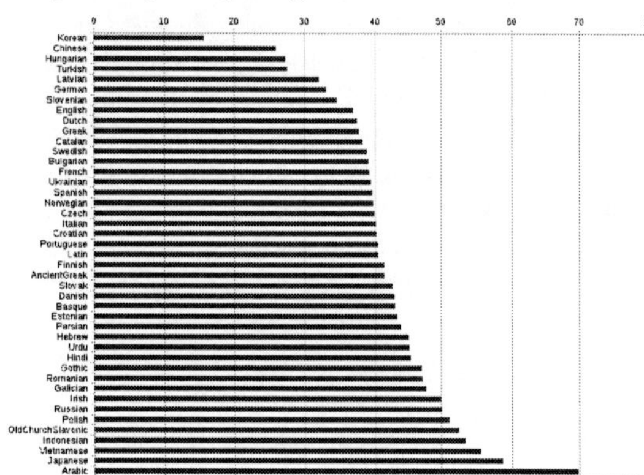

Figure 2: Languages
ordered by % of positive links

Although the two extremes (Korean and Arabic) are the same, the results correspond less to well-known language classifications. Observe how Japanese finds its natural position close to Korean, Turkish and Hungarian in the DDD measure, whereas the direction percentage measure places it right next to Arabic, presumably because of the high number of (postpositional) particles.[7]

---

⁶ Tesnière's language classification terminology (1959) precedes Greenberg's by 4 years but was not cited by the latter.

⁷ Although functionally analogous, equivalent postpositions are traditionally seen as morphological case-marking in Korean. This leads to quite diverse treebanks for structurally similar languages,

3.1 Corpus or Language differences?

A basic coherence measure of our data can be done by comparing not languages as a whole but treebanks which have usually been created by different groups of developers. If we encounter strong differences among treebanks of the same language that genre differences cannot account for, then this points to underspecification of guidelines – or possibly to systematic errors in one treebank.

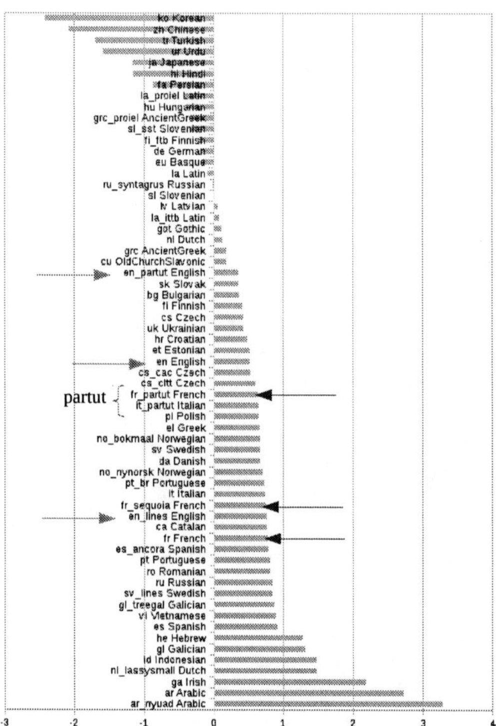

Figure 3: Treebanks ordered by dependency distance with positions for English and French.
The language names are preceded by the ISO language code and the complete treebank name if there is more than one treebank per language.

The separation of our data by treebank generally puts languages at similar positions independently of the treebank. Nevertheless, this also reveals some of the aforementioned incoherences of the current state of the annotations – and thus also the limits of our approach. The following figure indicates the different places taken by the English (left side, red arrows) and the French (right side, blue arrows) treebanks of UD 2.0. Although the absolute values are not as extremely different as the position suggests (en: 0.4, 0.5, 0.8; fr: 0.6, 0.8, 0.8), any derived typological

calling for a more precise tokenization specification.

classification seems to remain quite treebank dependent at the current state of UD. Note also that the treebanks from the ParTUT team coherently have a lower dependency direction than their counterparts for English, French, and Italian. It is tempting to attribute this difference to differences in the guidelines used by different teams in the annotation process, but for Italian, the other Italian treebank has also been created by the ParTUT team. So maybe the difference is rather due to the syntactic structure of "Translationese", that has shorter dependency links for the mostly head-initial languages included in ParTUT.

More generally, this shows how these methods also allow for detecting common ground and outliers in the process of treebank development. They can be used for error-mining the treebank.

4 Multi-dimensional clustering

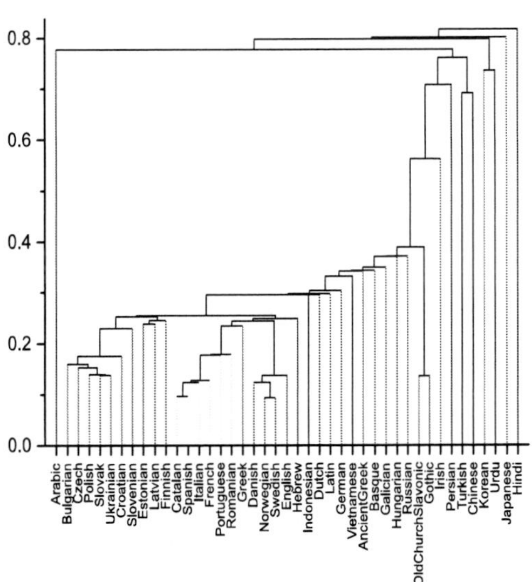

Figure 4: Dendrogram of DDD vectors per function

Measures on our set of treebanks that distinguish dependency relations give rise to multi-dimensional vectors. The clustering analysis can be done by the usual Principal Component (PCA[8]) and the Hierarchical Cluster Analysis (HCA[9]).

UD allows the introduction of idiosyncratic sub-classes of syntactic functions. English, for example has the *nmod:poss* function, the possessive subclass of nominal modifiers used for the

annotation of genitives. To make the values comparable, we are measuring the direction and distribution of simple functions, i.e. function names stripped of what follows the colon.

4.1 Directional Dependency Distance (DDD) by syntactic function

Instead of comparing the single DDD value, we can use the whole vector of DDDs, one for each of the 33 syntactic functions. Contrarily to what we have seen for the global DDD, the multi-dimensional HCA clustering of Figure 4 groups relatively correctly: the Slavic language family (red, except Russian), Romance (yellow, without Galician) and Germanic (green, without German and Dutch).

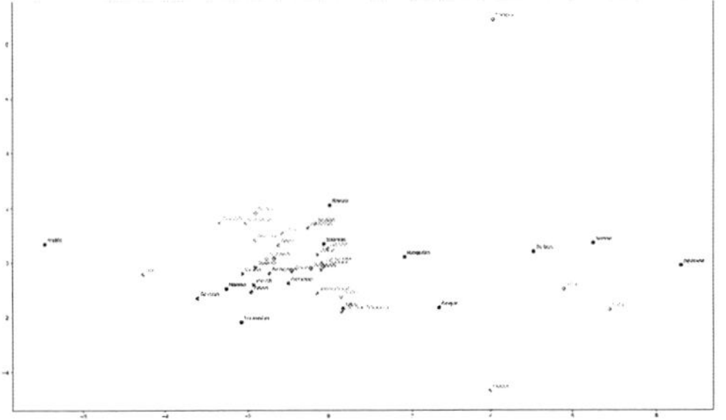

Figure 5: PCA of DDD vectors per function

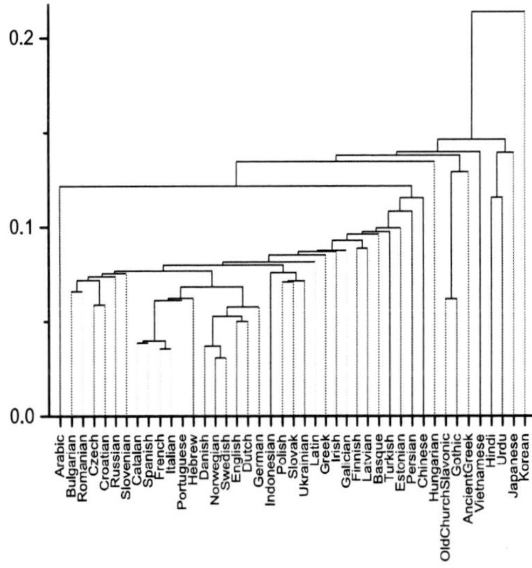

Figure 6: Dendrogram of relative frequencies of dependency relations

The PCA of the same data provides clustering of comparable quality, cf. Figure 5: Romance in blue, Germanic in turquoise, and, less clearly clustered, Slavic in green. Note also the rectangle containing Altaic languages in the following order but quite fare from one another: Hungarian, Turkish, Korean, and Japanese.

---

[8] The PCAs are performed with the decomposition package of the scikit-learn project. See github.com/scikit-learn/scikit-learn

[9] The HCA in this paper are conducted by OriginPro 9 (Cluster Method: Nearest neighbor, Distance Type: Euclidean).

4.2 Clustering relative frequency distributions

Do we actually need to take into account the length and direction of the dependency relation to obtain correct language families? Or will the simple frequency of dependency relation labels do? Figure 6, another clustering analysis, only on the relative frequency of each dependency label, shows that the analysis successfully distinguishes Indo-European languages and also obtains rather good results for three big sub-groups, namely the Germanic branch (in green color), Italic branch (in yellow color), and the Slavic branch (in red color). Although some intermingling of these three branches still exists, the result is slightly better than the result that we obtain based on simple dependency directions.

It is noteworthy that we cannot further simplify the underlying data and dispense with the tree structure altogether. If for example we only use relative POS frequencies, we obtain an PCA analysis where language groups are not coherent clusters (Figure 7).

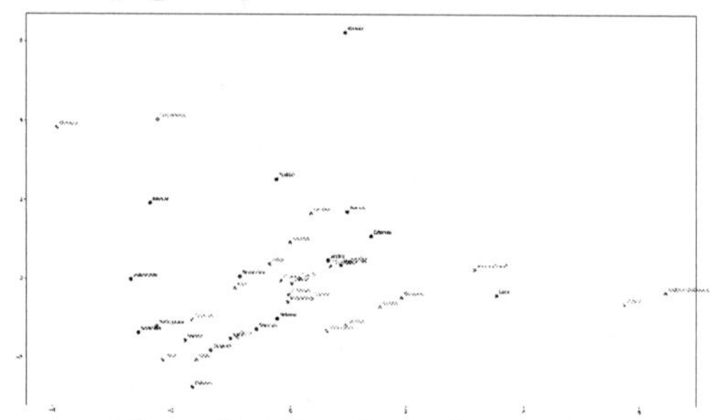

Figure 7: PCA of POS frequencies

Inversely, complexifying the features gives sparse data and unrecognizable results. If, for example, we combine function and category and measure the frequencies of function-category couples, one couple being for example (*nsubj→NOUN*), we obtain the following uninterpretable graph (Figure 8). Although many of UD's syntactic functions are actually redundant (*nsubj* contains the information that the dependent is a NOUN), the higher-dimensional space projects less clearly into two-dimensional space (~500 dimensions), presumably because of data sparsity. This experiment could be redone when some UD treebanks will have attained a significantly greater size.

Note that in both the pure POS and the function-POS analysis, the two ancient languages Gothic and Old Church Slavonic are strong outliers (on the right of the graph), not far from Ancient Greek and Latin. This suggests that the

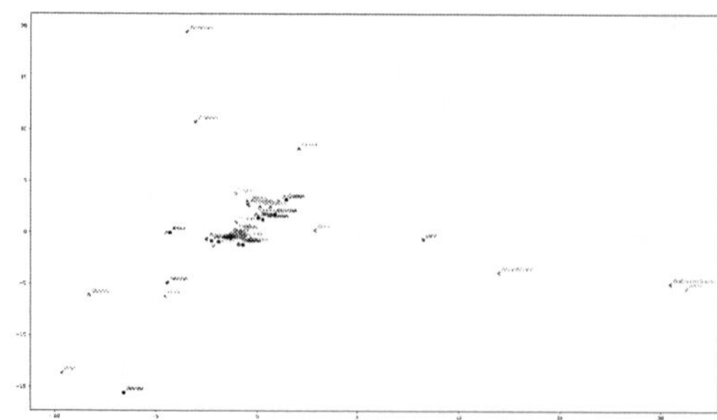

Figure 8: PCA of function-POS frequencies

POS annotations of these languages has been done by the same team or at least has been under mutual influence.

This shows that all measures are not created equal. The actual structural information of the treebank is crucial to obtain satisfying language groups.

4.3 DDD multiplied by relative frequency

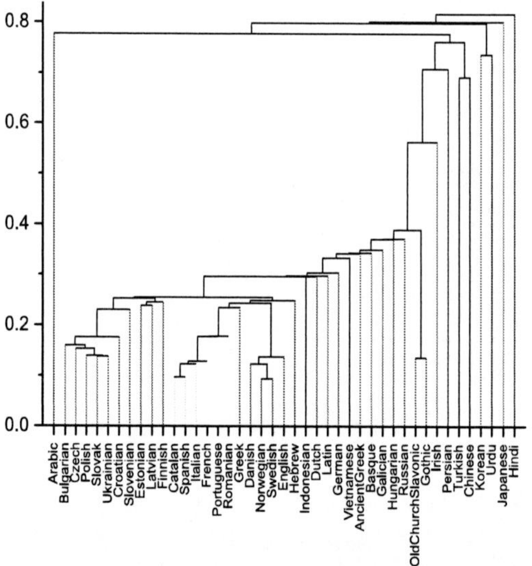

Figure 9: Dendrogram of distance × frequency clustering per language

Both the pure frequency measures and the directional dependency measures (DDD) measures give interesting results. When combining these two measures by multiplying the DDD by the relative frequencies, we obtain even more satisfying results: Figure 9 shows a first red subtree corresponding to Slavic langugaes, only Latvian, Russian, and Old Slavonic being outliers. The next yellow subtree hosts Romance language with Latin and Galician later following alone. The green sub-tree shows the proximity of the Germanic languages Danish, Norwegian, Swedish, and English – with Dutch and German following separately. As in the PCA analysis, Old Slavonic and Gothic form again a close subgroup – presumably due to a common annotation process.

Even when grouping by treebanks and not by languages, the subtrees cut neatly into the set of languages. In Figure 9, the red subtree on the left groups together nearly all Slavic languages, the yellow subtree contains nearly all Romance languages, and the green subtree most Germanic languages (see the Annex for the names of the language codes). Then there is another separate green subtree for German and Dutch and two more Germanic outliers: Gothic and another Dutch corpus. If this is not a genre difference, we can suppose that this Dutch Lassymal UD treebank follows different annotation guidelines. Note also how close are Finnish and Estonian (small light brown subtree). This subtree then groups together with Latvian, a language considered coming from a different group of languages. This structural similarity mimicking geographic proximity is an interesting result suggesting cross-language-group influences not only on the lexicon but also on the syntactic structure itself.

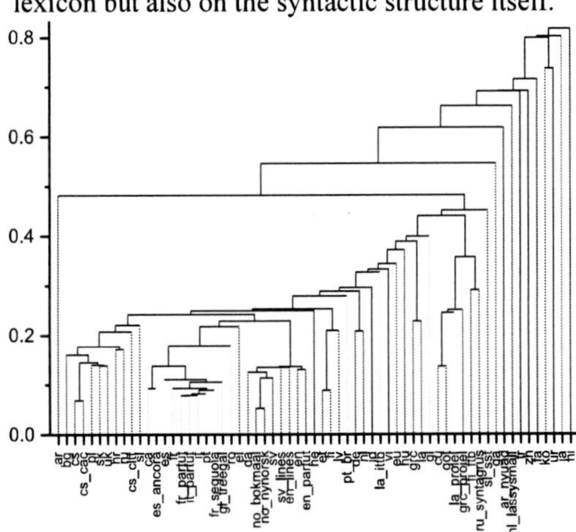

Figure 10: Dendrogram of distance × frequency clustering per corpus

Similarly, note that the distance × frequency measures consistently cluster Romanian in the Romance language group, but simple relative frequency measures show Romanian close to Bulgarian and other Slavic languages. In a sense, the simple frequency captured some features of language groups better than DDD and the multiplied values. We have to leave it to further research to determine which kind of proximity is better captured by which measure.

We can see that a well-chosen measure, here the combined frequency and distance measure, can abstract away from the many annotation errors and incoherences of the current UD.

Even using PCA on the language treebank data (Figure 11), we see that the right hand side of the PCA diagram contains the same languages as the most independent languages of the dendrogram: Japanese (black dot to the right) Chinese (red on top), Hindi, Korean, and Urdu stand out the furthest from the crowd in both projections, showing the relative robustness of the data concerning the actual choice of the clustering technique.

Figure 11: PCA of distance × frequency

5   Conclusion

The various data extraction and clustering techniques that we have carried out, only the most emblematic of which we could present in this paper, show that the UD treebanks succeed rather well for language classification even if we solely base our study on the delexicalized tree structures. The coherent cross-language annotation scheme makes it possible to split up the measures by dependency functions. Although modern language typology studies are mainly focused on word order, the different measures and methods we proposed show that the classical word order classification alone is no longer sufficient to classify languages based on authentic clustering data, which is a similar result to Liu (2012). Usually we get better results if we consider the actual dependency relations, no matter under which format: relative distribution, network, and network variations. For single parameters alone, the dependency relationship distribution is performing better than the dependency direction. However, combining the criteria provides us with the best language clustering results attainable on the sole basis of syntactic treebanks.

Meanwhile, it is necessary to further assess in future research the robustness of our clustering approach to typology across different annotation schemes, for instance by comparing the UD treebanks with data that can be obtained from crosslingual parsers (Ammar et al. 2016; Guo et al. 2016).

Since the distribution of dependency relationships is very uneven and the majority of links consists of a small subset of all types, it seems possible that the most frequent relations are sufficient for classifying languages. If they are, then some functions may have different effects on the clustering process. The decisive functions in the clustering represent language diversity, the others have a more universal character. This process transforms the categorical opposition between principles and parameters into a gradual scale where syntactic features and constructions can be positioned based on empirical data from treebanks.

A basic epistemological question arises from two types of results that we can obtain in our approach: We have measures that group languages according to well-known classes, and measures that show new groupings and relationships. Both results are interesting, the latter requiring further explorations and explanations – and, as in any truly empirical approach, it requires returning to the data to ascertain the actual causes of the observed distances between treebanks.

Here we encounter the difficulty of assessing the nature of the results: Are they possibly due to annotation errors and incoherences? Are they due to genre differences of the underlying texts? The methodology we propose will grow and improve with the coherence of the UD treebanks. – Or possibly with the emergence of other more syntactically oriented treebank collections, in particular if they are conceived as parallel treebanks, with identical genres. This would dispel any doubts on clustering results, as each cluster would solely and directly express an empirical typological relation.

References

Abramov, Olga, and Alexander Mehler. "Automatic language classification by means of syntactic dependency networks." *Journal of Quantitative Linguistics*, 18.4 (2011): 291-336.

Chen, Xinying, Haitao Liu, and Kim Gerdes. "Classifying Syntactic Categories in the Chinese Dependency Network." *Depling 2015* (2015): 74.

Croft, William. *Typology and universals*. Cambridge University Press, 2002.

De Marneffe, Marie-Catherine, et al. "Universal Stanford dependencies: A cross-linguistic typology." *LREC*. Vol. 14. 2014.

Dryer, Matthew S. "The Greenbergian word order correlations." *Language*, (1992): 81-138.

Ferrer-i-Cancho, Ramon, and Richard V. Solé. "The small world of human language." *Proceedings of the Royal Society of London B: Biological Sciences*, 268.1482 (2001): 2261-2265.

Gerdes, Kim, and Sylvain Kahane. "Dependency Annotation Choices: Assessing Theoretical and Practical Issues of Universal Dependencies." *LAW X (2016)*

Greenberg, Joseph H. "Some universals of grammar with particular reference to the order of meaningful elements." *Universals of language*, 2 (1963): 73-113.

Haspelmath, Martin. *The world atlas of language structures*. Vol. 1. Oxford University Press, 2005.

Ledgeway, Adam. "Syntactic and morphosyntactic typology and change." *The Cambridge history of the Romance languages*, 1 (2011): 382-471.

Liu, Haitao. "Dependency distance as a metric of language comprehension difficulty." *Journal of Cognitive Science*, 9. 2 (2008): 159-191.

Liu, Haitao. "Dependency direction as a means of word-order typology: A method based on dependency treebanks." *Lingua*, 120.6 (2010): 1567-1578.

Liu, Haitao, and Chunshan Xu. "Can syntactic networks indicate morphological complexity of a language?." *EPL (Europhysics Letters)*, 93.2 (2011): 28005.

Liu, Haitao, and Chunshan Xu. "Quantitative typological analysis of Romance languages." *Poznań Studies in Contemporary Linguistics PsiCL*, 48 (2012): 597-625.

Liu, Haitao, and Jin Cong. "Language clustering with word co-occurrence networks based on parallel texts." *Chinese Science Bulletin*, 58.10 (2013): 1139-1144.

Liu, Haitao, Richard Hudson, and Zhiwei Feng. "Using a Chinese treebank to measure dependency distance." *Corpus Linguistics and Linguistic Theory*, 5.2 (2009): 161-174.

Liu, Haitao, and Wenwen Li. "Language clusters based on linguistic complex networks." *Chinese Science Bulletin*, 55.30 (2010): 3458-3465.

Lucien Tesnière. 1959. *Éléments de syntaxe structurale*. Klincksieck, Paris.

Petrov, Slav, Dipanjan Das, and Ryan McDonald. "A universal part-of-speech tagset." *arXiv preprint arXiv:1104.2086*, (2011).

Sanguinetti M, Bosco C. "Building the multilingual TUT parallel treebank". *Proceedings of The Second Workshop on Annotation and Exploitation of Parallel Corpora* 2011 Sep 15 (p. 19).

Song, Jae Jung. *Linguistic typology: Morphology and syntax*. Routledge, 2014.

Zeman, Daniel. "Reusable Tagset Conversion Using Tagset Drivers." *LREC*. 2008.

Appendix A. *Selected Language Data*

Our study is based on the UD 2.0 treebanks of 43 languages combining 67 corpora.

As an example, we provide a table with the (alphabetically) first functions of rounded DDD data per language:

name	acl	advcl	advmod	amod	appos	aux
Arabic	3,37	9,87	3,42	1,39	3,43	-1,05
Bulgarian	5,07	2,73	-1,33	-1,09	2,58	-1,32
Catalan	5,51	7,41	-1,24	0,89	5,26	-1,45
Czech	5,58	1,72	-1,22	-0,97	4,83	-2,14
Old Church Slavonic	2,37	0,02	-0,97	0,66	1,63	0,79
Danish	5,42	5,15	-0,24	-0,63	2,59	-2,31
German	9,9	7,47	-1,84	-1,17	2,29	-4,54
Greek	4,25	4,01	-1,04	-1,08	5,67	-1,14
English	3,48	2,4	-0,93	-1,16	4,07	-1,58
Spanish	4,94	6,11	-1,16	0,7	3,45	-1,5
Estonian	2,07	3,39	-0,63	-1,04	2,84	-1,98
Basque	-1,83	-0,03	-1,93	0,43	4	0,78
Persian	7,81	-4,98	-5,66	0,95	2,81	-1,64
Finnish	1,4	2,24	-0,56	-1,19	2,96	-1,66
French	3,72	4,59	-1,17	0,65	3,2	-1,46
Irish	3,13	8,37	1,88	1,3	4,59	0
Galician	4,33	5,07	-1,06	0,78	5,14	-1,31
Gothic	3,35	1,04	-1,09	0,17	2,34	0,96
Ancient Greek	4,6	-0,52	-1,91	0,37	3,66	-1,73
Hebrew	4,53	2,83	-0,33	1,8	4,15	-1,96
Hindi	3,73	-5,67	-2,35	-1,32	0	1
Croatian	4,55	2,99	-1,48	-1,2	2,34	-1,54
Hungarian	8,67	4,22	-2,26	-1,39	3,67	0
Indonesian	3,81	4,65	-1,15	1,25	3,7	-1,33
Italian	3,84	2,46	-1,51	0,53	4,98	-1,32
Japanese	-6,35	0	-8,99	-1,43	0	1,76
Korean	-1,55	-5,22	-3,26	-1,08	-6,52	0
Latin	3,55	0,85	-2,33	0,1	3,5	0,55
Latvian	3,41	1,52	-1,5	-1,42	5,67	-1,11
Dutch	5	4,39	-1,67	-1,07	2,27	-2,62
Norwegian	3,77	3,71	-0,67	-0,94	4,79	-1,77
Polish	4,7	1,85	-1,13	-0,34	1,7	0,05
Portuguese	4,37	3,76	-1,29	0,46	3,68	-1,43
Romanian	4,13	3,37	-1,21	1	4,95	-1,21
Russian	4,19	3,07	-1,17	-1,05	2,31	-0,89
Slovak	4,57	1,73	-1,14	-1,06	3,68	-0,64
Slovenian	5,77	1,04	-1,28	-1,17	3,35	-2,35
Swedish	3,66	3,06	-0,64	-1,07	5,6	-1,95
Turkish	-2,46	0	-1,05	-1,9	2,11	1,35
Ukrainian	4,06	2,15	-1,28	-1,19	2,22	-0,65
Urdu	5,84	-3,73	-6,4	-1,43	0	1
Vietnamese	0	-3,61	-0,66	1,18	3,83	-0,77
Chinese	-4,88	-8,17	-2,5	-2,18	1,5	-2,67

The unabridged data used in this paper is available on https://gerdes.fr/papiers/2017/dependencyTypology/

code	Language	tokens
ar	Arabic	233, 712
ar_nyuad	Arabic	670, 612
bg	Bulgarian	123, 178
ca	Catalan	417, 453
cs	Czech	1, 174, 076
cs_cac	Czech	426, 274
cs_cltt	Czech	22, 000
cu	Old Church Slavonic	39, 394
da	Danish	80, 351
de	German	245, 524
el	Greek	47, 343
en	English	194, 428
en_lines	English	58, 223
en_partut	English	34, 195
es	Spanish	377, 020
es_ancora	Spanish	443, 951
et	Estonian	29, 051
eu	Basque	82, 516
fa	Persian	113, 699
fi	Finnish	152, 583
fi_ftb	Finnish	118, 747
fr	French	349, 973
fr_partut	French	16, 328
fr_sequoia	French	53, 635
ga	Irish	11, 627
gl	Galician	105, 844
gl_treegal	Galician	13, 819
got	Gothic	37, 931
grc	Ancient Greek	161, 184
grc_proiel	Ancient Greek	171, 524
he	Hebrew	127, 018
hi	Hindi	262, 007
hr	Croatian	161, 533
hu	Hungarian	27, 607
id	Indonesian	82, 588
it	Italian	254, 058
it_partut	Italian	38, 768
ja	Japanese	149, 147
ko	Korean	43, 921
la	Latin	15, 978
la_ittb	Latin	254, 683
la_proiel	Latin	134, 030
lv	Latvian	38, 476
code	Language	tokens
nl	Dutch	170, 665
nl_lassysmall	Dutch	73, 373
no_bokmaal	Norwegian	243, 529
no_nynorsk	Norwegian	240, 917
pl	Polish	63, 236
pt	Portuguese	196, 032
pt_br	Portuguese	260, 983
ro	Romanian	177, 755
ru	Russian	78, 025
ru_syntagrus	Russian	872, 362
sk	Slovak	79, 704
sl	Slovenian	113, 498
sl_sst	Slovenian	16, 389
sv	Swedish	65, 954
sv_lines	Swedish	56, 661
tr	Turkish	37, 167
uk	Ukrainian	11, 312
ur	Urdu	99, 024
vi	Vietnamese	25, 979
zh	Chinese	103, 614

A Dependency Treebank for Kurmanji Kurdish

Memduh Gökırmak
Department of Computer Engineering
Istanbul Technical University
Turkey
gokirmak@itu.edu.tr

Francis M. Tyers
School of Linguistics
Higher School of Economics
Russia
francis.tyers@uit.no

Abstract

This paper describes the development of
the first syntactically annotated corpus of
Kurmanji Kurdish. The corpus was used as
one of the *surprise* languages in the 2017
CoNLL shared task on parsing Universal
Dependencies. In the paper we describe
how the corpus was prepared, some Kurmanji specific constructions that required
special treatment, and we give results for
parsing Kurdish using two popular data-
driven parsers.

1 Introduction

With current end-to-end pipelines for tokenisation,
tagging and parsing, such as UDPipe (Straka et al.,
2016), a treebank is no longer simply a collection of
annotated sentences, but could be considered a vital
basic language resource. Given just the treebank
a statistical model can be trained which performs
everything up to dependency parsing.

This paper describes such a treebank for Kurmanji Kurdish, a language spoken in parts of Iran,
Iraq, Syria, Armenia and Turkey. The treebank
was created as one of the *surprise languages* for
the CoNLL 2017 shared task in dependency parsing (Zeman et al., 2017);[1] but it is hoped that it
provides a template for further development of language technology for Kurmanji.

The paper is laid out as follows, in Section 2 we
give a brief sociolinguistic and typological overview
of the Kurdish. Then in Section 3 we describe some
prior work on computational resources and tools for
Kurmanji. In Section 4 we describe the composition of the corpus, and in Section 5 we describe
some details of the annotation guidelines, paying attention to Kurmanji-specific phenomena. Section 6
reports on a small experiment with three popular

data-driven parsers, and is followed by some avenues for future work in Section 7 and conclusions
in Section 8.

2 Kurdish

Kurmanji Kurdish (also referred to in the literature as 'Northern Kurdish') is an Indo-Iranian language spoken by approximately 14 million people
throughout the Middle East. It is a recognised minority language in Armenia (Simons and Fennig,
2017). Kurmanji over the past century has become
the most prominent Kurdish language, partly due
to the fact that its speakers are a majority among
speakers of Kurdish languages, and partly due to intense cultural and political activity centered around
the Kurmanji language. Manuscripts in what could
be considered a precursor to Kurmanji have been
discovered from five centuries back or more, but
the most intense efforts in the creation of a literary
written standard of Kurmanji were in the 1920s and
30s onward throughout the 20th century. Through
the work of writers, academics and intellectuals like
Celadet Bedirxan and his colleagues at *Hawar*, the
Damascene Kurdish magazine where the Latin Kurdish alphabet was first adopted, Kurmanji has accu-
mulated a respectable literature and a standard reg-
ister has been created. Despite all of this activity
and possibly due to the 'prestige' status of other languages in the region,[2] many speakers of the various dialects of Kurmanji are not aware of a Kurdish
literature, and some are even shocked to learn that
Kurdish languages are written at all.

Kurmanji has two grammatical genders, masculine and feminine; four cases: nominative, oblique,
construct and vocative; and definiteness marked on
nouns. The language has prepositions and postpositions, and also combinations of these which form
circumpositions. Verbs are formed from two stems,
past and present.

---

[1]http://universaldependencies.org/
conll17/

[2]Such as Arabic, Persian and Turkish

Proceedings of the Fourth International Conference on Dependency Linguistics (Depling 2017), pages 64-72,
Pisa, Italy, September 18-20 2017

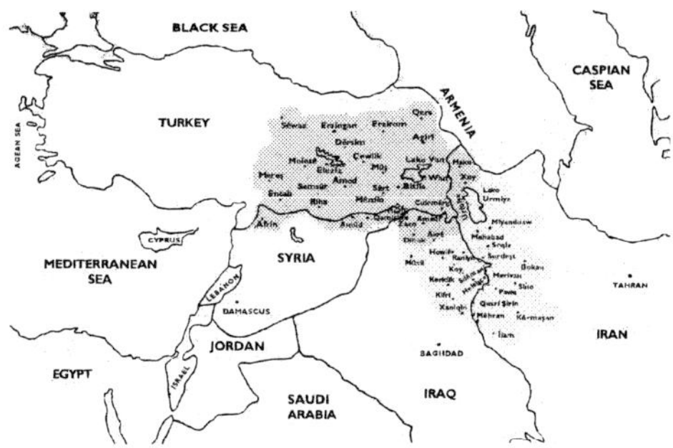

Figure 1: The Kurmanji speaking area (dark grey) within the wider Kurdish speaking area (light grey). The areas where Kurmanji is most widely spoken straddle the borders of Iran, Iraq, Syria and Turkey.

Regarding syntax, the language is primarily subject–object–verb, with auxiliaries following the main verb and split-ergative alignment, where past-tense transitive verbs agree with the person and number of the syntactic object rather than the subject. Noun phrases are largely head initial, with modifiers following the head noun, exceptions to this are determiners and numerals which precede the modified noun. The language has a fairly strict constituent order, and the morphology is of the fusional type with the complexity being similar to that of Icelandic.

3   Prior work

There are a number of reference grammars of Kurmanji available, the most widely-known being Thackston (2006). We also made use of the grammar by Bedirxan and Lescot (1990), and consulted the grammar by Aktuğ (2013). Many other grammars are available, including several different writings by Celadet Ali Bedirxan himself, in most languages of the Middle East, French and English. Many of these grammars are written for the purpose of teaching beginners, and most of these introductory grammars lack important details required for proper linguistic reference. Many grammars also have a good deal of influence from majority languages in the countries they were written. This particularly comes to light when the writer of a grammar describes and thinks about elements of Kurmanji with analogy to Turkish.

A text corpus of Kurmanji and Sorani Kurdish by the name of *Pewan* was introduced in Esmaili and Salavati (2013). Pewan is a plaintext corpus created for the purpose of information retrieval, and was the first publically-available digital corpus of Kurdish. The corpus is unfortunately not freely available, being based on texts under restrictive copyright provisions.

Another lexical resource for Kurdish, although again unfortunately not freely available, is KurdNet (Aliabadi et al., 2014). This is an effort to build a WordNet-like resource for all variants of Kurdish, including Kurmanji.

Walther et al. (2010) describes the rapid development of a morphological analyser and part-of-speech tagger for Kurmanji based on a raw corpus and Thackston's reference grammar (Thackston, 2006). They start by defining part-of-speech and morphological categories, and then build a morphological description of Kurmanji in their formalism. They train a maximum-entropy based tagger using a number of different unsupervised methods achieving an accuracy of 85.7% on a hand-tagged evaluation corpus of thirteen sentences. The semi-automatically created lexicon described was released under a free/open-source licence allowing it to be incorporated, after improvement in the Apertium morphological analyser for Kurmanji (see §4.2).

4   Corpus

The corpus comprises of text from two domains, the first is a short Sherlock Holmes story, *Dr. Rweylot*,[3] which was translated into Kurmanji by Segman (1944) and published in the *Rohanî* journal in Damascus.

The motivation behind choosing a story text as opposed to news text was threefold. First of all being published in 1944 by an author who died in 1951,[4] the text is out of copyright. Secondly, having a whole story annotated as opposed to individual sentences will be interesting when looking at problems such as co-reference resolution. Finally, the orthography is close enough to the modern orthography that any differences can be easily handled.

The text was available through the Kurdish Digital Library of the Paris Kurdish Institute[5] as a PDF file. The PDF had already been processed with an OCR system, and the resulting body of text was accurate enough to use with some manual fixing of errors resulting from the OCR process.

---

[3]Original title: *The Adventure of the Speckled Band*.

[4]Bişarê Segman is widely believed to be a nom de plume of Celadet Berdixan, who died in 1951.

[5]http://bnk.institutkurde.org/

Text	S	T	T/S	non-proj
Dr. Rweylot	339	4,717	13.9	17.9
Wikipedia	415	5,543	13.4	16.6
Total:	780	10,260	13.2	17.2

Table 1: Composition of the treebank. S is the number of sentences and T the number of tokens. T/S gives the average length of a sentence. The *non-proj* column gives the percentage of non-projective sentences.

The remainder of the treebank is made up of sentences selected randomly from the Kurdish Wikipedia.[6] From the randomly-selected sentences, we excluded those which were not in Kurmanji, those with too many orthographic errors and, for legal reasons, those dealing with topics considered *controversial* in Turkey.

4.1 Orthography

Kurmanji Kurdish, unlike Sorani Kurdish, is primarily written using the Latin script, rather than the Perso-Arabic script, ever since *Hawar* adopted the Latin script in the 1930s. Both, however, use *alphabets* as their primary writing system: Sorani uses a modified version of the Perso-Arabic abugida, by introducing mandatory vowels. Kurmanji's alphabet includes several letters with diacritics: circumflexes to mark long vowels, and cedillas to mark palato-alveolar affricates ş /ʃ/ and sibilants ç /tʃ/. The script was also devised by Celadet Bedirxan.

In both the Sherlock Holmes story and the Wikipedia sentences, the orthography was not standardised. This is an issue in written Kurmanji, where many can more or less write in a certain *literary* dialect but few will produce texts that overlap completely in terms of orthography. Depending on the writer's dialect, the word *ku* 'that' might be written *ko*, *heye* 'there is' might be written as *heya*, adpositions might have slight variations and spelling may vary to represent the differences in pronunciation. In order to be able to represent this variety in the treebank we have maintained the differently spelled words in the form column of the CoNLL-U file,[7] and used the variants that exist in the mor-

phological analyser in the lemma column, e.g. both *heya* and *heye* will have the lemma *hebûn* (the existential copula).

Another orthography issue becomes apparent in tokenisation. In the Sherlock story, in some cases negation is written analytically where it would be synthetic in a more modern text. Example (1a) shows negation written separately from the verb, while in example (1b) it is written together.[8]

(1) a. *Zimanê*   *wê*   **ne**
    Tongue-CON   she-OBL   NEG
    digeriya.
    turn-PROG.NARR.2SG

    'Her tongue was not turning.'

   b. *Zimanê*   *wê*
    Tongue-CON   she-OBL
    ne*digeriya.*
    NEG-turn-PROG.NARR.2SG

    'Her tongue was not turning.'

We have kept this syntactic variety as it is likely that many sentences parsed with any system based on this treebank will also have some non-standard syntactic elements, and standardising and fixing too much may lead to a less robust system.

Throughout the paper, we use { and } symbols to mark where contraction has taken place in the dependency trees, for example *Ezê* 'I will' will be shown as {Ez- -ê}. contracted with the first person singular pronoun.

4.2 Preprocessing

Preprocessing the corpus consists of running the text through the Kurmanji morphological analyser[9] available from Apertium (Forcada et al., 2011), which also performs tokenisation of multi-word units based on the longest match left-to-right. The morphological analyser returns all the possible morphological analyses for each word based on a lexicon of around 13,800 lexemes. After tokenisation and morphological analysis, the text is processed with a constraint-grammar (Bick and Didriksen, 2015) based disambiguator for Kurmanji consisting of 85 rules which remove inappropriate analyses in

---

[6]Database dump: `kuwiki-20150901-pages-articles.xml.bz2`

[7]CoNLL-U is the file format used in Universal Dependencies for storing treebanks. A description of the format can be found here: `http://universaldependencies.org/format.html`

[8]The tags used in the glosses are: CON = construct case, OBL = oblique case, PROG = progressive aspect, NARR = narrative tense, 2SG = second person singular.

[9]`https://svn.code.sf.net/p/apertium/svn/languages/apertium-kmr`

context. For example, there is a systematic ambiguity between the past participle and the second-person singular past tense of the verb. One rule removes the participle reading if there is no following auxiliary verb. Applying these rules reduces the average number of analyses per word from around 2.87 to around 1.47.

4.3 Formats

The native format of the treebank is the VISL format (Bick and Didriksen, 2015). This is a text-based format where surface tokens are on one line, followed by analyses on the subsequent line. The reason for choosing this format was that it was more convenient for hand-annotation, and was the format that the morphological analyser and constraint grammar output. In Appendix A we present, for reference, a sentence in VISL format.

4.3.1 CoNLL-U

In order to convert to the standard CoNLL-U format, we needed to do some additional processing:

- The morphological analyser sometimes tokenises two space-separated tokens into a single token, for example *li ber* 'in front of' is tokenised as a single token. When the surface form and the lemma had an equal number of spaces were split into multiple tokens.

- Parts of speech and morphological features were converted from Apertium standard to Universal Dependencies using a lookup table and set longest-overlap algorithm.

- In multiword tokens where there is a single surface form with multiple syntactic words, the sub-word tokens are created using a language-independent longest-common-subsequence algorithm with the surface form and the underlying lemma. For example, LCS(*ezê*, *ez*) = *ez* and LCS(*ezê*, *dê*) = *ê*.

- The special `SpaceAfter=No` feature, used in training tokenisers, was added automatically to the MISC column of CoNLL-U by a script.

After these transformations a valid CoNLL-U file is produced which can be used in training most popular statistical parsers.

5 Annotation guidelines

The annotation guidelines are based on Universal Dependencies (Nivre et al., 2016), an international collaborative project to make cross-linguistically consistent treebanks available for a wide variety of languages. The Kurmanji treebank is based on version 2.0 of the guidelines which were published in December, 2016.

We chose the UD scheme for the annotation as it provides ready-made recommendations on which to base annotation guidelines. This reduces the amount of time needed to develop bespoke annotation guidelines for a given language as where the existing *universal* guidelines are adequate they can be imported wholesale into the language-specific guidelines.

In the following subsections we describe some particular features of Kurmanji that are interesting or novel with respect to the Universal Dependencies annotation scheme.

5.1 Alignment

Kurmanji, like other Kurdish languages, is split ergative. This is similar to the languages of the (relatively) closely related Indo-Aryan family. Ergativity does not, however, exist in most other Indo-Iranian languages. With intransitive clauses and in non-past-tense transitive clauses, the verb agrees with the most agent-like argument (typically in nominative case). However in past-tense transitive clauses, the verb agree with the most patient-like argument, which is usually in nominative case, while the most agent-like is in the oblique case. This is different to the Indo-Aryan system, which primarily uses *aspect*, rather than tense, to assign ergativity.

The following sentence in the treebank provides a good example of the contrast between transitive and intransitive sentences in the past tense: *Ez kenîm û min got: …* 'I laughed and I said: …'

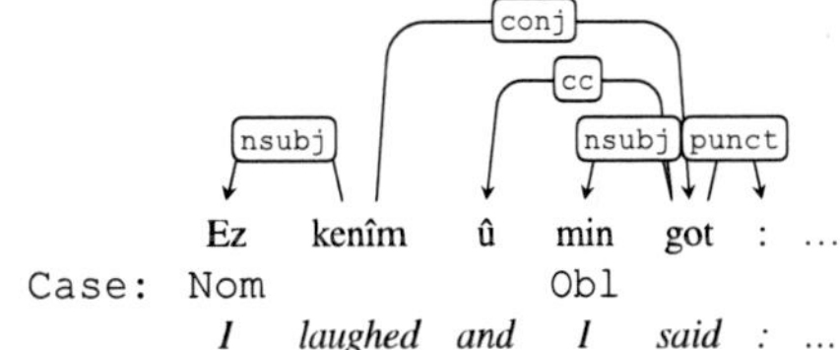

Note the intransitive verb *kenîm* 'laughed' has the subject in nominative, while the transitive verb *got* 'said' has the subject in the oblique.

5.2 Contracted prepositions

Similar to the preposition–pronoun combinations in the Celtic languages, and like the Spanish *contigo* 'with you', Kurmanji has four prepositions which contract with third-person singular complements.

These are *bi* 'with', *ji* 'from', *di* 'at/in' and *li* 'at/in'. They are dealt with in the annotation by assigning to syntactic words to the surface form, one representing the preposition and the other representing the pronoun.

5.3 Circumpositions

In addition to prepositions, Kurmanji also employs circumpositions, where a preposition and a postposition encircle the same noun phrase. In some situations, both the preposition and postposition *must* appear together, e.g. *di … de* 'in …'. In other situations the prepositions can be used on their own. In the latter situation the postposition either modifies or gives a more nuanced meaning to and thus refines the meaning of the preposition. Consider the following example, *Heq di destên we de ye.* 'The truth is in your hands'.

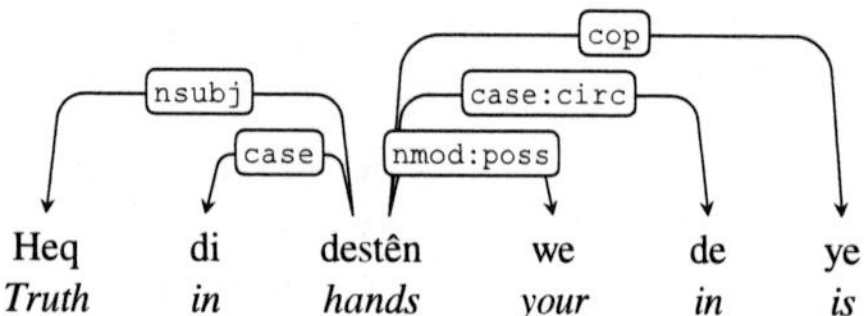

Either the preposition or the postposition can be elided, this phenomenon occurs more frequently in colloquial speech. The elided adposition is the *non-essential* one. If a postposition is part of a circumposition, we annotate it with the language-specific relation `case:circ`.

5.4 Construct case

The construct case in Kurdish is used to link a head noun to adjectival or nominal modifiers.

Construct inflection on the head noun signifies that the following word modifies the initial word. When more than one word modifies the initial word in a construct structure, a *construct extender* is used to show that the second modifier also modifies the initial noun, as opposed to modifying the last noun in the noun–noun structure.

If the phrase only has two elements, then sometimes the construct inflection can be dropped. In this case the head noun is inflected in the nominative case.

The construct case *overrides* any other inflection that the noun might have if it were not in a construct phrase. See Figure 2 for an example of how the construct inflection overrides the inflection from verbal subcategorisation.

5.5 "Light" verbs

We use the term *light verb* to refer to the complex predicates formed of a nominal plus a verb which is used as a single predicate. These are common in languages that Kurmanji is in close contact with, such as Persian and Turkish.

In the treebank we use the label `compound:lvc` to link the nominal part of the predicate to the verb, and consider them as forming a single unit. This is similar to the approach taken in other languages in Universal Dependencies which have this feature.

We use a number of diagnostics for determining if a given expression should be considered a light verb:

- "Is there another patient-like participant in the sentence aside from the nominal involved in the light verb construction?"

- "Is the nominal involved in the construction not inflected as if it were a simple argument to the verb? (i.e. is it inflected in the nominative case where it would otherwise be in the oblique?)"

- "Could this be considered a case of secondary predication?"

- "Are the constituents written together in the infinitive (e.g. in passive constructions, nominal use)"

An example is presented of a straightforward use of a light verb in Kurmanji. *Serokwezîr kuştina sivîlan şermezar dike.* "The Prime Minister condemns the killing of civilians." The word *şermezar*, "shame", is used together with the verb *kirin* to mean condemn, and the construction takes another argument as a direct object.

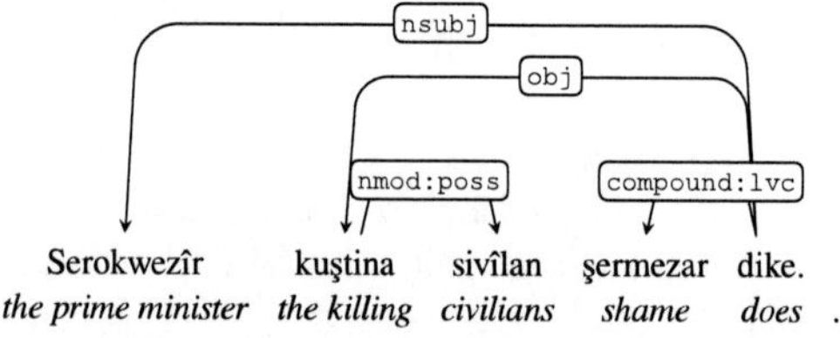

Unlike in some other languages, for example the Turkic languages, in Kurmanji these constructions may be discontinuous with an argument appearing between the verb and the nominal. For example: *Min bêriya te kiriye*, 'I missed you' (lit. I did a before **of you**), has a construct case on the nominal part of

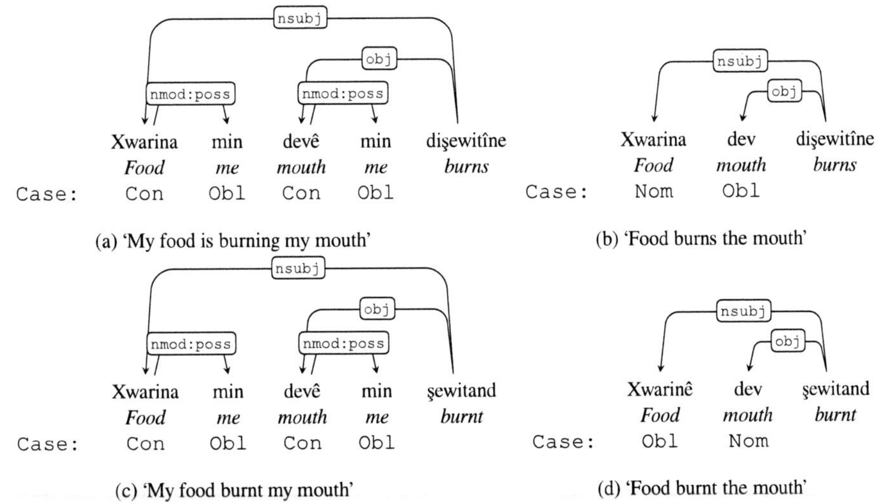

(a) 'My food is burning my mouth'

(b) 'Food burns the mouth'

(c) 'My food burnt my mouth'

(d) 'Food burnt the mouth'

Figure 2: Example of annotation of construct case. Note in (a) and (c) how the construct case overrides the verbal case government, which would have been nominative and oblique respectively (see §5.1).

the light verb construct, *bêriya* 'fore/before', which forms a noun phrase with the argument *te*, 'you'.

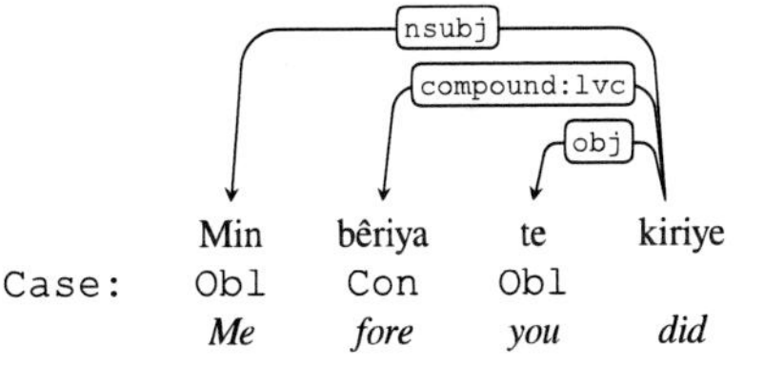

5.6 Future clitic

Future tense is expressed with present subjunctive inflection on the predicate and a *future clitic* after the subject. This clitic is usually in the form *dê*, which we consider to be its lemma in our annotation, but appears as *ê* after pronouns, and the pronoun and clitic often contract. For example compare examples (2a) and (2b).[10]

(2) a. *Hevalê   zilam   dê   min*
         Friend-CON man-OBL FUT me-OBL
         bibîne.
         see-FUT.3SG.

         'The man's friend will see me.'

     b. *Ezê   biçim   malê.*
         I-FUT go-FUT.1SG home.

         'I will go home.'

---

[10]The tag FUT stands for future tense, 3SG and 1SG stand for third and first person singular respectively.

The following example demonstrates the annotation of this feature for the sentence *Hûnê tê de çi bikin?* 'What will you do in there?'.

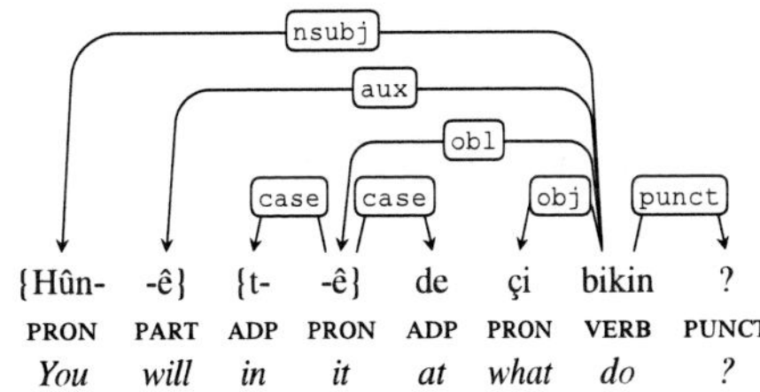

5.7 Pluperfect

The pluperfect tense is syntactically analytic but often contracts, e.g. *kirî bû* becomes *kiribû*. We currently represent this tense synthetically as this is how it is analysed by the morphological analyser. In the next version of UD Kurmanji we plan to split the tense up into its tokens of the main verb and the auxiliary *bûn*.

5.8 Subordination

Subordinate clauses are often formed with specific inflections, subjunctive in the present tense and what we have called 'optative' in the past.

5.8.1 Complement clauses

In some cases subordination of finite clauses also occurs, with or without a complementiser. In the sentence, *Tu ji xwe ewle yî **ko** te dengekî fîkandinê û yê zencîrê bihîst?*, 'Are you sure **that** you heard a sound of whistling and a chain?' subordination is done with the help of the complementiser *ku*, here written as *ko* as a result of dialect variation.

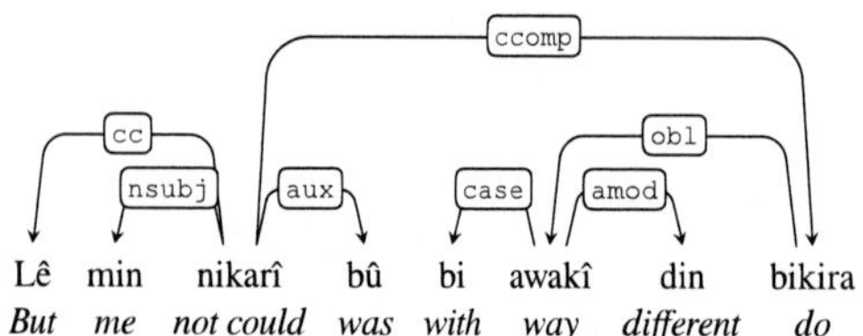

The verb form *bikira* in this sentence is an optative inflection of the verb *kirin*, 'to do'.

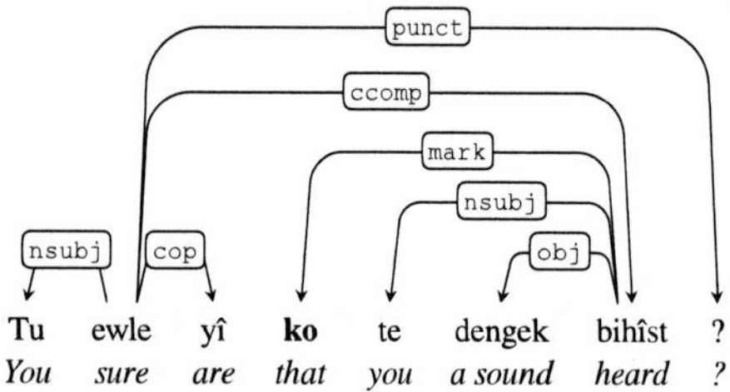

5.8.2 Relative clauses

Relative clauses can be introduced in three ways, which are not necessarily mutually exclusive.

Subjunctive mood: Here the mood of the subordinate clause indicates that the verb form is a nominal modifier. *Di xwezayê de bi hezaran tiştên mirov bixwin hene.* 'In nature things that people eat exist in thousands'.

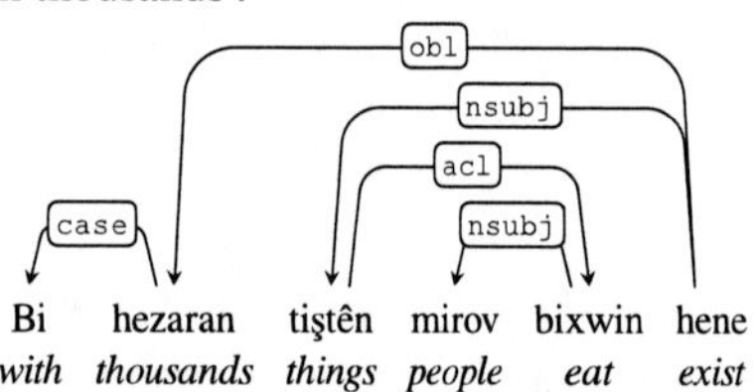

Relative pronoun: Very often a relative clause will be introduced with the use of a relative pronoun, usually *ku* 'that'/'who'. *Mirov ku dojeh nebîne*, 'a person who does not see hell'

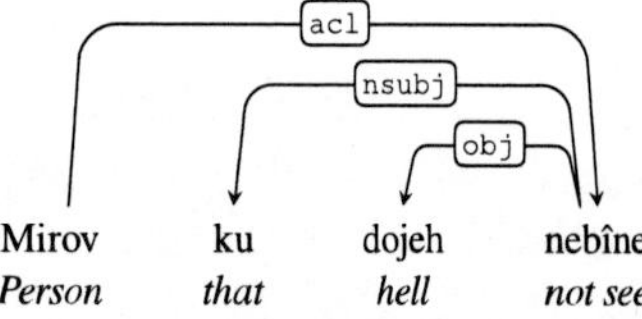

Note that like the English *that*, *ku* in Kurmanji is ambiguous between being a relative pronoun and a complementiser.

Construct case: A nominal in construct case is also a frequent way to introduce a relative clause.

Helbestên ku hatine nivisandin, 'poems that have been written'.

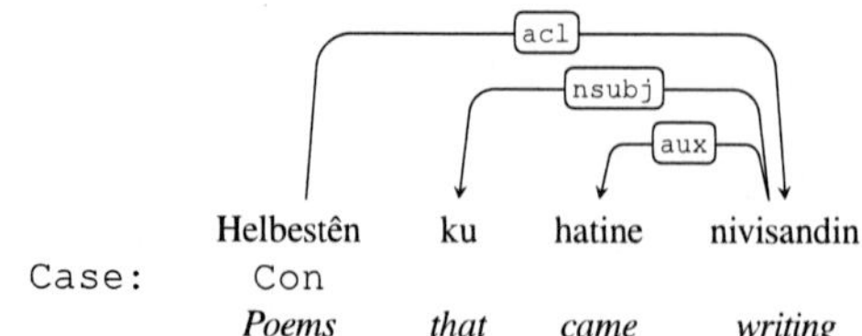

5.8.3 Adverbial clauses

As in other Indo-European languages, in Kurmanji, adverbial clauses are usually introduced by subordinating or adverbial conjunctions. In the following sentence, *Wextê Holmes vegeriya...saet jî bû bû yek,* "By the time Holmes returned, the clock had struck one', the subordinationg conjunction *wextê* 'by' introduces the adverbial clause.

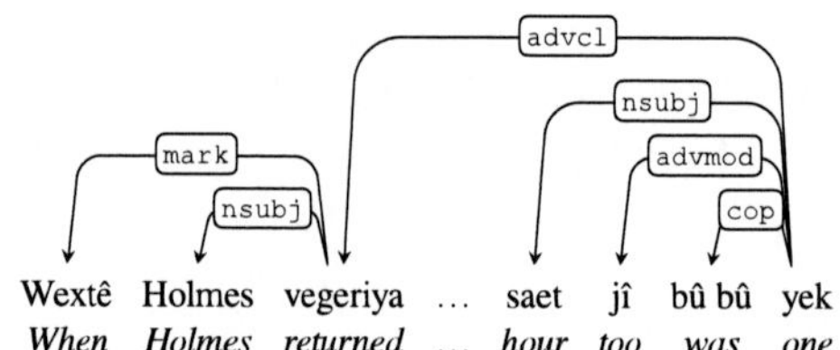

6 Parsing performance

In order to test the treebank in a real setting, we evaluated three widely-used popular dependency parsers: Maltparser (Nivre et al., 2007), UDPipe (Straka et al., 2016) and BiST (Kiperwasser and Goldberg, 2016). In addition we provide results for using the treebank for part-of-speech tagging using UDPipe, to be able to compare with Walther et al. (2010).

The BiST parser requires a separate development set for tuning. The set we used was the sample data from the shared task, this was 20 sentences, or 242 tokens. Both UDPipe and BiST parsers are also able to use word embeddings, we trained the embeddings using `word2vec` (Mikolov et al., 2013) on the raw text of the Kurdish Wikipedia. For Maltparser we used the default settings and for BiST parser we tested the MST algorithm.

We performed 10-fold cross-validation by randomising the order of sentences in the test portion of the corpus and splitting them into 10 equally-sized parts. In each iteration we held out one part for testing (75 sentences) and used the rest for training (675 sentences). We calculated the

Parser	UAS [range]	LAS [range]
Maltparser	69.4 [64.5, 76.7]	61.5 [57.3, 65.3]
BiST	71.2 [68.1, 74.4]	63.8 [60.7, 67.5]
UDPipe	73.1 [66.9, 77.6]	65.9 [59.6, 68.3]
Maltparser [+dict]	71.2 [67.8, 78.7]	64.0 [60.8, 69.3]
BiST [+dict]	72.7 [69.4, 74.5]	66.3 [63.7, 68.5]
UDPipe [+dict]	**74.3 [72.6, 77.2]**	**67.9 [65.6, 70.1]**

Table 2: Preliminary parsing results for UDPipe and Maltparser. The numbers in brackets denote the upper and lower bounds found during cross-validation.

System	Lemma	POS	Morph
UDPipe	88.3 [85.3, 89.6]	88.2 [85.5, 90.8]	78.6 [75.4, 80.1]
UDPipe [+dict]	94.6 [93.9, 95.7]	93.0 [91.8, 93.8]	85.9 [84.2, 87.6]

Table 3: Performance of UDPipe for lemmatisation, part-of-speech and morphological analysis with the default parameters, and with an external full-form morphological lexicon.

labelled-attachment score (LAS) and unlabelled-attachment score (UAS) for each of the models using the CoNLL-2017 evaluation script.[11] The same cross-validation splits were used for training all three parsers.

The morphological analyser and part-of-speech tagger in UDPipe was tested both with and without an external morphological dictionary. In this case the morphological dictionary, shown in Table 2 as `[+dict]`, consisted of a full-form list generated from the morphological analyserdescribed in §4.2 numbering 343,090 entries.

The parsing results are found in Table 2. UDPipe is the best model, and adding the dictionary helps both POS tagging and parsing, an improvement of 2% LAS over the model without a dictionary.

For calculating the results for part-of-speech tagging, morphological analysis and lemmatisation, we used the same experiment but just looked at the results for columns 3, 4, and 6 of the CoNLL-U file. The results presented in Table 3 can be compared with the 85.7% reported by Walther et al. (2010) on 13 sentences. Predictably, in all cases adding the full-form list substantially improves performance.

7 Future work

The most obvious avenue for future work is to annotate more sentences. A treebank of 10,000 tokens is useful, and can be used for bootstrapping, but in order to be able to train a parser useful for parsing unseen sentences we would need to increase the number of tokens 6-10 fold.

We also think that there are prospects for working on other annotation projects based on the treebank, for example a co-reference corpus based on the short story.

There are a number of quirks in the conversion process from VISL to CoNLL-U, for example the language-independent longest-common-subsequence algorithm could be replaced with a Kurmanji specific one that would be able to successfully split tokens like *lê* into *l* and *ê*.

8 Concluding remarks

We have described the first syntactically-annotated corpus of Kurmanji Kurdish, indeed of any Kurdish language. The treebank was used as one of the *surprise language* test sets in the 2017 CoNLL on dependency parsing and is now released to the public. The corpus consists of a little over 10,000 tokens and is released under a free/open-source licence.

Acknowledgements

Work on the morphological analyser was funded through the 2016 Google Summer of Code programme and Prompsit Language Engineering with a contract from Translators without Borders.

We would like to thank Fazil Enis Kalyon, Daria Karam, Cumali Türkmenoğlu, Ferhat Melih Dal, Dilan Köneş, Selman Orhan and Sami Tan for providing native speaker insight and assisting with grammatical and lexical issues.

We would also like to thank Dan Zeman and Martin Popel for insightful discussions and the anonymous reviewers for their detailed and helpful comments.

References

Halil Aktuğ. 2013. *Gramera Kurdî – Kürtçe Gramer*. Avesta Publishing.

Purya Aliabadi, Mohammad Sina Ahmadi, Shahin Salavati, and Kyumars Sheykh Esmaili. 2014. Towards building kurdnet, the kurdish wordnet. In *Proceedings of the 7th Global WordNet Conference*.

Celadet Bedirxan and Roger Lescot. 1990. *Rêzimana Kurdî*.

Eckhard Bick and Tino Didriksen. 2015. Cg-3 – beyond classical constraint grammar. In *Proceedings of*

---

[11] http://universaldependencies.org/conll17/evaluation.html

the 20th Nordic Conference of Computational Linguistics, NODALIDA, pages 31–39. Linköping University Electronic Press, Linköpings universitet.

Kyumars Sheykh Esmaili and Shahin Salavati. 2013. Sorani Kurdish versus Kurmanji Kurdish: An Empirical Comparison. In *Proceedings of the 51st Annual Meeting of the Association for Computational Linguistics*, pages 300–305.

M. L. Forcada, M. Ginestí-Rosell, J. Nordfalk, J. O'Regan, S. Ortiz-Rojas, J. A. Pérez-Ortiz, F. Sánchez-Martínez, G. Ramírez-Sánchez, and F. M. Tyers. 2011. Apertium: a free/open-source platform for rule-based machine translation. *Machine Translation*, 25(2):127–144.

Eliyahu Kiperwasser and Yoav Goldberg. 2016. Simple and accurate dependency parsing using bidirectional LSTM feature representations. *TACL*, 4:313–327.

Tomas Mikolov, Kai Chen, Greg Corrado, and Jeffrey Dean. 2013. Efficient estimation of word representations in vector space. In *Proceedings of Workshop at ICLR*.

J. Nivre, J. Hall, J. Nilsson, A. Chanev, G. Eryigit, S. Kübler, S. Marinov, and E. Marsi. 2007. MaltParser: A language-independent system for data-driven dependency parsing. *Natural Language Engineering*, 13(2):95–135.

Joakim Nivre, Marie-Catherine de Marneffe, Filip Ginter, Yoav Goldberg, Jan Hajič, Chris Manning, Ryan McDonald, Slav Petrov, Sampo Pyysalo, Natalia Silveira, Reut Tsarfaty, and Dan Zeman. 2016. Universal Dependencies v1: A Multilingual Treebank Collection. In *Proceedings of Language Resources and Evaluation Conference (LREC'16)*.

Bişarê Segman. 1944. Dr. Rweylot. *Ronahî*, 24. Trad. Doyle, A. C. (1892) *The Adventure of the Speckled Band*.

Gary F. Simons and Charles D. Fennig, editors. 2017. *Ethnologue: Languages of the World*. SIL International.

Milan Straka, Jan Hajič, and Jana Straková. 2016. UDPipe: trainable pipeline for processing CoNLL-U files performing tokenization, morphological analysis, pos tagging and parsing. In *Proceedings of the Tenth International Conference on Language Resources and Evaluation (LREC'16)*, Paris, France, May. European Language Resources Association (ELRA).

Wheeler M. Thackston. 2006. *Kurmanji Kurdish: A Reference Grammar with Selected Readings.* http://www.fas.harvard.edu/~iranian/Kurmanji/index.html.

Géraldine Walther, Benoît Sagot, and Karën Fort. 2010. Fast Development of Basic NLP Tools: Towards a Lexicon and a POS Tagger for Kurmanji Kurdish. In *International Conference on Lexis and Grammar*, September.

Daniel Zeman, Martin Popel, Milan Straka, Jan Hajic, Joakim Nivre, Filip Ginter, Juhani Luotolahti, Sampo Pyysalo, Slav Petrov, Martin Potthast, Francis Tyers, Elena Badmaeva, Memduh Gökırmak, Anna Nedoluzhko, Silvie Cinkova, Jan Hajic jr., Jaroslava Hlavacova, Václava Kettnerová, Zdenka Uresova, Jenna Kanerva, Stina Ojala, Anna Missilä, Christopher D. Manning, Sebastian Schuster, Siva Reddy, Dima Taji, Nizar Habash, Herman Leung, Marie-Catherine de Marneffe, Manuela Sanguinetti, Maria Simi, Hiroshi Kanayama, Valeria dePaiva, Kira Droganova, Héctor Martínez Alonso, Çağrı Çöltekin, Umut Sulubacak, Hans Uszkoreit, Vivien Macketanz, Aljoscha Burchardt, Kim Harris, Katrin Marheinecke, Georg Rehm, Tolga Kayadelen, Mohammed Attia, Ali Elkahky, Zhuoran Yu, Emily Pitler, Saran Lertpradit, Michael Mandl, Jesse Kirchner, Hector Fernandez Alcalde, Jana Strnadová, Esha Banerjee, Ruli Manurung, Antonio Stella, Atsuko Shimada, Sookyoung Kwak, Gustavo Mendonca, Tatiana Lando, Rattima Nitisaroj, and Josie Li. 2017. Conll 2017 shared task: Multilingual parsing from raw text to Universal Dependencies. In *Proceedings of the CoNLL 2017 Shared Task: Multilingual Parsing from Raw Text to Universal Dependencies*, pages 1–19, Vancouver, Canada, August. Association for Computational Linguistics.

Appendix A.   Format

Example sentence in VISL format, *Diviya bû tiştekî mihim qewimî biwa.* 'It must have been that something important had happened'

```
"<Diviya bû>"
        "divêtin" vblex plu p3 sg @root #1->0
"<tiştekî>"
        "tişt" n m sg con ind @nsubj #2->4
"<mihim>"
        "mihim" adj pst @amod #3->2
"<qewimî>"
        "qewimin" vblex iv pp @ccomp #4->1
"<biwa>"
        "bûn" vaux narr p3 sg @aux #5->4
"<.>"
        "." sent @punct #6->1
```

What are the limitations on the flux of syntactic dependencies?
Evidence from UD treebanks

Sylvain Kahane
Modyco
Université Paris Nanterre
CNRS – France
sylvain@kahane.fr

Chunxiao Yan
Modyco
Université Paris Nanterre
CNRS – France
yanchunxiao@yahoo.fr

Marie-Amélie Botalla
Lattice
Université Sorbonne Nouvelle
CNRS – France
marie-amelie.botalla
@sorbonne-nouvelle.fr

Abstract

The aim of this paper is to study some characteristics of dependency flux, that is the set of dependencies linking a word on the left with a word on the right in a given position. Based on an exploration of the whole set of UD treebanks (12M word corpus), we show that what we have called the flux weight, which measures center embeddings, is less than 3 in 99.62 % of the inter-word positions and is bounded by 6, which could be due to short-term memory limitations.

1 Introduction

It is generally recognized that speaker performance is limited by several factors and especially by short-term memory. Yngve (1960) was one of the first to take these limitations into account in language modeling, on the grounds that "although all languages have a grammar based on constituent structure, the sentences actually used in the spoken language have a depth that does not exceed a certain number equal or nearly equal to the span of immediate memory (presently assumed to be 7 ± 2)." This 7 ± 2 bound refers to the famous paper by Miller (1956). Miller (1962) and Chomsky and Miller (1963) stated that center-embedded constructions are limited. Very few studies have been conducted, however, on limitations on the syntactic structure. Gibson (1998) stated that "memory cost is hypothesized to be quantified in terms of the number of syntactic categories that are necessary to complete the current input string as a grammatical sentence", as well as the length during which "a predicted category must be kept in memory before the prediction is satisfied". Muratu et al. (2001) verified on a 20K word corpus of Japanese that the number of words on the left of a position that can have a dependent on the right (which will be called the left span of flux here) was bounded by 10. Liu (2008), Liu et al. (2009), and Liu (2010) expressed Gibson's hypothesis in terms of dependency length and studied it on Chinese data and on treebanks of 20 different languages.

In this paper, we will study *dependency flux*, that is the set of dependencies linking a word on the left with a word on the right in a given inter-word position. The notion of dependency flux was introduced in Kahane (2001:67) and previously studied on corpora of written French (Jardonnet 2009) and spoken French (Botalla 2014). This new study (Yan 2017) was conducted on the whole series of dependency treebanks provided by the Universal Dependencies (UD) project (Nivre et al. 2016), comprising 12M words and 630K sentences distributed in 70 treebanks of 50 languages.[1] Several features of the flux were measured: size, left and right spans, weight and density. Weight, which measures center embeddings and nested constructions, has stable properties: it seems to be distributed quite similarly in each corpus and language, and it is less than 3 in the overwhelming majority of the inter-word positions (99.62 %) and it never exceeds 6.

Dependency flux and its main characteristics are defined in Section 2 and studied on the UD treebanks in Section 3. A closer look at weight is proposed in Section 4.

---

[1] Our experiments have been done on UD v2 available in May 2017.

Proceedings of the Fourth International Conference on Dependency Linguistics (Depling 2017), pages 73-82,
Pisa, Italy, September 18-20 2017

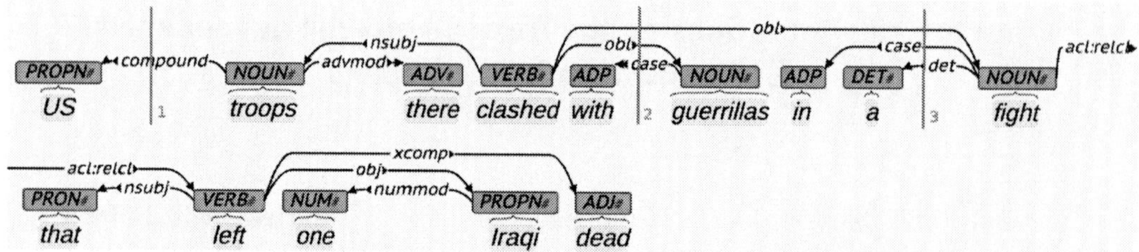

Figure 1. A UD dependency tree with three inter-word positions marked

2 Dependency flux and its characteristics

2.1 Definition and size

The *dependency flux* in a given inter-word position is the set of dependencies at this position, that is, linking a word on the left with a word on the right. In Fig. 1, the flux contains one dependency at position 1, three at positions 2 and 3.

The *size* of the flux is the number of dependencies belonging to it. The size of the flux is the most basic information about the flux. It is therefore a useful starting point for apprehending other concepts about flux.

Two dependencies are said to be *concomitant* if they belong to the same flux. The dependencies "with <case guerillas" and "clashed obl> fight" are concomitant at position 2.

The flux represents the set of pending syntactic relations that the speaker has to keep in mind after every word. One might expect it to be limited by the same boundary as that stated by Miller (1956) and not exceed 7 ± 2. We will see that this is not the case.

2.2 Spans and bouquets

Other characteristics of the flux can be considered. The *left span* (resp. *right span*) of the flux is the number of words on the left (resp. right) which are vertices of a dependency in the flux. For instance, the left span is 1 in position 1 (*US*), 2 in position 2 (*clashed, with*) and 3 in position 3 (*clashed, in, a*).

The left span in a given position corresponds to the number of words awaiting a governor or a dependent on the right of this position and the right span to the number of elements expected. In a transition-based parser (Bohnet & Nivre 2012, Dyer et al. 2015), it is the minimal number of words that must be stored in the stack.[2] Again,

one might expect the left span to be bounded due to short-term memory limitations, but it is not really the case. This can be illustrated by looking at what happens at position 3: the left span is 3 but the right span is only 1; all the words of the left span are linked to the same word (*fight*) on the right. This means that the information can be factorized and that the three words in the left span count more or less as one, which is their common target.

The flux configuration in position 3 is called a *left-branching bouquet*. A *bouquet* is a set of dependencies sharing the same vertex. When the common vertex is on the left, the bouquet is *right-branching*, and *left-branching* when the common vertex is on the right (Fig. 2).

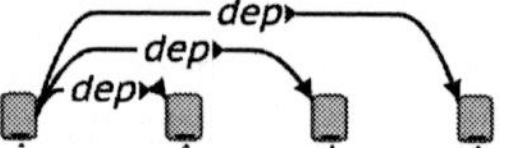

Figure 2. Right-branching bouquet

2.3 Disjoint dependencies and weight

We would like to measure the flux modulo the bouquets. This measure will be called the *weight* of the flux.

A set of dependencies is said to be *disjoint* if the dependencies do not share any vertex (Fig. 3). The *weight* is the size of the largest disjoint subset of dependencies in the flux.

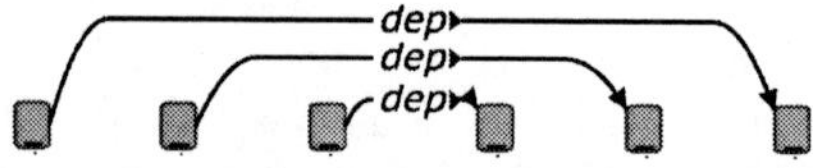

Figure 3. Disjoint dependencies

The weight of the flux is equal to 1 in position 3: it is not possible to find two disjoint dependencies. The weight is equal to 2 in position 2 because the subset { *with* <case *guerrillas*, *clashed* obl> *fight* } is disjoint but there is no disjoint subset with 3 elements.

---

[2] In practice all the nodes that are likely to have a dependent on the right are stored in the stack in arc-standard and arc-eager parsing strategies.

As we will see in the next section, the weight is clearly bounded. The weight measures more or less the center-embeddings: the fact that the dependency "*with* <case *guerrillas*" is disjoint from "*clashed* obl> *fight*" but concomitant means that the phrase *with guerrillas* headed by *guerrillas* is center-embedded in the phrase headed by *clashed*.[3] In other words, the weight is likely to measure the cognitive cost of parsing. This is noticeable if we compare the flux in positions 2 and 3. We saw earlier that the sizes of the flux at these two positions are equal: both have a value of 3. However, their weights are unequal: the weight at position 2 has a value of 2, whereas the weight at position 3 has a value of 1. Position 3 is simpler than position 2, because, as said before, the three dependencies at position 3 have a common target and requires less cognitive space than the disjoint dependencies at position 2.

We hypothesize that dependencies forming bouquets are cognitively less costly than dependencies forming disjoint subsets. This hypothesis is supported by the fact that the flux weight is clearly bounded while the size is not. We suppose that information can be factorized in case of dependencies sharing a same vertex. It is quite intuitive with right-branching bouquet, when the common vertex is on the left: only this vertex must be stored to analyze the bouquet. We postulate that the complexity is quite similar in case of left-branching bouquet, when two words are waiting for the same target word, but it remains to be proved by further studies.

Another advantage of the weight on the size is that it smooths out some idiosyncrasies of the UD scheme. For instance, coordination is analyzed in UD with every conjunct depending on the first conjunct, forming potentially very extended right-branching bouquets.

To calculate the weight, we have to find the biggest subset of disjoint dependencies in the flux. We can start with any dependency D in the flux with at least one vertex that is not shared with other dependencies in the flux (such a dependency exists because the structure is acyclic). Then we suppress all the dependencies that share a vertex with D and therefore cannot be disjoint from D. If the remaining flux is not empty we start over exactly the same process: choosing a dependency with at least one vertex that is not shared with other dependencies in the remaining

flux and deleting all the dependencies sharing a vertex with it. At the end we obtain one of the biggest sets of disjoint dependencies in the flux. This simple algorithm is linear in time.

2.4 R/L ratio and density

Note that the size of the flux is higher than the left and right span, which are both higher than the weight. Some ratios can be interesting to study.

Head-initial languages, such as Standard Arabic or Welsh, have right-branching dependency trees, while head-final languages, such as Japanese, Korean, or Turkish, have left-branching dependency trees. In other words, head-initial languages should have an *R/L ratio* (where R is the right span and L is the left span) higher than 1 and head-final languages an R/L ratio less than 1. Unfortunately, UD is not a very good resource to measure that due to some idiosyncrasies of the UD scheme, such as the right-branching analysis of coordination, which is particularly irrelevant for head-final languages.

The *density* of the flux is the W/S ratio, where W is the weight and S is the size. This ratio measures the proportion of bouquets in the flux: a disjoint flux, that is, a flux without bouquets, has a density of 1. The more bouquets the flux has, the lower the density is. For instance, the density in position 1 is 1, in position 2, 2/3, and in position 3, 1/3.

3 Results on UD

3.1 The UD corpus

We studied the flux on the whole collection of UD treebanks. The 70 dependency treebanks distributed by the UD project have all been corrected manually and they follow a common annotation scheme. Nevertheless, these treebanks were developed by different teams, who may have interpreted the guidelines differently and the coherence and quality of the different treebanks have not yet been verified. And as mentioned above, some of the decisions made for the UD annotation scheme are not very suitable for a study of flux. Despite the defects of this resource, however, it is the only available resource of this scale allowing a cross-linguistic study of 50 different languages.

3.2 List of measures

Table 1 gives the following measures of the flux for each UD treebank. Average values were

---

[3] In UD, prepositions are dependent on the noun they introduce. That is why the head of the PP *with guerrillas* is the noun in the dependency tree taken as an example here.

calculated on the values in each inter-word position.

- S-max: maximum size
- S-av: average size
- W-max: maximum weight
- W-av: average weight
- L-max: maximum left span
- R-max: maximum right span
- L-av: average left span
- R-ax: average right span
- R/L-av: average R/L ratio
- D-av: density = average W/S ratio

3.3 Sizes

The maximum size varies from 8 for Kazakh, Sanskrit, Uyghur, and Vietnamese, to 97 for Ancient Greek. The average size ranges from 1.92 for Polish to 3.61 for Czech-CLTT. As said before, the highest sizes are due to the bouquet-wise annotation of some constructions, such as coordination (`conj`), apposition (`appos`), flat (sic!) constructions (`flat`), and multiword expressions (`fixed`). We converted the annotations to obtain a string-analysis of these constructions, giving a maximum size between 6 for Sanskrit and 77 for Arabic-NYUAD and an average size between 1.89 for Polish and 3.44 for Persian.[4] Further investigations are needed to understand what could cause excessive flux sizes.

3.4 Weights

Compared to the size, the weight is more stable. The maximum weight ranges from 3 (only for Sanskrit) to 6. In the whole UD database only one occurrence with a weight of 7 was found, for Czech-CLTT. Most of the fluxes with a maximum weight that we checked were due to erroneous analysis. The average weight varied from 1.18 for Polish and Slovak to 1.77 for Czech-CLTT. Weight is studied in greater detail in the next section.

3.5 Spans

The left span is more stable among the various treebanks than the right span with values between 7 and 17 against values between 5 and 97. As expected, treebanks with the highest R/L ratio are head-initial languages: 1.31 for Old Church Slavonic, 1.37 for Irish, 1.55 and 1.32 for Arabic, 1.22 for Indonesian and 1.23 for Gothic. The first

exception is the value of 1.36 for Czech-CLTT, but this small corpus of Czech is atypical, the other two Czech treebanks having R/L ratios of 1.03 and 1.00. The second exception is that we have the value of 1.29 for Dutch-LassySmall, while the other Dutch treebank has an R/L ratio of 0.92 for Dutch.

The results for head-final languages are not relevant, as forecasted. Japanese has an R/L ratio of 1.17, Turkish, 1.04, and Korean 0.99, while the minimum ratio is 0.77 for Persian. The average ratio on the whole database is 1.05.

3.6 Densities

The density is quite stable with an average value between 57.00 % for Persian and 72.20 % for Polish, with 65.31 % for the whole database. This means that about 2/3 of dependencies in the flux form together disjoint sets and 1/3 are additional dependencies forming bouquets with the 2 other thirds. In fact, many fluxes have a density of 1 with only one element, as the flux at position 1 in Fig. 1, and form disjoint fluxes consequently.

4 A closer look at weight

4.1 Distribution of weight

Table 2 shows the distribution of the value of the weight of the flux for the 70 treebanks. For each treebank and each value between 1 and 6, we indicate the percentage of inter-word positions in the treebank with this value.

The first main result is that 99.62 % of interword positions in the whole UD database have a weight less than (or equal to) 3. Only 0.36 % have a weight of 4, 0.02 %, of 5, and 0.00 % of 6. For Polish, Sanskrit, Slovak and Vietnamese, 99.9 % of positions have a weight less than 3.

We have seen that some small corpora, such as Czech-CLLT, can have more exceptional values. If we put corpora with fewer than 1,000 sentences aside, Arabic, Chinese, and Korean are the three languages with more than 10% of positions with weight of 3.

Positions with a flux weight of 1 account for 62.15 % of positions in the whole database, and more than 80 % of positions in Finnish-FTB, Polish, and Slovak.

---

[4] The maximum size for Arabic is due to a sentence with 385 words and 77 nominal modifier (`nmod`) relations depending on the 5th word, which is likely to be a wrong analysis.

	Tokens	Trees	S-max	S-av	W-max	W-av	L-max	R-max	L-av	R-av	R/L-av	D-av
UD_Ancient_Greek	182030	12613	97	3,01	6	1,49	12	97	2,31	1,99	1,13	60,32%
UD_Ancient_Greek-PROIEL	198034	15865	31	2,89	6	1,49	12	29	2,19	1,99	1,14	61,96%
UD_Arabic	254120	6984	36	2,93	5	1,66	9	35	2,06	2,41	1,32	66,47%
UD_Arabic-NYUAD	738889	19738	78	3,12	6	1,66	12	78	1,95	2,74	1,55	64,65%
UD_Basque	97069	7194	13	2,25	5	1,36	9	11	1,86	1,63	1,05	70,68%
UD_Belarusian	6864	333	17	2,48	4	1,44	9	17	1,98	1,78	1,09	69,28%
UD_Bulgarian	140425	10022	14	2,24	5	1,28	9	14	1,90	1,50	0,97	67,67%
UD_Catalan	474069	14832	20	2,69	6	1,48	13	19	2,17	1,83	1,03	64,16%
UD_Chinese	111271	4497	27	3,24	6	1,65	14	25	2,77	1,86	0,84	61,28%
UD_Coptic	8519	320	9	2,74	4	1,43	8	8	2,23	1,74	1,00	60,08%
UD_Croatian	183816	8289	13	2,52	5	1,40	11	13	2,13	1,65	0,98	65,74%
UD_Czech	1332566	77765	56	2,43	6	1,37	17	56	2,03	1,63	1,00	67,23%
UD_Czech-CAC	483520	24081	47	2,50	6	1,39	11	47	2,04	1,71	1,03	66,49%
UD_Czech-CLTT	26781	814	28	3,61	7	1,77	10	24	2,36	2,83	1,36	62,24%
UD_Danish	90710	4947	16	2,61	4	1,34	16	12	2,20	1,61	0,97	63,32%
UD_Dutch	197925	13050	15	2,89	5	1,43	12	15	2,46	1,69	0,92	60,44%
UD_Dutch-LassySmall	91793	6841	29	2,74	4	1,33	10	29	2,06	1,87	1,21	61,32%
UD_English	229733	14545	18	2,58	6	1,35	13	17	2,19	1,58	0,92	63,01%
UD_English-LinES	67197	3650	25	2,54	5	1,35	10	24	2,13	1,61	0,95	63,89%
UD_English-ParTUT	38114	1590	15	2,63	5	1,39	9	14	2,26	1,60	0,89	62,79%
UD_Estonian	34628	3172	10	2,26	5	1,25	9	10	1,82	1,58	1,11	68,04%
UD_Finnish	180911	13581	33	2,31	6	1,31	10	33	1,89	1,63	1,06	68,53%
UD_Finnish-FTB	143326	16856	14	2,06	5	1,19	11	14	1,77	1,39	0,98	70,29%
UD_French	392230	16031	34	2,51	5	1,39	11	34	2,04	1,71	1,02	65,09%
UD_French-ParTUT	17927	620	11	2,70	5	1,44	11	10	2,31	1,68	0,91	62,86%
UD_French-Sequoia	60574	2643	31	2,63	5	1,44	12	31	2,15	1,75	1,00	64,58%
UD_Galician	109106	3139	15	2,56	5	1,41	11	15	2,04	1,80	1,08	64,54%
UD_Galician-TreeGal	15436	600	13	2,55	4	1,43	9	12	2,12	1,71	1,00	65,30%
UD_German	281974	14917	28	3,00	6	1,46	13	26	2,51	1,76	0,96	59,84%
UD_Gothic	45138	4372	21	2,53	4	1,38	10	20	1,87	1,91	1,23	65,96%
UD_Greek	51351	2065	13	2,51	5	1,41	10	9	2,12	1,65	0,95	65,57%
UD_Hebrew	149088	5725	62	2,56	5	1,48	11	61	2,01	1,86	1,11	66,99%
UD_Hindi	316274	14963	18	3,20	6	1,58	13	15	2,76	1,84	0,85	59,67%
UD_Hungarian	31584	1351	13	2,83	6	1,54	10	10	2,44	1,75	0,89	64,54%
UD_Indonesian	110143	5036	28	2,31	5	1,39	9	28	1,75	1,85	1,22	70,30%
UD_Irish	13826	566	18	2,88	5	1,56	7	18	1,94	2,34	1,37	64,95%
UD_Italian	282611	13402	35	2,50	5	1,39	10	34	2,10	1,65	0,96	65,69%
UD_Italian-ParTUT	42651	1590	14	2,59	5	1,43	9	14	2,20	1,66	0,93	64,46%
UD_Japanese	173458	7675	15	2,79	5	1,55	15	11	2,17	2,03	1,17	64,52%
UD_Kazakh	529	31	8	2,67	4	1,52	6	5	2,21	1,82	1,00	67,07%
UD_Korean	63426	5350	23	2,73	5	1,62	9	20	2,25	1,93	0,99	68,80%
UD_Latin	18184	1334	17	2,86	5	1,52	8	16	2,31	1,87	1,02	63,32%
UD_Latin-ITTB	280734	16508	11	2,67	6	1,46	10	10	2,30	1,65	0,89	64,10%
UD_Latin-PROIEL	159407	15324	28	2,77	6	1,47	14	28	2,15	1,91	1,12	64,14%
UD_Latvian	44795	3054	18	2,48	6	1,39	9	17	2,04	1,68	0,99	67,31%
UD_Lithuanian	5356	263	14	2,43	4	1,38	9	13	2,06	1,60	0,95	68,01%
UD_Norwegian-Bokmaal	280256	18106	38	2,44	5	1,30	11	38	2,08	1,54	0,96	64,18%
UD_Norwegian-Nynorsk	276580	16064	38	2,50	6	1,32	11	38	2,12	1,57	0,96	63,82%
UD_Old_Church_Slavonic	47532	5196	20	2,48	5	1,34	8	19	1,76	1,93	1,31	66,03%
UD_Persian	136896	5397	14	3,45	6	1,64	13	10	3,03	1,81	0,77	57,00%
UD_Polish	72763	7127	10	1,92	4	1,18	8	7	1,62	1,40	1,04	72,20%
UD_Portuguese	217591	8891	19	2,54	5	1,43	13	19	2,12	1,70	0,98	65,84%
UD_Portuguese-BR	287884	10874	38	2,54	5	1,45	10	38	2,05	1,77	1,04	66,46%
UD_Romanian	202187	8795	14	2,39	6	1,40	9	14	1,95	1,69	1,05	67,75%
UD_Russian	87841	4429	31	2,34	5	1,37	10	30	1,83	1,74	1,12	69,62%
UD_Russian-SynTagRus	988460	55398	18	2,34	6	1,37	10	17	1,94	1,63	1,01	68,64%
UD_Sanskrit	1206	190	8	2,23	3	1,29	6	5	2,05	1,39	0,82	68,76%
UD_Slovak	93015	9543	10	2,00	4	1,18	9	8	1,74	1,36	0,96	70,22%
UD_Slovenian	126593	7212	17	2,50	5	1,30	13	17	2,21	1,47	0,87	64,12%
UD_Slovenian-SST	19488	2137	14	2,77	4	1,33	12	8	2,34	1,62	0,94	60,51%
UD_Spanish	419587	15587	38	2,51	5	1,42	11	38	2,03	1,74	1,04	65,91%
UD_Spanish-AnCora	496953	15959	31	2,63	5	1,47	12	31	2,16	1,76	1,00	65,21%
UD_Swedish	76442	4807	31	2,58	5	1,32	10	31	2,07	1,68	1,04	62,95%
UD_Swedish-LinES	64787	3650	25	2,55	5	1,34	10	24	2,07	1,67	1,03	63,25%
UD_Tamil	9581	600	10	2,42	4	1,48	9	8	2,07	1,74	1,00	70,91%
UD_Turkish	48093	4660	13	2,44	6	1,48	9	13	2,00	1,77	1,04	71,20%
UD_Ukrainian	12846	863	11	2,19	4	1,27	8	9	1,85	1,49	0,98	69,22%
UD_Urdu	123271	4595	32	3,44	5	1,66	15	29	2,92	1,96	0,85	58,34%
UD_Uyghur	1662	100	8	2,93	5	1,73	7	6	2,75	1,80	0,77	67,31%
UD_Vietnamese	31799	2200	8	2,09	4	1,25	7	8	1,68	1,57	1,12	70,45%
Total	1E+007	630518	97	2,62	7	1,43	17	97	2,11	1,79	1,05	65,31%

Table 1: Size, weight, left and right spans, R/L ratio and density for the 70 UD treebanks available

	Tokens	Trees	1	2	3	4	5	6
UD_Ancient_Greek	182030	12613	57.77%	35.79%	5.96%	0.45%	0.02%	0.00%
UD_Ancient_Greek-PROIEL	198034	15865	57.81%	35.97%	5.74%	0.46%	0.02%	0.00%
UD_Arabic	254120	6984	47.15%	41.10%	10.60%	1.10%	0.05%	0.00%
UD_Arabic-NYUAD	738889	19738	47.16%	40.86%	10.67%	1.23%	0.08%	0.00%
UD_Basque	97069	7194	67.85%	28.28%	3.66%	0.21%	0.01%	0.00%
UD_Belarusian	6864	333	62.43%	31.70%	5.37%	0.50%	0.00%	0.00%
UD_Bulgarian	140425	10022	73.86%	24.20%	1.87%	0.06%	0.00%	0.00%
UD_Catalan	474069	14832	57.82%	36.58%	5.30%	0.30%	0.01%	0.00%
UD_Chinese	111271	4497	49.73%	37.35%	10.91%	1.78%	0.22%	0.01%
UD_Coptic	8519	320	61.76%	33.74%	4.37%	0.13%	0.01%	0.00%
UD_Croatian	183816	8289	64.46%	31.70%	3.66%	0.17%	0.01%	0.00%
UD_Czech	1332566	77765	66.78%	29.61%	3.42%	0.17%	0.01%	0.00%
UD_Czech-CAC	483520	24081	65.16%	30.82%	3.80%	0.22%	0.01%	0.00%
UD_Czech-CLTT	26781	814	42.78%	41.74%	12.19%	2.71%	0.53%	0.05%
UD_Danish	90710	4947	69.13%	27.85%	2.90%	0.12%	0.00%	0.00%
UD_Dutch	197925	13050	63.41%	31.12%	5.00%	0.44%	0.02%	0.00%
UD_Dutch-LassySmall	91793	6841	70.30%	27.04%	2.50%	0.15%	0.00%	0.00%
UD_English	229733	14545	68.45%	28.08%	3.29%	0.17%	0.00%	0.00%
UD_English-LinES	67197	3650	68.40%	28.16%	3.20%	0.23%	0.01%	0.00%
UD_English-ParTUT	38114	1590	64.99%	31.09%	3.77%	0.15%	0.00%	0.00%
UD_Estonian	34628	3172	77.26%	20.37%	2.21%	0.15%	0.01%	0.00%
UD_Finnish	180911	13581	72.60%	23.79%	3.28%	0.30%	0.03%	0.00%
UD_Finnish-FTB	143326	16856	82.77%	15.91%	1.22%	0.10%	0.00%	0.00%
UD_French	392230	16031	64.31%	32.23%	3.27%	0.17%	0.01%	0.00%
UD_French-ParTUT	17927	620	60.66%	34.99%	4.05%	0.26%	0.03%	0.00%
UD_French-Sequoia	60574	2643	61.25%	33.76%	4.69%	0.29%	0.01%	0.00%
UD_Galician	109106	3139	62.78%	33.73%	3.34%	0.14%	0.00%	0.00%
UD_Galician-TreeGal	15436	600	61.98%	33.75%	4.02%	0.25%	0.00%	0.00%
UD_German	281974	14917	59.60%	35.60%	4.46%	0.33%	0.01%	0.00%
UD_Gothic	45138	4372	65.83%	30.51%	3.46%	0.21%	0.00%	0.00%
UD_Greek	51351	2065	62.49%	33.73%	3.59%	0.19%	0.00%	0.00%
UD_Hebrew	149088	5725	58.04%	36.56%	5.17%	0.23%	0.00%	0.00%
UD_Hindi	316274	14963	49.02%	44.76%	5.65%	0.54%	0.03%	0.00%
UD_Hungarian	31584	1351	56.04%	35.24%	7.58%	0.99%	0.14%	0.02%
UD_Indonesian	110143	5036	64.82%	31.38%	3.61%	0.18%	0.01%	0.00%
UD_Irish	13826	566	53.11%	38.57%	7.47%	0.82%	0.03%	0.00%
UD_Italian	282611	13402	64.93%	31.55%	3.37%	0.16%	0.01%	0.00%
UD_Italian-ParTUT	42651	1590	61.56%	34.48%	3.78%	0.17%	0.00%	0.00%
UD_Japanese	173458	7675	50.98%	42.82%	6.03%	0.17%	0.00%	0.00%
UD_Kazakh	529	31	55.27%	37.42%	6.88%	0.43%	0.00%	0.00%
UD_Korean	63426	5350	51.30%	37.10%	10.24%	1.28%	0.09%	0.00%
UD_Latin	18184	1334	56.34%	35.90%	7.01%	0.69%	0.06%	0.00%
UD_Latin-ITTB	280734	16508	60.44%	33.25%	5.85%	0.45%	0.02%	0.00%
UD_Latin-PROIEL	159407	15324	61.30%	31.41%	6.27%	0.92%	0.10%	0.00%
UD_Latvian	44795	3054	67.21%	27.51%	4.75%	0.48%	0.05%	0.01%
UD_Lithuanian	5356	263	66.76%	28.97%	4.07%	0.21%	0.00%	0.00%
UD_Norwegian-Bokmaal	280256	18106	72.73%	24.95%	2.23%	0.08%	0.00%	0.00%
UD_Norwegian-Nynorsk	276580	16064	70.73%	26.67%	2.50%	0.10%	0.00%	0.00%
UD_Old_Church_Slavonic	47532	5196	69.31%	27.41%	3.15%	0.13%	0.00%	0.00%
UD_Persian	136896	5397	45.75%	45.14%	8.52%	0.59%	0.01%	0.00%
UD_Polish	72763	7127	82.46%	16.96%	0.57%	0.00%	0.00%	0.00%
UD_Portuguese	217591	8891	61.69%	33.94%	4.16%	0.21%	0.01%	0.00%
UD_Portuguese-BR	287884	10874	60.06%	35.50%	4.24%	0.20%	0.01%	0.00%
UD_Romanian	202187	8795	64.42%	31.62%	3.74%	0.22%	0.00%	0.00%
UD_Russian	87841	4429	66.76%	29.75%	3.28%	0.21%	0.00%	0.00%
UD_Russian-SynTagRus	988460	55398	67.30%	29.04%	3.42%	0.23%	0.01%	0.00%
UD_Sanskrit	1206	190	71.95%	27.07%	0.98%	0.00%	0.00%	0.00%
UD_Slovak	93015	9543	83.09%	16.24%	0.66%	0.01%	0.00%	0.00%
UD_Slovenian	126593	7212	72.12%	25.49%	2.31%	0.08%	0.00%	0.00%
UD_Slovenian-SST	19488	2137	70.09%	26.59%	3.17%	0.15%	0.00%	0.00%
UD_Spanish	419587	15587	61.54%	34.75%	3.56%	0.15%	0.01%	0.00%
UD_Spanish-AnCora	496953	15959	58.20%	36.45%	5.10%	0.25%	0.00%	0.00%
UD_Swedish	76442	4807	70.77%	26.62%	2.50%	0.10%	0.01%	0.00%
UD_Swedish-LinES	64787	3650	69.32%	27.51%	3.03%	0.13%	0.00%	0.00%
UD_Tamil	9581	600	58.14%	36.18%	5.23%	0.45%	0.00%	0.00%
UD_Turkish	48093	4660	60.71%	31.69%	6.69%	0.85%	0.06%	0.00%
UD_Ukrainian	12846	863	74.84%	23.60%	1.49%	0.06%	0.00%	0.00%
UD_Urdu	123271	4595	44.94%	45.09%	8.82%	1.04%	0.11%	0.00%
UD_Uyghur	1662	100	43.87%	42.16%	11.50%	2.12%	0.34%	0.00%
UD_Vietnamese	31799	2200	76.10%	22.71%	1.18%	0.01%	0.00%	0.00%
Total	1.2E+07	630518	62.15%	32.75%	4.71%	0.36%	0.02%	0.00%

Table 2: Percentage of inter-word positions for every possible value of the weight

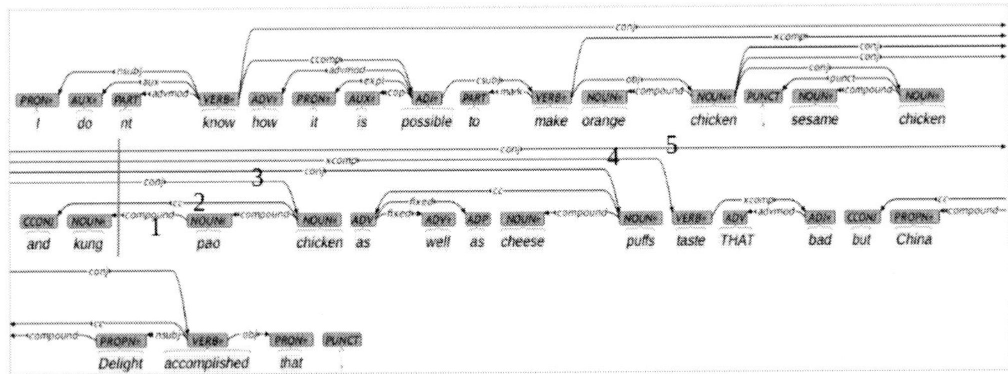

Figure 4. A dependency tree from UD-English with weight 5

We do not have enough metadata to know if the differences between treebanks are due to differences between languages or to differences between genres. It is highly likely that some kinds of texts (e.g. legal texts, specification sheets) are much more complicated than others. For 16 languages, there are two or three treebanks and noticeable divergences are observed in only three cases (Finnish, Dutch, and again Czech-CLTT). At first sight variations between languages appear to be greater than variations between corpora in the same language, but this point needs further investigation.

4.2 Examples

The only example of English with weight 6 was erroneously annotated. We give here two examples with weight 5. In all the examples, punctuation links (`punct`) have been removed and are not considered.

(1) *I dont know how it is possible to make orange chicken, sesame chicken and kung pao chicken as well as cheese puffs taste THAT bad but China Delight accomplished that.* (en-ud-train.conllu sent_id = reviews-235423-0012)

Sentence (1) has a weight of 5 between *kung* and *pao* (Fig. 4). A set of five disjoint dependencies at this point is:

1: kung <compound pao
2: and <cc chicken$_3$
3: chicken$_1$ conj> puffs
4: make xcomp> taste
5: know conj> accomplished

(2) *as an example they took payment for 5 out of 6 monthly plan premiums for a yearly policy and cancelled the contract for the remainder of the policy for reasons they stated was not receiving information on other licensed drivers in the household?* (en-ud-train.conllu sent_id = reviews-217359-0006)

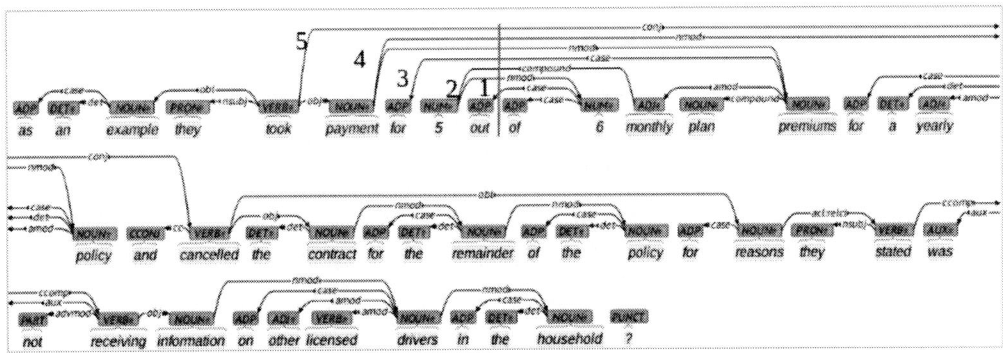

Figure 5. Another dependency tree from UD-English with weight 5

Sentence (2) has two positions with weight 5. We consider the flux between *out* and *of* (Fig. 5).

```
1: out case> 6
2: 5 <compound monthly
3: for <case premiums
4: payment nmod> policy
5: took conj> cancelled
```

If we except the two small corpora of Czech and Uyghur, Chinese appears to be the language with the largest number of positions with a weight higher than 5 (0.23 %). We will study an example with weight 6.

(3) 一 級 抗體 對於 檢測 如
   one   level antibody for   detect such_as

癌症、 糖尿 病、 帕金森 氏 症
cancer, diabetes disease, Parkinson 's disease

和 阿爾茨海默 氏 病 等 疾病
and Alzheimer ' 's disease etc. disease

所 特有 的 生物 標記
that specifically_have de(PART) biology marker

是 非常 有用 的。
be very useful de(PART).

(zh-ud-train.conllu id=21)

'Primary antibodies are useful for detecting biomarkers that diseases such as cancer, diabetes, Parkinson's disease, Alzheimer's disease, etc. specifically contain.'

The weight 6 appears between the noun 阿爾茨海默 'Alzheimer' and the case particle 氏 ('s). This flux contains 9 dependencies and can be separated into 6 disjoint bouquets of dependencies:

1: 阿爾茨海默 'Alzheimer' <case:suff 氏
2: 和 'and' <cc 病 'disease'
3: 癌症 'cancer' conj> 病 'disease'
   癌症 'cancer acl> 等 'etc.'
   癌症 'cancer appos> 疾病 'disease'
4: 如 'such_as' <csubj 特有 'specifically_have'
5: 檢測 'detect' obj> 疾病 'disease'
   檢測 'detect' xcomp> 有用 'useful'
6: 抗體 'antibody' <nsubj 有用 'useful'

The complexity of this Chinese sentence, compared to its English translation, is in great part due to word order differences.

1. In Chinese, adverbs and adverbial modifiers are placed before the verb. As a result, 有用 'useful' is at the end of the sentence and the long adverbial modifier 'for detecting …' is between the subject and the verb.

2. Noun modifiers are placed before the noun and '[diseases [such as cancer, diabetes, Parkinson's disease, and Alzheimer's disease, etc.]' becomes '[[such as cancer, diabetes, Parkinson's disease, and Alzheimer's disease, etc.] diseases]').

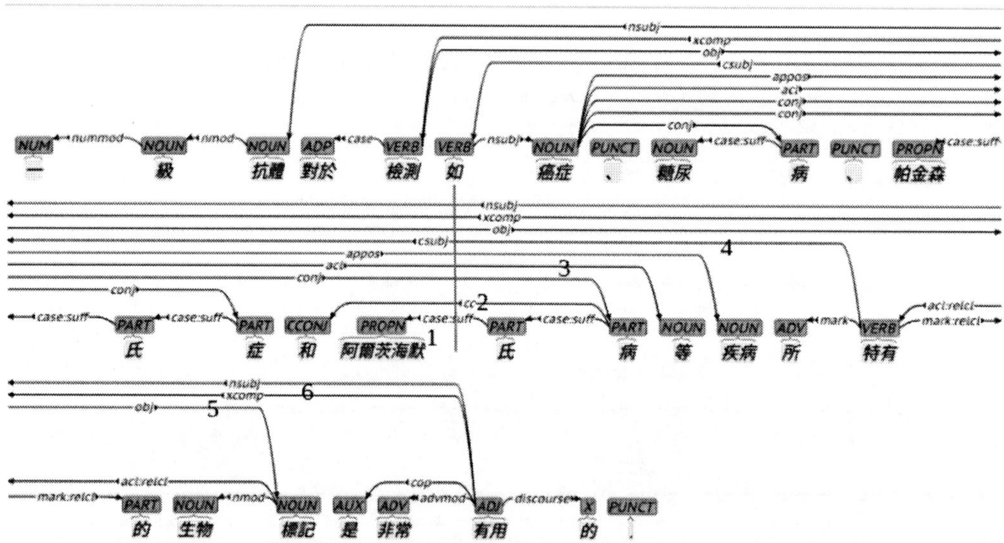

Figure 6. A dependency tree from UD-Chinese with weight 6

3. Relative clauses are also placed before the noun, which is a source of complexity discussed in Hsiao & Gibson (2003): "A key word-order difference between Chinese and other Subject-Verb-Object languages is that Chinese relative clauses precede their head nouns. Because of this word order difference, the results follow from a resource-based theory of sentence complexity, according to which there is a storage cost associated with predicting syntactic heads in order to form a grammatical sentence."

In any case, [biomarkers [(that are) specific to[diseases [such as cancer, diabetes, Parkinson's disease, and Alzheimer's disease etc.]]]] becomes [[[[such as cancer, diabetes, Parkinson's disease, and Alzheimer's disease etc.] disease] (that) specifically have] biomarkers].

5   Conclusion

We have studied different parameters concerning the dependency flux on a set of treebanks in 50 languages. We saw that the size, as well as the left and right spans, of the flux can vary considerably depending on the corpus and its language, and that they are not clearly bounded. Moreover, these values are quite heavily dependent on certain annotation choices. For instance the fact that UD proposes a bouquet-based analysis (rather than a string-based analysis) of coordination (and other similar constructions) significantly increases the size and the right span of the dependency flux.

Conversely, the dependency flux weight appears to be more homogeneous across languages and much less dependent on particular annotation choices (such as bouquet vs. string-based analysis of coordination). Weight measures what is traditionally called center embedding in constituency-based formalisms. We observe that weight is bounded by 5 except for very few positions (less than 1 position for 10,000 with weight of 6), which could be related to short-term memory limitations.

What now remains is to study all the data we have collected to determine, language after language, genre after genre, what are the most complex constructions and under which conditions they can appear. In particular, a comparison between weight and dependency distance (Liu 2010) is needed to determine how they are correlated and which one is the best predictor of the complexity.[5]

---

[5]   Fluxes with important weight or size tend to contain long dependencies and long dependencies to belong to large fluxes, but the two measures are quite different and remain partly independent.

Acknowledgments

We acknowledge our three reviewers for their comments. We could not answer their numerous suggestions but we hope to do that in further works.

References

Maria Babyonyshev, Edward Gibson. 1999. The Complexity of Nested Structures in Japanese, *Language, 75*(3), 423-450.

Bernd Bohnet, Joakim Nivre. 2012. A transition-based system for joint part-of-speech tagging and labeled non-projective dependency parsing. *Proceedings of EMNLP,* 1455-1465.

Marie-Amélie Botalla. 2014. Analyse du flux de dépendance dans un corpus de français oral annoté en microsyntaxe. Master thesis. Université Sorbonne Nouvelle.

Noam Chomsky. 1965. *Aspects of the Theory of Syntax.* Cambridge MA: MIT Press.

Chris Dyer, Miguel Ballesteros, Wang Ling, Austin Matthews, Noah A. Smith. 2015. Transition-based dependency parsing with stack long short-term memory. *Proceedings of ACL*, Beijing.

Edward Gibson. 1998. Linguistic complexity: Locality of syntactic dependencies. *Cognition, 68*(1), 1-76.

Franny Hsiao, Edward Gibson. 2003. Processing relative clauses in Chinese. *Cognition, 90*(1), 3-27.

Ugo Jardonnet. 2009. Analyse du flux de dépendance. Master thesis. Université Paris Nanterre.

Sylvain Kahane. 2001. Grammaires de dépendance formelles et Théorie Sens-Texte. Tutorial. *Proceedings of TALN*, vol. 2, 17-76.

Haitao Liu. 2008. Dependency distance as a metric of language comprehension difficulty. *Journal of Cognitive Science, 9*(2), 159-191.

Haitao Liu, Richard Hudson, Zhiwei Feng. 2009. Using a Chinese treebank to measure dependency distance. *Corpus Linguistics and Linguistic Theory, 5*(2), 161-174.

Haitao Liu. 2010. Dependency direction as a means of word-order typology: A method based on dependency treebanks. *Lingua, 120,* 1567-78.

Igor Mel'čuk. 1988. *Dependency Syntax: Theory and Practice.* The SUNY Press, Albany, N.Y.

G. A. Miller. 1956. The magical number seven, plus or minus two: Some limits on our capacity for pro-

belong to large fluxes, but the two measures are quite different and remain partly independent.

cessing information. *Psychological review*, *63*(2), 81-97.

G. A. Miller. 1962. Some psychological studies of grammar. *The American Psychologist, 17,* 748-762.

G. A Miller, Noam Chomsky. 1963. Finitary models of language users. In D. Luce (ed.), *Handbook of Mathematical Psychology*. John Wiley & Sons. 2-419.

M. Murata, K. Uchimoto, Q. Ma, H. Isahara. 2001. Magical number seven plus or minus two: Syntactic structure recognition in Japanese and English sentences. *International Conference on Intelligent Text Processing and Computational Linguistics.* Lecture notes in computer science, Springer, 43-52.

Joakim Nivre, Marie-Catherine de Marneffe, Filip Ginter, Yoav Goldberg, Jan Hajič, Christopher D. Manning, Ryan McDonald, Slav Petrov, Sampo Pyysalo, Natalia Silveira, Reut Tsarfaty, Daniel Zeman. 2016. Universal Dependencies v1: A Multinlingual Treebank Collection. *Proceedings of LREC*.

Lucien Tesnière. 1959. *Éléments de syntaxe structurale*. Klincksieck, Paris.

Chunxiao Yan. 2017. Étude du flux de dépendance dans 70 corpus (50 langues) de UD. Master thesis. Université Sorbonne Nouvelle.

V. H. Yngve.1960. A model and an hypothesis for language structure. *Proceedings of the American philosophical society*, *104*(5), 444-466.

Fully Delexicalized Contexts for Syntax-Based Word Embeddings

Jenna Kanerva
TurkuNLP Group
University of Turku
Graduate School (UTUGS)
Turku
Finland
jmnybl@utu.fi

Sampo Pyysalo
Language Technology Lab
DTAL
University of Cambridge
United Kingdom
sampo@pyysalo.net

Filip Ginter
TurkuNLP Group
University of Turku
Finland
figint@utu.fi

Abstract

Word embeddings induced from large amounts of unannotated text are a key resource for many NLP tasks. Several recent studies have proposed extensions of the basic distributional semantics approach where words form the context of other words, adding features from e.g. syntactic dependencies. In this study, we look in a different direction, exploring models that leave words out entirely, instead basing the context representation exclusively on syntactic and morphological features. Remarkably, we find that the resulting vectors still capture clear semantic aspects of words in addition to syntactic ones. We assess the properties of the vectors using both intrinsic and extrinsic evaluations, demonstrating in a multilingual parsing experiment using 55 treebanks that fully delexicalized syntax-based word representations give a higher average parsing performance than conventional word2vec embeddings.

1 Introduction

The recent resurgence of interest in neural methods for natural language processing involves a particular focus on neural approaches to inducing representations of words from large text corpora based on distributional semantics approaches (Bengio et al., 2003; Collobert et al., 2011). The methods introduced by Mikolov et al. (2013a) and implemented in their popular word2vec tool have been proven both effective and a good foundation for further exploration. In addition to representing word contexts as sliding windows of words in linear sequence, recent work has included efforts of building the word vectors using dependency-based approaches (Levy and Gold-

berg, 2014), where the context is based on nearby words in the syntactic tree.

In this paper, we set out to study dependency-based contexts further, exploring word embeddings derived from fully delexicalized syntactic contexts, and in particular the degree to which models induced using such context representations are dependent on word forms.

2 Methods

Our study builds on the seminal work introducing word2vec and later efforts generalizing it from a linear representation of context words to arbitrary contexts. We next present these methods and our proposed formulation of delexicalized syntax-based word embeddings.

2.1 Word2vec embeddings

The word2vec tool[1] implements two related approaches for inducing word representations – continuous bag-of-words (CBOW) and skip-grams – as well as a number of ways to train and parametrise them (Mikolov et al., 2013a; Mikolov et al., 2013b). Of these variants, the skip-gram with negative sampling (SGNS) model has been shown to be particularly effective and has become a *de facto* standard for neural word vector induction and the basis for many recent studies in the field. While the original work of Mikolov et al. explored different model architectures and approaches to learning, they all shared the property that the contexts of words in the model consisted of words.

2.2 Dependency-based word embeddings

Observing that the SGNS model is not inherently restricted to working with contexts consisting of words, Levy and Goldberg (2014) extended the model to work with arbitrary contexts, focusing

---

[1] https://code.google.com/p/word2vec/

83

Proceedings of the Fourth International Conference on Dependency Linguistics (Depling 2017), pages 83-91,
Pisa, Italy, September 18-20 2017

in particular on dependency-based contexts consisting of combinations of a neigbouring word in the dependency graph and its dependency relation to the target word (e.g. `scientist/nsubj`). Compared to embeddings based on linear contexts of words, they showed dependency-based embeddings to emphasize functional over topical similarity and to have benefits in distinguishing word relatedness from similarity. Levy and Goldberg released their generalized version of `word2vec` allowing arbitrary contexts as `word2vecf`.[2]

2.3 Delexicalized syntax-based embeddings

Although the context definition of Levy and Goldberg incorporates dependency information, it remains lexicalized, including also the surface form of the dependent or head word. Here, we consider whether it is possible to induce useful word embeddings with *delexicalized* contexts that omit the word form entirely. Specifically, we define the context of a target word as 1) the set of all dependency relations headed by the target word, 2) the relation where the target word is the dependent, marked to differentiate it from those in set 1), 3) the part-of-speech tag of the target word, and 4) the set of morphological features assigned to the target word. This context definition is illustrated in Figure 1. We use the `word2vecf` implementation to create embeddings using this context definition.

3 Experimental setup

We next present the sources of the unannotated texts and their syntactic analyses used as input and the methods and resources applied to create word embeddings and evaluate them.

3.1 Texts and dependency analyses

The texts used to induce word vectors are derived from the multilingual text collection recently introduced by Ginter et al. (2017) covering 45 languages. This resource consists primarily of texts collected through a combination of Internet crawl and extraction from Wikipedia data. The sizes of the 45 language-specific subcorpora range from 29,000 tokens for Old Church Slavonic to 9.5 billion tokens for English, averaging approximately 2B tokens with roughly half of the languages staying under the 1B token range. In addition to

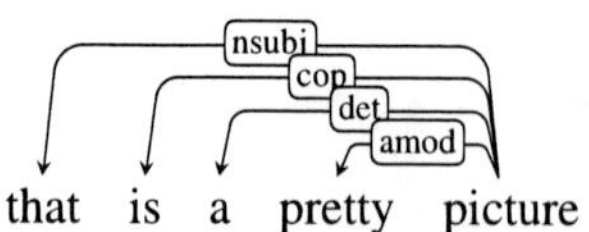

word	context	word	context
that	PRON	a	PronType=Art
that	PronType=Rel	a	det
that	nsubj	pretty	ADJ
is	AUX	pretty	Degree=Pos
is	Mood=Ind	pretty	amod
is	Number=Sing	picture	NOUN
is	Person=3	picture	Number=Sing
is	Tense=Pres	picture	root
is	VerbForm=Fin	picture	Dep_nsubj
is	cop	picture	Dep_cop
a	DET	picture	Dep_det
a	Definite=Ind	picture	Dep_amod

Figure 1: Delexicalized context for words in an English sentence.

plain texts, the resource provides also full syntactic analyses following Universal Dependencies (UD) (Nivre et al., 2016) version 2.0 guidelines, including tokenization, lemmatization, full morphological analyses and parses produced with the UDPipe pipeline (Straka et al., 2016). We note that even though many languages in the UD collection are covered by more than one treebank (and analyses may differ across treebanks for a single language), only one set of automatic analyses are provided per language in this resource.

3.2 Embeddings

We use the `word2vec` embeddings provided together with the CoNLL 2017 Shared Task automatically analyzed corpora (Ginter et al., 2017) as a baseline in our experiments. These models are trained on tokenized and lowercased text using the SGNS approach with a window size of 10, minimum word frequency count 10, and 100-dimensional vectors. Our new delexicalized `word2vecf` embeddings are created using the same, identically tokenized and lowercased texts, where the UDPipe morphological and syntactic analyses are used to generate our syntax-based contexts. We use the same minimum word frequency count 10 and vector dimensionality of 100 for our `word2vecf` models.

---

[2]`https://bitbucket.org/yoavgo/word2vecf`

france	jesus	xbox	reddish	scratched	megabits
belgium	christ	playstation	brownish	knicked	megabit
luxembourg	jesus.	ps3	yellowish	bruised	kilobits
nantes	god	ps4	greenish	nicked	gigabits
marseille	ahnsahnghong	xbox360	pinkish	scuffed	mbps
bretagne	jesuschrist	wii	grayish	chewed	mbits
boulogne	y'shua	xbla	bluish	sandpapered	terabits
poitou	christ	psvita	-orange	scratches	mbit
rouen	christ.	titanfall	orangish	brusied	kbits
paris	jesus	xboxone	greyish	scraped	kilobit
toulouse	yeshua	gamecube	mid-brown	thwacked	megabytes

Table 1: Nearest neighbours in <code>word2vec</code> embeddings

3.3 Intrinsic evaluation

Word vectors are frequently evaluated by assessing how well their distance correlates with human judgments of word similarity. Although these intrinsic evaluations have known issues (see e.g. Batchkarov et al. (2016), Chiu et al. (2016), Faruqui et al. (2016)) and we agree with the criticism that they are frequently poor indicators of the merits of representations, we include this common form of intrinsic evaluation here for reference purposes. We provide results using a comprehensive collection of English datasets annotated for word similarity and relatedness. Specifically, we used the evaluation service introduced by Faruqui and Dyer (2014) to evaluate on the 13 datasets available on the service[3] at the time of this writing. The datasets are summarized below in Table 3.

3.4 Extrinsic evaluation

Our primary evaluation is based on dependency parsing, where we evaluate parsing accuracy using different pre-trained word embeddings during parser training. We use the UDPipe pipeline[4] for tokenizing, tagging, lemmatizing and parsing Universal Treebanks (Straka et al., 2016). In all experiments, we use system parameters optimized on baseline models separately for each treebank,[5] keeping the parameters fixed in the comparative evaluations of the different word representations. We note that any possible bias introduced by this parameter selection strategy would favour the baseline model rather than one using the delexicalized syntax-based representations proposed here.

Parsing results are reported for all UD v2.0 treebanks in the CoNLL 2017 Shared Task release[6] that have a separate development set which can be used for testing and raw data for training embeddings. Of the 64 treebanks in the release, 9 do not fulfill these criteria (French-ParTUT, Galician-TreeGal, Irish, Kazakh, Latin, Slovenian-SST, Ukrainian and Uyghur do not have development data, Gothic does not have raw data) and are not included in the evaluation. Models are trained on the training section of a treebank and tested on the development section.[7]

4 Results

We next informally illustrate the characteristics of the English word vectors using nearest neighbours and give the intrinsic evaluation results for these vectors before presenting the results of our primary multilingual parsing experiments.

4.1 Nearest neighbours

Table 1 shows nearest neighbours in the conventional `word2vec` embeddings using the cosine similarity metric for a somewhat arbitrary selection of English words.[8] As has been well established in previous work, near words in `word2vec` representations are commonly (near) synonyms (e.g. *jesus/christ*, *scratched/scuffed*), cohyponyms (*france/belgium*, *xbox/playstation*), or topically related (*france/paris*, *scratched/sandpaper*).

We expected that the use of delexicalized contexts would eliminate much of the ability of the

---

[3] `http://wordvectors.org/`
[4] `http://ufal.mff.cuni.cz/udpipe`
[5] Optimized UDPipe parameters for UD v2.0 treebanks are released in the supplementary data of UDPipe models at `http://hdl.handle.net/11234/1-1990`.

[6] `http://hdl.handle.net/11234/1-1983`
[7] The test sections of the treebanks were held out for the final shared task evaluation and were thus not available for our experiments.
[8] The choice of words follows a similar illustration by Collobert et al. (2011).

france	jesus	xbox	reddish	scratched	megabits
lebanon	osama	vbox	greenish	snatched	megabytes
australia	napoleon	whitesox	grayish	touched	microseconds
england	ophelia	matchbox	bluish	punched	hectares
bolivia	gautama	firefox	greyish	deflected	tonnes
scotland	scipio	wmp	pinkish	warmed	microns
estonia	sauron	audiovox	yellowish	levelled	micrograms
switzerland	chandragupta	virtualbox	brownish	booted	litres
finland	claudius	equinox	blackish	stalked	megawatts
slovenia	jamarcus	rotax	temperate	ditched	gallons
algeria	olivia	hmp	redish	swallowed	bushels

Table 2: Nearest neighbours in delexicalized syntax-based word embeddings

embeddings to organize words by factors such as synonymy, cohyponymy, and topic and that nearest neighbours in our delexicalized syntax-based representations would be associated much more loosely, by syntactic behaviour rather than any aspect of meaning. Of the words illustrated in Table 2, *scratched* and *xbox* can be seen as broadly following this expected pattern in neighbouring past form verbs and singular nouns (respectively) with little semantic coherence. However, by contrast, all ten words nearest to *france* are countries, the neighbours of *jesus* are first names, nine out of ten nearest to *reddish* have the form color*ish*, and *megabits* is nearest ten different units. This unexpected result suggests that the syntactic structures and morphological features associated with a word can generate surprisingly useful word representations even in the absence of any lexical information. We also note the concerning (and systematic) tendency for nearest neighbours to end with the same characters (e.g. 8/10 nearest *xbox* in *x*). Although this may seem very surprising, we ruled out the possibility of leaking any word-suffix information by obtaining the same results when only word hashes were used during the model training. Our explanation is to note that the effect is strongest for rare words and that the parses are generated with a complex statistical model with access to word surface forms which are indirectly reflected in the predicted morphological and syntactic structures. In particular, the POS and morphological tagger naturally uses word suffix information, and we hypothesize that the vector model is able to pick this weak signal from the output of the morphological tagger and syntactic parser.

4.2 Intrinsic evaluation results

The results for the intrinsic evaluation based on the comparison of word pair similarity ranking with human judgments on 13 datasets are summarized in Table 3. The correlations seen for the `word2vec` embeddings are in line with those for previously released representations generated using the algorithm (e.g. (Mikolov et al., 2013a)), confirming that the texts used to induce these representations are appropriate for generating high-quality word embeddings.

The results for the delexicalized syntax-based embeddings are, as expected, much lower and far from competitive on any of the datasets. Nevertheless, the correlations remain positive in all 13 evaluations, providing support for the proposition that delexicalized contexts representations can identify similarities in word meaning.

4.3 Dependency parsing results

Parsing performance for the 55 treebanks is summarized in Table 4. We report labeled attachment scores evaluated using gold standard word segmentation with predicted part-of-speech tags and morphological features for parsers trained using three different pre-trained word embeddings: `word2vec` embeddings trained on the texts of the manually annotated UD treebanks (baseline), `word2vec` embeddings trained on the large unannotated corpora, and our delexicalized syntax-based embeddings trained on the automatically analyzed corpora.

`word2vec` embeddings trained on the large unannotated corpora yield on average a +0.16% point improvement over the baseline model. Somewhat surprisingly, incorporating standard `word2vec` embeddings trained on the larger cor-

Dataset	Correlation		Pairs		Reference
	word2vec	word2vecf	Found	Total	
WordSim-353	0.7083	0.2350	353	353	Finkelstein et al. (2001)
WordSim-353-SIM	0.7677	0.4033	203	203	Agirre et al. (2009)
WordSim-353-REL	0.6691	0.1318	252	252	Agirre et al. (2009)
MC-30	0.7028	0.2929	30	30	Miller and Charles (1991)
RG-65	0.6801	0.0593	65	65	Rubenstein and Goodenough (1965)
Rare-Word	0.4250	0.1998	2006	2034	Luong et al. (2013)
MEN	0.7397	0.2027	3000	3000	Bruni et al. (2012)
MTurk-287	0.6958	0.3474	287	287	Radinsky et al. (2011)
MTurk-771	0.6406	0.1336	771	771	Halawi et al. (2012)
YP-130	0.3882	0.0464	130	130	Yang and Powers (2006)
SimLex-999	0.3376	0.1004	999	999	Hill et al. (2016)
Verb-143	0.3633	0.2425	144	143	Baker et al. (2014)
SimVerb-3500	0.2175	0.0476	3500	3500	Gerz et al. (2016)

Table 3: Intrinsic evaluation results. The numbers of found pairs are identical for the two methods.

pora produces notably worse results compared to the baseline model for a number of languages. For Old Church Slavonic, the over 2% point drop in performance can likely be attributed to the modest size of the unannotated corpus available for that language: only 29,000 words are available in the raw data collection, compared to 37,500 words in the treebank training set. Otherwise, the differences range between -1.55% points and +6.28% points, with 31 treebanks showing positive results and 23 negative results. While some of these negative effects may be attributable to domain mismatches between the treebanks and the web-crawled and Wikipedia-derived texts, further study is required to analyze these findings in detail.

The delexicalized syntax-based embeddings yield an average 0.88% point improvement. Excluding Old Church Slavonic, which behaves similarly as with `word2vec` embeddings, the difference to the baseline ranges between -0.80% points and +7.30% points, with 45 treebanks showing a positive effect and 9 negative results. Overall, our results indicate the surprising conclusion that delexicalized syntactic embeddings lead to higher performance than conventional `word2vec` embeddings as well as generalize better across languages when evaluated in this closely related task.

4.4 Analysis

Given the positive effects of delexicalized syntax-based embeddings on the parsing task, it is natural to ask how the baseline parser performance affects the quality of the word embeddings. We set out to test this on Finnish, where our syntax-based embeddings have a clear positive effect compared to conventional `word2vec` embeddings and where our baseline parser accuracy is relatively low compared to the state-of-the-art parsers.

We first study whether the better parsing model showing a 1.65% point improvement in labeled attachment score can be used in a bootstrapping setup to generate yet better embeddings and parsers. We parsed the Finnish raw data with this better model, induced word vectors on the newly parsed data, and trained a UDPipe parsing model with the newly created word vectors. The results of this experiment are shown in Table 5. In terms of LAS, the second iteration model is +0.23% points better than the model from the first iteration.

We note that UDPipe may not be the optimal parsing pipeline for this experiment: our syntax-based embeddings are trained using both morphological features and syntactic trees, but while the UDPipe parser (Parsito (Straka et al., 2015)) uses pre-trained embeddings, the morphological tagger (MorphoDiTa (Straková et al., 2014)) does not, thus leaving part-of-speech tags and morphological features intact in newly parsed data. This means that the difference between old and new vector training data is relatively small.

A second consideration is that the 75.7% accuracy of the baseline parser used is not competitive with state-of-the-art parsers, where best reported labeled attachment scores for Finnish are in the range of 83-84% (Alberti et al., 2017; Bohnet et al., 2013). To investigate the effect of using higher-quality parses, we trained our syntax-based embeddings on the Finnish Internet Parsebank (Luotolahti et al., 2015), a 3.6 billion token collection of web crawled data. Finnish Internet Parsebank is analyzed with the Finnish de-

language	baseline	word2vec	diff to baseline	syntax-based	diff to baseline
Ancient_Greek	56.61	57.93	+1.32	58.18	+1.57
Ancient_Greek-PROIEL	72.35	72.48	+0.13	72.67	+0.32
Arabic	72.88	73.91	+1.03	74.00	+1.12
Basque	69.02	69.74	+0.72	69.93	+0.91
Bulgarian	83.90	84.29	+0.39	85.18	+1.28
Catalan	85.15	85.01	-0.14	85.31	+0.16
Chinese	68.48	68.83	+0.35	69.06	+0.58
Croatian	76.08	75.98	-0.10	77.35	+1.27
Czech-CAC	83.75	83.58	-0.17	84.54	+0.79
Czech-CLTT	69.58	68.92	-0.66	72.19	+2.61
Czech	84.47	84.24	-0.23	84.69	+0.22
Danish	75.18	74.63	-0.55	74.99	-0.19
Dutch-LassySmall	75.67	75.01	-0.66	76.68	+1.01
Dutch	74.73	75.21	+0.48	75.00	+0.27
English	79.66	80.20	+0.54	80.64	+0.98
English-LinES	74.62	74.35	-0.27	75.59	+0.97
English-ParTUT	75.72	75.21	-0.51	76.20	+0.48
Estonian	60.65	61.89	+1.24	63.22	+2.57
Finnish	75.70	75.79	+0.09	77.35	+1.65
Finnish-FTB	76.42	76.68	+0.26	77.72	+1.30
French	86.08	85.71	-0.37	86.53	+0.45
French-Sequoia	82.30	82.58	+0.28	82.65	+0.35
Galician	77.58	77.34	-0.24	78.21	+0.63
German	73.10	73.12	+0.02	72.87	-0.23
Greek	79.04	77.93	-1.11	79.93	+0.89
Hebrew	76.88	77.38	+0.50	78.52	+1.64
Hindi	87.09	86.82	-0.27	87.38	+0.29
Hungarian	65.59	66.40	+0.81	68.44	+2.85
Indonesian	74.39	72.84	-1.55	73.59	-0.80
Italian	85.44	84.98	-0.46	84.96	-0.48
Italian-ParTUT	78.21	78.74	+0.53	79.92	+1.71
Japanese	93.09	93.09	+0.00	93.23	+0.14
Korean	56.42	62.70	+6.28	63.72	+7.30
Latin-ITTB	71.15	71.72	+0.57	72.98	+1.83
Latin-PROIEL	70.08	69.76	-0.32	69.89	-0.19
Latvian	64.01	64.56	+0.55	66.16	+2.15
Norwegian-Bokmaal	83.91	83.44	-0.47	84.18	+0.27
Norwegian-Nynorsk	82.32	81.65	-0.67	81.89	-0.43
Old_Church_Slavonic	73.56	71.22	-2.34	71.40	-2.16
Persian	80.38	79.56	-0.82	80.86	+0.48
Polish	79.42	80.62	+1.20	81.21	+1.79
Portuguese-BR	85.55	86.11	+0.56	86.26	+0.71
Portuguese	83.64	84.49	+0.85	84.93	+1.29
Romanian	79.82	79.77	-0.05	80.30	+0.48
Russian	75.41	76.00	+0.59	77.48	+2.07
Russian-SynTagRus	86.76	86.58	-0.18	87.71	+0.95
Slovak	75.39	75.65	+0.26	76.55	+1.16
Slovenian	80.62	80.87	+0.25	81.38	+0.76
Spanish-AnCora	84.17	84.55	+0.38	84.31	+0.14
Spanish	84.34	83.85	-0.49	84.11	-0.23
Swedish-LinES	74.35	74.72	+0.37	75.34	+0.99
Swedish	73.39	74.25	+0.86	74.75	+1.36
Turkish	56.00	56.24	+0.24	57.75	+1.75
Urdu	76.98	76.23	-0.75	76.26	-0.72
Vietnamese	55.85	56.26	+0.41	55.22	-0.63
Average	-	-	+0.16	-	+0.88

Table 4: Parsing results for Conll 2017 shared task UD treebanks using different pretrained word embeddings. Green colour identifies treebanks where the performance of delexicalized syntax-based embeddings is higher than standard word2vec embeddings and the difference to the baseline model is positive.

	baseline	iteration 1	iteration 2
Finnish	75.70	77.35	77.57

Table 5: Bootstrapping results for Finnish syntax-based embeddings.

pendency parsing pipeline[9] trained on the UD Finnish treebank (Pyysalo et al., 2015) version 1.2. The Finnish parsing pipeline uses the OMorFi rule-based morphological analyzer (Pirinen, 2008) converted to the UD scheme, the Marmot tagger (Müller et al., 2013) and the graph-based dependency parser of Bohnet (2010). The labeled attachment score of the pipeline is estimated to be 82% based on the experiments reported in Pyysalo et al. (2015).

Interestingly, when the UDPipe parser was trained with syntax-based word embeddings induced from Finnish Internet Parsebank, UDPipe performance improved to the general level of the original parser used, giving a LAS of 82.21%. It must be noted that this number is not comparable to our main parsing results as the version of the UD Finnish treebank is different (version 1.2 compared to version 2.0), and the raw text collection is more than three times bigger. With UDPipe using standard `word2vec` pre-trained embeddings trained on the same Finnish Internet Parsebank data, parsing accuracy was 78.35%. These preliminary results are very promising and indicate that with good pre-trained word embeddings, we are able to improve a fast and comparatively simple feedforward parser near the numbers of the new DRAGNN-based SyntaxNet (Kong et al., 2017; Alberti et al., 2017) parser, which is more complex and much slower. Currently, we were only able to "mimic" the numbers of a good parser as we needed a high-quality parsebank to achieve these results, and the question whether similar results could be obtained without the near state-of-the-art parser remains open.

5   Conclusions and Future Work

In this work, we proposed a fully delexicalized syntax-based context representation for inducing word vectors using the Levy and Goldberg (2014) generalization of the `word2vec` skip-gram with negative sampling (SGNS) model. Building on a recently developed large-scale multilingual re-source of texts automatically annotated with Universal Dependencies, we created delexicalized syntax-based word embeddings for 45 different languages. Examination of nearest neighbours and evaluation against 13 English datasets annotated for human judgments of word similarity suggested that the embeddings retained a substantial degree of information on not only the syntactic and morphological aspects of words but also on aspects of their meaning despite being induced through a process with no access to lexical information. An extensive extrinsic evaluation using the UDPipe parser and 55 CoNLL 2017 shared task corpora demonstrated that the addition of our syntax-based embeddings not only substantially improved the performance of the baseline UDPipe model on average, but also that this improvement was greater than when using standard `word2vec` SGNS embeddings. A detailed analysis on Finnish showed potential additional promise from approaches using bootstrapping as well as combinations of embeddings induced using parses generated using complex models in simpler and faster parsers.

Our initial exploration suggests that fully delexicalized syntax-based embeddings have intriguing properties and show promise for use in practical applications. In future work, we will further explore how delexicalized context representations can capture aspects of word meaning – both in terms of degree and mechanism – as well as explore their use in improving mono- and multilingual parsing performance in combination with state-of-the-art models.

References

Eneko Agirre, Enrique Alfonseca, Keith Hall, Jana Kravalova, Marius Paşca, and Aitor Soroa. 2009. A study on similarity and relatedness using distributional and wordnet-based approaches. In *Proceedings of HLT-NAACL'09*, pages 19–27.

Chris Alberti, Daniel Andor, Ivan Bogatyy, Michael Collins, Dan Gillick, Lingpeng Kong, Terry Koo, Ji Ma, Mark Omernick, Slav Petrov, et al. 2017. Syntaxnet models for the conll 2017 shared task. *arXiv preprint arXiv:1703.04929*.

Simon Baker, Roi Reichart, and Anna Korhonen. 2014. An unsupervised model for instance level subcategorization acquisition. In *Proceedings of EMNLP'14*, pages 278–289.

Miroslav Batchkarov, Thomas Kober, Jeremy Reffin, Julie Weeds, and David Weir. 2016. A critique of word similarity as a method for evaluating distributional semantic models. In *Proceedings of RepEval'16*.

Yoshua Bengio, Réjean Ducharme, Pascal Vincent, and Christian Jauvin. 2003. A neural probabilistic language model. *Journal of machine learning research*, 3(Feb):1137–1155.

Bernd Bohnet, Joakim Nivre, Igor Boguslavsky, Richrd Farkas, Filip Ginter, and Jan Haji. 2013. Joint morphological and syntactic analysis for richly inflected languages. *Transactions of the Association for Computational Linguistics*, 1:415–428.

Bernd Bohnet. 2010. Very high accuracy and fast dependency parsing is not a contradiction. In *Proceedings of the 23rd international conference on computational linguistics*, pages 89–97.

Elia Bruni, Gemma Boleda, Marco Baroni, and Nam-Khanh Tran. 2012. Distributional semantics in technicolor. In *Proceedings of ACL'12*, pages 136–145.

Billy Chiu, Anna Korhonen, and Sampo Pyysalo. 2016. Intrinsic evaluation of word vectors fails to predict extrinsic performance. In *Proceedings of RepEval'16*, pages 1–6.

Ronan Collobert, Jason Weston, Léon Bottou, Michael Karlen, Koray Kavukcuoglu, and Pavel Kuksa. 2011. Natural language processing (almost) from scratch. *Journal of Machine Learning Research*, 12(Aug):2493–2537.

Manaal Faruqui and Chris Dyer. 2014. Community evaluation and exchange of word vectors at word-vectors.org. In *Proceedings of ACL'14*.

Manaal Faruqui, Yulia Tsvetkov, Pushpendre Rastogi, and Chris Dyer. 2016. Problems with evaluation of word embeddings using word similarity tasks. In *Proceedings of RepEval'16*, pages 30–35.

Lev Finkelstein, Evgeniy Gabrilovich, Yossi Matias, Ehud Rivlin, Zach Solan, Gadi Wolfman, and Eytan Ruppin. 2001. Placing search in context: The concept revisited. In *Proceedings of WWW'01*, pages 406–414.

Daniela Gerz, Ivan Vulić, Felix Hill, Roi Reichart, and Anna Korhonen. 2016. SimVerb-3500: A large-scale evaluation set of verb similarity. In *Proceedings of EMNLP'16*.

Filip Ginter, Jan Hajič, Juhani Luotolahti, Milan Straka, and Daniel Zeman. 2017. CoNLL 2017 shared task - automatically annotated raw texts and word embeddings. LINDAT/CLARIN digital library at the Institute of Formal and Applied Linguistics, Charles University.

Guy Halawi, Gideon Dror, Evgeniy Gabrilovich, and Yehuda Koren. 2012. Large-scale learning of word relatedness with constraints. In *Proceedings of SIGKDD'12*, pages 1406–1414. ACM.

Felix Hill, Roi Reichart, and Anna Korhonen. 2016. Simlex-999: Evaluating semantic models with (genuine) similarity estimation. *Computational Linguistics*.

Lingpeng Kong, Chris Alberti, Daniel Andor, Ivan Bogatyy, and David Weiss. 2017. Dragnn: A transition-based framework for dynamically connected neural networks. *arXiv preprint arXiv:1703.04474*.

Omer Levy and Yoav Goldberg. 2014. Dependency-based word embeddings. In *Proceedings of ACL*.

Thang Luong, Richard Socher, and Christopher D Manning. 2013. Better word representations with recursive neural networks for morphology. In *Proceedings of CoNLL'13*, pages 104–113.

Juhani Luotolahti, Jenna Kanerva, Veronika Laippala, Sampo Pyysalo, and Filip Ginter. 2015. Towards universal web parsebanks. In *Proceedings of the International Conference on Dependency Linguistics (Depling'15)*, pages 211–220. Uppsala University.

Tomas Mikolov, Kai Chen, Greg Corrado, and Jeffrey Dean. 2013a. Efficient estimation of word representations in vector space. In *Proceedings of ICLR*.

Tomas Mikolov, Ilya Sutskever, Kai Chen, Greg S Corrado, and Jeff Dean. 2013b. Distributed representations of words and phrases and their compositionality. In *Proceedings of NIPS*, pages 3111–3119.

George A Miller and Walter G Charles. 1991. Contextual correlates of semantic similarity. *Language and cognitive processes*, 6(1):1–28.

Thomas Müller, Helmut Schmid, and Hinrich Schütze. 2013. Efficient higher-order crfs for morphological tagging. In *Proceedings of the 2013 Conference on Empirical Methods in Natural Language Processing*, pages 322–332.

Joakim Nivre, Marie-Catherine de Marneffe, Filip Ginter, Yoav Goldberg, Jan Hajic, Christopher D Manning, Ryan McDonald, Slav Petrov, Sampo Pyysalo, Natalia Silveira, et al. 2016. Universal dependencies v1: A multilingual treebank collection. In *Proceedings of the 10th International Conference on Language Resources and Evaluation (LREC 2016)*, pages 1659–1666.

Tommi Pirinen. 2008. Suomen kielen äärellistilainen automaattinen morfologinen jäsennin avoimen lähdekoodin resurssein. *University of Helsinki*.

Sampo Pyysalo, Jenna Kanerva, Anna Missilä, Veronika Laippala, and Filip Ginter. 2015. Universal dependencies for Finnish. In *Proceedings of NODALIDA 2015, May 11-13, 2015, Vilnius, Lithuania*, pages 163–172.

Kira Radinsky, Eugene Agichtein, Evgeniy Gabrilovich, and Shaul Markovitch. 2011. A word at a time: computing word relatedness using temporal semantic analysis. In *Proceedings of WWW'11*, pages 337–346.

Herbert Rubenstein and John B Goodenough. 1965. Contextual correlates of synonymy. *Communications of the ACM*, 8(10):627–633.

Milan Straka, Jan Hajič, Jana Straková, and Jan Hajič jr. 2015. Parsing universal dependency treebanks using neural networks and search-based oracle. In *Proceedings of Fourteenth International Workshop on Treebanks and Linguistic Theories (TLT 14)*, December.

Milan Straka, Jan Hajič, and Jana Straková. 2016. UDPipe: trainable pipeline for processing CoNLL-U files performing tokenization, morphological analysis, POS tagging and parsing. In *Proceedings of LREC'16*.

Jana Straková, Milan Straka, and Jan Hajič. 2014. Open-Source Tools for Morphology, Lemmatization, POS Tagging and Named Entity Recognition. In *Proceedings of 52nd Annual Meeting of the Association for Computational Linguistics: System Demonstrations*, pages 13–18, Baltimore, Maryland, June. Association for Computational Linguistics.

Dongqiang Yang and David MW Powers. 2006. Verb similarity on the taxonomy of wordnet. In *Proceedings of GWC'06*.

Universal Dependencies for Dargwa Mehweb

Alexandra Kozhukhar
National Research University Higher School of Economics
Faculty of Humanities
School of Linguistics
Russia
sasha.kozhukhar@gmail.com

Abstract

The Universal Dependencies (UD) project aims to create the unified annotation schemes across languages. With its own annotation principles and abstract inventory for parts of speech, morphosyntactic features and dependency relations, UD aims to facilitate multilingual parser development, cross- lingual learning, and parsing research from a language typology perspective. This paper provides the description for the way Dargwa Mehweb (East Caucasian language family) meets UD scheme.

1 Introduction

The Universal Dependencies (UD) (Nivre et al., LREC 2016) is a project dealing with consistent cross-linguistic morphological and syntactic mark-up. The UD is currently in version 2 and covers 52 languages with 10 more languages yet to be included. While UD covers 11 language families, it does not include languages of the Caucasus and, in particular, East Caucasian languages.

The guidelines of UD are based on the Google Universal Part-of-Speech Tagset (Petrov et al. 2012) for parts of speech, the Interset framework (Zeman 2008) for morphological features, and Stanford Dependencies (De Marneffe et al. 2006, De Marneffe et al. 2014) for syntactic relations. The approach aims at making typological features of the languages of the world scalable and at simplifying the cross-linguistic comparison.

The paper is structured as follows: Section 2 provides general information about the Dargwa Mehweb language – area of distribution, number of speakers, some sociolinguistic data and a short grammar overview; Section 3 describes part of speech mapping; Section 4 discusses relevant features of Dargwa Me-hweb; Section 5 explains the syntactic dependencies of Dargwa Mehweb in terms of the UD approach; Section 6 discusses the cases of the language change and grammaticalization; and Section 7 presents the conclusions.

2 Dargwa Mehweb: General Information

Mehweb belongs to Dargwa group of East Caucasian language family. It is often considered a dialect of Dargwa (Magometov 1982), although according to (Koryakov & Sumbatova 2004, Khaidakov 1985) Mehweb is a separate language rather than a dialect. For the following research we consider Mehweb a separate language. According to lexicostatistic analysis, Mehweb is a member of the north-central group of Dargwa languages (Koryakov 2013).

Dargwa Mehweb is spoken in the village Megeb (Republic of Daghestan, Russian Federation). The language is spoken by approximately 800 people but is not quite at risk of becoming endangered (Dobrushina et al. 2017). Megeb is the only Dargwa village in the area surrounded by Lak and Avar villages. The official language of the village is Avar, children are taught Avar in school. Most of the speakers are bi- or trilingual (Kozhukhar & Barylnikova 2013).

Dargwa Mehweb was first mentioned in (Uslar 1892). There are two reference grammars of Mehweb (Magometov 1982, Khaidakov 1985), both published in 1980s, and selected essays on different aspects of the Mehweb grammar (Dobrushina et al. 2017) published in 2017. Dictionaries and texts were obtained during field trips to Megeb in 1990s and 2010s organized by Lomonosov Moscow State University and Higher School of Economics.

Proceedings of the Fourth International Conference on Dependency Linguistics (Depling 2017), pages 92-99,
Pisa, Italy, September 18-20 2017

Mehweb is notliterate. Native speakers use Avar orthography that does not match completely the phonemic inventory of Mehweb. During the field trips in 2010s a new orthography based on the IPA was introduced. All previous texts were converted into new orthography. In the following paper we use the orthography invented in 2010s.

In terms of its features Dargwa Mehweb is a typical East Caucasian language. Mehweb demonstrates agglutinative morphology. Mehweb is ergative in terms of agreement and case marking. There are five non-spatial cases in Mehweb. Spatial forms are bimorphemic: the first morpheme defines the spatial domain ('on', 'near', 'in' etc.) and the second one defines the orientation (Goal, Source, Path). There are no adpositions in Mehweb – all spatial relations are expressed with spatial cases and directional prefixes on verbs. Most of the verbs have perfective and imperfective stems from which all the verbal forms are derived. The formal relation between the stems is irregular and involves alternations, infixation and loss of class agreement slots. Most of the verbs bear a class agreement marker referential to the absolute argument of the clause. Class agreement distinguishes feminine, masculine and neuter in singular, human and non-human in plural. Mehweb is a typical East Caucasian language with basic SOV order.

Most of the East Caucasian languages, and Mehweb as well, allow using non-finite forms as heads of simple clauses. Clausal coordination is encoded by joining clauses headed by non-finite verb forms and the matrix clause. Apart from citation and reported speech contexts, where finite verb form is obligatory, all subordinate clauses bear non-finite verb forms such as action nominals, infinitives, participles and converbs. There is no clausal coordination in Mehweb. Mehweb has reflexive pronouns which can also be used in logophoric function.

In the following paper we use Leipzig Glossing Rules (Comrie et al. 2008) to indicate grammatical features in the examples. The list of abbreviations used in the paper is given in Appendix A.

3   POS Mapping

POS mapping is simple since there are exclusively verbal (participle morpheme, TAM markers etc.) and exclusively nominal mor-

phemes (number, case). Cross-categorial morphemes are considered clitics (coded as PART), for example, additive clitic *=ra*, which functions as CCONJ 'and', class markers or emphatic clitic *=al*, which can be combined with pronouns and numerals.

Most of the adjectives in Mehweb are marked with attributivizing morpheme *-(i)l*. There is a closed set of adjectives that also bear a class marker of the head.

(1) *hunt'a-l   qul-le-šu*
    red-ATR house-PL-AD(LAT)

(2) *har-il*   *urši-li-s*
    each-ATR   boy-OBL-DAT

(3) *r=igu-l*
    F1-engaged-ATR

Adverbs derived from adjectives are marked with adverbalizing morpheme *-le*. All other adverbial meanings, especially spatial ones, are expressed with verbal prefixes or spatial cases. Mehweb has auxiliaries, they are used with adjectives in predicative position (*sa=b=i*) and analytical progressive verb forms (*le=w*). Mehweb uses negative copula *agwara* with affirmative auxiliaries.

There are four deictic pronouns that are mapped as DET. DETs can also be used as personal pronouns (cf. Table 1).

Meaning	Pronoun	Meaning	Pronoun
'near the hearer'	il	'higher than hearer'	ič'
'far from hearer'	it	'lower than hearer'	iχ

Table 1: Mehweb deictic pronouns

There are special pronouns that function as wh-words, for example, *sik'al* meaning 'what'. Wh-words can be used in affirmative sentences as well as in interrogative ones.

There are no CCONJ and SCONJ in Mehweb since all the subordinates are encoded by non-finite verb forms. Thus 'Ali-[ERG] hit-[finite] Fatima run away-[converb]' would mean that 'Ali hit Fatima and ran away' but not that 'Running away Ali hit Fatima'.

In Mehweb CCONJ and SCONJ are distinguished by the type of the converb used in the subordinate clause – for CCONJ general converbs are used, for SCONJ, specialized ones. We can assume that Mehweb had SCONJs since the texts from 40 years ago contain a special conjunction, but contemporary texts lack this conjunction. For further information see Section 6.

Table 2 gives the overview on the POS mapping for Mehweb.

POS	Mehweb	POS	Mehweb
ADJ	+	CCONJ	–
ADV	+	DET	+
NOUN	+	NUM	+
VERB	+	PART	+
ADP	–	SCONJ	–
AUX	+	PRON	+
INTJ	+	PROPN	+

Table 2. Overview on the parts of speech in Mehweb

4 Features Mapping

The following section deals with feature mapping for Dargwa Mehweb. Subsection 4.1. deals with nominal features; subsection 4.2. covers verbal features.

4.1 Nominal Features

Animacy feature with values Hum and Nhum is used for class agreement in plural since Mehweb does not distinguish female, masculine and neuter in plural. Table 2 presents clitics marking class (gender) in Mehweb. Gender feature with values Fem, Masc and Neut are used in singular.

	Sg	Pl	
M	*w*		
F	*d*	*b*	HPL
F1	*d-r*		
N	*b*	*d-r*	NPL

Table 3: Class markers in Mehweb

Case feature is used to distinguish between cases. There are five non-spatial cases, namely, absolutive, ergative, comitative, dative, genitive. Vocative case is formed by stress shift (Dobrushina et al. 2017). Spatial cases consist of two morphemes. We propose our own mapping for spatial cases, where each spatial form has marker of Localization and Orientation:

Localizations: Super ('On'), In ('In'), Inter ('Inside'), Apud ('Near');

Orientations: Lat ('Move towards'), Ess ('Staying in place'), El ('Move away from'), Trans ('Moving through').

All orientation markers are expressed by special suffix except the lative, which is zero in Mehweb. It worths noting that zero lative is very rare in East Caucasian languages. Usually it is the essive which is expressed by zero.

There are only singular (coded as Sing) and plural (coded as Plur) number. There are also *pluralia tantum* nouns in Mehweb.

The Person feature is polarity dependent. There is a distinction between the first person singular and second person singular: in affirmative clauses suffix -ra marks the first person singular, whereas in negative and interrogative clauses the same suffix marks second person singular. Polarity feature thus has to be coded using three values instead of two: Pos, Neg and Interrogative.

Mehweb pronouns can be coded using the following values: Dem, Rcp, Int, Neg, Ind. There are no separate personal pronouns in Mehweb — demonstratives (in matrix clauses) and reflexives (in subordinate clauses) are used instead.

There is a set of ordinal (coded as Ord) and cardinal numerals (coded as Card). Cardinal numerals are derived from ordinals using emphatic clitic =*al*.

4.2 Verbal Features

Aspect feature is used to distinguish between imperfective (coded as `Imp`) and perfective (coded as `Perf`) verb stems.

Mehweb demonstrates a wide range of moods, thus the Mood feature with the values `Ind, Imp, Cnd, Pot, Jus, Opt, Prp` is required. Some of the values of the Mood feature are encoded by special converbs, for example, apprehensive meaning is expressed by a separate morpheme, and it is still under discussion whether the values of the feature Mood should be used or it requires introducing some separate values.

All verb forms bear a tense marker: `Past, Fut, Pres`. The following verb forms are relevant for Mehweb: `Fin, Inf, Part, Conv, Vnoun`. There are also analytical verb forms which consist of an auxiliary and a general converb, for example, the for of progressive.

Table 4 gives an overview on the feature mapping in Mehweb.

Feature	Relevant Values
Animacy	Hum, Nhum
Aspect	Imp, Perf
Case	Abs, Erg, Com, Dat, Gen, Voc
Foreign	Yes
Gender	Fem, Masc, Neut
Mood	Ind, Imp, Cnd, Pot, Jus, Opt, Prp
NumType	Ord, Card
Number	Sing, Plur, Ptan
Person	1, 2
Polarity	Pos, Neg
Reflexive	Yes
Tense	Fut, Past, Pres
VerbForm	Fin, Inf, Part, Conv, Vnoun

Voice	Cau
PronType	Dem, Rcp, Int, Neg, Ind

Table 4: Feature mapping in Mehweb

5 Syntactic dependencies mapping

Syntactic structure of East Caucasian languages, and Darwa Mehweb as well, differs significantly from languages described in terms of UD approach earlier. In this section we discuss some cases of dependency relations mapping for Mehweb.

In Mehweb as in a language with ergative alignment `nsubj` is marked with ergative case in transitive clauses and with absolutive in intransitive clauses. The causer is also marked with ergative.

```
text: ʔaʕli w-ak'-ib
gloss: Ali(nom) m-come.pfv-aor
text[eng]: 'Ali came'.
ʔaʕli NSUBJ PROPN
wak'ib ROOT VERB
```

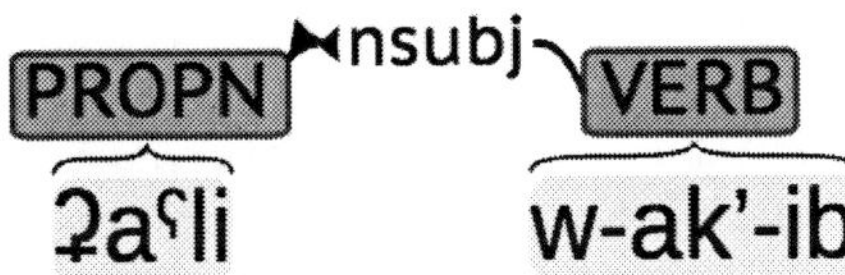

In the example above the `root` of the clause is the verb *wak'ib* 'came' which is intransitive. Ali is `nsubj` marked with absolutive case. Verb also bears a class agreement marker w- referring to Ali, i.e. masculine and singular (see Table 3).

However, there are cases where Mehweb does not fit the ergative logic. In the sentence with transitive and intransitive verb forms conjoined, since there is no coordination in Mehweb, transitive and intransitive verb forms have ergative argument as `nsubj`. Thus 'Ali-[ERG] hit-[transitive] Fatima-[ABS] and ran away-[intransitive]' would mean that 'Ali hit and Ali ran away' and not that 'Ali hit Fatima and Fatima ran away'.

There is also a list of experiential verbs that have subject marked with oblique cases such as `Dat` and `Inter:Lat`. Such cases will be marked as `obl:exprnc`.

The `obj` is always marked with Abs including the cases with transitive experiential verbs, for example, verb *gwes* 'to see' marks its `nsubj` with `Inter:Lat` and is `obj` with `Abs`. Transitive verbs get class agreement from OBJ. If the subordinate clause turns out to be a direct object of the verb, i.e. `ccomp`, the verb form gets `Neut` class agreement. `iobj` can be marked with oblique non-spatial cases and all spatial cases.

```
text: adaj-ni mašinka-li-če
muc'ur b-erč-ur
gloss: father-erg
hair.cutter-obl-super(lat)
beard(nom) n-cut.hair.pfv-aor
text[eng]: 'The father cut his
beard with a hair cutter'.
adajni NSUBJ NOUN
mašinkaliče OBL NOUN
muc'ur OBJ NOUN
berčur ROOT VERB
```

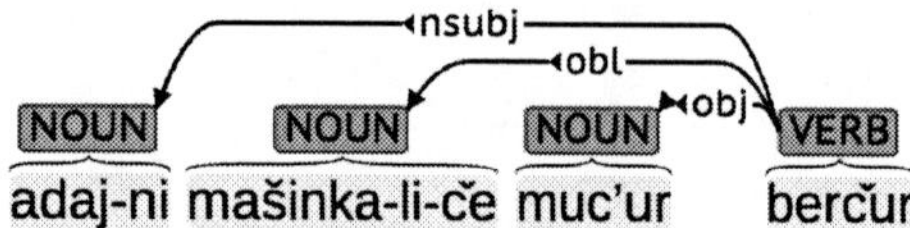

In the example above the `root` of the clause is transitive verb *berčur* 'shove'. Father ('adaj') is `nsubj` marked with ergative case. The verb bears an agreement marker *b-* (i.e. neuter, singular) referring to the beard ('muc'ur') which is in absolutive case, i.e. `obj`. The cutter ('mašinka-li-če') is marked with `Super:Ess` marker *-če* and a zero marker of lative, therefore it is considered an `obl`.

The relevance of `csubj` in Mehweb is under discussion since it was not directly tested yet. `advcl` and `acl` are the main strategies of the clause composition. In case subordinate clause is headed by the participle it is assigned `acl` label. In case subordinate clause is headed by the specialized or general converb it is assigned `advcl`. If the subordinate clause is headed by the infinitive or nomen actionis it is assigned `xcomp`. If the matrix verb bears a neuter singular class marker (*b-*) and there are no neuter singular `obj` in the matrix clause then b- is considered a subordinate clause agreement marker and the subordinate is assigned `ccomp` label.

In case of citation and indirect speech the cited phrase is headed by the finite verb. These types of clauses were labeled `parataxis`.

However, cited phrases can be connected with matrix clauses by reflexive pronoun used in subject position in the cited phrase and co-referential to the subject of the matrix clause. Thus the `parataxis` label is under discussion.

```
text: Ɂali-ze b-alh-an abaj iz-
uwe le-r-deš
gloss: Ali-inter n-know:ipf-hab
mother(abs) be.sick:ipf-cvb
cop-f-nmlz
text[eng]: 'Ali knows that mother
is sick.'
Ɂalize NSUBJ PROPN
balhan ROOT VERB
abaj NSUBJ NOUN
izuwe CCOMP VERB
lerdeš AUX AUX
```

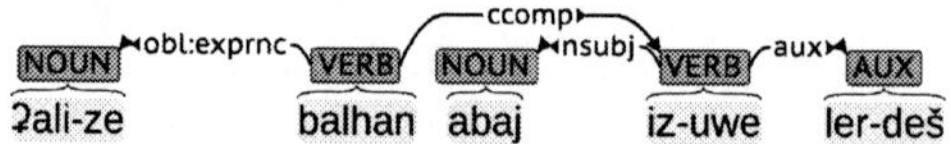

Example above consists of two clauses: *Ɂalize balhan* 'Ali knows' and *abaj izuwe lerdeš* 'mother is sick'. The `root` of the whole sentence is an experiential transitive verb balhan 'knows'. Since balhan is an experiential verb its `obl:exprn` is marked with interlative, i.e. `Inter:Lat`, case. The direct object of the root verb is a second clause abaj izuwe lerdeš, thus it is labeled `ccomp`. Root verb bears the class agreement marker *b-* (neuter, singular) which refers to the subordinate clause. The head of the second clause is an auxiliary verb lerdeš (being). Auxiliary verb bears the class agreement marker *-r-* (feminine, singular) referring to the `nsubj` of the ccomp mother ('abaj') and a nominalization suffix *-deš* since the second clause is subordinate and has to be non-finite. Subordinate clause contains also a converb *izuwe* 'being sick' which is a part of an analytic progressive form izuwe *lerdeš* standing for 'is being sick'. Converb *izuwe* is labeled VERB.

Mehweb does not allow to use more than one auxiliary in a single analytical verb form. However, Mehweb demonstrates so-called biabsolutive constructions with analytical verb forms:

(4) ʔali   kung
    Ali(ABS)   book(ABS)
    luč-uwe   le(=b/=w)
    read.IPF-CVB   aux(=N/=M)
    'Ali is reading a book'.

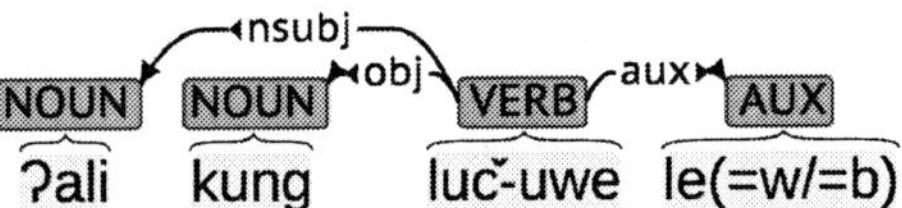

The preceding tree is impossible since Ali must be in ergative case in order to be considered `nsubj` of the transitive verb 'read'.

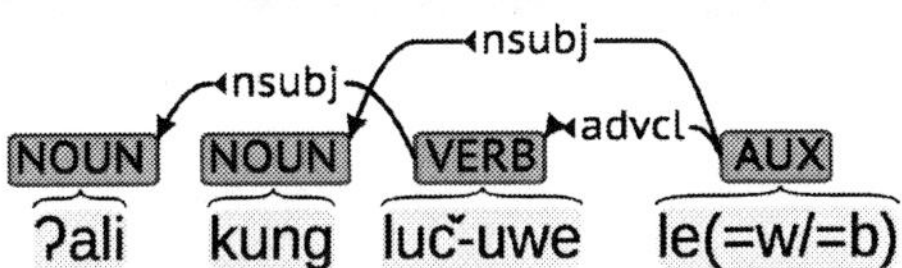

We propose treating biabsolutive constructions as if they were `advcl`s since they turn out to be two clauses: matrix clause headed by copula and subordinate clause headed by converb. Therefore (4) will be literally translated as 'The book is so that Ali reads it'.

Table 5 gives the overview on the syntactic dependencies mapping.

UD	Mehweb
nsubj	+
obj	+
iobj	+
csubj	not attested
ccomp	+
xcomp	+
obl	+
vocative	+
expl	−
acl	+
advcl	+
advmod	+
aux	+
cop	+
mark	−
nmod	+
det	+
clf	−

Table 5: Dependency relations (UD 2.0) as attested in Mehweb

Mehweb does not have mark tags since the clauses headed by converbs are encoded instead, marked as `advcl`. Mehweb also lacks expletive subject and classifiers. There is no `nmod` since there are no prepositional groups (the genitive case is used instead).

6 Language change and grammaticalization

Language material we are basing on is heterogeneous since half of the texts are contemporary and half of them is 40 years old. These two groups of texts demonstrate some differences in how conjunction is expressed. This was considered a case of a language change.

Texts from (Magometov 1982) have a special autonomous word form *wa* which functions as 'and' and is used as a conjunction between nouns and clauses. Contemporary texts lack *wa*. Instead of *wa* `acls` and `advcls`, i.e. subordinate clauses headed by non-finite verb forms, are used to conjoin clauses and *=ra* clitic is used to conjoin nouns. For cases with *wa* SCONJ POS label and `conj` dependency relation label are used, although conjoining clauses and nouns with *wa* is considered unnatural for Mehweb.

The following case is considered a grammaticalization of an non-finite verb form. In Mehweb when matrix clause is headed by the speech verb, e.g. 'say' or 'know', converb *ile* 'being said' occurs in the end of the subordinate clause. For majority of native speakers *ile* is optional. Some native speakers recognize *ile* as an autonomous verb form, whereas others do not provide a subtle translation for it.

We provide two ways of treating *ile*. The first one is treating it as an optional citation particle, i.e. PART. The second one is considering ile a separate `advcl` since it is a converb. Cited phrase that precedes *ile* then is considered its `ccomp` in that case.

7 Conclusion

In this paper we described how well the UD approach covers the features of one of the typical East Caucasian language, Dargwa Mehweb. Three types of guidelines were applied: POS mapping, feature mapping and dependency relations.

Some features were raised due to mapping. First is the way grammaticalization cases should be treated since there are more than one possible way of representing them on a dependency tree. Second is a clausal conjunction since Dargwa Mehweb use the sequence of non-finite clauses instead of expected SCONJs. Third is a lack of difference between moods and special converbs since there are special mood markers that can be combined with converbs only.

References

Bernard Comrie, Martin Haspelmath and Balthasar Bickel. 2008. *The Leipzig glossing rules: Conventions for interlinear morpheme-by-morpheme glosses.* URL: https://www.eva.mpg.de/lingua/resources/glossing-rules.php

Marie-Catherine de Marneffe, Bill MacCartney, Christopher D Manning, et al. 2006. *Generating typed dependency parses from phrase structure parses.* In Proceedings of 5th International Conference on Language Resources and Evaluation (LREC), volume 6, pages 449– 454.

Marie-Catherine de Marneffe, Timothy Dozat, Natalia Silveira, Katri Haverinen, Filip Ginter, Joakim Nivre, and Christopher D. Manning. 2014. *Universal Stanford Dependencies: a cross-linguistic typology.* In Proceedings of the 9th International Conference on Language Resources and Evaluation (LREC), Reykjavik, Iceland, May. European Language Resources Association (ELRA).

Nina Dobrushina, Michael Daniel, Dmitry Ganenkov, George Moroz , Daria Barylnikova, Marina Kustova, Alexandra Kozhukhar, Yuri Lander, Maria Sheyanova and Ilia Chechuro. 2017. *Mehweb. Selected essays on phonology, morphology and syntax.* Berlin: Language Science Press.

Said Khajdakov. 1985. *Darginskij i megebskij yazyki (printsipy slovoizmeneniya) [Dargwa and Mehweb languages].* Makhachkala.

Yuri Korjakov and Nina Sumbatova. 2007. *Darginskie jazyki [The Dargwa Languages]* In BRJe, tom 8. Moskva: Bol'shaja rossijskaja enciklopedija, pages 328–329.

Yuri Koryakov. 2013. *Convergence and divergence in the classification of Dargwa languages.* In 46th Annual Meeting of the Societas Linguistica Europaea (SLE 2013). 18–21 September 2013. Book of abstracts. Part 1. Split: University of Split.

Alexandra Kozhukhar and Daria Barylnikova. 2013. *Multilingualism in Dagestan.* Higher School of Economics Research Paper No. WP BRP, 4.

Alexander Magometov. 1982. *Megebskij dialekt darginskogo jazyka (Issledovanie i teksty) [The Mehweb Dialect of Darwga Language].* Tbilisi: Mecniereba.

Joakim Nivre, Marie-Catherine de Marneffe, Filip Ginter, Yoav Goldberg, Jan Hajič, Christopher D Manning, Ryan McDonald, Slav Petrov, Sampo Pyysalo, Natalia Silveira, et al. 2016. *Universal dependencies v1: A multilingual treebank collection.* In Proceedings of the 10th International Conference on Language Resources and Evaluation (LREC 2016).

Slav Petrov, Dipanjan Das, and Ryan McDonald. 2012. *A universal part-of- speech tagset.* In Proceedings of the 8th International Conference on Language Resources and Evaluation (LREC), pages 2089–2096.

Petr Uslar. 1892. *Etnografija Kavkaza. Jazykoznanie [Ethnography of the Caucasus].* V. Hjurkilinskij jazyk, Tiflis.

Daniek Zeman. 2008. *Reusable tagset conversion using tagset drivers.* In Proceedings of the 6th International Conference on Language Resources and Evaluation (LREC), pages 213–218.

Appendix A. List of abbreviations

ABS	absolutive
AD	localization ad
AOR	aorist
ATR	attributivized
AUX	auxiliary
CVB	converb
DAT	dative
F	feminine
F1	feminine
HPL	human plural
IPF	imperfective
LAT	lative
M	masculine
N	neuter
NMLZ	nominalization
NPL	non-human plural
OBL	oblique
PFV	perfective
PL	plural

Menzerath-Altmann Law in Syntactic Dependency Structure

Ján Mačutek

Comenius University in Bratislava

Faculty of Mathematics, Physics and Informatics

Department of Applied Mathematics and Statistics

Slovakia

jmacutek@yahoo.com

Radek Čech

University of Ostrava

Faculty of Arts

Department of Czech Language

Czech Republic

cechradek@gmail.com

Jiří Milička

Charles University, Prague

Faculty of Arts

Institute of Comparative Linguistics, and

Institute of the Czech National Corpus

Czech Republic

jiri@milicka.cz

Abstract

According to the Menzerath-Altmann law, there is a relation between the size of the whole and the mean size of its parts. The validity of the law was demonstrated on relations between several language units, e.g., the longer a word, the shorter the syllables the word consists of. In this paper it is shown that the law is valid also in syntactic dependency structure in Czech. In particular, longer clauses tend to be composed of shorter phrases (the size of a phrase is measured by the number of words it consists of).

1 Introduction

Some language properties can be considered a result of general mechanisms influencing human language behaviour. The mechanisms can be expressed by language laws which can have, in the ideal case, a form of a mathematic formula. The mathematical formalization allows to test the validity of a law statistically, and, in addition, it opens a door towards building a theory, i.e., a system of interconnected valid laws (see, e.g., Bunge, 1967; Altmann, 1978, 1993). In this paper, a particular instance of language laws, namely, the Menzerath-Altmann law

(MAL hereafter) in syntactic dependency structure is scrutinized. The MAL (Cramer, 2005a) is, in general, a law expressing a mechanism which controls mutual relations between sizes of language units belonging to "neighbouring" language levels (e.g., between lengths of words and syllables, clauses and words, etc.), see Section 2 for details. Our aim is to test the validity of the MAL in syntactic dependency structure; namely, we hypothesize that the relation between the size of the clause and the mean size of its parts (i.e., phrases; for details, see Section 3) follows the MAL. If the hypothesis is corroborated, syntactic dependency structure can be included among other linguistic "domains" which are substantially influenced by the very general mechanism expressed by the MAL. Consequently, in such a case the general status of the MAL in language is confirmed (and strengthened), and some fundamental properties of syntactic dependency structure can be seen (and possibly explained) from a new point of view.

The article is organized as follows. The MAL is introduced in Section 2 (with some basic examples). Section 3 describes the methodology applied in this study. The language material from which data are extracted is presented in Section 4. Section 5 summarizes the results

Proceedings of the Fourth International Conference on Dependency Linguistics (Depling 2017), pages 100-107,
Pisa, Italy, September 18-20 2017

achieved. Finally, the paper is concluded by Section 6, where also perspectives for future research are pointed to.

2 Menzerath-Altmann law

The MAL speaks, in general, about the relation between sizes of a construct and its constituents. It is named after two linguists: Paul Menzerath, who observed length of German words and length of syllables which the words consist of, and Gabriel Altmann, who contributed to a substantial generalization of the law.

The verbal formulation of the law changed over time. Its first version (the longer the word, the shorter syllables in the word, see Menzerath, 1954) was a description of the relation between length of words and syllables. The current version of the MAL (Altmann, 1980) is more general, expressing a relation between sizes of two language units which are "neighbours" in the language unit hierarchy, such as syllables and words, sentences and clauses, etc. (the greater the whole the smaller its parts). We note that the hierarchy of the units is a nested structure[1] (e.g., a sentence consists of clauses, which consist of words, which consist of syllables, which consist of phonemes[2]). Thus, one usually speaks about constructs and constituents (e.g., words and syllables). Furthermore, the formulation of the MAL from Altmann (1980) is not so strict with respect to the monotonicity of the relations between lengths of a construct and its constituents. In some cases, constituent's length does not achieve its maximum in constructs with length one, but its peak is shifted to the right. Hence, the MAL can be presented in its most general form as "the mean size of constituents is a function of the size of the construct".

The mathematical formula corresponding to the abovementioned general verbal expression of the MAL is

$$(1) \qquad y(x) = ax^b e^{-cx},$$

with $y(x)$ being the mean size of constituents if the size of the construct is x; a, b, c are parameters[3]. However, in many cases its special case of (1) for $c = 0$, i.e.,

$$(2) \qquad y(x) = ax^b,$$

fits data sufficiently well[4]. This special case describes a strictly decreasing trend of the constituent size. The goodness of fit is usually evaluated in terms of the determination coefficient R^2 (the higher R^2, the better fit). It is defined as

$$R^2 = 1 - \frac{\sum_{i=1}^{n}(S_i - y(i))^2}{\sum_{i=1}^{n}(S_i - \bar{S})^2},$$

where S_i is the observed mean size of constituents for constructs of size i, $\bar{S}$ is the mean of values S_i, $i = 1, 2, \dots, n$, and $y(i)$ are theoretical values from a model (which is given by (1) or (2) in this paper). A model is usually considered good enough if it achieves $R^2 \geq 0.9$, see Mačutek and Wimmer (2013).

The validity of the MAL was corroborated on relations between pairs of several language units in many languages (language material from both dictionaries and texts was used, i.e., the MAL seems to be valid for both types and tokens). We mention several examples which cover relations among some traditional language units[5]. Kelih (2010) investigated the relation between word length in syllables and syllable length in graphemes in Serbian. Gerlach (1982) chose word (in German) as the construct as well, but he measured word length in the number of morphemes (with morpheme length determined in the number of phonemes). Teupenhayn and Altmann (1984) showed that the MAL can be used also to describe the relation between sentence length (in clauses) and clause length (in words). An example of this relation, data from a German text together with a curve corresponding to the theoretical model of the MAL, can be seen in Figure 1. The data and the curve displayed in the figure can be considered typical for the MAL.

---

[1] In fact, there are several parallel nested structures. If word is taken as a construct, both syllables and morphemes can serve as its constituents; depending on whether one works directly with a written text or with its phonological or phonetic transcription, the size of a syllable can be measured in the number of graphemes, phonemes or sounds, etc. The choice of language units is conditioned by the technical tools available (e.g., a program for an automatic syllabification), by the researcher's aim, by the possibility to compare results with previous works, etc.

[2] One cannot a priori exclude the existence of some intermediate (maybe not so apparent) levels between the "traditional" ones, see the discussion in Section 5.
[3] Milička (2014) suggested an alternative mathematical model.
[4] Obviously, this special case of the MAL can be applied only under condition of a monotonous relation.
[5] See Altmann (2014) for a bibliography on the MAL.

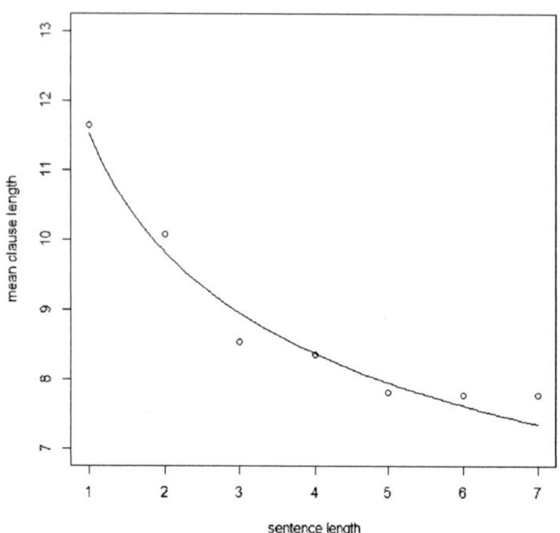

Figure 1. Sentence length (x-axis) and mean clause lengths (y-axis) in a German text (Teupenhayn and Altmann, 1984).

The data can be modelled by the simpler version of the MAL, i.e., by function (2). One obtains parameter values $a = 11.571$, $b = -0.229$. The determination coefficient for the model is $R^2 = 0.9659$, indicating thus a very good fit[6].

In general, the interpretation of the parameters of the MAL remains an open question. While Köhler (1984) suggested a very general interpretation, and parameter values resulting from relations between different language units were presented by Cramer (2005b), a connection between the numerical values of the parameters, language levels from which the values arise, and the general theoretical framework (such as a supposed processing capacity, structural information, and similar considerations, see Köhler 1984) is still an unsolved problem[7].

3   Methodology

The MAL predicts that there should be a systematic relation between the size of the clause and the size of its parts. As for the determination

of the clause, one can find a (more or less) general agreement among linguists about the character of this unit; e.g., Crystal (2008, p. 78) defines the clause as "a unit of grammatical organization smaller than the sentence, but larger than phrases, words or morphemes". According to the Prague Dependency Treebank annotation[8], which is used for the analysis in this study (see Section 4 for a very brief description, and Lopatková et al., 2009, for more details), clauses "are grammatical units out of which complex sentences are built. A clause typically corresponds to a single proposition expressed by a finite verb and all its arguments and modifiers (unless they constitute clauses of their own).". Regarding the MAL, the clause represents the *construct*.

It is less obvious how to determine parts of the clause which, in accordance to the theoretical background of the MAL (see Section 2), must be defined as its *constituents*. Following both the verb-centric character of dependency syntax traditionally used for Czech and the annotation of the Prague Dependency Treebank, we start with the assumption that the predicate represents the central element of the clause. Thus, the predicate is the highest unit of a hierarchical structure of the clause (see, e.g., Figure 2). Next, all phrases[9] directly dependent on the predicate, i.e. all its arguments and modifiers, are considered *constituents* of the clause (in the sense of the MAL); see Figure 2 where directly dependent phrases are bounded by dashed boxes. Finally, the size of the constituent (i.e., the size of a phrase which is directly dependent on the predicate) is measured by the number of words which the phrase consists of[10].

For an illustration, let us take the clause

My friend saw your sister from Pisa yesterday

depicted in Figure 2.

---

[6] The models in Sections 2 and 5 were fitted to the data by NLREG program.

[7] Another attempt to interpret the MAL – a modification of the ideas from the general approach suggested by Köhler (1984) – can be found in Milička (2014).

[8] http://ufal.mff.cuni.cz/pdt2.5/en/
documentation.html# clause

[9] We are aware that Tesnière (2015) used the term *node* (*nœud* in French); however, as the translators of his famous book notice, "[H]he first defines the node to be what modern theories of syntax take to be a phrase/constituent",

and "[H]his inconsistent use of the term is a source of confusion" (Tesnière, 2015, Translators' Introduction, p. xlv). We prefer the term phrase in the sense as it is used also by Meľčuk (1988) and Crystal (2008)

[10] We do not claim that this choice of the constituent is the only one possible, or the "right one" for clauses. In our opinion, it is quite probable that there are several "parallel" possibilities, analogous to the chains word – syllable – phoneme and word – morpheme – phoneme. Our approach is the first attempt to investigate the MAL in syntactic dependency structure, and it can be hoped it will be followed by other studies which will open other views.

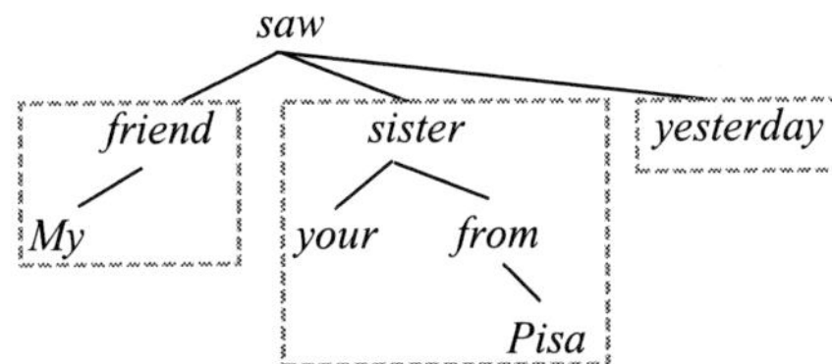

Figure 2. The hierarchical structure of the clause *My friend saw your sister from Pisa yesterday*. The dashed boxes represent phrases which are considered constructs of the clause.

There are three phrases directly dependent on the predicate *saw* (see Figure 2):

(Ph1) *My friend*;
(Ph2) *your sister from Pisa*;
(Ph3) *yesterday*.

Thus, the size of the clause is three. Next, the mean constituent size in the clause is determined as an average of sizes of particular phrases. Specifically, phrase (Ph1) consists of two words, (Ph2) of four words, and (Ph3) of one word. The mean size of the phrase in the clause considered is

$$(2 + 4 + 1) / 3 = 2.33.$$

This procedure is applied to each clause in the corpus (with mean phrase length computed from all clauses with a particular length in the corpus, e.g., we took all phrases which occur in clauses with length one and evaluated their mean length, then all phrases occurring in clauses with length two, etc.).

To sum up,

a) the clause represents the *construct*;
b) the size of the *construct* is determined by the number of phrases which are directly dependent on the predicate of the clause; each phrase represents a *constituent* of the clause;
c) the size of the *constituent* (i.e., of the phrase) is determined by the number of its words.

This approach satisfies the theoretical assumption of the MAL – language units which are in the relation of a construct and a constituent (clause – phrase – word) are used for the analysis.

4   Language material

In this study, dependency trees from the Prague Dependency Treebank 3.0 (Bejček et al., 2013; PDT 3.0 hereafter) were used; specifically, the data annotated on analytical lever (the treebank contains approximately 1.5 million words). Particular clauses from the corpus were determined in accordance with the annotation. Only main clauses were used for modelling because the analytical function "Predicate" is assigned only to the predicate of the main clause in the PDT 3.0[11]. We used tokenized sentences (see Section 3, Figure 2, for an example), with the tokenization from the PDT 3.0 taken without any adaptation. Punctuation is not considered.

Non-projective dependency trees were not filtered out. First, the (non-)projectivity of a dependency tree is irrelevant with respect to the validity of the MAL for the data from a treebank as whole[12]. Clauses consist of phrases regardless of properties of their tree representations. Second, non-projective trees do not present technical problems, as the determination of the predicate and phrases which are directly dependent on the predicate is not affected by the tree (non-)projectivity. Finally, crossings may be not so scarce as it is believed – it seems that they correlate with dependency length (the longer dependency length, the more crossings can be expected, see Ferrer-i-Cancho and Gómez-Rodríguez, 2016). A rejection of non-projective trees could thus lead to an underrepresentation of sentences with longer dependency lengths.

Because of the existence of technical nodes as well as specificities of the annotation in the PDT 3.0, we were forced to rearranged the original annotation to some extent; the whole procedure of the adjustment of the original annotation is described in detail in a technical report which is available online[13].

5   Results

The results – mean lengths of phrases which occur in clauses of particular lengths – are presented in Table 1. Only those clause lengths which occur in the corpus at least ten times, i.e.,

---

[11] In subordinate clauses, the predicate is not assigned by the analytical function "Predicate" but by a corresponding function of the subordinate clause (e.g., Attribute, Object, Subject).

[12] The validity of the MAL in a subcorpus consisting exclusively of non-projective trees is a different (albeit interesting) question, see a short discussion in Section 6.

[13] http://www.cechradek.cz/publ/
2017_macutek_etal_technical_report.zip

up to nine in our case, were analyzed (frequencies of clause lengths measured in the number of phrases in the corpus used can be found in Table 1 as well). Remarks on an irregular behaviour of constituents of long constructs[14] with low frequencies of occurrence can be found, e.g., in Kelih (2010), and in Mačutek and Rovenchak, (2011). The loss of data caused by neglecting longer clauses is minimal. We analyzed 56530 clauses from the corpus (see Section 4), only 18 of them (i.e., approximately 0.03%) consisted of more than nine phrases.

CL	f(CL)	MPL
1	7125	9.47
2	21508	5.04
3	16964	4.00
4	7858	3.51
5	2351	3.25
6	551	2.91
7	118	3.05
8	27	2.85
9	10	3.03

Table 1. Relation between clause length and mean phrase length (CL – clause length, f(CL) – frequency of clauses with the given length in the corpus, MPL – mean phrase length).

The relation can be modelled by the simpler form of the MAL (see Section 2), i.e., by function (2). The parameter values optimized with respect to the goodness of fit (expressed in terms of the determination coefficient) are $a = 8.96$, $b = -0.62$, with $R^2 = 0.9424$. The model fits the data sufficiently well[15] (see Section 2).

The tendency of the mean phrase length to decrease with the increasing clause length can clearly be seen in Figure 3, which depicts also the abovementioned function as the mathematical model for the MAL. We emphasize that the MAL – and all laws in linguistics, and all laws in empirical science in general – is of a stochastic rather than deterministic character, hence some minor local disturbances in the overall decreasing trend are admissible.

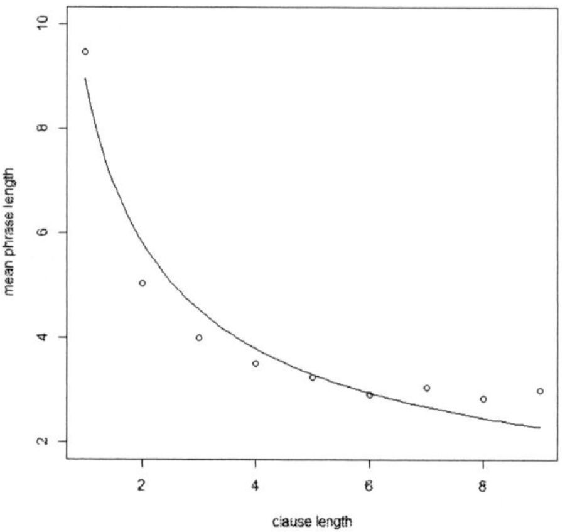

Figure 3. Relation between clause length and mean phrase length (see Table 1), with function (2) fitted to the data.

The result achieved is the first corroboration of the MAL in syntactic dependency structure (some hints towards the validity of the MAL in syntax in general can be found in Köhler, 2012, however, without specifying a wider framework, such as, e.g., dependency grammar in this paper).

6 Conclusion and perspectives

Our paper broadens the scope of the MAL. Based on the analysis of the Czech dependency treebank, it can be said, tentatively at least, that the law is valid also in syntactic dependency structure, with clauses being constructs and phrases (see Section 2, Figure 2) being constituents.

Naturally, further analyses must be postponed until results from several other languages are available. From a theoretical point of view, problems needed to be answered include, e.g., an interpretation of parameters of the mathematical model and relations with other language laws (Köhler, 2005). Another issue waiting to be studied more deeply is the question of non-projective dependency trees. Is the MAL valid for them as well? If yes, do the parameter values

---

[14] It remains unclear whether the irregular behavior is caused only by low frequencies of long constructs, in which the mean length of constituents then has than a higher variance, or whether there are also other factors at play, which have only a negligible influence on short constructs. Admittedly, if one includes rarely occurring longer constructs, the fit usually becomes worse (which is true also for data considered in this paper).

[15] The "full version" of the MAL, i.e., function (1) from Section 2, achieves a slightly better fit ($R^2 = 0.9970$, with $a = 8.11, b = -1.06, c = 0.15$), but it has one parameter more, making thus attempts to interpret the parameters more difficult.

differ from the ones typical for corpora in which projective trees prevail?

In more applied fields, parameters of the MAL parameters in dependency structure could perhaps strengthen the arsenal of tools used in authorship attribution, automatic text classification, and similar areas.

The parameters of the MAL in syntactic dependency structure offer themselves to be used in a syntactic language typology (see, e.g., Song, 2001; Whaley, 2010). It would be interesting to take some established typology and to check whether there are some typical parameter values for typologically similar languages. We remind that several attempts to build a language typology based on dependency grammar and on some characteristics of dependency relations appeared in recent years (Liu, 2010, Liu and Li, 2010; Liu and Xu, 2012; Jing and Liu, 2017).

In addition to bringing some results, the paper also opens several questions of theoretical and/or methodological character, some of which can be interesting not only within dependency grammar but also in mathematical modelling of language phenomena in general. We mention some of them in the following paragraphs.

The MAL is usually modelled across neighbouring levels in the language unit hierarchy. It seems that clauses and phrases (as defined in Section 2) are "neighbours" in this sense. The question is which is the next unit when one looks "downwards". We chose word as the constituent of a phrase, but the possibility that we skipped some level(s) cannot be a priori excluded. Will the MAL be valid also for the relation between phrases and "subphrases", i.e., units directly dependent on phrases? If yes, how many levels are there?

Up to our knowledge, there are no published results on the relation between sizes of clauses and words[16]. The paper by Buk and Rovenchak (2008), focusing mainly on the relation between sentence length and clause length (relation between clause length in words and word length in syllables can be reconstructed from the data for a narrow interval of clause size), does not bring any convincing results, it ends with a call for a clarification of the notion of clause. Can the reason be that clauses and words are not

neighbours in this sense[17], and that one should consider an intermediate level, such as phrase in this paper?

Nonetheless, the MAL is a good model (in terms of goodness of fit) for the relation between lengths of sentence (in clauses) and clause (in words). The validity of the law was corroborated in eight languages (Czech, English, French, German, Hungarian, Indonesian, Slovak, Swedish), see Köhler (1982), Heups (1983), and Teupenhayn and Altmann (1984). But, as it was mentioned above, clauses and words do not seem to be direct neighbours in the language unit hierarchy. These two facts – the assumed existence of some level(s) between clause and word on the one hand, and the validity of the MAL for the relation between lengths of sentences in clauses and of clauses in words – can be reconciled, e.g., if not one, but two levels (phrases and "subphrases") were omitted. Still another possible explanation is that we analyze parallel nested structures analogous to, e.g., the two chains of units mention in Section 2, one of which consists of words, syllables and phonemes, and the other of words, morphemes and graphemes. Dependency grammar, with its (relatively) clearly defined relations among words in a clause, can be a useful tool for determining "reasonable" (i.e., linguistically interpretable) language units "between" clause and word (if there are any) and for investigating relations among them.

It is our hope that our paper may serve as a stimulus towards future research in the areas of syntactic dependency structure and of relations among language units in general (especially with respect to their sizes and mutual influences).

Acknowledgment

Supported by the VEGA grant no. 2/0047/15 (J. Mačutek) and by the Charles University project Progress 4, Language in the shiftings of time, space, and culture (J. Milička).

---

[16] Similar discussions were opened by Chen and Liu (2016) on the relation between sizes of word and its constituents (i.e., one level lower than in this paper) in Chinese, and by Sanada (2016) on the relation between sizes of sentence, clause and argument (as defined in Sanada, 2016, pp. 259-260) in Japanese.

[17] According to Köhler (2012, p. 108), "an indirect relationship ... is a good enough reason for more variance in the data and a weaker fit".

References

Gabriel Altmann. 1978. Towards a theory of language. In Gabriel Altmann, editor, *Glottometrika 1*, pages 1-25. Brockmeyer, Bochum.

Gabriel Altmann. 1980. Prolegomena to Menzerath's law. In Rüdiger Grotjahn, editor, *Glottometrika 2*, pages 1-10. Brockmeyer, Bochum.

Gabriel Altmann. 1993. Science and linguistics. In Reinhard Köhler and Burghard B. Rieger, editors, *Contributions to Quantitative Linguistics*, pages 3-10. Kluwer, Dordrecht.

Gabriel Altmann. 2014. Bibliography: Menzerath's law. *Glottotheory*, 5(1):121-123.

Eduard Bejček, Eva Hajičová, Jan Hajič, Pavlína Jínová, Václava Kettnerová, Veronika Kolářová, Marie Mikulová, Jiří Mírovský, Anna Nedoluzhko, Jarmila Panevová, Lucie Poláková, Magda Ševčíková, Jan Štěpánek, Šárka Zikánová. 2013. *Prague Dependency Treebank 3.0.* Charles University, Praha.

Solomija Buk and Andrij Rovenchak. 2008. Menzerath-Altmann law for syntactic structures in Ukrainian. *Glottotheory*, 1(1):10-17.

Mario Bunge. 1967. *Scientific Research I, II.* Springer, Berlin.

Heng Chen and Haitao Liu. 2016. How to measure word length in spoken and written Chinese. *Journal of Quantitative Linguistics*, 23(1):5-29.

Irene M. Cramer. 2005a. Das Menzerathsche Gesetz. In Reinhard Köhler, Gabriel Altmann, and Rajmund G. Piotrowski, editors, *Quantitative Linguistics. An International Handbook*, pages 659-688. De Gruyter, Berlin / New York.

Irene M. Cramer. 2005b. The parameters of the Menzerath-Altmann law. *Journal of Quantitative Linguistics*, 12(1):41-52.

David Crystal. 2008. *A Dictionary of Linguistics and Phonetics.* Blackwell, Oxford.

Ramon Ferrer-i-Cancho and Carlos Gómez-Rodríguez. 2016. Crossings as a side effect of dependency lengths. *Complexity*, 21(S2):320-328.

Rainer Gerlach. 1982. Zur Überprüfung des Menzerath'schen Gesetzes im Bereich der Morphologie. In Werner Lehfeldt and Udo Strauss, editors, *Glottometrika 4*, pages 95-102. Brockmeyer, Bochum.

Gabriela Heups. 1983. Untersuchungen zum Verhältnis von Satzlänge zu Clauselänge am Beispiel deutscher Texte verschiedener Textklassen. In Reinhard Köhler and Joachim Boy, editors, *Glottometrika 5*, pages 113-133. Brockmeyer, Bochum.

Yingqi Jing and Haitao Liu. 2017. Dependency distance motifs in 21 Indoeuropean langauges. In Haitao Liu and Junying Liang, editors, *Motifs in Language and Text*, pages 133-150. De Gruyter, Berlin / Boston.

Emmerich Kelih. 2010. Parameter interpretation of Menzerath law: evidence from Serbian. In Peter Grzybek, Emmerich Kelih, and Ján Mačutek, editors, *Text and Language. Structures, Functions, Interrelations, Quantitative Perspectives*, pages 71-79. Praesens, Wien.

Reinhard Köhler. 1982. Das Menzeratsche Gesetz auf Satzebene. In Werner Lehfeldt and Udo Strauss, editors, *Glottometrika 4*, pages 103-113. Brockmeyer, Bochum.

Reinhard Köhler. 1984. Zur Interpretation des Menzerathschen Gesetzes. In Joachim Boy and Reinhard Köhler, editors, *Glottometrika 6*, pages 177-183. Brockmeyer, Bochum.

Reinhard Köhler. 2005. Synergetic linguistics. In Reinhard Köhler, Gabriel Altmann, and Rajmund G. Piotrowski, editors, *Quantitative Linguistics. An International Handbook*, pages 760-774. De Gruyter, Berlin / New York.

Reinhard Köhler. 2012. *Quantitative Syntax Analysis.* De Gruyter, Berlin / Boston.

Haitao Liu. 2010. Dependency direction as a means of word-order typology: a method based on dependency treebanks. *Lingua*, 120:1567-1578.

Haitao Liu and Wenwen Li. 2010. Language clusters based on linguistic complex networks. *Chinese Science Bulletin*, 55(30):3458-3465.

Haitao Liu and Chushan Xu. 2012. Quantitative typological analysis of Romance languages. *Poznań Studies in Contemporary Linguistics*, 48(4):597-625.

Markéta Lopatková, Natalia Klyueva, and Petr Homola. 2009. Annotation of sentence structure: capturing the relationship among clauses in Czech sentences. In *Proceedings of the Third Linguistic Annotation Workshop*, pages 74-81. ACL, Stroudsburg (PA).

Ján Mačutek and Andrij Rovenchak. 2011. Canonical word forms: Menzerath-Altmann law, phonemic length and syllabic length. In Emmerich Kelih, Viktor Levickij, and Yulia Matskulyak, editors, *Issues in Quantitative Linguistics 2*, pages 136-147. RAM-Verlag, Lüdenscheid.

Ján Mačutek and Gejza Wimmer. 2013. Evaluating goodness-of-fit of discrete distribution models in quantitative linguistics. *Journal of Quantitative Linguistics*, 20(3):227-240.

Igor A. Mel'čuk. 1988. *Dependency Syntax: Theory and Practice*. State University of New York Press, Albany (NY).

Paul Menzerath. 1954. *Die Architektonik des deutschen Wortschatzes*. Dümmler, Bonn.

Jiří Milička. 2014. Menzerath's law: the whole is greater than the sum of its parts. *Journal of Quantitative Linguistics*, 21(2):85-99.

Haruko Sanada. 2016. The Menzerath-Altmann law and sentence structure. *Journal of Quantitative Linguistics*, 23(3):256-277.

Jae J. Song. 2001. *Linguistic Typology: Morphology and Syntax*. Routledge, London / New York.

Lucien Tesnière. 2015. *Elements of Structural Syntax*. John Benjamins, Amsterdam.

Regina Teupenhayn and Gabriel Altmann. 1984. Clause length and Menzerath's law. In Joachim Boy and Reinhard Köhler, editors, *Glottometrika 6*, pages 127-138. Brockmeyer, Bochum.

Lindsay Whaley. 2010. Syntactic typology. In Jae J. Song, editor, *The Oxford Handbook of Linguistic Typology*, pages 465-486. Oxford University Press, Oxford.

Assessing the Annotation Consistency
of the Universal Dependencies Corpora

Marie-Catherine de Marneffe
Linguistics Department
The Ohio State University
Columbus, OH, USA
mcdm@ling.ohio-state.edu

Matias Grioni
Computer Science Department
The Ohio State University
Columbus, OH, USA
grioni.2@osu.edu

Jenna Kanerva and **Filip Ginter**
Turku NLP group
University of Turku
Finland
{jmnybl,figint}@utu.fi

Abstract

A fundamental issue in annotation efforts is to ensure that the same phenomena within and across corpora are annotated consistently. To date, there has not been a clear and obvious way to ensure annotation consistency of dependency corpora. Here, we revisit the method of Boyd et al. (2008) to flag inconsistencies in dependency corpora, and evaluate it on three languages with varying degrees of morphology (English, French, and Finnish UD v2). We show that the method is very efficient in finding errors in the annotations. We also build an annotation tool, which we will make available, that helps to streamline the manual annotation required by the method.

1 Introduction

In every annotation effort, it is necessary to make sure that the annotation guidelines are followed, and crucially that similar phenomena do receive a consistent analysis within and across corpora. Given the recent success of the Universal Dependencies (UD) project[1] which aims at building cross-linguistically consistent treebanks for many languages and the rapid creation of 74 corpora for 51 languages supposedly following the UD scheme, investigating the quality of the dependency annotations and improving their consistency is, more than ever, of crucial importance.

While there has been a fair amount of work to automatically detect part-of-speech inconsistent annotations (i.a., Eskin (2000), van Halteren (2000), Dickinson & Meurers (2003a)), most approaches to assess the consistency of dependency annotations are based on heuristic patterns (i.a., De Smedt et al. (2016) who focus on multi-word

expressions in the UD v1 corpora (Nivre et al., 2016)). There exists a variety of querying tools allowing to search dependency treebanks, given such heuristic patterns (i.a., SETS (Luotolahti et al., 2015); Grew (Bonfante et al., 2011); PML TreeQuery (Štěpánek and Pajas, 2010); ICARUS (Gärtner et al., 2013)). Statistical methods, such as the one of Ambati et al. (2011), are supplemented with hand-written rules. While approaches based on heuristic patterns work extremely well to look for given constructions (e.g., clefts) or check that specific guidelines are taken into account (e.g., auxiliary dependencies should not form a chain in UD), such approaches are limited to finding what has been defined a priori.

In this paper, we adapt the method proposed by Boyd et al. (2008) to flag potential dependency annotation inconsistencies, and evaluate it on three of the UD v2 corpora (English, French and Finnish). The original Boyd et al. method finds pairs of words in identical context that vary in their dependency relation. We show that this method works fairly well in finding annotation errors, within a given corpus. We further hypothesize that using lemmas instead of word forms would improve recall in finding annotation errors, without a detrimental effect on precision. We show that our intuition is valid for languages that are not too morphologically-rich, like English and French, but not for Finnish.

We also examine whether we can extend the method by leveraging the availability of large corpora which are automatically dependency-annotated to identify more inconsistencies than when restricting ourselves only to the given manually annotated corpus. We find that when based on automatic rather than manual annotation, the precision drops but not excessively so, but the gain in recall is rather moderate.

Finally, the Boyd et al. approach is semi-automatic, flagging potential inconsistencies

---

[1]http://universaldependencies.org

Proceedings of the Fourth International Conference on Dependency Linguistics (Depling 2017), pages 108-115,
Pisa, Italy, September 18-20 2017

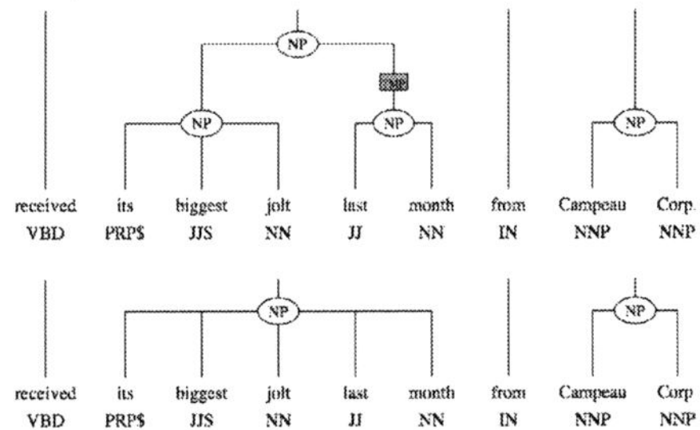

Figure 1: Example of variation nuclei for phrase-structure tree from (Boyd et al., 2008).

which require manual validation. To help streamline this manual validation process, we develop a visualization and annotation tool for the task, available to the UD community, with data for all UD treebanks.[2] Rather than a standalone tool such as ICARUS (Thiele et al., 2014), we provide an accessible browser-based interface.

2 Boyd et al. 2008: Variation nuclei

Boyd et al. (2008) extend, to dependency representation, the concept of *variation nuclei* developed by Dickinson and Meurers (2003b; 2005) for identifying inconsistent annotations in phrase-structure trees. Variation nuclei are elements which occur multiple times in a corpus with varying annotation. For phrase-structure trees, a variation nucleus is any n-gram for which bracketing or labeling varies, with one shared word of context on each side of the n-gram. Figure 1, from Boyd et al. (2008), shows an example of a 5-gram, *its biggest jolt last month*, which receives two different analyses in the Penn TreeBank.

For dependency representation, the basic elements are dependencies, i.e. pairs of words linked by a labeled dependency. Here variation nuclei are then pairs of words which are linked by different relations. However flagging any pairs of words linked by different relations would generate too many potential inconsistencies, most of which might be genuine ambiguities and not annotation errors. To restrict the number of potential inconsistencies, Boyd et al. add context restrictions. Their "non-fringe heuristic" requires the words in the nucleus to share the same context (one word to the left and one word to the right of the nucleus). Example (1) shows a variation

nucleus in a dependency representation, extracted from the UD English corpus, where the pairs of words *Here* and *examples* are linked differently. Boyd et al. also experimented with a "dependency context heuristic" requiring the governors of the dependency pairs to have the same incoming dependency relation. They also considered the case of pairs of words which are linked by a dependency relation in some instances and not linked by any relation in other instances, but required for those cases that the internal context between the two words be exactly the same.

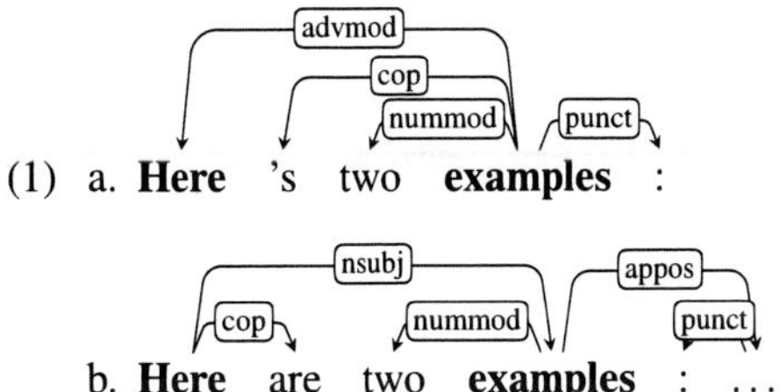

(1) a. **Here** 's two **examples** :

b. **Here** are two **examples** : ...

3 Extending to lemmas

Our goal in this paper is two-fold: evaluate the Boyd et al. method on the UD data, and increase recall of finding annotation errors without sacrificing precision. So far we have restricted our evaluation to words that are linked by different existing dependency relations, evaluating the "non-fringe" and "dependency context" heuristics. Boyd et al. applied their method to words (tokens). We hypothesized that to reduce data sparsity and thus find more errors, we could use lemmas instead of words, and contrary to Boyd et al., we do not require that the part-of-speech of the lemmas match. Note that the Boyd et al. method is independent of the dependency representation chosen.

4 Data

We evaluate our reimplementation and extension of the Boyd et al. method on three different languages: English, French and Finnish. We chose these three languages because they vary in their degree of morphology, and are therefore good candidates to properly evaluate the impact of using lemmas instead of words. We used the UD v2 corpora of English, French and Finnish. Table 1 gives the size of these corpora in terms of number of sentences and tokens. For the purpose of finding inconsistencies in the annotations, we collapse all the data sets (train, development, and test) available into one corpus for each language.

---

[2]`http://www.universaldependencies.org/fixud`

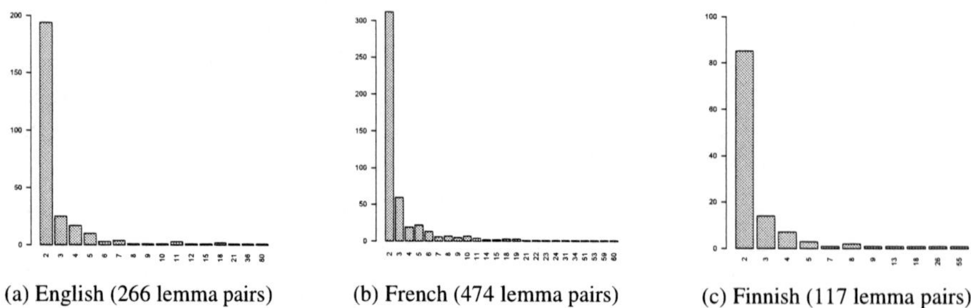

Figure 2: Number of lemma pairs (y-axis) displaying different numbers of potentially erroneous trees (x-axis).

UD v2	# sentences	# tokens
English	14,545	229,753
French	16,031	392,230
Finnish	13,581	181,138

Table 1: Size of the UD v2 English, French and Finnish corpora.

5 Evaluation

The method retrieves 266 pairs of lemmas displaying inconsistencies for English, 474 for French and 117 for Finnish, using the "non-fringe" heuristic (i.e., the pairs need to share context: same lemma to the left and same lemma to the right of the lemmas in the dependency pair). Each pair varies in the number of inconsistent trees they are associated with. But most pairs contain two trees, as can be seen in Figure 2 which shows the counts of pairs (y-axis) for the different numbers of trees they contain (x-axis).

For each language, to evaluate how many of the inconsistencies flagged are indeed annotation errors, we randomly sampled 100 of the pairs retrieved and annotated all the trees associated with these pairs, nevertheless limiting to 10 trees per dependency type.

5.1 Lemma-based approach

Table 2 gives the results. In the "non-fringe" column, we computed how many of the 100 pairs do contain erroneous trees. Thus these results indicate how precise the method is. Boyd et al. propose an additional, more stringent heuristic of "dependency context". This heuristic requires the word/lemma pairs to not only share the left/right context, but also the incoming relation type. As we did not implement this heuristic when select-ing the trees for annotation, we are able to evaluate its precision as well as its recall relative to the pairs retrieved when using only the "non-fringe" heuristic. Using the 100 pairs annotated in each language as a gold-standard, we calculated the precision and recall of the "dependency context" heuristic by examining which pairs are left when adding the further requirement of shared incoming relation to the governor.

For the method used on lemmas, the results are satisfying for both English and French, with a precision of 62% and 65%, respectively. However the method is not precise enough for Finnish, with only 19% of the pairs containing annotation errors. The use of lemmas for Finnish loses too much information: different inflections in Finnish can have completely different roles in many cases, and this leads to many false positives being retrieved. A good example of this is relative clauses, where the Finnish relativizer lemmas *joka* and *mikä* get different syntactic functions depending on the case inflection. For example, in the relative clauses "joka (Case=Nom) tarvitsee" *who needs*, "jota (Case=Par) tarvitsee" *what is needed* and "jossa (Case=Ine) tarvitsee" *where something is needed*, three different syntactic functions, "nsubj", "obj" and "obl" respectively, are correctly assigned for the same lemma pair.

The more stringent heuristic of "dependency context" leads to a loss in recall (especially for French with only 47%) without a clear boost in precision. These results are in line with the results from Boyd et al. who evaluated their method on Czech (one portion of the Prague Dependency Treebank, (Böhmová et al., 2003)), Swedish (Talbanken05, (Nivre et al., 2006)) and German (Tiger Dependency Bank, (Forst et al., 2004)). For the Czech data (38,482 sentences – 670,544 tokens),

| | LEMMAS | | | WORDS | |
| | "Non-fringe" | "Dependency context" | | "Non-fringe" | |
	Precision (%)	Precision (%)	Recall (%)	Precision (%)	Recall (%)
English	62	76	66	72	79
French	65	64	47	76	73
Finnish	19	21	81	72	75

Table 2: Results of the Boyd et al. method on 100 pairs in each corpus for the "non-fringe" and "dependency context" heuristics when using lemmas as well as for the "non-fringe" heuristic when using wordforms. Recall is always reported relative to the "non-fringe" lemma-based method.

Boyd et al. obtained 58% precision on 354 pairs retrieved, increasing precision slightly to 61% when adding the more stringent heuristic, but with a recall of 66%. For the Swedish data (11,431 sentences – 197,123 tokens), 210 pairs were retrieved, with a high precision of 92%. The more stringent heuristic yielded a slight increase in precision (95%) but an important drop in recall (48%). For German (1,567 sentences – 29,373 tokens) however, due to the small corpus size, only 3 pairs were retrieved, all containing annotation errors.

5.2 Wordform-based approach

Capitalizing on the fact that every identified pair of words is also among the pairs of lemmas, we can subset the manually annotated lemma pairs and compute the precision of the method using wordforms as well as its recall relative to the lemma-based method. The results of the method based on words (instead of lemmas) are shown in the last columns of Table 2. For English and French, we see a moderate gain in precision whereas for Finnish we see a dramatic gain in precision, from 19% to 72%. The recall of the wordform-based method is in the 70–80% range for all languages, meaning that the gain in precision is offset by a loss of 20–30% of identified annotation errors. As the task is to find as many annotation errors as possible, the loss of 20–30% of identified annotation errors might not be justified, especially for English and French where it is not accompanied by a major gain in precision.

5.3 Delexicalized approach

Seeing that for Finnish, new strategies need to be explored, we also test a delexicalized version of the method, whereby only pairs of morphological features are considered, rather than wordforms or lemmas, but constrained on the context lem-

mas. For instance, in Figure 3, instead of using the wordform or lemma, we work at the level of the morphological features: the elements in the pairs share the same features, and the left and right contexts have identical lemmas. For English and French, initial inspection of the results revealed a hopeless over-generation, but for Finnish this method outperforms the lemma-based approach both in precision and recall. While the lemma-based method identifies 117 pairs with precision of 19%, the delexicalized version identifies 353 pairs with precision of 25%. This shows that when applying the method to Finnish, the morphology is of primary consideration, even above the lemmas themselves. Nevertheless for Finnish, the more useful method is the original Boyd et al., which considers wordforms, given that it reaches a high enough precision.

5.4 Analysis of the errors retrieved

We give here a few examples of the pairs retrieved which accurately pointed to errors in the annotations. In all examples, we bold the words that constitute the word/lemma pairs. Examples in (2), (3), (4), (5) and (6) display trees in which two very different analyses have been given to the same construction. Such trees indicate that some specific constructions in the corpus need to be systematically checked: for instance, (3) shows that comparatives in the UD French corpus need to be checked for consistency in their analysis, and (4) shows that Fr. "ce qui" *that which* needs to be checked across the board. Similarly (5) shows that number constructions in the Finnish corpus are not consistent in the choice of the head. Thus the examples flagged are useful to write patterns to check the annotations of some constructions that we may not have been thinking of a priori. (6) shows a case where there is a disagreement in the

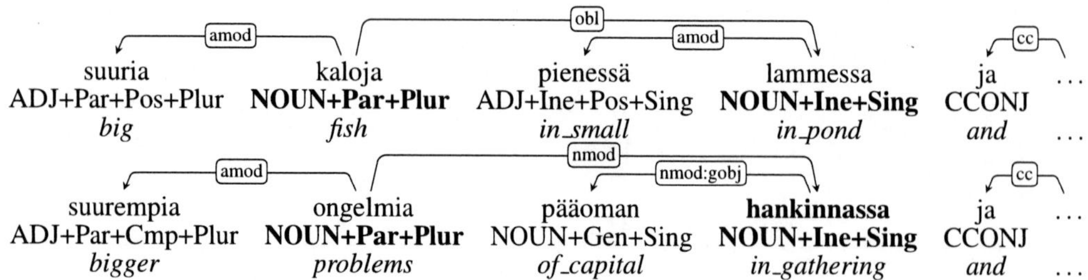

Figure 3: An example of an annotation error identified by the delexicalized method in the Finnish corpus. Here a pair of words is identified sharing a lemma-based context (*big, and*) such that the first word is a noun in plural partitive and the second word is a noun in singular inessive.

dependency type in identical phrase constructions. As the "obl" relation type has only been introduced in the recent version of the UD guidelines, it may be more error prone at this point.

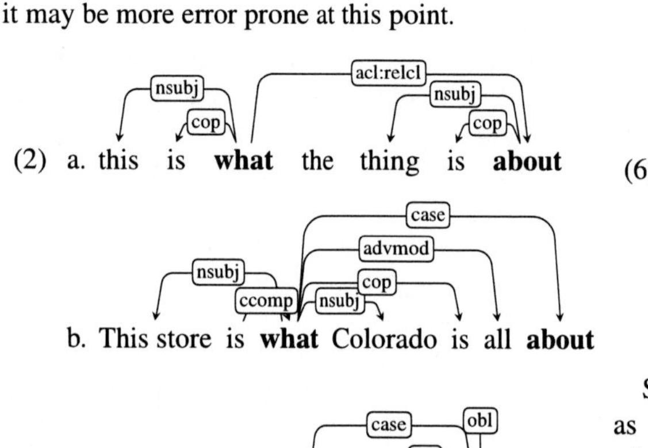

(2) a. this is **what** the thing is **about**

b. This store is **what** Colorado is all **about**

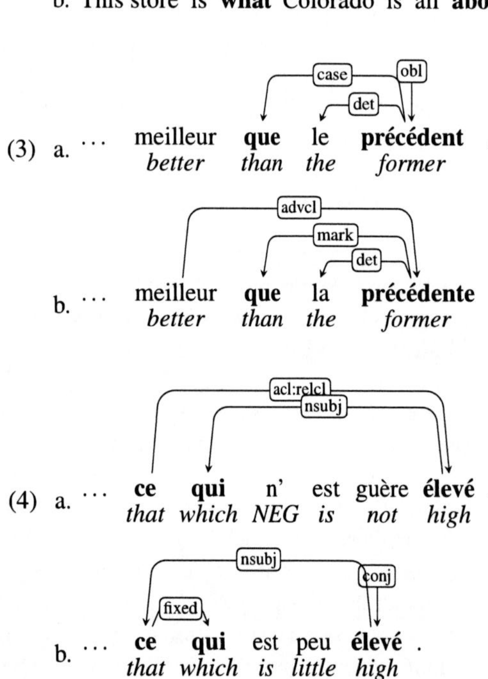

(3) a. ⋯ meilleur **que** le **précédent** .
    better   than the former

b. ⋯ meilleur **que** la **précédente** .
   better   than the former

(4) a. ⋯ **ce** **qui** n' est guère **élevé** .
    that which NEG is not   high

b. ⋯ **ce** **qui** est peu **élevé** .
   that which is little high

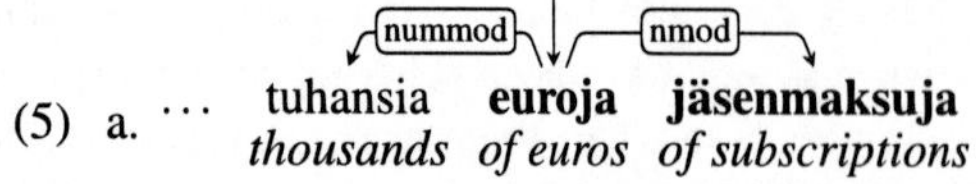

(5) a. ⋯ tuhansia **euroja** **jäsenmaksuja**
    thousands of euros of subscriptions

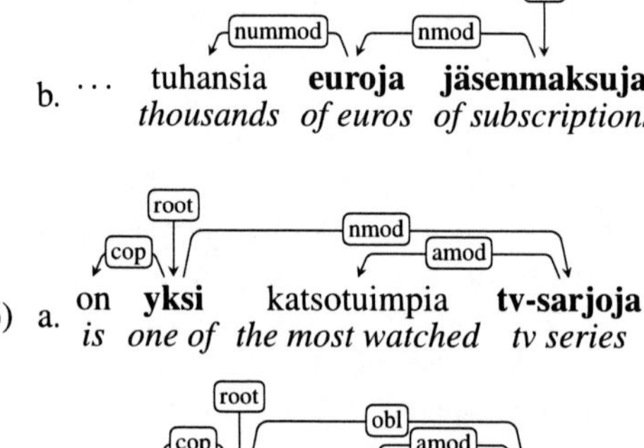

b. ⋯ tuhansia **euroja** **jäsenmaksuja**
   thousands of euros of subscriptions

(6) a. on **yksi** katsotuimpia **tv-sarjoja**
    is one of the most watched tv series

b. ⋯ on **yksi** pahimpia **ongelmia**
   is one of the worst problems

Some errors are due to wrong attachments, such as (7) in which *able* is wrongly attached to *had* with a "ccomp" relation instead of being attached to *idea*.

(7) We **had** a pretty good idea when we signed the contract that ECS would not be **able** to complete that by the contract start date, ⋯

The total number of annotation errors identified during the annotation of the 100 lemma pairs for each of the three corpora is summarized in Table 3. The annotation took a maximum of two hours per language and was carried out by annotators well versed in the task.

6 Extending with parsebank data

The Boyd et al. method is very useful to find annotation errors when there are similar contexts within the corpus. We examine whether we can take advantage of existing large parsebank data to find more contexts in which analyses differ, and thus hopefully catch more annotation errors in the UD data. We used the CoNLL'17 Shared Task supporting data (Ginter et al., 2017), comprising of up to several billions of words of web-crawled data

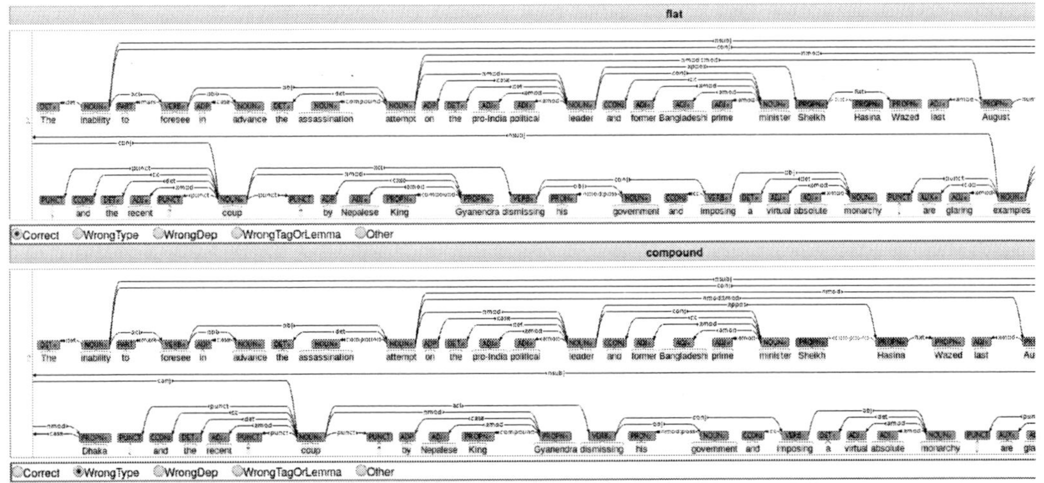

Figure 4: Example of the annotation tool.

	Erroneous		Correct
	Type	Structure	
English	63	13	223
French	56	45	241
Finnish	7	12	259

Table 3: The number of trees assessed as erroneous (incorrect relation type or incorrect structure), and the number of trees verified to be correct.

per UD language, parsed with the UDPipe 1.1 dependency parser (Straka et al., 2016). For each of the three UD corpora we analyze, we flag pairs if they appear in the corresponding parsebank data in the same context at least 5 times, but are a variation nucleus. Table 4 gives the number of trees which were manually assessed as annotation errors, as well as the percentage of trees which contain annotation errors (out of 100 pairs randomly sampled for French, all of them for English and Finnish). It also indicates how many of the erroneous trees are already found based on the treebank itself. The proportion of such erroneous trees ranges from 30% to 40% depending on the language, but this means that 60–70% of annotation errors found based on the parsebank data are not flagged by the Boyd et al. method, when operating only within the same corpus.

7 Annotation tool

The method retrieves pairs that display different analyses. However the pairs retrieved need to be checked manually: are they annotation errors or genuine ambiguities? To facilitate the annotation, we implemented a web-based tool which allows the annotation of the flagged inconsistencies to be carried out entirely in the browser in an intuitive manner. The tool is illustrated in Figure 4. First, the annotators are presented with a list of lemma pairs, sortable by various criteria. For each pair, a link is provided leading to visualizations of the trees involving the pair, which is highlighted in every tree. The trees are grouped by dependency relation, which very often results in consistent groups where every tree is correct or every tree is incorrect, thus streamlining the annotation. For each tree, the annotator can mark the

	# tree errors	"Non-fringe" Precision	% in Boyd
English	54	41%	38%
French	74	57%	36%
Finnish	10	16%	30%

Table 4: Results using parsebank data and lemmas: the number of trees that were manually assessed as annotation errors, the precision of the method, and the percentage of the erroneous trees which would be also found based on the treebank itself.

tree as *correct* or *incorrect* for three separate reasons (relation type, governor/dependent, or part-of-speech), or the catch-all category *other*. The choice is saved automatically, and retrieved in case the page with the trees is reloaded or reopened. A visual cue in the form of a green border is given to assure the annotator that the choice was successfully saved.

8 Conclusion

We evaluated the Boyd et al. (2008) method for finding annotation errors in dependency corpora on three of the UD v2 datasets (English, French and Finnish), and showed that this method performs fairly well.

We tried to adapt the Boyd et al. method to retrieve more errors, by working at the level of lemmas instead of wordforms. While results seem to indicate that this can work for languages with no case marking, it is clearly failing for a morphologically-rich language such as Finnish.

The parsebank-based method did not at present result in a large increase in recall, likely in part due to a too strict cut-off on the minimal number of parsebank instances needed in order to flag a treebank relation as inconsistent, and in part due to the noise in the automated parses of the web data. The winning system of the CoNLL'17 Shared Task[3] gains 8 percents in Labeled Attachment Score (LAS) over the baseline system which produced the parsebank analyses that we used, giving hope that this winning parser will lead to better results for the parsebank-based method.

We developed an easy and intuitive web interface for manual verification of the identified inconsistencies. Given our encouraging results on the three UD treebanks, we make both the interface and the automatically identified inconsistencies available to the UD community for all of the 70+ UD treebanks. This will allow us to expand the effort to the larger UD community and cover a number of languages and treebanks. For this, we will implement a light-weight user management so that multiple annotations for a single tree can be aggregated if necessary.

Our work is restricted to assessing the annotation consistency within a given corpus. However, moving forward, ensuring that similar constructions across corpora and languages are given the

---

[3] http://universaldependencies.org/conll17/results.html

same analysis will also need to be addressed.

Acknowledgments

We are grateful to Alane Suhr for her help on this project early on. We thank our anonymous reviewers for their useful feedback. The work was supported by a Google Faculty Award to the first author and by the KONE Foundation and the Finnish Academy.

References

Bharat Ram Ambati, Rahul Agarwal, Mridul Gupta, Samar Husain, and Dipti Misra Sharma. 2011. Error detection for treebank validation. *Proceedings of the 9th Workshop on Asian Language Resources*, pages 23–30.

Alena Böhmová, Jan Hajič, Eva Hajičová, and Barbora Hladká. 2003. The Prague dependency treebank. In *Treebanks*, pages 103–127. Springer.

Guillaume Bonfante, Bruno Guillaume, Mathieu Morey, and Guy Perrier. 2011. Modular graph rewriting to compute semantics. In *Proceedings of the Ninth International Conference on Computational Semantics*, pages 65–74.

Adriane Boyd, Markus Dickinson, and W Detmar Meurers. 2008. On detecting errors in dependency treebanks. *Research on Language & Computation*, 6(2):113–137.

Koenraad De Smedt, Victoria Rosén, and Paul Meurer. 2016. Studying consistency in UD treebanks with INESS-Search. In *Fourteenth Workshop on Treebanks and Linguistic Theories (TLT14)*.

Markus Dickinson and W. Detmar Meurers. 2003a. Detecting errors in part-of-speech annotation. In *Proceedings of the Tenth Conference on European Chapter of the Association for Computational Linguistics*, pages 107–114.

Markus Dickinson and W. Detmar Meurers. 2003b. Detecting inconsistencies in treebanks. In *Proceedings of the Second Workshop on Treebanks and Linguistic Theories (TLT-03)*.

Markus Dickinson and W. Detmar Meurers. 2005. Detecting errors in discontinuous structural annotation. In *Proceedings of the 43rd Annual Meeting of the Association for Computational Linguistics*, pages 322–329.

Eleazar Eskin. 2000. Detecting errors within a corpus using anomaly detection. In *Proceedings of the 1st North American Chapter of the Association for Computational Linguistics Conference*, pages 148–153.

Martin Forst, Núria Bertomeu, Berthold Crysmann, Frederik Fouvry, Silvia Hansen-Schirra, and Valia Kordoni. 2004. Towards a dependency-based gold standard for German parsers – the TiGer Dependency Bank. In *Proceedings of the COL-ING Workshop on Linguistically Interpreted Corpora (LINC04), Geneva, Switzerland.*

Markus Gärtner, Gregor Thiele, Wolfgang Seeker, Anders Björkelund, and Jonas Kuhn. 2013. ICARUS – An extensible graphical search tool for dependency treebanks. In *Proceedings of the 51st Annual Meeting of the Association for Computational Linguistics: System Demonstrations*, pages 55–60.

Filip Ginter, Jan Hajič, Juhani Luotolahti, Milan Straka, and Daniel Zeman. 2017. CoNLL 2017 shared task - automatically annotated raw texts and word embeddings. LINDAT/CLARIN digital library at the Institute of Formal and Applied Linguistics, Charles University.

Juhani Luotolahti, Jenna Kanerva, Sampo Pyysalo, and Filip Ginter. 2015. SETS: Scalable and efficient tree search in dependency graphs. In *NAACL Demo*, pages 51–55.

Joakim Nivre, Jens Nilsson, and Johan Hall. 2006. Talbanken05: A Swedish treebank with phrase structure and dependency annotation. In *Proceedings of the fifth international conference on Language Resources and Evaluation (LREC-06)*.

Joakim Nivre, Marie-Catherine de Marneffe, Filip Ginter, Yoav Goldberg, Jan Hajic, Christopher D Manning, Ryan McDonald, Slav Petrov, Sampo Pyysalo, Natalia Silveira, et al. 2016. Universal dependencies v1: A multilingual treebank collection. In *Proceedings of the 10th International Conference on Language Resources and Evaluation (LREC 2016)*, pages 1659–1666.

Jan Štěpánek and Petr Pajas. 2010. Querying diverse treebanks in a uniform way. In *Proceedings of the 7th International Conference on Language Resources and Evaluation (LREC 2010)*.

Milan Straka, Jan Hajič, and Jana Straková. 2016. UD-Pipe: Trainable pipeline for processing CoNLL-U files performing tokenization, morphological analysis, pos tagging and parsing. In *Proceedings of the Tenth International Conference on Language Resources and Evaluation (LREC'16)*, Paris, France, May. European Language Resources Association (ELRA).

Gregor Thiele, Wolfgang Seeker, Markus Gärtner, Anders Björkelund, and Jonas Kuhn. 2014. A graphical interface for automatic error mining in corpora. In *Proceedings of the Demonstrations at the 14th Conference of the European Chapter of the Association for Computational Linguistics*, pages 57–60. Association for Computational Linguistics.

Hans van Halteren. 2000. The detection of inconsistency in manually tagged text. In *Proceedings of the 2nd Workshop on Linguistically Interpreted Corpora*.

To what extent is Immediate Constituency Analysis dependency-based?
A survey of foundational texts

Nicolas Mazziotta
Université de Liège
Universität Stuttgart
Belgium, Germany
`nicolas.mazziotta@ulg.ac.be`

Sylvain Kahane
Modyco
Université Paris Nanterre
CNRS
France
`sylvain@kahane.fr`

Abstract

This paper investigates the seminal texts on Immediate Constituent Analysis and the associated diagrams. We show that the relations between the whole and its parts, that are typical of current phrase structure trees, were less prominent in the early diagramming efforts than the relationships between units of the same level. This can be observed until the beginning of the 1960's, including in Chomsky's *Syntactic Structures* (1957). We discuss whether such analyses could be said "dependency-based", according to an attempt to define this term.

1 Introduction

Chomsky's *Syntacic structures* (1957) is famous for the formalization of immediate constituent analysis (henceforth *ICA*) it introduces, using string-rewriting systems. After the first example of such a system, Chomsky introduces a corresponding diagram (reproduced here in fig. 1(a)) representing a set of equivalent derivations. Such a structure is now called a *derivation tree* and represented by tree, but it will appear later in this paper that Chomsky's first diagram was not exactly a tree. Let us compare fig. 1(a) with fig. 1(b), which should be an equivalent diagram, since it appears in the French translation of the same text (Chomsky, 1969(1957)). Fig. 1(b) is similar to phrase structure trees in (Chomsky, 1965): each internal node except the root, is linked to an upper node by a stroke encoding a part-whole relation. The original diagram (fig. 1(a)) does not display the same configuration of strokes.

Synctacticians of all kinds are familiar with diagrams, but most of the time, they use them without questioning their origins or the implications of the structural choices they represent. Studies on this subject, such as (Coseriu, 1980) on Tesnière's stemmas, (Stewart, 1976) on linguistic diagrams in general and (Mazziotta, 2016b) on the representation of syntactic knowledge, are not frequent, but we think they contribute to the definition of our epistemological field. Thus, the aim of this paper is to understand Chomsky's first diagram, as well as the other diagrams proposed for the formalization of ICA until tree-based diagrams become the norm in the mid 1960's. These diagrams will be compared with dependency trees and we will discuss whether such analyses can be deemed as "dependency-based".

Section 2 introduces the mathematical and graphical notion of *tree* as well as the notion of *reification*, that helps understanding how diagrams are conceptualized. Section 3 attempts to define the meaning of the term *dependency*, in connection with the usage of trees in dependency and phrase structure syntax. Chomsky 1957's diagram is analyzed in section 4 in order to evaluate to what extent it is "dependency-based". The same section surveys the foundational works in ICA in the light shed by those preliminary notions (Barnard, 1836; Bloomfield, 1933; Wells, 1947; Nida, 1943; Gleason, 1955; Hockett, 1958). In the conclusion, we point out what distinguishes dependency syntax from ICA.

2 Trees and reification

This section introduces the notion of *tree*, from an algebraic as well as a graphical perspectives (section 2.1). The notion of *reification*, i.e. the fact that conceptual elements are represented by discrete graphical entities in diagrams, is discussed under 2.2.

2.1 Algebraic and graphical notion of *tree*

To understand Chomsky's first diagram and other ICA diagrams, we need to bear in mind what a tree is. In graph theory, a tree T is algebraically de-

Proceedings of the Fourth International Conference on Dependency Linguistics (Depling 2017), pages 116-126,
Pisa, Italy, September 18-20 2017

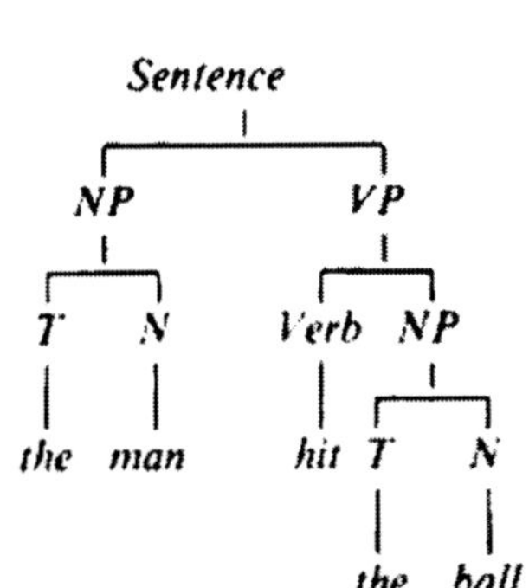
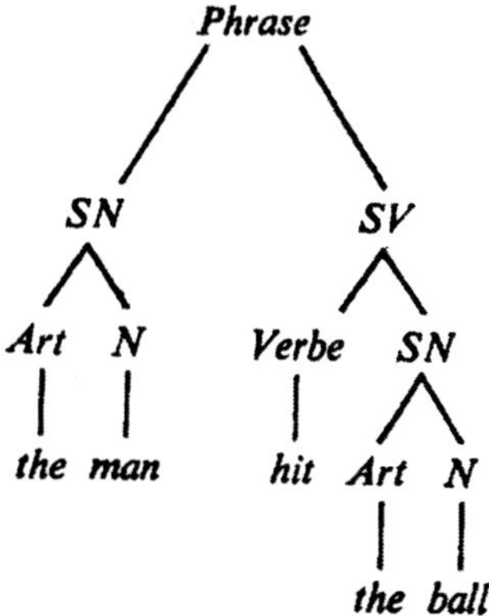

(a) Original diagram (Chomsky, 1957)   (b) Diagram in the French translation (Chomsky, 1969(1957))

Figure 1: Diagrams corresponding to the first derivation structure in (Chomsky, 1957)

fined as a kind of directed graph (with nodes and edges pairing them) that satisfies two additional constraints: it is connected and it does not contain any cycle. (1) is a simple example of the algebraic expression of a tree T, with N a set of nodes, E a set of edges, and π a map associating edges with their vertices, that is, ordered pairs in $N \times N$.

(1) $T = (N, E, \pi)$
$N = \{n1, n2, n3, n4\}$
$E = \{u, v, w\}$
$\pi : E \to N \times N$
with
$\pi(u) = (n1, n2),$
$\pi(v) = (n1, n3),$
$\pi(w) = (n3, n4)$

(1) is an *algebraic inscription* of a tree. Other inscriptions are possible; e.g. it is possible not to introduce the map π and to directly define E as a set of ordered pairs, i.e. as a *binary relation* on N.

Trees are often labeled, i.e. their nodes or their edges can be associated with labels; e.g. the nodes of (1) could be labeled using a labelling map λ as follow: $\lambda(n1) = a$, $\lambda(n2) = b$, $\lambda(n3) = c$, $\lambda(n4) = d$.

Fig. 2 depicts three alternate *graphical inscriptions* of the labeled structure of (1), where strokes or arrows correspond to edges. Nodes are either represented by discs or by their labels. Other variants are of course possible.

In an algebraic inscription, it is possible to part the expression of the binary relation that symmetrically links nodes and the direction of this relation, e.g. by using unordered pairs to encode

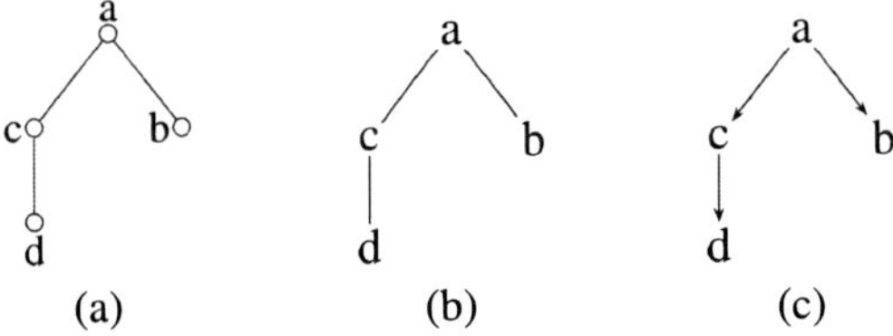

Figure 2: Graphical inscriptions of a tree

edges and a typing of the vertices to encode direction. The use of arrows in a graphical inscription (fig. 2(c)) is similar to this typing operation, but direction can be expressed by other means. When directed edges correspond to bare strokes without arrows, direction can be expressed by the verticality of the diagram: the source of the edge is placed at a higher level than the target (fig. 2(a,b)).

2.2 Reification

In graphical trees, nodes and edges are turned into discrete graphical objects. This encoding operation is called *reification* (from Lat. *rēs* 'thing'; hence *to reify* 'to turn into a thing'). Theoretical objects can be expressed by graphical objects, in which case, they are indeed reified (Kahane and Mazziotta, 2015; Mazziotta, 2016b). However, as illustrated by the alternative between the use of arrows or the use of vertically ordered strokes, the fact that diagrams are drawn on a bidimensional plane allows for the configurational expression of theoretical objects. Configurational expression competes with reification – e.g. in phrase structure trees (henceforth *PST*), words are often linearly ordered, which is a configurational means of expression of their precedence relations; this precedence could be reified by arrows instead.

As an example of linguistic entities that are conceived as distinct notions in the argumentation but not reified in the diagrams, one can introduce S.W. Clark's diagrams. The diagrams in his *Practical grammar* (1847), a pedagogical handbook on the grammar of English, do not reify the relations between the words – see Mazziotta's comprehensive study (2016a), although the text acknowledges that some words *modify* or *complete* others. In the diagrams, words are depicted as labeled bubbles that are but aggregated to one another (fig. 3).

Figure 3: Bubble diagram (Clark, 1847, 23)

It is clear in Clark's diagrams that bubbles in contact correspond to word in syntagmatic relation (cf. section 3.2). Their configuration conveys information about the syntactic analysis they encode. It is possible to reify these contacts and we obtain a diagram that, intuitively, is very similar to a classical dependency tree (fig. 4) – the only difference is that the connection between the verb and the subject and between the verb and the object are not directed.

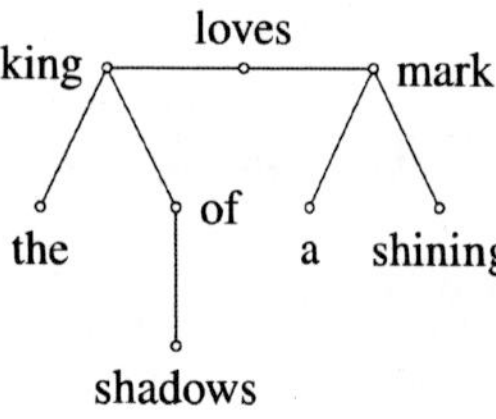

Figure 4: Clark's diagram, reified

In the diagrams, the choice of what is reified and what is not is closely bound to the theoretical stance chosen, but, as it will appear, some options are not always taken in full awareness.

3 What does dependency-based mean?

The difference between constituency and dependency is presented through their use of tree structures under 3.1 and the definitional attributes of dependency trees are reviewed under 3.2.

3.1 Phrase structure trees vs. dependency trees

Since trees are pure formal objects, they imply no *a priori* interpretation as such. The formal objects in a tree (or a graph) can represent different kinds of relations, with respect to the theoretical framework they are conventionally correlated to. The edges of PST do not represent the same information as the edges of dependency trees.

Bloomfield does not provide any ICA diagram, but he quite clearly defines constituents in terms of part-whole relations (1933, § 10.2):

> A linguistic form which bears a partial phonetic-semantic resemblance to some other linguistic form, is a *complex form*. The common part of any (two or more) complex forms is a linguistic form; it is a *constituent* (or *component*) of these complex forms. The constituent is said to be *contained in* (or to be *included in* or to *enter into*) the complex form.

Accordingly, in a PST, edges represent part-whole relations between a phrase and one of its immediate constituent.[1] This kind of relation can be called a *constituency relation*. Consequently, diagrams containing constituency relations will be said *constituency-based* (Kahane and Osborne, 2015, lv).

In a classical dependency tree, such as fig. 5, edges represents *dependencies* between pairs of words. The rationales at work are not the same at all: dependency trees match the five definitional attributes described in section 3.2.

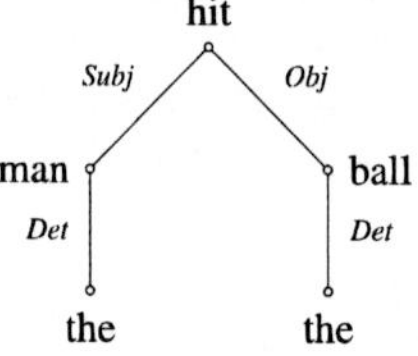

Figure 5: Dependency tree

---

[1]The widespread use that consists in calling constituents the nodes of a phrase structure tree (cf. "constituency tests") rather than to use the term *constituent* as a relational term denoting an (immediate) constituent of a phrase is confusing at best. The term *constituent* will be used in this latter sense, as it is in the first works on constituency, since we think it fits ICA better.

3.2 Dependency trees: definitional attributes

Dependency trees have five theoretical attributes that distinguish them from phrase structure trees, namely: *connection-basedness*, *binarity*, *headedness*, *flatness*, and *node-to-word mapping*.

As a preliminary remark, word order is abstracted away from the following discussion. It is generally assumed that PSTs encode word order: many of them actually represent the order of the words by sequentially organizing their terminal nodes from left to right (or the opposite, depending on the language). By contrast, dependency trees often encode other pieces of information by the same means – e.g., in Tesnière's stemmas, the dependents of the verb are linearly organized with respect to their status (the subject comes first, then the object, etc.). However, the correspondance between the order of the words and the sequence of terminals in a PST necessitates the tree to be projective.[2] Additionally, a genuine dependency tree can encode word order with the same restrictions as a PST (Groß and Osborne, 2009).

Connection-basedness. Words combine pairwise, they are in a *syntagmatic* relationship in the sense of de Saussure (2013(1916), 170):

> Words as used in discourse, strung together one after another, enter into relations based on the linear character of languages. Linearity precludes the possibility of uttering two words simultaneously. They must be arranged consecutively in spoken sequence. Combinations based on sequentiality may be called *syntagmas*. The *syntagma* invariably comprises two or more consecutive units: for example, *re-lire* ('re-read'), *contre tous* ('against all'), *la vie humaine* ('the life of man'), *Dieu est bon* ('God is good'), *s'il fait beau temps, nous sortirons* ('if it's fine, we'll go out').

Since the term *syntagma* has been led astray – this is especially the case in French linguistic: Fr. *syntagme* has been used to translate *phrase* (Chomsky, 1969(1957)) –, we suggest to use the term *connection* introduced by Tesnière (2015(1959), ch. 1, § 3-5):

> Each word in a sentence is not isolated as it is in the dictionary. The mind perceives **connections** between a word and its neighbors. The totality of these connections forms the scaffold of the sentence. [...] [A] sentence of the type *Alfred speaks* is not composed of just the **two** elements, *Alfred* and *speaks*, but rather of **three** elements, the first being *Alfred*, the second *speaks*, and the third the connection that unites them – without which there would be no sentence.

Elaborating from this quotation, we call *connection* the undirected relation underlying any dependency.[3] Hence, in a dependency tree, syntagmatic relations are encoded by edges. By contrast, in a PST, edges represent constituency relations – see also (Mel'čuk, 1988, 13-14). Analyses and diagrams that make use of connections to describe the syntactic structure of constructions are *connection-based*.

Binarity. In a dependency tree, a connection always involves exactly two words. In a PST, a phrase can have more than two immediate constituents. Binarity is a central property of ICA until the 60's and still remains preeminent.[4] It seems that binarity is the consequence of the connection-basedness of these ICAs. Non-binary structures appear later, cf. fig. 6 (Chomsky, 1965, 65).[5]

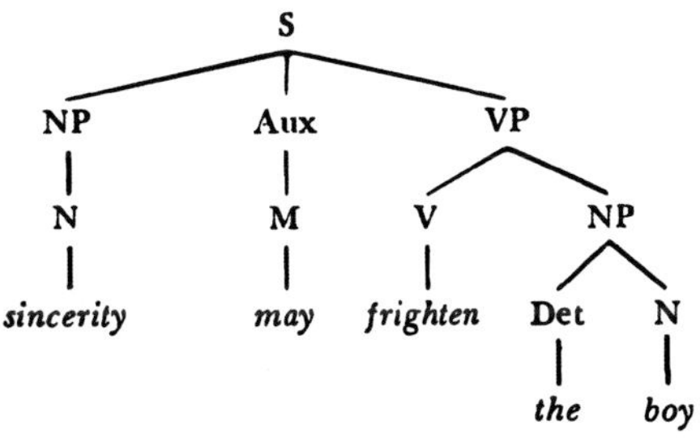

Figure 6: First PST in (Chomsky, 1965)

Headedness. Connections are directed, as explained by Tesnière (2015(1959), ch. 2, § 1-3):

---

[2] See (Gerdes, 2006) for an in-depth discussion on the relation between X-bar syntax and word order and its consequences.

[3] Tesnière's theory actually lacks a term to designate such a general undirected relation: his *connexion structurale* is equivalent to a dependency.

[4] Some ternary constructions are considered, such as the coordination (Wells, 1947, § 53 sqq.) and (Hockett, 1958).

[5] This first diagram in (Chomsky, 1965) is a tree containing unary, binary, and ternary branchings.

Structural connections establish **dependency** relations between words. In principle, each connection unites a **superior** term and an **inferior** term. The superior term is called the **governor**, and the inferior term the **subordinate**. Thus in the sentence *Alfred speaks* (Stemma 1), *speaks* is the governor and *Alfred* is the subordinate. We say that the subordinate depends on the governor and that the governor governs the subordinate. Thus in the sentence *Alfred speaks* (Stemma 1), *Alfred* depends on *speaks*, and *speaks* governs *Alfred*.

We call this property *headedness*.

It is noteworthy to mention that although the notion of *head* is absent from (Chomsky, 1957), headedness is considered as a central notion in many early ICA-based presentations, and especially in (Bloomfield, 1933). Bloomfield's work emphasizes constituency relations, but connections are also considered: "Every syntactic constructions shows us two (or sometimes more free forms combined in a phrase, which may call the *resultant* phrase." (§ 12.10) This last definition allows Bloomfield to oppose *endocentric* vs. *exocentric* constructions, according to the fact that the resultant phrase may belong or not to the "form-class" (i.e. distributional class) of one of the constituents (called the *head*). In a dependency tree, every construction is *endocentric*, i.e. connections are directed from a governor to a dependent. In a PST, endocentric constructions can be encoded by marking one of their constituents as the head.

Flatness (i.e. absence of stratification). In a dependency tree, dependents that have the same governor are not hierarchized. In a PST, phrases are embedded: if a head word has several complements (or specifiers, or adjuncts), each of them can belong to a different stratum (Kahane, 1997; Kahane and Mazziotta, 2015). E.g., the dependency tree of a sentence such as *Mary gives Peter a book* represents *Mary*, *Peter* and *a book* as co-dependents of *gives* that belong to the same level, whereas a PST of the same sentence can attach *Mary*, *Peter* and *a book* at different levels. Stratification remains the main difference between dependency syntax and ICA-based syntax. This point will be developed in Section 4.

Node-to-word mapping. Dependency trees do not encode connections by the means of nodes: these are used exclusively to encode words.[6] As a result, one can state:

> A dependency structure for a sentence is a one-to-one mapping between the nodes of a tree (the dependency tree) and the words of the sentence. (Kahane, 1996, 45)

By contrast, classical PST use nodes to encode words as well as constituents. Thus the mapping between nodes and words is not one-to-one. As it will appear in the next section, node-to-word mapping does not imply flatness.

As soon as additional nodes are introduced, labels on these nodes can be used to reify other information. E.g., X-bar syntax (Chomsky, 1970) uses *XP* vs. *X* labels to express headedness.

Summary. The definitional attributes can be summarized in a table (tab. 1). In the next section, ICA diagrams wil be evaluated in comparison with this table.

	Connection	Binarity	Headedness	Flatness	Node-to-word
Dependency tree (fig. 5)	✓	×	×	×	×

Table 1: Definitional attributes of dependency trees.

4 Interpreting ICA diagrams

Chomsky's commentary on the diagram of fig. 6 deserves to be mentioned: "The interpretation of such a diagram is transparent, and has been frequently discussed elsewhere." (Chomsky, 1965, 64). The assumed "transparency" of syntactic diagrams in general could lead to overlook important characteristics that only emerge when the graphical elements are scrutinized.

A stroke, an arc, or an arrow in a diagram generally correspond to an edge of a binary rela-

---

[6] It should be noted that the very definition of the term *word* has to be stated precisely. We assume that, in a dependency tree, words are abstract units. Depending on the descriptive stance chosen, they can be "zero" forms as well as elements of amalgamated complexes, such as Fr. *au = à* 'to' + *le* 'the' (Mel'čuk, 1988, 15).

tion.[7] From the perspective of a linguistic analysis, such an edge in a syntactic diagram reifies a constituency relation or a connection.

4.1 Chomsky, 1957

Chomsky's first diagram (fig. 1(a)) displays a continuous arc between NP and VP nodes and a small stroke between the S node and this arc. The diagram is introduced in the text. Chomsky first introduces the rewriting rules in the first page of ch. 4, entitled "Phrase structure":

> As a simple example of the new form for grammars associated with constituent analysis, consider the following: (13) (i) *Sentence* → *NP* + *VP* [...] Suppose that we interpret each rule $X \to Y$ of (13) as the instruction "rewrite X as Y". [...] [T]he second line of (14) is formed from the first line by rewriting *Sentence* as *NP + VP* in accordance with rule (i) of (13) [...] We can represent the derivation (14) in an obvious way by means of the following diagram.

It seems reasonable to interpret the arc between the NP node and the VP node in fig. 1(a) as a notation of the relation between the nodes: they combine to form *NP + VP*. Moreover, the operation corresponding to this connection is noted down in the rewriting rule (i.e. the algebraic inscription) by the symbol "+". Accordingly, the arc between NP and VP would reify the syntagmatic combination of *NP* and *VP*, i.e. a connection edge. The small stroke that stands between the S node and this arc reifies the rewriting operation: *Sentence* is rewritten as *NP + VP*. This corresponds to the symbol "→" in the algebraic inscription. According to this interpretation, the small stroke and the arc are to be considered as the reifications of two distinct elements that encode two binary relations: the connection between the ICs and the rewriting operation.

Headedness is partially encoded in an indirect way: by using similar labels for *NP* and *N*, the diagram shows that *N* is the most important element in the NP.

The diagram is not a dependency tree, but it shares some of the definitional attributes of such structures (as shown in tab. 2).

	Connection	Binarity	Headedness	Flatness	Node-to-word
Chomsky, 1957 (fig. 1(a))	×	×	?		

Table 2: Description of fig. 1(a) with respect to definitional attributes of dependency trees.

Constituency relations are not reified in the diagram, whereas connections are. Could it be that previous ICA diagrams share this characteristic? To answer this question, the rest of this section scrutinizes previous and contemporary ICA diagrams in a chronological order.

4.2 Barnard, 1836

To our knowledge, the first diagram representing an ICA (fig. 7) appears in Frederick A. P. Barnard's *Analytic Grammar with Symbolic Illustrations* (1836). Syntactic categories of units are represented by special symbols and braces that indicate in a configurational way that a list of units combine together to form another unit. In his text, Barnard compares *man* and *a rational animal* or *quadruped* and *a four-footed animal* and says (Barnard, 1836, 243-244):

> We thus construct *phrases* standing in the *places of nouns*, and answering all their purpose. [...] Contemplating, then, a noun and its adjective, we say that they constitute, together, a compound noun. Contemplating an adjective and its accompanying adverb, we say, in like manner, that they constitute a compound adjective.

E.g., in fig. 7, *in* and *disposition* form together a unit with the same category as *very* and *who is mild* and *in disposition* form together a unit with the same category as *many*.[8]

Barnard's diagrams have no discrete means to express individual part-whole relations: the brace

---

[7]It is not always the case. For instance, (Reed and Kellogg, 1876) makes use of syntactic diagrams where words are represented as labeled strokes, which connect to each other to represent the way they combine. See also the discussion on Nida's diagrams below (section 4.3).

[8]Categories are represented by symbols in Barnard's diagrams. These symbols are probably inspired by symbols used for sign language writing systems, since Barnard was a 27-year-old professor of English in a deaf institute when his book was published. The fact that he taught deaf people is likely to be the reason for the use of diagrams in his book.

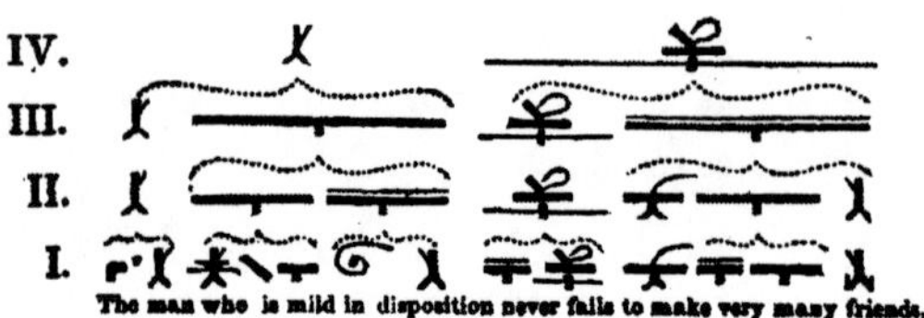

Figure 7: Barnard's diagram (1836)

is equivalent to Chomsky's rewriting operator as well as the "+" symbol, linking a phrase with the entire set of its immediate constituents. There is no independent reification for the two operations. Syntagmatic relations are not represented in a discrete way either. The brace inscribes the whole construction. According to our terms (section 3), such a diagram is thus neither exactly connection-based nor exactly constituency-based.

As shown in tab. 3, the diagram is very different from a canonical dependency tree: not a single definitional attribute firmly holds.

	Connection	Binarity	Headedness	Flatness	Node-to-word
Barnard, 1836 (fig. 7)	?				

Table 3: Description of fig. 7 with respect to definitional attributes of dependency trees.

4.3 Nida, 1943; 1966

It seems that Barnard's diagram was overlooked by his contemporaries. More than one century passed between this attempt and the next ICA diagram.[9] It appears in Nida's *Morphology* (1949(1943), 87).[10] Fig. 8 shows the first ICA diagram published by Nida and fig. 9 is a diagram from (Nida, 1966).

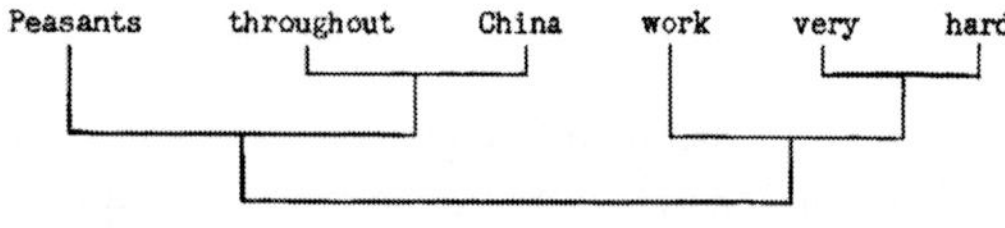

Figure 8: Nida's first diagram (1949(1943))

---

[9]In the mid time, other diagrams, which are much more dependency-based and that will not be discussed here, have been proposed by several authors (Clark, 1847; Reed and Kellogg, 1876; Kern, 1883; Tesnière, 1934).

[10]We could not access the fist edition of Nida's *Morphology* (1943).

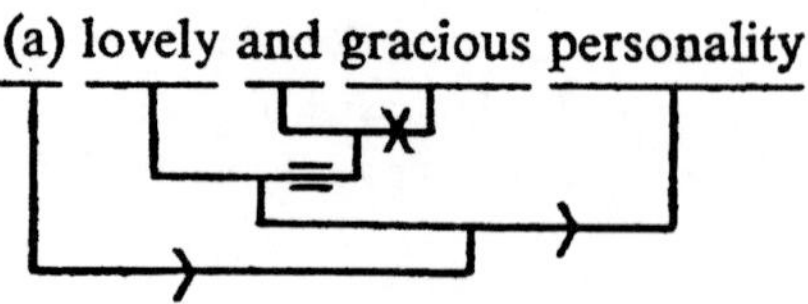

Figure 9: Nida's diagram (1966)

At first glance, it would seem that Nida's first diagram could be interpreted as a PST. It is tempting to consider that fig. 8 is completely equivalent to fig. 10, where constituency relations are reified as distinct graphical entities.

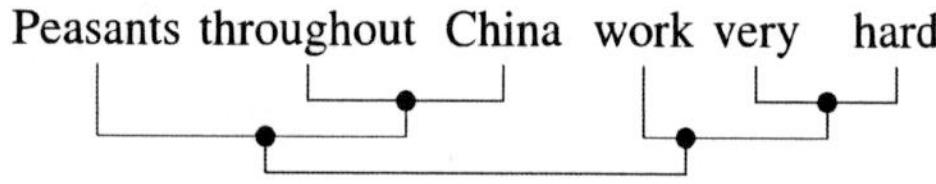

Figure 10: Nida, 1943's diagram, reified

However, fig. 9, which elaborates on the same rationales as fig. 8, demonstrates that it is not the case. Both diagrams consist of arcs between words and arcs between words and other arcs. Every single node in these diagrams corresponds to a word. Thus, the contact point between strokes are not equivalent to reifications, since they are not discrete graphical entities and they possibly allow for several interpretations.

To fully understand fig. 9, let us recall that Nida's work was preceded by Bloomfield's seminal text on constructions (section 3.1). Hence, in his fig. 9, arcs bear additional symbols (">", "×", "=") and the accompanying text clearly explains how to interpret them (Nida, 1966, 17):

> In addition to the usual set of lines used to show relationships between immediate constituents, an additional set of symbols has been employed to mark exocentric, endocentric, and paratactic relationships.

Consequently, the labels over the strokes reify the headedness of the connections. Nida's diagrams are connection-based and not constituency-based. Such a diagram is close to a dependency tree. The only difference between classical dependency trees and Nida's diagrams is that the later are not flat, but stratified: connections are ordered and hierarchized. The consequence of such an analysis is that connections can be connected to one another.

From a mathematical perspective, this means that edges can have other edges as vertices – see (Kahane and Mazziotta, 2015) for a formalization of such a structure, that can be called a *polygraph*.

Tab. 4 shows that the evolution between fig. 8 and fig. 9 consists in encoding headedness in the diagram. Fig. 9 is almost a dependency tree: the only attribute that does not hold is flatness.

	Connection	Binarity	Headedness	Flatness	Node-to-word
Nida, 1943 (fig. 8)	×	✓			×
Nida, 1966 (fig. 9)	×	×	×		×

Table 4: Description of fig. 8 and 9 with respect to definitional attributes of dependency trees.

4.4 Wells, 1947

Rulon S. Wells (1947) is more interested in constituency relations than in constructions seen as wholes. The term *construction* itself is used in another meaning – "The reader must constantly bear in mind that our definition of this term is not the same as Bloomfield's" (Wells, 1947, note 19). He proposes a linear diagram (fig. 11).

the ‖ king ⦀ of ⦀⦀ England ∣ open ⦀ ed ‖ Parliament

Figure 11: Well's diagram (1947)

This diagram (Wells uses this very term to designate this inscription) corresponds to the following analysis (Wells, 1947, 84):

> Let us call the ICs of a sentence, and the ICs of those ICs, and so on down to the morphemes, the CONSTITUENTS of the sentence; and conversely whatever sequence is constituted by two or more ICs let us call a CONSTITUTE. Assuming that the ICs of *The king of England opened Parliament* are *the king of England* and *opened Parliament*, that those of the former are *the* and *king of England* and those of the latter are *opened* and *Parliament*, and that *king of England* is divided into *king* and *of England*, *of England* is divided into the morphemes *of* and *England*, and *opened* is divided into *open* and *-ed*-all of which

facts may be thus diagrammed [by fig. 11]"

Although this analysis is purely based on the decomposition of wholes ("constitutes") into parts ("constituents"), the symbols made of "I" in Wells's diagrams reify the combination/separation operations (according to the perspective, that can be deductive or inductive) of the elements around them. In a sense, they correspond more to connections than to constituency relations.

Tab. 5 shows that Wells's diagram is equivalent to Nida's first diagram (fig. 8).

	Connection	Binarity	Headedness	Flatness	Node-to-word
Wells, 1947 (fig. 11)	×	×			×

Table 5: Description of fig. 11 with respect to definitional attributes of dependency trees.

4.5 Gleason, 1955

H. A. Gleason's handbook (1961(1955)) also contains interesting diagrams.[11] Gleason has a clear bottom-up vision of the ICA. Considering the sentence *The old man who lives there has gone to his son's house*, he says (Gleason, 1961(1955), § 10.3):

> We may, as a first hypothesis, consider that each of [the words] has some statable relationship to each other word. If we can describe these interrelationships completely, we will have described the syntax of the utterance in its entirety. [...] At a second step in our procedure, let us assume that these pairs of words function in the utterance as single units. [...] If this procedure is valid, there is no reason why it cannot be repeated as many times as may be useful. Something like the following [diagram] might result.

In the mentionned diagram (fig. 12), braces indicates the units that combine together as in Barnard's diagrams (cp. fig. 7).

A characteristic of Gleason's handbook is that it introduces alternate diagrams to inscribe the same

---

[11] We could only manage to access the 1961 edition and we don't know if diagrams have been changed.

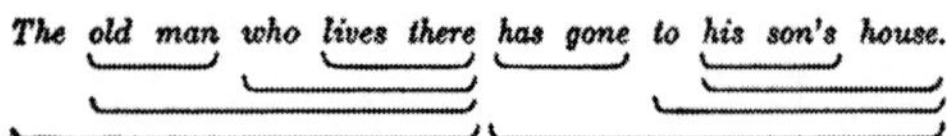

Figure 12: Gleason's first ICA diagram

analysis. Fig. 13 is similar to Wells's diagrams, but where the hierarchy of frontiers is inverted. Gleason, who starts from the bottom, use thin stroke for the most embedded connection, while Wells, who starts from the top, use them for main segmentation of the sentence.

The | old ⋮ man ‖ who | lives ⋮ there ❙ has ⋮ gone | to ‖ his ⋮ son's | house.

Figure 13: Gleason's second ICA diagram

Gleason introduces a third concurrent diagram (fig. 14) as follows (Gleason, 1961(1955), *ibid.*):

> The procedure which we have just sketched will be useful to us, if it serves as a framework within which all the relationships of the utterance can be effectively and economically described.

This is done in the following diagram, where the heavier line is "intended to indicated the most direct relationship between *old* and *house* [...] describable in terms of a chain of relationships each of which individually seems significant."

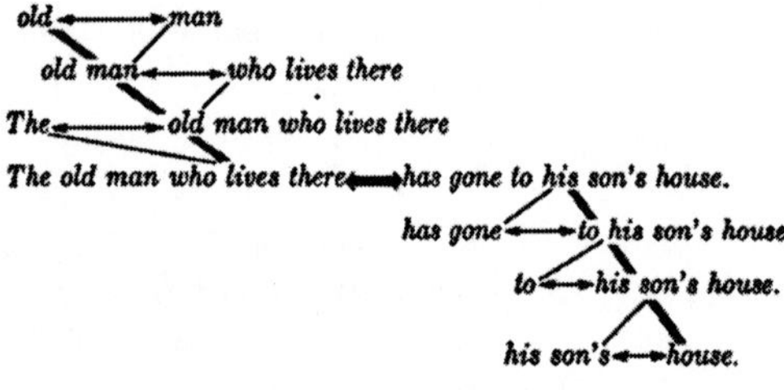

Figure 14: Gleason's third ICA diagram

This last diagram clearly provides both constituency relations (reified by mere strokes) and connections (reified by double arrows). The book does not contain any diagram that is exactly a tree.

The attributes of Gleason's diagrams are summarized in tab. 6.

4.6 Hockett, 1958

Hockett (1958) formalizes the concept of *construction* by the means of diagrams consisting of embeddable three-compartment boxes (fig. 15). Two compartments represent immediate constituents and the lower compartment represents the resultant phrase. These boxes can be embedded to give the whole ICA of a sentence (Hockett, 1958, 160-161):[12]

> Sentence A consists of only two ultimate constituents (morphemes), which are therefore also the ICs of the whole sentence: 3 and 2 are the ICs of 1. Sentence B consists of more than two *ultimate* constituents, but, once again, of only two *immediate* constituents: 3 and 2 as in A, are the ICs of 1. Similar remarks apply to sentences C and D. Furthermore, the relationship between the two ICs of each whole sentence is the same. Thus, if we make just one IC-cut in each sentence, ignoring any smaller constituents for the moment, then all four sentences conform to pattern X.

Hockett's boxes can be typed by an additional symbol, "<" or ">", "placed at each junction of ICs, pointing from attribute to head" (fig. 16).

We can observe that, in Hockett's diagrams, constituency relations and connection are indissociable and none of them is favored, although the additional symbols ("<" or ">"), similar to Nida's (1966), are clearly connection-based.

	Connection	Binarity	Headedness	Flatness	Node-to-word
Gleason, 1955 (fig. 12)	×	×			×
Gleason, 1955 (fig. 13)	×	×			×
Gleason, 1955 (fig. 14)	×	✓			

Table 6: Description of fig. 12 to 14 with respect to definitional attributes of dependency trees.

	Connection	Binarity	Headedness	Flatness	Node-to-word
Hockett, 1958 (fig. 16)	?	×	×		

Table 7: Description of fig. 16 with respect to definitional attributes of dependency trees.

---

[12] Numbers in the text correspond to numbers in the lower right-hand corners of compartments.

	Binarity	Connection	Node-to-word	Headedness	Flatness
Barnard, 1836 (fig. 7)		?			
Chomsky, translated (fig. 1(b))	×				
Gleason, 1955 (fig. 14)	×	×			
Chomsky, 1957 (fig. 1(a))	×	×		?	
Hockett, 1958 (fig. 16)	×	?		×	
Gleason, 1955 (fig. 12)	×	×	×		
Wells, 1947 (fig. 11)	×	×	×		
Nida, 1943 (fig. 8)	×	×	×		
Nida, 1966 (fig. 9)	×	×	×	×	
Dependency tree (fig. 5)	×	×	×	×	×

Table 8: Comparison of the diagrams with respect to definitional attributes of dependency trees (rows and columns are arranged for better visualization).

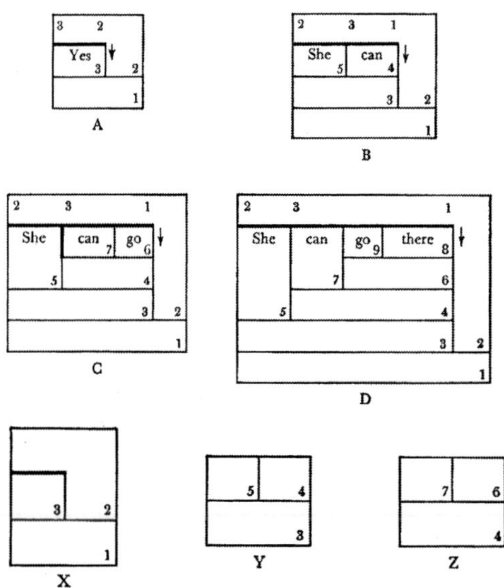

Figure 15: Hockett's boxes (1958)

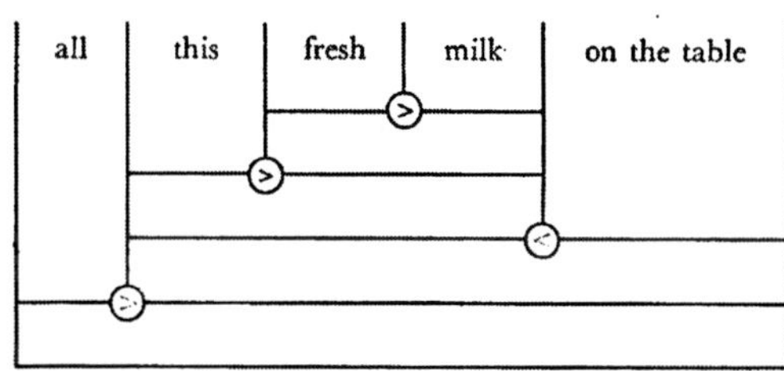

Figure 16: Endocentric construction in Hockett's diagram (1958)

5 Conclusion

Immediate constituent Analysis has been modeled by phrase structure trees only from the middle of the 1960's on. Chomsky's first derivation diagrams is not a genuine modern phrase structure tree; it is partly connection-based and it also contains other edges. Previous ICA diagrams by Nida are totally connection-based. Contemporary diagrams by Hockett or Gleason are more connection-based than constituency-based.

Tab. 8, which merges all previous tables, clearly shows that: (i) until fig. 1(b), all ICA diagrams encoded connections to a certain extent; (ii) the only constant difference between a dependency tree and a PST is the flatness of the former (opposed to the stratification of the later).[13]

These connection-based diagrams are very close to dependency trees, since they (at least partially) consist of reified connections rather than reified constituency relations. By contrast, modern PSTs do not reify connections directly: one has to infer them from specific configurations. The seemingly trivial differences between the diagrams in fig. 1 are actually very important from the perspective of the history of linguistics. The diagrammatic habits led their users to ignore connections. In consequence, original diagrams were reinterpreted. Fig. 1(b) was already understood as a faithful copy of fig. 1(a) at the time the book was translated into French, and the interpretation of fig. 6 was considered completely transparent by its author. This progression demonstrates that the tools we use to model and to inscribe knowledge about language have a dramatic epistemological impact.

Acknowledgements

The authors would like to thank Kim Gerdes, Timoty Osborne and the anonymous reviewers of the Depling conference for their comments, suggestions and debates.

References

Frederick Augustus Porter Barnard. 1836. *Analytic Grammar, with symbolic illustration*. French, New York.

---

[13] It is possible to use PSTs for diagramming flat structures, but there is no obvious advantage in using PSTs instead of dependency trees.

Leonard Bloomfield. 1933. *Language*. The University of Chicago Press.

Noam Chomsky. 1957. *Syntactic structures*. Mouton, The Hague.

Noam Chomsky. 1965. *Aspects of the Theory of Syntax*. The MIT Press, Cambridge.

Noam Chomsky. 1969(1957). *Structures syntaxiques,* translation of (Chomsky, 1957) by M. Braudeau. Seuil, Paris.

Noam Chomsky. 1970. Remarks on nominalization. In *On the Nature of Grammatical Relations*, pages 184–221. Ginn and Co., Waltham, Mass.

Stephen W. Clark. 1847. *The science of the English language. A practical grammar; in which words, phrases, and sentences are classified according to their offices, and their relation to each other. Illustrated by a complete system of diagrams*. A. S. Barnes & Co. and Derby, Bradley & Co., New York and Cincinnati.

Eugenio Coseriu. 1980. Un pécurseur méconnu de la syntaxe structurale, H. Tiktin. In *Recherches de linguistique: hommage à Maurice Leroy*, pages 48–62. Bruxelles.

Kim Gerdes. 2006. Sur la non-équivalence des représentations syntaxiques: Comment la représentation en x-barre nous amène au concept du mouvement. *Cahiers de grammaire*, 30:175–192.

Henry A. Gleason. 1961(1955). *An Introduction to Descriptive linguistics*. Holt, Rinehart and Winston.

Henry A. Gleason. 1969. *An Introduction to Descriptive Linguistics*. Holt, Rinehart & Winston, New York, revised edition.

Thomas Groß and Timothy Osborne. 2009. Toward a practical dependency grammar theory of discontinuities. *SKY Journal of Linguistics*, 22:43–90.

Charles F. Hockett. 1958. *A course in modern linguistics*. The MacMillan Company.

Sylvain Kahane and Nicolas Mazziotta, 2015. *Proceedings of the 14th Meeting on the Mathematics of Language (MoL 2015)*, chapter Syntactic Polygraphs. A Formalism Extending Both Constituency and Dependency, pages 152–164. Association for Computational Linguistics.

Sylvain Kahane and Timothy Osborne. 2015. Translators' introduction. In *Elements of structural syntax* (Tesnière, 2015(1959)), pages xxix–lxxiv.

Sylvain Kahane. 1996. If hpsg were a dependency grammar... In *Actes de TALN, Marseille*, pages 45–49.

Sylvain Kahane. 1997. Bubble trees and syntactic representations. In *Proceedings of Mathematics of Language (MOL5) Meeting*, pages 70–76.

Franz Kern. 1883. *Zur Methodik des deutschen Unterrichts*. Nicolai, Berlin.

Nicolas Mazziotta. 2016a. Drawing syntax before syntactic trees. Stephen Watkins Clark's sentence diagrams (1847). *Historiographia Linguistica*, 43(3):301–342.

Nicolas Mazziotta. 2016b. *Représenter la connaissance en linguistique. Observations sur l'édition de matériaux et sur l'analyse syntaxique. Habilitation à diriger des recherches, mémoire de synthèse*. Université Paris-Ouest, Nanterre – La Défense, Paris. http://hdl.handle.net/2268/204408.

Igor Mel'čuk. 1988. *Dependency syntax: theory and practice*. State University of New York, Albany.

Eugene Nida. 1949(1943). *Morphology: the descriptive analysis of words*. University of Michigan press, Ann Arbor, 2nd edition.

Eugene Nida. 1966. *A synopsys of English Syntax*. Mouton and Co., London, The Hague, Paris, 2 edition.

Alonzo Reed and Brainerd Kellogg. 1876. *Graded Lessons in English*. Clark and Maynard, New York.

Ferdinand de Saussure. 1916. *Cours de linguistique générale*. Payot, Paris.

Ferdinand de Saussure. 2013(1916). *Course in general linguistics,* translation and annotations of (Saussure, 1916) by Roy Harris, with a new introduction by Roy Harris. Bloomsbury, London and New York.

An Harleman Stewart. 1976. *Graphic representation of models in linguistic theory*. Indiana university press, Bloomington and London.

Lucien Tesnière. 1934. Comment construire une syntaxe. *Bulletin de la Faculté des Lettres de Strasbourg*, 7:219–229.

Lucien Tesnière. 1959. *Éléments de syntaxe structurale*. Klincksieck, Paris.

Lucien Tesnière. 2015(1959). *Elements of structural syntax,* translation by Timothy Osborne and Sylvain Kahane of (Tesnière, 1959). Benjamins, Amsterdam/Philadelphia.

Rulon S. Wells. 1947. Immediate constituents. *Language*, 23(2):81–117.

Dependency Structure of Binary Conjunctions

(of the IF…, THEN… Type)

Igor Mel'čuk
University of Montreal
Department of Linguistics and Translation
Observatoire de linguistique Sens-Texte
Canada

`igor.melcuk@umontreal.ca`

Abstract

The dependency surface-syntactic structure is proposed, within the Meaning-Text framework, for binary conjunctions of the IF–THEN type; e.g.:

IF→Y, THEN←X

A universal typology of conjunctions is sketched, and three examples of English binary conjunctions are given. Binary conjunctions are "discontinuous" phrasemes-idioms, collocations and formulemes that have to be considered together with their actants, since there are no direct syntactic links between their components. Full lexical entries for two Russian binary conjunctions are presented, supplied with linguistic comments, and deep-syntactic rules ensuring the expansion of a deep-syntactic binary conjunction node into the corresponding surface-syntactic tree are illustrated.

1 The Syntactic Structure of a Binary Conjunction

This paper examines subordinating and coordinating binary conjunctions (or correlative subordinators/coordinators, as they are known in the literature: Quirk *et al.* 1991: 935–941, 999–1001). The typical examples are the subordinating conjunction IF…, THEN… and the coordinating conjunction EITHER…, OR… The discussion is carried out within the Meaning-Text approach (see Mel'čuk 1974, 2012, 2016b).

In sentence (1) dependency relations between lexemes are obvious, except for THEN, the second component of the conjunction IF…, THEN…:

(1) *If A→and→B are→equal,* **then** *B←follows→C.*

The dependency for THEN is proposed in what follows.

Without THEN the superordinate clause can linearly precede or follow the subordinate clause with IF; but with THEN it can only follow. This gives the idea to make this THEN dependent on IF: IF–**r**→THEN; as a result, the binary conjunction IF…, THEN… can be stored in the lexicon exactly in the form of this syntactic subtree. Such a description had been tacitly accepted for almost half a century:

• In Mel'čuk 1974: 231, No. 31, (e), the surface-syntactic relation [SSyntRel] **r** between IF and THEN was called "1ˢᵗ auxiliary."

• In Mel'čuk & Pertsov 1987: 331, No. 19.1, it was rebaptized "binary-junctive."

• In Iomdin 2010: 43, it appears under the name of "correlative SSyntRel."

• In Mel'čuk 2012a: 143, No. 51, it is "correlative-auxiliary."

However, this syntactic description of binary conjunctions contradicts the definition of surface-syntactic dependency (or, more precisely, that of surface-syntactic relation), which was advanced in Mel'čuk 1988: 130–144 and has been used as such since; see its newer formulations, for instance, in Mel'čuk 2009: 25–40 and Mel'čuk 2015b: 411–433. In order to lay bare this contradiction, only the first part of this definition—namdely Criterion A—is needed, strictly speaking. Nevertheless, to facilitate the task of the reader I will cite here the whole definition—that is, the full set of criteria for SSyntRels. (Of course many substantial explanations and interesting special cases have to be bypassed.)

Proceedings of the Fourth International Conference on Dependency Linguistics (Depling 2017), pages 127-134,
Pisa, Italy, September 18-20 2017

2 Criteria for Surface-Syntactic Dependencies (= Surface-Syntactic Relations)

NB: Given the limitations of space and time, the formulations below are approximate and controversial cases are not considered; for important details, see the above references.

Criterion A: PRESENCE of a syntactic dependency between two lexemes in an utterance (prosodic unity of and linear arrangement in the configuration L_1–**synt**–L_2)

In a given utterance, the lexemes L_1 and L_2 can have a direct Synt-dependency link (= they can form a configuration L_1–**synt**–L_2), if and only if both Conditions 1 and 2 are simultaneously satisfied:

Condition 1

(a) General case

L_1 and L_2 can form a phrase of **L**, such as

N—V, V—N, ADJ—N, PREP—N, ADV—ADJ, etc.

(b) Special case

L_1 and L_2 cannot form a phrase, but the lexemes L_1, L_2 and configurations of lexemes of the set $\{L_i\}$ appearing in the same utterance can, such that the following are also phrases of **L**:

- $L_1 \rightarrow \{L_{i-1}\}\ L_2 \rightarrow \{L_{i-2}\}$
- $L_1 \rightarrow \{L_{i-1}\}\ L_2 \leftarrow \{L_{i-2}\}$
- $L_1 \rightarrow \{L_{i-1}\}$
- $L_2 \rightarrow \{L_{i-2}\}$
- $L_2 \leftarrow \{L_{i-2}\}$

Condition 2

The linear position of one of the lexemes L_1 and L_2 in the utterance under consideration must be specified with respect to the other.

Examples

Case (b) covers configurations of three types:

(i) $L_1 \rightarrow L_{(PREP)2} \rightarrow L_{(N)\{i-2\}}$, as in $one_{L_1}\ of_{L_2}\ them_{L_{\{i-2\}}}$

Here, **one→of* cannot be a phrase, while the utterances *of→them* and *one→of→them* are phrases, having *of* and *one* as their heads.

(ii) $L_1 \rightarrow \{L_{\{i-1\}}\}\ L_{(CONJ)2} \rightarrow \{L_{\{i-2\}}\}$, as in

It←became$_{L_1}$→{*obvious*}$_{\{L_{i-1}\}}$ *that*$_{L_2}$→{*he was there*}$_{\{L_{i-2}\}}$.[1]

(the relation *became*→*obvious* marked *pseudo-subjectival*)

Here, **became→that* cannot be a phrase, while *became→obvious* and *that→{he was there}* are phrases, with *became* and *that* as their heads.

(iii) $L_{(CONJ\_SUB)1} \rightarrow \{L_{\{i-1\}}\}\ L_{(PARTICLE)2} \leftarrow \{L_{\{i-2\}}\}$, as in

If$_{L_2}$→{*John is here,*}$_{\{L_{i-2}\}}$ *then*$_{L_1}$←{*we go*}$_{\{L_{i-1}\}}$.

(the relation *If*→{*John is here*} marked *circumstantial*)

Here, **if→then* cannot be a phrase, while the utterances *If→{John is here}* and *then←{we go}* are phrases, having *if* and *go* as their heads.

Condition 1 of Criterion A requires that, in order to have a direct syntactic link in the given utterance, two lexemes L′ and L″ could form a phrase of the language.

Condition 2 of Criterion A requires that, in order for two lexemes L′ and L″ to have a direct syntactic link in the given utterance, one of them must determine the linear position of the other.

These conditions are logically independent:

—In *He took in his* **knapsack** *a book* **full** *of vowels* [Keats], Condition 1 allows the adjective FULL to depend on KNAPSACK *(full knapsack* is a phrase of English), but Condition 2 does not.

—In *I wish I was* **either** *in your arms,* **or** *that a thunderbolt would strike me* [Keats], Condition 2 allows the particle EITHER to depend on OR *(either* has to precede the governor of *or*), but Condition 1 does not.

Criteria B1-B3: DIRECTION of the syntactic dependency between two lexemes in an utterance

Criterion B1 (passive syntactic valence[2] of the phrase L_1–**synt**–L_2)

In a phrase L_1–**synt**–L_2 the lexeme L_1 is the syntactic governor of L_2, or the head of the phrase L_1–**synt**–L_2, if L_1 determines the passive syntactic valence of the phrase to a greater extent than L_2.

Example

The passive valence of the phrase *John—and—Mary* is that of a noun (it can be the subject and the direct object of a verb, the object of a preposition, an apposition, etc.); the passive valence of the phrase *and—Mary* is determined by AND; therefore,

$$MARY\text{–synt}\rightarrow AND\text{–synt}\rightarrow JOHN.$$

This is actually the general schema for coordinating conjunctions:

$$L_1\text{–synt}\rightarrow CONJ_{(coord)}\text{–synt}\rightarrow L_2.$$

Criterion B2 (morphological contact point in the phrase L_1–**synt**–L_2)

In a phrase L_1–**synt**–L_2, where both L_1 and L_2 have the same syntactic properties (and influence the

---

[1] For the surface-syntactic relations mentioned in this paper, see Mel'čuk 2015c and 2016a.

[2] Passive syntactic valence of an LU L is the set of all possible syntactic governors of L.

passive valence of L_1–synt–L_2 to the same degree), the lexeme L_1 is the syntactic governor of L_2, or the head of the phrase L_1–synt–L_2, if L_1 determines the morphological behavior of the phrase to a greater extent than L_2.

Example

In the French phrase *Bibliothèque Mitterand* 'Mitterand Library' the head is BIBLIOTHÈQUE since the phrase imposes the agreement of the adjective in the feminine gender (the gender of BIBLIOTHÈQUE): *La Bibliothèque Mitterand est spaci+euse*(fem) 'The Mitterand Library is spacious'.

Criterion B3 (denotation of the phrase L_1–synt–L_2)

In a phrase L_1–synt–L_2, where both L_1 and L_2 have the same syntactic and morphological properties (and influence the passive valence and morphological behavior of L_1–synt–L_2 to the same degree), the lexeme L_1 is the syntactic governor of L_2, or the head of the phrase L_1–synt–L_2, if L_1 determines the denotation of L_1–synt–L_2 to a greater extent than L_2.

Example

The denotation of the phrase *[the American] writer–Dos_Pasos* is a real person (an American writer having a particular name), not the name *Dos_Pasos*; therefore, we have

$$\text{WRITER–synt}\rightarrow\text{DOS\_PASOS}.$$

Criteria B1–B3 form a hierarchy:

$$B1 > B2 > B3$$

This means that if Criterion B1 is applicable, it determines the syntactic governor; otherwise, Criterion B2 is pressed into action, and if applicable, it determines the syntactic governor; if it also fails, Criterion B3 is supposed to solve the problem.

Criteria C1-C3: TYPE of the syntactic dependency between two lexemes in an utterance

Criterion C1 (presence of semantic contrast: Minimal Pair test)

Notation: $w_i(L)$ is a wordform of lexeme L.

A hypothetical SSyntRel **r** should not describe two phrases
$$w_1(L_1)\text{–}\mathbf{r}\rightarrow w_2(L_2) \text{ and } w_3(L_1)\text{–}\mathbf{r}\rightarrow w_4(L_2),$$
if 1) they contrast semantically
$$['w_1(L_1)\text{–}\mathbf{r}\rightarrow w_2(L_2)' \neq 'w_3(L_1)\text{–}\mathbf{r}\rightarrow w_4(L_2)'],$$
and
2) they formally differ only by some syntactic means of expression—i.e., by word order, syntactic prosody, or syntactic grammemes.

In such a case, **r** should be split into two different SSyntRels, $\mathbf{r_1}$ and $\mathbf{r_2}$.

Example

Rus. *žena*–synt→*druga* 'wife of.friend' and *žena*–synt→*drug* 'wife, who is a friend' should be described by two different SSyntRels (**actantial-attributive** and **qualifying-appositive**), since these phrases semantically contrast and formally differ only by the case of DRUG: the genitive in the first phrase and the same case as that of ŽENA in the second.

Criterion C2 (syntactic substitutability: Substitution test)

A SSyntRel **r** must have a prototypical dependent that is allowable with any governor.

Example

have–synt→*been* and *be*–synt→*going* should be described by two different SSyntRels (**perfect-analytical** and **progressive-analytical**) since there is no word-class whose element is possible as a dependent both with HAVE and BE within an analytical form.

Criterion C3 (no limited repeatability: Cooccurrence test)

A SSyntRel **r** must be either unlimitedly repeatable or non-repeatable—that is, it cannot be limitedly repeatable.

Example

write–synt→*after the lunch*, *write*–synt→*on the next line*, *write*–synt→*over the door* etc. can all be described by the same SSyntRel: **circumstantial**, since the number of these dependents is theoretically unlimited. On the contrary, *[They] returned*–synt→*all* and *[They] returned*–synt→*drunk* require two different SSyntRels (**floating-copredicative** and **subject-copredicative**), since otherwise the dependent will be repeatable exactly twice.

Now we are fully equipped to take on the problem formulated in Section 1: What is the dependency structure of a binary conjunction?

3 The Dependency Description for Binary Conjunctions

Consider the expression "IF Y, THEN X":

—The expression *IF THEN is not a phrase of English;

—IF$_{L_2}$ forms a phrase with the subordinate clause $Y_{\{L_{i-2}\}}$, and THEN$_{L_1}$, with the superordinate clause $X_{\{L_{i-1}\}}$;

—IF$_{L_2}$ subordinates the Main Verb of Y and is itself subordinated to the Main Verb$_1$ of $X_{\{L_{i-1}\}}$:

$$MV(X_{\{L_{i-1}\}})\rightarrow IF_{L_2}\rightarrow MV(Y_{\{L_{i-2}\}}),$$

thus corresponding to Case (b) of Condition 1 of Criterion A;

—THEN is subordinated to the Main Verb of $X_{\{L_{i-1}\}}$.

As a result, we have the following SSynt-structure for a subordinating binary conjunction (both of its components depend on the Main Verb of the superordinate clause):

$$\text{IF}{\rightarrow}\text{Y, THEN}{\leftarrow}\text{X.}$$

This proposal is aimed at correcting a mistake that has been being perpetrated for many years; it concerns all the binary conjunctions and a motley set of expressions similar to them.

4   Conjunctions: A Typology

A sketch of conjunction typology will give the discussion a certain depth:, it will make clear that the proposed solution is typologically plausible.

• According to their meaning/function, conjunctions are divided in two major families: subordinating *vs.* coordinating. These two families are very different in their properties and behavior—as different as two major opposed ways of syntactic linking: subordination and coordination.

• According to their form, conjunctions are classified along two independent axes:

—the number of components: single (just one component) *vs.* binary (two components) *vs.* repeated (theoretically unlimited repetition of the second component);

—the structure of components: simple (all components are monolexemic) *vs.* compound (at least one component is plurilexemic).

A binary or repeated conjunction is necessarily linearly discontinuous—its components cannot be in linear contact. (In a sentence like *He is an **either-or** person* we do not have a binary conjunction used as such, but its meta-linguistic name as a premodifier.)

Since repeated conjunctions can be only co-ordinating, there are 10 logically possible classes of conjunctions, see Table 1 below. (Since there are no English examples for Class 10, Russian conjunctions are supplied; raised semi-brackets ˹ ˺ enclose idioms.)

5   Binary Conjunctions in English

Here is a (non-exhaustive) list of English binary conjunctions.

Subordinating	Coordinating
IF..., (THEN)...	˹BOTH... AND...˺
˹NO SOONER..., THAN²...˺	˹EITHER... OR...˺
˹THE³..., THE²...˺	˹NEITHER... NOR...˺
	NOT ONLY..., BUT ALSO...
	NOT SO MUCH..., AS...

The first component of a coordinating binary conjunction and the second component of a subordinating binary conjunction are themselves not conjunctions, but, respectively, adjectives or particles, which depend on an element in the corresponding clause—via the **modificative**, the auxiliary or the restrictive SSyntRel (according to the conjunction).

	simple		compound	
	simple conjunctions		**compound conjunctions**	
	subordinating	**coordinating**	**subordinating**	**coordinating**
single	**1** IF, WHEN, ALTHOUGH	**2** AND, OR, BUT	**3** ˹AS SOON AS˺	**4** ˹AS WELL AS˺, ˹LET ALONE˺
binary	**5** IF..., (THEN)... ˹THE..., THE...˺	**6** ˹BOTH... AND...˺, ˹EITHER... OR...˺, ˹NEITHER... NOR...˺	**7** ˹NO SOONER..., THAN²...˺	**8** NOT SO MUCH..., AS... NOT ONLY..., BUT ALSO...
repeated	———	**9** ˹EITHER..., OR..., OR..., OR...˺ ˹NEITHER..., NOR..., NOR..., NOR...˺	———	**10** Rus. ˹TO LI..., TO LI..., TO LI...˺ 'whether..., or..., or...'

Table 1: Classes of conjunctions

The following three examples will be helpful.

⌐NO SOONER – THAN²⌐:
deep binary subordinating conjunction, consisting of the surface subordinating conjunction ⌐NO SOONER⌐ and the particle THAN² (THAN¹ is a comparative conjunction).

        ┌──────circumstantial──────┐
        │   ┌──auxiliary──┐ │
        ▼   ▼   ▼

(2) *No←sooner→had I arrived than the kids rushed towards me.*

⌐THE³ – THE²⌐:
deep binary subordinating conjunction, consisting of the surface subordinating conjunction THE³ and the particle THE² (THE¹ is the definite article).

(3) a.

  ┌──────────────────── comparative ───┐
  │ ┌─subord-conjunct─┐   │
  ▼ ▼   ▼   ▼

The higher you climb the←auxil–colder it←gets.

The surface-syntactic structure [SSyntS] for a synonymous sentence with a different ordering of the superordinate and subordinate clauses is almost the same as the SSyntS for sentence (3a), but with THE² omitted:

    ┌comparative┐ ┌subord-conjunct┐
            ▼   ▼

b. *It←gets→colder the higher you climb.*

⌐EITHER – OR⌐:
deep binary coordinating conjunction, consisting of the surface coordinating conjunction OR and the particle EITHER.

(4) *I'll have either←auxiliary–tacos–coord→or–[a]– –coord-conjunctional→pizza.*

6 Phraseological Nature of Binary Conjunctions

A binary conjunction is a plurilexemic expression that is not free: it is a phraseme (Mel'čuk 2015b: 263–362). However, it is quite an uncommon phraseme: its components are not directly syntactically linked. Such syntactically discontinuous phrasemes have not been considered before. Indeed, a phraseme is "a phrase that…," while IF – THEN or EITHER – OR are obviously not phrases. Therefore, one has to consider ta binary conjunction together with the lexical expressions (in this case, clauses) that implement its actants: IF Y, THEN X and EITHER Y OR X are *bona fide* phrases. It is under this form that they must be stored in the lexicon. (For more on the semantic, deep-syntactic and surface-syntactic representation of binary conjunctions, see Section 8.)

But if binary conjunctions are phrasemes, what type of phraseme are they?

Five of the English binary conjunctions—⌐NO SOONER Y, THAN² X⌐; ⌐THE³ Y, THE² X⌐; ⌐BOTH X AND Y⌐; ⌐EITHER X OR Y⌐ and ⌐NEITHER X NOR Y⌐ —are idioms: they are non-compositional.

The conjunctions NOT SO MUCH X, AS Y and NOT ONLY X, BUT ALSO Y are formulemes (a subtype of cliché; Mel'čuk 2015a)—compositional, but completely fixed expressions.

And the binary conjunction IF Y, THEN X is a collocation, although of an unusual type: there is no direct syntactic link between the base and the collocate. In this collocation, the base is the first component (IF), which controls the use of the second component (the collocate THEN); the latter can be optional, must follow the base and occupies the initial linear position in the superordinate clause.

Binary conjunctions are characterized by syntactic discontinuity: they form phrases only together with their actants, since their own components are syntactically not directly linked to each other. In this, they are unlike almost all other phrasemes. However, they share this feature with a few idioms, which it seems worthwhile to quote here:

      ┌──────┐
⌐NOTHING→IF NOT←X_(ADJ)⌐ ≈ 'extremely':
    Barbara was nothing if not feminine.

        ┌────┐
Rus. ⌐PRI VSËM←X-e⌐ 'despite X' (Apresjan 2014):
pri vsëm ego talante 'despite [lit. 'with all'] his talent'

        ┌────r─┐
Rus. ⌐TO LI EŠČË←X_(V)⌐ 'I signal that X_(V) will take place, TO referring to something very bad': *To li ty togda eščë uvidiš'!* 'I signal that what you will then see will be very bad' [lit. 'That whether you then still will.see!'].

      ┌────┐
Fr. ⌐EN TOUT←X_(N)⌐
'while being completely ADJ(X)':
Je te le dis en toute amitié
'I tell you this being completely [your] friend [lit. 'in all friendship']'.

7 An Illustration: Russian Binary Conjunctions KAK…, TAK I… lit. 'as…, so also…'

To demonstrate my proposal in action, I will offer here the lexicographic descriptions—that is, lexical entries—for two Russian binary compound conjunctions:

the coordinating ⌐KAK X, TAK I Y¬**¹** ≈ 'both X and Y', see (5), and

the subordinating ⌐KAK Y, TAK (I) X¬**²** ≈ 'as Y, X', see (6).

First, two illustrative sentences and their surface-syntactic structures.

(5) Russian
On čitaet **kak** *anglijskie,* **tak i** *francuzskie knigi.*
he reads as English so also French books
'He reads both English and French books'.

Figure 1:
Surface-Syntactic Structure of Sentence (5)

In (5), KAK 'as' is not a conjunction, but a particle depending on the following adjective. Similarly, I is a particle meaning 'also', homonymous with the coordinating conjunction I 'and'. But TAK 'so' appears here as a coordinating conjunction (*anglijskie*–coord→*tak*–(*i*)–coord-conjunct→*francuzskie* by analo-gy with *anglijskie*–coord→*i*–coord-conjunct→*francuzskie*).

(6) Russian
Kak sidel on nad stat´ëj, **tak** *on* **i** *zasnul.*
as worked he on paper so he also fell.asleep
'As he was.working on [his] paper, he fell asleep'.

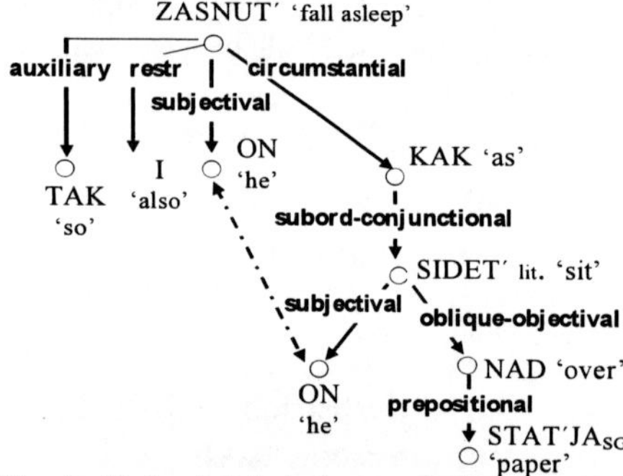

The double-headed dashed arrow indicates core-ference; it is part of the referential structure, one of the four structures composing the surface-syntactic representation of a sentence.

Figure 2:
Surface-Syntactic Structure of Sentence (6)

In (6), TAK 'so' is not a manner adverb, but a component of the second part of a binary compound conjunction; it is semantically empty and is positioned always at the beginning of the superordinate clause. This is why it needs a special auxiliary SSyntRel. It links the second component of some binary subordinating con-junctions to the head of the superordinate clause, cf. (2).

The conjunctions ⌐KAK X TAK I Y¬**¹** and ⌐KAK Y, TAK I X¬**²** are:
• homonymous and belong to two different vocables;
• idioms, since their meanings are by no means compositional;
• syntactically discontinuous in that **kak tak i* is not a phrase of Russian: only *kak X, tak i Y* is a phrase.

Here are the lexical entries of both Russian binary compound conjunctions. (For the organization of a lexical entry of the *Explanatory Combinatorial Dictionary*—a special lexicon of the Meaning-Text approach, see, among others, Mel'čuk 2013: Ch. 11.)

⌐**KAK X, TAK I Y**¬**¹** ≈ 'both X and Y': idiom, deep binary compound coordinating conjunction (Sannikov 2008: 302–303); written language.

Definition
⌐kak X, tak i Y¬**¹**: 'i X, i Y'
[lit. 'as X, so also Y']

Government Pattern

X ™ I	Y ™ II
1. L	1. L

("L" stands for 'lexeme'[3])

1) L ≠ ?ADJ$_{(short)}$, ?PREDICATIVE
   (Sannikov 2008: 303)
?*On byl kak bolen, tak i goloden*
'He was both sick and hungry'
(*bolen* and *goloden* are short adjectives).

Surface-Syntactic Structure
KAK←auxil–Y–coord→TAK–coord-conjunct→X–restr→I

Lexical Functions
Syn : i X, i Y ≈ 'both X and Y'
Anti : ni X, ni Y ≈ 'neither X nor Y'

Examples
V ètoj proporcii izmenjaetsja **kak** *cena,* **tak,** *razumeetsja,* **i** *bogatstvo*
lit. 'In this proportion changes as price, so, of course, also wealth'.
Tam vy smožete **kak** *vinogradnogo soka vypit´,* **tak i** *černiki poest´*
lit. 'There you will.be.able as grape juice drink, so also blackberries eat'.

---

[3] Thus, X and Y cannot be expressed by clauses.

*Ja **kak** sebe takogo ne pozvoljal, **tak i** ne pozvoljaju* lit. 'I as to.myself such.things didn't allow, so also don't allow' = 'As I didn't allow this to myself before, so I do not now'.

*Oba filosofa izučali **kak** fiziku, **tak i** kosmologiju*
lit. 'Both philosophers studied as physics, so also cosmology'.

⸢**KAK Y, TAK (I) X**⸣^{2} ≈ 'as Y, X': idiom, deep binary compound subordinating conjunction; colloquial style.

Definition
⸢kak Y, tak i X⸣^{2}: 'immediately at/since the
        moment of Y, X'
[lit. 'as Y, so also X']

Government Pattern

X ™ **I**	Y ™ **II**
1. CLAUSE	1. CLAUSE

Surface-Syntactic Structure

KAK—subord-conjunctional→Y TAK←—auxil–X—restr→I
(circumstantial)

Linear Order

1. The particle TAK is initial in the superordinate clause.

2. The subordinate clause introduced by KAK precedes the superordinate clause.

3. The conjunction KAK is not necessarily initial in the subordinate clause, but it necessarily precedes its Main Verb.

4. If the particle I is omitted, there must be at least one full lexeme between TAK and the Main Verb of the superordinate clause.

Examples
***Kak** pervyj raz sxodil ja v ataku, **tak** ot very **i** otpal*
lit. 'As first time went I in attack, so from faith [I] also fell.away' = 'After my first attack I lost my faith'.

***Kak** on rodilsja v Armavire, **tak** tam **i** vyros*
lit. 'As he was.born in Armavir, so there [he] also grew.up'.

*Èta dama **kak** podnjala ruku "za", **tak i** ne opustila eë, kogda golosovali "protiv"*
lit. 'This lady as rose hand *for*, so [she] also didn't lower it when [people] were voting *against*'.

***Kak** budeš′ s nej govorit′, **tak** vsë (**i**) pojmëš′*
lit. 'As [you] will with her talk, so everything [you] also will.understand'.

8   Deep-Syntactic Rules for Binary Conjunctions

Finally I would like to illustrate the Sem-rules and DSynt-rules that ensure the treatment of a binary conjunction. Two examples will be given: for a binary conjunction that is an idiom (⸢NO SOONER Y, THAN^2 X⸣) and for one that is a collocation (IF Y, THEN X).

Example 1

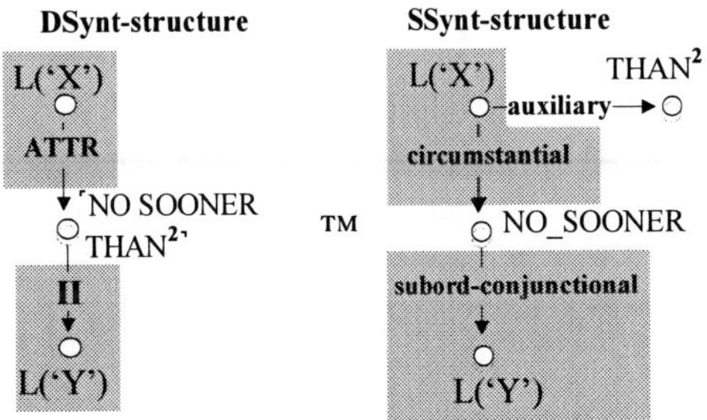

Shading indicates the context: that part of the rule that is not manipulated by it but whose presence is necessary for the rule to apply. L('X') stands for «lexical expression L of meaning 'X'».

The correspondence between these two structures constitutes a DSynt-rule for the binary compound conjunction ⸢NO SOONER Y, THAN^2 X⸣. In other words, this rule, as as part of its lexical entry, is exploited during the transition from the deep-syntactic structure of a sentence with this conjunction to its surface-syntactic structure.

A binary conjunction that is an idiom exists as such only in the DSynt-structure, where it appears on one node. This reflects its semantic unity.

Example 2

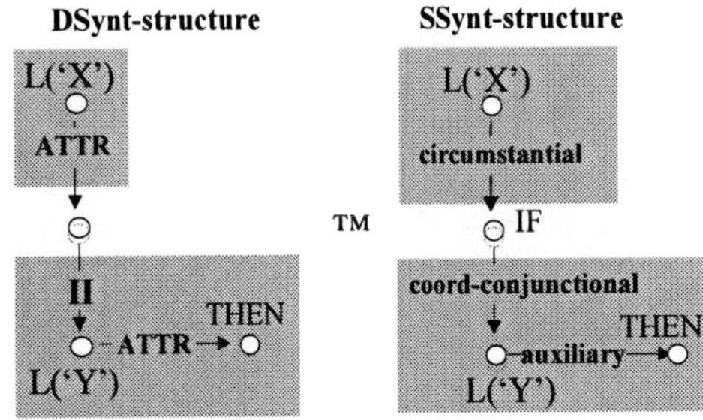

9   Conclusions

1. A dependency syntactic structure is proposed for binary conjunctions, both subordinating and coordinating.

2. A universal typology of conjunctions is sketched, and three examples are given of English binary conjunctions.

3. Binary conjunctions are "discontinuous" phrasemes—phrasemes that have to be considered together with their actants.

4. The full lexical entries are presented for two Russian binary compound conjunctions: the coordinating ⌐KAK X, TAK I Y^1 ≈ 'both X and Y' and the subordinating ⌐KAK Y, TAK (I) X^2 ≈ 'as Y, X'.

5. Two sample DSynt-rules for introducing a binary conjunction into the SSynt-subtree are presented for the binary conjunctions ⌐NO SOONER Y, THAN^2 X⌐ and IF Y, THEN X.

Acknowledgments

My most heartfelt thanks go to Margarita Alonso Ramos, David Beck, Lidija Iordanskaja, Sébastien Marengo and Jasmina Milićević, who read the preliminary versions of this text. Thanks as well to the three anonymous reviewers for Depling-2017.

References

Valentina Apresjan. 2014. Syntactic Idioms across Languages: Corpus Evidence from Russian and English. *Russian Linguistics*, 38: 2, 187–203.

Leonid Iomdin. 2010. Sintaksičeskie otnošenija [Syntactic Relations]. In: Apresjan, Ju., Boguslavskij, I., Iomdin, L., Sannikov, V., *Teoretičeskie problemy russkogo sintaksisa: vzaimodejstvie grammatiki i slovarja*, Moskva: Jazyki slavjanskix kul´tur, 21–43.

Igor Mel'čuk. 1974. *Opyt teorii lingvističeskix modelej «Smysl ⇔□Tekst». Semantika, sintaksis [Outline of a Theory of Linguistic Meaning-Text Models. Semantics, Syntax]*. Moskva: Nauka.

Igor Mel'čuk. 1988. *Dependency Syntax: Theory and Practice*. Albany, N.Y.: State University of New York Press.

Igor Mel'čuk. 2009. Dependency in Natural Language. In: Polguère & Mel'čuk (eds) 2009: 1–110.

Igor Mel'čuk. 2012a. *Jazyk: ot smysla k tekstu [Language: from Meaning to Text]*. Moskva: Jazyki slavjanskoj kul´tury.

Igor Mel'čuk. 2012b. *Semantics: From Meaning to Text*. [Vol. 1.] Amsterdam/Philadelphia: John Benjamins.

Igor Mel'čuk. 2013. *Semantics: From Meaning to Text*. Vol. 2. Amsterdam/Philadelphia: John Benjamins.

Igor Mel'čuk. 2015a. Clichés, an Understudied Subclass of Phrasemes. *Yearbook of Phraseology*, 6: 55–86.

Igor Mel'čuk. 2015b. *Semantics: From Meaning to Text*. Vol. 3, Amsterdam/Philadelphia: John Benjamins.

Igor Mel'čuk. 2015c. A General Inventory of Surface-Syntactic Relations in World Languages. Part One. *Moscow Linguistic Journal*, 17: 2, 75–103.

Igor Mel'čuk. 2016a. A General Inventory of Surface-Syntactic Relations in World Languages. Part Two. *Moscow Linguistic Journal*, 18: 1, 94-120.

Igor Mel'čuk. 2016b. *Language: From Meaning to Text*. Moskva/Boston: Academic Studies Press.

Igor Mel'čuk. 2017. KAK ..., TAK I ...: čto èto za? [KAK..., TAK I...: What Kind of Stuff is It?]. *Russkij jazyk v naučnom osvesčenii*, No. 1 (33), 67–85.

Igor Mel'čuk and Nikolaj Pertsov. 1987. *Surface Syntax of English. A Formal Model within the Meaning-Text Framework*. Amsterdam: John Benjamins.

Alain Polguère and Igor Mel'čuk (Eds.) 2009. *Dependency in Linguistic Description*. Amsterdam/Philadelphia: John Benjamins.

Randolph Quirk, Sydney Greenbaum, Geoffrey Leech, Jan Svartvik. 1991. *A Comprehensive Grammar of the English Language*. London/New York: Longman.

Vladimir Sannikov. 2008. *Russkij sintaksis v semantiko-pragmatičeskom prostranstve [Russian Syntax in Semantic-Pragmatic Space]*. Moskva: Jazyki slavjanskix kul´tur.

Non-Projectivity in Serbian: Analysis of Formal and Linguistic Properties

Aleksandra Miletic
CLLE, CNRS & University of Toulouse
France
aleksandra.miletic@univ-tlse2.fr

Assaf Urieli
CLLE, CNRS & University of Toulouse
and Joliciel Informatique
France
assaf.urieli@gmail.com

Abstract

This paper presents insights into non-projective relations in Serbian based on the analysis of an 81K token gold-standard corpus manually annotated for dependencies. We provide a formal profile of the non-projective dependencies found in the corpus, as well as a linguistic analysis of the underlying structures. We compare the observed properties of Serbian to those of other languages found in existing studies on non-projectivity.

1 Introduction

This contribution presents an initial analysis of formal and linguistic properties of non-projective structures in Serbian. The work is based on the first freely available gold-standard corpus for parsing Serbian. Previous experiments in parsing this language (Agić et al., 2013; Jakovljević et al., 2014; Agić and Ljubešić, 2015) did not lead to the creation of a gold-standard corpus, and whereas a Universal Dependency treebank is under construction (Samardžić et al., 2017), it has not yet been made available at the project website at the time of writing this paper[1]. We therefore (tentatively) consider that the corpus used in the present contribution is the first freely available gold-standard corpus of this kind for Serbian. The corpus was developed as part of the ParCoLab project, aimed at the constitution of a Serbian-French-English parallel treebank, and it can be downloaded from the project's resource page (http://parcolab.univ-tlse2.fr/en/about/resources/).

The existence of this resource makes it possible to examine the properties of non-projectivity in Serbian. Non-projectivity reflects syntactic structures in which a dependant is separated from its governor by an element of a different subtree, leading to crossing edges in the dependency tree. Typically, languages with richer morphology and flexible word order tend to have more non-projective structures. Since Serbian fits this category, it can be expected to be an interesting object of study from this point of view. This hypothesis is further supported by the findings for other related languages, such as Czech and Slovene, in both of which over 2% of dependency edges are non-projective, occurring in over 20% of sentences (Havelka, 2007).

The phenomenon of non-projectivity holds interest both for theoretical linguistics and for parsing. Constituency-based theories approach it through the notion of movement and traces (in transformational grammars), or through that of feature passing mechanisms (in the non-transformational ones), whereas dependency-based theories address it, for example, as rising (Groß and Osborne, 2009), emancipation (Gerdes and Kahane, 2001), or climbing (Duchier and Debusmann, 2001). In parsing, handling non-projective structures increases computational complexity, and this type of processing cannot be done by linear-complexity transition-based parsers. For these reasons, non-projectivity has been examined accross a number of languages (Hajičová et al., 2004; Kuhlmann and Nivre, 2006; Havelka, 2007; Bhat and Sharma, 2012; Mambrini and Passarotti, 2013). In these works, several formal properties of dependency trees are used to describe non-projectivity, such as well-nestedness, maximum edge degree and maximum gap degree (Kuhlmann and Nivre, 2006). There is also an effort to identify the linguistic structures giving rise to non-projective syntactic relations: see (Hajičová et al., 2004) for Czech, (Bhat and Sharma, 2012) for Hindi, Urdu and

---

[1] http://universaldependencies.org/#upcoming-ud-treebanks. Last access: May 12, 2017.

Proceedings of the Fourth International Conference on Dependency Linguistics (Depling 2017), pages 135-144,
Pisa, Italy, September 18-20 2017

Bangla, (Mambrini and Passarotti, 2013) for Ancient Greek. This allows for different types of comparisons between languages. For example, Mambrini and Passarotti (2013) underline the role of clitics in non-projective structures in Ancient Greek: these forms account for more than 40% of words creating non-projectivity. Since the enclitics in Serbian behave the same way as those in Ancient Greek (they follow Wackernagel's law and tend to occupy the 2nd position in the clause), we can expect to find a comparable effect in our corpus. Another example involves the fact that both in Czech (Hajičová et al., 2004) and in Hindi (Bhat and Sharma, 2012), non-projective nodes can be caused by dependants of infinitives in control constructions moving out of their clause. The same structure is possible in Serbian. An in-depth analysis of non-projectivity in our corpus would therefore allow us to draw parallels between Serbian and other languages, which could be informative both from the processing perspective (tools and resources best suited for these languages) and from the typological one (types of non-projective syntactic structures represented in these languages).

Our goal in this contribution is to establish a non-projectivity profile for Serbian: we examine the formal properties of non-projective structures in our corpus and accompany this account with an analysis of the underlying linguistic phenomena. We use this information to compare Serbian to a number of different languages and bring forward observations on both levels of analysis. The remainder of this paper is organized as follows: in section 2, we offer a brief presentation of our working corpus, section 3 is dedicated to the analysis of the formal properties of non-projectivity in the corpus and section 4 offers a linguistic analysis of structures resulting in non-projectivity. Lastly, in section 5, we give our conclusions and perspectives for future work.

2 Working Corpus

The gold-standard treebank used in this work contains 81K tokens annotated manually for POS-tags, lemmas and syntactic dependencies. It is based on two original literary texts in Serbian from the 2nd half of the 20th century. It was developed as part of the ParCoLab project, which goal is to create a parallel treebank in Serbian, French and English. The corpus is available at the following address: `http://parcolab.univ-tlse2.fr/en/about/resources/`.

Some basic corpus statistics are given in Table 1. Morphosyntactic annotation is done on 2 levels: POS tags, and detailed morphosyntactic descriptions (MSDs) including features such as case, gender, number, person, tense, and degree of comparison. Given the relatively rich inflectional morphology of Serbian, there are over 1000 possible MSDs in our tagset, 647 of which occur in the corpus.

Our syntactic annotation uses a project-specific dependency set and annotation scheme[2]. The dependency label set contains 50 basic labels, and 17 additional ones for treating ellipsis[3]. The labels for core functions (subject, direct and indirect object, predicatives) are based on the traditional Serbian syntax (cf. (Stanojčić and Popović, 2012; Ivić, 2005)). However, existing theoretical descriptions of verbal dependants other than the ones cited above, as well as those of noun, adjective and adverb dependants, are often based on semantic rather than syntactic criteria, which are ill-suited for parsing. We therefore introduce a set of underspecified labels based on surface properties of these elements: they identify the element as a dependant, and indicate the morphosyntactic nature of the head and dependant of the relation. They correspond to the following pattern: *Dep(V|N|Adj|Adv)(Cas|Prep|Adj|Adv)*. For instance, a dependant of a verb in form of a prepositional group is marked as DepVPrep, whereas a nominal dependant in form of another noun in an oblique case is given as DepNCas. Our goal is to establish a reliable initial annotation of these elements that will allow for a corpus-based analysis of their properties and lead to the creation of more informative labels based on their syntactic characteristics.

It is worth noting that the average sentence

---

[2]An alternative possiblity would have been to use the Universal Dependency annotation scheme. However, we agree with some of the criticisms of the UD annotation scheme pointed out by Groß and Osborne (2015) and prefer the functional head approach to the lexical head one proposed by UD. Furthermore, we found it relevant to keep a native language-specific approach, especially given that there was no other treebank for Serbian available at the beginning of this project. Nonetheless, given the usefulness of the UD annotation scheme for a wide range of NLP research, automatic conversion of the corpus into a UD-style resource is part of the project's perspectives

[3]We adopt the treatment for ellipsis used in Prague Dependency Treebank (Hajič et al., 1999), p. 204-221.

Tokens	81204	Sentences	2949
Wordforms	19681	Lemmas	10223
POS tags	15	MSDs	647
Dependency labels		67 (50+17)	
Aver. sent. length		27.53 tokens	
Aver. max. tree depth		7.23	
Long-distance relations		5.78%	
Non-projective trees		503	
Non-projective edges		658	
Non-projective nodes		725	

Table 1: Gold corpus information

length in the corpus is relatively high. This is also the case with the average maximum tree depth. For this measure, we consider the node that is the deepest in the tree and calculate its distance from the root. The value given here is the average for all the trees in the corpus. For the long-distance relationships, we used a threshhold of 7: 5.78% of the edges in the corpus link nodes that are separated by 7 or more tokens in the linear ordering of the sentence.

3 Formal Analysis of Non-Projectivity in Corpus

When defining projectivity, we follow the formal definitions presented in (Kuhlmann and Nivre, 2006). We will now briefly describe the main concepts used in this contribution less formally. A sentence is formed of a sequence of tokens. A syntactic tree drawn over a sentence is a connected acyclic directed graph rooted at an artificial root node. The tokens represent the **nodes** of this graph, and each directed arc from a governing node to its dependant is an **edge**. A node is said to **dominate** another node if the other node is its descendent. A node is considered **projective** if the subtree dominated by it contains no gaps, where a **gap** occurs any time two adjacent nodes in the subtree are separated by one or more tokens from a different subtree—these tokens are then said to be contained within the gap. A tree is projective if all of its nodes are projective.

Over time, mechanisms for quantifying and qualifying the non-projectivity in a language have developed. In addition to direct indicators, such as the percentage of non-projective nodes and trees in a corpus, Kuhlmann and Nivre present various other formal properties of projectivity, including well-nestedness, maximum gap degree, and max-

imum edge degree. A **well-nested** tree is one in which, for any two nodes A and B, if node A does not dominate node B, then node A does not dominate any gaps in node B's subtree. A node's **gap degree** is the number of distinct gaps in its subtree (regardless of each gap's size). A node's **edge degree** is the number of edges originating outside the lower and upper boundaries of the node's sub-tree, and governing tokens contained in the node's gaps. For trees, these degrees are taken to be the maximum degree among the tree's nodes. As in (Havelka, 2007), we also consider non-projective edges (as opposed to nodes). A **non-projective edge** is an edge from token i to j, where at least one token between i and j is not dominated by i. A single non-projective edge can be responsible for multiple non-projective nodes, as in example 1: here we have a single non-projective edge, $Tok5 \rightarrow Tok2$, where $Tok3$ and $Tok4$ are not dominated by $Tok5$. This edge is responsible for two non-projective nodes, $Tok5$ (with $Tok3$ and $Tok4$ in the gap), and $Tok4$ (with $Tok3$ in the gap).

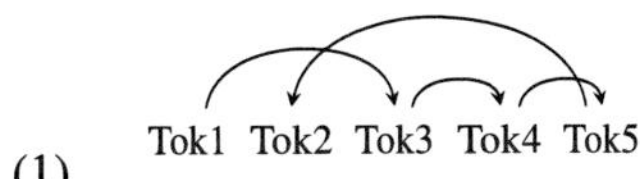

(1)

The frequency of non-projective edges, non-projective trees and ill-nested trees in our corpus is given in Table 2, whereas Table 3 gives details on gap degree and edge degree. For comparison, we provide data for other languages based on existing works[4]. We give data for Czech and Slovene, as they are related to Serbian and it is reasonable to expect comparable results for the three languages, for Danish and Dutch, as European languages with well-known non-projective structures, for Hindi as a relatively distant language, and for Ancient Greek, as the language for which the existing works indicate the most prominent levels of non-projectivity.

Based on the results in Table 2, we can see that Serbian has a smaller percentage of non-projective edges compared to other Slavic languages (Slovene and Czech), but the percentage of non-projective trees is comparable. Ill-nested trees

---

[4]The data for Czech, Slovene and Dutch in Table 2 were taken from (Havelka, 2007), whereas those for Czech and Danish in Table 3 are from (Kuhlmann and Nivre, 2006). The data for Ancient Greek and Hindi in both tables come from (Mambrini and Passarotti, 2013) and (Bhat and Sharma, 2012), respectively.

Language	Edges		Trees		
	Tot. edges	Non-proj.(%)	Tot. trees	Non-proj.(%)	Ill-nested (%)
Serbian	81204	0.81	2949	17.06	0.17
Czech	1105437	2.13	72703	23.15	0.11
Slovene	25777	2.13	1534	22.16	0.20
Dutch	179063	5.90	13349	36.44	0.11
Hindi	NA	1.65	20497	14.85	0.19

Table 2: Non-projective edges, non-projective and ill-nested trees in Serbian and other languages

Language	Trees	Gap degree (%)				Edge degree (%)					
		Gd0	Gd1	Gd2	Gd3	Ed0	Ed1	Ed2	Ed3	Ed4	Ed5
Serbian	2949	82.94	16.58	0.44	0.03	82.94	15.36	1.66	0.03	-	-
Czech	73088	76.85	22.72	0.42	0.01	76.85	22.69	0.35	0.09	0.01	<0.01
Danish	4393	84.95	14.89	0.16	-	84.95	13.29	1.32	0.39	0.05	-
Hindi	20497	85.14	14.56	0.28	0.02	85.14	14.24	0.45	0.11	0.03	-
A. Greek	24825	25.20	68.33	6.17	0.28	25.20	43.73	14.15	7.07	3.88	-

Table 3: Gap-degree and edge-degree in Serbian and other languages

comprising <1% of the trees in the corpus, well-nestedness proves to be a useful relaxation of the projectivity constraint for Serbian, as is the case for all other languages considered.

Among the languages compared in Table 3, Serbian has a similar profile to other modern languages (in contrast to Ancient Greek), with over 99% of the trees having a gap degree of 0 or 1, and 98.30% of the trees with an edge degree of 0 or 1. Serbian and Danish are the only two modern languages where over 1.5% of the trees have an edge degree ≥ 2.

4 Underlying Linguistic Structures

A corpus-based linguistic analysis of non-projective structures has been done for several languages. Hajičová et al. (2004) analyze Czech using Prague Dependency Treebank. They identify 12 different non-projective constructions on the surface syntax level and classify them according to their underlying deep syntax structure. Mannem et al. (2009) worked on Hindi using a pilot treebank of 35K words. They describe 9 different non-projective structures, while giving special attention to the identification of the constructions allowing for projective reordering. Bhat and Sharma (2012) used an expanded version of the same treebank and extended their analysis to 3 more Indian languages (Urdu, Bangla and Telugu). They analyze 8 specific constructions with respect to the type of discontinuity observed (topicalization, extraposition, NP extraction, quantifier float, scrambling, or inherent non-projectivity). Mambrini and Passarotti (2013) classify the non-projective structures in Ancient Greek according to the type of the head (verb or noun) and analyze in more detail the role of clitics.

In this section, we present the most prominent non-projective structures identified in our corpus and draw parallels when possible with the findings in the works cited above. Most of the non-projective structures found in our corpus belong to well-established discontinuity types such as wh-fronting, extraposition, topicalization and long-distance scrambling[5]. Serbian also allows for split constructions, which are mostly (but not exclusively) nominal. We analyse the detachment of the prefix of the negative pronouns form the base inside a PP as a separate category, as it does not seem to belong to any of the types cited above.

Here a clarification is due as to the annotation scheme of the corpus on which this work was done, more specifically, about the status of the auxiliary verbs. In our working corpus, auxiliary verbs are annotated as dependants to lexical verbs, meaning that in a sentence with a complex verb form, it is the lexical verb that is annalyzed as the root of the sentence. Milićević (2009) argues that clitic auxiliary verbs in Serbian should have this role, and this is also the case in a number of studies on other languagues (cf. (Abeillé

Non-projectivity type	%
Splitting	33.7%
Wh-fronting	20.4%
Scrambling	17.0%
Extraposition	15.9%
Negative pronoun split	1.9%
Topicalization	1.5%
Other	9.8%
Text issues	0.4%
Annotation errors	0.8%

Table 4: Distribution of non-projectivity by type

and Godard, 2002) for French, (Kupść and Tseng, 2005) for Polish, (Krapova, 1995) for Bulgarian). However, we chose to consider the lexical verb as the governor, as this allows for a more immediate representation of the argument structure of the verb, with the subject and all other arguments depending directly on the lexical verb. The same choice was made in, e.g., French Dependency Treebank (cf. (Candito et al., 2009), p.9) and Prague Dependency Treebank (cf. (Hajič et al., 1999), p.19). The examples hereafter containing non-projectivity linked to the auxiliaries (i.e., examples 2a, 3, 7d) would still be non-projective if the auxiliary verb was considered the root of the sentence, although the syntactic trees would not be the same. It is also possible that the counts of non-projective structures in the corpus would be slightly different with this approach.

A total of 658 non-projective edges were identified in the corpus. The distribution of the non-projective relations given the type of non-projectivity is shown in Table 4. Some of the non-projective edges identified in the corpus were due to irregularities inherent to the text (i.e., subordinate clauses missing their verb), and some were due to manual annotation errors. All other examples were analyzed with respect to the types of discontinuity cited above. The category "Other" represents non-systematic cases with too few occurrences to allow for a meaningful analysis, such as extrapredicative elements or reported speech. We will discuss in more detail the four most represented types of non-projectivity - splitting, wh-fronting, scrambling, and extraposition, and briefly present the negative pronoun split.

Serbian has a very flexible order of the base syntactic relations: even though the SVO ordering is the canonical one, all 6 permutations (SVO, SOV, OVS, OSV, VOS and VSO) are grammatical, with each of them expressing a different topicalization of the sentence.

Another important property of the word-order in Serbian is the behaviour of the enclitics: they follow the so-called Wackernagel's law and occupy the second position in the prosodic structure. Corbett (1987) identifies an enclitic cluster containing 6 slots, dedicated to different auxiliary and pronoun enclitics and the interrogative particle *li*. The morpho-syntactic structure of the cluster is analyzed in (Groß, 2011). For the scope of this contribution, their most important characteristic is that the Wackernagel constraint can be strong enough to lead to the splitting of the phrase occupying the sentence-initial position by the enclitic cluster. They are therefore an important factor in the non-projective structures in Serbian. Their effect will be shown throughout the following subsections.

Also, one property of Serbian that is not typical of other Slavic languages, but is shared with other languages of the Balkans, is that the control constructions (with two verbs sharing the same subject) can be expressed by the typical infinitival construction, but also by a full completive clause, introduced by the conjunction *da* 'that' and having a verb in present tense. The sentences such as *Filip želi kupiti knjigu* 'Filip wants to buy a book' and *Filip želi da kupi knjigu* lit. 'Filip wants that he buys a book', are both grammatical, and have the same meaning. Both of these constructions participate in a number of non-projective structures, which will be discussed below.

4.1 Split Constructions

Split constructions involve cases in which a head of a group is separated from its dependant by an element of a different node's subtree. This type of non-projectivity is the most productive in our corpus, accounting for 33% of all non-projective edges. Split nominal groups are an important source of non-projectivity in Czech, too : Hajičová et al. (2004) indicate that this construction represents 11% of non-projective edges observed in Prague Dependency Treebank.

In our corpus, split constructions typically involve an enclitic or an enclitic cluster occupying the 2nd position in the sentence, immediately after the left-most element of the sentence-initial group, thus detaching this element from the rest of the group. Since the enclitics typically depend on the main verb, this often leads to non-projective edges in the tree (see example 2a).

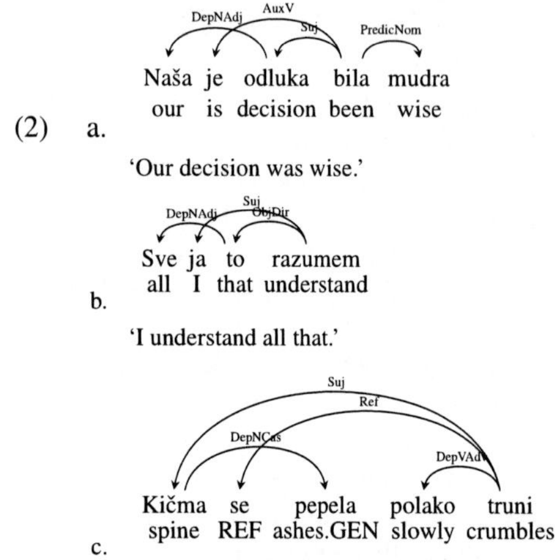

(2) a.

'Our decision was wise.'

b.

'I understand all that.'

c.

'The spine of the ashes is slowly crumbling.'

Splitting can also be created by a non-clitic word as in example 2b: *ja* 'I' is the full form of the pronoun, and not a clitic. The split can also occur between the head and its right branch, as in 2c, where the genitive noun *pepela* (from *pepeo* 'ashes') is the right dependant of the subject noun *kičma* 'spine'. And nominal heads are not the only ones concerned: even though it is much less frequent, the splitting can also happen inside an AP or and AdvP, following the same principles. These examples represent 16.4% of all the occurrences of splitting found in the corpus.

An interesting specific case of splitting involves NPs that are inside a sentence-initial PP. The preposition being a proclitic, it forms a prosodic unit with the content immediately after it. The enclitic (or the enclitic cluster) therefore cannot insert itself immediately after the preposition and rather occupies the position after the first element of the NP. This leads to double non-projectivity, since both the subtree dominated by the preposition and the one dominated by the preposition's complement contain gaps (cf. crossing arcs in example 3).

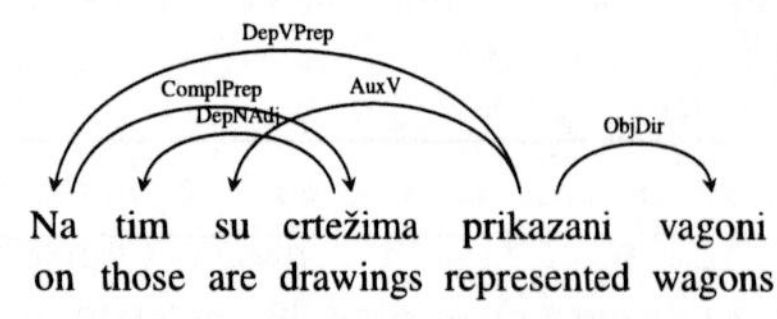

(3)

'There are train wagons on those drawings.'

In the above examples, non-projectivity is optional: the enclitic (cluster) can also occupy a position next to the verb without a major meaning shift. Thus, the sentence in 3 can be reformulated as *Na tim crtežima su prikazani vagoni* or as *Na tim crtežima prikazani su vagoni*. On the other hand, non-projectivity seems to be obligatory if the enclitic causing the split is the main verb (cf. 4).

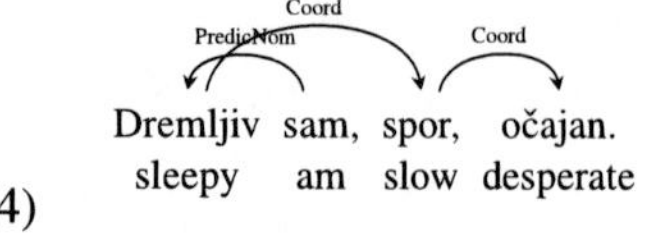

(4)

'I am sleepy, slow, desperate.'

Here, the only way to resolve non-projectivity would be for the verb to occupy either the sentence-initial or the sentence-final position. The former is impossible since the verb is an enclitic and must be preceded by an accented form. The latter receives aggramaticality judgments from our informants, probably due to the fact that the verb is a much "lighter" element than the predicative and is therefore blocked from the sentence-final position.

As mentioned in section 1, Mambrini and Passarotti (2013) draw attention to the fact that the 5 most frequent words occuring in gaps are postpositives (mostly clitics), accounting for nearly 40% of words found in gaps. Clitic-related observations were also made on Czech: Hajičová et al. (2004) indicate that the interrogative particle *li* occupying the second position and leading to non-projectivity appears in 5.1% of dependencies in a sample of 615 sentences. Our own observations presented above confirm that the behaviour of clitics subject to Wackernagel's law is an important source of non-projectivity.

4.2 Wh-fronting

Like in many other languages, the wh-words in Serbian tend to occupy the sentence-initial position, be it in direct or indirect questions, or in relative clauses. Note that the Left Branch Condition (Ross, 1967) does not hold in Serbian: unlike in English, in Serbian an interrogative adjective can be detached from its governor and fronted alone. This makes both 5a and 5b possible, the difference between them being that in the former it is the whole NP that is topicalized, whereas in the latter it is only the wh-word. In the latter, non-projectivity occurs.

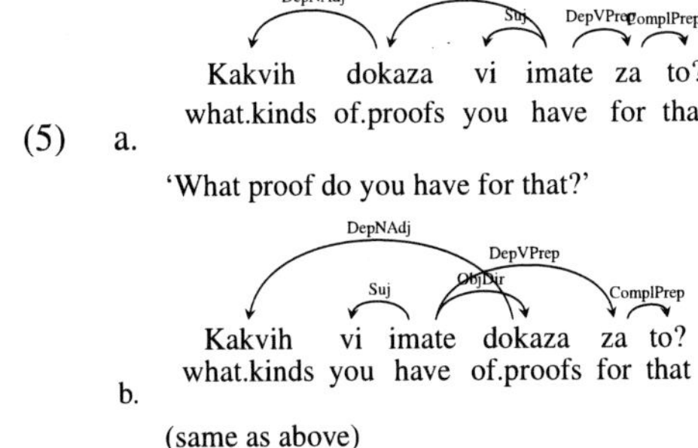

(5) a.

'What proof do you have for that?'

b.

(same as above)

This is another trait that Serbian shares with Czech: following (Hajičová et al., 2004), wh-words in Czech can also be fronted without pied-piping, and this construction accounts for 1.6% of non-projective relations in their corpus.

Stranding prepositions being impossible in Serbian, if a wh-word is inside a PP, pied-piping of the preposition is obligatory (cf. 6a). On the other hand, the NP that is the complement of the preposition can be split, as in example 6b. This leads to double non-projectivity following the same principles as in 3.

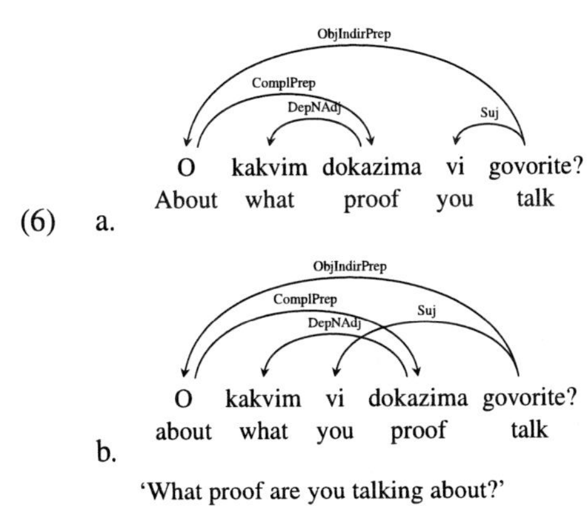

(6) a.

b.

'What proof are you talking about?'

In the case of infinitival and *da*+V$_{pres}$ clauses, the wh-word occupies the position in front of the verb introducing those clauses (cf. 7a and 7b).

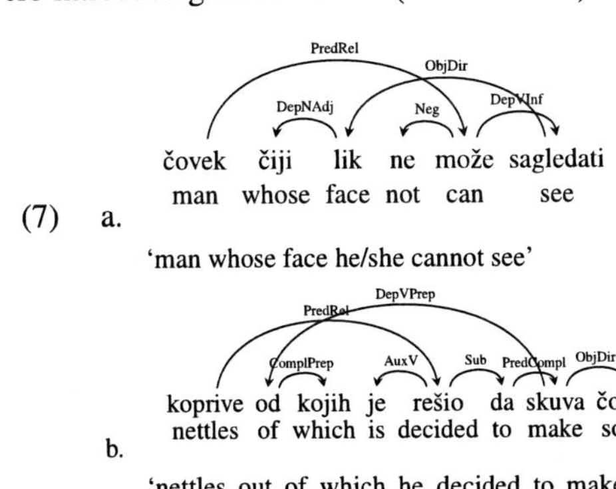

(7) a.

'man whose face he/she cannot see'

b.

'nettles out of which he decided to make a soup'

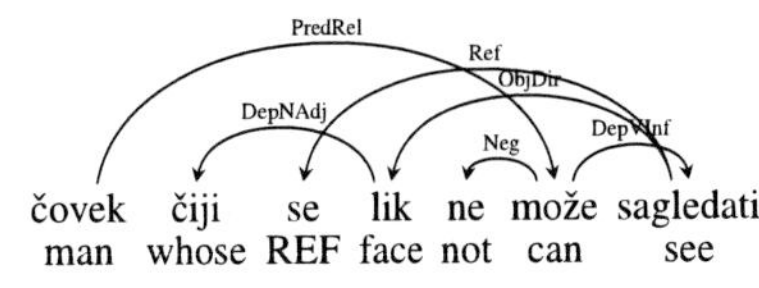

c.

'man whose face cannot be seen'

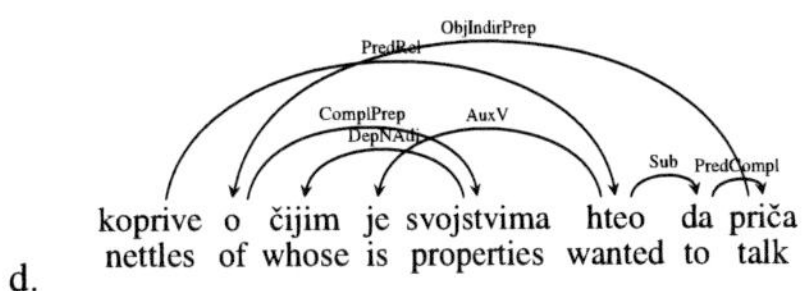

d.

'nettles of whose properties he wanted to talk'

This leads to non-projectivity even with structures that would not be discontinuous in a simple clause (i.e., with relative pronouns depending directly on the verb or in cases of pied-piping). This type of non-projectivity is obligatory: there is no alternative way to obtain wh-fronting with an embedded or an infinitival clause.

Furthermore, these contexts do not exclude splitting, cf. examples 7c and 7d. This is not a rare occurrence: it appears in 31% of the wh-fronting-related non-projective constructions in our corpus. This additionally complexifies the syntactic structure of the sentence and can potentially make the processing of the relative clauses even more difficult.

4.3 Long-Distance Scrambling

A dependant of an infinitival or *da*+V$_{pres}$ clause can appear outside of it independently of wh-fronting. In other words, Serbian allows for long-distance scrambling.

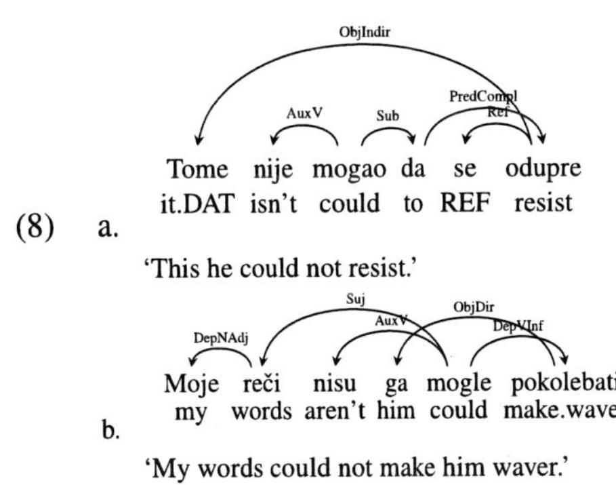

(8) a.

'This he could not resist.'

b.

'My words could not make him waver.'

The scrambling of the dependants of an infinitive was also observed by Hajičová et al. (2004) in Czech, and it accounted for 9% of the non-projective relations in their corpus. This property is also shared by Hindi; however, in this language it only represents 1.5% of non-projective structures. Since in our corpus it covers 17%, it seems that Serbian has a higher propensity for these constructions than the other two languages.

Whereas this type of discontinuity was obligatory in the case of wh-fronting, it is not in the case of scrambling, at least for the embedded clauses: the extracted indirect object *tome* in 8a can easily occupy its canonical place inside the embedded clause: *Nije mogao da se odupre tome*. The scrambled order contributes to topicalize the element that appears out of its canonical position. However, it is less evident with the infinitival clauses: both *Moje reči nisu mogle ga pokolebati* and *Moje reči nisu mogle pokolebati ga* receive marginality judgements from our informants. This seems to be due to the enclitic nature of the pronoun *ga* 'him': if the full form *njega* is used, both sentences become grammatical, but the pronoun receives a topicalized reading: *Moje reči nisu mogle njega pokolebati* and *Moje reči nisu mogle pokolebati njega* both translate as 'Him, my words could not make waver'.

4.4 Extraposition

Examples of typical extraposition, with an informationally heavy element being positioned further to the right, were found in the corpus (cf. example 9a). There were also two specific constructions that can be analysed as cases of extraposition. The first one, illustrated in 9b, is the correlative structure involving a demonstrative word in the main clause and a consecutive clause. The adverb here occupies the canonical position of an adverbial dependant of an adjective to the left of its head. However, the consecutive clause it introduces is too heavy to appear immediately after it; the clause is therefore moved to the right, making the adverb node non-projective. A projective version of this construction is possible, with the adverb moving to the right of the adjective: *Nisam bio bezuman toliko da poverujem*. But in this sentence, the adverb is topicalized: 'I was not so mindless as to believe her'.

(9) a.

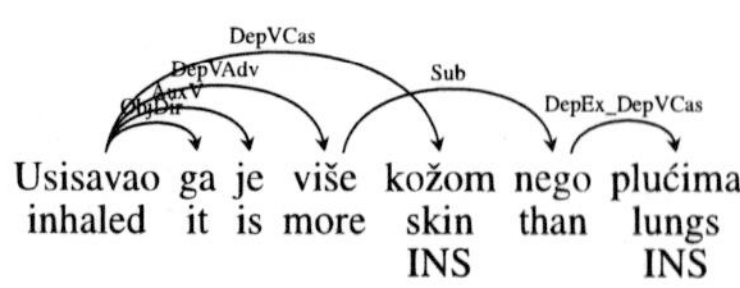

'He was inhaling it more with his skin than with his lungs.'

The second specific construction involves the comparative forms and their dependant introduced by *nego* 'than' (ex. 9c). Once again, a projective version is possible if the adverb is placed to the right of the noun (*Udisao ga je kožom više nego plućima*), but this gives a topicalized reading for the first element of the comparison. This construction was also observed in Prague Dependency Treebank and it was the source of 2.7% of all non-projective structures (Hajičová et al., 2004).

4.5 Negative Pronouns in PPs

This type of non-projectivity does not have a high incidence in our corpus, but we present it as a specific type of non-projectivity on the frontier between the morphosyntax and syntax. It is all the more interesting since we did not encounter descriptions of a similar phenomenon for another language.

Negative pronoun split occurs when a so-called negative pronoun appears inside a PP. Negative pronouns such as *niko* 'nobody' and *ništa* 'nothing' derive respectively from interrogative pronouns *ko* 'who' and *šta* 'what', prefixed with a negative prefix *ni*. If such a pronoun appears inside a PP, the prefix detaches itself and is placed in front of the preposition, leaving only the inflected part of the pronoun to the right of the preposition (ex. 10). At present, in our annotation scheme this prefix is annotated as a part of the polylexical unit and attached to the inflected part of the pronoun, which is in turn governed by the preposition. Therefore, this structure generates non-projective edges.

(10) a.

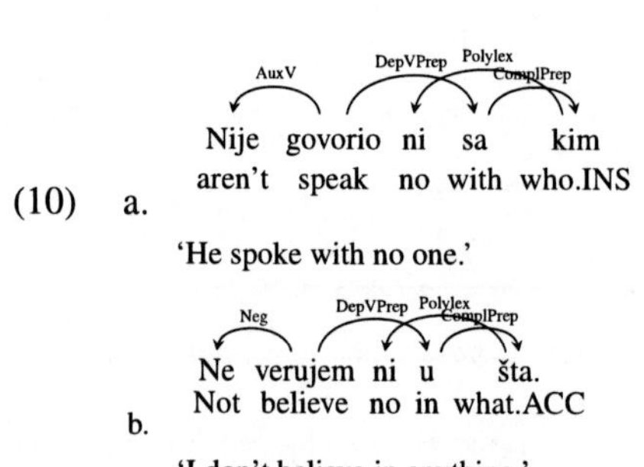

'He spoke with no one.'

b.

'I don't believe in anything.'

This type of non-projectivity is sometimes ignored in spoken language: *Ne verujem u ništa* lit. 'I don't believe in nothing'. However, the pronoun split is considered as the correct form from the normative point of view, and it seems to be observed systematically in our corpus.

5   Conclusions and Future Work

In this work, we offered a formal and linguistic profile of non-projectivity in Serbian based on the first freely available gold-standard treebank for this language. The analysis showed that even though Serbian has less non-projective edges than other Slavic languages, it has a comparable proportion of non-projective trees. Another interesting feature of this language is that it has a higher edge degree than the other languages examined, implying that Serbian allows more easily for discontinuities created by disjoint subtrees. The analysis of the underlying linguistic structures showed that non-projectivity in Serbian belongs to well-known discontinuity types, such as wh-fronting, extraposition, long-distance scrambling, and splitting. We also saw that some of the non-projectivity types found in Serbian exist in other languages: split constructions were also found in Czech, and both Czech and Hindi allow for the long-distance scrambling of the dependants in control constructions. In a more general way, the remarks of Mambrini and Passarotti (2013) regarding the importance of clitics behaviour for non-projective structures in Ancient Greek were found to be relevant for Serbian too: in our corpus, clitics had a significant role in different non-projectivity types, most notably in split constructions and wh-fronting.

Given these initial observations on clitics, we will continue examining their properties with the goal of determining more precisely the proportion of non-projectivity in Serbian that is caused by the behaviour of these forms. Also, the work presented in this contribution was carried out on a corpus containing only literary texts. Our analysis will be expanded to other text genres in order to see if the non-projectivity properties observed here are stable accross genres. We will also be investigating these questions from the point of view of parsing: our future works will focus on conducting parsing experiments and comparing performances of different algorithms on different types of non-projective structures found in Serbian.

References

Anne Abeillé and Danièle Godard. 2002. The syntactic structure of French auxiliaries. *Language*, 78(3):404–452.

Željko Agić and Nikola Ljubešić. 2015. Universal Dependencies for Croatian (that work for Serbian, too). In *The 5th Workshop on Balto-Slavic Natural Language Processing (BSNLP 2015)*.

Željko Agić, Danijela Merkler, and Daša Berović. 2013. Parsing Croatian and Serbian by using Croatian dependency treebanks. In *Proceedings of the Fourth Workshop on Statistical Parsing of Morphologically-Rich Languages*.

Riyaz Ahmad Bhat and Dipti Misra Sharma. 2012. Non-projective structures in Indian language treebanks. In *Proceedings of the 11th Workshop on Treebanks and Linguistic Theories (TLT11)*, pages 25–30.

Marie Candito, Benoît Crabbé, and Mathieu Falco. 2009. Dépendances syntaxiques de surface pour le français. Technical report, Paris 7.

Greville Corbett, 1987. *The World's Major Languages*, chapter Serbo-Croat, pages 391–490. Oxford University Press.

Denys Duchier and Ralph Debusmann. 2001. Topological dependency trees: A constraint-based account of linear precedence. In *Proceedings of the 39th Annual Meeting on Association for Computational Linguistics*, pages 180–187. Association for Computational Linguistics.

Kim Gerdes and Sylvain Kahane. 2001. Word order in German: A formal dependency grammar using a topological hierarchy. In *Proceedings of the 39th annual meeting on association for computational linguistics*, pages 220–227. Association for Computational Linguistics.

Thomas Groß and Timothy Osborne. 2009. Toward a practical dependency grammar theory of discontinuities. *SKY Journal of Linguistics*, 22:43–90.

Thomas Groß and Timothy Osborne. 2015. The Dependency Status of Function Words: Auxiliaries. In *Proceedings of the 3rd International Conference on Dependency Linguistics (DepLing2015)*, pages 111–120.

Thomas Groß. 2011. Clitics in Dependency Morphology. In *Proceedings of the 1st International Conference on Dependency Linguistics (DepLing 2011)*.

Jan Hajič, Jarmila Panevová, Eva Buráňová, Zdeňka Urešová, and Alla Bémová. 1999. Annotations at analytical level. Instructions for annotators. *UK MFF ÚFAL, Praha, Czech Republic. URL http://ufal. mff. cuni. cz/pdt2. 0/doc/manuals/en/a-layer/pdf/a-man-en. pdf (2012-03-18)*.

Eva Hajičová, Jiří Havelka, Petr Sgall, Kateřina Veselá, and Daniel Zeman. 2004. Issues of Projectivity in the Prague Dependency Treebank. *Prague Bull. Math. Linguistics*, 81:5–22.

Jiří Havelka. 2007. Beyond Projectivity: Multilingual Evaluation of Constraints and Measures on Non-Projective Structures. In *ANNUAL MEETING-ASSOCIATION FOR COMPUTATIONAL LINGUISTICS*, volume 45, page 608.

Milka Ivić, editor. 2005. *Sintaksa savremenog srpskog jezika*. Institut za srpski jezik SANU, Beograd.

Bojana Jakovljević, Aleksandar Kovačević, Milan Sečujski, and Maja Marković. 2014. A dependency treebank for Serbian: Initial experiments. In *International Conference on Speech and Computer*, pages 42–49. Springer.

Iliyana Krapova. 1995. Auxiliaries and complex tenses in Bulgarian. In W. Browne, E. Domisch, N. Kondrašova, and D. Zec, editors, *Annual workshop on Formal approaches to Slavic linguistics. The Cornell meeting*, pages 320–344. Ann Arbor: Michigan Slavic Publications.

Marco Kuhlmann and Joakim Nivre. 2006. Mildly Non-Projective Dependency Structures. In *Proceedings of the COLING/ACL on Main conference poster sessions*, pages 507–514. Association for Computational Linguistics.

Anna Kupść and Jesse Tseng. 2005. A new HPSG approach to Polish auxiliary constructions. In S. Müller, editor, *Proceedings of the 12th International Conference on Head-Driven Phrase Structure Grammar*, pages 253–273. Stanford: CSLI Publications.

Francesco Mambrini and Marco Passarotti. 2013. Non-Projectivity in the Ancient Greek Dependency Treebank. In *Proceedings of the 2nd Internanctional Conference on Dependency Linguistics (DepLing 2013)*, volume 177.

Prashanth Mannem, Himani Chaudhry, and Akshar Bharati. 2009. Insights into non-projectivity in Hindi. In *Proceedings of the ACL-IJCNLP 2009 Student Research Workshop*, pages 10–17. Association for Computational Linguistics.

Jasmina Milićević. 2009. Serbian Auxiliary Verbs: Syntactic Heads or Dependents? In W. Cichocki, editor, *Proceedings of the 31st Annual Conference of the Atlantic Provinces Linguistics Association*, pages 43–53. PAMAPLA 31.

John Robert Ross. 1967. *Constraints on variables in Syntax*. Ph.D. thesis, MIT.

Tanja Samardžić, Mirjana Starović, Željko Agić, and Nikola Ljubešić. 2017. Universal Dependencies for Serbian in Comparison with Croatian and Other Slavic Languages. In *The 6th Workshop on Balto-Slavic Natural Language Processing (BSNLP 2017)*.

Živojin Stanojčić and Ljubomir Popović. 2012. *Gramatika srpskog jezika*. Zavod za udžbenike.

Prices go up, surge, jump, spike, skyrocket, go through the roof…
Intensifier Collocations with Parametric Nouns of Type PRICE

Jasmina Milićević
Department of French,
Dalhousie University
Halifax
Canada
jmilicev@dal.ca

Abstract

The paper looks into the expression of intensification with parametric nouns such as PRICE, COST, FEE, RATE, etc., focusing on collocations these nouns form with intensifying adjectives, inchoative and causative intensifying verbs and corresponding de-verbal nouns. Degrees of intensification possible with these nouns are discussed, as well as analytical vs. synthetic expression of intensification (*a steep increase in prices* ~ *a spike in prices*). Sample lexicalization rules are proposed—namely, rules that map semantic representations of intensifier collocations headed by nouns of this type to their deep-syntactic representations. The theoretical framework of the paper is Meaning-Text linguistic theory.

1 The Problem Stated

The paper looks into the expression of intensification with parametric nouns such as PRICE, COST, FEE, RATE, etc., hereafter *PRICE type nouns*, or {N_{PRICE}} for short (see Table 1, Section 3 below). More precisely, it describes collocations these nouns form with intensifying adjectives, as well as with inchoative and causative intensifying verbs and corresponding de-verbal nouns. A cursory comparison is provided with antonymic, i.e., attenuating, expressions entering in collocations with {N_{PRICE}}.

A parametric noun (cf. Mel'čuk, 2013: 214) corresponds to (at least) a two-place predicate, 'P of X is α', with X being the thing parameterized and α, the value of the parameter: *the price$_P$ [of gas]$_X$ is [$1.85 per gallon]$_α$, the*

speed$_P$ [of the vehicle]$_X$ is [70 miles per hour]$_α$, the quantity$_P$ [of oil]$_X$ is [30 tons]$_α$, etc.[1]

The α value may not be explicitly quantified, but characterized as being big or small (on some scale): *The price of gas is high. | The speed of the vehicle is low. | The quantity of oil is huge. | Etc.*

I will be interested namely in the case where α of an N_{PRICE}, without being explicitly quantified, is qualified as high, or 'big' [STATIVE], or rising—'getting bigger'—[INCHOATIVE], or else being caused to rise [CAUSATIVE]. These cases are illustrated, respectively, in (1), (2) and (3); the examples come from Google searches (some have been slightly modified).

(1) STATIVE: '⟦P of X being α,⟧ α is (very) big', etc.

   a. *Post-paid service plans often charge* **steep** ⟨**astronomical, prohibitive**⟩ *overage FEES.*

   b. *California divorce COST is* **high** ⟨**whooping high, exorbitant**⟩.

(2) INCHOATIVE: '⟦P of X being α,⟧ α begins to be bigger than α′ by β (β being big)'

   a. *Electricity COSTS* **went up** ⟨**rose sharply, surged, skyrocketed**⟩ *in August.*

   b. *Make sure your mortgage payments do not increase1 if there is a* **rise** ⟨**a major hike, a spike**⟩ *in interest RATES.*

---

[1] An N_{PRICE} parametric noun typically has additional dependents; thus, the person who determines the price of something corresponds to an argument (in our terms, semantic actant) of PRICE; similarly, the person who incurs the cost of something corresponds to a semantic actant of COST; FEE has two additional semantic atants: the one who sets it and the one who pays it; and so on. These actants are not directly relevant for the present discussion.

Proceedings of the Fourth International Conference on Dependency Linguistics (Depling 2017), pages 145-153,
Pisa, Italy, September 18-20 2017

(3) CAUSATIVE: '[[P of X being α,]] α is caused to begin to be bigger …'

   a. *Massive regulation of the health care industry **causes** the PRICES to **increase**1 ⟨to **go way up**, to **go through the roof**⟩.*

   b. *Higher mortgage rates **spurred** an **increase** ⟨a **jump**, a **surge**⟩ in home SALES.*

   c. *If you're running for office you don't want to be known as the person **who increased**2 ⟨**hiked up**⟩ TAXES.*[2]

The paper will focus on two phenomena, observed in the examples above:

1) Varying degrees of intensification expressed by {N$_{\text{PRICE}}$} collocates.

Thus, *steep < astronomical*; *go up < skyrocket << go through the roof*; *a rise < a spike*; *raise < hike up*; and so on.

2) Synthetic vs. analytical expression of intensification in collocations headed by {N$_{\text{PRICE}}$}.

High(er) degree of intensification can be expressed either by an N$_{\text{PRICE}}$ collocate itself or by a separate lexeme (underlined in the examples below), which gives rise to approximate equivalences: [cost is] *exorbitant* ⟨*whooping high*⟩; [costs] *skyrocket* ⟨*rise <u>sharply</u>*⟩; *hike up* [prices] ⟨*cause a <u>substantial</u> rise* [in prices]⟩; etc. When intensification is expressed analytically, the collocate of an N$_{\text{PRICE}}$ is itself intensified, serving as the base of the corresponding collocation of "second order", as it were.

These phenomena will be described from the viewpoint of Meaning-Text linguistic theory [MTT], in particular, its lexicological branch, *Explanatory Combinatorial Lexicology* (Mel'čuk, 2006), and its dependency-based semantics and syntax (Mel'čuk, 2012, 2013 and 2015).

The rest of the paper is structured as follows: a brief review of formal means used in the Meaning-Text approach to describe intensification: the lexical function Magn 'big'/'intense' and other related lexical functions (Section 2); an overview of {N$_{\text{PRICE}}$} and intensifying expressions with which they combine (Section 3); degrees of intensification expressed by collocates of {N$_{\text{PRICE}}$} and their lexicographic treatment (Section 4); a sketch of lexicalization rules for analytical vs. synthetic expression of intensification with {N$_{\text{PRICE}}$}, i.e., rules that map semantic representations of the corresponding collocations to their deep-syntactic representations (Section 5); conclusion (Section 6).

Data used in the paper come from a collocation database that Igor Mel'čuk kindly let me use, *Longman Dictionary of Contemporary English* [LDOCE, www.ldoce.online.com], and the WWW.

The collocation database consists of over 15,000 entries (entry count is per collocate, not per headword). The number of intensifier collocations is some 4,000; only a small proportion of those are headed by {N$_{\text{PRICE}}$}. For the purposes of this paper, collocations were added and data complemented from the two other sources.

Linguistic literature on intensification is extremely rich and even a cursory survey thereof is impossible here; some of the works I consulted are Greenbaum (1970), Quirk *et al.* (1985: 589*ff*), Altemberg (1991), Kennedy & McNally (2005), Cacchiani (2004), Gallardo (2008), Méndez-Naya, ed. (2008), Fleischhauer (2013), Bertinetto & Civardi (2015) and van Der Wouden & Foolen (2017). Within Meaning-Text approach, various aspects of intensification were treated, for instance, in Boguslavskij & Iomdin (2000), Iordanskaja & Polguère (2005), Grossman & Tutin (2007) and Milićević & Timošenko (2014).

2   Meaning-Text Description of Intensification: Magn and Related Lexical Functions

2.1   Collocations and Lexical Functions

In the MTT framework, collocations are described in terms of lexical functions [LFs]. Since LFs are quite well known, there is no need to introduce them here (the interested reader may consult, for instance, Wanner, ed., 1996 and Mel'čuk, 2015: 155-279) and we can pass directly to the LFs relevant for the present discussion: Magn, Plus, IncepPredPlus, and CausPredPlus. But first, two important facts, holding for all LFs, should be noted.

• The meaning of an LF is actually a cluster of several related meanings, similar to the meaning of a grammeme, which also "stands for" a cluster of several meanings; for instance, the grammeme 'plural' can mean 'more than one' [*three books*], 'a kind of' [*three cheeses*], 'a big quantity of' [*the sands of the desert*], and so on. This explains the recourse to several glosses

---

[2] INCREASE1 'become bigger' is an intransitive verb, and INCREASE2 the corresponding causative verb.

indicating the meaning of some LFs, such as Magn (see immediately below).

• Elements of the value that an LF returns for a given headword are not perfectly synonymous (this may be the case even if we consider just one particular meaning of the LF, as mentioned in the preceding paragraph); in fact, sometimes they display obvious semantic differences, which in case of intensifiers may go beyond varying degrees of intensification. Thus, for instance, [a] *spike* [in prices] is not only more intense than [a] *rise* but also quicker, [prices] *go through the roof* means that they rise very high from an already high starting level, and so on (for more on this, see Section 3). However, such differences can be ignored in contexts where precision and attention to detail are not paramount, i.e., in most everyday discourse situations.

2.2 Lexical Functions Magn and Plus

The LF Magn is an adjectival/adverbial modifier whose meaning is 'intense(ly)', 'big', 'much'/'many'.

Here are examples of Magn type collocations as they would appear in an English *Explanatory Combinatorial Dictionary* [ECD] (where collocates are listed in the entries of their headwords):

NUMBER$_{(N)}$ 'quantity'
Magn: *large, sizeable, //myriad, << huge, << record-breaking, << unprecedented, << //gazillion*

FIGURE$_{(N)}$ 'number'
Magn: *high, << huge, << staggering*

SHORTAGE
Magn: *severe, acute*
Magn^{temp}: *chronic*

INFLATION
Magn^{quant}: *widespread, rampant*
impossible to control Magn: *<< runaway*

COST$_{(N)}$
Magn: *high, significant, < huge, << astronomical, << exorbitant*

SPENDING$_{(N)}$
Magn$_2$: *strong*
[AntiBon+Magn$_2$]: *lavish*

The symbol "//" precedes a fused element of the value of an LF, expressing together, i.e., in one word, the meaning of the headword and the intensification; thus, *myriad* means 'huge number'.

Degrees of intensification are indicated by the symbols "<" (more) and "<<" (much more). (Another way to specify intensification degrees is to use degree Roman superscripts; see Section 4.)

Superscripted semantic features, such as ^{temp} and ^{quant} above, identify the dimension of the meaning of the headword that is being intensified. Subscripted Arabic numerals, as in Magn$_2$, indicate the semantic actant of the headword on which the intensification bears. (In this particular case, these are the things for which the spending takes place; cf. *military* ⟨*defense, capital*⟩ *spending*).

Non-standard components, such as impossible to control, capture the additional meaning carried by a given collocate with respect to the basic meaning of the relevant LF; we will see more of these in Section 3.

The last example features a configuration of LFs, made up of a complex LF AntiBon 'not good according to the Speaker', and the already seen Magn$_2$. Intensifying LFs often enter into such configurations. For some examples of the LF AntiMagn, see Table 2 in Section 3.

Like Magn, the LF Plus is a quantitative modifier, a comparison marker meaning 'to a greater extent'; its antonym is Minus 'to a lesser extent'. Both appear only in complex LFs, either with Magn (e.g., PlusMagn(ALERT): *heightened*; PlusMagn(CONCERN): *growing*; MinusMagn(DISCIPLINE): *failing*) or with Incep and Pred (see immediately below).

2.3 Lexical Functions IncepPredPlus and CausPredPlus

These are complex verbal LFs, made up of the following simple LFs: the verb Pred 'to.be', the already seen comparison marker Plus 'more', and the verb Incep 'begin', respectively Caus 'to.cause'. Thus, IncepPredPlus means 'begin to be bigger (than before/than something else by some value)' and IncepPredPlus—'cause something [to begin] to be bigger (than before/than something else by some value)'. For instance:

NUMBER$_{(N)}$ 'quantity'
IncepPredPlus: *grow*
quickly IncepPredPlus: *<< explode*

COST$_{(N)}$
IncepPredPlus: *go up, rise, increase1*
very quickly IncepPredPlus: *<< (sky)rocket*
CausPredPlus: *drive up* [ART ~], *push* [ART ~] *up/higher*

Caus$_2$PredPlus: *raise* [ART ~][3]

For some examples of the antonyms of these two LFs, the attenuators `IncepPredMinus` and `CausPredMinus`, see Tables 4 & 5 below.

3 Intensification with PRICE-type Parametric Nouns

{N$_{PRICE}$} have a "natural" and very rich co-occurrence with expressions of intensification (this is why they have been selected for this study). The nouns are presented first, and then their intensifying (and some of attenuating) collocates.

3.1 The Domain of {N$_{PRICE}$}

Here are some nouns belonging to the set {N$_{PRICE}$}:

amount	*deficit*	**interest**	**rate**
budget	**expense(s)**	*investment*	*sales*
business	*fare*	*level*	*spending*
charge(s)	**fee**	**mortgage**	**stock(s)**
cost(s)	*figure*	*number*	**tax(es)**
debt	**inflation**	**price(s)**	*wage(s)*

Table 1. Some members of {N$_{PRICE}$}

The bolded nouns are the core items of the set; the co-occurrence data supplied below applies in the first place to these nouns and is shared to a somewhat lesser extent, albeit quite robustly, with the remaining items (for more on this, and for some frequency data, see the end of this section).

Other, semantically more distant nouns such as *employment, enrolment, turnout*, etc., share some co-occurrence with {N$_{PRICE}$}.

Some of the nouns in Table 1 are used (in the relevant sense) only in the plural (e.g. *sales*) or are much more frequently used in the plural (those with the plural marker in parentheses). In some cases, there is a meaning difference between the plural and the singular form (i.e., they represent two different lexemes); for instance, *costs* 'expenses' vs. *cost* = 'price'.

The underscored nouns can combine with some other nouns from the set, as in **Inflation levels** *are high*; **Mortgage rates** *went up*; *The* **amount of sales** *increased*ı; etc., but they easily

undergo ellipsis: **Inflation** *is high*; **Mortgage** *went up*; *The* **sales** *increased*ı. Conversely, there are instances where these nouns are used alone, such as *The* **rate(s)** *increased*ı; *The* **figures/numbers** *are up*; etc.[4]

3.2 Intensifiers of {N$_{PRICE}$}

Tables 2-5 show the most common intensifying collocates of {N$_{PRICE}$}; attenuating collocates are indicated as well, for comparison.

In the tables, the non-standard components of an LF meaning (`abruptly & quickly, from a high level, impossible to control`, etc.) precede the elements of LF value which express them; these components are based on LDOCE's definitions of the corresponding lexical units. Intensification levels are tentatively indicated as Degree I and Degree II/III.

Magn 'big'	
Degree I	Degree II/III
high; *steep*	*astronomical*; *exorbitant*; `making Oper1 impossible` *prohibitive*; `impossible to control` *runaway*; *staggering*
Plus 'to a greater extent'	
Degree I	Degree II/III
growing	*galloping*
AntiMagn 'small'	
Degree I	Degree II/III
low < modest	*negligible*
Minus 'to a smaller extent'	
Degree I	Degree II/III
falling	*dwindling*

Table 2. Degree adjectives combining with {N$_{PRICE}$}

Two adjectival modifiers non-specific to {N$_{PRICE}$}, **colloq.** *whooping* 'very large [physically]' and **colloq.** *jaw-dropping* 'very impressive or surprising' are indiscriminately used as higher-level intensifiers or attenuators.[5]

---

[3] Examples for the last two LFs: *Increasing fuel prices also drive up the cost of food* (the Cause is external, i.e., not an actant of the headword, so `Caus` bears no actantial subscripts); *Apple quietly raised the cost of some of its machines* (the Causer is internal, coinciding with the SemA 2 of the headword, i.e., the person who determines the cost, which is shown by the actantial superscript accompanying `Caus`).

[4] These are of course two different types of ellipsis. The first ellipsis type is seen also in the expressions such as *The* ~~(exchange) rate of the~~ *US dollar fell/rose against the Japanese Yen*.

[5] Examples: *Nike debuts a pair of sunglasses at the Rio Olympics for a jaw-dropping cost of $1,200* [by anyone's standard, this must be 'very high']. | *The price is jaw-dropping, 9 dollars per bottle*. [For quality wine, this means 'very low'.] | *Yet another whopping pay raise* ['very big', or, ironically, 'very small'].

IncepPredPlus 'become +'	
Degree I	Degree II/III
gradually creep *up; go up; grow; increase*1*; rise*	to a very high level *go through the roof;* abruptly *jump, surge, shoot up, spike, zoom;* abruptly & quickly *balloon, escalate, explode;* quickly, to a high level *soar;* quickly, by a large amount *(sky)rocket*
IncepPredMinus 'become –'	
Degree I	Degree II/III
gradually cool; decrease; for a short time *dip; drop; fall; go down*	abruptly, to a very low level *crash;* gradually, to a very low level *dwindle;* abruptly, by a large amount *plummet, plunge, tumble*

Table 3. Inchoative degree-verbs combining with {N$_{PRICE}$}

CausPredPlus 'cause to become +'	
Degree I	Degree II/III
*boost; drive up; increase*2*; push up/higher; put up; raise; send up*	deliberately *hike up, ramp up; send sky-high/soaring, send through the roof*
CausPredMinus 'cause to become –'	
Degree I	Degree II/III
cut; drive down; push down/lower; reduce; send down	*slash*

Table 4. Causative degree-verbs combining with {N$_{PRICE}$}

S$_0$IncepPredPlus	
Degree I	Degree II/III
growth; increase(N)*; rise*(N)	*jump*(N)*; escalation; explosion; spike*(N)*; surge*(N)
S$_0$IncepPredMinus	
Degree I	Degree II/III
drop(N)*; dip*(N)	*crash*(N)
S$_0$CausPredPlus	
Degree I	Degree II/III
raise(N)	*hike*(N)*; rump-up*
S$_0$CausPredMinus	
Degree I	Degree II/III
cut(N)*; reduction*	

Table 5. Degree nouns combining with {N$_{PRICE}$}

Many collocates (both intensifiers and attenuators) are metaphorically derived from independent lexical units denoting basic spatial positions (up/down) or changes thereof (rise/fall, jump/dip; hike up/push down), as well as violent physical phenomena (explosion/crash).

As mentioned at the beginning of this section, most of the collocates listed in Tables 2-5 combine with the nouns in Table 1, but some of them fit some nouns better than others. For example, in a cursory www search, *ballooned* was most frequently found in combination with

costs (40,700 hits), significantly less so with *prices* (6,210) and infrequently with *fees* (1,230). Similarly, *crashed* was found co-occurring most often with *prices* (61,100 hits), more rarely with *stock* (19,100), and hardly ever with *fees* (349). On the other hand, some nouns have more specific collocates, not used with other nouns.

Degree I intensity collocates seem to fit virtually all nouns from {N$_{PRICE}$}, those of Degree II/III may have a less close fit with some of the nouns.

Table 6 features common intensifiers of some (for the most part) Degree I intensifying and attenuating collocates of {N$_{PRICE}$}.

Magn of Magn/AntiMagn	
Degree I	Degree II/III
very	*extremely,* **colloq.** *whooping*
Magn of IncepPredPlus/Minus	
Degree I	Degree II/III
a lot; considerably; markedly; significantly; sharply; steeply; substantially; **colloq.** *way*	abruptly, by a large amount *dramatically*
Magn of S$_0$IncepPredPlus/Minus	
Degree I	Degree II/III
considerable; major; sharp; steep; substantial	abrupt, by a large amount *dramatic*

Table 6. Intensifiers of {N$_{PRICE}$} degree collocates

The same intensifiers combine with high- and low degree expressing collocates of {N$_{PRICE}$}; for instance, ***very*** ⟨***extremely, whooping***⟩ *low/high* **prices**; **Stocks** *rose/fell* **sharply** ⟨***considerably, dramatically***⟩; and so on.

To sum up, while some interesting generalizations over collocates of {N$_{PRICE}$} are possible, it is still necessary to describe the co-occurrence for each noun individually. More on this will be said in Conclusion.

4 Degrees of Intensification with PRICE-type Parametric Nouns

As mentioned previously, *ECD* lexicographers use three degrees of intensification with Magn type LFs: 'intense', 'very intense, and 'very very intense'. Some data from the collocation database I consulted are presented in Table 7, next page.

The 3-way distinction is based on linguistic intuition and has not been specifically theorized within this framework.

In the linguistic literature on intensification, some authors use three degrees (e.g., Cacchiani, 2004), as above, and others, two: relative and high (e.g., Gallardo, 2009).[6] However, the theoretical bases of or linguistic evidence for these distinctions are hardly ever discussed.

	Magn	Magn <	Magn <<
DANGER	*big, grave, great*		*mortal*
DIFFER-ENCE	*big, fundamental, significant, sharp, stark, striking, vast*	*crucial, enormous, huge, key*	
DIFFER-ENT	*basically, distinctly, dramatically, markedly, starkly, strikingly*		*completely, entirely, //poles apart, radically, totally*
EPIDEM-IC(N)	*major, vast*	*sweeping*	
EVI-DENCE	*quant ample, clear, cogent, compelling, convincing, dramatic, quant mountainous, strong, unambiguous*	*conclusive, incontrovertible, irrefutable*	
FACT	*True*	*well-established, well-known*	*irrefutable*
PAIN	*keen, temp-nagging, searing, severe, sharp, temp unrelenting*	*killer-*	*excruciating, extreme, gut-wrenching*
SPEED(N)	*High*	*breathtaking, lightning*	*breakneck*
TIRED	*//exhausted, to the bone, very, //washed out*	*completely, extremely*	
TOLL	*heavy*	*devastating*	

Table 7. Degrees of Magn in an ECD database (excerpts)

In domains such as ours, degrees of intensification could be determined rather objectively, by reference to numerical values of the parameters in question. That is, we could try and find

conceptual correlates for intensification degrees admitted by {N_PRICE}.

Let us assume the following Semantic Structure [SemS] for the LF IncepPredPlus (on semantic representations in MTT, see, for instance, Mel'čuk, 2012: 161-394):

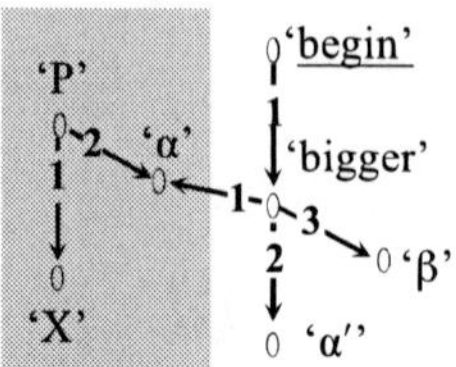

Figure 1. SemS of the LF IncepPredPlus

NB: The semanteme configuration in the shaded area of *Figure 1* is not the part of the meaning of the LF IncepPredPlus: it represents the context (or conditions) in which the configuration 'begin being bigger ...' can be implemented, at the deep-syntactic level, by the LF in question. (This context is actually a generalized SemS of the corresponding collocation base with its SemA 1.) See the lexicalization rules in *Figure 3*.

A note on the actants of the semanteme 'bigger' is in order: in 'α is bigger than α′ by β, 'α' is the value [of something] that is being compared with 'α′', which is either 'α' at some previous time point or the value of another parameter; the meaning 'β' is obvious—the value representing the difference between 'α' and 'α′'. Thus, *Prices go up* means 'prices [of something] are α, α being bigger than α′ [= α before the change] by β', and *Prices of wheat are higher than prices of barley* means 'prices of wheat are α, α being bigger than α′, prices of barley, by β'.

Some possible instantiations of the SemS in Figure 1 follow:

(4) a. *Between 1850 and 1854 prices_P of wheat_X jumped by 60%* [β].

   b. *The price_P of natural gas_X rose above $5 per mcf* [α].

   c. *Gasoline_X prices_P will increase1 by 10%* [β], *to 1.65 euros per liter* [α].

   d. *Crude oil_X prices_P spiked from $13* [α′] *to roughly $34 per barrel* [α], *i.e., by some 38%* [β].

As we can see, specific lexicalizations of the meaning of IncepPredPlus correlate with actual numerical values of the parameter P. Therefore, we could posit that higher degree inchoative verbs are used if the value of β exceeds a

---

certain percentage point or if α is bigger than α' by certain amount, and so on. The same reasoning could be used to determine whether a two- or three-degree distinction is necessary for degrees of intensification.

This kind of precision would be in order if we were to elaborate entries for a terminological database or a lexicon to be used in some NLP applications. For our purposes, however, it is enough to determine the relative values of the parameter.

Speaking about linguistic evidence, it is clearly there to corroborate a two-degree distinction; cf., for instance, the incompatibility of higher degree nouns and verbs with *slight(ly)/a bit* (a *slight increase/*surge*; *costs rose/*spiked slightly*) or the incompatibility of higher degree adjectives with VERY/A LOT (*very high ⟨steep⟩* vs. *very *staggering*). However, the evidence is hard to come by when it comes to distinguishing between (the putative) Degrees II and III.

For the time being, I will refrain from making too fine distinctions and will use two degrees of intensification: high, and very high, which will be indicated by degree superscripts accompanying the relevant LFs: $\mathtt{Magn^I}$ vs. $\mathtt{Magn^{II}}$, $\mathtt{IncepPredPlus^I}$ vs. $\mathtt{IncepPredPlus^{II}}$, and $\mathtt{CausPredPlus^I}$ vs. $\mathtt{CausPredPlus^{II}}$. (The same superscripts can be used with attenuating LFs).[7]

Thus, the SemS in Figure 1 above is actually good for $\mathtt{IncepPredPlus^I}$, and that of $\mathtt{IncepPredPlus^{II}}$ looks like this:

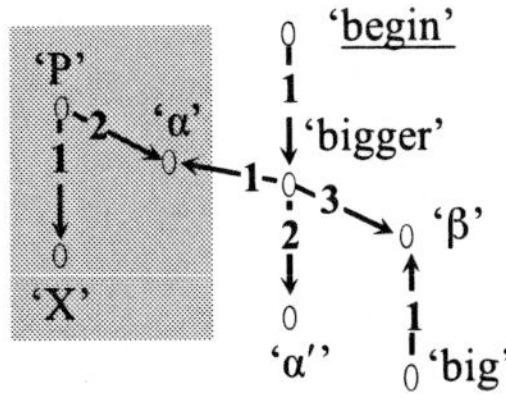

Figure 2. SemS of the LF $\mathtt{IncepPredPlus^{II}}$

This is a generalized representation, capturing the core meaning of this LF; in actual fact, either α or α' (or both) can also be characterized as 'big', which will trigger specific lexicalizations: if α is 'big' (plus the non-standard component 'quickly' is present), then *soar* is an appropriate lexicalization, if both α and α' are big, ⌜*go through the roof*⌝ is OK, and so on.

---

[7] While the Roman superscript notation is sporadically found (in the MTT literature) with $\mathtt{Magn}$ type LFs, it is standardly used with realization LFs to indicate "degrees" of realization.

5 Sample Lexicalization Rules for Intensifiers of PRICE-type Parametric Nouns

As indicated in Section 1, higher degree of intensification with $\{\mathrm{N_{PRICE}}\}$ nouns can be expressed synthetically, within an $\mathrm{N_{PRICE}}$ collocate, or analytically, by a separate lexical unit forming a collocation with the $\mathrm{N_{PRICE}}$ collocate as the headword; this gives rise to equivalences such as these:

(5) a. *Alberta crop crisis **sent** wheat PRICES **through the roof**$_{\mathtt{CausPredPlus^{II}}}$.*

   b. *Alberta crop crisis **caused**$_{\mathtt{Caus}}$ wheat PRICES **to shoot up**$_{\mathtt{IncepPredPlus^{II}}}$.*

   c. *Alberta crop crisis **spurred**$_{\mathtt{Caus}}$ a sharp-$_{\mathtt{Magn}}$ **increase**$\mathtt{1_{S0\,IncepPredPlus^I}}$ in wheat PRICES.*

   d. *Wheat PRICES **spiked**$_{\mathtt{IncepPredPlus^{II}}}$ ⟨**rose**$_{\mathtt{IncepPredPlus^I}}$ **steeply**$_{\mathtt{Magn^I}}$, **got**$_{\mathtt{Incep}}$ **much**$_{\mathtt{Magn^I}}$ **higher**$_{\mathtt{Plus}}$⟩ ⌜in the wake of⌝$_{\mathtt{Adv_2Caus}}$ Alberta crop crisis.*

These sentences are mutual paraphrases: they express the same meaning—'Alberta crop crisis caused wheat prices to begin being much bigger'—but they do so more and more analytically, as it were, as we go from (5a) to (5d).

In MTT framework, there are two ways to produce these sentences:

1) by alternative lexicalizations from their common semantic structure, through application of semantic-to-deep syntax mapping rules (e.g., Mel'čuk, 2013: 188-259);

2) by meaning-preserving reformulations of the deep-syntactic structure of any of these sentences, through application of deep-syntactic equivalence, or paraphrasing, rules (e.g., Mel'čuk, 2013: 137-188).

In what follows, I will illustrate the first rule type.

Sample rules for synthetic vs. analytic implementation of inchoative high intensity verbs are given in Figure 3, next page. (Some lexicalization rules for the FL $\mathtt{Magn}$ can be found in Mel'čuk 2013: 213-214.)

These rules are needed (among others) to produce paraphrases such as those in example (5d) above.

Similar lexicalization rules can be written for other intensifying (and attenuating) LFs.

6 Conclusion

The paper discussed intensifier collocations of parametric nouns of type PRICE, in particular degrees of intensification and analytical vs. synthetic expression of intensification possible with these nouns.

While all the nouns considered share to a considerable extent the co-occurrence with intensifiers—in particular Degree I intensifiers, they also have their own, idiosyncratic, collocates, a finding consistent with the collocation phenomenon in general. Thus, a generalized lexicographic entry for the nouns belonging to {N_PRICE} can be envisaged, but this does not obviate the need for recording intensifier collocations for each member of the set, in their respective lexicographic entries.

Two degrees of intensification, high and very high, were suggested for these nouns' collocates, along with the corresponding formal lexicographic treatment within the Meaning-Text paradigm.

Sample lexicalization rules for intensifier collocation headed by members of {N_PRICE} were proposed, taking into account the possibility of analytical and synthetic expression of intensification, i.e., by a separate lexeme, a collocate of an {N_PRICE} intensifier (*a **steep rise** in PRICES ⟨TAXES, FEES⟩; SALES ⟨STOCKS⟩ **rose dramatically***), or within the intensifier itself (*a **hike** in PRICES ⟨TAXES, FEES⟩; SALES ⟨STOCKS⟩ **went through the roof***).

Attenuating collocates of {N_PRICE} were considered in a cursory way, insofar as they provided a basis for comparison with the intensifying collocates. Preliminary findings point to two differences: attenuators are not as numerous as intensifiers, and they are even less prone to a three-degree distinction of intensity.

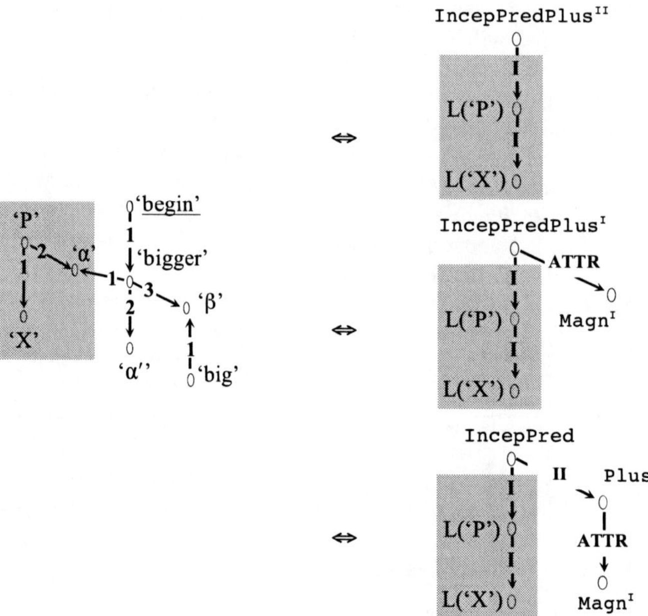

Figure 3. Lexicalization rules for the FL IncepPredPlus^II

Future work could focus on determining, based on a larger corpus of data, if two degrees of intensification are enough to cover all the cases of intensification (as tentatively suggested here) or, on the contrary, a three-degree distinction is necessary. Other topic to explore include factors determining the choice of intensifier collocates of PRICE type nouns (e.g., how high a rise in prices should be in order for it be called *a spike*, etc.), as well as preference rules for analytical vs. synthetic expression of intensification with the nouns of this type. Plus, of course, a closer look at attenuation, along the same lines.

Acknowledgments

I am grateful to Igor Mel'čuk for generously letting me use his database of lexical functions for English, as well as for his most helpful remarks on a pre-final version of this paper. Thanks are also due to three anonymous reviewers, whose comments allowed me to improve some aspects of the paper.

References

Altemberg, Bengt. 1991. Amplifier Collocations in Spoken English. In Johanson, S. & Stenström, A.-B., eds, *English Computer Corpora. Selected Papers and Research Guide*, Mouton de Gruyter, Berlin/New York, p. 127-149.

Bertinetto, Pier Marco & Civardi, Eugenio. 2015. The Semantics of Degree Verbs and the Telicity Issue. *Borealis: An International Journal of Hispanic Linguistics*, 4(1): 57-77.

Boguslavskij, Igor & Iomdin, Leonid. 2000. Semantika medlennosti [The Semantics of Slowness]. *Slovo v tekste i v slovare. Sbornik stat'ej k 70-letiju akademika Ju. D. Apresjana*. Jazyki russkoj kul'tury, Moskva, p. 52-60.

Cacchiani, Silvia, 2004. Towards a Model for Investigating Predicate-Intensifier Collocations. *Proceedings of EURALEX 2004*, p. 943-947.

Fleischhauer, Jens. 2013. Interaction of Telicity and Degree Gradation in Change of State Verbs. In Arsenijević, B., Gehrke, B. & Marín, R., eds, *Studies in the Composition and Decomposition of Event Predicates*. Springer, Dordrecht, p. 125-152.

Gallardo, Catherine. 2009. L'intensification dans les expressions figées françaises à coordination interne. *Lingvisticæ Investigationes*, 32(2): 238-252.

Greenbaum, Sidney. 1970. *Verb-Intensifier Collocations in English: An Experimental Approach*. Mouton, The Hague/Paris.

Grossmann, Francis & Tutin, Agnès. 2007. Motivation of Lexical Functions in Collocations: The Case of Intensifiers Denoting 'Joy'. In Wanner, Leo, ed., *Selected Lexical and Grammatical Issues in the Meaning-Text Theory. In Honour of Igor Mel'čuk*. Benjamins, Amsterdam/Philadelphia, p. 140-165.

Iordanskaja, Lidija & Polguère, Alain. 2005. Hooking up Syntagmatic Lexical Functions to Lexicographic Definitions. In Apresjan, Ju. & Iomdin, L., eds, *East-West Encounter: Second International Conference on Meaning-Text Theory*. Slavic Culture Languages Publishing House, Moscow, p. 176-186.

Kennedy, Christopher & McNally, Louise. 2005. Scale Structure, Degree Modification, and the Semantics of Gradable Predicates. *Language*, 81, p. 345–381.

Mel'čuk, Igor. 2012, 2013, 2015. *Semantics. From Meaning to Text*, vols 1-3. John Benjamins, Amsterdam/Philadelphia.

Mel'čuk, Igor. 2006. Explanatory Combinatorial Dictionary. In Sica, G., ed., *Open Problems in Linguistics and Lexicography*. Polimetrica, Monza, p. 225–355.

Méndez-Naya, Bélen, ed. 2008. *Intensifiers, Special Issue of English Language and Linguistics*, 12(2).

Milićević, Jasmina & Timošenko, Svetlana. 2014. Towards a Fine-grained Description of Intensifying Adjectives for Text Processing. *Computational Linguistics and Intellectual Technologies. Proceedings of the Annual International Conference on Computational Linguistics, DIALOG 2014*, p. 427-440.

Quirk, Randolph, Greenbaum, Sidney, Leech, Geoffrey & Svartvik, Jan. 1985. *A Comprehensive Grammar of the English Language*. Longman, London.

Van Der Wouden, Ton & Foolen, Ad. 2017. A Most Serious and Extraordinary Problem. Intensification of Adjectives in Dutch, German, and English. *Leuvense Bijdragen*, 101: 82-100.

Wanner, Leo, ed. 1996. *Lexical Functions in Lexicography and Natural Language Processing*. Benjamins, Amsterdam/Philadelphia.

Chinese Descriptive and Resultative V-*de* Constructions
A Dependency-based Analysis

Ruochen Niu
Zhejiang University
Hangzhou
China
niuruochen@126.com

Abstract

This contribution presents a *dependency grammar* (DG) analysis of the so-called *descriptive and resultative V-de constructions* in Mandarin Chinese (VDCs); it focuses, in particular, on the dependency analysis of the noun phrase that intervenes between the two predicates in a VDC. Two methods, namely chunking data collected from informants and two diagnostics specific to Chinese, i.e. *bǎ* and *bèi* sentence formation, were used. They were employed to discern which analysis should be preferred, i.e. the ternary-branching analysis, in which the intervening NP (NP2) is a dependent of the first predicate (P1), or the small-clause analysis, in which NP2 depends on the second predicate (P2). The results obtained suggest a flexible structural analysis for VDCs in the form of "NP1+P1-*de*+NP2+P2". The difference in structural assignment is attributed to a semantic property of NP2 and the semantic relations it forms with adjacent predicates.

1 Introduction

The aim of this paper is to assign dependency structures to a familiar construction of Chinese, the *descriptive and resultative V-de constructions* (abbreviated as VDCs in following discussions). Having attracted considerable interest both at home in China and abroad, VDC has also been referred to as 得字句、得句型 '*de* construction', 状态补语 'stative complement' and 得字补语 '*de* complement' according to different scholars.

Until now, research efforts concerning VDCs have centered on the origin and lexical properties of *de* (e.g., Jinxi Li, 2000/1924, p. 178-181;

Chao, 1968, p. 350-358; Wang, 1985, p. 98-100, 103-105; Lin, 2011/1957, p. 69-71), categorization and typology (e.g., Li and Thompson, 1981; Zhu, 1982, p. 133; Chao Li, 2015), and semantic, syntactic, and pragmatic properties of the construction (e.g., Linding Li, 1986, p. 225-255; Huang, 1988; Yen-hui Audrey Li, 1990; Fan, 1993; Yafei Li, 1999; Gouguet, 2006; Zhang, 2006, p. 47-66, 155-161; Loar, 2011, p. 331-367). The big picture is that although many aspects of VDC have been studied, little agreement has been reached. This observation is particularly true of the hierarchical analysis.

Examples (1) and (2) are illustrations of the widely-assumed dichotomy between the *descriptive* and *resultative* VDCs (c.f., Li and Thompson, 1981; Yen-hui Audrey Li, 1990; Huang et al., 2009; Chao Li, 2015):

(1) (from Huang, 1988, p. 274)

Wǒ pǎo de hěn kuài.
I run DE very (be)fast
'I run very fast.'
我跑得很快。

(2) (EM=Emphasis)

Wǒ pǎo de xiédài   dōu diào le.
I run DE shoelaces EM loosen LE
'I ran to the extent that even my shoelaces got loose'
我跑得鞋带都掉了。

That *de* is the marker of this construction is easy to see, but a proper analysis of *de* is much more difficult to produce. There are three distinct stances in this regard: *De* has been treated as a preposition (e.g., Jinxi Li, 2000/1924, p. 178), as a suffix (e.g., Zhu, 1982, p. 32), and as a 结构助词 'structural function word', as opposed to a content word (e.g., Fan, 1993, p. 60; Zhang, 2006, p. 156). Following the majority position on this issue, i.e. the last of the three, the discussion

Proceedings of the Fourth International Conference on Dependency Linguistics (Depling 2017), pages 154-164,
Pisa, Italy, September 18-20 2017

here takes *de* as a function word that "clings to" its preceding predicate P1, and it is glossed as *-de* in the syntactic structures.

A notable feature of VDCs is the presence of two predicates.[1] For instance, in (1), the verb *pǎo* 'run' is a predicate that takes NP1 *wǒ* 'I' as its agent; on the other hand, the adjective *kuài* '(be)fast' is also a predicate that takes either the entity *wǒ* 'I' or the proposition *wǒ pǎo* 'I run' as its argument. In example (2), where there is an intervening NP *xiédài* 'shoelaces', NP1 *wǒ* 'I' is the agent of the first predicate *pǎo* 'run', and *xiédài* 'shoelaces' is the theme of the second predicate *diào* 'loosen'. The question, then, is which of the two predicates involved, the first predicate (P1) to the left or the second (P2) to the right, is the root of the sentence?

There has been a longstanding debate on the basic structural analysis just sketched (e.g., Li and Thompson, 1981; Huang, 1988; Osborne and Ma, 2015). Researchers in this area have attempted to address this problem by examining the forms of the two predicates during question formation, aspect marking and sentence negation. In particular, Huang (1988) has contributed to the establishment of the *Secondary Predication hypothesis* (in which P1 is the main predicate over P2) by reinvestigating the arguments for the opposite viewpoint and rebutting them cogently. Since the status of P1 and P2 is not the focus of this study, the discussion here takes Huang's claim for granted (also following Ding, 1961; Linding Li, 1986; Gouguet, 2006; Loar, 2011). Thus sentence (1) has the following dependency analysis, where P2 is a dependent of P1:

(3)

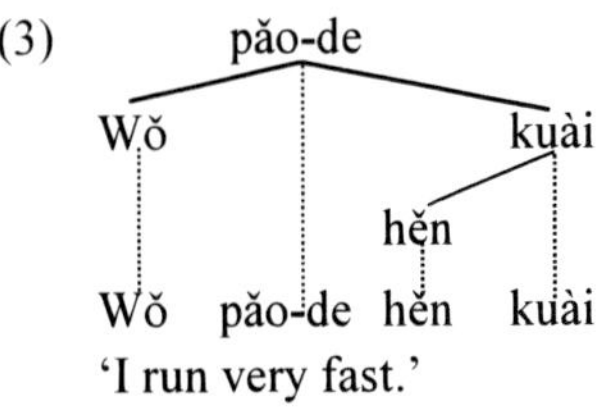

Difficulty arises when one attempts to assign structures to VDCs such as sentence (2), in which an intervening NP (NP2) appears between P1-*de* and P2. In previous studies regarding the status of NP2, a series of diagnostics were employed to discern to which predicate the intervening NP is closer in meaning and structure. These tests include: pause and interjection insertion (e.g., Ding 1961, p. 65; Zhu 1982, p. 136; Yafei Li, 1999, p. 458; Huang et al., 2009, p. 85), *bǎ* and *bèi* constructions (see section 3.2), adverbial insertion (e.g., Zhu, 1982, p. 135; Yafei Li, 1999, p. 459) and topicalization (e.g., Zhu, 1982, p. 136). Given that the diagnostics at times deliver contradictory results and that the validity of some of the tests are debatable (e.g., Chao Li 2015), no consensus has been reached about the best hierarchical analysis.

One noteworthy study that is directly related to VDCs with an intervening NP is Sun (2005). By examining how each type of construction behaves, Sun claims that there are four varying structures that have the form of "NP1+P1+'de'+NP2+P2". Insightful as it is, Sun's analysis does not include any diagrams. Thus, it is difficult to see what his interpretations of hierarchical structures might be.

Adopting DG as the theoretical framework, the account presented here strives to address the thorny issue just outlined: When there is an NP2 in the Chinese V-*de* constructions, should it be analyzed as a dependent of P1, or of P2? Compared to other theories of syntax, dependency grammar is by nature more straightforward and efficient in assigning hierarchical structures to natural languages. Nonetheless, there are few theoretically-oriented DG accounts of this construction (e.g., Osborne and Ma, 2015), let alone an analysis on the particular issue of the intervening NP.

To address the problem raised by contradictory diagnostics, the current study also employed chunking data to discern the best hierarchical analysis. The results suggest that VDCs with an

---

[1] To be precise, a small handful of adverbials can appear where P2 normally would be, adding intense extent to the statement denoted by P1. These degree adverbs, as noted by Chao Li (2015), are not predicative. Such adverbials include *hěn* 'very', *duō* 'much', *yuǎn* 'far', *yàomìng* 'almost killed sb', *lìhài* 'severely' and *bùxíng* 'not ok', e.g.,

(i) Wǒ   kùn   de   bùxíng
   I   (be)sleepy   DE   not ok
   'I am extremely sleepy.'
   我困得不行。

intervening NP enjoy flexible structures. Actual structure assignment, either as a ternary-branching analysis (in which NP2 is a dependent of P1) or a small-clause analysis (in which NP2 is dependent on P2), is determined by predicate-argument relationships between NP2 and the two predicates, results of the *bǎ* and *bèi* tests, and a semantic property of NP2.

2 Dependency grammar

2.1 Some principles

This subsection briefly introduces the theoretical framework adopted in this manuscript. Three principles of syntactic organization are assumed:

1. One-to-one mapping,
2. Strict headedness, and
3. Projective syntax

Like many other DGs, the current approach assumes one-to-one mapping whereby each atomic syntactic unit, i.e. each word, is mapped to exactly one node in the syntactic structure, and vice versa (e.g., Mel'čuk and Pertsov, 1987, p. 48, 57–8; Kahane, 1996, p. 45; Hudson, 2007, p. 183). In addition, the syntactic structures adopted in this DG are entirely headed, meaning that exocentric units are not possible. The current DG also agrees that the root of a sentence is the (finite) verb (in Chinese just verb), and it allows ternary branching, as opposed to the strict binarity of branching associated with many modern phrase structure grammars (PSGs).

At the same time, the current DG is different from many other DGs in that it is projective (or mono-stratal) in syntax. This means that linear order (precedence) and vertical order (dominance) are both considered as primitive, as opposed to linear order being secondary to hierarchical order (e.g., Tesnière, 2015/1959; Mel'čuk and Pertsov, 1987). The structures assumed in the study therefore always encode actual word order.

2.2 Dependency grammar and Chinese

The modern history of dependency grammar begins primarily with the posthumously published oeuvre of Lucien Tesnière (1893–1954), *Elements of Structural Syntax* (2015/1959). While constituency-based grammars have been dominant in the study of syntax and grammar, DG has enjoyed a following in Europe, particularly in Germany, likely because the verb centrality of Tesnière's approach was more compatible with the verb second (V2) principle of word order in German and other Germanic languages. In China, it was not until the late 1970s and early 1980s that the first work introducing DG was published (e.g., Feng, 1983). Due to easily accessible and readily applicable structures, DG has become the widely-assumed approach for parsing in machine translation and natural language processing (e.g., Liu, 1997; Feng, 1998; Feng, 2008).

In the last decade, work on DG concerning Chinese has been increasing in great number due to the development of computational linguistics. Focusing on the functional side of the grammar, Chinese computational linguists have made attempt to deepen our understanding of human languages and cognition on the basis of their self-built DG tree banks (e.g., Liu, 2008; Jiang and Liu, 2015). At present, there are three true-born large-scale dependency tree banks of Chinese, one from Zhejiang University, one from Peking University, and another is the HIT-CIR from Harbin Institute of Technology.

While there have been many computational and quantitative investigations into the nature of Chinese, purely linguistic questions about Chinese have received less attention. It is therefore warranted that DG be employed to address syntactic issues of the sort mentioned above, and to shed light on the potential structural analyses of various constructions, such as the VDCs.

3 Methodology

This section establishes the validity of the two means for discerning the best structural analysis, namely the chunking experiment and the *bǎ* and *bèi* diagnostics. It starts with the introduction of the experiment in which informants were asked to chunk sentences according to their intuition, and then moves to the illustration of how the widely-used *bǎ* and *bèi* tests are employed to help discern the status of the intervening NP.

3.1 Chunking handouts

Informants' chunking responses were collected and used as guidance to discern the best hierarchical analysis for VDCs with an intervening NP.

In this regard, the following claims are put forth for orientation:

1. Native speakers of a language intuitively know how words in a sentence are organized into meaningful groups, and these groups can be identified using chunking data collected from informants.

2. Words connected in meaning are more likely to be included within one chunk. i.e. dependents should be grouped together with their head, as opposed together with one or more words that do not include their head (think *projectvity*, e.g., Hays, 1964; Gaifman, 1965; Robinson, 1970).

By asking informants to divide sentences into chunks, the researcher is actually inviting them to group words together that are closely connected in meaning and accordingly in structure. Take sentence (1) as an example, i.e. *Wǒ pǎo-de hěn kuài* 'I run very fast'. The prediction is that informants will prefer to include *hěn* 'very' with *kuài* 'fast' rather than with *pǎo* 'run', because *hěn* is an adverb that modifies *kuài*, not *pǎo*. Similarly, if a significant majority of participants include the intervening NP and a particular predicate within one chunk, then the intervening NP is more likely to a dependent of that predicate, rather than the other one.

All together thirty sentences were tested via three rounds of data collection at a major university in China. The chunking handout was arranged in such a manner that it contained mainly V-*de* sentences as well as a small number of filler sentences, such as *bǎ* sentences. At the beginning of each handout, the chunking concept was introduced and illustrated with examples. The handout then prompted the participants to chunk the sentences according to their intuition.

All the handouts were collected in the classroom with the permission of the teacher. The researcher arrived several minutes before class to explain the instruction. Students were encouraged to ask questions if they did not understand. At the end of the handout, participants were prompted to write down their suggestions as well.

The results were recorded using Microsoft Excel 2007. Handouts that contained responses that are not consistent with the requirements of participation, i.e. containing sentences that are not chunked into three chunks, were excluded from recording. The number of meaningful set of results obtained from each round of data collection was 43 (two excluded), 47(one excluded), and 43, respectively.

3.2 The *bǎ* and *bèi* diagnostics

The *bǎ* and *bèi* diagnostics are two related, widely-used tests in the study of Mandarin grammar (e.g., Zhu, 1982, p. 135; Linding Li, 1986, p. 241-242, 245-246; Huang, 1988, p. 297-300; Yafei Li, 1999, p. 449-451; Loar, 2011, p. 364-366). Compatible with previous analyses that take *bǎ* and *bèi* as object markers (e.g., Liang, 1971; Wang, 1985, p. 82-92; Goodall, 1986; Jinxi Li, 2000/1924, p. 37), the assumption of these tests is that what can follow *bǎ* or what precedes *bèi* in corresponding structures is the direct object of the main predicate in the normal active counterpart.

Acknowledging that some doubt the assumption behind these dignostics (e.g., Xue, 1987; Shen, 1997; Chao Li, 2015), the discussion here focuses on the dependency relations that the test is able to reveal. If a VDC with an intervening NP (NP2) can be transformed into *bǎ* and *bèi* constructions, then it seems plausible to assume NP2 as a dependent of P1, because P1 denotes how NP2 is "disposed of",[2] whereas P2 describes the result or the extent.

Take (4) as an example:

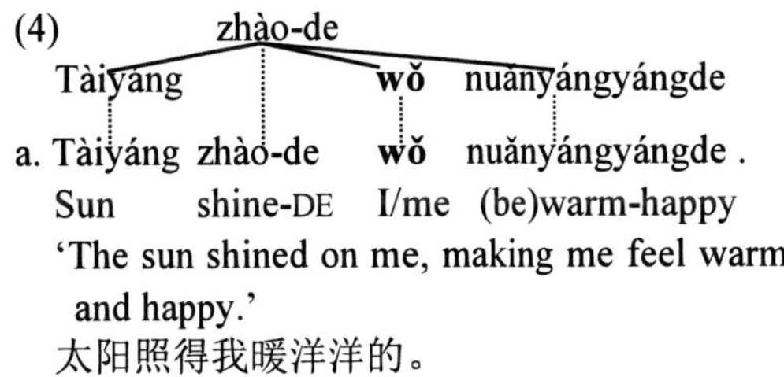

a. Tàiyáng zhào-de   wǒ   nuǎnyángyángde .
Sun   shine-DE I/me (be)warm-happy
'The sun shined on me, making me feel warm and happy.'
太阳照得我暖洋洋的。

---

[2] "The *bǎ* construction is often called the 'disposal' construction, a term due to Wang (1947), who writes, 'The disposal form states how a person is handled, manipulated , or dealt with; how something is disposed of; or how an affair is conducted.' (translation by Y.-C. Li, 1974) " (from Bender, 2000, p. 106).

b. Tàiyáng **bǎ wǒ** zhào-de nuǎnyángyángde.
Sun BA me shine-DE (be)warm-happy
'The sun shined on me, making me feel warm
and happy.'
太阳把我照得暖洋洋的。

c. **Wǒ bèi** tàiyáng zhào-de nuǎnyángyángde.
Me BEI sun shine-DE (be)warm-happy
'I was shone by the sun, and as a result, I felt
warm and happy.'
我被太阳照得暖洋洋的。

The semantic relations in the sentence do not provide any clue about the best hierarchical analysis: *Wǒ* 'I/me' is the object argument of P1 *zhào* 'shine' that is acted upon; it is also the subject argument of P2 *nuǎnyángyángde* '(be)warm-happy' that experiences the change.

That NP2 can be passivized in (4b) and (4c) suggests that it should be analyzed as the dependent of P1 instead of P2, supporting the ternary-branching analysis shown in (4a).

This use of the *bǎ* and *bèi* tests is also supported by another observation:

(5) 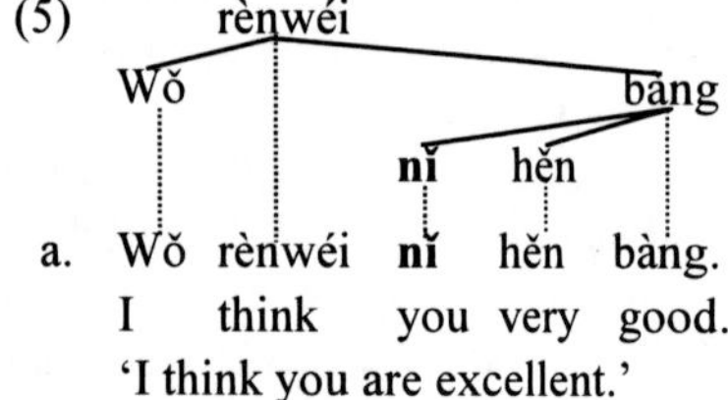

a. Wǒ rènwéi **nǐ** hěn bàng.
I think you very good.
'I think you are excellent.'
我认为你很棒。

b. *Wǒ **bǎ nǐ** rènwéi hěn bàng.
I BA you think very excellent
Intended: 'I think you are excellent.'
我把你认为很棒。

c. *Nǐ **bèi** wǒ rènwéi hěn bàng.
You BEI I think very excellent
Intended: 'You are thought by me to be excellent.'
你被我认为很棒。

Example (5a) is a sentence with a bridge verb *rènwéi* 'think'.[3] As the root of the sentence, *rènwéi* 'think' takes the clause *nǐ hěn bàng* 'you are excellent' as its complement. NP2 *nǐ* 'you' is clearly a dependent of the root of the object

clause *bàng* 'good' rather than of the matrix root *rènwéi* 'think'. Taking the position of *nǐ* into consideration, the assumption is that it should indeed not be accessible for building the *bǎ* and *bèi* constructions. Attempts to form such sentences support this prediction, as shown in (5b) and (5c). Note that similar attempts to form the passive in English also fail, e.g., *You are thought by me are excellent.*

The inference is thus that if an intervening NP can survive the *bǎ* and *bèi* tests, it seems more plausible to analyze it as a dependent of P1 than of P2.

4 Discussion of results

The discussion in this section focuses only on the thorny issue of the hierarchical analysis of the VDCs with an intervening NP. Based on their predicate-argument relationships, VDCs were divided into three groups:

1. The intervening NP is an argument of P1 only,

2. The intervening NP is an argument of both P1 and P2 at the same time, and

3. The intervening NP is an argument of P2 only.

Chunking results obtained for each type of VDCs are reported and discussed in the following subsections.

4.1 Argument of P1 only

When NP2 is semantically selected just by P1, P2 generally needs to be predicated of the other NP in the sentence, i.e. the matrix subject, forming *subject control* (e.g., Sun, 2005, p. 125; Chao Li, 2015, p. 27). Take *Wǒ děng-de tā hǎoxīnjiāo* as an example. The matrix subject *wǒ* 'I' is the agent of the first predicate *děng* 'wait'.

(6) (from Chao Li, 2015, p. 25)

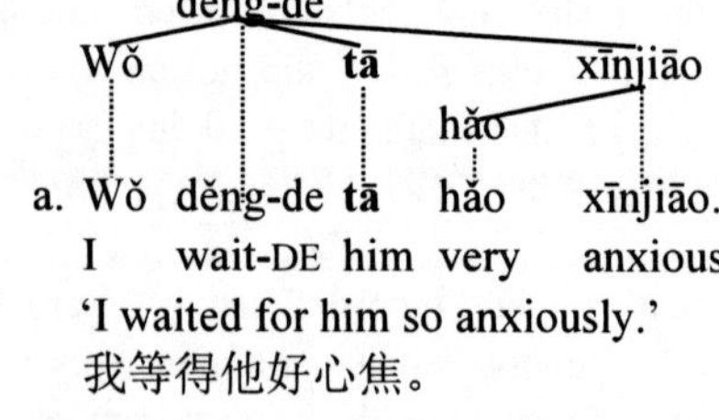

a. Wǒ děng-de **tā** hǎo xīnjiāo.
I wait-DE him very anxious
'I waited for him so anxiously.'
我等得他好心焦。

---

[3] A bridge verb is a predicate of speaking and thinking that typically takes an object clause, e.g., *rènwéi* 'think', *shuō* 'say', and *zhīdào* 'claim'.

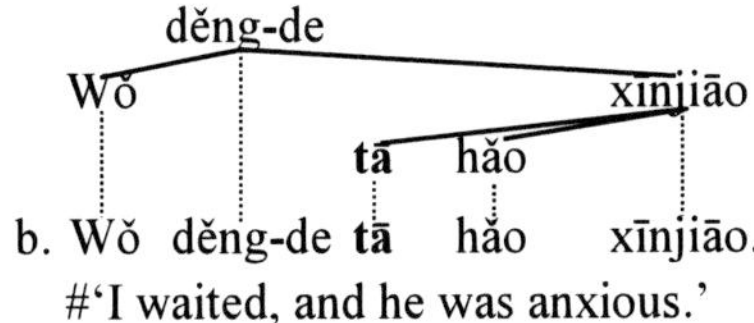

b. Wǒ děng-de **tā** hǎo xīnjiāo.
#'I waited, and he was anxious.'

In the ternary-branching analysis given as (6a), the intervening NP is the patient of P1. P2 *xīnjiāo* 'anxious', on the other hand, is predicated of the matrix subject *wǒ* 'I', denoting the agent's anxious state from the action of *děng tā* 'waiting for him'. In the small-clause analysis shown in (6b), however, P2 seems to take NP2 as its subject argument, resulting in a pragmatically strange reading of *tā* 'he' being anxious while *wǒ* 'I' was the one who waited. The prediction is therefore that the ternary-branching analysis will be preferred for this type of VDC.

Results obtained from chunking handouts confirmed the prediction. For sentence (6), informants produced the following responses:

(7)   I   wait-DE him very anxious

   a. Wǒ | děng-de **tā** | hǎo xīnjiāo.   − 35
   b. Wǒ děng-de **tā** | hǎo | xīnjiāo.   − 3
   c. Wǒ | děng-de | **tā** hǎo xīnjiāo.   − 2
   d. Wǒ děng-de | **tā** | hǎo xīnjiāo.   − 3

'I waited for him so anxiously.'

As stated in the previous section, dependents are normally grouped together with their head according to the principle of *projectivity*. The fact that a significant majority of informants chose to chunk the sentence as in (7a) and (7b) in which P1 and NP2 are in one chunk excluding P2 supports the ternary-branching analysis that positions NP2 as a dependent of P1 as shown in (6a).

Concerning the other sentence containing subject control that was tested, i.e. *Wǒ xiǎng-de tā shuì-bù-zháo jiào* 'I missed her so much that I cannot fall asleep',[4] the results were similar:

----

[4] It should be pointed out that, although all sentences tested are well-accepted Chinese, the use of this type of subject control VDCs that put NP2 directly after *−de*, as shown in (7) and (8), is decreasing (e.g., Linding Li, 1986, p. 244). The preferred way to express this meaning is the verb-copying construction (e.g., Chao Li, 2015, p. 27). For example, sentence (8) would be *Wǒ xiǎng tā xiǎng-de shuì-bù-zháo jiào* 'I miss her miss-*de* that I cannot fall asleep'.

(8)   I   miss-DE her sleep-not-touch

   a. Wǒ | xiǎng-de **tā** | shuì-bù-zháo jiào. − 39
   b. Wǒ xiǎng-de **tā** | shuì-bù-zháo | jiào. − 1
   c. Wǒ xiǎng-de | **tā** | shuì-bù-zháo jiào. − 3

'I missed her so much that I cannot fall asleep.'

While a significant majority of informants (40 out of 43) grouped NP2 *tā* 'he/him' with P1 *xiǎng* 'miss', no one grouped it with P2 *shuì-bù-zháo jiào* 'cannot fall asleep' (0 out of 43). Once again, three informants chose to chunk the sentence in a manner that NP2 alone appears as one chunk, which was not in favor of either one of the analyses.

The conclusion is therefore that when NP2 is selected just by P1, a ternary-branching analysis should be preferred over the small-clause analysis.

4.2 Argument of both P1 and P2

While the structure of *subject control* VDCs matched expectation, it is hard to predict which analysis should be preferred for the second type of VDC, in which NP2 is selected by both P1 and P2.

(9) (from Zhang, 2006, p. 47; gloss and translation mine)

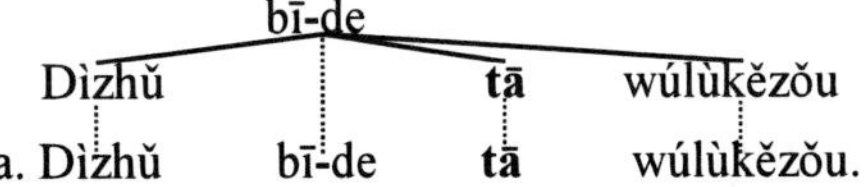

a. Dìzhǔ   bī-de   **tā**   wúlùkězǒu.
landowner force-DE he/him no-way-can-go
'The landowner drove him into a desperate situation. '
地主逼得他无路可走。

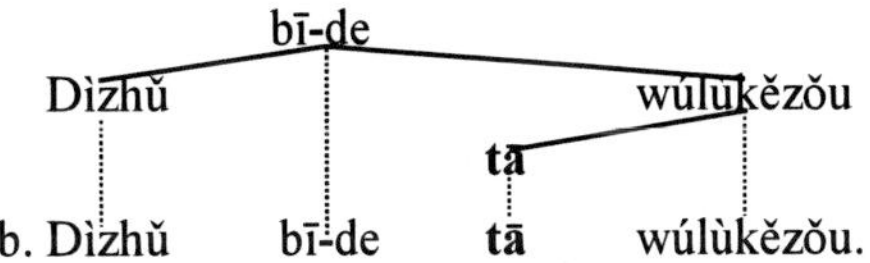

b. Dìzhǔ   bī-de   **tā**   wúlùkězǒu.
'The landowner drove him into a desperate situation.'

(10) (CL = classifier)

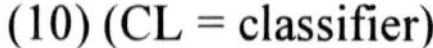

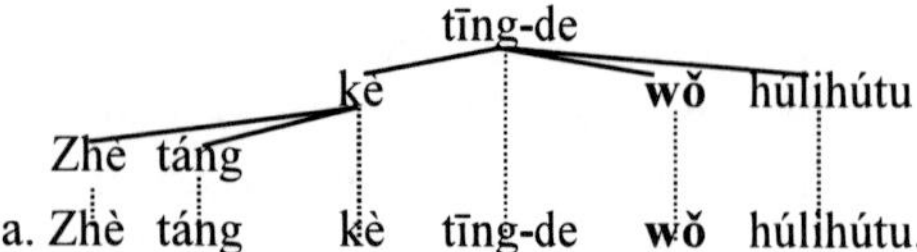

a. Zhè táng   kè   tīng-de   wǒ   húlihútu.
   This CL   class listen-DE I/me confused
   'I listened to the class, and as a result, I was confused.'

这堂课听得我胡里胡涂。

(10)

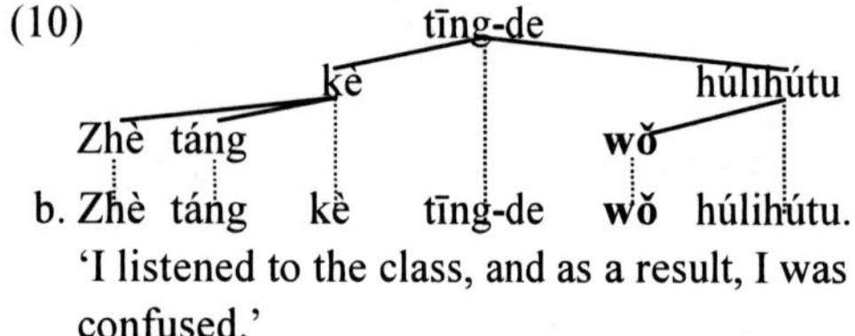

b. Zhè táng   kè   tīng-de   wǒ   húlihútu.
   'I listened to the class, and as a result, I was confused.'

Sentences (9) and (10) demonstrate the case where NP2 is selected by both predicates. In (9), the intervening NP *tā* 'he/him' is the patient of P1 *bī* 'force' and the experiencer of P2 *wúlùkězǒu* 'no-way-can-go'. In (10), the syntactic subject of P1, i.e. NP1, is the patient of P1 and NP2 is both the agent of P1 and the experiencer of P2 (c.f., Huang, 1988, p. 299; Sun, 2005, p. 149-151; 450-452).

Six of the sentences tested contained an intervening NP that is semantically related to both predicates. Among them, two were "active" VDCs such as (9), and four were "passive" VDCs like (10).

The two active sentences were sentence (9) and *Tàiyáng zhào-de wǒ nuǎnyángyángde* 'The sun shined on me, making me feel warm and happy', as illustrated in (4). The results obtained for sentence (9) were as follows:

(11)   landowner force-DE him no-way-can-go

   a. Dìzhǔ | bī-de   **tā** | wúlùkězǒu. − 37
   b. Dìzhǔ | bī-de | **tā**   wúlùkězǒu. − 3
   c. Dìzhǔ   bī-de | **tā** | wúlùkězǒu. − 3

   'The landowner drove him into a desperate situation.'

Two potential structural analyses of the sentence are illustrated in (9) above. Example (9a) is the ternary-branching analysis and (9b) shows the small-clause analysis. Given the informants' responses, it is possible to discern the best analysis.

The chunking results in (11) reveal that informants were more willing to group the inter-

vening NP with P1 rather than with P2, supporting the ternary-branching analysis given as (9a).

Concerning the other active sentence that was tested, i.e. *Tàiyáng zhào-de wǒnuǎnyángyáng-de* 'The sun shined on me, making me feel warm and happy', the results were similar: 40 out 43 participants chunked the sentence in such a manner that supports the ternary-branching analysis that views NP2 as a dependent of P1.

The four "passive" sentences that were tested are listed next: *Zhè táng kè tīng-de wǒ húlihútu* 'I listened to the class, and as a result, I was confused', *Shǔ jià fàng-de wǒ bù xiǎng kāixué* 'I had a summer vacation, and as a result, I did not feel like going to school', *Zhè dùn fàn chī-de wǒ bù kāixīn* 'I had the meal, and as a result, I was unhappy', and *Zhè diànyǐng kàn-de wǒ hěn gāoxìng* 'I watched the movie, and as a result, I was pleased'. The results for the first sentence i.e. sentence (10), are provided here for discussion. The informants were, again, invited to divide these sentences into three chunks, the following results obtained:

(12)   This CL class listen-DE I/me confused

   a. Zhè táng kè | tīng-de **wǒ** | húlihútu. − 35
   b. Zhè táng kè | tīng-de| **wǒ** húlihútu. − 4
   c. Zhè táng kè   tīng-de | **wǒ** | húlihútu. − 4

   'I listened to the class, and as a result, I was confused.'

The preferred way of chunking again supports the ternary-branching analysis given as (10a) over the small-clause analysis given as (10b). While thirty-five informants chose to group the intervening NP with P1, four of them grouped it with P2. The results given in (12c) are not in favor of either one of the analyses.

The results for the other three passive sentences were similar. Although there was a small minority of informants that chunked the sentence in a manner that contradicts the ternary-branching analysis, it was usually the case, however, that a large majority of informants chunked the sentence in a manner that supports it.

The conclusion so far is therefore that as long as the intervening NP is an argument of P1 (regardless of its relation with P2), a ternary-branching analysis in which the intervening NP is a dependent of P1 should be pursued.

4.3 Argument of P2 only

The feature of the third type of VDC is that the intervening NP is selected by P2 only. Unlike subject control VDCs, the hierarchy of which is predictable, the structure of this group of VDCs is hard to predict for two reasons:

1. The arguments for the two competing analysis both seem well-motivated (e.g., Huang, 1988; Sun, 2005);

2. The diagnostics used in the literature, e.g., the pause test and *ya* insertion, sometimes yield inconsistent results.

By collecting informant responses to chunking tasks, it has become possible to shed light on this group of VDCs. A pilot test containing a couple of sentences was conducted first. Based on the results obtained, a ternary-branching analysis is preferable for sentences that can survive *bǎ* and *bèi* tests, whereas for those sentences that do not allow the insertion of *bǎ* and *bèi*, a small-clause analysis seems more plausible. These matters are illustrated with the following examples:

(13) (from Yafei Li, 1999, p. 459; translation mine)

a. Tāmen chàng-de **wǒ** bù xiǎng kàn shū.
   They sing-DE I not want read book
   'They sang, and as a result, I did not feel like reading.'
   他们唱得我不想看书。

b. Tāmen **bǎ wǒ** chàng-de bù xiǎng kàn shū.
   They   BA me sing-DE not want read book
   'They sang, and as a result, I did not feel like reading.'
   他们把我唱得不想看书。

c. **Wǒ bèi** tāmen chàng-de bù xiǎng kàn shū.
   I/me BEI they sing-DE   not want read book
   'I did not not feel like reading because they sang.'
   我被他们唱得不想看书。

(14) (adapted from Sun 2005: 141)

a. Zhè háizi zhǎng-de **wǒ** dōu bú rènshi   le.
   This child grow-DE I even not recognize LE
   'The child has grown so much that I did not even recognize him.'
   这孩子长得我都不认识了。

b.*Zhè háizi **bǎ wǒ** zhǎng-de dōu bú rènshi le.
   This child BA I grow-DE even not recognize
   Intended: 'The child has grown so much that I did not even recognize him.'
   *这孩子把我长得都不认识了。

c.* **Wǒ bèi** zhè háizi zhǎng-de dōu bú rènshi le.
   I   BEI this child grow-DE even not recognize
   Intended: 'I did not even recognize the child because he has grown so much.'
   *我被这孩子长得都不认识了。

Sentence (13) and sentence (14) both contain an intervening NP that is semantically selected just by P2: in (13) the verb *chàng* 'sing' is used intransitively; in (14) *zhǎng* 'grow' is an intransitive verb. As illustrated in (13b) and (13c), *Tāmen chàng-de wǒ bù xiǎng kàn-shū* can be transformed into *bǎ* and *bèi* constructions. Sentence (14), however, failed to form the corresponding *bǎ* and *bèi* constructions, as in (14b) and (14c). Their chunking results are listed as follows:

(15) (=sentence (13))

   They sing-DE I not want read book

a. Tāmen | chàng-de **wǒ** | bù xiǎng kàn shū.–24
b. Tāmen chàng-de **wǒ**| bù xiǎng | kàn shū –1
c. Tāmen |chàng-de| **wǒ** bù xiǎng kàn shū.–9
d. Tāmen chàng-de |**wǒ** bù xiǎng| kàn shū.–2
e. Tāmen chàng-de |**wǒ** bù xiǎng kàn| shū. –1
f. Tāmen chàng-de | **wǒ** | bù xiǎng kàn shū. –6

'They sang, and as a result, I did not feel like reading.'

(16) (=sentence (14))

   This child grow-DE I EM not recognize LE

a. Zhè háizi |zhǎng-de| **wǒ** dōu bú rènshi le. –30
b. Zhè háizi |zhǎng-de **wǒ** | dōu bú rènshi le. –1
c. Zhè háizi zhǎng-de| **wǒ** dōu| bú rènshi le. –7
d. Zhè háizi zhǎng-de| **wǒ** | dōu bú rènshi le. –5

'The child has grown so much that I did not even recognize him.'

While the chunking results for sentence (13), a sentence that can be transformed into the *bǎ* and *bèi* constructions, suggest a ternary-branching analysis, the results in (16) imply that for sentences like (14) that cannot survive the *bǎ* and *bèi* diagnostics, a small-clause analysis should be pursued.

To test this observation, more sentences of the two types sketched above were tested. Sentences that can form corresponding *bǎ* and *bèi* constructions include *Wǒ pǎo-de xiédài dōu diào le* 'I ran to the extent that even my shoelaces got loose', *Tāmen bèng-de fángzi dōu kāishǐ huàng le* 'They jumped to the extent that the house has started to shake' and *Tāmen chàng-de wǒ yilián sān-tiān dōu bù xiǎng kàn shū* 'They sang, and as a result, I did not feel like reading for three days in a row' (adapted from (13)). Sentences that failed the *bǎ* and *bèi* diagnostics were *Zhè yì qiú tī-de guānzhòng liánshēng jiàohǎo* 'The kick ['goal'] was so good that the audience broke into loud cheers' (from Sun, 2005, p. 141) and *Zhè wénzhāng xiě-de shéi yě kàn bù dǒng* 'The article is written in such a way that no one can understand' (adapted from Zhu, 1982, p. 135).

Chunking results for the sentences that failed the *bǎ* and *bèi* tests were consistent with the small-clause analysis. Take *Zhè wénzhāng xiě-de shéi yě kàn bù dǒng* as an example; the following results obtained (*Zhè wénzhāng* 'this article' is abbreviated as NP1)

(17) NP1 write-DE who also see not understand

    a. NP1 | xiě-de | **shéi** yě kàn bù dǒng. −31
    b. NP1 | xiě-de **shéi** yě | kàn bù dǒng.   −1
    c. NP1 xiě-de | **shéi** | yě kàn bù dǒng. −3
    d. NP1 xiě-de | **shéi** yě | kàn bù dǒng. −8

'This article is written in such a way that no one can understand'

The fact that a significant majority of participants, 31 of them, chose to group the intervening NP with P2 to the exclusion of P1 implies that NP2 is a dependent of P2. Results obtained for the other sentence containing an intervening NP that fail the *bǎ* and *bèi* tests were similar, i.e. supportive of the small-clause analysis.

Results for the other subgroup of sentences that survived the *bǎ* and *bèi* diagnostics, however, were unexpected. For instance, the results for *Wǒ pǎo-de xiédài dōu diào le* 'I ran to the extent that even my shoelaces got loose' were as follows:

(18) (=sentence (2))

    I   run-DE shoelaces EM loosen LE

    a. Wǒ | pǎo-de| **xiédài** dōu diào le. −18
    b. Wǒ | pǎo-de **xiédài** | dōu diào le. −5
    c. Wǒ pǎo-de **xiédài** | dōu | diào le. −1

    d. Wǒ pǎo-de | **xiédài** | dōu diào le. −16
    e. Wǒ pǎo-de | **xiédài** dōu | diào le. −3

'I ran to the extent that even my shoelaces got loose'

While 18 participants grouped NP2 together with P2, only five grouped it together with P1. Note that results shown in (18d) are not in favor of either analysis (because *xiédài* 'shoelace' is grouped neither with P1 nor with P2). The result for *Tāmen bèng-de fángzi dōu kāishǐ huàng le* 'They jumped to the extent that the house has started to shake' were similar, i.e. in favor of the small-clause analysis in which the intervening NP is a dependent of P2 rather than of P1. The chunking results for the sentence with an animate NP support the ternary-branching analysis, however.

The contradictory results for this type of VDC are accommodated in terms of a semantic property of the intervening NP (NP2): (in)animacy.[5] The success of the *bǎ* and *bèi* tests suggests that NP2 can be interpreted as an entity that is disposed of or affected by the matrix predicate P1, even though P1 is intransitive. When NP2 is animate, it is more accessible to P1 allowing P1 to influence its, i.e. NP2's, relationship with P2. When NP2 is inanimate, however, despite the success of the *bǎ* and *bèi* diagnostics, its semantic property prevents P1 from establishing a syntactic relation with it.

The conclusion is therefore that when the intervening NP is an argument of P2 only, a flexible structural analysis should be pursued. When a VDC can survive the *bǎ* and *bèi* tests and has an animate NP2, a ternary-branching

---

[5] One may object that this difference is not caused by a property of NP2, but rather by the features of predicates. For example, two of the tested VDCs with an inanimate NP2 (in favor of a small-clause analysis) both had an intransitive P1, i.e. *bèng* 'jump' and *pǎo* 'run'. Two other examples with an animate NP2, on the other hand, had an unergative P1, i.e. *chàng* 'sing'. To test this, one V-*de* sentence containing the same intransitive P1 *bèng* 'jump' and the same animate NP2 *wǒ* 'I/me' was chunked by 20 informants. The results were supportive of the stance assumed here, namely that the (in)animacy of NP2 is the decisive factor: More informants chose to chunk NP2 with P1 this time, consistent with the results obtained for the VDCs that has an animate NP2 but a different P1.

analysis is warranted; otherwise, i.e. when it survives the *bǎ* and *bèi* tests but has an inanimate NP2 or when it fails the tests, a small-clause analysis is preferred.

5 Summary and conclusion

This study has assigned dependency structures to the descriptive and resultative V-*de* constructions (VDCs) in Mandarin Chinese. The focus has been on the status of the intervening NP (NP2) between the two predicates. The analyses arrived at above are visualized with the following syntactic diagrams:

(19)

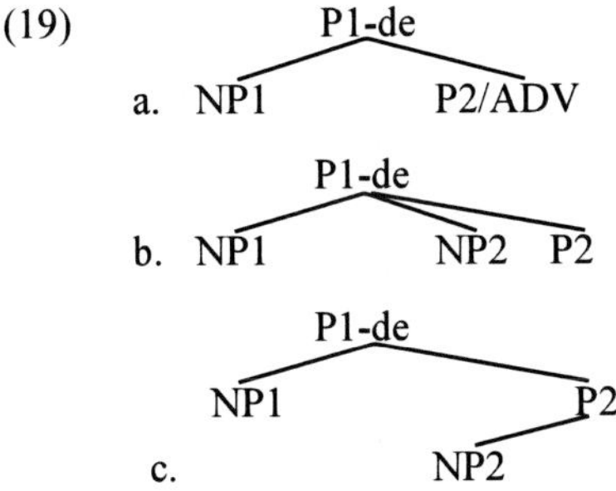

Tree (19a) shows that when there is no intervening NP in the construction, P2 is viewed as a direct dependent of the first predicate (P1), in accordance with the *Secondary Predication hypothesis* (e.g., Huang, 1988). In addition to predicates (verbs and predicative adjectives), some adverbials can also appear in the position of P2, expressing a high degree of the action or event denoted by P1 (see footnote 1).

The structure becomes much more complicated when an NP intervenes between P1 and P2. As shown in (19b) and (19c), there are two possible dependency analyses concerning this matter. The structure in (19b) demonstrates the ternary-branching analysis in which NP2 is a dependent of P1, and (19c) shows the small-clause analysis in which NP2 is a dependent of P2. Based on chunking results collected from native speakers of Chinese, the account above proposed a flexible analysis for VDCs with an intervening NP, whereby the actual structure assignment is determined by predicate-argument relationships, results of the *bǎ* and *bèi* tests and a semantic property of NP2 ((in)animacy).

According to the predicate-argument structures that NP2 forms with P1 and P2, VDCs are divided into three groups:

1. The intervening NP is an argument of P1 only (e.g., (6), (8));

2. The intervening NP is an argument of both P1 and P2 (e.g., (4), (9), (10)), and;

3. The intervening NP is an argument of P2 only (e.g., (2), (13), (14), (17)).

For the first two types, a ternary-branching analysis should be preferred. For the last type, however, some flexibility of analysis is necessary to accommodate all the data.

Acknowledgement

The research presented in this article was funded by the Ministry of Education of the People's Republic of China, Grant # 15YJA74001.

References

Emily Bender. 2000. The syntax of Mandarin *bǎ* : reconsidering the verbal analysis. *Journal of East Asia Linguistics*, volume 9 (2), 105-145.

Yuen Ren Chao. 1965. *A Grammar of Spoken Chinese*. Oakland, California: University of California Press.

Shengshu Ding. 1961. *Xiàndài hànyǔ yǔfǎ jiǎnghuà [Lectures on the Modern Chinese Grammar]*. Beijing: The Commercial Press.

Xiao Fan. 1993. Fù dòng V-de jù [The verb-copying V-de construction]. *Yǔyán jiàoxué yǔ yánjiū [Language Teaching and Linguistic Studies]* 4, 57-74.

Zhiwei Feng. 1983. Tesnière de cóngshǔ guānxī yǔfǎ [The dependency grammar of Tesnière]. *Dāngdài yǔyánxué [Contemporary Linguistics]* 1, 63-65.

Zhiwei Feng. 1998. Cóngshǔ guānxī yǔfǎ duì jīqì fānyì yánjiū de zuòyòng [The role dependency grammar plays in machine translation research]. *Wàiyǔ xuékn [Foreign Language Research]* 1, 18-21.

Zhiwei Feng. 2008. Zìrán yǔyán chǔlǐ de lìshǐ yǔ xiànzhuàng [The past and present of natural language processing]. *Zhōngguó wàiyǔ [Foreign Languages in China]* 1, 14-22.

Chaim Gaifman. 1965. Dependency systems and phrase-structure systems. *Information and Control* 8, 304-337.

Grant Goodall. 1986. On argument Structure and L-marking with Mandarin Chinese *Ba*. *Proceedings of NELS17*, volume1, 232-242.

Jules Gouguet. 2006. Adverbials and Mandarin argument structure. *Empirical Issues in Syntax and Semantics* 6, 155-173.

David Hays. 1964. Dependency theory: A formalism and some observations. *Language* 40, 511–525.

James Huang. 1988. *Wǒ pǎo de kuài* and Chinese phrase structure. *Language* 2, 274-311.

James Huang, Yen-hui Audrey Li, and Yafei Li. 2009. *The Syntax of Chinese.* Cambridge: Cambridge University Press.

Richard Hudson. 2007. *Language Networks: The New Word Grammar.* Oxford: Oxford University Press.

Jinyang Jiang and Haitao Liu. 2015. The effects of sentence length on dependency distance, dependency direction and the implications–based on a parallel English–Chinese dependency treebank. *Language Sciences* 50, 93-104.

Sylvain Kahane. 1996. If HPSG were a dependency grammar… *Actes de TALN*, Marseille, 22–24, 45–49.

Chao Li. 2015. On the V-DE construction in mandarin Chinese. *Lingua Sinica* 1: 6, 1-40.

Linding Li. 1986. *Xiàndài hànyǔ jùxíng [The Modern Chinese Constructions].* Beijing: The Commercial Press.

Jinxi Li. 2000/1924. *Xīnzhù guóyǔ wénfǎ [The Grammar of Mandarin Chinese: New Edition].* Beijing: The Commercial Press.

Yafei Li. 1999. Cross-componential Causativity. *Natural Language & Linguistic Theory* 17 (3), 445-497.

Yen-hui Audrey Li. 1990. *Oder and Constituency in Mandarin Chinese.* Dordrecht: Kluwer Academic Publishers, 41-59.

James Chaoping Liang. 1971. *Prepositions, Co-verbs or Verbs? A Commentary on Chinese Grammar Past and Present.* PhD dissertation, University of Michigan, Ann Arbor.

Tao Lin. 2011/1957. Xiàndài hànyǔ bǔzúyǔ lǐ de qīngyīn xiànxiàng [Grammatical and semantic issues revealed by phonetic reductions in modern Chinese complements], *Journal of Peking University* 03, 61-74.

Haitao Liu. 1997. Yīcún yǔfǎ hé jīqì fānyì [Dependency grammar and machine translation]. *Yǔyán wénzì yìngyòng [Applied Linguistics]* 3, 91-95.

Haitao Liu. 2008. Dependency distance as a metric of language comprehension difficulty. *Journal of Cognitive Science* 2, 159-191.

Jian Kang Loar. 2011. *Chinese Syntactic Grammar.* New York: Peter Lang.

Igor Mel'čuk and Nikolai Pertsov. 1987. *Surface Syntax of English: A Formal Model with the Meaning-Text Framework.* Amsterdam: Benjamins.

Timothy Osborne and Shudong Ma. 2015. A DG account of the descriptive and resultative de-constructions in Chinese. *Depling 2015*, 261-270.

Jane Robinson. 1970. Dependency structures and transformational rules. *Language* 46, 259–285.

Yang Shen. 1997. Míngcí duǎnyǔ de duōchóng yíwèi xíngshì jí bǎ zì jù de gòuzào guòchéng yǔ yǔyì jiěshì [Formation process of *bǎ*-constructions and its semantic interpretation] *Zhōngguó yǔwén [Studies of the Chinese Language]* 6, 402-414.

Yinxin Sun. 2005. Tóngxíngyìgòu de "NS + V + 'de' + NP + VP" jù [Four structures of the "NS + V + 'de' + NP + VP"]. *Lìyún yǔyán xuékān [Academic Journal of Liyun (Language Volume)]* 1, 125-159.

Lucien Tesnière. 2015/1959. *Elements of structural syntax* (translated by Timothy Osborne and Sylvain Kahane). Amsterdam & Philadelphia: John Benjamins.

Li Wang. 1985. *Zhōngguó xiàndài yǔfǎ [China Modern Grammar].* Beijing: The Commercial Press.

Fengsheng Xue. 1987. Shì lùn bǎ zì jù de yǔyì tèxìng [Study on the semantic features of bǎ-constructions]. *Yǔyán jiàoxué yǔ yánjiū [Language Teaching and Linguistic Studies]* 1, 4-22.

Yufeng Zhang. 2006. *Xiàndài hànyǔ jùzi yánjiū [Research on Modern Chinese Sentences].* Shanghai: Xuelin Press.

Dexi Zhu. 1982. *Yǔfǎ jiǎngyì [Lectures on Grammar].* Beijing: The Commercial Press.

The Component Unit
Introducing a Novel Unit of Syntactic Analysis

Timothy Osborne
Zhejiang University
Hangzhou
China
tjo3ya@yahoo.com

Ruochen Niu
Zhejiang University
Hangzhou
China
niuruochen@126.com

Abstract

This contribution introduces a novel unit of syntactic analysis, which is called the *component*. The validity and utility of the component unit are established in terms of *chunking*. When informants organize the words of sentences into groups, they are creating *chunks*, and these chunks then qualify as components in dependency syntax. By acknowledging the nature of chunking and the component unit, it is possible to cast light on controversial aspects of dependency hierarchies. In particular, the component unit, informant data, and the reasoning based on these provide an argument in favor of the traditional DG assumptions about hierarchical status of many function words (auxiliary verbs, prepositions, subordinators, etc.), and in so doing, they contradict the Universal Dependencies (UD) annotation scheme. The data discussed here are from English, but the methodology and reasoning employed are easily extendable to other languages.

1 Introduction

The purpose of this manuscript is to probe the extent to which dependency syntax provides a basis for discerning how words are grouped together into units of meaning. The words that constitute sentences are of course not arranged arbitrarily, but rather they are grouped in such a manner that phrases and clauses can be acknowledged. According to the principle of *projectivity* (Hays,1964; Gaifman, 1965; Robinson,1970; Melčuk, 1988), dependents should be grouped together with their head, as opposed to together with one or more words that do not include their head. For instance, given a three-word string such as *walk really fast*, a straightforward assumption is that the adverb *really* modifies the adverb *fast* and should hence be grouped together with *fast* before being grouped with *walk*. We therefore have *walk [really fast]*, not *[walk really] fast*.

While this analysis of *walk really fast* is not controversial, there are other cases where intuition about how the words should be grouped is not as clear. For instance, should an auxiliary verb be grouped first with the subject or with what follows it, e.g. *[I am] having lunch* vs. *I [am having lunch]*. Most phrase structure grammars (PSGs) would of course prefer the latter analysis. However, what does dependency syntax say about such examples? A DG analysis that subordinates both the subject *I* and the auxiliary verb *am* to the content verb *having* also predicts that the latter analysis, i.e. *I [am having lunch]*, should, for a reason discussed below, be preferred, whereas the alternative DG analysis, which positions both the subject *I* and the light verb *having* as immediate dependents of the finite auxiliary *am* predicts that neither one of the two groupings shown should be significantly preferred.

This manuscript makes and defends three major claims concerning the issue just sketched:

Claim 1
Exactly how speakers of a language organize the words of sentences into groups can be determined by simple chunking data collected from informants.

Claim 2
There is a novel unit of dependency syntax that helps predict how informants will chunk sentences. This unit is the *component*.

Proceedings of the Fourth International Conference on Dependency Linguistics (Depling 2017), pages 165-175,
Pisa, Italy, September 18-20 2017

Claim 3

One can use the component unit as a basis for motivating analyses of sentence structure. One can thus resolve areas of debate about the best hierarchical analysis.

Returning to the phrase *walk really fast*, informants can, for example, be prompted to divide the phrase into two chunks. The prediction in this area is that a significant majority of them will prefer to chunk the phrase as in (1a) rather than as in (1b):

(1) a. walk | really fast
      b. walk really | fast.

The same experiment can be conducted on the sentence *I am having lunch*, whereby there are three potential responses:

(2) a. I | am having lunch.
      b. I am | having lunch.
      c. I am having | lunch.

If a large majority of informants chunk the sentence as in (2a), one could then conclude that the auxiliary verb *am* can be grouped together with *having lunch* to the exclusion of *I*. If, in contrast, a large majority opts for the analysis in (2b), then one could conclude that *am* can be grouped with *I* to the exclusion of *having lunch*. If the sentence is chunked as in (2c) or there is a more even distribution of informant choices across (2a–c), then it is more difficult to acknowledge a clear grouping of the words in the sentence.

The component unit is the means by which the chunks just indicated in (1–2) can be interpreted. Our hypothesis is that informants prefer to chunk sentences in such a manner that the resulting chunks are components, whereby a component is *a word or a combination of words that form a string and are linked together by dependencies*.[1] This manuscript employs the component as the basis for shedding light on areas in which there is some disagreement among dependency grammarians about the best hierarchical analysis. In particular, it scrutinizes aspects of the Universal Dependencies (UD) annotation scheme.

2   Units of structure

The current DG is like many other DGs in understanding dependency as a one-to-one mapping of words to nodes and vice versa (e.g. Mel'čuk and Pertsov, 1987: 48, 57–8; Kahane, 1996: 45; Schubert,1987: 78–86, 129; Engel, 1994: 25, 28; Bröker, 2003: 297; Hudson, 2007: 183). In addition, the current DG assumes trees and is monostratal in syntax, which means linear order (precedence) and hierarchical order (dominance) are both primitive – as opposed to just hierarchical order being primitive and linear order being derived from hierarchical order. What this means is that the dependency trees assumed here always encode actual word order.

Given these assumptions about the nature of dependency syntax, key units of syntax can be defined as follows:

String
A word or a combination of words that are continuous with respect to precedence

Catena
A word or a combination of words that are continuous with respect to dominance

Component
A word or a combination of words that are continuous with respect to both precedence and dominance

Constituent
A component that is a complete subtree

These units are illustrated using the following dependency tree:

(3)
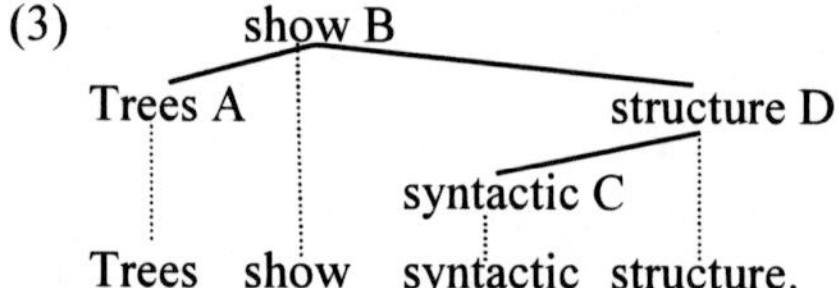

The capital letters abbreviate the words. All the distinct strings, catenae, components, and constituents in (3) are listed next:

10 distinct strings in (3)
A, B, C, D, AB, BC, CD, ABC, BCD, and ABCD

---

[1] Another, more principled definition of the component unit is given in the next section.

10 distinct catenae in (3)
A, B, C, D, AB, BD, CD, ABD, BCD, and ABCD

8 distinct components in (3)
A, B, C, D, AB, CD, BCD, and ABCD

4 distinct constituents in (3)
A, C, CD, and ABCD

Of these four units, the focus below is on the component. The reason the other three are presented here together with the component is the desire to increase understanding of the one through comparison with the other three.

Most theories of syntax acknowledge strings, and the validity of the catena unit as just defined has been thoroughly established in a series of articles (e.g. O'Grady, 1998; Osborne et al., 2012). The constituent is generally viewed as a unit of phrase structure grammar. However, some DGs have also acknowledged constituents as just defined over dependency structures (e.g. Hudson, 1984: 92; Starosta, 1988: 105; Hellwig, 2003: 603; Anderson, 2011: 92).

While the component has been acknowledged in the DG literature (Osborne and Groß, 2016: 117), it has not been the focus of particular research efforts until now. It is therefore necessary to establish a solid understanding of this unit. To do this here now, the two examples discussed in the introduction above are examined more carefully. The first example:

(4) 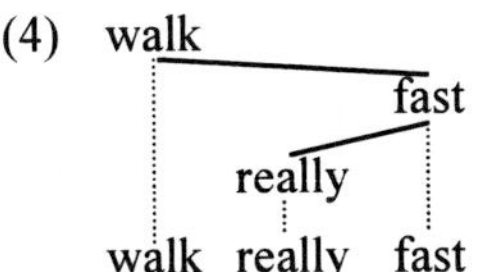
walk really fast

This hierarchical analysis is, as stated above, not controversial. Each individual word is a component by definition. The word combinations that are strings and consist of two words are of particular interest in this case, since predictions made about chunking apply directly to them. There are two two-word strings: *walk really* and *really fast*. The former of these is not a component according to the hierarchy in (4), whereas the latter is.

The prediction concerning chunking, then, is that informants will prefer to chunk this phrase in a manner that the two resulting chunks are component strings, as opposed to one of them being a

non-component string. In other words, informants will NOT chunk this phrase as *walk really | fast* because the chunk *walk really* would not be a component. They will instead chunk the phrase as *walk | really fast*, because the chunk *really fast* is a component (and so is the one-word string *walk*, of course).[2]

Turning to the second example, i.e. *I am having lunch*, there are two conceivable structural analyses that DGs are likely to pursue:

(5) 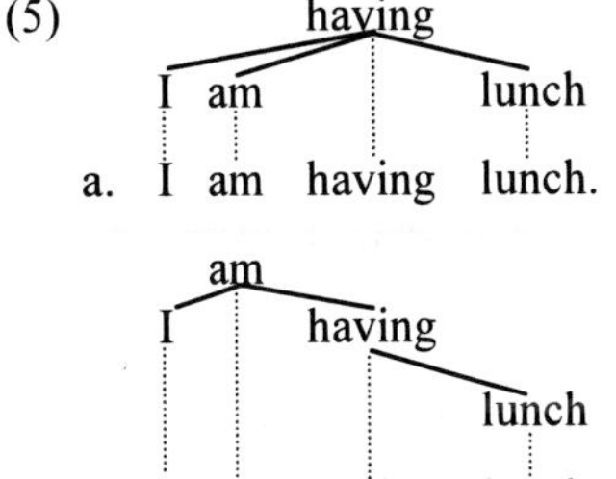

a. I am having lunch.

b. I am having lunch.

The analysis in (5b) has a long tradition in DG, reaching back to Franz Kern (1883, 1884). This tradition positions the finite verb as the clause root and then subordinates the subject to the finite verb. The type of analysis in (5a) has recently gained many adherents; it is the one advocated by the Universal Dependencies (UD) annotation scheme (e.g. de Marneffe et al., 2014).[3] This scheme systematically subordinates function words such as the auxiliary *am*, to the content words with which they co-occur.

The account of chunking in terms of components predicts that if the hierarchical analysis in (5a) is correct, then informants will prefer to chunk the sentence as *I | am having lunch* because the chunk *am having lunch* would then be a component; they would not chunk the sentence as *I am | having lunch*, because according to the hierarchy in (5a), *I am* would not be a component. The hierarchical analysis in (5b), in contrast, predicts that informants will chunk the sentence

---

[2] In our original rounds of data collection, we did not test the phrase *walk really fast*. In a follow-up round of data collection, however, we did test it. The informant responses strongly verified expectation:

  (i)   walk | really fast   – 30 responses
  (ii) walk really | fast   – 1 response

[3] At the time of writing this manuscript (April 2017), an over view of the Universal Dependencies project and of its annotation scheme were available at the following web address: http://universaldependencies.org/.

as *I | am having lunch* or *I am | having lunch* or *I am having | lunch* because in all three cases, each of the chunks shown would be a component.

The informant responses we have collected resolve this issue and others. The hierarchical analysis in (5b), which corresponds to the more traditional stance towards the hierarchical status of auxiliary verbs, receives support. Auxiliary verbs are heads over the content verbs with which they co-occur.

3 Methodology

Two rounds of handouts were designed to obtain data that reveal how speakers chunk sentences. The instructions at the beginning of each handout provided an introduction to the chunking concept as well as illustrations of how a sentence might be divided into chunks. The handout then prompted the informants to chunk a number of sentences.

The first round of data collection, i.e. the pilot test, consisted of ten English sentences that varied in length and type. The handout was arranged in such a way that sentences of the same type and in the same length were randomly scattered. Participants were invited to divide the sentences into three chunks by using two dividers "|".

The second round of data collection via a handout obtained participants' responses to sentences of which the hierarchical structure is under debate. It consisted of two parts: part one was composed of five sentences containing auxiliary and content verbs, where informants were asked to divide the sentence into two chunks by inserting only one divider "|"; part two had fifteen sentences concerning controversial issues, such as the status of auxiliary verbs, the status of prepositions, and the status of object predicatives. Informants were invited to divide each sentence into three chunks.

All the informants involved in the surveys were undergraduate students learning English at a major university in China.[4] Their level of Eng-

lish was evaluated as intermediate to advanced, CET3 (College English Test Band 3). The simple sentences in each handout were easy for them to read and understand.

All the responses obtained from the informants were recorded using Microsoft Office Excel 2007. Exactly how informants divided each sentence and how many informants did so in that way, i.e. the tokens, were recorded below each sentence. Handouts containing responses that did not follow the requirements were excluded from recording. The number of handouts recorded for the pilot test and the second round was 46 (two excluded) and 43 (one excluded), respectively.

4 Discussion of results

4.1 Auxiliary verbs

As stated above, there are two competing analyses within DG regarding the status of auxiliary verbs. There is the traditional analysis that is assumed in DG frameworks such as Lexicase Grammar (Starosta,1988), Word Grammar (Hudson, 1990, 2007) and Meaning-Text Theory (Mel'čuk, 1988), and in numerous prominent DG works such as as Kunze (1975), Schubert (1987), Heringer (1996), Eroms (2000). The central status of the finite verb, which is an auxiliary verb if an auxiliary verb is present, reaches back to the earliest works in DG, namely to the treatises of Franz Kern (e.g. 1883, 1884) – Kern emphasized time and again the central role that the finite verb plays as the sentence root. The competing analysis is more recent; it is associated mainly with the annotation scheme of Universal Dependencies (UD) – see footnote 3.

Of the 26 initial sentences we tested on informants, 15 of them contained an auxiliary verb. The tendency in this area is that informants prefer to chunk the sentence immediately before the auxiliary verb if the subject is a noun (phrase) or immediately after the auxiliary verb if the subject

---

[4] Since we were testing English sentences, native speakers of English would have been preferred as informants, of course. We unfortunately did not have access to large numbers of English native speakers at this stage of our project. Two important factors moderate this weakness in the informant responses. The first is that the sentences we tested were simple sentences of English of the sort that certainly none of the informants had difficulty reading and understanding. The second is that we did a smaller, follow-up round of data collection from native informants, testing most of the key sentences presented in this manuscript. With one exception, the results we obtained from the native informants were similar to the results obtained from the much larger number of Chinese informants. This issue is acknowledged and discussed briefly in the concluding section.

is a pronoun. This variation is best accommodated on the structural analysis illustrated above with (5b), where the finite auxiliary verb is the sentence root. If the finite auxiliary verb is the sentence root, both strings – the string consisting of the subject and the finite auxiliary as well as the string consisting of the finite auxiliary and everything following the finite auxiliary – qualify as components.

To make this point concrete, the results we obtained for the example sentence discussed above, i.e. *I am having lunch,* are presented next. When informants were asked to divide this sentence into two chunks, the following results obtained:

(6) a. I am | having lunch.   – 26 responses
    b. I | am having lunch.   – 10 responses
    c. I am having | lunch.   – 7 responses

These data reveal three things about how the words are organized into groups. The first is that they refute the initial binary division of the clause associated with most PSGs. Phrase structure syntax typically divides the clause into a subject NP and a predicate VP. If that division were real, the expectation would have been for a greater number of informants to chunk the sentence as in (6b). The fact that a significant majority of informants chose to chunk the sentence as in (6a) refutes the NP-VP division of most PSGs.

The second thing that the data in (6a–c) reveal is that the string *I am* is likely a component. This then refutes the UD analysis of auxiliary verbs. The two competing structural analyses are repeated here as (7a–b):

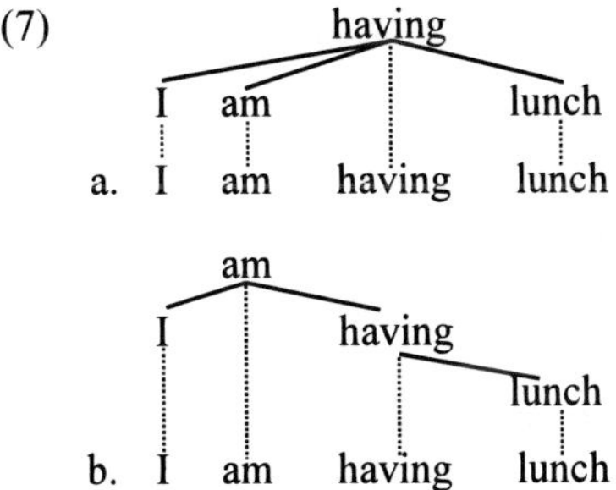

On the UD analysis given as (7a), the string *I am* is NOT a component. Accordingly, the prediction is that informants should not choose to chunk the sentence in a way that produces this chunk. The fact that 26 of the informants, a significant majority, did choose to chunk the sentence in this

manner refutes the UD annotation scheme concerning auxiliary verbs.

The third thing that the data in (6a–c) reveal is that the traditional analysis given as (7b) receives support. On that analysis, the relevant strings (*I, I am, having lunch, am having lunch, I am having,* and *lunch*) are all components. Most importantly, the string *I am* is a component on that analysis, and so is *having lunch.* This dovetails with the fact that those two strings were the chunks chosen by a majority of the informants, 26 of them.

An objection that can be raised at this point concerns the fact that the subject *I* in (6) is a prosodically weak definite pronoun and that this prosodic weakness might be more responsible for the status of *I am* as a chunk than anything in the syntax. In a follow-up round of data collection, we tested this possibility. The additional sentence we tested in this area and the informant responses we collected are given next:

(8) a. Sam | has arrived.   – 28 responses
    b. Sam has | arrived.   – 3 responses

These results support the insight that prosodic strength is indeed likely a factor influencing how informants chunk sentences. In this case, the preferred analysis was to grant the prosodically strong proper noun *Sam* alone the status of a chunk.

This insight, however, does not contradict the central claim in this contribution, namely that the chunks informants produce are components. In fact, it seems likely that both avenues of addressing chunking data are valid. In other words, there is a positive correlation between prosodic phrases and components. Prosodic phrases tend to be chunks and chunks tend to be components, which means prosodic phrases tend to be components.

Concerning example (8), a traditional analysis that positions the finite auxiliary *has* as the sentence root sees both of the strings *Sam* and *has arrived* as components:

(9)
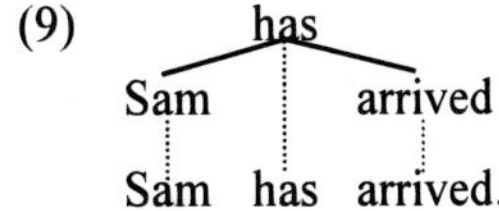

This means that the informant responses given in (8) do not contradict our hypothesis that informants chunk sentences in such a manner that the resulting chunks are components. What they do do, however, is reveal that prosodic factors influence which particular components will be chosen as chunks.

4.2 Subject-auxiliary inversion

Four of the sentences tested contained subject-auxiliary inversion. The responses we received in this area reveal that informants are reluctant to chunk between the subject and auxiliary verb. This reluctance again supports the traditional analysis which maintains a direct dependency between the subject and finite verb.

The four sentences we tested containing subject-auxiliary inversion are listed next: *Have you told them the truth?*, *Why did he quickly leave?*, *Did you send it out?*, and *Where did you go?*. The results for the first of these four sentences are provided here for discussion. The informants were invited to divide the sentence into three chunks. We received the following responses:

(8) a. Have you | told them | the truth?   − 39

    b. Have you told | them | the truth?   − 4

    c. Have | you told them | the truth?   − 2

    d. Have you | told | them the truth?   − 1

The two relevant and competing structural analyses of this sentence are as follows:

(9)

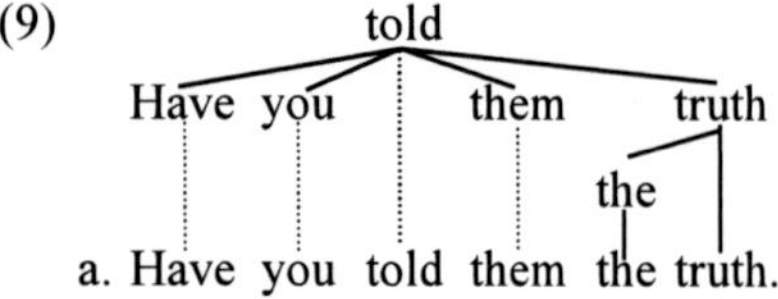

a. Have you told them the truth.

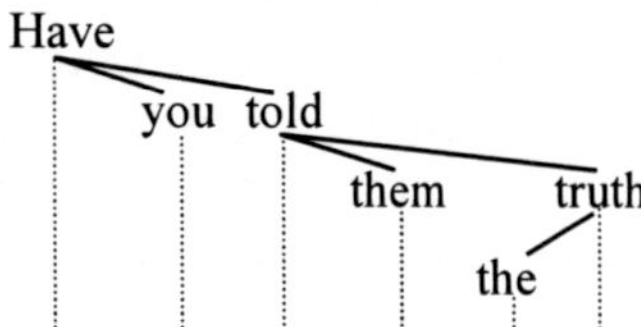

b. Have you told them the truth.

The analysis given as (9a) is that of UD; both the subject *you* and the auxiliary *have* appear as a dependent of the content verb *told*. The more traditional analysis is given as (9b); the finite verb, which is the auxiliary verb, is the root of the sentence there.

The fact that a large majority of the informants, 39 of 46, chose to chunk the sentence as in (8a) supports the traditional analysis given as (9b) over the UD analysis given as (9a). This conclusion follows from the status of the string *Have*

you as a non-component in (9a), but as a component in (9b). Observe also that each of the five chunks indicated in (8a) and (8b) is a component.

Worth considering in this area is that only 3 of the 46 informants chunked the sentence in a manner that was inconsistent with the traditional analysis given as (9b). The chunk *you told them* in (8c) is a not a component on the analysis in (9b), and the chunk *them the truth* in (8d) is also not a component on the analysis in (9a) and (9b). Anomalous responses like these were not unusual. For most of the sentence we tested, there was a small minority of informants that chunked the sentence at hand in a manner that contradicted the traditional analysis. It was usually the case, however, that a large majority of informants chunked the sentence at hand in a manner that contradicted the UD annotation scheme.

The results for the other three sentences containing subject-auxiliary inversion were similar. The results we obtained were more consistent with an analysis that takes the subject and auxiliary verb as forming a component than with one where the two do not form a component.

4.3 Sentence negation

We tested two sentences containing an auxiliary verb and the standard clausal negation *not*. The results we obtained again support the traditional hierarchical analysis of auxiliary verbs over the UD approach. Further, the results we obtained also support an analysis that positions the negation *not* as a postdependent of the auxiliary verb.

The two sentences containing *not* that we tested were *Jill did not laugh* and *I may not help them*. The informants were invited to divide these sentences into three chunks. The results we obtained for the latter sentence were as follows:

(10) a. I | may not | help them.   − 27

    b. I may not | help | them.   − 7

    c. I may | not | help them.   − 6

    d. I | may not help | them.   − 5

    e. I may | not help | them.   − 4

Four potential structural analyses of this sentence are as follows:

(11)

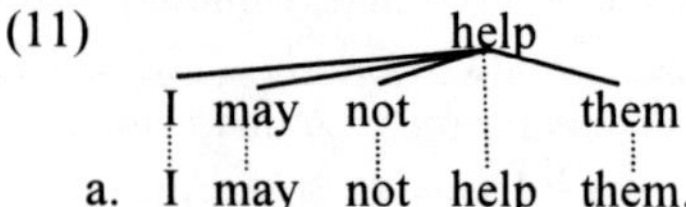

a. I may not help them.

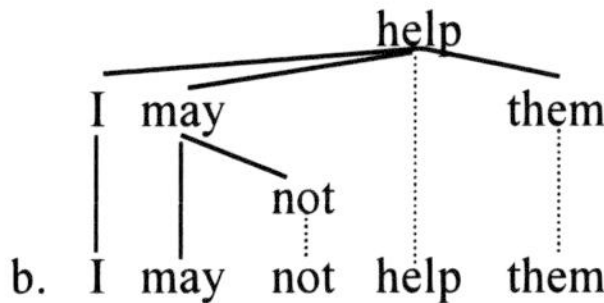

b. I may not help them.

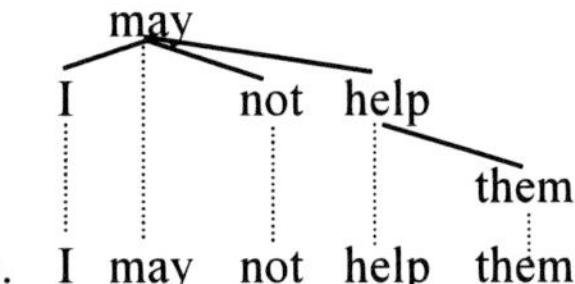

c. I may not help them.

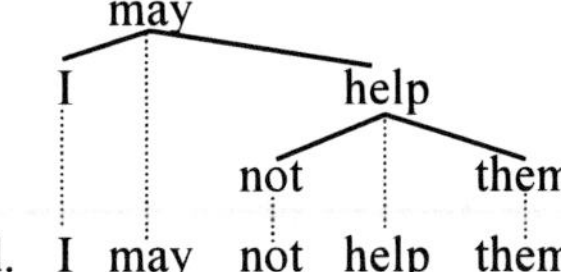

d. I may not help them.

The UD annotation scheme would likely pursue the analysis in (11a) or (11b), whereas more traditional assumptions would be along the lines of (11c) or (11d). Given the component unit and chunking data, it is possible to discern which of the four analyses is the best.

The chunking in (10a) and (10b) reveal first and foremost that *may not* and *I may not* should have component status. Since the analysis in (11c) is the only one of the four that grants both of these strings component status, it is preferable. Observe as well that the chunks indicated in (10c) and (10d) are also all components on the analysis in (11c). Only the chunking in (10e), which was produced by just four informants, contradicts the hierarchical analysis given as (10c), because the chunk *not help* in (10e) is not a component in (11c).

Concerning the other sentence containing *not* that we tested, i.e. *Jill did not laugh*, the results we obtained were as follows:

(12) a. Jill | did not | laugh.   − 44
      b. Jill did | not | laugh.   − 1
      c. Jill | did | not laugh.   − 1

These results are uninteresting insofar they do not clearly support one analysis over another, for if the negation *not* here is interpreted as a postdependent of the auxiliary verb *did*, similar to the analyses shown in both (11b) and (11c), then *did not* is a component on both accounts, the UD account and the traditional account.

4.4 Prepositions

Most DGs acknowledge prepositional phrases, that is, they view prepositions as heads over the nouns with which they co-occur. The UD annotation scheme, in contrast, positions prepositions as dependents of the nouns with which they co-occur. To shed light on these alternative analyses of prepositions, we included sentences containing prepositional phrases in our test sentences. The informant responses we obtained again support the traditional analysis over the UD approach.

Six of the sentences we tested contained a prepositional phrase. These six sentences are listed next: *Friends of mine are arriving now, I am in the classroom, One of the people protested, We are looking out for the teacher, He sleeps on his bed, We waited for Susan.* When invited to divide the last of these sentences into three chunks, the informants responded as follows:

(13) a. We | waited for | Susan.   − 32
      b. We | waited | for Susan.   − 6
      c. We waited | for | Susan.   − 5

The two relevant and competing hierarchical analyses of this sentence are given next:

(14)
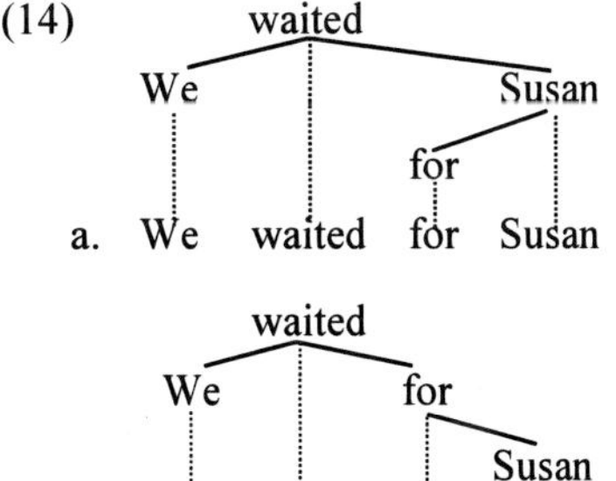

a. We waited for Susan

b. We waited for Susan.

The UD analysis is shown as (14a), and the more traditional analysis as (14b). The difference lies with the hierarchical position of the preposition.

The preferred way to chunk the sentence supports the traditional analysis. A large majority of informants, 32 of them, chunked the sentence in such a manner that *waited for* appears as a chunk. Since *waited for* is not a component on the UD analysis in (14a) but is a component on the traditional analysis in (14b), the traditional analysis is again more consistent with predictions based upon the component unit.

The results for the other five sentences containing a preposition were similar. While there were a few anomalies, the informants by and large chunked the sentences in ways that support the existence of prepositional phrases. Note that an important caveat concerning the data in (13) is mentioned in the conclusion below.

4.5 Determiners

The status of determiners has been controversial since the term *determiner phrase* (DP) first became established in the mid 1980s (e.g. Abney 1987). While the dominant view among DGs was and still is that determiners are dependents of their nouns, there have been exceptions. Most notably, Richard Hudson has argued in a number of works (e.g. 1984: 90–2, 1990: 268–276), that determiners are heads over their nouns. The component unit and chunking tasks can be brought to bear on this issue. The results we have obtained support the traditional NP analysis of nominal groups over the DP analysis.

Of the sentences we tested, eight of them contained a determiner, e.g. *Give me a call tomorrow*. Concerning the nominal group *a call* in this example, the two competing views about the hierarchical nature of nominal groups are present in the following analyses of the sentence:

(15)

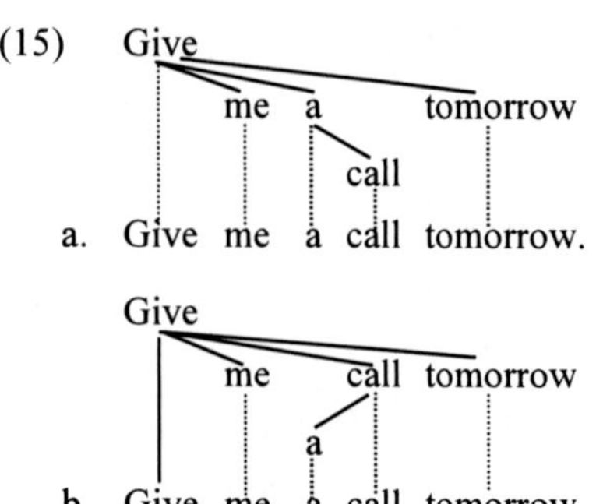

a. Give me a call tomorrow.

b. Give me a call tomorrow.

The DP analysis of *a call* shown in (15a) predicts that some informants would choose to chunk between *a* and *call*, since the structure in (15a) shows *Give me a* as a component. The NP analysis of *a call* shown in (15b), in contrast, predicts that informants will not chunk between *a* and *call*, because on that account, *Give me a* and *me a* would not be components.

The informant responses in this area were mostly consistent. With only 13 exceptions (among hundreds of responses), the informants chunked the eight sentences containing deter-

miners in such a manner that the determiner was grouped together with the following noun. For instance, sentence (15) was chunked as follows:

(16) a. Give me | a call | tomorrow. − 44

    b. Give | me | a call tomorrow. − 2

Not one of the informants who chunked this sentence chose to chunk between *a* and *call*. The three chunks shown in (16a) are components. The latter chunk in (16b), i.e. *a call tomorrow*, is the exception, since it is not a component in (15b) (and 15a).

The conclusion concerning determiners is therefore that informants prefer to group determines together with the nouns that follow them. This fact supports the traditional NP analysis of nominal groups over the DP analysis.

4.6 Object predicatives ("small clauses")

The hierarchical status of object predicative expressions, e.g. *I judged him to have lied*, has been a source of much debate among syntacticians. A ternary-branching analysis has been in competition with a strictly binary branching analysis. From the DG point of view, there are two conceivable analyses of these predicatives. The component unit and chunking task can be brought to bear on this issue. They reveal that the ternary-branching analysis should be preferred.

We tested four sentences that contained object predicatives: *I judged him to have lied*, *My parents expect me to become a doctor*, *We believe Sam to be upset*, and *They want you to go home*. Three possible structural analyses of the first of these four sentences are given next:

(17)

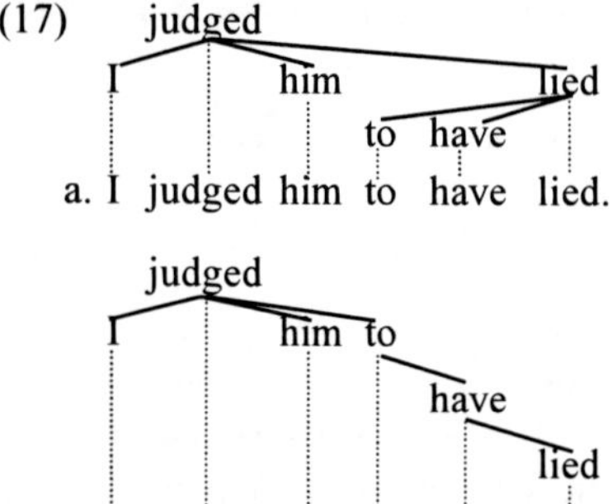

a. I judged him to have lied.

b. I judged him to have lied.

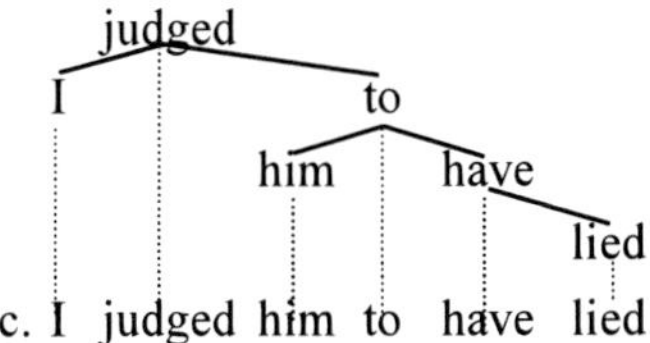

c. I judged him to have lied.

The UD approach is likely to pursue (17a). A "small clause" analysis would be along the lines of (17c). Analysis (17b) can be viewed as the traditional analysis of object predicatives in DG (see Kunze, 1975: 111–2; Schubert, 1987: 94–6; and Heringer, 1996: 76–7).

The informant responses we received for this sentence are listed next:

(18) a. I | judged him | to have lied. – 25
    b. I judged him | to | have lied. – 4
    c. I | judged him to | have lied. – 4
    d. I judged | him | to have lied. – 3
    e. I judged | him to | have lied. – 3
    f. I | judged | him to have lied. – 3
    g. I judged | him to have | lied. – 1

The fact that a majority of informants preferred to chunk this sentence immediately after the object *him* provides guidance about the structure. The small clause analysis (17c) can be immediately rejected because it does not grant the chunk *judged him* component status. Choosing between (17a) and (17b) is more difficult based on the informant responses. The informants that chunked the sentence as in (18c) did, however, provide some guidance insofar as the chunk *judged him to* is a component in (17b) but not in (17a).

Other considerations allow the approach to more confidently choose between (17a) and (17b). The discussion of auxiliary verbs above in Sections 4.1, 4.2, and 4.3 established that auxiliary verbs are plausibly viewed as heads over the content verbs with which they co-occur. This fact hence points to (17b) as the best analysis, since (17b) does, but (17a) does not, position the auxiliary verb *have* as head over *lied*.

The informant responses we received for the other four sentences that contained an object predicative further support the conclusion. The traditional, ternary-branching analysis of object predicatives, as in (17b), is well motivated based upon the reasoning from chunking and the component unit.

5 Overall relevance of component unit

Given the aspects of sentence structure established in the previous sections, it has become possible to put everything together in order to arrive at a motivated analysis of the overall structures discussed. We calculated the overall component to non-component ratio given traditional structures as opposed to structures corresponding to the UD annotation scheme. These overall numbers provide a cumulative argument in favor of the traditional structures.

The following points were established above:

1. Auxiliary verbs are heads over content verbs.

2. The nature of subject-auxiliary inversion further supports the stance that auxiliary verbs are heads over content verbs.

3. The sentence negation *not* is typically a postdependent of the auxiliary verb that precedes it.

4. Prepositional phrases exist, that is, the preposition is the head of the phrase it introduces.

5. The traditional NP analysis of nominal groups is preferable over the DP analysis.

6. Object predicatives are best analyzed with a ternary-branching structure that positions the object as an immediate dependent of the matrix verb.

To illustrate all of these points in one structure, we offer the following example:

(19) 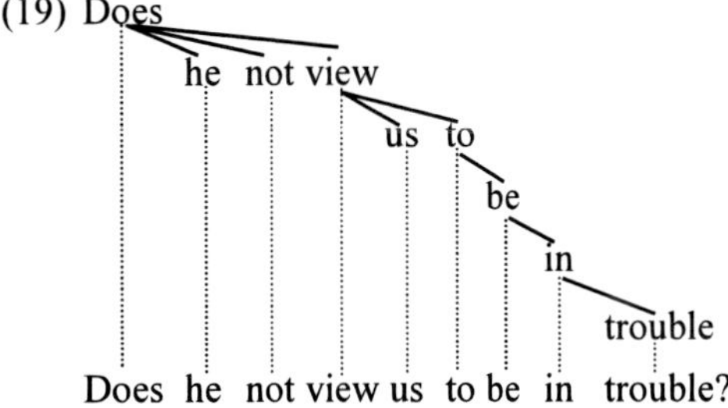

Does he not view us to be in trouble?

If one produces hierarchical analyses of this sort for all 25 of the original sentences we tested on informants, one can then check to see how many of the chunks (consisting of two or more words) produced by informants were and were not components.[5] By doing so, one arrives at an overall number that can be used to summarize the validity of varying assumptions about syntactic structure (e.g. traditional analysis vs. UD).

We obtained a total of 2,252 chunks from informants that consisted of two or more words. Among these 2,252 chunks, 2,124 of them were identified as components on traditional assumptions about sentence structure (as illustrated with 19). Thus, the ratio of component strings to total strings (abbreviated as R_C) reached 94%. In contrast, a smaller number of these chunks, i.e. 1,632 of them, were components on competing UD assumptions about sentence structure, rendering R_C at 72%.

The results just mentioned are given visually with the following pie charts:

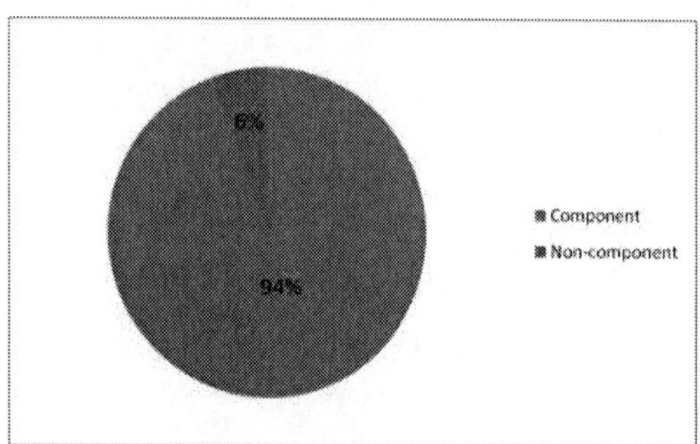

Figure 1. Component to non-component chunks on traditional analysis; R_c = 94%

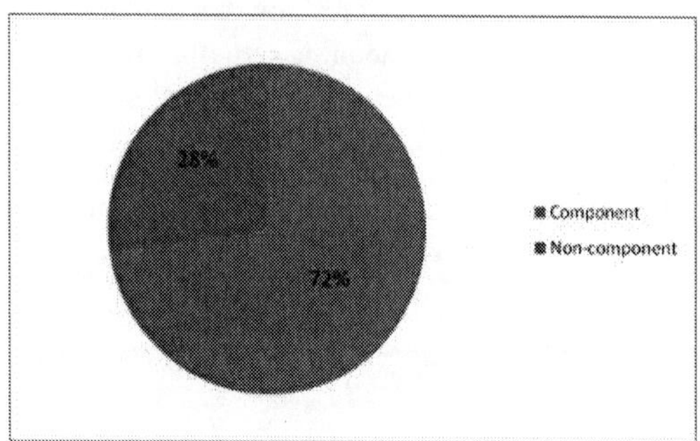

Figure 2. Component to non-component chunks on UD annotation scheme; R_c = 72%

The higher number of component chunks on the traditional analysis supports traditional DG

---

[5] The qualification "consisting of two or more words" is important. Individual words are always components by definition (regardless of the hierarchical analysis assumed). They were therefore excluded from the calculations in order to more strongly draw out the contrasts in the numbers across the two competing hierarchical analyses.

assumptions about the structure of sentences in English over the UD annotation scheme.

6   Concluding comments

This manuscript has employed the component unit, which is a novel unit of dependency syntax, to shed light on aspects of sentence structure in English. It should be evident that the simple methodology and reasoning employed can be easily extended to other languages. As long as one has access to a significant number of speakers of the language under investigation, the relevant data can be easily collected and analyzed to resolve issues about the hierarchical structures of that language. Indeed, the methodology and reasoning we have employed in this study are currently being extended to Chinese to resolve issues about the hierarchical analysis of Chinese sentences.

The principle objection that can be raised against the message delivered in this contribution concerns the informants – see note 4. Native speakers of Chinese may chunk English sentences differently than native speakers of English. In an effort to address this objection, a follow-up round of data collection was conducted on 13 native speakers of English. Most of the sentences presented and discussed above were tested. The results obtained matched those of the Chinese informants, with one exception.

The exception is present in the following numbers:

f.   We | waited | for Susan.   – 9
     We | waited for | Susan.   – 3
     We waited | for | Susan.   – 1

Comparing these numbers with the numbers for sentence (13) above, there is an obvious difference. These numbers from native informants are more congruent with the UD analysis, which subordinates the preposition *for* to the proper noun *Susan*.

Caution is therefore warranted concerning the greater conclusion. Solid claims about syntactic structure of English sentences will become possible only after the project has been extended to include data from large numbers of native informants.

Acknowledgement

The research presented in this article was funded by the Ministry of Education of the People's Republic of China, Grant # 15YJA74001.

References

Paul Steven Abney. 1987. The English noun phrase in its sentential aspect. Doctoral dissertation, MIT, Cambridge, MA.

John Anderson. 2011. *The substance of language volume I: The domain of syntax*. Oxford University Press.

Norbert Bröker. 2003. Formal foundations of dependency grammar. In Vilmos Ágel et al. (eds.), *Dependency and valency: An international handbookof contemporary research*, vol. 1, 294–310. Walter de Gruyter, Berlin.

Ulrich Engel. 1994. *Syntax der deutschen Gegenwartssprache*, 3rd ed. Erich Schmidt Verlag, Berlin.

Hans-Werner Eroms. 2000. *Syntax der deutschen Sprache*. Walter de Gruyter, Berlin.

Chaim Gaifman. 1965. Dependency systems and phrase-structure systems. *Information and Control* 8, 304–337.

Thomas Groß and Timothy Osborne. 2009. Toward a practical dependency grammar theory of discontinuities. *SKY Journal of Linguistics* 22, 43–90.

David Hays. 1964. Dependency theory: A formalism and some observations. *Language* 40, 511–525.

Peter Hellwig. 2003. Dependency Unification Grammar. *Dependency and valency: An international handbook of contemporary research*, ed. by Vilmos Ágel et al., 593–635. Walter de Gruyter, Berlin.

Hans Jürgen Heringer. 1996. *Deutsche Syntax: Dependentiell*. Stauffenburg, Tübingen.

Richard Hudson. 1984. *Word Grammar*. Basil Blackwell, Oxford.

Richard Hudson. 1990. *An English Word Grammar*. Basil Blackwell, Oxford.

Richard Hudson. 2007. *Language networks: The new Word Grammar*. Oxford University Press.

Sylvain Kahane. 1996. If HPSG were a dependency grammar... *Actes de TALN*, Marseille, 22–24, 45–49.

Franz Kern. 1883. *Zur Methodik des deutschen Unterrichts*. Nicolaische Verlags-Buchhandlung, Berlin.

Franz Kern. 1884. *Grundriss der Deutschen Satzlehre*. Nicolaische Verlagsbuchhandlung, Berlin.

Jürgen Kunze. 1975. *Abhängigkeitsgrammatik*. Series: *studia grammatika XII*. Akademie-Verlag, Berlin.

Marie-Catherine de Marneffe, Timothy Dozat, Natalia Silvaire, Katrin Haverinen, Filip Ginter, Joakim Nivre, Christopher D. Manning. 2014. Universal Stanford Dependencies: A cross-linguistic typology. *LREC* 14.

Igor Mel'čuk. 1988. *Dependency syntax: Theory and practice*. Albany: State University of New York Press.

Igor Mel'čuk and Nikolai Pertsov. 1987. *Surface syntax of English: A formal model with the Meaning-Text Framework*. Benjamins, Amsterdam.

William O'Grady 1998. The syntax of idioms. *Natural Language and Linguistic Theory* 16, 79–312

Timothy Osborne and Thomas Groß. 2016. The *do-so*-diagnositc: Against finite VPs and for flat non-finite VPs. *Folia Linguistica* 50, 1, 97-35

Timothy Osborne, Michael Putnam, and Thomas Groß. 2012. Catenae: Introducing a novel unit of syntactic analysis. *Syntax* 15, 354-396.

Jane Robinson. 1970. Dependency structures and transformational rules. *Language* 46, 259–285.

Klaus Schubert. 1987. *Metataxis: Contrastive dependency syntax for machine translation*. Foris Publications, Dordrecht.

Stanley Starosta. 1988. *The case for Lexicase: An outline of Lexicase grammatical theory*. Pinter Publishers, London.

Control vs. Raising in English
A Dependency Grammar Account

Timothy Osborne
Zhejiang University
Hangzhou
China
tjo3ya@yahoo.com

Matthew Reeve
Zhejiang University
Hangzhou
China
mjreeve@zju.edu.cn

Abstract

This contribution presents a dependency grammar (DG) account of control and raising in English. Due to the minimalism of DG analyses of sentence structure, the difference between control and raising cannot be captured in the syntactic structure alone. The situation forces the DG account to reach to some other aspect of dependency syntax other than the raw hierarchies of structure to account for the differences between control and raising. This other aspect is valency. Valency has, of course, been a central subtheory of dependency syntax since Tesnière (1959/2015: Book D). By augmenting the valency frames of predicates to distinguish between valents that are and are not semantic arguments of the predicate at hand, the differences between control and raising can be acknowledged and accommodated.

1 Control vs. raising

The distinction between control and raising predicates in English and related languages is well established. These two types of predicates have a combinatory potential that appears to be essentially the same at first blush, e.g.

(1) a. Sam preferred to stop.

    b. Sam seemed to stop.

The control predicate *preferred* and the raising predicate *seemed* both combine with a *to*-infinitive. This similarity obscures the fact that there are important differences in how the two behave semantically.

Consider in this regard that many DGs would produce structural analyses of these two sentences that are hierarchically the same, e.g.

(1)

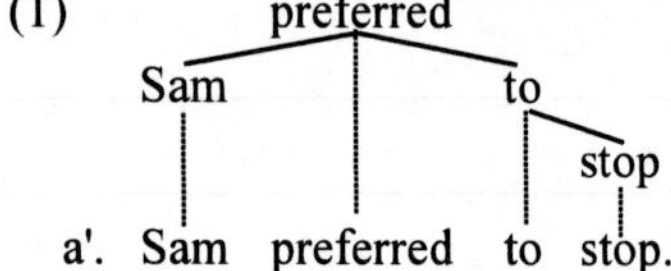

a'. Sam preferred to stop.

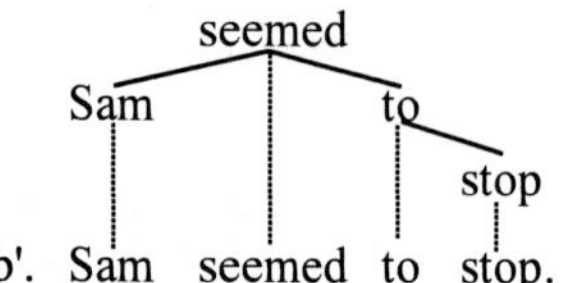

b'. Sam seemed to stop.

The finite verb in these cases is clearly the clause root, and the subject and *to*-infinitive are then dependents of the root. Given this state of affairs, it might seem that DG has nothing to say about the differences between these two classes of predicates.

The differences between control and raising predicates are substantial. For instance, one can often form the passive of a control predicate, but not of a raising predicate, e.g.

(2) a. To stop was preferred (by Sam).

    b. *To stop was seemed (by Sam).

The expletive *there* can often combine with a raising predicate, but not with a control predicate, e.g.

(3) a. *There preferred to be objections.

    b. There seemed to be objections.

Further, raising often allows the alternative formulation with expletive *it* and a full clause or *to*-infinitive, e.g.

(4) a. *It preferred that Sam stopped.

    b. It seemed that Sam stopped.

The aspect of control and raising predicates that helps one understand how these differences exist lies with the (in)ability of the predicate at hand to semantically select (one of) the valent(s) that it takes. Control predicates semantically select their valent(s), whereas raising predicates do not semantically select (one of) their valent(s).

Semantic selection is indeed the concept necessary for accounting for examples (2–4). The control predicate *prefer* semantically selects an experiencer valent (*Sam* in 1a). The raising predicate *seem* does not, in contrast, place any semantic restrictions on its subject valent, but rather its subject valent must be compatible with the embedded

Proceedings of the Fourth International Conference on Dependency Linguistics (Depling 2017), pages 176-186,
Pisa, Italy, September 18-20 2017

predicate. This means that just the embedded predicate *to stop* in (1b) semantically selects the subject *Sam*, whereas both the matrix predicate *preferred* and the embedded predicate *to stop* in (1a) semantically select the subject predicate *Sam*. The primary difference between control and raising predicates therefore resides with the locus of semantic selection, i.e. matrix predicate and/or embedded predicate.

Acknowledging that there are indeed important differences between control and raising predicates, DG would seem to be challenged, since the structural analyses DGs produce of such predicates cannot distinguish any significant hierarchical difference between them, as illustrated with the trees (1a'–b').

The greater goal of this manuscript is to investigate the distinction between control and raising predicates from a DG perspective. The message delivered is that the differences between the two predicate types indeed cannot be captured in the hierarchy of structure, but rather it should be located in the subtheory of valency. Valency frames that are sufficiently augmented to distinguish between argument and non-argument valents can capture the differences between control and raising.

2 Terminology

A control predicate such as *prefer* involves so-called *subject control*, because the matrix subject is also the understood subject of the embedded predicate. A raising predicate such as *seem* is known as a *raising-to-subject* verb because it appears as though the subject of the embedded predicate has been raised into the position of the matrix subject. We build on this sort of terminology here, although the specific terms we employ to denote these predicate types are more exact: *prefer* is called a *subject-to-subject (S-to-S)* control predicate, and *seem* a *subject-from-subject (S-from-S)* raising predicate.

The motivation for this use of terminology is illustrated schematically as follows:

S-to-S control

(4) a. Bill prefers __ to nap in the afternoon.

S-from-S raising

   b. Bill seems __ to nap in the afternoon.

The arrows now show the distinction between control and raising. The appearance of *to* or *from* in the two terms captures the fundamental distinction just sketched in the previous section. The subject valent of the matrix predicate *prefers* in (4a) is conveyed *to* the embedded predicate, so that it can serve as the subject of that predicate. In contrast, the raising predicate *seems* in (4b) raises its subject valent *from* the subject position of the embedded predicate.

Note that our use of terminology should be understood metaphorically. We do not, namely, advocate a transformational understanding of these structures, but rather we are employing the terminology in a manner that we think is accessible to the widest possible audience. The type of DG we advocate is decidedly monostratal in syntax.

The schematic notions just employed can be extended to denote other types of control and raising predicates. Cases of so-called *object control* and *raising-to-object* can be denoted more exactly as *object-to-subject (O-to-S) control* and *object-from-subject (O-from-S) raising*, e.g.

O-to-S control

(5) a. Sue asked Jim __ to stay.

O-from-S raising

   b. Sue expected Jim __ to stay.

The *there*-diagnostic verifies that *ask* is a control predicate, and *expect* a raising predicate: **Sue asked there to be a problem* vs. *Sue expects there to be a problem*.

The dependency hierarchies for these sentences are as follows:

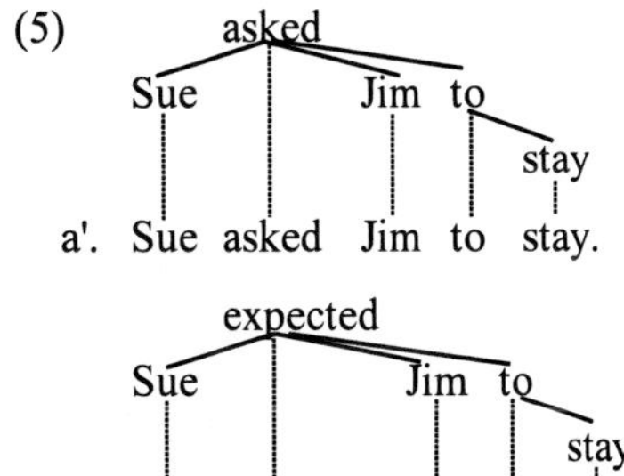

These trees demonstrate again that from the DG perspective, there is no hierarchical difference in the syntactic structure across control and raising predicates. The differences lie, rather, in the lexicon with the combinatory potential of the distinct predicate types.

The types of control and raising predicates mentioned so far are widely acknowledged and have been studied a lot, as is apparent in textbook accounts (e.g. Haegeman 1991: 237–70, 282–95, Radford 2013: 431–50, Carnie 2013: 431–56). The terminology adopted here suggests, however, that the typology goes further, that is, that additional types of control and raising predicates can be discerned. This is indeed the case. One can also identify *S-to-O* and *O-to-O* control predicates as well as *S-from-O* and *O-from-O* raising predicates. The following tables provide an overview of all eight predicate types with representative examples given.

Control predicates	
S-to-S	*ask, attempt, begin, eager, expect, happy, have, hope, refuse, reluctant, start, stop, try, too*+adjective, *want, willing*
S-to-O	*available, heavy, light, pretty, ready, soft, tasty, too*+adjective
O-to-S	*ask, encourage, force, hear, help, listen, persuade, tell*
O-to-O	*bring, build, buy, create, give, take*

Raising predicates	
S-from-S	*appear, apt, certain, happen, have, likely, prove, seem, tend, threaten, unlikely*
S-from-O	*bad, easy, difficult, fun, good, hard, tough,*
O-from-S	*assess, believe, consider, deem, expect, judge, make, need, see, view, want*
O-from-O	*have, get, want*

Four of these predicate types have already been mentioned and illustrated above. The status of the remaining four as control and raising predicates is less known and certainly controversial. They are illustrated and discussed below in Section 8.

Observe that some predicates appear in more than one category. Many predicates can license control or raising based on context, e.g. *expect, want*. This points to an important aspect of these categories. Most control and raising verbs and adjectives (and nouns) have a combinatory potential that is to a greater or lesser degree flexible, hence often two or more (often many more) distinct valency frames characterize the combinatory potential of a given verb or adjective (or noun).[1]

3 Structural analysis

The dependency trees (1a'–b') and (5a'–b') have demonstrated that the basic structural analyses that DGs produce do not distinguish between control and raising in the hierarchy of structure. This fact seems problematic in view of the differences across the two. One might expect, namely, that given the differing behaviors with respect to passivization, *there*-insertion, and *it*-extraposition that significantly different structures for each would obtain.

Indeed, one might strive to accommodate the differences by pursuing distinct structural analyses. For instance, sentences (5a–b) could be analyzed as follows:

(5)

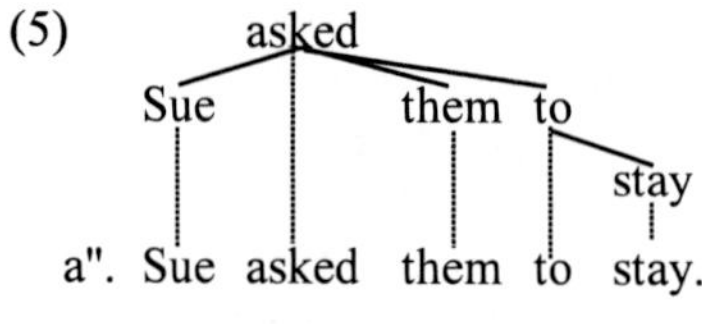

a". Sue asked them to stay.

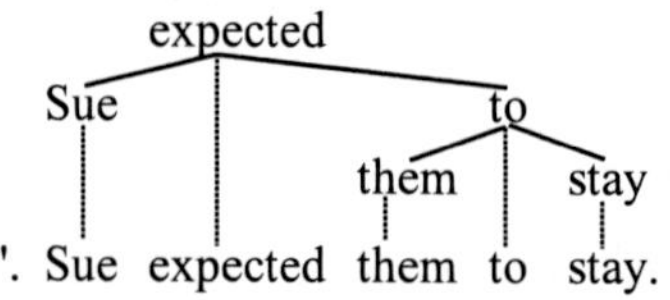

b". Sue expected them to stay.

The analysis given as (5a") is the same as (5a'). The analysis given as (5b"), however, is different from (5b'); the object *Jim* has been subordinated to the particle *to* in a manner that suggests a small-clause-type account. Certainly, other variations on the analysis given as (5b") are also conceivable. The point to be established next, though, is that there are good reasons to reject analyses along the lines of (5b"). The ternary branching analysis given as (5b') is in fact well motivated (cf. Kunze 1975: 111–2, Schubert 1987: 94–6, and Heringer 1996: 76–7)).

O-to-S control predicates like *ask* and O-from-S raising predicates like *expect* actually behave the same with respect to a battery of other diagnostics, as illustrated next:

Topicalization

(6) a. *…but **Jim to stay**, Sue did ask.

   b. *…but **Jim to stay**, Sue did expect.

   c. …but **Jim** Sue did ask to stay.

---

[1] That nouns license control and/or raising is evident with NPs such as *These hot wings are bitch to enjoy*. Due to space limitations, however, nouns in this role are not examined in this contribution.

d. …but **Jim** Sue did expect to stay.

Clefting

(7) a. *It was **Jim to stay** that Sue asked.
   b. *It is **Jim to stay** that Sue expected.

   c. It was **Jim** who Sue asked to stay.
   d. It was **Jim** who Sue expected to stay.

Passivization

(8) a. ***Jim to stay** was asked (by Sue).
   b. ***Jim to stay** was expected (by Sue).

   c. **Jim** was asked (by Sue) to stay.
   d. **Jim** was expected (by Sue) to stay.

Reflexivization

(9) a. *Sue$_1$ did ask **her**$_1$ to stay.

   b. *Sue$_1$ did expect **her**$_1$ to stay.

   c. Sue$_1$ did ask **herself**$_1$ to stay.
   d. Sue$_1$ did expect **herself**$_1$ to stay.

Each of these four data sets illustrates an aspect of control and raising predicates that supports the relatively flat, ternary-branching analyses given as (5a'–b').

The topicalization data illustrate that *Jim to stay* cannot be fronted, whereas *Jim* alone can be. Similarly, the clefting data illustrate that *Jim to stay* cannot be focused as the pivot of cleft sentence, whereas *Jim* alone can be. The passivization data demonstrate that *Jim to stay* cannot become the subject of a passive sentence, but *Jim* alone can; and the reflexivization data show that if co-reference obtains across the subject and object, then the object must appear as a reflexive; this fact is, then, congruent with the flat analysis, where the object is a dependent of the matrix predicate. In sum, the four diagnostics are consistent with the flat analysis, where *Jim to stay* does not form a constituent (i.e. a complete subtree) and both *Jim* and *to stay* are immediate dependents of the matrix predicate.²

There is a fifth observation that further strengthens the ternary branching analysis given as (5a–b). It is possible to insert an adverb that modifies the matrix predicate between the object nominal and the embedded predicate, e.g.

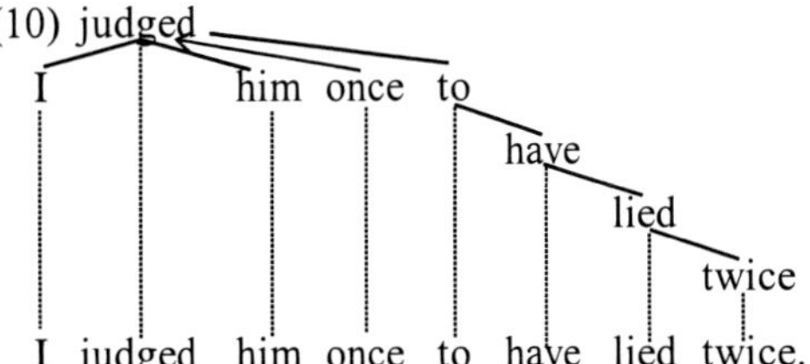

The arrow dependency edge (pointing from *once* to *judged*) marks *once* as an adjunct. Using a particular visual convention like this in the dependency tree to identify adjuncts has precedent, although the specific convention used varies (e.g. Tarvainen 1981: 61, Engel 1994: 44, Eroms 2000: 85–6).

The position of the adverb *once* between the object *him* and the *to*-infinitive phrase is accommodated if the structural analysis shown is assumed. There is no semantic contradiction, since the adverb *once* modifies the 'judging', and the adverb *twice*, the 'lying'. The alternative analysis that positions *him* as a dependent of *to* (or *have*) would incur a projectivity violation, since *once* would still necessarily be a modifier, i.e. a dependent, of *judged*.

In sum, the fact that control and raising structures receive the same structural analysis here is well motivated and should therefore not be construed as a problem for DG more generally. It does, though, raise the basic question about how DGs can capture the distinction in an insightful way. The point established below is that a DG can do this in terms of the combinatory potential of the relevant predicates. This combinatory potential is captured with valency frames.

4   Phrase structure accounts

Before proceeding to the discussion of valency frames, it is worth considering how the control vs. raising distinction is addressed in some phrase structure grammars (PSGs). The Government and Binding framework explored the distinction between control and raising extensively (e.g. Chomsky 1981: 55–92). It captured the distinction in terms thematic marking and null elements. The null element PRO was put forth as a means of understanding control, and in cases of raising, a trace t was placed in the base position of the raised constituent.

---

² See Hays (1960:261, 1964:520) and Kunze (1975:13) for the use of the term *complete subtree* of dependency syntax as being analogous to the constituent of phrase structure syntax.

Given the null elements PRO and t, control and raising predicates were analyzed along the following lines:

<u>Subject control</u>
(11) a. Neil₁ refused PRO₁ to slow down.

<u>Object control</u>
b. They forced Neil₁ PRO₁ to slow down.

<u>Raising-to-subject</u>
(12) a. Neil₁ appeared t₁ to slow down.

<u>Raising-to-object</u>
b. They need Neil₁ t₁ to slow down.

Hence the fundamental insight that control predicates do, but raising predicates do not, semantically select (one of) their valent(s) is captured via the presence of distinct types of null elements and, in the case of raising, the assumption that movement occurs.

Stepping back for a moment, positing the existence of null elements such as PRO and t is independent of the dependency vs. phrase structure distinction. In this regard, nothing prevents a DG from also addressing the control vs. raising distinction in terms of null elements and movement. One could, for example, advocate for the following structural analyses of the examples just given:

(11)
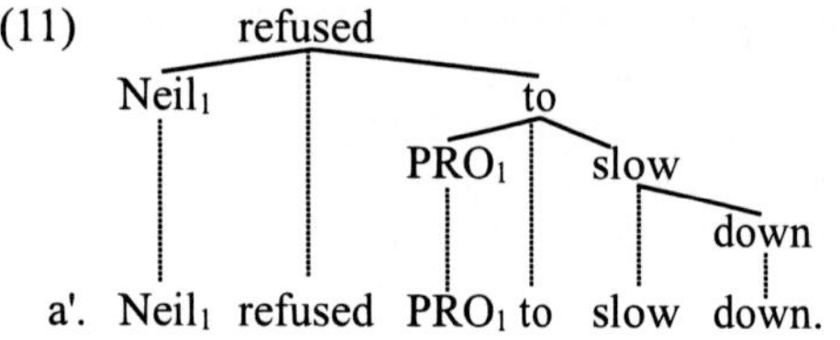

a'. Neil₁ refused PRO₁ to slow down.

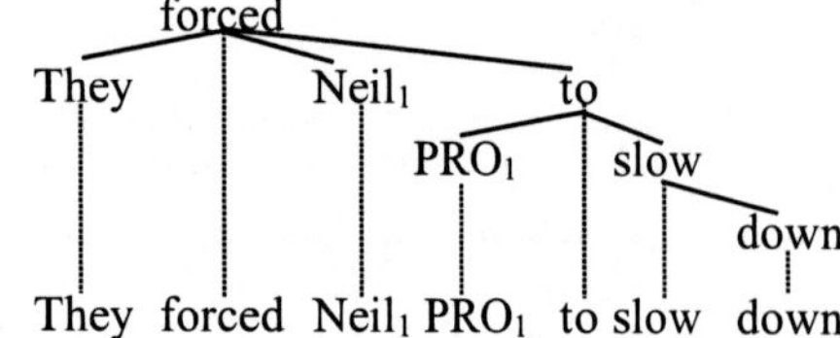

b'. They forced Neil₁ PRO₁ to slow down.

(12)
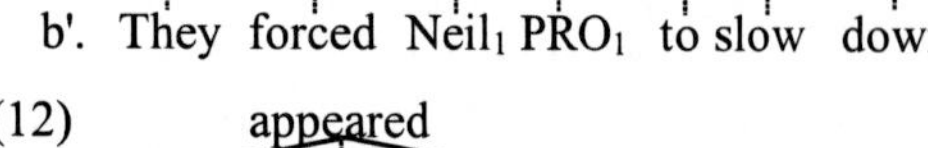

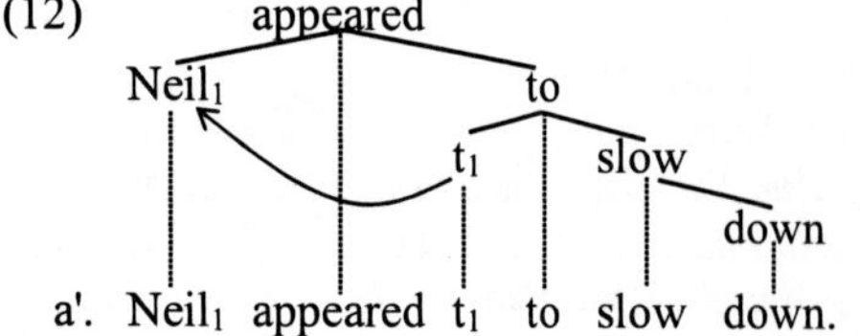

a'. Neil₁ appeared t₁ to slow down.

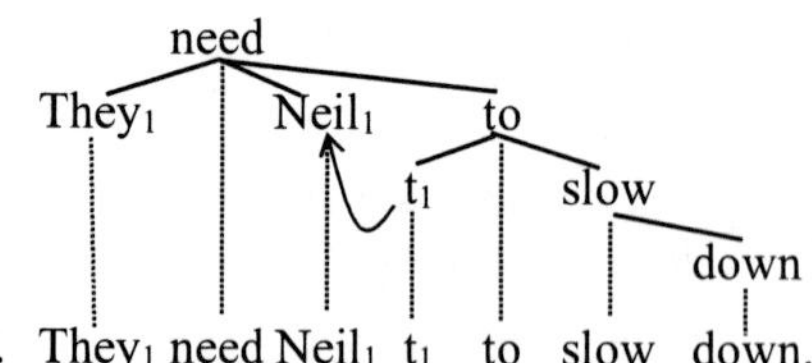

b'. They₁ need Neil₁ t₁ to slow down.

A theory of syntax that acknowledges such null elements takes the control vs. raising distinction to be a phenomenon of syntax. This is particular true of traces, since their existence is contingent upon the occurrence of movement, a transformational notion that is located entirely in syntax.

While nothing prevents a DG from positing the existence of null elements and movement, DGs have traditionally been loath to do so. DG by nature is strongly lexical. This is in fact a necessity, since the minimalism of dependency structures cannot accommodate the richness of category distinctions associated with some PSGs. For instance, DGs are incapable of locating in the rich hierarchy functional categories posited by the Minimalist Program (MP), e.g. Focus Phrase (FP), Agreement Phrase (AgrP), Tense Phrase (TP), Topic Phrase (TopP), etc.

What all this means for the DG analysis of control and raising predicates is that an approach that looks to the lexicon is more consistent with the spirt of dependency syntax. The distinction between control and raising predicates resides with the combinatory potential of the relevant predicates, and this combinatory potential is captured via valency frames.

5   Three options

There are three basic options for addressing control and raising in dependency syntax:

1. Networks,
2. An augmented inventory of syntacitc relations, and/or
3. Augmented valency frames

The first option, i.e. networks, stipulates additional dependencies to show the extent to which control and raising predicates designate one of their valents to serve as the valent of a lower predicate. The second option adds more syntactic relations and then addresses the difference between control and raising in terms of these additional relations. The third option locates control and raising entirely in the lexicon and distinguishes between them in terms of valency frames. The third option is the one pursued below.

Most DGs conceive of syntactic structure in terms of trees. Trees are not a necessity, however. When a dependency grammar allows a given word to have more than a single parent word, it assumes networks. Word Grammar (e.g. Hudson 1990) is perhaps the most prominent DG to assume networks. The Word Grammar analysis of control and raising structures is along the following lines:

(13)

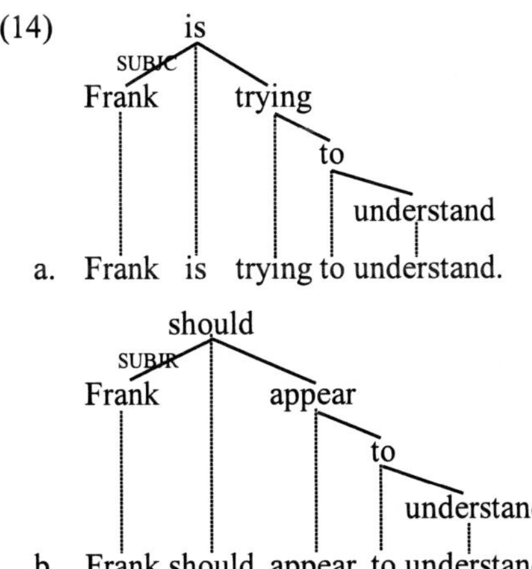

The fact that *Frank* is the logical subject of both the matrix and the embedded predicate is indicated directly in these cases by the fact that both *tried/appeared* and *understand* are shown as the parent of *Frank*.

While these networks accommodate the fact that *Frank* is the valent of two predicates at the same time, the presence of the additional dependency does not alone distinguish between control and raising. Something more is needed to this end. This necessity brings the discussion to the second option, namely an augmented inventory of syntactic relations.

Many DGs take the syntactic relations to be primitive and grant them an important role in the theory of syntax. In this regard, the distinction between control and raising might be addressed in terms of an augmented list of syntactic relations – cf. Mel'čuk and Persov (1987). The additional relations would be such that they would discern when control or raising is present. One might, for instance, posit distinct syntactic relations along the following lines (SUBJC = subject control, SUBJR = subject raising):

(14)

The presence of the labels indicating the pertinent syntactic relations in these two cases would discern and distinguish between control and raising. Note, however, the presence of the auxiliary verbs, *is* in (14a) and *should* in (14b). Their presence combined with the fact that the subject is an immediate dependent of the finite verb obscures the insight that it is the content verbs *tried* and *appeared* that are responsible for the presence of the syntactic realtions SUBJC and SUBJR.

The points just established reveal difficulties associated with the first two options for discerning and distinguishing between control and raising in dependency syntax. The first option, i.e. networks, is rejected here in part because we believe trees are a simpler and more principled basis for dependency syntax. The second option, i.e. an augmented inventory of syntactic relations, is also deemed insufficient for capturing the distinction between control and raising because they alone do not make clear that control and raising phenomena are closely linked to specific predicates.

The third option, namely valency frames, avoids networks at the same time that it it ties control and raising closely to specific predicates. The discussion now turns to these valency frames.

6   Valency frames

There is a long tradition of using valency frames, especially in the German language literature. In German, a valency frame is often called a *Satzmuster* 'sentence pattern'. Dictionaries of German provide dozens of Satzmuster as a guide to correct use of verbs and adjectives (and other types of predicates), e.g. *dtv Wörterbuch der deutschen Sprache* (1978: 30–3). To my knowledge, however, these dictionaries do not distinguish between control and raising predicates in a consistent and principled manner. The discussion here henceforth demonstrates how these frames can distinguish between control and raising predicates in English.

Table 3 gives the symbols employed in the valency frames below. The table is intended to serve as a quick reference guide to the valency frames introduced and discussed further below.

Symbol	What the symbol means
ᵃ	Marks an argument valent; the absence of this subscript indicates that the valent is not an argument of its governor

f, nf	valency frame given is valid for the finite/nonfinite form of the verb
N	Nominal (noun, pronoun, or noun phrase)
Pa	(Passive) perfect participle, e.g. *eaten, understood, worked*
T	*to*-infinitive phrase, e.g. *to stay*
R	R indicates that that valent is to be understood in terms of **raising**; the valency carrier does not syntactically select that valent
$\underline{N}$, $\underline{\underline{N}}$	Single underline marks that valent as the subject argument of a predicate lower in the structure; double underline marks that valent as the object argument of a lower predicate
↑	Up-arrow indicates that the valent does not appear as a dependent of the predicate, but rather it appears elsewhere in the structure or situational context

The valents of a predicate are enclosed in square brackets […] and the predicate itself is put in small caps and positioned to the immediate left of the brackets, e.g. *Harry loves Harriet* – LOVEf [Na, Na].

The machinery given in the table is just enough to address control and raising and distinguish between them. The list of categories and labels necessary for a full account of valency patterns in English would be much larger, of course.

7 *To/from*-subject predicates

The following four subsections provide examples of the four types of control and raising predicates already mentioned above. These predicates have the/a matrix valent serving as the subject argument of the embedded predicate. In order to have more space for the discussion for the more controversial types of control and raising discussed in Section 8, the discussion in this section is very brief.

7.1 S-to-S control

S-to-S control predicates are numerous and they occur frequently. Both verbs and adjectives can establish S-to-S control, e.g.

(15) 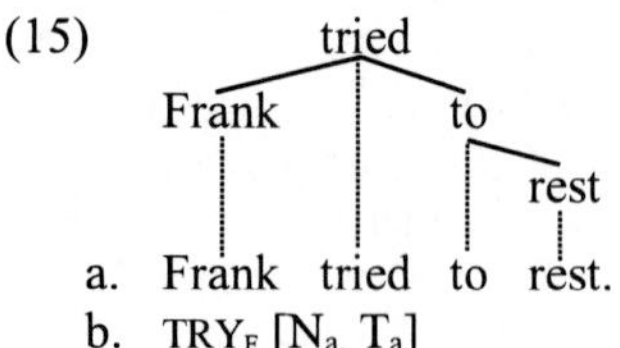

a. Frank tried to rest.
b. TRYF [Na, Ta]

(16) 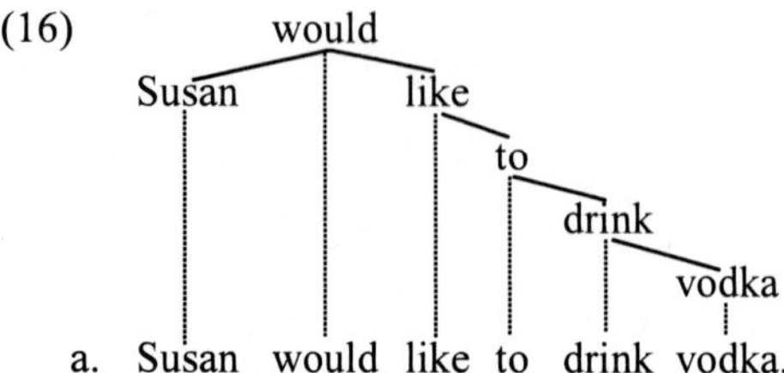

a. Susan would like to drink vodka.
b. LIKEnf [Na↑, Ta]

(17) 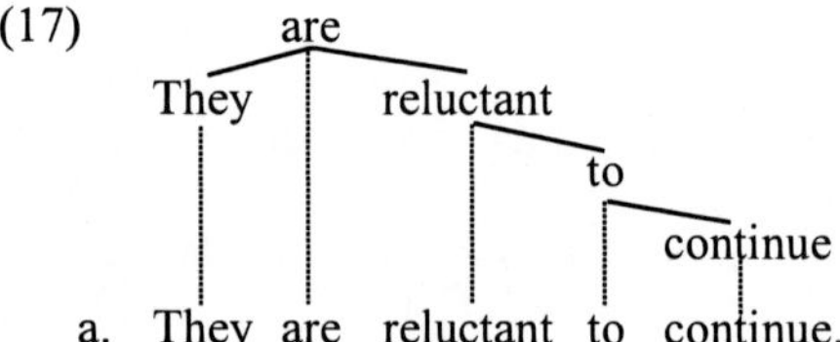

a. They are reluctant to continue.
b. RELUCTANT [Na↑, Ta]

The single underline under N marks that valent as controlling the embedded *to*-infinitive predicate. Hence the single underline marks that valent as the understood subject valent of the *to*-infinitive. The up-arrow in (16b) indicates that that valent is not a dependent of the nonfinite *like*, but rather it appears higher in the structure – in this case, as a dependent of the root verb *would*.

The up-arrow is a convention that helps characterize the primary combinatory difference between finite verbs and other nonfinite forms of predicates. For the use of similar means to indicate that the subject valents are typically not dependents of nonfinite forms, see Heringer (1996: 44, 62) and Starosta (2003: 275–6).

7.2 S-from-S raising

S-from-S raising also occurs with both verbs and adjectives, e.g.

(18) 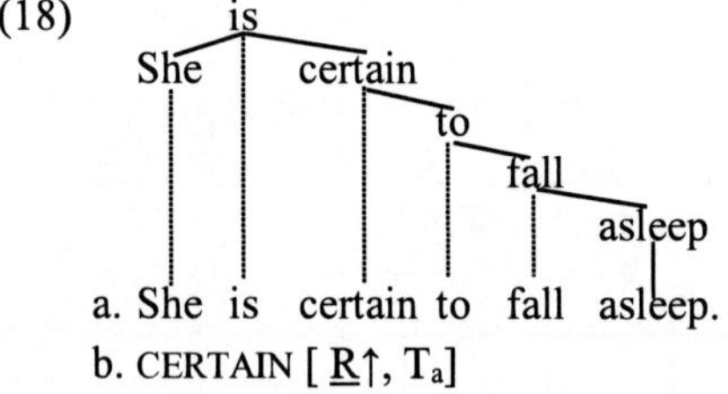

a. She is certain to fall asleep.
b. CERTAIN [R↑, Ta]

(19) a. The fridge is threatening to explode.
b. THREATENnf [R↑, Ta]

(20) a. They are unlikely to succeed.

    b. UNLIKELY [R↑, T$_a$]

These valency frames differ from those just given in the previous section regarding the presence of R and the absence of the $_a$ subscript on R. The R indicates that that valent is not syntactically selected by its parent, and the absence of the $_a$ subscript always indicates that that valent is also not semantically selected by its parent. At the same time, the single underline continues to indicate that that valent serves as the subject argument of the embedded infinitival predicate.

7.3   O-to-S control

O-to-S control predicates are also numerous, and they occur frequently as well. Examples follow:

(21)

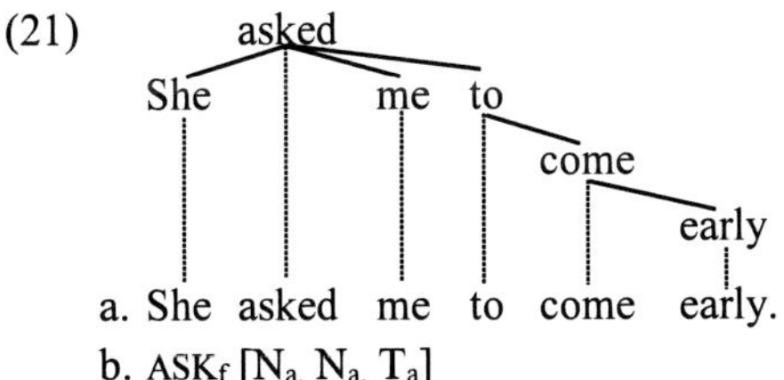

    a. She asked me to come early.

    b. ASK$_f$ [N$_a$, N̲$_a$, T$_a$]

(22) a. They have forced him to try it.

    b. FORCE$_{nf}$ [N$_a$↑, N̲$_a$, T$_a$]

(23) a. Jill told us to start immediately.

    b. TELL$_f$ [N$_a$, N̲$_a$, T$_a$]

The object now controls the embedded *to*-infinitive, functioning as its subject argument. The single underline continues to indicate that that valent serves as the understood subject valent of the embedded predicate.

7.4   O-from-S raising

O-from-S raising predicates have the matrix object, as opposed to the matrix subject, being semantically selected by the embedded nonfinite predicate. Only verbal predicates can do this, e.g.

(24)

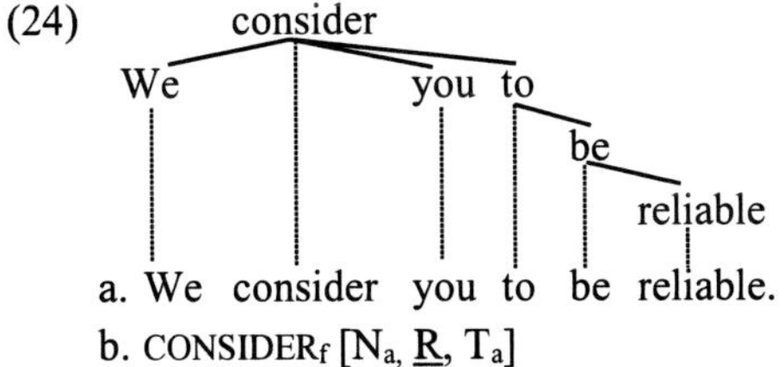

    a. We consider you to be reliable.

    b. CONSIDER$_f$ [N$_a$, R̲, T$_a$]

(25) a. They will need us to help them.

    b. NEED$_{nf}$ [N$_a$↑, R̲, T$_a$]

(26) a. He wants them to leave.

    b. WANT$_f$ [N$_a$, R̲, T$_a$]

The R and the absence of the $_a$ subscript on the R are again the means by which raising is indicated. The single underline continues to show that that valent serves as the subject valent of the embedded predicate.

8   To/from-object predicates

The following four subsections consider S-to-O and O-to-O control predicates as well as S-from-O and O-from-O raising predicates. The extent to which the predicates discussed are indeed control or raising predicates is less acknowledged and/or controversial. This, then, is arguably the merit of the current account; it discerns generalizations about control and raising predicates that have been overlooked.

8.1   S-to-O control

The typical S-to-O control predicates is an adjective, e.g. *available, fit, heavy, light, pretty, ready, soft, tasty, ugly, unavailable*:

(27)

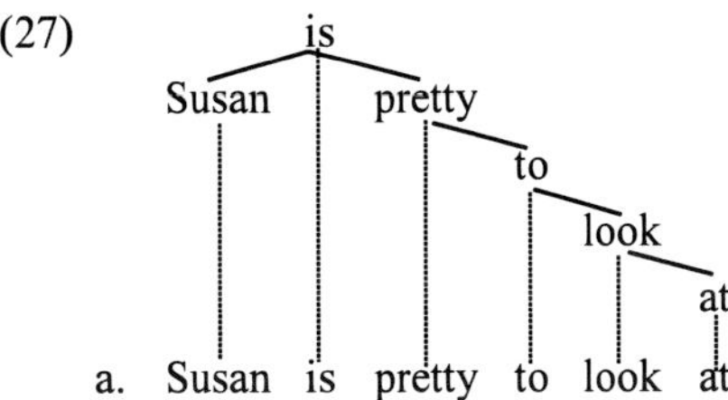

    a.   Susan is pretty to look at.

    b.   PRETTY [N̲$_a$↑, T$_a$]

    c.   *It is pretty to look at Susan.

(28) a.   These nuts are tasty to snack on.

    b.   TASTY [N̲$_a$↑, T$_a$]

    c.   *It is tasty to snack on these nuts.

(29) a.   This coat is soft to touch.

    b.   SOFT [N̲$_a$↑, T$_a$]

    c.   *It is soft to touch this coat.

The unacceptability of the c-sentences here reveal that *pretty*, *tasty*, and *soft* are not raising predicates. The b-examples show how the combinatory potential of these predicates is captured in valency frames. The double underline marks the subject valent as controlling an object that appears lower in the structure. The fact that the subject N bears the $_a$ subscript indicates that raising is not involved.

An interesting aspect of S-to-O control is that many adjectives can be coerced into becoming such predicates by the appearance of *too*, e.g.

(30)

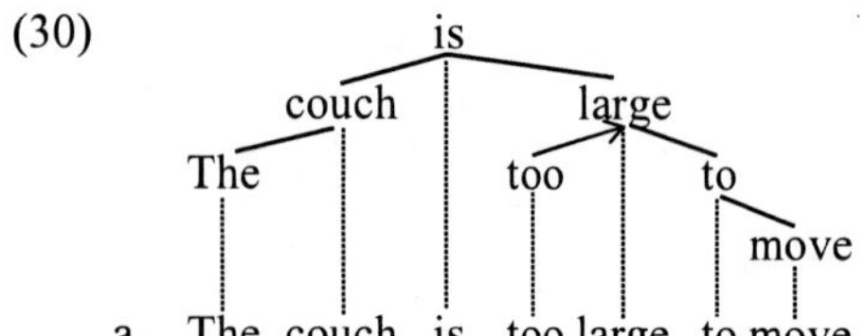

   a. The couch is too large to move.
   b. TOO LARGE [$\underline{\underline{N}}_a\uparrow$, T_a]

(31) a. Tom is too clever to fool.
      b. TOO CLEVER [$\underline{\underline{N}}_a\uparrow$, T_a]

(32) a. This essay is too long to read.
      b. TOO LONG [$\underline{\underline{N}}_a\uparrow$, T_a]

Without *too*, the adjectives *large*, *clever*, and *long* are not control predicates. The ability of the degree adverb *too* to coerce adjectives that alone are not control predicates is also true in cases of S-to-S control, e.g.

(33) a. Frank is too lazy to get up early.
      b. TOO LAZY [$\underline{\underline{N}}_a\uparrow$, T_a]

(34) a. Larry is too slow to catch us.
      b. TOO SLOW [$\underline{\underline{N}}_a\uparrow$, T_a]

(35) a. Harriet is too careful to get caught.
      b. TOO CAREFUL [$\underline{\underline{N}}_a\uparrow$, T_a]

The combinatorial difference across (30–32) and (33–35) is captured with the underlines, double vs. single.[3]

8.2   S-from-O raising

S-from-O raising is more widely known under the rubric of *tough-movement* – a reference to the adjective *tough* as the typical predicate that licenses such movement (e.g. McCawley 1998: 107–10, Culicover and Jackendoff 2005: 342–47). The double underline again serves to indicate that the valent serves as the object of a lower predicate, e.g.

(36)

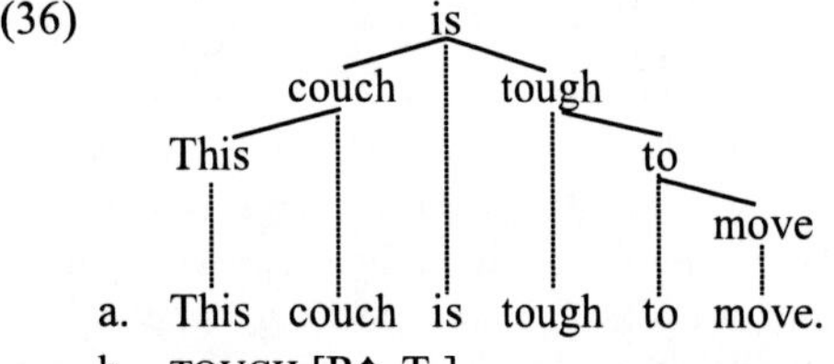

   a. This couch is tough to move.
   b. TOUGH [$\underline{\underline{R}}\uparrow$, T_a]
   c. It is tough to move this couch.

(37) a. The floor is easy to clean.
      b. EASY [$\underline{\underline{R}}\uparrow$, T_a]
      c. It's easy to clean this floor.

(38) a. A break is good to get.
      b. GOOD [$\underline{\underline{R}}\uparrow$, T_a]
      c. It's good to get a break.

The double underline shows that that valent serves as the object of the/a predicate appearing lower in the structure. The R and the absence of the $_a$ subscript on the R valent indicate that that valent is neither syntactically nor semantically selected by the predicate.

    The valency frames just introduced to capture the combinatory potential of S-from-O raising are also capable of characterizing these predicates when they are used attributively – although an additional assumption is necessary, e.g.

(39)

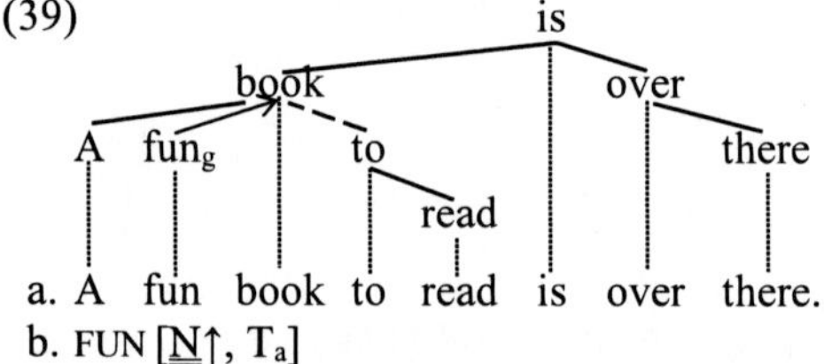

   a. A fun book to read is over there.
   b. FUN [$\underline{\underline{N}}\uparrow$, T_a]

The attributive adjective *fun* clearly governs the *to*-infinitive *to read*. The word order is such, however, that a non-projective structure should obtain due to the intervening noun *book*. To overcome this non-projective structure, rising is assumed, as indicated with the dashed dependency edge and the $_g$ subscript (see Groß and Osborne 2009). Note that in such cases of a predicate used attributively, the up-arrow in the valency frame continues to capture the fact that the subject valent of the predicate is not a dependent of that predicate. Note also that the R valent does not occur. In cases of attributive use, the subject valent is always a nominal.

8.3   O-to-O control

Cadidates for an analysis in terms of O-to-O control are listed next: *bring, build, buy, create, find, give, take*, e.g.

---

[3] An anonymous reviewer points out that combinations such as *too large*, *too lazy*, etc. are not stored in the lexicon as single lexical items and that an account of such data in terms of valency is hence problematic. This matter is open issue.

(40)

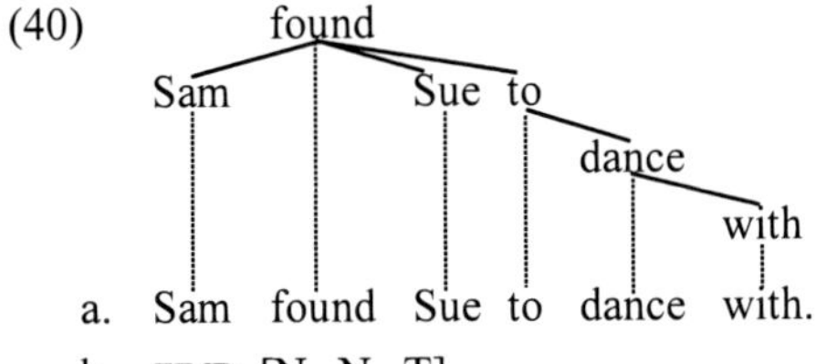

a. Sam found Sue to dance with.

b. FIND$_f$ [N$_a$, <u>N</u>$_a$, T]

(41)

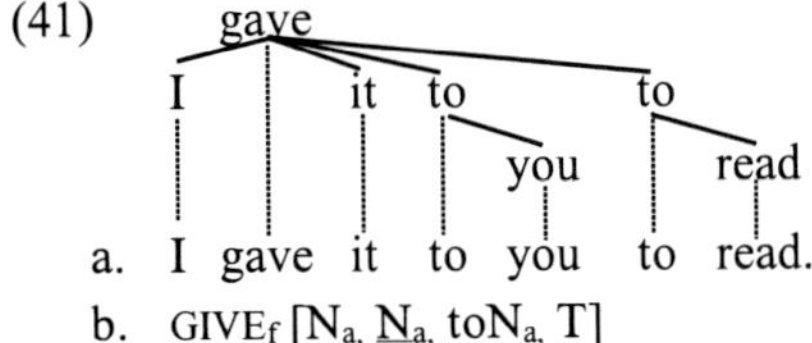

a. I gave it to you to read.

b. GIVE$_f$ [N$_a$, <u>N</u>$_a$, toN$_a$, T]

(42)

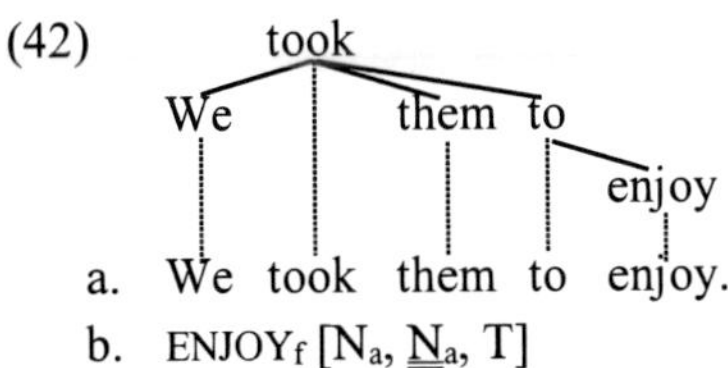

a. We took them to enjoy.

b. ENJOY$_f$ [N$_a$, <u>N</u>$_a$, T]

The flatness of structure here is motivated by diagnostics for constituents – see examples (6–9). These diagnostics reveal that, for instance, *Sue to dance with* in (40) is not a constituent, e.g. topicalization: **...and Sue to dance with Sam found*; clefting: **It is Sue to dance with that Sam found*. In addition, we know that the *to*-infinitive phrases are not dependents of the objects *Sue, it,* and *them* because definite nouns and pronouns do not typically take dependents. Furthermore, the fact that *to read* in (41a) is separated from *it* by *to you* refutes the notion that *it* and *to read* could form a constituent (i.e. a complete subtree).

Another noteworthy aspect of these examples is the absence of $_a$ subscript on the T valent. This indicates that those valents are not arguments of the parent predicate; they are, rather, secondary predications the presence of which is optional. Their actual status is a difficult issue (valent or adjunct?) that cannot be addresssed here appropriately due to limited space.

Finally, observe that control is doubly present in these cases, since the subject of the *to*-infinitive is also a matter of control – although of nonobligatory control, as example (41a) reveals, where the understood subject of the *to*-infinitive is the *to*-argument, not the subject. That nonobligatory control is involved is also evident in the fact that insertion of a *for*-phrase in these examples can shift the controller from the subject to the object of *for*, e.g. *For the kids, we took the snacks to enjoy* – the kids will enjoy the snacks.

8.4 O-from-O raising

The final type of raising is O-from-O raising. This type of raising occurs infrequently. We are aware of just a couple of verbs that qualify as such predicates: *have, get,* and *want*, e.g.

(43)

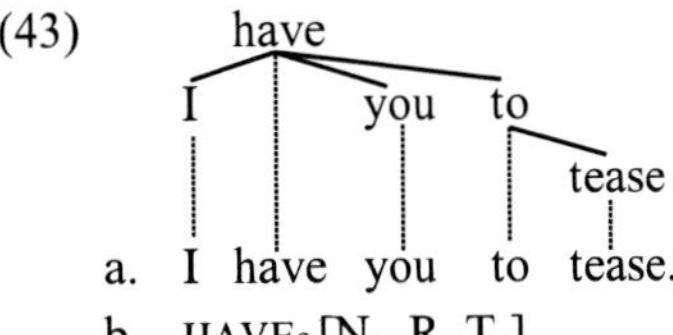

a. I have you to tease.

b. HAVE$_f$ [N$_a$, <u>R</u>, T$_a$]

(44)

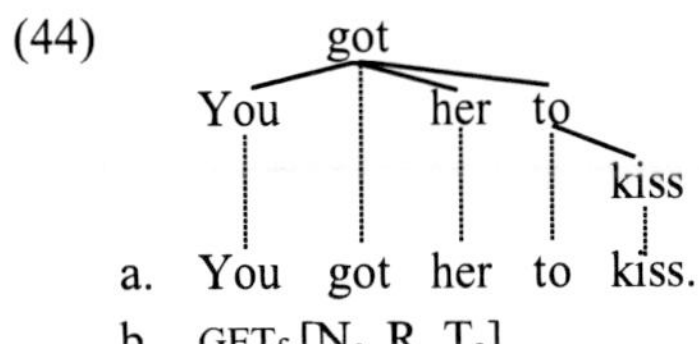

a. You got her to kiss.

b. GET$_f$ [N$_a$, <u>R</u>, T$_a$]

(45)

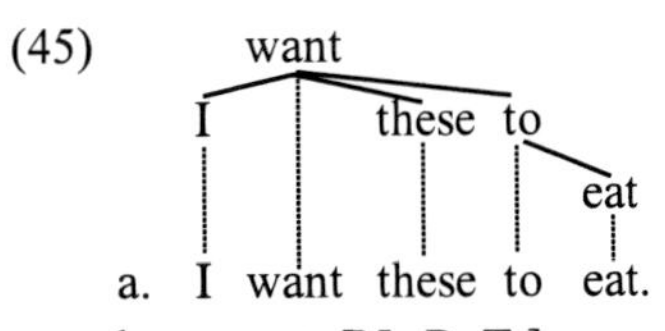

a. I want these to eat.

b. WANT$_f$ [N$_a$, <u>R</u>, T$_a$]

Observe as well that the object R in these examples is a definite pronoun. This fact again supports the flat analysis shown, since it contradicts the alternative analysis that positions the *to*-infinitive as a dependent of the object – definite pronouns do not accept postdependents. Observe that as with the examples of O-to-O control in the previous section, nonobligatory subject control is also present in these examples. We again know that control is pragmatically determined in such cases because it is possible to vary the understood subject of the *to*-infinitive, e.g. *For my kids, I want these to eat*.

Another interesting aspect of these predicates is that they also alternatively license O-from-S raising, e.g.

(46)

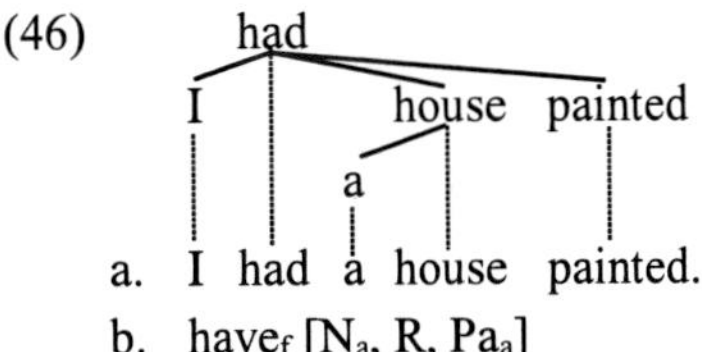

a. I had a house painted.

b. have$_f$ [N$_a$, <u>R</u>, Pa$_a$]

(47) a. I got my paper corrected.

 b. GET$_f$ [N$_a$, <u>R</u>, Pa$_a$]

(48) a. They wanted it revised.

 b. WANT$_f$ [N$_a$, <u>R</u>, Pa$_a$]

Used in this way, the predicates *have, get,* and *want* no longer involve control. The appearance of the passive participle forces the account to assume that the object functions as the subject of the embedded participle, rather than as its object.

9   Conclusion

This contribution has presented a DG account of obligatory control and raising. Due to the minimal nature of dependency structures, the distinction cannot be captured in the hierarchy of words; it can, rather, be captured in valency frames. The valency frames introduced here distinguish between control and raising mainly via the presence/absence of the $_a$ subscript and the R valent. When $_a$ subscript is absent, the valent is not semantically selected by the predicate. A particular merit of the approach is its ability to distinguish between various types of control and raising predicates, eight in all.

References

Andrew Carnie. 2013. *Syntax: A Generative Introduction*, 3rd edition. Wiley-Blackwell, Malden, MA.

Noam Chomsky. 1981. *Lectures on Government and Binding: The Pisa Lectures*. Foris Publications, Dordrecht.

Peter Culicover and Ray Jackendoff. 2005. *Simpler Syntax*. Oxford University Press.

dtv Wörterbuch der deutschen Sprache. 1978. Herausgegeben von Gerhard Wahrig. Deutscher Taschenbuch Verlag GmbH, München.

Ulrich Engel. 1994. *Syntax der deutschen Gegenwartssprache*, 3rd fully revised edition. Erich Schmidt, Berlin.

Hans-Werner Eroms. 2000. *Syntax der deutschen Sprache*. de Gruyter, Berlin.

Thomas Groß and Timothy Osborne. 2009. Toward a practical dependency grammar theory of discontinuities. *SKY Journal of Linguistics* 22, 43–90.

Liliane Haegeman. 1991. Introduction to Government .& Binding Theory. Blackwell, Oxford, UK.

David G. Hays. 1964. Dependency theory: A formalism and some observations. *Language* 40, 511–25.

Hans Jürgen Heringer. 1996. *Deutsche Syntax Dependentiell*. Staufenberg, Tübingen.

Richard Hudson. 1990. *English Word Grammar*. Basil Blackwell, Oxford, UK.

Jürgen Kunze. 1975. *Abhängigkeitsgrammatik. Studia Grammatica* 12. Akademie Verlag, Berlin.

James McCawley. 1998. *The Syntactic Phenomena of English*, 2nd ed. The University of Chicago Press.

Igor Mel'čuk and Nikolai Pertsov. 1987. *Surface syntax of English: A formal model with the Meaning-Text Framework*. John Benjamins, Amsterdam.

Klaus Schubert. 1987. *Metataxis: Contrastive dependency syntax for machine translation*. Foris Publications, Dordrecht.

Stanley Starosta. 2003. *Dependency grammar and lexicalism*. In Vilmos Ágel et al. (eds.), *Dependency and Valency: An International Handbook of Contemporary Research*, vol. 1, pp. 270–81. Walter de Gruyter, Berlin.

Kalevi Tarvainen. 1981. *Einführung in die Dependenzgrammatik*. Max Niemeyer Verlag, München.

Lucien Tesnière. 1959. *Éléments de syntax structurale*. Klincksieck, Paris.

Lucien Tesnière. 2015 (1959). *Elements of structural syntax*, translated by Timothy Osborne and Sylvain Kahane. John Benjamins, Amsterdam.

Segmentation Granularity in Dependency Representations for Korean

Jungyeul Park
Department of Linguistics
University of Arizona
jungyeul@email.arizona.edu

Abstract

Previous work on Korean language processing has proposed different basic segmentation units. This paper explores different *possible* dependency representations for Korean using different levels of segmentation granularity — that is, different schemes for morphological segmentation of tokens into syntactic words. We provide a new Universal Dependencies (UD)-like corpus based on different levels of segmentation granularity for Korean. The corpus contains 67K words in 5,000 sentences which are split into training, development and evaluation data sets. We report parsing results using the new dependency corpus for Korean and compare them with the previous Korean UD corpus.

1 Dependency Parsing and the Korean Language

Language processing including morphological analysis for Korean has traditionally been based on the *eojeol*, which is a basic segmentation unit delimited by a blank in the sentence. Let us consider the sentence in (1), which contains ten eojoels (the corresponding morphological analysis is found in Figure 1). The number of eojoels is entirely based on the blank space character and the tenth eojeol in (1) also includes the punctuation mark. Almost all natural-language processing systems that have been previously developed for Korean have used the eojeol as a fundamental unit of analysis. As Korean is an agglutinative language, joining content and functional morphemes is very productive and they can be combined exponentially. For example, *yeoghal* ('role') is a content morpheme (a common noun) and -*eul*, a case marker ('ACC', accusative), is a functional

morpheme.[1] They form together a single eojeol *yeoghal-eul* ('role + ACC'). A predicate *gangjo-ha-ass-da* ('focused') also consists of the content morpheme *gangjo-ha* ('focus') and its functional morphemes, -*ass* ('PAST', past tense) and -*da* ('IND', indicative), respectively.

In this paper, we analyze different levels of segmentation granularity in dependency representations for syntactic annotation (§2). We then propose a scheme to build a new Universal Dependencies (UD)-like corpus for Korean based on segmentation granularity (§3). UD has been developed cross-linguistically using a consistent treebank annotation scheme for many languages.[2] We provide 5,000 sentences based on each of the segmentation granularity possibilities described in this paper. We also present its UD parsing results, compare them with previously proposed UD for Korean (§4), and discuss future perspectives of dependency annotation and parsing for Korean (§5).

2 Segmentation Granularity for Korean

We define the following four different levels of segmentation granularity for Korean. These granularity levels have been independently proposed in previous work on Korean language processing as different basic segmentation units.

2.1 Eojeols

Most language processing systems and corpora developed for Korean have used the eojeol as a fundamental unit of analysis (Figure 2). For example, the Sejong corpus, the most widely-used corpus for Korean, uses the eojeol as the basic unit of analysis as presented in (1). Most morphological analysis systems have been developed based

---

[1] For convenience sake, we add the hyphen-minus (-) at the beginning of functional morphemes, such as -*eul* to distinguish boundaries between content and functional morphemes. The accusative case marker -*eul* or -*leul* vary depending on the preceding character.

[2] http://universaldependencies.org

Proceedings of the Fourth International Conference on Dependency Linguistics (Depling 2017), pages 187-196,
Pisa, Italy, September 18-20 2017

(1) 황석영을 비롯해 도서전에 참가한 한국 작가들도 이구동성으로 번역자의 역할을 강조했다.

hwangseogyeong-eul   *bilos-ha-a*   *doseojeon-e*   *chamga-ha-n*   *hangug*   *jagga-deul-do*
Hwang Seok-young-ACC including   book exhibition-LOC participated   Korean   other authors-ALSO
igudongseong-eulo   *beonyeogja-ui*   *yeoghal-eul*   *gangjo-ha-ass-da.*
with one voice   translators-GEN   role-ACC   emphasize-PAST-IND-.

'Hwang Seok-young and other Korean authors who participated in the book exhibition emphasized the role of translators with one voice.'

1	황석영을	황석영/NNP+을/JKO	*hwangseogyeong-eul*
2	비롯해	비롯/XR+하/XSA+아/EC	*bilos-ha-a*
3	도서전에	도서/NNG+전/NNB+에/JKB	*doseojeon-e*
4	참가한	참가/NNG+하/XSV+ㄴ/ETM	*chamga-ha-n*
5	한국	한국/NNP	*hangug*
6	작가들도	작가/NNG+들/XSN+도/JX	*jagga-deul-do*
7	이구동성으로	이구동성/NNG+으로/JKB	*igudongseong-eulo*
8	번역자의	번역자/NNG+의/JKG	*beonyeogja-ui*
9	역할을	역할/NNG+을/JKO	*yeoghal-eul*
10	강조했다.	강조/NNG+하/XSV+았/EP+다/EF+./SF	*gangjo-ha-ass-da.*

Figure 1: Sejong corpus-style POS tagging example

on eojeols as input and can yield morphologically analyzed results, in which a single eojeol can contain several morphemes. The dependency parsing systems described in Oh and Cha (2010) and Park et al. (2013) use eojeols as an input token to represent dependency relationships between eojeols. Interestingly, Oh et al. (2011) presented a system of phrase-level syntactic label prediction for eojeols based on morpheme information. Petrov et al. (2012) proposed Universal POS tags for Korean based on the eojeol and Stratos et al. (2016) worked on POS tagging accordingly.

2.2 Separating words and punctuation

As eojeols have been used as a basic analysis unit in Korean corpora, the tokenization task is often ignored for Korean. However, there are corpora which use an English-like tokenization (Figure 3). Words in these corpora are already preprocessed: for example, the Penn Korean treebank (Han et al., 2002), in which punctuation marks are separated from words. Note that among existing corpora for Korean, only the Sejong treebank separates quotation marks from the word. Other Sejong corpora including the morphologically analyzed corpus do not separate the quotation marks. While the Korean Penn treebank separates all punctuation marks, quotation marks are the only symbols that are separated from words in the Sejong treebank. Chung and Gildea (2009) used this granular-

ity of separating words and symbols for a baseline tokenization system for a machine translation system. Park et al. (2014) also used this granularity to develop Korean FrameNet lexicon units.

2.3 Separating case markers

The Sejong corpus has been criticized for the scope of the case marker, in which only a final noun (usually the lexical anchor) in the noun phrase is a modifier of the case marker. For example, *Emmanuel Ungaro-ga* in the Sejong corpus is annotated as *(NP (NP Emmanuel) (NP Ungaro-ga))*, in which only *Ungaro* is a modifier of *-ga* ('NOM'). The Korean Penn treebank does not explicitly represent this phenomenon. It just groups a noun phrase together: *e.g. (NP Emmanuel Ungaro-ga)*. Collins' preprocessing for parsing the Penn treebank adds intermediate NP terminals for the noun phrase (Collins, 1997; Bikel, 2004), and NPs in the Korean Penn treebank will have a similar NP structure in the Sejong corpus (Chung et al., 2010). To fix the problem in the previous treebank annotation scheme, there are other annotation schemes proposed in the corpus and lexicalized parsing grammars for the purpose to correctly express the scope of the case marker (Figure 4).

Park (2006) considered case markers (or postpositions) as independent elements in Tree adjoining grammars (Joshi et al., 1975). Therefore, he defined case markers as an auxiliary tree to be ad-

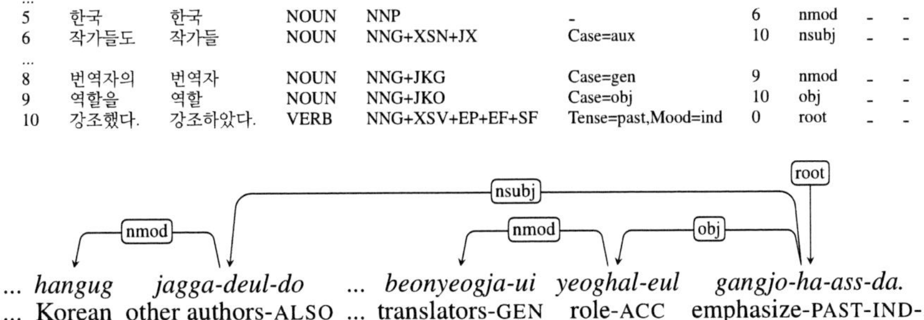

Figure 2: CoNLL-U format for eojeols: the basic elements of dependency relationships are based on eojeols delimited by a blank space character in the sentence. While the actual CoNLL-U data that we provide in this paper contain the results of morphological analysis (such as 강조/NNG+하/XSV+았/EP+다/EF+./SF for line 10) to conserve the original structure of a combination of the word, for simplicity's sake we do not present them here.

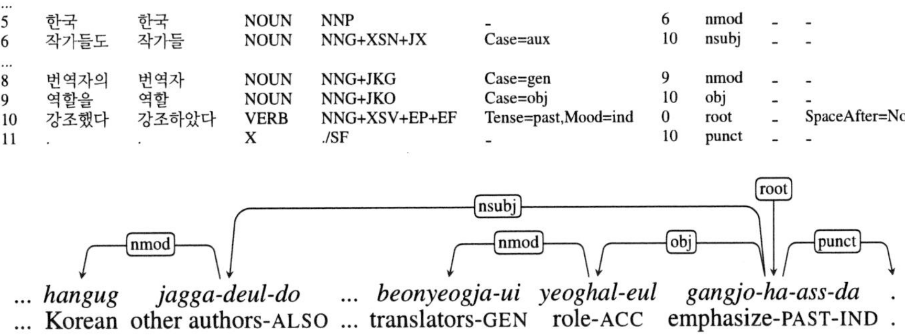

Figure 3: CoNLL-U format for English-like tokenization by separating punctuation marks: it separates the punctuation mark from the word *gangjo-ha-ass-da* ('focused') with `punct`. Otherwise, it still keeps the original structure of the eojeols.

joined to a noun phrase. For example, the single token *jagga-deul-do* becomes two tokens, *jagga-deul* ('author') and *-do* ('also'). However, verbal endings on the inflected forms of predicates are still in the eojoel and they are represented as initial trees for Korean TAG grammars. The lemma of the predicate and its verbal endings are dealt with as inflected forms instead of separate functional morphemes.

2.4 Separating verbal endings

Government and binding (GB) theory for Korean often proposed a syntactic analysis, in which the entire sentence depends on verbal endings. For example, *gangjo-ha-ass-da* becomes *gangjo-ha* ('emphasize'), *-ass* ('PAST'), and *-da* ('IND')

as described in Figure 5.

The Kaist treebank (Choi et al., 1994), the first treebank created for Korean adapted this type of analysis (Figure 6). While the Kaist treebank separates case markers and verbal endings with their lexical morphemes, punctuation marks are not separated and they are still a part of the preceding token. Therefore, strictly speaking, this granularity level is not exactly same as in the Kaist treebank.

2.5 Discussion

The different levels of segmentation granularity described in this section have been proposed mainly because of different syntactic analysis in several previously proposed Korean treebank

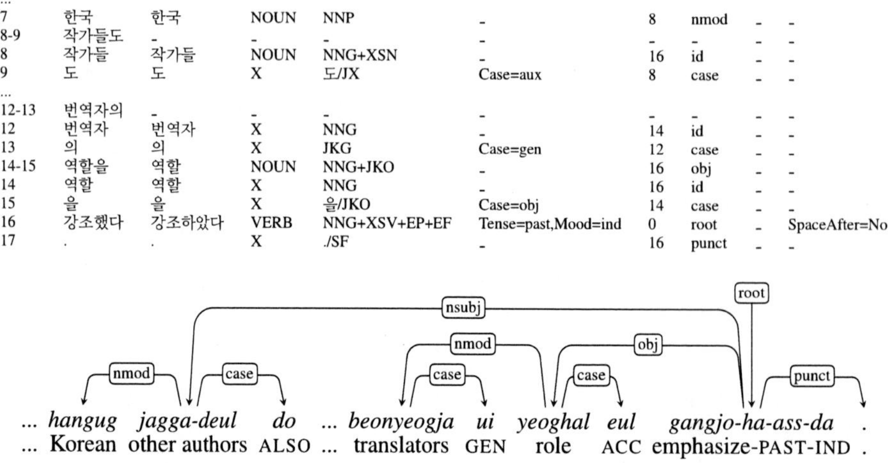

...									
7	한국	한국	NOUN	NNP	-		8	nmod	-	-
8-9	작가들도	-	-	-	-		-	-	-	-
8	작가들	작가들	NOUN	NNG+XSN	-		16	id	-	-
9	도	도	X	도/JX	Case=aux		8	case	-	-
...									
12-13	번역자의	-	-	-	-		-	-	-	-
12	번역자	번역자	X	NNG	-		14	id	-	-
13	의	의	X	JKG	Case=gen		12	case	-	-
14-15	역할을	역할	NOUN	NNG+JKO	-		16	obj	-	-
14	역할	역할	X	NNG	-		16	id	-	-
15	을	을	X	을/JKO	Case=obj		14	case	-	-
16	강조했다	강조하았다	VERB	NNG+XSV+EP+EF	Tense=past,Mood=ind		0	root	-	SpaceAfter=No
17	.	.	X	./SF	-		16	punct	-	-

Figure 4: CoNLL-U format by separating case markers, which requires a dependency relationship between the noun phrase and the case marker (`case`), for example *yeoghal* ('role') and *eul* ('ACC').

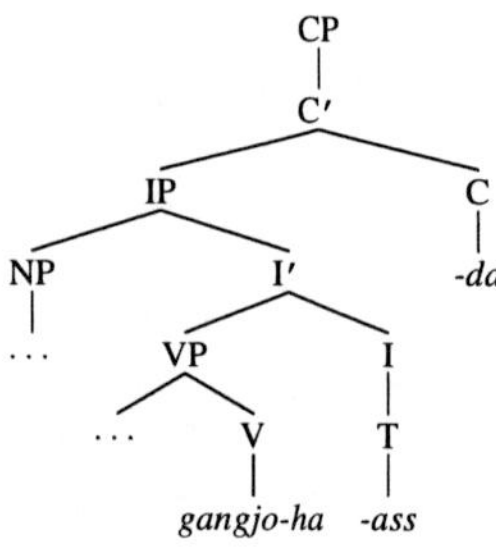

Figure 5: X-bar schema for *gangjo-ha*, *-ass*, and *-da* in Korean

datasets: Kaist (Choi et al., 1994), Sejong[3], and Penn (Han et al., 2002) treebanks. Even for the segmentation granularity which we deal with, syntactic theory is implicitly presented in the corpus for Korean words. Granularity described in §2.1 and §2.3 is based on the Sejong treebank. Granularity described in §2.2 and §2.4 is based on the Korean Penn treebank and the Kaist treebank, respectively.

Many applications for Korean language processing are based on another level of segmentation granularity, in which all morphemes are separated: phrase-structure parsing (Choi et al., 2012; Park et al., 2016) and statistical machine translation (SMT) (Park et al., 2016), etc. Such morpheme-based analysis for the word can be generated by a morphological analysis system, and most POS tagging systems such as Hong (2009) and Park et al. (2011) can produce all morpheme-based analysis. For example, *jagga-deul-do* ('authors-ALSO') is separated into *jagga* ('author'), *deul* ('PLUR'), and *do* ('ALSO'). However, we do not deal with this granularity to represent dependencies. It shows rather how words are formed, and it should include the fine-grained relationships between morphemes. This type of representation of words does not conform with the current dependency schemes for other languages and especially, neither with UD best practices.

3   UD for Korean

Since Universal Dependencies (UD) has been released (Nivre et al., 2016), several studies have been published, both theoretical (Schuster and Manning, 2016) and practical (Zeman et al., 2017). As for other morphologically rich languages, specific Universal Dependencies for Japanese were introduced relatively recently to meet the requirement of UD's cross-linguistically consistent treebank annotation (Tanaka et al., 2016). In the current UD, other morphologically rich languages such as Kazakh (Tyers and Washington, 2015) and Turkish (Sulubacak et al., 2016) are also available. In this section, we describe how to build UDs for Korean based on the different levels of segmentation granularity.

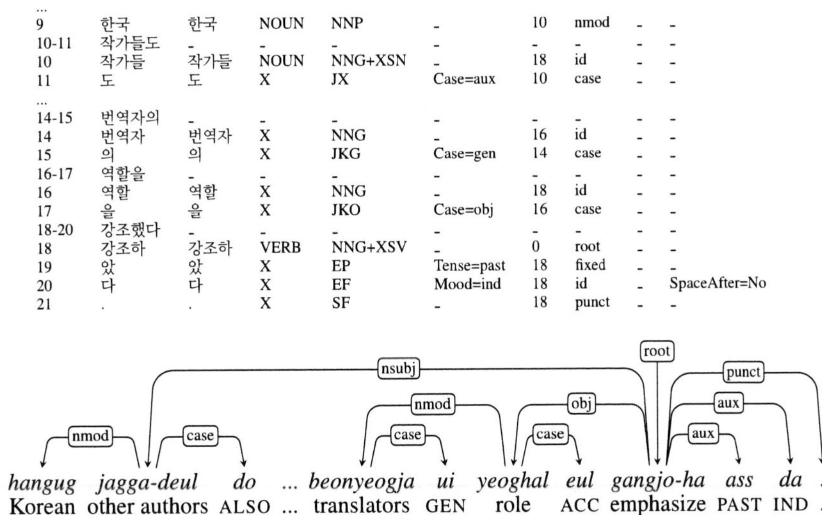

...									
9	한국	한국	NOUN	NNP	-	10	nmod	-	-
10-11	작가들도	-	-	-	-	-	-	-	-
10	작가들	작가들	NOUN	NNG+XSN	-	18	id	-	-
11	도	도	X	JX	Case=aux	10	case	-	-
...									
14-15	번역자의	-	-	-	-	-	-	-	-
14	번역자	번역자	X	NNG	-	16	id	-	-
15	의	의	X	JKG	Case=gen	14	case	-	-
16-17	역할을	-	-	-	-	-	-	-	-
16	역할	역할	X	NNG	-	18	id	-	-
17	을	을	X	JKO	Case=obj	16	case	-	-
18-20	강조했다	-	-	-	-	-	-	-	-
18	강조하	강조하	VERB	NNG+XSV	-	0	root	-	-
19	았	았	X	EP	Tense=past	18	fixed	-	-
20	다	다	X	EF	Mood=ind	18	id	-	SpaceAfter=No
21	.	.	X	SF	-	18	punct	-	-

Figure 6: CoNLL-U format that separates verbal endings, which requires a dependency relationship between the verbal head and the verbal ending (`aux`), for example a verb *gangjoha* ('focus'), and two verbal endings *ass* ('PAST') and *da* ('IND') for tense and mood.

3.1 Universal POS

Using the eojeol and morpheme level mapping tables to Universal POS tags for the Sejong tagset proposed in Petrov et al. (2012) and Park et al. (2016), we can convert the single tags (morphemes) and the sequences of tags (eojeols and tokens) in the Sejong corpus into Universal POS tags. We also use additional mapping rules by using the approach to find Universal POS tags described in Oh et al. (2011) in which they predict phrase tags for the eojeol. In addition, the Sejong tags (morphemes) and the sequence of tags (tokens and eojeols) represented as immediate non-terminal nodes in the eventual parse tree can be used as a language-specific part-of-speech tag in the CoNLL-U format. Figure 7 shows example mapping rules for each segmentation granularity level. Tagsets in the Sejong corpus are mapped to the Universal POS tag sets either individually (NNP → PROPN) or by a sequence of the POS tags (NNP+JKS → PROPN). Figure 8 represents the 1-to-1 mapping from the POS tags in the Sejong corpus to Universal POS tags described in Park et al. (2016). These 1-to-1 mapping rules are used throughout segmentation granularity schemes described §2.1 to §2.4 if the eojeol is composed only by a single morpheme.

3.2 Universal features

Park (2006) detailed an approach to extract features from the Sejong treebank. Syntactic tags and morphological analysis allow us to extract syntactic features automatically and to develop universal features. For example, NP-SBJ syntactic tag is changed into NP and a syntactic feature `Case=Nom` is added. Syntactic tags which end with -sbj (subject), -obj (object) and -CMP (attribute), we extract `Case` features which describe argument structures in the sentence. Alongside `Case` features, we also extract `Mood` and `Tense` from the morphological analyses in the Sejong treebank. Since however morphological analyses for verbal and adjectival endings in the Sejong treebank are simply divided into ep (non-final endings), ef (final endings) and ec (conjunctive endings), `Mode` and `Tense` features can not be extracted directly. Park (2006) analyzed 7 non-final endings and 77 final endings used in the Sejong treebank to extract automatically `Mood` and `Tense` features. In general, ef carries `Mood` inflections, and ep carries `Tense` inflections. Conjunctive endings are not concerned with `Mood` and `Tense` features and we only extract ec features with their string value. We also add `Hor` for the honorific feature, which we can extract from lexical information of non-final endings

		참가한 *chamga-ha-n* ('participated')	작가들도 *jagga-deul-do* ('authors')	강조했다. *gangjo-ha-ass-da.* ('emphasize-PAST-IND-.')
eojeol	§2.1 (S)	*chamga-ha-n*/NNG+XSV+ETM	*jagga-deul-do*/NNG+XSN+JX	*gangjo-ha-ass-da.*/NNG+XSV+EP+EF+SF
	(U)	*chamga-ha-n*/VERB	*jagga-deul-do*/NOUN	*gangjo-ha-ass-da.*/VERB
separating	§2.2 (S)	*chamga-ha-n*/NNG+XSV+ETM	*jagga-deul-do*/NNG+XSN+JX	***gangjo-ha-ass-da*/VV+EP+EF /SF**
symbols	(U)	*chamga-ha-n*/VERB	*jagga-deul-do*/NOUN	***gangjo-ha-ass-da*/VERB /PUNCT**
separating	§2.3 (S)	*chamga-ha-n*/NNG+XSV+ETM	***jagga-deul*/NNG+XSN *-do*/JX**	*gangjo-ha-ass-da*/VV+EP+EF /SF
case markes	(U)	*chamga-ha-n*/VERB	***jagga-deul*/NOUN *-do*/ADP**	*gangjo-ha-ass-da*/VERB /PUNCT
separating	§2.4 (S)	***chamga-ha*/NNG+XSV *-n*/ETM**	*jagga-deul*/NNG+XSN *-do*/JX	***gangjo-ha*/VV *-ass*/EP *-da*/EF /SF**
verbal endings	(U)	***chamga-ha*/VERB *-n*/PRT**	*jagga-deul*/NOUN *-do*/ADP	***gangjo-ha*/VERB *-ass*/PRT *-da*/PRT /PUNCT**

Figure 7: Example of the tag sequences at each granularity level. We show the examples for the converting mapping table between Sejong and Universal POS tag sets described in §3.1: *e.g.* NNG+XSV+ETM is converted into VERB in §2.1. (S) and (U) are for the Sejong and Universal POS tag sets.

such as *-si*.

3.3 Universal dependency representations

We use basic dependencies (core, non-core, noun dependents) for eojeols for segmentation granularity in §2.1. We add `punct` between word and punctuation marks (§2.2), and `case` between noun phrase and case markers (§2.3). We also employ `fixed` for verbal endings (§2.4). Initial dependency labels are based on phrase information in the Sejong treebank such as `np-sub`, `np-obj`, etc. We create conversion rules to conform to Universal Dependency relations.

`nsubj` (nominal subject) and `csubj` (clausal subject) can be assigned in which `np-sbj` occurs and nouns ended with either `jks` (nominative marker) or `jx` (topic marker). We distinguish `nsubj` and `csubj` as follows:

- if a subject `noun` is a derivational noun from the verb or the adjective, which are usually ended with `etn+jks` or `etn+jx` (where `etn` is a derivational morpheme for the noun), then `csubj`.

- otherwise, `nsubj`.

(2)   a. *unggaro-ga ... naseo-eoss-da*
        Ungaro-jx ... become-PAST-IND
        'Ungaro became ...'

     b. *unggaro-ga naseo-gi-ga ... sib-eoss-da*
        Ungaro-NOM become-etn-jx ... easy-PAST-IND
        'Ungaro's becoming ... was easy'

While the previous UD for Korean uses `nsubj:pass` for the passive construction in Korean, we do not use it for the following two reasons: First, passive and causative verbs are often in the same form if they use passive or causative derivational morphemes such as *-i*, *-hi*, etc. and they are very ambiguous. Second, intransitive verbs are also allowed in the passive construction unlike in English.

`obj` (direct object) can be assigned in which `np-obj` occurs and nouns ended with `jko` (accusative marker). There are several cases where nouns can be ended with `jx` (topic marker). There are also some cases where nouns can be ended with `jx` (topic marker) for `obj`. `iobj` (second core dependent) can be assigned when `np-alt` (NP adjunct) occurs and nouns ended with `jkb` (auxiliary marker) such as *-ege*, *-e*, *-gge* (dative markers).

(3)   *... sagoa-leul unggaro-ege ju-eoss-da*
      ... apple-jko Ungaro-jkb give-PAST-IND
      '... gave an apple to Ungaro'

`ccomp` (clausal complement) can be assigned when `vp-cmp` or `vnp-cmp` occurs. `ccomp` normally ends with `ec` and we identify 71 verbal

Sejong POS (S)	description	Universal POS (U)
NNG, NNB, NR, XR	Noun related	NOUN
NNP	Proper noun	PROPN
NP	Pronoun	PRON
MAG,	Adverb	ADV
MAJ	Conjunctive adverb	CCONJ
MM	Determiner	DET
VV, VX, VCN, VCP	Verb related	VERB
VA	Adjective	ADJ
EP, EF, EC, ETN, ETM	Verbal endings	PRT
JKS, JKC, JKG, JKO, JKB, JKV, JKQ, JX, JC	Postpositions (case markers)	ADP
XPN, XSN, XSA, XSV	Suffixes	PRT
SF, SP, SE, SO, SS	Punctuation marks	PUNCT
SW	Special characters	X
SH, SL	Foreign characters	X
SN	Number	NUM
NA, NF, NV	Unknown words	X

Figure 8: POS tags in the Sejong corpus and their 1-to-1 mapping to Universal POS tags.

ending (among 410) in the Sejong treebank for `ccomp`. Otherwise, if `vp` or `vnp` occurs, and a phrase ends with `ec`, we consider it as a non-core dependent clause and assign `advcl` (adverbial clause modifier).

(4)   ... *unggaro-ga* ... *naseo-eoss-**dago*** *malha-eoss-da*
      ... Ungaro-NOM ... become-PAST-ec tell-PAST-IND
      '... told that Ungaro became ...'

`acl` (adnominal clause) and `amod` (adjectival modifier) for Korean, in which `vp-mod` occurs, are defined as follows:

- if a `verb` ends with `etm` (verbal/adjectival ending for the relative clause) and it modifies a `noun`, we assign `acl`.

- if a `adj` ends with `etm` and it modifies a `noun`, we assign `amod`.

UD for Korean annotates `acl:rel` instead of `acl` to specify a relative clause for the verb ended with `etm`. `ajt` (adjunct) or `nmod` (nominal dependents) can be assigned where `np-ajt` or `np` occurs, respectively. `det:poss` is assigned for `noun` ended with `jkg` (genitive marker). Other UD relations such as `advmod`, `det`, etc can be assigned as a 1-to-1 mapping table by using Sejong POS labels as described in Table 1.

4 Experiments and Results

We collected sentences from news articles in one of Korean News websites published during 2016.[4] We select the length of sentences in which there

Sejong POS	UD relations
mag	advmod
maj	cc
mm	det
sn	nummod

Table 1: Miscellaneous conversion between Sejong POS labels and UD representations

are words (eojeols) between 10 and 20 and the sentence should end with the final verbal ending such as *-da* (IND) or *-gga* (INT) and the punctuation mark such as *period* or *question mark* (`sf`).[5] We perform initial automatic preprocessing tasks using existing tools for Korean such as POS tagging (Hong, 2009), assigning Universal POS labels (Petrov et al., 2012; Park et al., 2016), and MaltParser-based dependency parsing (Park et al., 2016). We manually correct the initial preprocessing tasks especially focused on dependency relation as described in §3.3.[6] First, we build a corpus as described in §2.1, then convert it into other levels of segmentation granularity as described in from §2.2 to §2.4. As a result, we provide a new UD for Korean which contain 5,000 sentences. We split them into 3K-1K-1K sentences for training, development, and evaluation data sets. Table 2 shows the brief statistics of the new UD for Korean. The number of words indicates the number of eojeols as described in §2.1. We train and evaluate four different dependency segmen-

---

[4] `http://hani.co.kr`

[5] Similar criteria for selecting sentences are used for the Kaist and the Penn Korean treebank.

[6] Manual verification was done by two linguists in a month.

	sentences	words
training	3,000	40,648
dev	1,000	13,492
eval	1,000	13,623
total	5,000	67,763

Table 2: Statistics of the new UD for Korean. A number based on granularity §2.1)

	eojeol §2.1	symbol §2.2	case marker §2.3	verbal ending §2.4
UPOS	93.04	94.13	97.12	98.31
XPOS	82.59	85.22	90.63	95.19
UAS	62.08	65.72	76.19	79.59
LAS	40.51	48.44	71.29	78.07

Table 3: POS tagging and parsing results using UDPipe trained with four different UDs for Korean.

tation schemes based on segmentation granularity for Korean. Table 3 shows results produced by UDPipe (Straka et al., 2016). Upper granularity (towards granularity described in §2.4) generally gives better results than lower granularity (towards §2.1) because lexical items with functional morphemes in lower granularity can yield data sparseness. Bengoetxea and Gojenola (2010) presents a system that also changes segmentation granularity. They converted back the result of parsing to the original granularity to decide whether the new representation is effective for parsing. Additionally, the usual attachment score metrics used to evaluate dependency parsers are biased as described in Nivre and Fang (2017) for the cross-lingual setting. This bias can be equally applied to different segmentation granularity for Korean. We leave the evaluation as future work.

The current Universal Dependencies treebank for Korean used for the *CoNLL 2017 UD Shared Task* (Zeman et al., 2017)[7] uses the same segmentation granularity as described in §2.2. We obtain 59.64% (UAS) and 51.05% (LAS) using the current version of UD for Korean (Nivre et al., 2017). While the current UD for Korean has a more sentences in the training data (4400 sentences vs. 3000), its results are comparable with the results by our corpus of §2.2 where we obtain 65.72% (UAS) and 48.44% (LAS).

5 Conclusion

The different levels of segmentation granularity described in this paper are mainly due to different representations of syntactic structure in the various Korean treebank datasets. They have used different word segmentation depending on their linguistic and computational requirements. While a certain segmentation granularity may be well suited for some linguistic phenomena or applications, it does not mean that this granularity is a better representation than the other in general. We need to find the most adequate segmentation granularity to adapt to our requirements for Korean language processing. The UDs corpus for Korean based on different levels of segmentation granularity will be publicly available.

Acknowledgement

We thank Francis Morton Tyers, Loïc Dugast, and the anonymous reviewers for their helpful comments and suggestions.

References

[Bengoetxea and Gojenola2010] Kepa Bengoetxea and Koldo Gojenola. 2010. Application of Different Techniques to Dependency Parsing of Basque. In *Proceedings of the NAACL HLT 2010 First Workshop on Statistical Parsing of Morphologically-Rich Languages*, pages 31–39, Los Angeles, CA, USA. Association for Computational Linguistics.

[Bikel2004] Daniel M. Bikel. 2004. Intricacies of Collins' Parsing Model. *Computational Linguistics*, 30(4):479–511.

[Choi et al.1994] Key-Sun Choi, Young S Han, Young G Han, and Oh W Kwon. 1994. KAIST Tree Bank Project for Korean: Present and Future Development. In *Proceedings of the International Workshop on Sharable Natural Language Resources*, pages 7–14.

[Choi et al.2012] DongHyun Choi, Jungyeul Park, and Key-Sun Choi. 2012. Korean Treebank Transformation for Parser Training. In *Proceedings of the ACL 2012 Joint Workshop on Statistical Parsing and Semantic Processing of Morphologically Rich Languages*, pages 78–88, Jeju, Republic of Korea. Association for Computational Linguistics.

[Chung and Gildea2009] Tagyoung Chung and Daniel Gildea. 2009. Unsupervised Tokenization for Machine Translation. In *Proceedings of the 2009 Conference on Empirical Methods in Natural Language*

---

[7] http://hdl.handle.net/11234/1-1983

Processing, pages 718–726, Singapore. Association for Computational Linguistics.

[Chung et al.2010] Tagyoung Chung, Matt Post, and Daniel Gildea. 2010. Factors Affecting the Accuracy of Korean Parsing. In *Proceedings of the NAACL HLT 2010 First Workshop on Statistical Parsing of Morphologically-Rich Languages*, pages 49–57, Los Angeles, CA, USA. Association for Computational Linguistics.

[Collins1997] Michael Collins. 1997. Three Generative, Lexicalised Models for Statistical Parsing. In *Proceedings of the 35th Annual Meeting of the Association for Computational Linguistics*, pages 16–23, Madrid, Spain. Association for Computational Linguistics.

[Han et al.2002] Chung-Hye Han, Na-Rae Han, Eon-Suk Ko, Heejong Yi, and Martha Palmer. 2002. Penn Korean Treebank: Development and Evaluation. In *Proceedings of the 16th Pacific Asia Conference on Language, Information and Computation*.

[Hong2009] Jeen-Pyo Hong. 2009. *Korean Part-Of-Speech Tagger using Eojeol Patterns*. Master's thesis. Changwon National University.

[Joshi et al.1975] Aravind K. Joshi, Leon S. Levy, and Masako Takahashi. 1975. Tree Adjunct Grammars. *Journal of Computer and System Sciences*, 10(1):136–163.

[Nivre and Fang2017] Joakim Nivre and Chiao-Ting Fang. 2017. Universal Dependency Evaluation. In *Proceedings of the NoDaLiDa 2017 Workshop on Universal Dependencies (UDW 2017)*, pages 86–95, Gothenburg, Sweden. Association for Computational Linguistics.

[Nivre et al.2016] Joakim Nivre, Marie-Catherine de Marneffe, Filip Ginter, Yoav Goldberg, Jan Hajic, Christopher D. Manning, Ryan McDonald, Slav Petrov, Sampo Pyysalo, Natalia Silveira, Reut Tsarfaty, and Daniel Zeman. 2016. Universal Dependencies v1: A Multilingual Treebank Collection. In Luis von Ahn, editor, *Proceedings of the Tenth International Conference on Language Resources and Evaluation (LREC 2016)*, Portorož, Slovenia. European Language Resources Association (ELRA).

[Nivre et al.2017] Joakim Nivre, Željko Agić, Lars Ahrenberg, et al. 2017. Universal dependencies 2.0 – CoNLL 2017 shared task development and test data. LINDAT/CLARIN digital library at the Institute of Formal and Applied Linguistics, Charles University.

[Oh and Cha2010] Jin-Young Oh and Jeong-Won Cha. 2010. High Speed Korean Dependency Analysis Using Cascaded Chunking. *Korean Simulation Journal*, 19(1):103–111.

[Oh et al.2011] Jin-Young Oh, Yo-Sub Han, Jungyeul Park, and Jeong-Won Cha. 2011. Predicting Phrase-Level Tags Using Entropy Inspired Discriminative Models. In *International Conference on Information Science and Applications (ICISA) 2011*, pages 1–5.

[Park et al.2011] Jungyeul Park, Jeong-Won Cha, and Seok Woo Jang. 2011. Korean POS Tagging using Noisy Channel Model with Syllable Lattice Based OOV Words Resolution. *Information - an international interdisciplinary journal*, 14(8):2835–2843.

[Park et al.2013] Jungyeul Park, Daisuke Kawahara, Sadao Kurohashi, and Key-Sun Choi. 2013. Towards Fully Lexicalized Dependency Parsing for Korean. In *Proceedings of The 13th International Conference on Parsing Technologies (IWPT 2013)*, Nara, Japan.

[Park et al.2014] Jungyeul Park, Sejin Nam, Youngsik Kim, Younggyun Hahm, Dosam Hwang, and Key-Sun Choi. 2014. Frame-Semantic Web : a Case Study for Korean. In *Proceedings of ISWC 2014 : International Semantic Web Conference 2014 (Posters and Demonstrations Track)*, pages 257–260.

[Park et al.2016] Jungyeul Park, Jeen-Pyo Hong, and Jeong-Won Cha. 2016. Korean Language Resources for Everyone. In *Proceedings of the 30th Pacific Asia Conference on Language, Information and Computation (PACLIC 30)*, pages 49–58, Seoul, Korea.

[Park2006] Jungyeul Park. 2006. *Extraction automatique d'une grammaire d'arbres adjoints à partir d'un corpus arboré pour le coréen*. Ph.D. thesis, Université Paris 7 - Denis Diderot.

[Petrov et al.2012] Slav Petrov, Dipanjan Das, and Ryan McDonald. 2012. A Universal Part-of-Speech Tagset. In *Proceedings of the Eighth International Conference on Language Resources and Evaluation (LREC-2012)*, pages 2089–2096, Istanbul, Turkey. European Language Resources Association (ELRA).

[Schuster and Manning2016] Sebastian Schuster and Christopher D. Manning. 2016. Enhanced English Universal Dependencies: An Improved Representation for Natural Language Understanding Tasks. In *Proceedings of the Tenth International Conference on Language Resources and Evaluation (LREC 2016)*, Paris, France, 5. European Language Resources Association (ELRA).

[Straka et al.2016] Milan Straka, Jan Hajic, and Jana Straková. 2016. UDPipe: Trainable Pipeline for Processing CoNLL-U Files Performing Tokenization, Morphological Analysis, POS Tagging and Parsing. In *Proceedings of the Tenth International Conference on Language Resources and Evaluation (LREC 2016)*, Paris, France, 5. European Language Resources Association (ELRA).

[Stratos et al.2016] Karl Stratos, Michael Collins, and Daniel Hsu. 2016. Unsupervised Part-Of-Speech Tagging with Anchor Hidden Markov Models. *Transactions of the Association for Computational Linguistics*, 4:245–257.

[Sulubacak et al.2016] Umut Sulubacak, Memduh Gökırmak, Francis M. Tyers, Çağrı Çöltekin, Joakim Nivre, and Gülşen Eryiğit. 2016. Universal dependencies for Turkish. In *Proceedings of COLING 2016*.

[Tanaka et al.2016] Takaaki Tanaka, Yusuke Miyao, Masayuki Asahara, Sumire Uematsu, Hiroshi Kanayama, Shinsuke Mori, and Yuji Matsumoto. 2016. Universal Dependencies for Japanese. In *Proceedings of the Tenth International Conference on Language Resources and Evaluation (LREC 2016)*, Paris, France, 5. European Language Resources Association (ELRA).

[Tyers and Washington2015] Francis Morton Tyers and Jonathan North Washington. 2015. Towards a Free/Open-source Universal-dependency Treebank for Kazakh. In *Proceedings of the 3rd International Conference on Turkic Languages Processing (TurkLang 2015)*, pages 276–289.

[Zeman et al.2017] Daniel Zeman, Martin Popel, Milan Straka, Jan Hajič, Joakim Nivre, Filip Ginter, Juhani Luotolahti, Sampo Pyysalo, Slav Petrov, Martin Potthast, Francis Tyers, Elena Badmaeva, Memduh Gökırmak, Anna Nedoluzhko, Silvie Cinková, Jan Hajič jr., Jaroslava Hlaváčová, Václava Kettnerová, Zdeňka Urešová, Jenna Kanerva, Stina Ojala, Anna Missilä, Christopher Manning, Sebastian Schuster, Siva Reddy, Dima Taji, Nizar Habash, Herman Leung, Marie-Catherine de Marneffe, Manuela Sanguinetti, Maria Simi, Hiroshi Kanayama, Valeria de Paiva, Kira Droganova, Héctor Martínez Alonso, Hans Uszkoreit, Vivien Macketanz, Aljoscha Burchardt, Kim Harris, Katrin Marheinecke, Georg Rehm, Tolga Kayadelen, Mohammed Attia, Ali Elkahky, Zhuoran Yu, Emily Pitler, Saran Lertpradit, Michael Mandl, Jesse Kirchner, Hector Fernandez Alcalde, Jana Strnadova, Esha Banerjee, Ruli Manurung, Antonio Stella, Atsuko Shimada, Sookyoung Kwak, Gustavo Mendonça, Tatiana Lando, Rattima Nitisaroj, and Josie Li. 2017. CoNLL 2017 Shared Task: Multilingual Parsing from Raw Text to Universal Dependencies. In *Proceedings of the CoNLL 2017 Shared Task: Multilingual Parsing from Raw Text to Universal Dependencies*. Association for Computational Linguistics.

Universal Dependencies for Portuguese

Alexandre Rademaker
IBM Research and EMAp/FGV
Brazil
alexrad@br.ibm.com

Fabricio Chalub
IBM Research
Brazil
fchalub@br.ibm.com

Livy Real
University of São Paulo
Brazil
livyreal@gmail.com

Cláudia Freitas
PUC-Rio
Brazil
claudiafreitas@puc-rio.br

Eckhard Bick
University of Southern Denmark
Denmark
eckhard.bick@mail.dk

Valeria de Paiva
Nuance Communications
USA
valeria.depaiva@nuance.com

Abstract

This paper describes the creation of a Portuguese corpus following the guidelines of the Universal Dependencies Framework. Instead of starting from scratch, we invested in a conversion process from the existing Portuguese corpus, called Bosque. The conversion was done by applying a context-sensitive set of Constraint Grammar rules to its original deep linguistic analysis, which was carried out by the parser PALAVRAS, with some additional manual corrections. Universal Dependencies offer the promise of greater parallelism between languages, a plus for researchers in many areas. We report the challenges of dealing with Portuguese, a Romance language, hoping that our experience will help others.

1 Introduction

The Universal Dependencies (UD) project,[1] in its ambitious and encompassing mission of providing a single set of tags and parallel analyses common to several different languages, not only provides for a multilingual natural language processing (NLP) framework, but also allows the representation of specific features of each language and this motivates our interest in participating in the project. Since it is a well documented project, we asked ourselves to which extent the general UD guidelines were enough to represent the features of each individual language, in particular we asked

ourselves whether they were enough to properly represent the grammatical features of Portuguese.

The release of the UD treebanks version 1.2, in November 2015, was the first release to include a Portuguese treebank. The UD_Portuguese treebank is based on the corpus Bosque, part of the Floresta Sintá(c)tica project (Afonso et al., 2002), version used in the CoNLL-X Shared Task in dependency parsing (2006); the CoNLL version was taken and converted to the Prague dependency style as a part of HamleDT (since 2011). Later versions of HamleDT added a conversion to the Stanford dependencies (2014) and to Universal Dependencies (HamleDT 3.0, 2015). The conversion path from the original Bosque still goes through the CoNLL-X format and the Prague dependencies, which may occasionally lead to loss of information. In the release 1.3 of UD, in May 2016, one additional Portuguese treebank was added, the UD_Portuguese-BR, a conversion of the original work of (McDonald et al., 2013), as per the description in (et al., 2016).

This paper describes the consolidation of the UD_Portuguese treebank in the UD Framework. For that, between September 2015 and March 2016, a set of UD conversion rules for the CG input was written, as described in (Bick, 2016), and applied to the updated version of the dependency-style Bosque (Linguateca version 7.5 of March 2016). For a team effort starting in October 2016, we were given a version of the this converted corpus, and through consistency-checking and discussion, aiming at full compatibility with UD specification, converged to a further round of · manual treebank corrections and conversion rules

---

[1]http://universaldependencies.org

Proceedings of the Fourth International Conference on Dependency Linguistics (Depling 2017), pages 197-206,
Pisa, Italy, September 18-20 2017

changes. The first version of our data, fully UD 1.4 compliant, was include it in the UD release 1.4 with the name `UD_Portuguese-Bosque`. Latter, motivated by the inclusion of Portuguese language on the 'Multilingual Parsing from Raw Text to Universal Dependencies' CoNLL 2017 Shared Task, we accepted the challenge to update `UD_Portuguese-Bosque` to UD 2.0 guidelines and replace the previous `UD_Portuguese` corpus. This paper describes the technical and linguistics hurdles of the conversion and of the management of the different versions of the corpus Bosque available. The Conference on Computational Natural Language Learning (CoNLL), has a long history of shared tasks in which training and test data are provided by the organizers, allowing participating systems to be evaluated and compared in a systematic way.

Many reasons supported our decision to re-use the Bosque corpus, instead of creating an entire new corpus from scratch. The Bosque corpus -- created and maintained by Linguateca [2] — was already annotated with dependencies and was manually revised, saving us time. Besides, it was already used in previous editions of CONLL – CONLL-X Shared task on Multilingual Dependency Parsing (Buchholz and Marsi, 2006) –, and it is distributed in different versions, annotated with different tagsets and formats.[3] The existence of different versions of the same material fosters the study about different tagsest and its impacts in NLP systems. Finally, the fact that we had on the team two researchers who had already worked on previous versions of Bosque also contributed to this choice. However, the conversion to UD scheme was much more complicated than initially planned.

Different tagsets usually correspond to different reifications of grammars, which indicates different conceptualizations of a language. For this reason, a conversion of tagsets is rarely a purely mechanical task of substitution. In our improved conversion, we address both structural links (dependencies labels) and part-of-speech tagsets, following the Universal Dependencies guidelines for

version 2.0. This conversion also deals with phenomena that needs manual revision, such as apposition, copular sentences and multiword expressions (MWE) structures, among others.

We first describe how and why we chose the corpus we decided to work from, then we describe the process we used to improve this data. Very many small and not so small decisions were taken along the way, and we try to recap and explain the main ones, why they are important for the specific language we are dealing with (Portuguese) and how they impact our continued plans for Portuguese NLP. We finish with preliminary conclusions on the state of this data and the the tasks ahead.

2 The Bosque versions

The Bosque corpus is a subset of the Floresta Sintá(c)tica (*syntactic forest*) treebank, first described in (Afonso et al., 2002). 'Bosque' means 'woods' in Portuguese. It consists of news running text from both Portugal and Brazil, chunked into sentences, syntactically analyzed in tree structures, making use of both automatic parsing, PALAVRAS (Bick, 2014) and fully revised by linguists.

Over its 15-year history, the corpora from Floresta Sintá(c)tica have spawned several format conversions, resulting in a somewhat complex mix of editions. The original text corpora were processed with PALAVRAS, a rule-based Constraint Grammar (CG) system (Karlsson, 1990) designed specifically for Portuguese. The parser produces deep linguistic analyses, with tags at the morphological, syntactic and semantic levels. Despite CG's native dependency tags, the first published version of the Floresta treebank opted for constituent trees.

From 2006–2008, the Floresta treebank were enriched with additional tags for cross-token morphology (e.g. definiteness and complex tenses) and some semantics, derived from a re-annotation with an improved PALAVRAS parser. The PALAVRAS native dependency annotation was retained, and aligned with the hand-corrected constituent version. The constituent version was then revised up to version 8.0 (Freitas et al., 2008),[4] while the dependency version was used for ongoing experiments. The first `UD_Portuguese` treebank (published in 2006, UD 1.2) was also de-

---

[2] http://www.linguateca.pt

[3] There is the original Bosque tagset and the CONLL 2006 tagset; there is also the CG (constraint grammar, (Karlsson, 1990)) format, the AD format (phrase structure tree), the graphical and tgrep format, the Penn TreeBank and TIGER fomat. All these versions are available from http://www.linguateca.pt/Floresta/download.html and http://corpora.di.uminho.pt/linguateca/FS/fs.html.

[4] http://www.linguateca.pt/floresta/corpus.html

rived from Bosque, as said before, but it was independently converted from the constituent version 7.3 to a dependency version, and it is this version (i.e. without the later revisions in the treebank project itself) that went through a Penn treebank dependency-style conversion as part of HamleDT (2011), then Stanford Dependencies and then UD conversion (HamleDT 3.0).

For our own work, we opted to use the original Bosque treebank from Floresta, converted to UD by (Bick, 2016), rather than the existing CoNLL-U edition of the Bosque (the `UD_Portuguese` released in the UD 1.2), in part because we wanted to: (a) incorporate changes and additions made to the dependency version of the original treebank after 2006; (b) circumvent possible information loss due to previous conversions; and (c) because we thought that a comparison of the results of two different conversions might yield interesting insights. The most important reason, however, was methodological: we wanted to build a framework where manual revision work and consistency checks could be coordinated with automatic parser annotation and conversion rules. On the one hand, this would allow us to save work by addressing systematic errors, and thus fix them automatically, based on a few examples, rather than repeatedly fixing the same kind of error manually. On the other hand, and more importantly in the long run, we intend to enlarge the treebank, and therefore deem it important to be able to maintain a close link between live parser output and the UD conversion method. One of us is building a parser pipeline with an integrated UD conversion grammar, to support a semi-automatic system of manual revisions and consistency checks, which should allow for an efficient text-to-dependencies creation of new treebank material in the future. We also believe that having the corpus revised by native Portuguese linguists guarantees a better annotation quality, since the conversion from the original Bosque tagset to the UD tagset and relations is far from obvious.

2.1 Annotations: similarities and differences

The conversion grammar ultimately used for the first conversion of Bosque to UD contained some 530 rules. Of these 70 were simple feature mapping rules, and 130 were local MWE splitting rules, assigning internal structure, POS and features to the MWEs from Bosque. The remain-

der of the rules handled UD-specific dependency and function label changes in a context-dependent fashion (Bick, 2016). The main issues were raising of copula dependents to subject complements, inversion of prepositional dependency and a change from syntactic to semantic verb chain dependency. In one respect, punctuation attachment, the grammar actually went beyond conversion, identifying meaningful head tokens for commas, parenthesis etc., that all had been left unattached in the original Bosque. Figure 1 shows an example of sentence with the original PALAVRAS dependencies (top, simplified) and the resulting UD encoding after the conversion (bottom). The complete PALAVRAS annotation of the same sentence in the *niceline* format is presented below.

```
Esse [esse] <*> <dem> DET M S @>N #1->2
carro [carro] <V> N M S @SUBJ> #2->3
foi [ser] <fmc> <aux> V PS 3S IND VFIN @FS-STA #3->0
achado [achar] <vH> <mv> V PCP M S @ICL-AUX< #4->3
em [em] <sam-> PRP @<ADVL #5->4
o [o] <-sam> <artd> DET M S @>N #6->7
início [início] <temp> N M S @P< #7->5
de [de] <sam-> <np-close> PRP @N< #8->7
a [o] <-sam> <artd> DET F S @>N #9->10
tarde [tarde] <per> N F S @P< #10->8
em [em] <np-close> PRP @N< #11->10
Engenheiro Marcilac [Engenheiro=Marcilac] <civ> <*>
  <heur> <foreign> PROP M S @P< #12->11
. #13->0
```

The new UD treebank retains the additional tags for NP definiteness and complex tenses, as well as the original syntactic functions tags and secondary morphological tags, which makes it a more informative treebank. This way, the treebank keeps its original linguistic focus, but in addition it can be used for the new machine learning scenarios targeted by the CoNLL-U format. To give an example of the usefulness of having the deep, old annotations and the the new ones together, we could mention that, for instance, Bosque tags roots of sentences for their functions, such as question, command or statement. We retain these tags in our conversion. It would be very hard for a shallow dependency representation to recover these differences were they to be erased to begin with and for a question answering application these tags are very useful.

In some cases, the stored original function tags allow the user to recover a valency relation otherwise lost in the underspecified UD edge label, such as the distinction between free adverbial prepositional phrases (e.g. *trabalhar em* (ADV) 'work at' and valency-bound adverbial (e.g. *morar em* (ARG) 'live at').

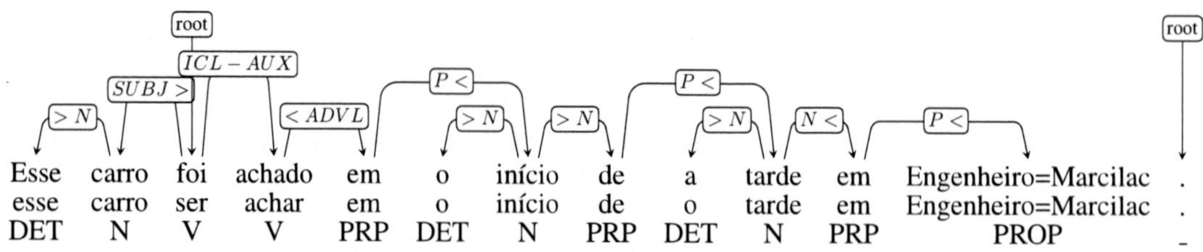

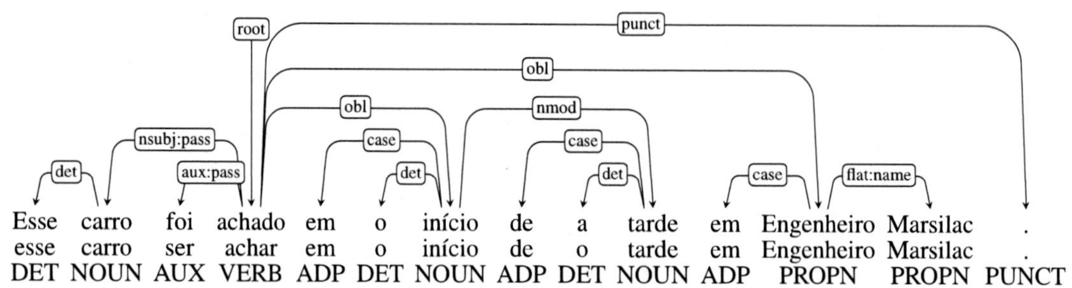

Figure 1: The sentence 'Esse carro foi achado no início da tarde em Engenheiro Marsilac/This car was found in the beginning of the evening at 'Engenheiro Marsilac' (location)' annotated with the parser PALAVRAS and UD scheme.

2.2 Improving the data

Having a version of the corpus committed to a common repository, work started on checking first basic code conventions: do we have empty CoNLL-U representations? Do we have the same number of columns for all sentences? Are we allowed to have many values for a single tag? Do all sentences have a "root" node? Can we enforce the UD requirement that representations are trees?

Then more linguistic questions began to emerge. For example, gender is one of the hallmarks of Romance languages and annotation can be complicated, as some words appear to have an underspecified gender. There are adjectives such as *grande* ('big') or *feliz* ('happy') that have only one form for both genders. So we cannot tell whether they are masculine or feminine unless we see the context they appear in. In many cases, even looking at the full sentence, one cannot tell if the word is masculine or feminine. For example, in the sentence:

CP652-3 Por enquanto, estamos *felizes* só com o reconhecimento implícito ('For now, we are happy with only the implicit recognition')

we have no way of knowing what is the gender of *felizes*. How should these expressions be annotated? After some discussion, it was decided that these cases would be annotated as 'Unsp' (for "unspecified" value) and that a similar annotation would be used for unspecified number too.

Then the first main issue with the MWEs and the different approaches to their annotation had to be tackled. The PALAVRAS annotation has MWEs tokenized as a single word, but this is not the UD recommendation. The UD version 1 guidelines proposed the dependency relations 'mwe' or 'compound', so a process of dismembering these single token MWEs and assigning each of their components a POS-tag was initiated. Things changed in UD version 2, different tags for MWE are used ('flat', 'fixed' and 'name'), but this conversion could be done automatically.

How to deal with participles was also a challenging issue. PALAVRAS tags all participles as verbs, with the 'PCP' (participle) feature. However, UD guidelines state: "Note that participles are word forms that may share properties and usage of adjectives and verbs. Depending on language and context, they may be classified as either VERB or ADJ."

We followed the criteria discussed in (Truggo, 2016) to define participles acting as verbs or adjectives and worked on a set of linguistic rules to semi-automatically re-tag participles.

Another change from UD version 1 to 2 is the

treatment of ellipsis. In version 1, ellipsis cases were dealt with via a 'remnant' dependency relation. This relation linked the core arguments of the ellipsis clause to their corresponding arguments in the complete clause. In the sentence bellow (CF349-2 – 'Opala lasted 23 years, Chevette, 20 [. . .]'), the token *Chevette* was related to *Opala* and the token *20* to *23*.

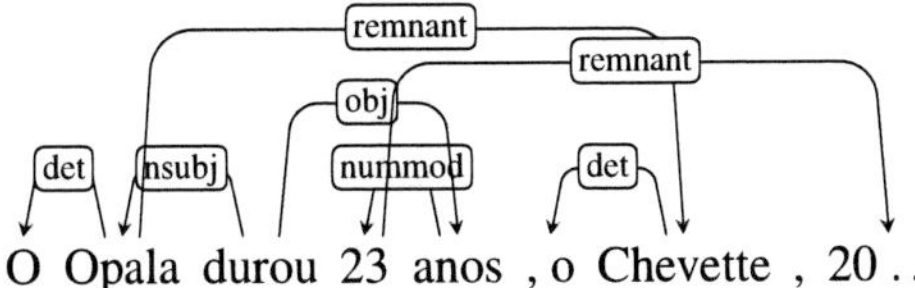

In UD version 2.0, the 'remnant' relation was discarded and a new treatment was proposed, using a new relation 'orphan'. With this proposal, only the first core argument of the ellipsis clause is related to the main clause and the other core arguments are related to it via the 'orphan' relation. In the example above, *Chevette* is related to *durou* 'lasted' (the root of the main sentence) via 'parataxis' and *20* is related to *Chevette* via 'orphan'. All 'remnant' cases were manually fixed.

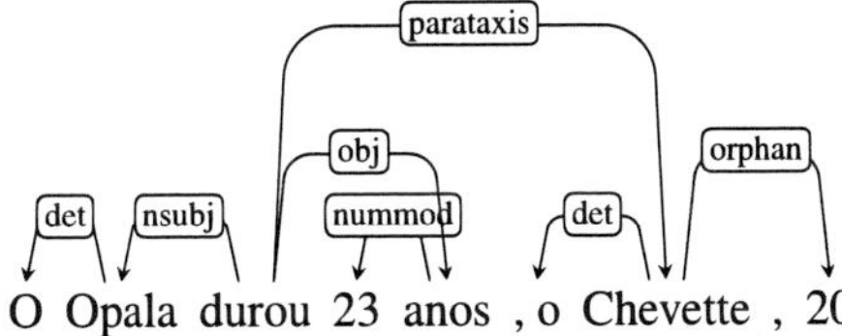

Also there were many minor discrepancies, like Bosque used 'pret' (for preterite), while UD used 'past', so we had some "unknown attribute-value pairs" to translate. Using the UD provided scripts and manual checking, the validator script was satisfied with the representations and we could start thinking about similarities and differences to the other version of the Bosque, which we discuss in the next section.

3   Portuguese annotation choices

Clear and detailed guidelines are the crucial data in annotation projects. It is reasonable to expect that the UD guidelines would be, as they are, less specific than we would like them to be. Their main motivation is to be universal, so special characteristics of the target language are to be down-played, for the sake of being able to compare features in other languages. However, this lack of specificity of the guidelines makes somewhat more explicit the interpretative dimension of linguistic analysis.

In this section we discuss some of the issues that we consider interesting, either because they were not sufficiently described in the guidelines, or because they are issues that seem mainly important for Portuguese.

3.1   Tokenization

While the first conversion grammar did convert syntactic to semantic (UD) dependencies and function-based edge labels to form-based (UD) edge labels, it did not handle UD's space-based tokenization, maintaining the original treebank's MWE (e.g. complex conjunctions, prepositions and named entities) and its - syntactically motivated - splitting of Portuguese contractions (preposition plus article/determiner/pronoun, e.g *neste* to *em + este* ('in this'). Linguistically, the problem in token-splitting is the need to assign (a) partial POS tags, (b) additional internal dependency links and (c) new internal hook-up points for existing outgoing and incoming dependency links. Unlike simple label conversion for, say, morphological features, this cannot be achieved with a systematic conversion table only.

Our solution was to use CG-based retokenization rules. Its most recent implementation (Bick and Didriksen, 2015) offers context-based manipulation (removal, substitution, addition etc.) of not only tags, but also of entire (annotated) tokens. We used this feature to split MWE tokens into their sub-words, while at the same time adding the missing POS, features, edge labels and dependency links to the individual parts.

This solves the problem that while the UD treatment of MWEs considers each part of an MWE as a single POS, the set of words that compose a given MWE may not contain a word that has the same POS tag as the MWE as a whole. The MWE *ao vivo* ('live'), for instance, is an ADV as a whole, while 'ao' is a contraction (ADP 'a' + DET 'o') and 'vivo' 'live' is an ADJ. Since it is clear that the most important information for the entire sentence structure is the POS tag of the whole MWE, and not the POS tag of each of its constituents, we keep a tag for the whole MWE in our representation. Then, at least for the Portuguese UD corpus, both the internal structure and the functional POS tag of a MWE are available. In the same fashion, CG rules can be used to fuse Portuguese contractions that were split in Bosque (*dos* 'of the', *pelas* 'by the', *nisto* 'in this'), assigning them a compound pos and joint external dependency links.

Another issue related to tokenization is the problem of clitics in Portuguese. As other Romance languages, Portuguese has enclisis and proclisis. Moreover, in Portuguese we have mesoclitics, that is, clitics that come inside the verb and change the verbal structure:

CP895-1 *Poder-se-á* dizer que o estilo resulta da sua profissão, fotojornalista. ('It can be said that the style results from his profession, photojournalist.')

After some discussion, we decided to follow the traditional Portuguese grammars. Mesoclitics seem to us a language specific issue that maybe each group dealing with an UD specific language corpus should manage on their own. Guidelines seem to be emerging that consider mesoclisis as two syntactic words: a verb plus a pronoun. In the example above, *poder-se-á* is *poderá*/VERB followed by *se*/PRON ('it can' in the future plus the reflexive). The surface form *poder-se-á* is still present in the tree analysis as a multi-word token.

3.2 The particle 'se'

The analysis of the particle 'se' is well-known as a complex phenomenon in Portuguese. Traditionally, besides being a conjunction, the particle appears in:

(*a*) **reflexive and reciprocal constructions** *CF314-2 Você se acha louca?* (Do you think you are crazy?);

(*b*) **pronominal verbs** *CF340-2 O ciclista espanhol, 48, se suicidou em Caupenne d'Armagnac, no sul da França com um tiro.* (The Spanish cyclist, 48, killed himself in Caupenne d'Armagnac, south of France, with a single shot.);

(*c*) **pronominal passive voice** *CF32-2 - Primeiro aprova-se o texto enxuto e depois negocia-se a aprovação, sem prazo definido, das leis complementares e ordinárias.* (First, the short text is approved and then, without a definite deadline, the approval of the complementary and ordinary statutes is negotiated.);

(*d*) **undeterminate subject constructions** *CP263-3 Pense-se em Kingsley Amis, Malcolm Bradbury e Albert Finney.* (One can think of Kingsley Amis, Malcolm Bradbury and Albert Finney.)

The difference between (*c*) and (*d*) above, discussed in traditional grammars and textbooks, has gradually been substituted for an analysis that takes as primary the non-determination of the subject in both cases. The example in (*c*) corresponds to *Primeiro, alguém aprova o texto e depois alguém...* ('First someone approves the text and after that someone...'). This is to be compared to *Primeiro, o texto é aprovado e depois a aprovação é negociada...* ('First the text is approved and then the approval is negotiated...'). This means that we consider equivalent the analyses where 'se' assumes the function of the subject, which one cannot or does not want to make explicit. A strong argument for this interpretation is the lack of verbal concordance, the verb remaining in the singular form, even in formal registers, in some traditional examples such as *Vende-se casas* 'Houses are sold'. In this case, the verb *vender* ('sell') must be a plural form (*vendem*), to agree with the plural *casas* 'houses', but the actual use is *Vende-se casas*.

In the context of the universal dependencies this indicates that in both cases (*c*) and (*d*) we could have the particle *se* as the subject of the verb, although the subject remains non-explicit. This analysis would have the advantage of making uniform constructions that the speakers of Portuguese tend to consider the same. Nonetheless, according to UD guidelines, this analysis should be avoided: "The 'nsubj' role is only applied to semantic arguments of a predicate. When there is an empty argument in a grammatical subject position (sometimes called a pleonastic or expletive), it is labeled as 'expl'. If there is then a displaced subject in the clause, as in the English existential 'there is' construction, it will be labeled as 'nsubj'. The UD annotation creates a certain uniformity between the cases (*b*), (*c*) and (*d*). Since we consider relevant the distinction between (*b*) (which has an explicit subject) and (*c*) and (*d*) (which do not), we keep this information. Thus, to keep the additional information, cases (*c*) and (*d*) carry the label SUBJ_INDEF in the MISC field.

3.3 Additional annotations

In the corpus, we use extra fields to keep the linguistic information that we have from the parsing analysis and that we would not like to lose, even if this information is not used by the UD project presently. The CoNNL-U field MISC (miscellaneous) is also used to keep any information that is not reported in the other fields. The indefinite subject, cited above, is one example of use of that field. Another information we keep in the MISC is the POS tags of MWE, which we had to unpack for this annotation task as described in the Section 3.1.

The indication of the POS tags in the case of 'fixed' MWEs is particularly relevant, as these expressions are crystallized in such way that their components can have completely different POS tags from the total expression. Having the information about the POS-tag of the entire MWE in the MISC field helps to justify some dependency relations. In the example already mentioned, the expression *ao vivo* is a MWE with POS-tag 'adv', although it is not composed by adverbs.

3.4 Negation

The treatment of negation has changed from UD version 1 to 2. In the earlier version, a dependency relation 'neg' was used to link a negative word, such as *não* ('not'), to its head. In the UD version 2, a polarity feature was introduced ('Polarity=Neg') to keep the negative information and the 'neg' relation was removed from the set of universal relations.

We give negation in Portuguese a different treatment than other UD corpora. In Portuguese, negation is commonly expressed with the word *não*. This word cannot be contracted and it behaves exactly like any other adverb. Traditional grammars of Portuguese state that *não* is always an adverb and we agree with this analysis. Because of this, the negation treatment we propose is slightly different from the one proposed by the universal guidelines. We understand *não* – and other words as some uses of *nada* ('nothing') – as adverbs. Therefore one should be prepared to find in the corpus fewer words tagged with the POS tag PART than in other corpora, such as the English and the French tree banks.

Another interesting aspect of negation in Portuguese is the issue of double negation, which is pervasive in Portuguese. For example in the sentence:

CP153-4 Não estava nada à espera disto. ('[I] was not waiting nothing for it.')

We tagged both the main negation, *não* in the sentence above and the second element of the negation *nada* as adverbs. Sometimes we tag the second negative in a double negation as a pronoun, depending on the kind of structure they are in. In the example above, *nada* was tagged as an adverb, since *nada* here could be replaced by another adverb, for example *pouco* ('little') or *muito* ('much'). In other cases of double negation, the second element of the negation can be seen as a direct object of the negated verb:

CP778-11 A coincidência de funerárias e queijarias na nossa circunstância não significava nada [...] ('The coincidence of mortuaries and cheesemakers in our circumstances did not mean nothing [...]')

In those cases, *nada* ('nothing') is indeed the direct object of the verb, and therefore it was tagged as a pronoun (PRON) and it has the 'obj' relation with the verb.

For those interested in double negations in Portuguese, the best way to look for them in the current UD_Portuguese corpus will be to check for the polarity feature ('Polarity=Neg') expressed in words that surround the verbs. We expect that the consistent use of the polarity feature in adverbs, pronouns, conjunctions, as *nem* ('neither'), and others will provide us with a full analysis of this phenomenon without loosing the surface syntactic analysis provided by the UD relations.

3.5 Appositives

In our conversion process, we have chosen – so far – to take into account the classic and comprehensive notion of appositives (non-restrictive and restrictive) (Biber et al., 1999), since a) this was already the original analysis provided by PALAVRAS; b) this is a gray area of the UD guidelines; c) in our view, the decision favors consistent analysis. According to UD guidelines, the 'appos' relation "serves to define, modify, name, or describe that noun" [5]. Combinations like *president Obama* would be 'appos' (restrictive appositive), if we agree that *Obama* describes, defines or modifies *president*. Yet UD guidelines explicit state that cases like *president Obama*, or *state senator Paul Mnuchin* should not be considered appositives, since the impossibility of the reversal

---

[5]It is interesting to note how this definition, essentially semantic, overlaps with the 'amod' definition ("serves to modify the meaning of the noun."). But we will not explore this point here.

(*_Paul Mnuchin state senator_) indicates the presence of one and only nominal. However, guidelines also recognize that there are always borderline cases. In the sentences _I met the French actor Gaspard Ullie_ and _I met Gaspard Ulliel the French actor_, the reversal indicates, in both sentences, the presence of apposition between _actor_ and _Gaspar Ulliel_. It is not clear to us why _I met the president Obama_ should receive a different analysis. So this cases were also tagged as 'appos' in our corpus, but we recognize the issue is still open.

4 Bosque UD in numbers

The Bosque corpus consists of 9.368 sentences and 227.653 tokens, with 18.140 unique lemmas. In Table 1 we present the frequency of all 17 UD POS tags in the corpus. The POS tag 'X' is used for foreign words. At the moment we still have 957 'dep' relations (Table 2), which we want to investigate, since this dependency is mostly used when no other relation is applicable. We also plan to check the coverage of the classes of verbs, nouns, adjectives and adverbs, against OpenWordNet-PT.[6]

5 Improving Bosque analyses

To allow us to analyze the representations and the effects of the automatically applied choices in the pipeline, we feed the result of processed sentences to the interface developed and distributed by the Turku BioNLP Group (Luotolahti et al., 2015).[7] This has been very helpful, as one can tell immediately how big the issues are within the corpus.

The UD project provides a validation script that allows us to check some basic generic facts, such as that every sentence has a root and that CoNLL representations have always the same number of fields or that there are no multiple values for the same tag. Some of these are mandatory, a corpus needs to be validated to be part of the distribution. But more sophisticated constraints, both on the level of POS tags and of dependencies, can also be checked. The Turku search tools make use of a sophisticated query language, with Boolean operators that helps ascertain whether the treebank satisfies some more semantic properties too.

In the course of the project, we have also started developing our own library for dealing with

tag	count	examples
ADJ	11560	grande, novo, primeiro, bom, último, político, pequeno, próximo, segundo, passado
ADP	36614	de, em, a, por, para, com, como, entre, sobre, sem
ADV	8742	não, mais, já, também, ainda, ontem, como, só, quando, depois
AUX	6315	ser, estar, ter, poder, ir, dever, vir, continuar, começar, acabar
CCONJ	5222	e, mas, ou, nem, quer, mais, &, tampouco
DET	35076	o, um, seu, este, todo, outro, esse, muito, algum, mesmo
INTJ	43	não, rarará, é, adeus, ah, ai, alô, basta, bem, bingo
NOUN	41353	ano, dia, milhão, país, presidente, empresa, pessoa, vez, tempo, estado
NUM	4312	um, dois, três, mil, cento, quatro, cinco, 15, 30, seis
PART	4	anti, ex, pré, pós
PRON	7236	que, se, ele, o, eu, ela, isso, quem, eles, tudo
PROPN	18984	Paulo, Portugal, Brasil, José, Porto, Governo, Nacional, Lisboa, EUA
PUNCT	29983	, , . , , , (,), , , :, ?, ;
SCONJ	2201	que, se, porque, embora, pois, como, caso, assim, e, senão
SYM	415	%, US, R, CR$
VERB	19482	ter, fazer, dizer, haver, dar, ser, ficar, ver, ir, querer
X	136	in, pole, position, body, dream, jet, shopping, art, center, centers

Table 1: POS tags in Bosque

---

[6] The open wordnet for Portuguese available at http://openwordnet-pt.com/.

[7] https://github.com/fginter/dep_search

rel	count	rel	count
acl	2930	flat	11
acl:relcl	2562	flat:foreign	71
advcl	2440	flat:name	5832
advmod	8461	iobj	236
amod	8732	mark	4724
appos	3272	nmod	26493
aux	2444	nmod:npmod	473
aux:pass	1125	nmod:tmod	193
case	33170	nsubj	10958
cc	5263	nsubj:pass	976
ccomp	1567	nummod	2853
compound	536	obj	8211
conj	6145	obl	4933
cop	2748	obl:agent	727
csubj	376	orphan	8
dep	957	parataxis	463
det	34942	punct	29986
discourse	13	reparandum	1
dislocated	9	root	9368
expl	948	vocative	14
fixed	607	xcomp	1900

Table 2: The dependency relations in Bosque

CoNLL-U files. The `cl-conllu` library is implemented in Common Lisp, it is open-source and freely available.[8] Since we have not yet decided in our group to use any particular dependencies editor, we also implemented an online CoNLL-U validation service.[9]

6   Comparison and Assessment

As we said in the introduction, one of the reasons for working with the same Bosque corpus, already available in UD release 1.2, was to be able to compare conversions. Some big discrepancies in numbers, as computed by the statistics script, were easy to see. For instance, it was clear that in our version had many more cases of auxiliary verbs than `UD_Portuguese` in UD 1.2. The difference is probably due to the fact that, in Portuguese, verbs like *continuar* (to continue), *começar* (to start) and *acabar* (to end) can also be seen as modal auxiliaries, and that was our decision. In the previous `UD_Portuguese` corpus from UD 1.2, such verbs were considered full verbs:

CP269-3 O soldado disparou para o ar, mas o in-

[8]https://github.com/own-pt/cl-conllu
[9]https://github.com/own-pt/conll-workbench

divíduo **continuou** a avançar e foi atingido mortalmente. (The soldier fired into the air, but the individual continued to advance and was struck deadly.)

On the other hand, we found that our version of the Bosque had many more cases of apposition dependencies ('appos'). In addition to our choice to include restrictive appositives under the tag 'appos', the main difference in numbers reflects different choices in the alignment-conversion process. In the annotation provided by PALAVRAS, the syntactic function @N<PRED (non-identifying apposition) can and should be converted into *appos* but, in the `UD_Portuguese` UD 1.2, all these cases were converted into 'nmod' (see Table 3). In the sentence below, there is an 'appos' relation between *diretor* (director) and *Ailton Reis*, but in the first automatic conversion, the relation was 'nmod'.

CF103-4 Os documentos foram encontrados em papel ou retirados de disquetes apreendidos em a casa de **Ailton Reis**, **diretor** da Odebrecht. (The documents were found on paper or removed from diskettes seized at Ailton Reis' house, director of Odebrecht.)

When we looked for the 'appos' relation, considering the possible cases of different POS tags pairs being related, we were surprised to find around 50 possibilities of POS tag pairs being related through the 'appos' relation.

Corpus UPOSTAG	UD PT 2.0 (appos)	UD PT 1.2 (nmod)
PROPN	234	218
NOUN	961	935

Table 3: Cases of @N<PRED from PALAVRAS annotation.

One relevant difference between our version and the previous `UD_Portuguese` version is that all contractions are introduced also as a multiword token, allowing one to know the surface structure of the sentence easily. The process of re-tokenization of these contractions made us realize many mistakes in the annotation of these contractions. For example, 'a' is a preposition but also a determiner (definite article) and, in Portuguese, two definite articles do not occur contiguously, so we could easily correct, in contractions, all cases where the preposition 'a' (that should be annotated as ADP) was wrongly annotated as a determiner ('det'). Our version also keeps the raw text of all annotated sentences.

7 Conclusions

We described how we took an existing corpus, produced for us by a careful, context-sensitive conversion process using a Constraint Grammar framework, and managed to validate it, using the UD guidelines versions 1 and 2.

This required extensive work, mainly dealing with contractions (a widespread phenomenon in Portuguese) and with multiword expressions (a universal problem). We had to re-annotate many sentences and make some tough decisions. Some of these decisions are far-reaching (like the one on the treatment of negation), others are less so, but cumbersome. We had to re-annotate all proper nouns that were originally simply considered multiword expressions, to provide them with individual POS-tags and structural dependencies. This showed us how useful it would be to have a lexical resource like the English Multiword Expression Lexicons from CMU,[10] which does not exist for Portuguese, yet.

We should note that this work is not finished. While our treebank once again is syntactically validated by the UD script, we are sure that many errors remain. First because, like other treebanks, we still have so-called "semantic" failures, as described by the UD second level of validation.[11] But mostly because we know that many phenomena are not as yet susceptible of validation. Coordination, ellipsis and negation remain big issues.

References

Susana Afonso, Eckhard Bick, Renato Haber, and Diana Santos. 2002. Floresta sintá(c)tica: a treebank for Portuguese. In *Proceedings of the 3rd International Conference on Language Resources and Evaluation (LREC)*, pages 1698–1703, Las Palmas, Spain.

Douglas Biber, Stig Johansson, Geoffrey Leech, Susan Conrad, and Edward Finegan. 1999. *The Longman grammar of spoken and written English*. Longman, London.

Eckhard Bick and Tino Didriksen. 2015. Cg-3—beyond classical constraint grammar. In *Proceedings of the 20th Nordic Conference of Computational Linguistics, NODALIDA 2015, May 11-13, 2015, Vilnius, Lithuania*, pages 31–39. Linköping University Electronic Press.

Eckhard Bick. 2014. PALAVRAS – a constraint grammar-based parsing system for portuguese. In Tony Berber Sardinha and Thelma de Lourdes São Bento Ferreira, editors, *Working with Portuguese Corpora*, pages 279–302. Bloomsbury Academic.

Eckhard Bick. 2016. Constraint grammar-based conversion of dependency treebanks. In *Proceedings of the 13th International Conference on Natural Language Processing (ICON)*, pages 109–114, Varanasi, India, Dec. NLP Association of India (NLPAI).

Sabine Buchholz and Erwin Marsi. 2006. Conll-x shared task on multilingual dependency parsing. In *Proceedings of the Tenth Conference on Computational Natural Language Learning*, CoNLL-X '06, pages 149–164, Stroudsburg, PA, USA. Association for Computational Linguistics.

Joakim Nivre et al. 2016. Universal dependencies v1: A multilingual treebank collection. In *Proceedings of the Tenth International Conference on Language Resources and Evaluation (LREC 2016)*.

Cláudia Freitas, Paulo Rocha, and Eckhard Bick. 2008. Floresta sintá (c) tica: bigger, thicker and easier. In *International Conference on Computational Processing of the Portuguese Language*, pages 216–219. Springer.

Fred Karlsson. 1990. Constraint grammar as a framework for parsing running text. In *Proceedings of the 13th conference on Computational linguistics-Volume 3*, pages 168–173. Association for Computational Linguistics.

Juhani Luotolahti, Jenna Kanerva, Sampo Pyysalo, and Filip Ginter. 2015. Sets: Scalable and efficient tree search in dependency graphs. In *Proceedings of the 2015 Conference of the North American Chapter of the Association for Computational Linguistics: Demonstrations*, pages 51–55. Association for Computational Linguistics.

R. McDonald, J. Nivre, Y. Quirmbach-Brundage, Y. Goldberg, D. Das, K. Ganchev, K. Hall, S. Petrov, H. Zhang, O. Tckström, D. Bedini, N. Castelló, and J. Lee. 2013. Universal dependency annotation for multilingual parsing. In *Proceedings of the ACL 2013*. Association for Computational Linguistics, August.

Luiza Frizzo Truggo. 2016. Classes de palavras - da grécia antiga ao google: um estudo motivado pela conversão de tagsets. Master's thesis, PUC-Rio.

---

[10] http://www.cs.cmu.edu/~ark/LexSem/

[11] http://universaldependencies.org/svalidation.html

UDLex: Towards Cross-language Subcategorization Lexicons

Giulia Rambelli and **Alessandro Lenci**
Computational Linguistics Laboratory
Department of Philology, Literature, and
Linguistics
University of Pisa
Pisa, Italy
`g.rambelli1@studenti.unipi.it`
`alessandro.lenci@unipi.it`

Thierry Poibeau
LATTICE
CNRS, École normale supérieure and
Université Sorbonne nouvelle
PSL Research University and USPC
Paris, France
`thierry.poibeau@ens.fr`

Abstract

This paper introduces *UDLex*, a computational framework for the automatic extraction of argument structures for several languages. By exploiting the versatility of the Universal Dependency annotation scheme, our system acquires subcategorization frames directly from a dependency parsed corpus, regardless of the input language. It thus uses a universal set of language-independent rules to detect verb dependencies in a sentence. In this paper we describe how the system has been developed by adapting the *LexIt* (Lenci et al., 2012) framework, originally designed to describe argument structures of Italian predicates. Practical issues that arose when building argument structure representations for typologically different languages will also be discussed.

1 Introduction

The argument structure of predicates is a key research area in Natural Language Processing (NLP), as verb valency has a decisive impact on sentence structure. Since including information about the syntactic-semantic realization of predicate arguments in a lexicon proved to benefit many NLP applications, e.g. recognition of textual entailment, information retrieval, machine translation and word-sense disambiguation (Korhonen, 2009), research in the (semi-)automatic acquisition of argument structure information from corpora has become widespread. Meanwhile, the last years have also witnessed a growing interest in multilingual studies and evaluation campaigns to test the quality and the robustness of parsing software.

By combining these two computational linguistic topics, our work is oriented towards the elaboration of a cross-language subcategorization lexicon, i.e. an automatically-built resource that encodes combinatorial properties of verbs at the syntax-semantics interface. This resource will in turn help the comparison of results among languages. In this paper, we describe the first steps into the realization of this resource, consisting in proposing a general framework to automatically derive verb subcategorization frames regardless of the specificities of the input language. For our purpose, we decided to exploit Universal Dependencies[1] (UD) annotations: UD is developed by the UD community with the final goal of creating a cross-linguistically consistent treebank annotation scheme for many languages (Nivre, 2015). The actual UD design combines the (universal) Stanford dependencies (de Marneffe and Manning, 2008; de Marneffe et al., 2014), the Google universal part-of-speech tags (UPOS) (Petrov et al., 2012) and the Interset interlingua for morpho-syntactic tag sets (Zeman and Resnik, 2008).

The aim of our project is twofold: on the one hand, we want to test if UD relations are sufficient to describe argument structure for some representative languages, and on the other hand we want to create a multilingual subcategorization lexicon to carry out a contrastive study regarding argument structures, i.e., the analysis of the syntactic realization patterns of verbs arguments across languages. For instance, we would like to know if synonymous predicates across languages occur with similar or different morpho-syntactic frames, or if the same valency frame in two languages is instantiated or not by similar constructions. Our aim is so to exploit UD treebanks to explore possible language universals concerning the relationship between form and meaning in argument structures. This work is the first step into building a unique database where all languages are aligned,

---

[1] www.universaldependencies.org

Proceedings of the Fourth International Conference on Dependency Linguistics (Depling 2017), pages 207-217,
Pisa, Italy, September 18-20 2017

in order to facilitate the comparison among lexica, using *FrameNet* (Fillmore, 1982; Fillmore, 1985) with links between verbs expressing similar semantic frames across different languages. A frame is a schematic representation of the situations that characterizes human experience, constituted by a group of participants in the situation (Frame Elements), and representing the possible syntactic realizations of the Frame Elements for every word (Fillmore and Atkins, 1992).

The paper is organized as follows: in section 2, we summarize related works on automatic lexical acquisition; in section 3, we describe the key characteristics of the *LexIt* framework and we then focus on the adaptation of the original module to the UD annotation scheme (section 4). We then describe the resulting lexica for English, Italian, French, German and Finnish. We conclude with a general discussion about argument representation (section 5). Ongoing work will be discussed in section 6.

2 Previous work

Automatic lexical acquisition, that is the research area that develops methodologies to automatically build large-scale, wide coverage lexical resources, is constantly growing and lots of resources have been built for several languages. Among the several kinds of information that can be acquired from a corpus, it is worth mentioning the intrinsic relation between the semantics of a predicate and the morpho-syntactic realization of its arguments, embracing the theoretical assumption described by (Levin, 1993; Bresnan, 1996; Roland and Jurafsky, 2002; Levin and Rappaport-Hovav, 2005).

In the last two decades, automatic methods have been developed for the identification of verb subcategorization frames (SCFs) (Korhonen, 2002; Messiant et al., 2010; Schulte im Walde, 2009), selectional preferences (Resnik, 1996; Light and Greiff, 2002; Erk et al., 2010) and diathesis alternation (McCarthy, 2001). The approach consists in automatically infering subcategorization frames directly from the corpus, with or without a predefined list of possible frames. The literature reports a large number of automatically built subcategorization lexica, among which *VALEX* for English verbs (Korhonen et al., 2006), *LexSchem* (Messiant et al., 2008) and *LexFr* (Rambelli et al., 2016) for French verbs, *LexIt* for Italian verbs, nouns and adjectives (Lenci et al., 2012). SCFs acquisition has been investigated also for languages such as Chinese (Han et al., 2004) and Japanese (Marchal, 2015). These resources have been of particular interest to classify verbs on the basis of their syntactic and semantic properties, producing several taxonomies comparable to *VerbNet* (Kipper-Schuler, 2005).

Despite the importance of these resources, existing lexica only focus on a single language with a specific syntactic frame representation, strongly dependent on the corpus used for acquisition. Few studies tried to automatically build multilingual SCFs lexica. To the best of our knowledge, there have been few experiments in multilingual verb lexicon with syntactic and semantic information, mostly establishing multilingual links manually (Civit et al., 2005; Hellan et al., 2014).

3 The *LexIt* Framework

LexIt (Lenci et al., 2012) is a computational framework whose aim is to automatically extract distributional information about the argument structure of predicates. It was originally developed to extract information on Italian verbs, nouns and adjectives from "La Repubblica" (Baroni et al., 2004) corpus (ca. 331 millions tokens) and from a "dump" of the Italian section of Wikipedia (ca. 152 millions of tokens). The database resulting from this previous work is freely browsable.[2] The whole framework aims at processing linguistic information from a dependency-parsed corpus and then storing the results into a database where each predicate is associated with a distributional profile, i.e. a data structure that combines several statistical information about the combinatorial behaviour of the lemma. This profile is articulated into:

1. a *syntactic profile*, specifying the syntactic arguments (a.k.a. syntactic *slots*: e.g. subject, complements, modifiers, etc.) and the subcategorization frames (SCFs) associated with the predicate;

2. a *semantic profile*, composed of:

   - the *lexical set* of the most typical lexical items that occur in each syntactic slots;
   - the *semantic classes* characterizing the selectional preferences of the different syntactic slots.

---

[2]http://lexit.fileli.unipi.it/

This framework was designed to be open and adaptable to novel languages and domains. For example, the most salient frames can be identified directly from corpora in an unsupervised manner, without the need to provide a pre-compiled list of valid SCFs (contrary to what was done for the VALEX model for example). Besides, there is no formal distinction between arguments and adjuncts: a SCF is represented as an unordered pattern of syntactic dependencies whose combination is strongly associated to the target predicate. But the key aspect is that the system consists of a pipeline of three modules:

Dependency extractor The first module extracts the syntactic dependencies of each predicate in a sentence along with the lexical elements realized in the slots. The inventory of slots for verbs comprehends subject (`subj`), object (`obj`), complements (`comp`$_*$), finite clauses (`fin`$_*$) and infinitives (`inf`$_*$), including the presence of the reflexive pronoun (`se`) and predicative complements (`cpred`). The design of the algorithm is strictly dependent on the output of a specific parser.

SCF Identifier The main goal of this step is to identify SCFs licensed by each verb in a sentence using filtering techniques to remove possible noisy frames. Given a list of allowed SCFs, our algorithm identifies the SCF licensed by each predicate in each sentence as the longest and most frequent unordered concatenation of argument slots. The resulting frames are represented as a list of syntactic slots concatenated with the symbol "#". For instance, a subject-object transitive SCF is marked as `subj#obj`.

Profiler Finally, the system categorizes lexical elements into WordNet (Fellbaum, 1998) supersenses and compute selectional preferences by following the methodology described by Resnik (1996). The module builds the final profiles by computing for each predicate its joint frequency and strength of association with each SCF, each slot, each lexical element for a given slot (in isolation or in each SCF) and semantic class (in isolation or in each SCF).

The final *LexIt* dataset encodes 3,873 verbs, 12,766 nouns and 5,559 adjectives for "La Repubblica" corpus and 2,831 verbs and 11,056 nouns for Wikipedia dump. The resulting syntactic information has been evaluated by comparing the SCF frames available in three gold standard dictionaries against those automatically extracted from the "La Repubblica" corpus, filtered by exploiting either a MLE-based threshold or a LMI-based threshold. In the MLE-based setting, the authors reported 0.69-0.78 precision, 0.91-0.97 recall and 0.78-0.82 F-measure; while in the LMI-based setting the system obtained 0.77-0.82 precision, 0.92-0.96 recall and 0.84-0.85 F-measure.

The system adaptability was also tested by using different existing modules for French. The result was the *LexFr* lexicon (Rambelli et al., 2016), representing information for 2,493 verbs, 7,939 nouns and 2,628 adjectives extracted from *FrWaC* web corpus of 90M token (Baroni et al., 2009). The evaluation of the automatically acquired frames against a gold standard dictionary was in line with the state-of-the-art (0.74 precision, 0.66 recall and 0.70 F-measure), thus supporting the cross-lingual adaptability of the *LexIt* framework.

4 UDLex: Adapting the *LexIt* Framework to UD

As said above, the dependency extractor is the only module of the *LexIt* framework to be strictly dependent on the annotation scheme of the input corpus. Therefore, a set of rules must be developed each time the system has to process a new language or a corpus with a different annotation scheme. To overcome this limitation, we decided to adapt the extractor algorithm to the Universal Dependency annotation scheme, a cross-linguistically consistent grammatical annotation. We also focused on some specific linguistic phenomena which vary from language to language and for this reason are treated in a specific way depending on the reference theoretical framework.

4.1 Universal Dependencies

As Manning (2015) states, the UD scheme was designed to optimize subtle trade-off between a satisfactory analysis on linguistic grounds and an annotation scheme that can be automatically applied to several languages with good accuracy. UD is not proposed as a linguistic theory, but rather as a good compromises in the interest of practical NLP applications, i.e., multilingual parser development, cross-lingual learning, and parsing research from a language typology perspective (Nivre, 2015). Therefore, the representations adopted by UD are oriented towards surface syntax with a simple, lexically shallow approach that primarily focuses on transparently encoding predicate-argument structure.

The latest version 2.0 uses a more consistent and efficient annotation, even if UD teams still work on language-specific issues (there are still lots of inconsistencies in the migration from UD v1 and UD v2, for example regarding reflexive pronouns). The last release of UD treebanks covers 45 different languages. For what concerns syntactic relations, UD v2 contains 37 universal grammatical relations that re-arrange previous dependencies based on the *core-oblique* distinction (for more details, see (Thompson, 1997)). As stated in UD guidelines, this distribution is grounded on the assumption that all languages have some prototypical way of encoding the arguments of intransitive and transitive verbs, often referred to as S (for the subject of an intransitive verb), A (for the subject/agent of a transitive verb) and O or P (for the object/patient of a transitive verb). Each language has its own way to establish what is the prototypical encoding: it often involves some combination of case-marking (nominative-accusative or ergative-absolute) and/or indexing on the verb (agreement) and/or linear position in the clause (typically relative to the verb). We can add to this the possibility to undergo certain grammatical transformations, such as relativization and passivization. In UD, the notion of core argument (nsubj, iobj, obj plus argument clauses) is reserved to those dependents of the verb that exhibit all or most of this prototypical encoding.

Accordingly, all other dependents of the verb are oblique, a fuzzy concept which entails different things for different languages. For example, in English it means having a prepositional marker and/or occurring in a different position relative to the verb than core arguments. For case languages, obliques may either be accompanied by adpositions or occur with cases that are not prototypical for core arguments (often referred to as oblique cases). Exactly which cases are regarded as oblique can again vary between languages, and typical borderline cases are dative, partitive and (less commonly) genitive[3]. Note also that a specific linguistic property, such as the presence of an adpositional marker, cannot be considered as a universally valid criterion for obliqueness. The core-oblique distinction should not correspond to

---

[3] And of course, each language uses this terminology differently. We are well aware that a Finnish genitive has very little to do with a Latin genitive, for example.

argument-adjunct distinction. In a language like Italian or French, for example, prepositions are used in the prototypical encoding of indirect objects and prepositional complements can occur as arguments into a subcategorization frame.

4.2 Selected phenomena tackled by UDLex

4.2.1 Indirect object

In the UD scheme, the core argument *iobj* identifies a noun phrase that is generally the indirect object of a verb. In German and in languages distinguishing morphological cases, the indirect object is often marked by the dative case (even if it may take other forms as well). For these languages, we decided to include into the list of argument slots a new label `iobj`. So, sentences in (4) refers to a unique frame `subj#obj#iobj`). As English have also a double object construction, its frame list will admit both a `subj#obj#iobj` e `subj#obj#comp`$_{to}$ (examples in (1)). However, in Italian and French this relation only appears when the indirect object is a clitic pronoun, while if the indirect object is realized as a prepositional phrase it is marked with `obl` relation. In this perspective, sentences in (2) should be both represented with frame `subj#obj#comp`$_a$ and sentences in (3) with `subj#obj#comp`$_à$ slots, to avoid double object construction for these two languages.

(1)   a. *The woman gives <u>him</u> an apple.*

      b. *The woman gives an apple <u>to the child</u>.*

(2)   a. *La donna <u>gli</u> dà una mela.*

      b. *La donna dà una mela <u>al bambino</u>.*

(3)   a. *La femme <u>lui</u> donne une pomme.*

      b. *La femme donne une pomme <u>à l'enfant</u>.*

(4)   a. *Die Frau gibt <u>ihm</u> einen Apfel.*

      b. *Die Frau gibt <u>dem Kind</u> einen Apfel .*

4.2.2 Reflexive pronoun

The UD has a specific morphological feature *Reflex* that tells whether a given word is reflexive, i.e. refers to the subject of its clause. However, not all languages that have a reflexive pronoun use this label, preferring more elaborated kinds of annotation. For example, the team developing the Italian UD Treebank did not choose to include into the feature list this specific label, since this information does not seem to add relevant information for training a syntactic parser, and it is quite redundant with the presence of the language-specific label *Clitic*.

For Italian, we designed a simple rule that identifies into a sentence all pronouns that are 1) clitics (with the morphological feature `Clitic=Yes` and 2) the objects of verbs (`obj` relation). We also use a whitelist of admitted pronouns forms to avoid clitics that are real object of the verb.

> (5)   a. *Maria si lava.* "Mary washes herself".
>   b. *Maria li lava.* "Mary washes them".

In sentence (5), verb *lavare* ("wash") occurs with two clitic pronouns that are marked with the same label `obj`. However, the verb is reflexive only in (a) (`subj#si#0`, while it has the transitive frame `subj#obj` in (b). The algorithm detects the two forms by verifying that the form of the pronoun is included in the whitelist and that the verb and the pronoun agree in number and person. The Italian treebank still has lots of inconsistent annotations regarding the possible values of a clitic, e.g. the dependency `expl` that marks the impersonal form of a verb is sometimes used to label the reflexive pronouns.

French also uses this label in a different way, to identify the combination of the personal pronouns with the adjective "même/s" to emphasize on the person ("myself, yourself..."), while the reflexive pronoun is detected using the dependency relation *expl*. The expletive relation can be used for reflexive pronouns attached to inherently reflexive verbs, i.e. verbs that cannot occur without the reflexive pronoun (see Figure 1).

We have to clarify that actually the nature of these clitics is underspecified, so we do not distinguish among verbs which have lexicalized pronoun (e.g. *s'amuser* "to have fun"), verbs which alternate reflexive form with a transitive one (e.g. *se raser* and *raser* "to shave (one self)"), and verbs whose reflexive form expresses a reciprocal action between more than one person, (e.g. *s'aimer* "to love each other" or *se parler* "to talk to each other").

4.2.3 Passive voice

Our system takes into account a traditional argument syntactic alternation: the relation between active sentence and its passive counterpart. Following Chomsky (1957; 1965), the two forms of verbs actually rely on the identical subcategorization frame and share the same selectional prefer-

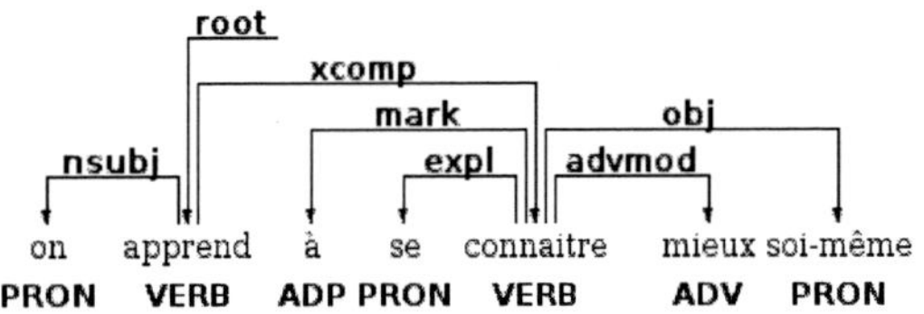

Figure 1: A French sentence with the reflexive pronoun ("We learn to know ourselves better").

ences (in the so called *underlying semantic structure*), but they differ in their syntactic derivation (or *surface structure*). Given this assumption, our system tries to reduce the two forms into a single SCF entry, converting the subject of passive sentences into the verb object and the agent complement into the subject. Concerning languages that have a grammaticalized passive transformation (among all English, Italian, French, German), the subject of this passive sentences is labelled with the subtype *nsubj:pass*. More complex is inferring the subject of the active form from a passive sentences: for example, in Italian this is generally conveyed by the prepositional phrase introduced by *da* ("by"), as illustrated in figure 2. In this case, the algorithm identifies the verb *provocare*("to cause") and extracts the frame `subj#obj` instead of `subj#comp`$_{da}$.

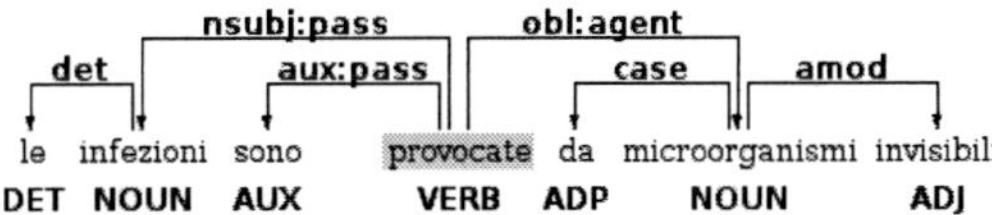

Figure 2: An Italian example of a passive sentence ("The infections are caused by invisible microorganisms").

However, the preposition *da* can express other complements, e.g. a locative or a temporal ones. In case the algorithm does not succeed in extracting the correct dependency of the verb, a subject slot with empty lexical is added to the resulting frame.

Note that the Finnish passive works quite differently and cannot be directly connected to an active form.

4.2.4 Co-reference in relative clauses

Our framework does not only detect the type of arguments of a given verb, but also store the lexical element in each slot. In order to store as many information as possible, it is useful to detect reference chains and try to re-annotate each pronoun with the appropriate antecedents. We consider in particular the case of relative pronoun. The UD created a specific relation *acl:relcl* for identifying the lexical antecedent of a relative clause. This label is used in 17 languages: Chinese, Danish, English, Estonian, Finnish, French, Greek, Hebrew, Hindi, Irish, Italian, Norwegian, Persian, Portuguese, Russian, Spanish, Swedish.

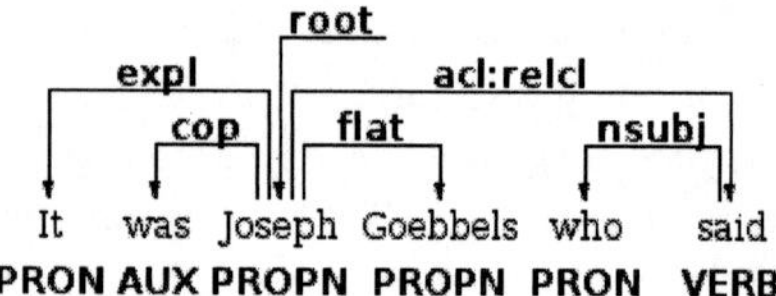

Figure 3: An example of relative clause annotation in English.

4.3 Resulting resources

The final system, *UDLex*, was run to extract syntactic frames and its lexical realization from Universal Dependencies 2.0 treebanks. As the corpora were released for the CoNLL 2017 shared task[4], we performed our experiments on available training sets. As a starting point, we tested *UDLex* on four languages: English, Italian, French and Finnish. Table 2 summarizes the characteristics of the input corpora.

	Tokens	Predicates	Lexical elements
English	229753	364	914
Italian	356912	481	1448
French	483781	543	1602
Finnish	181138	419	765

Table 1: Statistics in selected UD treebanks.

The resulting lexica mostly preserve the distributional profile format exploited in *LexIt* and *LexFr*. A verb syntactic profiles lists all the SCFs sorted by their salience, while the lexical set returns all the lexemes occurring in each slot of a SCFs. To identify prototypical or salient contexts of verbs (e.g. a SCF, a slot, a lexical realization of an argument), the system uses Local Mutual Information (Evert, 2009, LMI). In general, for a target word w_j and a context c_i, LMI is computed as follows:

---
[4]http://universaldependencies.org/conll17/

$$LMI(c_i, w_j) = f(c_i, w_j) + log_2 \frac{p(c_i, w_j)}{p(c_i) * p(w_j)}$$

LMI is an association measure which corresponds to the verb-SCF joint frequency $f(c_i, w_j)$ weighted with Pointwise Mutual Information (PMI) between the v_j and the SCF scf_i. PMI quantifies the discrepancy between the probability $p(c_i, w_j)$ of verb-SCF coincidence and the probability $p(c_i)$ and $p(w_j)$ of their individual distributions, assuming independence. Unlike PMI, LMI reduces the risk of overestimating the significance of low-frequency events.

A slight difference compared to *LexIt* regards the presence of `iobj` label among admitted syntactic slots (see Table 2). This argument was included for those languages that need to mark the indirect object (section 4.2.1).

Label	Argument Slot
0	zero argument construction
subj	subject
si	reflexive pronoun
cpred	predicative complement
obj	direct object
iobj	indirect object
comp$_*$	prepositional phrases
fin$_*$	finite clauses
inf$_*$	infinitive clauses

Table 2: SCF argument slots.

Tables 3a–3c report the SCFs associated to the English verb *play* and its translation for Italian (*giocare*) and French (*jouer*). As the number of occurrences in the corpora is quite low (50, 58 and 141 respectively), there are very few really associated frames, while most of them occurs once with it the target predicate. However, it is possible to see some syntactic correspondences among the three tables, e.g. the presence of locative complement in several frames.

Table 4 instead lists extracted lexical items that occur as objects of target predicates. The English and French lexemes can be connected to three different semantic field: competition (*chess* in English vs *match*, *finale* in French), cause noise/music (*song* vs *chanson*) and perform a role (*role, part, movie* vs *rôle, personnage*). However, Italian verb *giocare* is not polysemic, in fact lexemes occurring in its context all refer to the com-

SCF	LMI
subj#obj#comp$_{in}$	14.10
subj#obj	9.56
subj#0	5.54
subj#comp$_{in}$#comp$_{with}$	3.13
subj#comp$_{with}$	1.80
subj#comp$_{in}$	

(a)

SCF	LMI
subj#comp$_{con}$	24.03
subj#comp$_{in}$	15.84
subj#comp$_{a}$	4.40
subj#comp$_{contro}$	4.29
subj#comp$_{per}$	3.38
subj#obj#comp$_{con}$	0.53

(b)

SCF	LMI
subj#obj#comp$_{dans}$	22.46
subj#obj#comp$_{avec}$	18.38
subj#comp$_{avec}$	17.74
subj#comp$_{dans}$	17.35
subj#comp$_{pour}$	16.81
subj#0	-13.77

(c)

Table 3: Syntactic profile of the verb *play*, *giocare* and *jouer*.

petition field (*ruolo* has to be intended as the role into a team).

A major limitation of this first experiment was the small dimension of existing treebanks. By filtering infrequent lemmas we obtained a narrow group of verbs, and the relative frequencies and association measures between a target verb and its SCFs are really lower, as shown in Tables 3a–3c. Moreover, the lexical sets consist of very few lexical item with a very low joint frequency.

English	Italian	French
role (86.8)	*partita* (78.7)	*rôle* (238.4)
chess (16.3)	*ruolo* (11.9)	*match* (58.1)
part (9.5)	*incontro* (6.9)	*personnage* (17.8)
song (6.6)	*gioco* (6.6)	*morceau* (11.8)
couple (5.9)		*chanson* (8.8)
movie (5.9)		*performance* (6.0)
version (5.4)		*finale* (4.1)

Table 4: Lexical sets of the object of *to play*, *giocare* and *jouer*. Between parentheses, the LMI values between each verb and the lexical filler.

4.3.1 Evaluation

The standard methodology for testing the accuracy of an automatically acquired subcategorization lexicon is to evaluate extracted SCFs against a manual annotated gold standard (Preiss et al., 2007). Although this approach may not be ideal (Poibeau and Messiant, 2008) in our case as we work with small corpora (so a dictionary may include a significant number of SCFs not attested in our data), it can provide a useful starting point.

For our purposes, the gold standard is represented by the valence patterns extracted from three manually-built lexical resources:

- *Valency Patterns Leipzig* (ValPaL) – an on-line database[5] that stores valency information for a small sample of verbs of 36 different languages, including English (Goddard, 2013) and Italian (Cennamo and Fabrizio, 2013). The aim of the project is to carry a cross-linguistic study of valency classes, choosing verbs that have the same meanings and encoding the valency information in a standard way.

- *Dicovalence* (Mertens, 2010) – a valency lexicon containing information for more than 3,700 French verbs. It is based on the pronominal approach (Eynde and Mertens, 2003), a linguistic theory that treats pronouns as semantic primitives due to the purely linguistic nature and a finite inventory of this lexical class. Accordingly, in this resource valence slots are characterized by the set of accepted pronouns, which subsume the possible lexicalizations of that slot.

For each language, we selected the most frequent 20 verbs among those attested in both the gold standards and in the resulting lexicons. There are many differences in the way valence patterns are represented in gold standard and in *UDLex*, so checking which extracted frames also appear in the lexical resources is not a straightforward operation. Accordingly, we manually verified for each SCF whether it was attested in the gold standard or not. For example, ValPaL and *Dicovalence* use a general label for locative complements, with no information about the type of preposition involved, while *UDLex* considers all prepositions heading a slot as a distinctive feature for frames. In these cases, we regarded the extracted frames as correct, if the gold standard contains a frame with an acceptable prepositional phrase looking at the exam-

---

[5] http://valpal.info

ple sentences in the lexical resources (if available) or at corpus examples.

The standard practice to evaluate automatically-acquired SCFs is to filter frames with respect to some statistical score so as to exclude "noisy" frames caused by tagging or parsing errors. In particular, only SCFs with a score above a certain threshold are evaluated. We followed the same procedure resorting to Maximum Likelihood Estimation (Korhonen, 2002), that corresponds to the relative frequency of a scf_i with a verb v_j and it is calculated as follows:

$$freq_{rel}(scf_i, v_j) = \frac{f(scf_i, v_j)}{f(v_j)}$$

We then computed precision (the proportion of extracted SCFs that are attested in the gold standard), recall (the proportion of gold SCFs that have been extracted by our system) and F-measure (i.e., the harmonic mean of precision and recall) over the three gold-standards for increasing thresholds of MLE in order to reach the best scores (Lenci et al., 2012).

Results are generally a bit lower than the state-of-the-art (see Table 5). For the three resources we obtained very high recall but low precision. The precision score is mostly affected by the fact that in *UDLex* our approach do not consider the argument/adjunct distinction, as it extracts all SCFs in an unsupervised way. On the contrary, the three gold standard resources (in particular Val-PaL) code only core verb argument, ignoring possible adjuncts or circumstantial slots that could be meaningful in the description of the frame verb. This also explains why recall is higher than precision in all settings. To better understand the differences between the gold standard and the lexicons, we then performed a manual analysis (Poibeau, 2011).

	Precision	Recall	F-measure
En_ValPaL	0.49	0.62	0.55
Dicovalence	0.37	0.63	0.47
It_ValPaL	0.55	0.51	0.53

Table 5: Top scores with MLE thresholds.

UDLex has the best performance for English, because ValPaL encodes a very small set of possible SCFs (only 21 distinct and very basic frames can be extracted from the resource). All ValPaL frames are attested in our resource, but our system

extracts a large number of other frames. For instance, *to call* is associated with only one frame in ValPal `subj#cpred#obj`, while 17 SCFs can be found in our lexicon, most of them being without doubt relevant like `subj#comp_for` (*I called for assistance*), `subj#obj` (*I called the hotel*), etc.

Another example is provided by the Italian reflexive pronoun *si*. ValPal encodes very fine-grained distinctions between different uses of *si*, such as true reflexive constructions, impersonal uses, pronominal intransitives, etc. Capturing these differences goes well beyond the expressive capability of our lexicon. As a matter of fact, for each languages our approach only distinguishes verb frames containing a reflexive pronoun (e.g., `subj#si#0`), from those not containing any (e.g., `subj#0`). Consistently, we decided to not consider more fined-grained distinctions in the present evaluation.

Among all languages, French obtains the worst results. *Dicovalence* is very different from ValPaL since it is based on a more fined-grained representation, leading to a number of 386 distinct subcategorization frames. For example, in *Dicovalence* there is a distinction between the verb *appeler* (to call) and the construction *en appeler*, that has the specific meaning "to appeal" (cf. *J'en appelle à votre bonté pour lui donner une deuxième chance.* "I appeal to your kindness to give him a second chance"). Obviously, this kind of information is difficult to automatically detect, and our resource does not contain this construction (although it is also questionable whether these are really two different, unrelated word senses).

5 Perspectives

The previous section introduced the distributional profiles resulting of the application of *UDLex* to English, Italian and French, i.e. closely related languages from a typological point of view. However we still have to further investigate whether the actual syntactic frame representation is sufficient for all kinds of languages , or if we should take into account additional morpho-syntactic phenomena when dealing with other, typologically-different, languages.

We need in particular to have a closer look at non Indo-European languages. In order to do this, we chose as a starting point to test our framework on Finnish, which is characterized by several interesting linguistic phenomena such as, inter alia, "differential object marking", which means that the object of a given verb may be marked by different cases (esp. nominative, genitive, accusative or partitive), depending on the verb, the noun and the overall meaning one wants to convey (for a more detailed description, see Karlsson (2008)). Chaminade and Poibeau (2017) studied this phenomenon by automatically extracting Finnish predicative structures from corpora. They then categorized verbs into three categories: verbs subcategorizing exclusively the partitive case, verbs subcategorizing exclusively the accusative/genitive case and verbs subcategorizing both cases.

(6) *Poika lukee kirjaa.* "the boy is reading a/the book" (as opposed to *Poika lukee kirjan.*, where *kirjan* is the genitive form and the whole sentence is resultative).

Sentence (6) is a simple example of a sentence with a transitive verb and a partitive complement. Thanks to UD annotation, our actual system induces a frame `subj#obj`, where the subject is *poika* and the object is *kirjaa*. However, an alternative possible representation of the frame would be `subj#obj+partitive`, including information about the case of the object. In this example, the partitive case means that the action is not completed, but the same sentence with `subj#obj+genitive` (*kirjan*) would also be entirely valid, with emphasis on the finiteness and totality of the clarification. As this distinction refers to the verbal aspect, we need to decide whether we want to include the representation of object cases or not.

Other features should be studied in greater detail. For example, Finnish has a so-called passive form (*Luetaan kirja/kirjaa*), but it can hardly be analyzed as being the transformation of a corresponding active form. The Finnish passive is available only for the 3rd person singular, and in fact corresponds to an active form with an unspecified subject. Moreover this form is used in various contexts, and can be either an injunction to do something ("let's read a book!") or can just be used instead of the 1st person plural in speech and dialogue. All this is of course known from traditional grammars but a general framework like UD may help us reconsider terminological issues and thus clarify the linguistic analysis of frequent word forms.

Passive is not the only example one can give when considering a language as different from Indo-European as Finnish. One should also consider null subjects used for "generic sentences expressing a general truth or law or state of affairs" (Karlsson, 2008) (Karlsson gives the following examples: *Usein kuulee, että...* "One often hears that..." or *Siellä saa hyvää kahvia.* "One gets good coffee there"). One should also consider sentences expressing an obligation, where the person affected is expressed through a genitive (*Miesten on pakko poistua.* "The men have to leave") or other sentences expressing a transformation (*Hänestä tuli lääkäri* "He has become a doctor", where the source of the transformation is expressed through a special case called elative). All this should be taken into account when processing Finnish corpora and it is not fully clear yet what should be taken into consideration during the analysis (as opposed to language idiosyncrasies that should be left apart), what is part of the dictionary (as opposed to a more general syntactic level) and how to deal with all this in a multilingual framework.

6 Conclusion

In this paper, we have proposed a general framework making it possible to build SCF lexicons for all the languages with a UD annotated corpus. The main purpose of our work was to understand how the UD annotation scheme represents information about verb dependencies in different languages. Our preliminary results show that our main algorithm is able to detect essential information about subcategorization frames for every languages exploiting general UD relations. Furthermore, the modularity of the framework makes it possible to process different language, taking ionto account language specificities with minimal changes.

Ongoing work includes the development of strategies to link lexica for different languages using the notion of "shared semantic frames". Our approach is based on a contextualized distributional analysis of argument structures, that is, we plan to exploit the distribution of lexical items in the different SCFs of a given verb to cluster verb senses, as already explored by Rumshisky (2008). Furthermore, we plan to link SCFs of verbs from different languages by combining bilingual dictionaries with information about the semantics of their respective arguments.

Finally, we are considering a practical evaluation through the integration of this resource into specific natural language applications. The results presented in this study can be seen as a first step in creating a multilingual subcategorization lexicon based on a pure distributional approach rather than a manually-built resource.

Acknowledgments

This work was partially funded by the ANR ERA-NET ATLANTIS project. Giulia Rambelli has benefited from an Erasmus grant while visiting the Lattice Lab.

References

Marco Baroni, Silvia Bernardini, Federica Comastri, Lorenzo Piccioni, Alessandra Volpi, Guy Aston, and Marco Mazzoleni. 2004. Introducing the La Repubblica Corpus: A Large, Annotated, TEI(XML)-Compliant Corpus of Newspaper Italian. In *Proceedings of the 4th International Conference on Language Resources and Evaluation (LREC'04)*:1771–1774.

Marco Baroni, Silvia Bernardini, Adriano Ferraresi, and Eros Zanchetta. 2009. The WaCky Wide Web: A Collection of Very Large Linguistically Processed Web-Crawled Corpora. *Language Resources and Evaluation*, 43(3):209–226.

Joan Bresnan. 1996. Lexicality and Argument Structure. In *Paris Syntax and Semantics Conference*.

Michela Cennamo and Claudia Fabrizio. 2013. Italian Valency Patterns. In I. Hartmann, M. Haspelmath and B. Taylor (Eds.), *Valency Patterns Leipzig*. Max Planck Institute for Evolutionary Anthropology, Leipzig.

Guersande Chaminade and Thierry Poibeau. 2017. Preliminary Experiments in the Extraction of Predicative Structures from a Large Finnish Corpus. In *Proceedings of the Workshop 3rd International Workshop for Computational Linguistics of Uralic Language*:37–55.

Noam Chomsky. 1957. *Syntactic Structures*. Mouton, The Hague.

Noam Chomsky. 1965. *Aspects of the Theory of Syntax*. MIT Press, Cambridge, MA.

Montserrat Civit, Joan Castelvi, Roser Morante, Antoni Oliver, and Joan Aparicio. 2005. 4LEX: a Multilingual Lexical Resource. In *Cross-Language Knowledge Induction Workshop*:39–45.

Katrin Erk, Sebastian Padó, and Ulrike Padó. 2010. A flexible, corpus-driven model of regular and inverse selectional preferences. *Computational Linguistics*, 36(4):723–763.

Stefan Evert. 2009. Corpora and Collocations. In A. Lüdeling et M. Kytö (Eds.), *Corpus Linguistics. An International Handbook*, chapter 58. Mouton de Gruyter, Berlin.

Karel van den Eynde and Piet Mertens. 2003. La valence: l'approche pronominale et son application au lexique verbal. *Journal of French Language Studies*, 13:63–104.

Christiane Fellbaum. 1998. *WordNet An Electronic Lexical Database*. The MIT Press, Cambridge, MA.

Charles J. Fillmore and Beryl T. (Sue) Atkins. 1992. Towards a frame-based lexicon: The semantics of RISK and its neighbors. In A. Lehrer and E.F. Kittay (Eds.), *Frames, fields and contrasts*:75–102. Lawrence Erlbaum Associates, Hillsdale, NJ.

Charles J. Fillmore. 1982. Frame Semantics. In *Linguistics in the Morning Calm: Selected Papers from SICOL 1981*:111–137.

Charles J. Fillmore. 1985. Frames and the semantics of understanding. *Quaderni di semantica*, 6:222–254.

Cliff Goddard. 2013. English Valency Patterns. In I. Hartmann, M. Haspelmath and B. Taylor (Eds.), *Valency Patterns Leipzig*. Max Planck Institute for Evolutionary Anthropology, Leipzig.

Xiwu Han, Tiejun Zhao, Haoliang Qi, and Hao Yu. 2004. Subcategorization acquisition and evaluation for Chinese verbs. In *Proceedings of the 20th International Conference on Computational Linguistics (COLING'04)*.

Lars Hellan, Dorothee Beermann, Tore Bruland, Mary Esther Kropp Dakubu, and Montserrat Marimon. 2014. MultiVal towards a multilingual valence lexicon. In *Proceedings of the 9th Edition of the Language, Resources and Evaluation Conference (LREC'14)*:2478–2485.

Fred Karlsson. 2008. *Finnish: An Essential Grammar*. 2nd edition. Routledge Essential Grammars, London.

Karin KipperSchuler. 2005. VerbNet: A Broadcoverage, Comprehensive Verb Lexicon. PhD thesis, University of Pennsylvania, Philadelphia, PA. .

Anna Korhonen, Yuval Krymolowski, and Ted Briscoe. 2006. A Large Subcategorization Lexicon for Natural Language Processing Applications. In *Proceedings of the 5th Edition of the Language, Resources and Evaluation Conference (LREC'06)*:1015–1020.

Anna Korhonen. 2009. Automatic Lexical Classification - Balancing between Machine Learning and Linguistics. In *Proceedings of the 23rd Pacific Asia Conference on Language, Information and Computation (PACLIC 23)*:19–28.

Anna Korhonen. 2002. *Subcategorization acquisition*. PhD thesis, University of Cambridge.

Alessandro Lenci, Gabriella Lapesa, and Giulia Bonansinga. 2012. LexIt : A Computational Resource on Italian Argument Structure. In *Proceedings of the 8th International Conference on Language Resources and Evaluation (LREC12)*:3712–3718.

Beth Levin and Malka Rappaport-Hovav. 2005. *Argument Realization*. Cambridge University Press, Cambridge, UK.

Beth Levin. 1993. *English Verb Classes and Alternations*. The University of Chicago Press, Chicago, IL.

Marc Light and Warren Greiff. 2002. Statistical models for the induction and use of selectional preferences. *Cognitive Science*, 26(3):269–281.

Christopher D. Manning. 2015. The case for universal dependencies. In *Proceedings of the Third International Conference on Dependency Linguistics (Depling 2015)*:1.

Pierre Marchal. 2015. *Acquisition de schmas prdicatifs verbaux en japonais*. PhD Thesis, INaLCO.

Marie-Catherine de Marneffe and Christopher D. Manning. 2008. The Stanford typed dependencies representation. In *Proceedings of COLING 2008 Workshop on Cross-framework and Cross-domain Parser Evaluation*.

Marie-Catherine de Marneffe, Timothy Dozat, Natalia Silveira, Katri Haverinen, Filip Ginter, Joakim Nivre, and Christopher D. Manning. 2014. Universal Stanford Dependencies: A cross-linguistic typology. In *Proceedings of the Ninth International Conference on Language Resources and Evaluation (LREC'14)*:4585–4592.

Diana McCarthy. 2001. *Lexical Acquisition at the Syntax-Semantics Interface: Diathesis Alternations, Subcategorization Frames and Selectional Preferences*. Ph.D. thesis, University of Sussex.

Piet Mertens. 2010. Restrictions de sélection et réalisations syntagmatiques dans DICOVALENCE. Conversion vers un format utilisable en TAL. In *Actes TALN 2010*.

Cédric Messiant, Thierry Poibeau, and Anna Korhonen. 2008. Lexschem: a large sub-categorization lexicon for French verbs. In *Proceedings of the International Conference on Language Resources and Evaluation (LREC'08)*:142–147.

Cédric Messiant, Kata Gábor, and Thierry Poibeau. 2010. Lexical acquisition from corpora: the case of subcategorization frames in French. *Traitement Automatique des Langues*, 51(1):65–96.

Joakim Nivre. 2015. Towards a Universal Grammar for Natural Language Processing. In: Alexander Gelbukh (Ed.), *Computational Linguistics and Intelligent Text Processing. CICLing 2015*:3–16. Springer, Cham.

Slav Petrov, Dipanjan Das, and Ryan McDonald. 2012. A universal part-of-speech tagset. In *Proceedings of the 8ht International Conference on Language Resources and Evaluation (LREC'12)*:2089–2096.

Thierry Poibeau and Cdric Messiant. 2008. Do we still need gold standard for evaluation ? In *Proceedings of the 6th International Conference on Language Resources and Evaluation (LREC'08)*.

Thierry Poibeau. 2011. *Traitement automatique du contenu textuel*. Lavoisier. Paris.

Judita Preiss, Ted Briscoe, and Anna Korhonen. 2007. A system for large-scale acquisition of verbal, nominal and adjectival subcategorization frames from corpora. In *Proceedings of the 45th Meeting of the Association for Computational Linguistics (ACL'07)*:912–918.

Giulia Rambelli, Gianluca E. Lebani, Alessandro Lenci and Laurent Prévot. 2016. LexFr: adapting the LexIt framework to build a corpus-based French subcategorization lexicon. In *Proceedings of the 10th Edition of the Language, Resources and Evaluation Conference (LREC'16)*:930–937.

Philip Resnik. 1996. Selectional constraints: an information-theoretic model and its computational realization. *Cognition*, 61(1-2):127-159.

Douglas Roland and Daniel Jurafsky. 2002. Verb sense and verb subcategorization probabilities. In Paola Merlo and Suzanne Stevenson (Eds.), *The Lexical Basis of Sentence Processing: Formal, Computational, and Experimental Issues*:325–346. John Benjamins, Amsterdam.

Anna Rumshisky. 2008. Resolving polysemy in verbs: Contextualized distributional approach to argument semantics. In *Distributional Models of the Lexicon in Linguistics and Cognitive Science, special issue of Italian Journal of Linguistics / Rivista di Linguistica*.

Sabine Schulte im Walde. 2002. A subcategorisation lexicon for German verbs induced from a lexicalised PCFG. In *Proceedings of the 3rd Conference on Language Resources and Evaluation (LREC'02)*:1351–1357.

Sabine Schulte im Walde. 2009. The induction of verb frames and verb classes from corpora. In A. Lüdeling et M. Kytö (Eds.), *Corpus Linguistics. An International Handbook*, chapter 61. Mouton de Gruyter, Berlin.

Sandra A. Thompson. 1997. Discourse Motivations for the Core-Oblique Distinction as a Language Universal. In Akio Kamio (Ed.), *Directions in Functional Linguistics*:59–82. Benjamins, Amsterdam.

Daniel Zeman and Philip Resnik. 2008. Cross-Language Parser Adaptation between Related Languages. In *Proceedings of IJCNLP 2008 Workshop on NLP for Less Privileged Languages*.

Universal Dependencies are hard to parse – or are they?

Ines Rehbein♣, Julius Steen⋆, Bich-Ngoc Do⋆, Anette Frank⋆
Leibniz ScienceCampus
Institut für Deutsche Sprache Mannheim♣
Universität Heidelberg⋆
Germany
{rehbein,steen,do,frank}@cl.uni-heidelberg.de

Abstract

Universal Dependency (UD) annotations, despite their usefulness for cross-lingual tasks and semantic applications, are not optimised for statistical parsing. In the paper, we ask what exactly causes the decrease in parsing accuracy when training a parser on UD-style annotations and whether the effect is similarly strong for all languages. We conduct a series of experiments where we systematically modify individual annotation decisions taken in the UD scheme and show that this results in an increased accuracy for most, but not for all languages. We show that the encoding in the UD scheme, in particular the decision to encode content words as heads, causes an increase in dependency length for nearly all treebanks and an increase in arc direction entropy for many languages, and evaluate the effect this has on parsing accuracy.

1 Introduction

Syntactic parsing, and in particular dependency parsing, is an important preprocessing step for many NLP applications. Many different parsing models are available for many different languages, and also a number of annotation schemes that differ with respect to the linguistic decisions they take. One of them is the Universal Dependencies (UD) scheme (Nivre et al., 2016) that has been developed to support cross-lingual parser transfer, and cross-lingual NLP tasks in general, and to provide a foundation for a sound cross-lingual evaluation.

While the value of the UD framework for multilingual applications is beyond doubt, it has been discussed that the annotation decisions taken in the UD framework are likely to decrease parsing accuracies, as most dependency-based parsers do prefer a chain representation of shorter dependencies over the UD-style encoding of dependencies where content words are heads, with function words attached as dependent nodes (*content-head* encoding). This is especially relevant for the encoding of coordinations, copula, and prepositions (Marneffe et al., 2014) (see figure 1). Several studies have addressed this problem and presented experiments on converted trees, offering evidence that a function-head encoding might increase the learnability of the annotation scheme (Schwartz et al., 2012; Popel et al., 2013; Silveira and Manning, 2015; Rosa, 2015; Versley and Kirilin, 2015; Kohita et al., 2017).

Evaluating the learnability of annotation frameworks, however, is not straightforward and attempts to do so have often resulted in an apples-to-oranges comparison as there are multiple factors that can impact parsing performance, including the language, the annotation scheme, the size of the treebank, and the parsing model. Even text-intrinsic properties such as domain and genre of the texts that are included in the treebank can influence results (Rehbein and van Genabith, 2007). It is not possible to control for all of them and this has made it extremely difficult to come to conclusions concerning the learnability of syntactic representations for different languages or annotation frameworks.

In the paper, we show that the design decisions taken in the UD framework have a negative impact on the learnability of the annotations for many languages, but not for all. We do this by evaluating three important design decisions made in the UD scheme and compare their impact on parsing accuracies for different languages.

The contributions of the paper are as follows. We test the claim that content-head dependencies are harder to parse, using three parsers that implement different parsing paradigms. We present a conversion algorithm that transforms the content-

Proceedings of the Fourth International Conference on Dependency Linguistics (Depling 2017), pages 218-228,
Pisa, Italy, September 18-20 2017

head encoding of the UD treebanks for coordination, copula constructions and for prepositions into a function-head encoding and show that our conversion algorithm yields high accuracies (between 98.4% and 100%) for a back-and-forth conversion of *gold* trees.

We run parsing experiments on the original and the converted UD treebanks and compare the learnability of the annotations across 15 different languages, showing that language-specific properties play a cruicial role for the learning process. We further show that the changes in *dependency length* that result from the different encoding styles are *not* responsible for the changes in parsing accuracy.

The paper is structured as follows. We first review related work (§2) and present our conversion algorithm (§3). The data and setup for our experiments as well as the results are described in section §4. After a short discussion (§5) we conclude (§6).

2 Related work

It is well know from the literature that the linguistic framework used for a particular task has a great impact on the learnability of the annotations. Several studies have tried to evaluate and compare annotation schemes for syntactic parsing of one language (Kübler, 2005; Schwartz et al., 2012; Husain and Agrawal, 2012; Silveira and Manning, 2015) or across languages (Mareček et al., 2013; Rosa, 2015; Kohita et al., 2017), or have investigated the impact of a particular parsing model on the learnability of specific phenomena encoded in the framework (McDonald and Nivre, 2007; Goldberg and Elhadad, 2010).

Popel et al. (2013) present a thorough crosslingual investigation of different ways to encode coordination in a dependency framework. They did, however, not address the issue of learnability of the different encodings. This has been done in Mareček et al. (2013), who reach the somewhat disenchanted conclusion that the observed results of their experiments are "unconvincing and not very promising" (Mareček et al., 2013).

Versley and Kirilin (2015) look at the influence of languages and annotation schemes in universal dependency parsing, comparing 5 different parsers on 5 languages using two variants of UD schemes. They state that encoding content words as head has a negative impact on parsing results and that PP attachment errors account for a large portion of the differences in accuracy between the different parsers and between treebanks of varying sizes.

Recent work by Gulordava and Merlo (2016) has looked at word order variation and its impact on dependency parsing of 12 languages. They focus on word order freedom and dependency length as two properties of word order that systematically vary between different languages. To assess their impact on parsing accuracy, they modify the original treebanks by minimising the dependency lengths and the entropy of the head-direction (whether the head of dependent *dep* can be positioned to the left, to the right, or either way), thus creating *artificial* treebanks with systematically different word order properties. Parsing results on the modified treebanks confirm that a higher variation in word order and longer dependencies have a negative impact on parsing accuracies. These results, however, do not hold for all languages.[1]

The work of Gulordava and Merlo (2016) can not be used to compare the impact of different encoding schemes on the learnability of the annotations, as the modifications applied by the authors do result in *artificial* treebanks and cannot be traced back to specific design decisions, thus making the results hard to interpret for our purposes.

Kohita et al. (2017) overcome this problem by providing a conversion algorithm for the three functional labels *case, dep, mark* from the UD scheme. They convert the representations for those labels into function-head encodings and present parsing experiments on 19 treebanks from the UD project. Their results corroborate earlier findings and show that the conversions improve results for 16 out of 19 languages, using two graph-based parsers (MST and RBG) with default feature templates.

Our work is similar in spirit to the one of Kohita et al. (2017). We do, however, address partly different linguistic phenomena, namely the encoding of adpositions, copula verbs and coordinations. In contrast to Kohita et al. (2017), we do not back-transform the parser output but evaluate the converted trees against a converted version of the gold trees, as it has been shown that the back-conversion results in error propagation, which is reflected in lower parsing accuracies (Silveira and

---

[1] For German, for instance, word order variability seems to have a much stronger impact on parsing results while optimising dependency length resulted in a lower LAS.

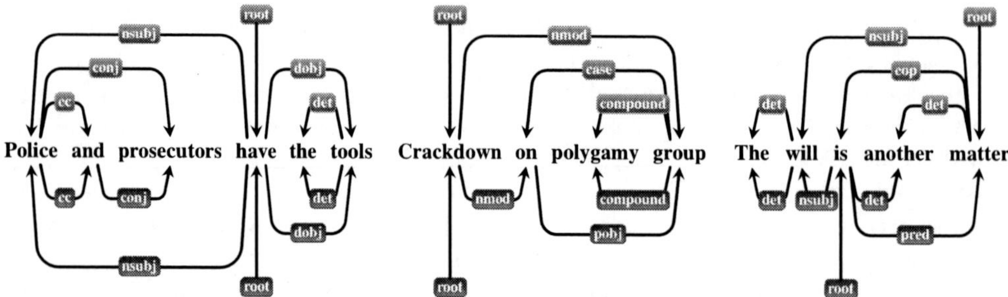

Figure 1: Dependency trees for conversion of coordination (left), prepositions (middle) and copula (right); UD encoding (brown, above) and modified trees with function words as heads (green, below).

Manning, 2015).[2]

Another difference to Kohita et al. (2017) concerns the parsers used in the experiments. While Kohita et al. (2017) use two graph-based parsing algorithms, we choose three parsers that represent different parsing paradigms, namely a transition-based parser, a graph-based parser and a head-selection parser. The latter is a neural parsing model that simply tries to find the best head for each token in the input. While the first two parsers use rich feature templates (and thus might be biased towards one particular encoding scheme), the head-selection parser does not use any pre-defined feature templates but learns all information directly from the input (§4.1).[3]

This allows us to test whether the previous results hold for parsers implementing different parsing paradigms and, crucially, whether they are independent of the feature templates used by the parsers. Finally, we are interested in the interaction between language, parser bias, and encoding scheme.

3 Conversion algorithm

The phenomena we consider in our experiments concern the encoding of copula verbs, coordinations and adpositions. All three address an important design decision taken in the UD project, namely to encode content words as heads.

We choose these because they are highly frequent in all the languages considered here and there is preliminary work discussing their impact

on statistical parsing (Schwartz et al., 2012; Marneffe et al., 2014), claiming that encoding content words as heads has a negative impact on parsing accuracy, as has the UD way of encoding coordinations.

To compare the impact on parsing scores across different languages, we develop a conversion algorithm that transforms the original UD trees (figure 1, trees above) into a function-head style encoding (figure 1, trees below).[4] We first use our conversion algorithm to transform the encodings for individual constructions (**cop**ula, **prep**ositions, **co-ord**inations) and the combination of all the three (**c-p-c**) and then transform the converted trees back to the original encoding, using our conversion method. We then evaluate the trees that have been converted back and forth between UD style and function-head style against the original UD gold trees.

Table 1 shows results for a back-and-forth conversion of the original gold UD trees for 15 languages. Languages are ordered according to how many tokens in the test set are affected by the conversion. This ranges from 20.9% for Chinese (zh) to 45.7% for Farsi (fa), with an average of 34.7% over all 15 languages.[5] We can see that at least for gold trees, our conversion algorithm is able to transform between the two encodings without substantial loss of information.[6]

Errors in the back-conversion are partly due to inconsistencies in the annotations that are not always compliant with the UD scheme. Some of these issues have already been addressed in the

---

[2]The main goal of Kohita et al. (2017) was to increase parsing accuracy for UD parsing, thus making a back-conversion necessary. We, instead, are interested in a comparison of the learnability of the different schemes and thus can skip the back-conversion step.

[3]We do not use pretrained word embeddings in the experiments but learn the embeddings from the training data.

[4]Our code is available for download at http://wisscamp.de/en/research-2/resources.

[5]For comparison, the average ratio of converted tokens in the study of Kohita et al. (2017) is 6.3%.

[6]An exception is Farsi, where we observe a slightly higher LAS error rate, in particular for the conversion of coordinations.

					LAS			UAS	% affected
		size	cop	prep	coord	c-p-c	c-p-c	c-p-c
Chinese	**zh**	3,997	100.0	100.0	99.9	99.9	100.0	20.9
Estonian	**et**	14,510	99.9	100.0	100.0	99.9	100.0	23.6
Turkish	**tr**	3,948	99.9	99.8	99.8	99.4	99.8	27.9
Russian-SynTagRus	**ru**	48,171	100.0	100.0	100.0	100.0	100.0	30.6
German	**de**	14,118	99.8	100.0	99.8	99.6	100.0	33.2
Czech	**cs**	68,495	100.0	100.0	99.7	99.7	100.0	35.3
Romanian	**ro**	7,141	99.9	99.9	99.8	99.7	100.0	36.4
English	**en**	12,543	100.0	99.8	99.9	99.6	99.9	37.6
Croatian	**hr**	5,792	100.0	100.0	99.8	99.8	100.0	38.5
French	**fr**	14,554	100.0	99.8	99.9	99.8	99.9	38.5
Catalan	**ca**	13,123	99.9	99.5	99.9	99.4	99.8	38.8
Italian	**it**	12,837	100.0	100.0	99.9	100.0	100.0	40.3
Spanish	**es**	14,187	99.8	99.9	99.9	99.6	99.9	40.3
Bulgarian	**bg**	8,907	100.0	100.0	99.9	99.9	100.0	43.7
Farsi	**fa**	4,798	99.6	100.0	98.8	98.4	100.0	45.7
avg.		*16,475*	*99.9*	*99.9*	*99.8*	*99.6*	*99.9*	*35.4*

Table 1: LAS (excluding punctuation) on the test sets after round-trip conversion for individual transformations and for the combination of all (c-p-c: copula, prep, coord), evaluated against the original UD trees, and UAS for all conversions (c-p-c) (languages are ordered according to the amount of tokens affected by the combination of all conversions; zh: 20.9% – fa: 45.7%).

new release of the UD 2.0.[7] Other errors are due to language-specific constructions. A case in point are compositional preposition in Catalan (e.g. *per a*) where both parts are attached to the same head, while other sequences of prepositions have a chain-like attachment. Our conversion algorithm does not pay attention to language-specific properties that are neither encoded on the pos level nor in the dependency labels. It would, however, be straightforward to extend the algorithm to include these.

A final cause of errors in the back-conversion concerns coordinations with more than two conjuncts, where we have embedded coordinated constituents of the type *(A and B and (C and D))*. Here the back-conversion from the chain-like representation to UD looses information. In practice, however, these structures are not very frequent. For instance, in the English test set less than 0.8% of all sentences include a coordination of that particular type.

4 Experiments

We now want to use our conversion method to assess the impact of the content-head encoding in general and of individual, construction-specific

encodings on parsing accuracies across different languages. In contrast to Kohita et al. (2017), our objective is *not* to improve UD parsing accuracies by using the conversion before parsing to increase the learnability of the representations and then convert the *parser output* back to the UD scheme. Our main goal is to use the conversion on *gold* trees in order to compare the impact it has for different languages and thus learn more about how to encode languages with different typological properties to improve monolingual dependency parsing results.

To rule out the influence of extrinsic factors such as data size or text type, we do not compare results across different treebanks and languages but modify specific annotation decisions and compare parsing accuracies for the original treebanks with the ones obtained on modified versions of the *same* treebank. Figure 1 illustrates the UD encoding (trees above) and the modified trees with function words as heads and a chain-like encoding of coordinations (trees below).

4.1 Data and setup

The data we use in our experiments comes from the UD treebanks (Nivre et al., 2016) v1.3. The selected 15 languages cover different language families and a range of typological properties. We

---

[7]The sixth release of the Universal Dependencies treebanks, v2.0, is available at http://universaldependencies.org.

		LAS			CNC		
		IMS	RBG	HSEL	IMS	RBG	HSEL
germanic	de	**84.3**	83.8	82.0	**79.7**	78.9	77.1
	en	**86.4**	86.3	86.0	**82.8**	82.2	82.3
iranian	fa	83.4	83.1	**83.9**	80.5	79.5	**80.8**
romance	ca	**89.5**	88.8	89.1	**84.0**	82.7	83.6
	es	**85.6**	85.2	85.2	**78.6**	77.5	78.0
	fr	**85.6**	84.4	85.2	**79.4**	77.6	78.6
	it	**89.6**	88.8	89.3	**84.3**	82.9	83.9
	ro	**79.9**	79.6	78.6	**75.4**	74.6	73.3
slavic	bg	**86.9**	84.9	85.6	**83.7**	80.8	81.7
	cs	**87.8**	86.1	85.7	**86.1**	83.9	83.5
	hr	79.9	**80.7**	78.1	77.2	**77.6**	74.9
	ru	**89.5**	**89.5**	86.8	**88.0**	87.8	84.4
sinitic	zh	**81.8**	79.4	80.4	**80.6**	77.9	79.1
finnic	et	**84.1**	83.9	75.3	**83.0**	82.6	73.0
turkic	tr	73.5	**75.1**	62.5	71.9	**73.4**	59.1

Table 2: LAS (excluding punctuation) and CNC (content dependencies only) on the test sets of the original treebanks.

choose three different non-projective parsers to assess the impact of specific parsing frameworks on the results, namely the graph-based RBG parser (Lei et al., 2014), the transition-based IMSTrans parser of Björkelund and Nivre (2015) (IMS), and our reimplementation of the head-selection parser of Zhang et al. (2017) (HSEL).

The RBG parser uses tensor decomposition and greedy decoding and the IMSTrans parser implements the (labeled) ArcStandard system, including a swap transition that can generate non-projective trees. The head-selection parser generates unlabeled trees by identifying the most probable head for each token in the input and then assigns labels to each head-dependent pair in a post-processing step. In contrast to the other two parsers, the head-selection parser does not use any predefined feature templates but selects the most probable head for each token based on word representations learned by a bidirectional long-short memory model (LSTM) (Hochreiter and Schmidhuber, 1997). Despite its simplicity and the lack of global optimisation, Zhang et al. (2017) report competitive results for English, Czech, and German.

For the first two parsers, we use default settings and the provided feature templates (for the RBG parser we use the *standard* setting *without* pretrained word embeddings), with no language-specific parameter optimisation.[8] We use the coarse-grained universal POS (Petrov et al., 2012) for all languages. The RBG and IMSTrans parser

are trained on gold POS and morphological features provided by the UD project, the head-selection model is trained *without* morphological information, using word and POS embeddings only.

We choose the head-selection model to test whether a potential positive impact of the conversion might simply be a bias introduced by the feature templates, which might favour one particular encoding scheme. If we see the same improvements for all three parsers, we can be sure that the results are robust and not just an artefact of the feature templates used in the experiments.

For our experiments we systematically modify the input data and run parsing experiments on the original and on the converted treebanks. We have 15 settings per language (3 parsers x 5 treebank versions x 15 languages), which results in a total of 225 experiments. We hypothesize that the different modifications have a different effect on each language, which will be reflected in the changes in parsing accuracy when training and testing the parser on the different treebank versions.

4.2 Results for the original treebanks

Table 2 shows results for the three parsers on the original treebanks. We use the CNC metric proposed by Nivre (2016) and Nivre and Fang (2017) for UD evaluation. The metric excludes function words and punctuation from the evaluation and reports results only for *core* and *non-core* grammatical functions, thus providing a more informative and also more robust evaluation across different

---

[8] Please note that our goal is not to improve, or compare, results for individual languages but to assess the impact of different encoding decisions on the parsing accuracy for one language.

	lang	IMS		RBG		HSEL	
		CNC	Δ	CNC	Δ	CNC	Δ
ger	de	81.0	1.3	81.2	2.3	78.0	0.9
	en	83.6	0.8	83.4	1.2	83.6	1.3
ira	fa	84.2	3.7	83.4	3.9	83.6	2.8
rom	ca	85.6	1.6	85.0	2.3	84.9	1.3
	es	80.5	1.9	80.8	3.3	79.9	1.9
	fr	81.9	2.5	80.7	3.1	80.4	1.8
	it	86.1	1.8	86.1	3.2	85.5	1.6
	ro	75.7	0.3	75.3	0.7	73.6	0.3
sla	bg	85.4	1.7	83.8	3.0	83.8	2.1
	cs	87.3	1.2	85.2	1.3	84.2	0.7
	hr	77.4	0.2	77.3	-0.3	73.2	-1.7
	ru	89.2	1.2	88.7	0.9	82.1	-2.3
sin	zh	81.9	1.3	78.9	1.0	79.2	0.1
fin	et	84.4	1.4	82.8	0.2	74.7	1.7
tur	tr	71.6	-0.3	71.8	-1.6	58.3	-0.8

Table 3: CNC for the converted treebanks and differences Δ to the CNC obtained on the original treebanks.

metric	orig	cop	prep	coord	c-p-c	Δ
			Turkish			
with punc	77.4	76.9	76.6	76.7	76.4	-1.0
w/o punc	75.1	74.4	74.1	74.2	73.8	-1.3
CNC	73.4	72.9	72.6	71.9	71.8	-1.6
core	65.9	65.3	65.9	64.7	**67.1**	+1.2
non-core	75.5	74.9	74.4	73.9	73.2	-2.3
func	85.6	84.2	83.4	**88.2**	**86.0**	+0.4
			Croatian			
with punc	80.2	78.7	79.4	**81.0**	80.1	-0.1
w/o punc	80.7	79.0	80.0	**81.5**	80.5	-0.2
CNC	77.7	75.5	76.9	**78.6**	77.3	-0.4
core	81.1	**81.5**	81.0	**81.7**	**81.9**	+0.7
non-core	76.8	74.0	75.9	**77.8**	76.1	-0.9
func	88.5	87.9	87.9	**89.1**	**88.7**	+0.2

Table 4: Results for different label sets for Turkish and Croatian (RBG parser) and difference (Δ) between original and converted treebank (**cop**-**prep**-**coord**).

languages.[9] Our evaluation does not provide a fair comparison between the parsers, as the different parsers do not have access to the same information (the head-selection parser, for instance, has no access to morphological information) and were not optimised for specific languages. Instead, our goal is to test whether the results of our conversion are robust across different languages and parsing models.

From the table we can see that the parsers perform differently well on the different treebanks. The transition-based parser provides best results for most languages and is only outperformed by the tensor-based RBG parser on Turkish (tr) and Croatian (hr) and by the head-selection parser on Farsi (fa), all three languages with rather small training sets.

It comes at not surprise that the head-selection parser, which has no access to morphological information or subword representations, has problems with Turkish (tr) and Estonian (et), which are both agglutinative languages. Despite the simplicity of the head-selection model, however, the parser produces competetive results for many languages and even outperforms the other two parsers on Farsi (fa).[10]

---

[9]Please note that the CNC metric considers the same number of tokens for evaluation in the original and converted treebanks, which is crucial for comparability.

[10]The head-selection model can easily be extended to include character-based embeddings or morphological embeddings, which will increase its performance on morphologically rich languages, but this is out of scope of the present study.

4.3 Results for the converted treebanks

We now want to assess the impact of our conversions on the different languages. Table 3 shows CNC scores for the three parsers trained on the converted treebanks as well as the difference (Δ) to the results we get when training on the original treebanks.[11]

Our results confirm previous results from the literature (Schwartz et al., 2012; Marneffe et al., 2014) and show that our conversions are beneficial for nearly all languages. One exception is Turkish where CNC scores for all three parsers decrease. For Croatian, we observe only a minor increase for the IMSTrans parser and a decrease in results for the other two parsers.

To better understand the results for Turkish, we compare accuracies for the different label sets for the RBG parser which obtained best results on the Turkish treebank (Table 4). Most interestingly, we see that our conversions do indeed increase results for the core arguments (+1.2% labelled accuracy; improvements for csubj and ccomp) and also for the function tags (+0.4%), but all three conversions result in lower scores for the non-core dependency labels, especially for coordinations. These results highlight the importance of a detailed error analysis and show that overall parsing scores might be misleading.

Considering the small size of the Turkish treebank and the fact that the data has been converted automatically without manual correction, we can

---

[11]LAS and CNC scores for all parsers and each individual conversion are shown in table 7 in the appendix.

not rule out that the negative impact of the conversion on the non-core dependencies is merely an artefact of low data quality. This issue requires further investigation.

Looking at the results for Croatian, we see that the chain-like encoding of coordinations in our conversion experiments brings improvements for all subsets of grammatical functions. The other two conversions, however, result in a decrease in accuracy, which is also reflected in the results for the combined conversion (c-p-c). While for Turkish all three conversions on their own seem to decrease results and only the combination of all three converted encodings yields an improvement, for Croatian we get best results when changing the annotation of coordinations only and keeping the remaining representations in UD style. This increases CNC scores for RBG from 77.7% to 78.6% (+0.9). Our last finding suggests that a language-specific optimisation of annotation schemes for parsing might be worthwhile, and that there is a complex interaction between encoding styles, data properties (e.g. the size of the treebank) and language properties.

We also observe a correlation between language family and the degree to which the conversion improves performance. For all three parsers, we observe a similar ranking.[12] At the top is Farsi which benefits most from the conversion, while for Croatian and Turkish the results decrease. In general, the romance languages (fr, es, it, ca) seem to profit more from the transformations than the germanic and slavic languages. Romanian, however, an easter romance language, seems to behave different from the italo-western romance languages and shows only a slight increase in CNC.

In the next section, we turn to the question what it is that determines whether and how much a particular language will benefit from a specific choice of encoding. To that end, we focus on two language-specific properties, namely on dependency length and on the direction of the relations, i.e. head-initial versus head-final dependencies.

4.4 Dependency length

Previous work has discussed the different factors that might impact parsing accuracies across

	Lang	orig	cop	prep	coord	c-p-c
ger	de	3.4	0.98	1.01	1.03	1.03
	en	2.9	1.00	1.04	1.03	1.07
ira	fa	3.5	0.97	0.99	1.02	0.97
rom	ca	3.1	1.00	1.06	1.03	1.09
	es	2.8	0.99	1.07	1.04	1.11
	fr	2.8	0.99	1.07	1.03	1.09
	it	2.7	1.00	1.05	1.02	1.08
	ro	2.7	1.00	1.04	1.04	1.07
sla	bg	2.5	1.01	1.05	1.02	1.08
	cs	2.8	1.00	1.58	1.03	1.06
	hr	2.8	1.00	1.03	1.04	1.08
	ru	2.7	1.00	1.02	1.03	1.05
sin	zh	3.6	1.00	0.98	1.01	1.00
fin	et	2.6	1.00	1.00	1.03	1.02
tur	tr	2.6	1.00	1.01	1.01	1.02

Table 5: Avg. dependency length in the original treebank and DLM ratio for each modification

languages, such as word order properties, the high amount of unknown words for morphologically rich languages, ambiguity due to case syncretism, non-projectivity, ambiguity in head direction, and dependency length (Tsarfaty et al., 2010; Schwartz et al., 2012; Gulordava and Merlo, 2016).

Gulordava and Merlo (2016) have investigated the influence of dependency length and arc direction entropy on parsing results, using *artificially created* treebanks. We adopt their measures to find out more about the impact of different encodings on natural languages. Following Gulordava and Merlo (2016), we compute the overall ratio of Dependency Length Minimisation (DLM) in the modified treebanks (as compared to the original treebanks), based on the data in the training set, as follows.

$$DLMRatio = \sum_s \frac{DL_s}{|s|^2} / \sum_s \frac{ModDL_s}{|s|^2} \quad (1)$$

The dependency length DL for each sentence s in the original treebank is calculated as the sum of the length of all arcs in the tree for sentence s,[13] and $ModDL$ refers to the dependency length in the modified treebank. A DLM ratio above 1 means that the treebank conversion resulted in a decreased dependency length in the data.[14]

---

[12] We obtain highly significant results for Spearman's rank correlation, computed on the differences Δ in CNC (see table 3), between all possible parser pairs (IMS-RBG, IMS-HSEL, RBG-HSEL) (all $p < 0.0006$).

[13] For the rightmost UD tree in Figure 1 DL_s is 7 while the length for the modified tree ($ModDL_s$) is 5.

[14] Please note that in contrast to Gulordava and Merlo (2016), who computed the DLM ratio between the original treebanks and an artificially created version of the same data where the order of the tokens had been modified, we compute the DLM ratio between two different encodings of the *same* data and thus their DLM ratios are not directly comparable to ours.

We can see that the modifications have quite a different effect on the average dependency length in the different treebanks (Table 5). While for many languages the combination of all modifications results in a minimisation of dependency length, this does not hold for Farsi and Chinese, and only slightly for Turkish, German and Estonian. It does not seem that the minimisation in dependency length is the responsible factor for the improvements in CNC. To test this, we fitted a linear regression model to the data and, as expected, did not find a significant correlation between dependency length and the changes in CNC accuracy for any of the parsers (IMSTrans: p=0.604, RBG: p=0.463, HSEL: p=0.943).[15]

We were thus not able to replicate the findings of Gulordava and Merlo (2016) who optimised UD trees for dependency length, thus generating artificial trees that were allowed to violate language-specific word order restrictions. They concluded that an increase in dependency length has, in general, a negative impact on parsing scores. This conclusion does not hold for our data. However, Gulordava and Merlo (2016) also found that minimising dependency length e.g. for German did not improve parsing accuracies the same way as it did for other languages.

Even if our conversion does result in a minimisation of dependency length in the treebanks, we conclude that the improvements in parsing accuracy are not due to the shorter dependencies. This raises the question what it is that makes the converted trees easier to learn and whether the differences are due to typological properties or merely reflect idiosyncrasies in the treebanks.

4.5 Arc direction entropy

We now look at the variation in the linear ordering between a head and its dependent as a potential factor that might impact parsing accuracy. Languages can be distinguished with regard to the proportion of head-initial versus head-final dependencies, which reflect typological differences between language families (Liu, 2010). Different treebank annotation schemes, however, can also influence the variation in arc direction, independent from the specific language of the treebank content.

To quantify this variation, we compute arc-direction entropy (ADE) (Gulordava and Merlo,

	lang	Δ cop	Δ prep	Δ coord	Δ c-p-c
ger	de	-0.26	-0.03	0.03	-0.23
	en	-0.56	-0.19	-0.01	-0.72
ira	fa	-0.73	0.07	0.02	-0.60
rom	ca	0.09	0.07	-0.01	0.16
	es	-0.19	-0.19	0.02	-0.36
	fr	-0.16	-0.15	0.04	-0.27
	it	-0.22	-0.11	0.02	-0.29
	ro	-0.13	0.17	0.04	0.09
sla	bg	-0.31	-0.10	0.05	-0.34
	cs	-0.30	0.20	0.07	0.03
	hr	0.16	0.21	0.03	0.41
	ru	0.17	0.19	0.05	0.41
sin	zh	-0.25	-0.00	0.03	-0.19
fin	et	-0.37	0.16	0.04	-0.16
tur	tr	0.19	0.28	0.03	0.50

Table 6: Difference (Δ) between avg. unlexicalised arc direction entropy (ADE) in the original treebank and in the modified treebanks

2016) in a treebank by iterating over all dependents in each individual arc and summing up the probability of the arc, represented by the POS of the dependent, the relation and the POS of the head, times the conditional entropy of the head direction, given the arc (Equation (2)).[16] An increase in ADE means that a particular modification introduced more variation with respect to the linear order of head and dependent for a specific relation.

$$H(Dir|Rel, H, D) = \sum_{rel,h,d} p(rel, h, d) H(Dir|rel, h, d)$$

(2)

For most languages, the conversion from content-head to function-head dependencies decreases ADE (Table 6). For some languages, we see a slight increase (Czech, Romanian, Catalan) while for Croatian, Russian and Turkish, the increase in entropy is substantial with 0.4 and 0.5, respectively. When fitting a linear regression model to the data, this time we see a significant effect on parsing accuracy (CNC) for the IMSTrans parser ($p = 0.01$) and the RBG parser ($p = 004$). For the head-selection parser, the correlation is even stronger with $p = 0.0002$.

We also experimented with lexicalised arc entropy but found no improvement over the unlexicalised model, probably due to data sparseness (see the discussion in Futrell et al. (2015)).

---

[15]We used R's lm function to predict the changes in CNC for each modified treebank version, based on the DLMratio.

[16]Futrell et al. (2015) discuss a methodological problem for using entropy for estimating word order properties, namely its sensitivity to sample size. We adress this by measuring variation in arc direction over n equally-sized random samples from each treebank (with replacement, $n = 1000$), and then report the average over all samples.

5 Discussion

Our findings suggest that it is not so much an increase in dependency length that goes along with the content-head representation implemented in the UD treebanks, but rather the increase in entropy for the position of the head that causes the loss in parsing accuracy when training a parser on UD-style dependencies.

Kohita et al. (2017) also discuss another property, namely the *head word vocabulary entropy*, as a potential factor that impacts parsing scores. Their measure is an implementation of an idea described in Schwartz et al. (2012). However, Kohita et al. (2017) did not observe a significant correlation between improvements in parsing accuracy (obtained by the RBG parser) and head word vocabulary entropy.

Our results show that the improvements we get through the conversion of content-head to function-head dependencies are not only due to the feature templates used by the parsers, which might introduce a bias towards one particular encoding, as we get similar improvements for the head-selection parser, a neural parser which does *not* use any predefined feature templates but learns its features directly from the input representations.

6 Conclusions

We presented a systematic investigation of the impact of specific annotation design decisions for statistical dependency parsing. We showed that claims that have been made for English (Schwartz et al., 2012) also hold for many other languages, but that the effect strength varies considerably.

We also showed that the UD encoding of adpositions, coordination and copula increases dependency length for all the languages we investigated except Persian and Chinese. This increase, however, does not directly translate to lower parsing scores. Head direction entropy, on the other hand, seems to have a stronger impact on parsing. This finding is consistent with the observations of Gulordava and Merlo (2016) obtained on *artificially* created data and their suggestion that at least for German, word order variability might have a higher impact on parsing difficulty than dependency length.

Finally, our results suggest that there is an interaction between typological properties and the effect strength of the improvments obtained by the treebank conversion. This provides interesting avenues for future research, as language generalisations might help us to design treebank encoding schemes that are optimised for specific languages, without having to repeat the same effort for each individual language.

Acknowledgments

We would like to thank the anonymous reviewers for their valuable comments and suggestions. This research has been conducted within the Leibniz Science Campus "Empirical Linguistics and Computational Modeling", funded by the Leibniz Association under grant no. SAS-2015-IDS-LWC and by the Ministry of Science, Research, and Art (MWK) of the state of Baden-Württemberg.

References

Anders Björkelund and Joakim Nivre. 2015. Nondeterministic oracles for unrestricted non-projective transition-based dependency parsing. In *Proceedings of the 14th International Conference on Parsing Technologies*, IWPT '15, pages 76–86, Bilbao, Spain, July.

Richard Futrell, Kyle Mahowald, and Edward Gibson. 2015. Quantifying word order freedom in dependency corpora. In *Proceedings of the Third International Conference on Dependency Linguistics*, Depling 2015, pages 91–100.

Yoav Goldberg and Michael Elhadad. 2010. Inspecting the structural biases of dependency parsing algorithms. In *Proceedings of the Fourteenth Conference on Computational Natural Language Learning*, CoNLL '10, pages 234–242, Uppsala, Sweden.

Kristina Gulordava and Paola Merlo. 2016. Multilingual dependency parsing evaluation: a large-scale analysis of word order properties using artificial data. *Transactions of the Association for Computational Linguistics*, 4:343–356.

Sepp Hochreiter and Jürgen Schmidhuber. 1997. Long short-term memory. *Neural Computing*, 9(8):1735–1780.

Samar Husain and Bhasha Agrawal. 2012. Analyzing parser errors to improve parsing accuracy and to inform tree banking decisions. In *The 10th International Workshop on Treebanks and Linguistic Theories*, TLT.

Ryosuke Kohita, Hiroshi Noji, and Yuji Matsumoto. 2017. Multilingual back-and-forth conversion between content and function head for easy dependency parsing. In *Proceedings of the 15th Conference of the European Chapter of the Association for Computational Linguistics*, EACL'17, pages 1–7, Valencia, Spain.

Sandra Kübler. 2005. How do treebank annotation schemes influence parsing results? Or how not to compare apples and oranges. In *Proceedings of Recent Advances in Natural Language Processing*, RANLP '05.

Tao Lei, Yu Xin, Yuan Zhang, Regina Barzilay, and Tommi Jaakkola. 2014. Low-rank tensors for scoring dependency structures. In *Proceedings of the 52nd Annual Meeting of the Association for Computational Linguistics*, ACL '14, pages 1381–1391.

Haitao Liu. 2010. Dependency direction as a means of word-order typology: A method based on dependency treebanks. *Lingua*, 120(6):1567–1578.

David Mareček, Martin Popel, Loganathan Ramasamy, Jan Štěpánek, Daniel Zeman, Zdeněk Žabokrtský, and Jan Hajič. 2013. Cross-language study on influence of coordination style on dependency parsing performance. Technical report, UFAL.

Marie-Catherine De Marneffe, Timothy Dozat, Natalia Silveira, Katri Haverinen, Filip Ginter, Joakim Nivre, and Christopher D. Manning. 2014. Universal Stanford dependencies: a cross-linguistic typology. In *Proceedings of the Ninth International Conference on Language Resources and Evaluation*, LREC '14, Reykjavik, Iceland.

Ryan T. McDonald and Joakim Nivre. 2007. Characterizing the errors of data-driven dependency parsing models. In *Proceedings of the 2007 Joint Conference on Empirical Methods in Natural Language Processing and Computational Natural Language Learning, June 28-30, 2007, Prague, Czech Republic*, EMNLP-CoNLL '07, pages 122–131, Prague, Czech Republic.

Joakim Nivre and Chiao-Ting Fang. 2017. Universal dependency evaluation. In *Proceedings of the NoDaLiDa 2017 Workshop on Universal Dependencies*, pages 86–95, Gothenburg, Sweden.

Joakim Nivre, Marie-Catherine de Marneffe, Filip Ginter, Yoav Goldberg, Jan Hajic, Christopher D. Manning, Ryan McDonald, Slav Petrov, Sampo Pyysalo, Natalia Silveira, Reut Tsarfaty, and Daniel Zeman. 2016. Universal dependencies v1: A multilingual treebank collection. In *Proceedings of the Tenth International Conference on Language Resources and Evaluation*, LREC '16, Portorož, Slovenia.

Joakim Nivre. 2016. Universal dependency evaluation. Technical report, Uppsala University, Sweden.

Slav Petrov, Dipanjan Das, and Ryan McDonald. 2012. A universal part-of-speech tagset. In *Proceedings of the Eight International Conference on Language Resources and Evaluation*, LREC '12, Istanbul, Turkey.

Martin Popel, David Marecek, Jan Stepánek, Daniel Zeman, and Zdenek Zabokrtský. 2013. Coordination structures in dependency treebanks. In *Annual Meeting of The European Chapter of The Association of Computational Linguistics*, EACL '13, pages 517–527.

Ines Rehbein and Josef van Genabith. 2007. Why is it so difficult to compare treebanks? TIGER and TüBa-D/Z revisited. In *The Sixth International Workshop on Treebanks and Linguistic Theories*, TLT '07, pages 115 – 126, Bergen, Norway.

Rudolf Rosa. 2015. Multi-source cross-lingual delexicalized parser transfer: Prague or Stanford? In *Proceedings of the Third International Conference on Dependency Linguistics*, DepLing '15, pages 281–290, Uppsala, Sweden.

Roy Schwartz, Omri Abend, and Ari Rappoport. 2012. Learnability-based syntactic annotation design. In *Proceedings of the 24th International Conference on Computational Linguistics*, COLING '12, pages 2405–2422, Mumbai, India.

Natalia Silveira and Christopher D. Manning. 2015. Does universal dependencies need a parsing representation? an investigation of english. In *Proceedings of the Third International Conference on Dependency Linguistics*, DepLing'15, pages 310–319, Uppsala, Sweden.

Reut Tsarfaty, Djame Seddah, Yoav Goldberg, Sandra Kübler, Marie Candito, Jennifer Foster, Yannick Versley, Ines Rehbein, and Lamia Tounsi. 2010. Statistical Parsing of Morphologically Rich Languages (SPMRL): What, How and Whither. In *Proceedings of the first workshop on Statistical Parsing of Morphologically Rich Languages*, SPMRL'10, Los Angeles, CA, USA.

Yannick Versley and Angelika Kirilin. 2015. What is hard in universal dependency parsing? In *The 6th Workshop on Statistical Parsing of Morphologically Rich Languages*, SPMRL '15.

Xingxing Zhang, Jianpeng Cheng, and Mirella Lapata. 2017. Dependency parsing as head selection. In *Proceedings of the 15th Conference of the European Chapter of the Association for Computational Linguistics*, EACL'17, pages 665–676, Valencia, Spain.

Appendix A. Supplemental Material

		IMS (LAS)					IMS (CNC)				
		orig	cop	prep	coord	c-p-c	orig	cop	prep	coord	c-p-c
germanic	de	84.3	85.0	84.3	84.9	**85.2**	79.7	80.9	79.9	80.5	**81.0**
	en	86.4	86.0	86.5	**87.0**	86.7	82.8	82.5	83.2	83.5	**83.6**
iranian	fa	83.4	85.6	84.6	84.5	**86.4**	80.5	83.0	81.9	82.0	**84.2**
romance	ca	89.5	89.5	89.2	**90.1**	89.9	84.0	84.3	84.1	85.3	**85.6**
	es	85.6	85.4	85.6	86.7	**86.8**	78.6	78.2	78.7	80.3	**80.5**
	fr	85.6	86.1	85.3	86.1	**87.0**	79.4	80.6	79.2	80.2	**81.9**
	it	89.6	89.9	90.1	**90.7**	90.5	84.3	85.0	85.1	86.0	**86.1**
	ro	79.9	79.4	79.6	**80.7**	80.0	75.4	74.8	75.1	**76.4**	75.7
slavic	bg	86.9	87.6	87.0	87.5	**88.0**	83.7	84.8	84.0	84.5	**85.4**
	cs	87.8	88.2	88.2	88.2	**88.8**	86.1	86.5	86.6	86.5	**87.3**
	hr	79.9	79.8	79.5	**82.2**	80.4	77.2	77.0	76.8	**79.3**	77.4
	ru	89.5	89.5	89.8	**90.6**	90.6	88.0	88.0	88.3	**89.2**	89.2
sinitic	zh	81.8	81.5	82.3	82.1	**82.9**	80.6	80.5	81.1	80.9	**81.9**
finnic	et	84.1	84.9	84.1	84.8	**85.5**	83.0	83.8	83.0	83.7	**84.4**
turkic	tr	73.5	73.8	**74.0**	73.3	73.6	71.9	72.3	**72.5**	71.1	71.6

		RBG (LAS)					RBG (CNC)				
		orig	cop	prep	coord	c-p-c	orig	cop	prep	coord	c-p-c
germanic	de	83.8	84.2	84.0	84.0	**85.4**	78.9	79.6	79.3	79.0	**81.2**
	en	86.3	86.0	86.2	86.4	**86.8**	82.2	82.1	82.5	82.5	**83.4**
iranian	fa	83.1	84.6	83.8	83.3	**86.1**	79.5	81.2	80.6	79.9	**83.4**
romance	ca	88.8	88.6	88.9	89.4	**89.6**	82.7	82.5	83.6	83.9	**85.0**
	es	85.2	85.4	85.9	85.8	**86.8**	77.5	77.9	78.9	79.0	**80.8**
	fr	84.4	85.1	84.8	85.6	**86.3**	77.6	78.9	78.5	78.8	**80.7**
	it	88.8	89.1	89.7	89.3	**90.8**	82.9	83.3	84.3	83.6	**86.1**
	ro	79.6	79.1	79.3	79.8	**79.9**	74.6	74.1	74.4	74.9	**75.3**
slavic	bg	84.9	85.2	85.5	85.3	**86.9**	80.8	81.4	81.8	81.4	**83.8**
	cs	86.1	86.0	86.3	85.9	**87.1**	83.9	83.9	84.2	83.8	**85.2**
	hr	80.7	79.0	80.0	**81.5**	80.5	77.7	75.5	76.9	**78.6**	77.3
	ru	89.5	88.8	89.4	90.0	**90.1**	87.8	87.1	87.8	88.3	**88.7**
sinitic	zh	79.4	78.7	79.6	78.6	**80.2**	77.9	77.3	78.4	77.0	**78.9**
finnic	et	83.9	83.3	83.4	**84.2**	84.1	82.6	81.9	82.2	**83.0**	82.8
turkic	tr	**75.1**	74.4	74.1	74.2	73.8	**73.4**	72.9	72.6	71.9	71.8

		HSEL (LAS)					HSEL (CNC)				
		orig	cop	prep	coord	c-p-c	orig	cop	prep	coord	c-p-c
germanic	de	82.0	82.6	82.2	82.5	**82.8**	77.1	**78.0**	77.2	77.6	**78.0**
	en	86.0	86.2	86.1	86.5	**86.8**	82.3	82.7	82.6	82.9	**83.6**
iranian	fa	83.9	85.2	84.3	84.3	**86.1**	80.8	82.4	81.3	81.2	**83.6**
romance	ca	89.1	89.4	89.1	**89.9**	89.6	83.6	84.1	83.8	**84.9**	84.9
	es	85.2	85.6	86.0	85.8	**86.3**	78.0	78.7	79.3	79.1	**79.9**
	fr	85.2	**86.2**	85.3	85.7	**86.2**	78.6	80.1	78.8	79.5	**80.4**
	it	89.3	89.5	89.4	89.7	**90.4**	83.9	84.0	83.8	84.3	**85.5**
	ro	78.6	78.2	78.1	**79.2**	78.7	73.3	73.2	72.7	**74.2**	73.6
slavic	bg	85.6	86.5	85.9	86.0	**87.0**	81.7	83.3	82.2	82.6	**83.8**
	cs	85.7	86.1	85.8	86.0	**86.5**	83.5	83.8	83.5	83.7	**84.2**
	hr	78.1	75.4	77.9	**79.6**	76.8	74.9	72.4	74.9	**76.7**	73.2
	ru	86.8	86.6	86.6	**87.6**	84.7	84.4	84.2	84.2	**85.2**	82.1
sinitic	zh	80.4	79.7	**80.7**	79.7	80.4	79.1	78.5	**79.4**	78.6	79.2
finnic	et	75.3	76.5	74.9	75.8	**77.0**	73.0	74.3	72.7	73.4	**74.7**
turkic	tr	**62.5**	61.7	62.3	62.3	62.2	**59.1**	58.4	59.0	58.2	58.3

Table 7: LAS (excluding punctuation) and CNC (content dependencies only) on the test sets for the original UD treebanks and for individual conversions (cop: copula, prep: prepositions, coord: coordination, c-p-c: combination of all three conversions).

Annotating Italian Social Media Texts in Universal Dependencies

Manuela Sanguinetti
Cristina Bosco
Alessandro Mazzei
Università di Torino
Dipartimento di Informatica
Torino, Italy
{msanguin,bosco,mazzei}@di.unito.it

Alberto Lavelli
Fondazione Bruno Kessler
Trento, Italy
lavelli@fbk.eu

Fabio Tamburini
Università di Bologna
FICLIT
Bologna, Italy
fabio.tamburini@unibo.it

Abstract

Social media texts have been widely used in recent years for various tasks related to sentiment analysis and opinion mining; nevertheless, they still feature a wide range of linguistic phenomena that have proved to be particularly challenging for automatic processing, especially for syntactic parsing. In this paper, we describe a recently started project for the development of PoSTWITA-UD, a novel Italian Twitter treebank in Universal Dependencies. In particular, the paper focuses on its development steps, and on the challenges such work entails, both for automatic systems and human annotators, by discussing the errors produced, by parsers in particular, and the guidelines we adopted for manual revision of annotated tweets. Such guidelines aim to bring to the reader's attention the most critical cases (in themselves, but also in a UD perspective) encountered so far and stemming from the specific characteristics of the texts we are dealing with.

1 Introduction

In the last few years, the interest for automatic evaluation of social media texts has grown considerably; thanks to the various APIs available from the platform, Twitter in particular has been considered a valuable source of data that can be used for different computational linguistics studies and applications. Nevertheless, the annotation and exploitation of Twitter corpora are currently mainly referred to sentiment analysis and opinion mining or other semantic-oriented forms of processing, see e.g. tasks in SemEval 2017[1]

and EVALITA (Barbieri et al., 2016). Only a few experiments have been done for developing treebanks and datasets from social media annotated with Part-of-Speech tags and other morphological features (see Section 2).

Regardless of the irregularities of Twitter language, human beings do not seem to find it excessively troubling to understand each other when communicating via social media. Therefore, among the research question that we would like to address, there is also how much this performance depends on human morpho-syntactic ability or on other parts of linguistic competence.

Considering that the availability of a full or partial syntactic analysis can improve the results of semantic and pragmatic-oriented techniques, we propose the development of PoSTWITA-UD, a collection of social media texts annotated according to a well-known dependency-based annotation format: the Universal Dependencies (Nivre et al., 2016)[2].

The goal of this work is twofold. On one hand, it consists in making available a resource currently missing, for Italian in particular, which can be exploited for training NLP systems in order to enhance their performance on social media texts. On the other hand, it may also contribute to the wider debate about social media texts and their analysis, for example by showing how much syntactic information can be helpful for a given NLP task or downstream application; we refer in particular to phenomena such as negation and coordination scope, which, if not correctly detected, can strongly undermine the results obtained e.g. by a sentiment analysis engine in classifying the polarity of a message (Bosco et al., 2013b).

From a methodological point of view, our choice to adopt the UD scheme stems from the interest in a dependency-based representation for-

---

[1] http://alt.qcri.org/semeval2017/task4/

[2] http://universaldependencies.org/

Proceedings of the Fourth International Conference on Dependency Linguistics (Depling 2017), pages 229-239,
Pisa, Italy, September 18-20 2017

mat that has gained full acceptance from the research community over a few years, especially regarding Italian resources. The goal of creating this resource goes hand in hand with that of sharing it and validating its annotation according to a shared standard, such as the one UD projects aims to provide. In addition, UD format allows to extend the inventory of morphological features and syntactic relations with further subtypes, according to the language, genre or linguistic construction peculiarities. For all these reasons Universal Dependencies proved to be the optimal representation choice.

This project benefits from the availability of a Twitter corpus used as dataset for the task of Part-of-Speech tagging on social media texts (PoSTWITA) held at the 2016 edition of EVALITA, the evaluation campaign for Italian NLP tools[3]. For our current purpose, we further enriched the corpus by adding the missing annotation layers, i.e. lemmas, morphological features and syntactic relations, all in compliance with the annotation scheme and principles of Universal Dependencies.

The content of this paper is thus organized as follows. Next section briefly surveys the literature on syntactic analysis of social media texts, and Section 3 introduces the dataset used for our project. Sections 4, 5 and 6 describe the various annotation steps, while in Section 7 we discuss the creation of the gold standard set. In particular, in Section 7.2 we discuss the annotation guidelines we followed for manual revision. Finally, Section 8 closes the paper with some considerations on the current state of the project.

2 Related Work

Considering their increasing importance in NLP, several efforts have been made to annotate, manually or semi-automatically, social media texts. However, the use of typical NLP tools and techniques has proved critical, essentially by virtue of the unconventional use of the language norms at all levels (orthography, lexicon, morphology and syntax) and the amount of noise such non-standard linguistic behaviors and meta-textual elements can bring about. Although various attempts to produce such kind of specialized resources and tools are described in literature (e.g. (Gimpel et al., 2011; Owoputi et al., 2013; Lynn et al., 2015; Rei et al., 2016)), most of these attempts mainly focus on

PoS-tagged corpora, while few of them deal with syntactic annotation as well. One of such works is that of Foster et al. (2011), who built a dataset containing 1,000 sentences including tweets and forum posts, with the specific aim of investigating the problems of parsing social media texts. Later on, other works attempted to overcome such limits by creating *ah hoc* resources to be used as training data for parsing. This is the case of the French Social Media Bank (Seddah et al., 2012), a set of 1,700 sentences from various types of user-generated content (among those, tweets), annotated using an adapted version of the French Treebank (Abeillé et al., 2003) scheme, and TWEEBANK (Kong et al., 2014), built by manually adding dependency parses to tweets drawn from the PoS-tagged Twitter corpus of Owoputi et al. (2013).

Finally, it is worth mentioning the English Web Treebank (Silveira et al., 2014), a collection of more than 16k sentences taken from various Web media, including blogs, emails, reviews and Yahoo! answers, and also available in UD format.

To the best of our knowledge, however, the one presented here is the first work devoted to create a Twitter treebank annotated according to UD specifications, and is almost certainly the first resource of this kind created for Italian.

3 The Dataset

PoSTWITA-UD was not built from scratch, but it has been developed by processing and further enriching an already existing resource, that is the dataset used for the EVALITA 2016 task on Part-of-Speech tagging of social media, i.e. PoSTWITA (Bosco et al., 2016). Therefore, data and content are the same as those of the PoSTWITA corpus released to the task participants, which includes a development set composed of 6,438 tweets (114,967 tokens), and a test set of 300 tweets (4,759 tokens).

Its content, in turn, comes from the SENTIPOLC corpus, i.e. the dataset used for the EVALITA SENTIment POLarity Classification (SENTIPOLC) task in 2014 (Basile et al., 2014) and 2016 (Barbieri et al., 2016). Furthermore, within the EVALITA 2016 campaign, the same core dataset was made available with semantic-oriented annotations for two other tasks as well: the Named Entity Recognition and Linking in Italian Tweets (NEEL-IT) (Basile et al., 2016)

---

[3]http://www.evalita.it

and the Event Factuality Annotation (FactA) task (Minard et al., 2016). Working on this treebank thus collocates our current activity in the perspective of the development of a benchmark where a full pipeline of NLP tools can be applied and tested in the future evaluation campaigns.

Considering its use for EVALITA, the PoSTWITA dataset has already been automatically pre-processed, tokenized and PoS tagged, as well as entirely revised by human annotators, in order to remove duplicate tweets and provide a gold annotation. Such gold set is the starting point of the PoSTWITA-UD project, whose development steps are described in the next sections.

4 Tokenization and Part-of-Speech Tags: from PoSTWITA to PoSTWITA-UD

For what concerns tokenization and tagging principles, the PoSTWITA task organizers followed the strategy proposed in the Italian section of the UD guidelines, though applying some minor changes. Assuming, as usual and more suitably in PoS tagging, a neutral perspective with respect to the solution of parsing problems (more relevant in building treebanks), PoSTWITA format differs from the one applied in UD, in that it leaves tokens unsplitted in the two following cases:

- articulated prepositions (e.g. *dalla* ('from-the [fem]'), *nell'* ('in-the'), *al* ('to-the'), ...)

- clitic clusters, which are composed by one or more clitic pronouns attached to the end of a verb form (e.g. *regalaglielo* ('offer-it-to-him'), *dandolo* ('giving-it'), ...)

For this reason, and according to the strategy assumed in previous EVALITA PoS tagging evaluations, two novel specific tags were assigned in these cases: ADP_A and VERB_CLIT, for articulated prepositions and verbs with clitics respectively.

Furthermore, all the Internet and Twitter-specific tokens that, according to UD specifications, should be classified as SYM (symbol) were further specified based on the token type. As a result, all the categories that typically occur in social media texts, like emoticons, Internet addresses, email addresses, hashtags and Twitter mentions had their own tag, i.e. EMO, URL, EMAIL, HASHTAG and MENTION.

For the development of PoSTWITA-UD, we had to restore the initial UD tokenization format, thus re-splitting all ADP_A and VERB_CLIT cases into the corresponding UD PoS tags (upos) ADP+DET and VERB+PRON respectively. We also had to restore all the Twitter-specific tags into SYM.

Finally, it should be pointed out that no modification on the sentence splitting has been carried out. Just like the original PoSTWITA dataset, the reference unit is always the tweet in its entirety – which may thus consist of multiple sentences – not the sentence alone.

5 Lemmas and Morphological Features

In order to produce a correctly formatted corpus in CoNLL-U format, we also inserted information about lemmas and morphological features associated to each word. To speed up the process, we relied on AnIta (Tamburini and Melandri, 2012), an Italian morphological analyzer based on a large lexicon (about 110,000 lemmas) able to analyze the various word forms and produce all the possible lemmas and morphological features for these forms. A two-step semi-automatic conversion between the different annotation schemes ensured a full compatibility with the UD specifications.

In the first step we added lemmas and language-specific PoS tags (xpos). As mentioned above, the insertion was done partly with a script that converts AnIta output into a UD-compatible form, and matches the word forms on the PoSTWITA-UD side with the lemmas provided by AnIta for the respective upos. While the xpos tags (the same used in UD_Italian) were added with *ad hoc* heuristics and manual disambiguation.

The insertion of lemmas was also performed manually, by revising the automatic results of the script and adding the missing lemmas. The choice we made in this manual stage represented a guiding principle for syntactic annotation as well (see Section 7.2), i.e what is understandable by a human should be annotated accordingly. With regard to lemmatization in particular, this means that whenever possible, we assigned to a non-standard form the lemma of the respective standard form (though leaving the word form unchanged). Following this principle, we thus assigned the corresponding lemma to the various cases of abbreviation, capitalization, typos and grammatical errors, and word lengthening.

An exception is made for punctuation, non-intelligible word forms, dialectal forms and foreign words, in which cases the lemma remained the same as the word form.

In the second step we then added the morphological features by following the same strategy described above for lemmatization, that is by matching the proper morphological features with a given word form based on its lemma, upos and xpos tag. The feature insertion step involved the following parts of speech: adjectives, adverbs, determiners, nouns, numerals, pronouns and verbs.

In order to preserve a higher consistency among resources, we also used the language-specific features introduced in UD_Italian for clitic pronouns (`Clitic=Yes`) and possessives (`Poss=Yes`).

6 Syntactic Analysis

The last step included the syntactic annotation of the tweets according to UD specifications. We carried out this task by running different parsers and developing proper annotation guidelines. In this and the next section we describe both aspects.

6.1 Data Parsing

Similar to the previous steps, we first automatically analyzed the texts with state-of-the-art dependency parsers, and then we manually revised the annotation.

As regards Italian UD-compliant resources, the only dataset that was suitable for training is UD_Italian (Bosco et al., 2013a)[4], version 2, which includes texts from newspapers, Wikipedia and legal Italian and European Community sources. Therefore, we performed an out-of-domain parsing experiment, by training different systems on this treebank, though being aware that the result would be undermined by the deep differences between the text types included in such resources.

For the automatic annotation we used some of the parsers that obtained the best performance in a recent comparative study concerning an Italian dependency treebank (Lavelli, 2016), in particular:

- the MATE tools, that include both a graph-based (Bohnet, 2010) and a transition-based parser (Bohnet and Nivre, 2012; Bohnet and

---

Parser	-LX	-F	-UD
MATE graph-based	62.53	67.05	91.26
MATE transition-based	64.92	66.65	91.44
RBG full	64.36	67.07	90.16

Table 1: Results of the parsers after the different annotation stages, i.e. with lemmas and language-specific PoS tags (-LX), and with morphological features as well (-F). The parser outputs were evaluated against the gold standard of the test set (300 tweets, -LX and -F columns) but also against the UD_Italian test set (489 sentences, -UD column).

Kuhn, 2012); they were run using standard parameters;

- RBG (Lei et al., 2014; Zhang et al., 2014b; Zhang et al., 2014a), which is based on a low-rank factorization method that enables to map high dimensional feature vectors into low dimensional representations; the full model was chosen.

For the near future, we also plan to extend the experiment to other state-of-the-art parsers as well (namely TurboParser (Martins et al., 2013) and ZPar (Zhang and Nivre, 2011)), and to combine all the outputs produced to obtain an improved parsing quality (Hall et al., 2010).

In order to get an overall picture of the parsing results after each of the steps described in Section 5, we parsed both development and test set *a*) after the insertion of lemmas and language-specific PoS tags, and *b*) after the morphological features were also added.

To get a measure of how much parsing quality differs between standard and Twitter texts, in Table 1 we report also the results of the parser on the UD_Italian test set (489 sentences). For the evaluation step we used the script made available for the CoNLL 2017 Shared Task[5] with the default setting (i.e. by reporting the Labelled Attachment Score, *LAS* F_1 score only).

The overall parsing results are discussed in the next section.

6.2 Results and Discussion

The reported results actually show what we were already expecting: the performance of the three

---

[4]The other resource is the Italian section of the parallel treebank ParTUT (UD_Italian-ParTUT), but it has many overlapping sentences with UD_Italian, and it is much smaller.

[5]`http://universaldependencies.org/conll17/evaluation.html`

parsers improves when we add linguistic information. Overall, however, the parsing quality for the PoSTWITA test set is relatively poor considering both the results on UD_Italian test set and the fact that the systems start from partially annotated and corrected texts, rather than raw ones[6]. The explanation we can give is also the most obvious, that is, parsers have to deal with texts from a different domain than those of the training set, and what is more, having very specific - and challenging - features. As a proof of this, we observed the behavior of the three parsers on single relations, assuming that their performance would remain stable on well-known cases and decrease on poorly-covered phenomena in the training set.

To verify this assumption, we observed the F-score obtained by parsers on two sub-sets of relations that reflect two different, though in a sense complementary, aspects: the first one includes the 10 most frequent relations in UD_Italian[7], and the second one comprises three of the relations where parsers get the lowest results, i.e. `discourse`, `parataxis` and `vocative`. These relations are summarized in Table 2, along with their F-score averaged over the three parsers and their distribution both in UD_Italian training set and on PoSTWITA-UD test set.

As it can be seen, just three relations exceed the 90% threshold (`advmod`, `amod` and `cc`), and just one is between 80% and 90%, i.e. the relation linking the direct object to its predicate (`obj`). The relation with the lowest F-score, among the most frequent in UD_Italian, is the one representing adverbial clauses (`advcl`). This can be explained by the fact that most of the relations labeled by the parsers as adverbial clauses were rather considered as paratactic constructions in the gold set.

Interestingly enough, a quite low F-score is reported for the `nsubj` relation, and the cases where it was erroneously annotated are quite systematic on all three parsers. They correspond to cases of nouns that in the gold set we have chosen to consider as the root of the whole tweet, because they are followed by paratactic elements (see Section 7.2), or as addressees of a given utterance (hence

UD relation	F **score**	% train	% test
acl	58.00	1.18	0.46
advcl	50.98	1.26	1.05
advmod	96.85	3.52	6.22
amod	90.27	5.45	2.25
cc	97.27	2.74	2.43
conj	66.74	3.39	3.26
obj	82.75	3.41	4.72
obl	72.46	5.74	4.23
nmod	72.62	8.06	5.23
nsubj	65.37	4.26	3.62
discourse	0	0.02	3.18
parataxis	11.18	0.14	5.29
vocative	0	0.07	3.83

Table 2: Averaged results of the three parsers, in terms of F-score, along with the relative frequency in UD_Italian training set ('train') and PoSTWITA-UD test set ('test'), of individual relations: the 10 most frequent relations in UD_Italian (upper part), and three of the relations with poorer parsing results (lower part).

as `vocative`). This aspect, in turn, raises the issue of the use, within the gold set, of labels such as `parataxis`, `vocative` and `discourse`. For the reasons outlined in Section 7.2, these three relations are much more frequent in the PoSTWITA-UD gold set than in UD_Italian, as also reported in Table 2. The far lower frequency of these relations in the training set and, as a result, in parsers outputs, compared to the gold set, leads to the extremely poor parsing quality with respect to these three phenomena.

7 Towards the gold standard

In this section we describe the creation of a fully corrected PoSTWITA-UD, from the manual revision of parsing output to the definition of the guidelines for the annotators. The annotation methodology, as conceived and tested so far for the test set only, will also be applied to the development set in the next project phase.

7.1 Manual revision and Inter-Annotator Agreement

The manual post-processing of annotated texts, while it was useful for parsers evaluation, represented the first step towards the goal of our work: obtaining a reference gold standard for the further manual annotation, for the current evaluation

---

[6]This is also true for the UD_Italian test set, which was parsed starting from the CoNLL-U files with gold PoS tags, rather than from raw texts.

[7]Excluding `punct`, `det` and `case`, which are poorly indicative of the challenging aspects of this out-of-domain parsing experiment.

of parsers and for their future training on Twitter texts.

The revision was made by two trained annotators who were familiar with the UD format and using DGAnnotator[8] as tree editor. Although their work proceeded independently, some particularly critical phenomena were previously discussed. This allowed to come up with shared guidelines (see Section 7.2). In order to take into account the fact that the outputs of the different parsers can be affected by different errors, the two annotators used as starting dataset the output files from two (of the three used) different parsers, randomly selected.

As a result of the first correction phase, the degree of inter-annotator agreement (on relations alone) was calculated, using Cohen's kappa as the reference index (Carletta, 1996). The agreement at this stage was $k = 0.83$.
Based on this result, and in particular on cases with higher disagreement, a consistency check on the application of the guidelines and a further revision were made (after which the agreement went up to $k = 0.92$); finally, the corrections of both annotators were merged into a single final file.

7.2 Annotation Guidelines

Several phenomena featuring social media texts are poorly treated by existing morphological analyzers and parsing systems. In fact, it can be quite difficult to decide their collocation within a single layer of analysis (syntax, semantics or pragmatics), since they better collocate in the broader area of communication dynamics taking place in social media conversation. In computer-mediated communication, and specifically on Twitter, users often resort to a language type that is closer to speech, rather than written language. Narrowing it down to Italian, this is found at various levels, from orthography, with forms and expressions that imitate the verbal face-to-face conversation, to lexis (colloquialisms and vulgar language) and syntax, with the prevalence of simple sentences or paratactic forms, clefting, dislocations and syntactic structures that do not respect the typical SVO order of constituents (Zaga, 2012). The continuous shift from written to spoken language and *vice versa*, on the other hand, is also found in the absence (at least in our corpus) of those typical

mechanisms of spoken language, such as repairs and restarts.
The absence of these phenomena, and, at the same time, the presence of others (mentioned later in this section) that are typical of the medium used, make Twitter language a unique, for which - unlike written and speech treebanks[9] - we were not able to find clear and shared guidelines.

For the purposes of our project, we had to face the challenge of classifying all these Twitter-specific phenomena within a syntactic framework – rather than within pragmatics or semantics – more specifically the one conceived for Universal Dependencies. For that purpose, we drafted some tentative guidelines and followed them while preparing the gold standard.

In the remainder of this section we briefly discuss these principles by showing some practical annotation examples[10].

Emoticons, emojis and similar aspects. As regards these iconic elements, and emojis in particular, a wide debate has opened on whether they should be considered as an emerging language in itself[11] or just a powerful communication tool that does not substitute language, but rather complements it. While going into the substance of this debate is well beyond the scope of this paper, and of our project in general, we equally had to face the issue on what status we should attribute to these so-called pictograms, in an attempt to draw a line between what should or should not be annotated on the syntactic layer. In fact, emoticons and emojis are typically used to express feelings and emotions, reproduce facial expressions or even convey the intonation of spoken language. Although performing on a more pragmatic, than merely syntactic level, they seem to function in a language-like fashion[12]. In this sense, they could then be compared to interjections and other discourse particles. Bearing in mind what UD guidelines suggest for

---

[9]Regarding, in particular, UD-based speech treebanks, we mention here the resource available for Slovenian (Dobrovoljc and Nivre, 2016), and that for French (upcoming) (Gerdes and Kahane, 2017).

[10]For the sake of readability, we kept just the more relevant dependency edges and the corresponding relations.

[11]See, for example, the study on emojis in Italian language (Chiusaroli, 2015) and the EmojitalianoBot and EmojiWorldBot experiments (Monti et al., 2016)

[12]http://blog.oxforddictionaries.com/2015/11/emoji-language/

[8]http://medialab.di.unipi.it/Project/QA/Parser/DgAnnotator/

such particles[13], we labelled also emoticons and emojis as `discourse` items, as in example (1).

(1)

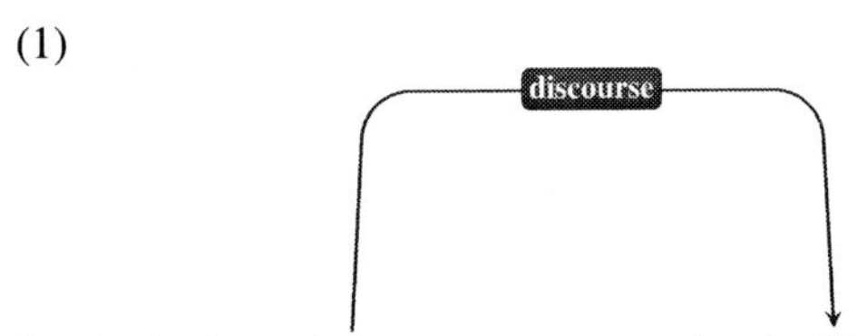

i risultati usciranno tra quattro giorni :)))
(*the results will-be-out in four days :))))*)

On the other hand, we also found few cases where the tweet ends with an expression (typically a verb) between asterisks that, conversely, substitutes an iconic element (perhaps an emoji). Despite the similar pragmatic function these verbs seem to have with respect to emoticons and emojis, we considered them as independent clauses, therefore as paratactic elements, and annotated as shown in (2).

(2)

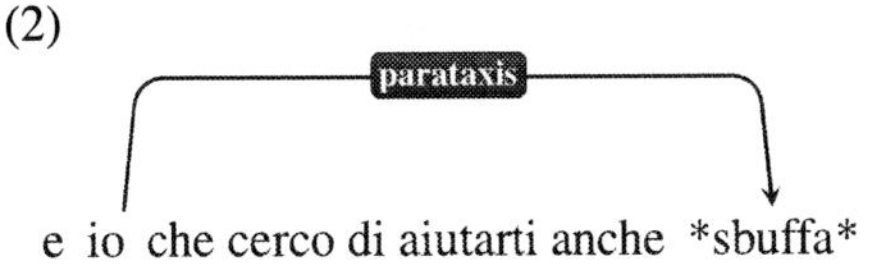

e io che cerco di aiutarti anche *sbuffa*

Hashtags, mentions and replies. These are meta-language items with manifold purposes.
The @ symbol that characterizes the so-called mentions and replies is used to call out usernames in tweets. Usernames preceded by the sign become links to the respective Twitter profiles, and can be used mainly in two ways: to just mention another user or to reply another user/s' tweet[14]. The act of addressing to other users by resorting to such conventions can be compared to a typical vocative function, which made us lean on annotating these cases with the `vocative` relation, by attaching the addressee to its host sentence, as in example (3).

---

[13]http://universaldependencies.org/u/dep/discourse.html
[14]https://support.twitter.com/articles/464314

(3)

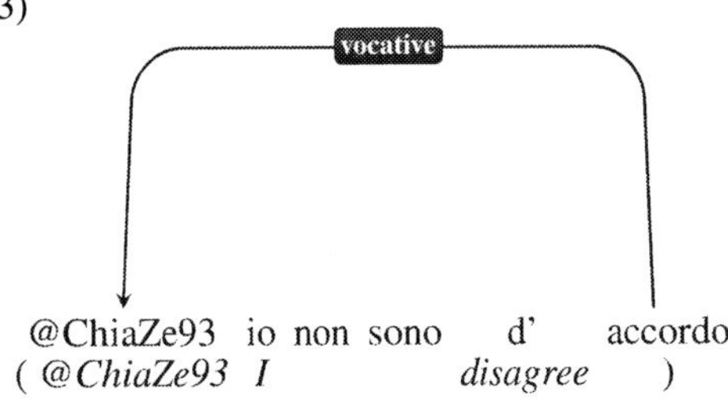

@ChiaZe93 io non sono d' accordo
(*@ChiaZe93 I disagree*)

Hashtags are key words or phrases preceded by the # symbol. They serve different purposes, often depending on their position within the tweet. When placed in prefix (example (4)) or suffix position (example (5)), they are mainly used to describe and/or comment the main topic of the tweet, making it more intelligible to other users; in most cases they do not modify any word in particular, nor they reflect any explicit coordination, subordination, or argument relation with a given head word. Similar to other run-on sentences, hashtags are are not integrated into the sentence, rather being joined to the latter without any conjunction or punctuation mark; therefore, we consider them as paratactic elements

(4)

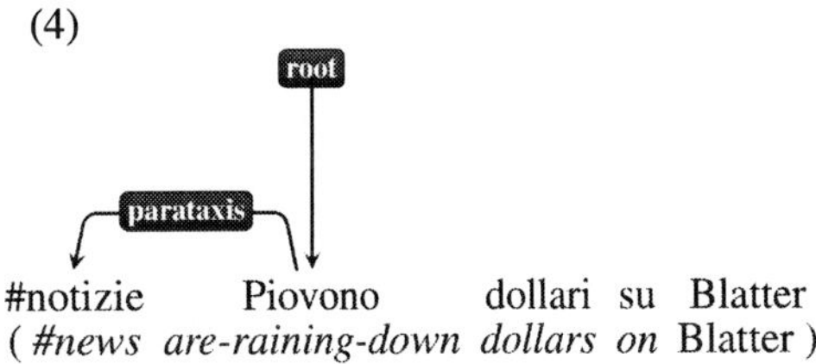

#notizie Piovono dollari su Blatter
(*#news are-raining-down dollars on* Blatter)

(5)

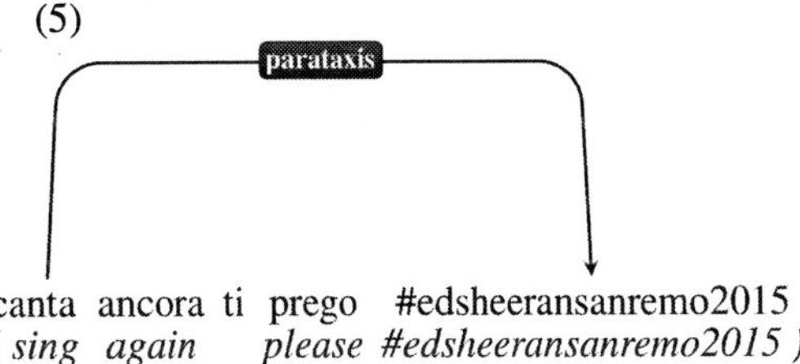

canta ancora ti prego #edsheeransanremo2015
(*sing again please #edsheeransanremo2015*)

Hashtags and mentions, however, can also be placed in infix position, i.e. by adding their respective sign to the word/phrase or username within the tweet, even just to keep it simple and save character space. In these cases they can be considered as fully syntactically-integrated elements, whose removal could potentially make the sentence ungrammatical (Chiusaroli, 2014); we thus assign them their corresponding syntactic role. In tweets

(6) and (7), shown below, the tokens *@matteorenzi* and *#Boldrini* are the actual subjects of the predicates *arriva* and *ha*, respectively.

(6)

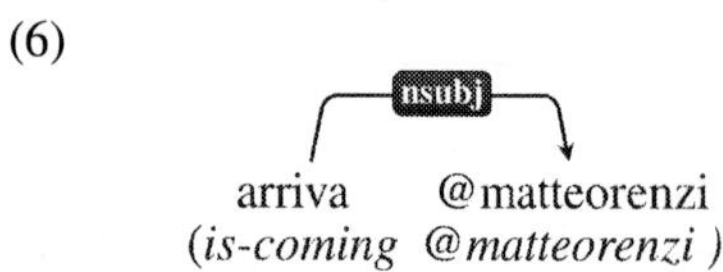

arriva   @matteorenzi
(*is-coming @matteorenzi*)

(7)

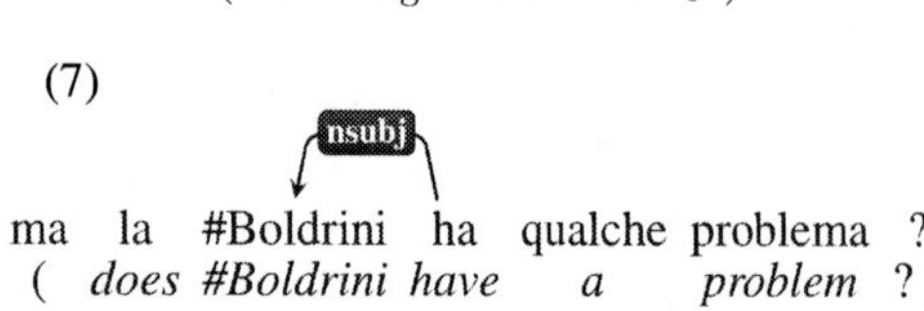

ma   la   #Boldrini   ha   qualche   problema   ?
(*does #Boldrini have   a   problem   ?*)

Unknown or mispelled words. Sometimes tweets can also contain a whole host of unconventional elements that substitute actual words: abbreviations, homophones, conflations, or just spelling errors. Whenever we can guess what that element stands for, we assign it the corresponding syntactic role. In the example tweet (8), the adverb *perché* is abbreviated to *Xché* (which is a quite common form in any kind of informal communication), while the two auxiliaries *è stata*, the predicate *premiata* and the determiner *una* were capitalized and conflated into a single token. Considering, however, that among these words, there is one, i.e. the predicate, that can be promoted as the head of the remaining words, we took this item as the sentence root.

(8)

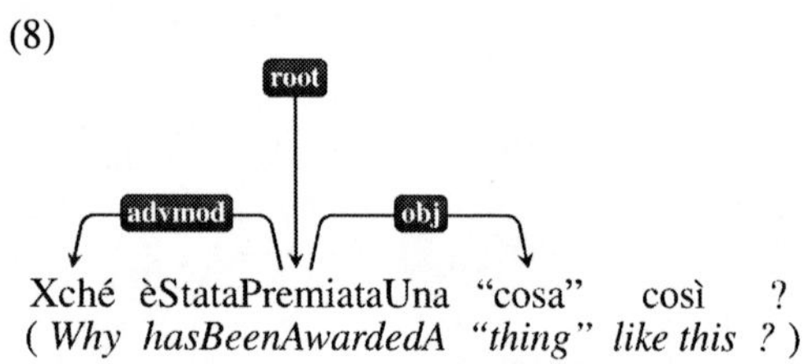

Xché   èStataPremiataUna   "cosa"   così   ?
(*Why   hasBeenAwardedA   "thing"   like this   ?*)

There are cases, however, where we cannot determine which category the word belongs to, nor its syntactic or pragmatic role: in the absence of such information, the word is attached to the nearest head with the dep relation, as shown in tweet (9).

(9)

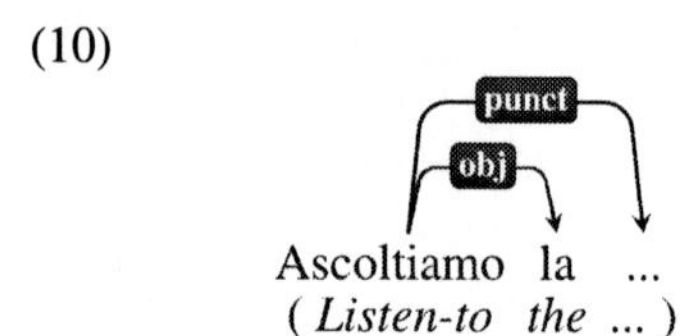

quanto   sono   bravi ,   fdgjdkjgd
(*they're   so   good ,   fdgjdkjgd*)

Incomplete tweets. Because of the 140-character limit imposed to Twitter users, it often appears that tweets are incomplete, and the elided part is represented by an ellipsis ("..."). In such cases, the full text can usually be read by clicking on the URL that is appended to the tweet; however, once the tweet is collected and processed, the elided part is lost. Despite this, most of the times, such part is quite predictable by the reader/annotator, either because of the way the remaining sentence is structured or because even one word was partially replaced by the ellipsis, as in example (11). We treat these two cases a bit differently, though. In sentence (10), for example, the fact that the ellipsis points occur after the predicate *Ascoltiamo* and the determiner *la* suggests that there may be a noun depending on that predicate, and, in turn, representing the head of the determiner. We then treat cases like this as typical noun ellipsis, by promoting one of its overt dependents (such as the determiner, in the example) as head word, following the order suggested in UD guidelines[15].

(10)

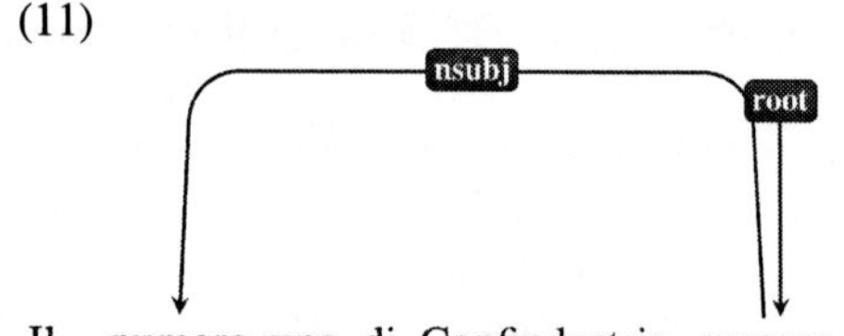

Ascoltiamo   la   ...
(*Listen-to   the   ...*)

However, if the suspension ellipsis is used to replace also part of a word that has been cut off, and considering that - in these cases - the dots are part of the word itself[16], the word is treated as it is, without any head promotion of its dependents.

(11)

Il   numero   uno   di   Confindustria   comme...
(*The number one of Confindustria comme...*)

In tweet (11), for example, the word *comme...* is likely to stand for the predicate *commenta* (*(he) comments*); therefore we annotate it as the head.

[15] http://universaldependencies.org/u/
overview/specific-syntax.html/ellipsis

[16]This is a tokenization principle adopted from the beginning of the corpus development for the PoSTWITA task and that were left unchanged.

URLs. Another common practice in microblogging, and in Twitter posts in particular, is to incorporate links to Web pages, blog entries or even other tweets. These links are usually appended at the end of the tweet and they are not part of its syntactic structure. Therefore, we always consider them as generic dependents of the root, using the `dep` relation (see tweet (12)).

(12)

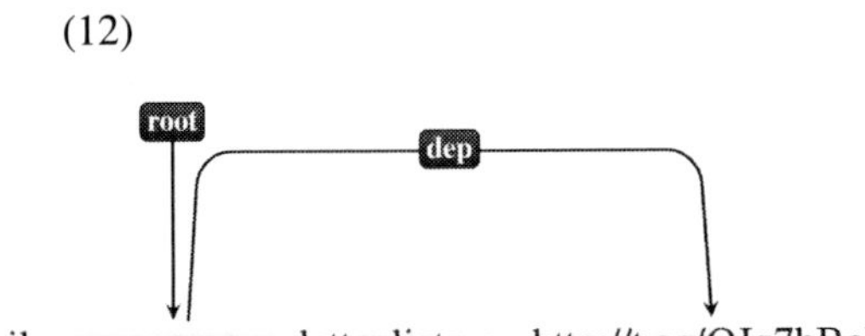

il   programma dettagliato :   http://t.co/OJq7hBcH
(*the   program   detailed   : http://t.co/OJq7hBcH*)

On the other hand, a URL may also happen to occur within the sentence, as a syntactically-integrated element. Although we have not encountered similar cases in our treebank yet, we consider the URL as a proper noun and apply the same annotation criteria described above for hashtags and mentions, i.e. we assign the proper syntactic label according to the actual role the URL plays within the sentence.

As mentioned before, these guidelines are preliminary and refer to the trickiest phenomena encountered in the test set. It is not to be ruled out, however, that in the manual revision of the development set there will be other cases that will lead us either to revise the criteria adopted so far or to extend the inventory of uncertain cases. A final version of the guidelines, to be considered as an integration of those conceived for UD_Italian, will be released in the UD repository along with the fully annotated PoSTWITA-UD treebank, by November 2017, that is with the release of UD version 2.1.

8   Conclusion and Future Work

In this paper we presented a recently started project of an Italian Twitter treebank in Universal Dependencies to be released as gold standard for training and testing NLP tools on social media texts. What we achieved so far is the complete annotation of the entire corpus on morphological and syntactic levels, and the manual revision of the test set (300 tweets) by two independent annotators. In parallel with the annotation correction, we also developed some guidelines to properly deal with the genre-specific most critical issues.

As stated above, the project is at an early stage, therefore much work has to be done. First of all, the complete revision of the development set as well (approximately 6,000 tweets), which is planned to be ready for the next release of Universal Dependencies, with a further revision and/or extension of the annotation manual, if necessary. Then we aim to train statistical parsers using this newly-created gold standard and compare their results with the ones obtained in other similar experiments (see, e.g. Petrov and McDonald (2012)).

We are aware of the debate on the nature of NLP results obtained with Twitter-based datasets and their poor generalization with other social media texts (Darling et al., 2012; Eisenstein, 2013). Therefore, in the future we could also attempt to incorporate texts from different social media sources and provide a more balanced resource.

Finally, we would also like to widen the debate on social media text processing by opening this work to a multilingual comparison, which would be made possible by the UD format, specifically designed for that purpose. This would allow us to asses the applicability of our annotation proposal to other languages, thus further encouraging cross-linguistic studies on social media communication.

References

Anne Abeillé, Lionel Clément, and François Toussenel. 2003. Building a treebank for French. In Anne Abeillé, editor, *Treebanks: Building and Using Parsed Corpora*, pages 165–187. Springer Netherlands, Dordrecht.

Francesco Barbieri, Valerio Basile, Danilo Croce, Malvina Nissim, Nicole Novielli, and Viviana Patti. 2016. Overview of the Evalita 2016 SENTIment POLarity Classification Task. In *Proceedings of Evalita 2016*.

Valerio Basile, Andrea Bolioli, Viviana Patti, Paolo Rosso, and Malvina Nissim. 2014. Overview of the Evalita 2014 SENTIment POLarity Classification Task. In *Proceedings of Evalita 2014*.

Pierpaolo Basile, Annalina Caputo, Anna Lisa Gentile, and Giuseppe Rizzo. 2016. Overview of the EVALITA 2016 Named Entity rEcognition and Linking in Italian Tweets (NEELIT) task. In *Proceedings of Evalita 2016*.

Bernd Bohnet and Jonas Kuhn. 2012. The best of both worlds – a graph-based completion model for transition-based parsers. In *Proceedings of the 13th Conference of the European Chapter of the Association for Computational Linguistics*, pages 77–87, Avignon, France. Association for Computational Linguistics.

Bernd Bohnet and Joakim Nivre. 2012. A transition-based system for joint part-of-speech tagging and labeled non-projective dependency parsing. In *Proceedings of the 2012 Joint Conference on Empirical Methods in Natural Language Processing and Computational Natural Language Learning*, pages 1455–1465, Jeju Island, Korea. Association for Computational Linguistics.

Bernd Bohnet. 2010. Top accuracy and fast dependency parsing is not a contradiction. In *Proceedings of the 23rd International Conference on Computational Linguistics (Coling 2010)*, pages 89–97, Beijing, China. Coling 2010 Organizing Committee.

Cristina Bosco, Simonetta Montemagni, and Maria Simi. 2013a. Converting Italian treebanks: Towards an Italian Stanford Dependency treebank. In *Proceedings of the 7th Linguistic Annotation Workshop and Interoperability with Discourse*, pages 61–69.

Cristina Bosco, Viviana Patti, and Andrea Bolioli. 2013b. Developing corpora for sentiment analysis: The case of irony and Senti-TUT. *IEEE Intelligent Systems*, 28(2):55–63.

Cristina Bosco, Fabio Tamburini, Andrea Bolioli, and Alessandro Mazzei. 2016. Overview of the EVALITA 2016 Part Of Speech on TWitter for ITALian task. In *Proceedings of Evalita 2016*.

Jean Carletta. 1996. Assessing agreement on classification tasks: The kappa statistic. *Computational Linguistics*, 22(2):249–254, June.

Francesca Chiusaroli. 2014. Sintassi e semantica dell-hashtag: studio preliminare di una forma di scritture brevi. In *Proceedings of the 1st Italian Conference on Computational Linguistics (CLiC-it 2014)*, pages 117–121, Pisa, Italy.

Francesca Chiusaroli. 2015. La scrittura in emoji tra dizionario e traduzione. In *Proceedings of the 2nd Italian Conference on Computational Linguistics (CLIC-It 2015)*, pages 88–92, Trento, Italy.

William M. Darling, Michael J. Paul, and Fei Song. 2012. Unsupervised part-of-speech tagging in noisy and esoteric domains with a syntactic-semantic bayesian hmm. In *Proceedings of the Workshop on Semantic Analysis in Social Media*, pages 1–9, Stroudsburg, PA, USA. Association for Computational Linguistics.

Kaja Dobrovoljc and Joakim Nivre. 2016. The Universal Dependencies treebank of spoken Slovenian. In *Proceedings of the Tenth International Conference on Language Resources and Evaluation LREC 2016, Portorož, Slovenia, May 23-28*, pages 1566–1571. European Language Resources Association (ELRA).

Jacob Eisenstein. 2013. What to Do About Bad Language on the Internet. *Proceedings of the North American Chapter of the Association for Computational Linguistics : Human Language Technologies (NAACL-HLT)*, pages 359–369.

Jennifer Foster, Özlem Çetinoglu, Joachim Wagner, Joseph Le Roux, Stephen Hogan, Joakim Nivre, Deirdre Hogan, and Josef van Genabith. 2011. #hardtoparse: POS tagging and parsing the twitterverse. In *Analyzing Microtext, Papers from the 2011 AAAI Workshop, San Francisco, California, USA, August 8, 2011*.

Kim Gerdes and Sylvain Kahane. 2017. Trois schémas d'annotation syntaxique en dépendance pour un même corpus de français oral: le cas de la macrosyntaxe. In *Actes de l'atelier "ACor4French - Les corpus annotés du français"*, pages 1–9, Orléans, France.

Kevin Gimpel, Nathan Schneider, Brendan O'Connor, Dipanjan Das, Daniel Mills, Jacob Eisenstein, Michael Heilman, Dani Yogatama, Jeffrey Flanigan, and Noah A. Smith. 2011. Part-of-speech tagging for twitter: Annotation, features, and experiments. In *Proceedings of the 49th Annual Meeting of the Association for Computational Linguistics: Human Language Technologies: Short Papers - Volume 2*, HLT '11, pages 42–47, Stroudsburg, PA, USA. Association for Computational Linguistics.

Johan Hall, Jens Nilsson, and Joakim Nivre. 2010. Single malt or blended? a study in multilingual parser optimization. In Harry Bunt, Paola Merlo, and Joakim Nivre, editors, *Trends in Parsing Technology: Dependency Parsing, Domain Adaptation, and Deep Parsing*, pages 19–33. Springer Netherlands.

Lingpeng Kong, Nathan Schneider, Swabha Swayamdipta, Archna Bhatia, Chris Dyer, and Noah A. Smith. 2014. A dependency parser for tweets. In *Proceedings of the 2014 Conference on Empirical Methods in Natural Language Processing (EMNLP)*, pages 1001–1012, Doha, Qatar. Association for Computational Linguistics.

Alberto Lavelli. 2016. Comparing state-of-the-art dependency parsers on the Italian Stanford Dependency Treebank. In *Proceedings of the Third Italian Computational Linguistics Conference (CLiC-it 2016)*.

Tao Lei, Yu Xin, Yuan Zhang, Regina Barzilay, and Tommi Jaakkola. 2014. Low-rank tensors for scoring dependency structures. In *Proceedings of the 52nd Annual Meeting of the Association for Computational Linguistics (Volume 1: Long Papers)*, pages 1381–1391, Baltimore, Maryland. Association for Computational Linguistics.

Teresa Lynn, Kevin Scannell, and Eimear Maguire. 2015. Minority language twitter: Part-of-speech tagging and analysis of Irish tweets. In *Workshop on Noisy User-generated Text*, Beijing, China.

Andre Martins, Miguel Almeida, and Noah A. Smith. 2013. Turning on the turbo: Fast third-order non-projective turbo parsers. In *Proceedings of the 51st Annual Meeting of the Association for Computational Linguistics (Volume 2: Short Papers)*, pages 617–622, Sofia, Bulgaria. Association for Computational Linguistics.

Anne-Lyse Minard, Manuela Speranza, and Tommaso Caselli. 2016. The EVALITA 2016 Event Factuality Annotation Task (FactA). In *Proceedings of Evalita 2016*.

Johanna Monti, Federico Sangati, Francesca Chiusaroli, Martin Benjamin, and Sina Mansour. 2016. Emojitalianobot and emojiworldbot - new online tools and digital environments for translation into emoji. In *Proceedings of Third Italian Conference on Computational Linguistics (CLiC-it 2016) & Fifth Evaluation Campaign of Natural Language Processing and Speech Tools for Italian. Final Workshop (EVALITA 2016)*, volume 1749 of *CEUR Workshop Proceedings*, Napoli, Italy. CEUR-WS.org.

Joakim Nivre, Marie-Catherine de Marneffe, Filip Ginter, Yoav Goldberg, Jan Hajič, Christopher D. Manning, Ryan T. McDonald, Slav Petrov, Sampo Pyysalo, Natalia Silveira, Reut Tsarfaty, and Daniel Zeman. 2016. Universal dependencies v1: A multilingual treebank collection. In *Proceedings of the Tenth International Conference on Language Resources and Evaluation LREC 2016, Portorož, Slovenia, May 23-28, 2016*.

Olutobi Owoputi, Brendan OConnor, Chris Dyer, Kevin Gimpel, Nathan Schneider, and Noah A Smith. 2013. Improved part-of-speech tagging for online conversational text with word clusters. In *Proceedings of NAACL 2013*, pages 380–390.

Slav Petrov and Ryan McDonald. 2012. Overview of the 2012 Shared Task on Parsing the Web. Notes of the First Workshop on Syntactic Analysis of Non-Canonical Language (SANCL).

Luis Rei, Dunja Mladenić, and Simon Krek. 2016. A multilingual social media linguistic corpus. In *Proceedings of the 4th Conference on CMC and Social Media Corpora for the Humanities*, Ljubljana, Slovenia.

Djamé Seddah, Benoît Sagot, Marie Candito, Virginie Mouilleron, and Vanessa Combet. 2012. The French social media bank: a treebank of noisy user generated content. In *COLING 2012, 24th International Conference on Computational Linguistics, Proceedings of the Conference: Technical Papers, 8-15 December 2012, Mumbai, India*, pages 2441–2458.

Natalia Silveira, Timothy Dozat, Marie-Catherine De Marneffe, Samuel Bowman, Miriam Connor, John Bauer, and Chris Manning. 2014. A gold standard dependency corpus for English. In *Proceedings of the Ninth International Conference on Language Resources and Evaluation (LREC'14)*, Reykjavik, Iceland. European Language Resources Association (ELRA).

Fabio Tamburini and Matias Melandri. 2012. AnIta: a powerful morphological analyser for Italian. In *Proceedings of Language Resources and Evaluation Conference 2012*, pages 941–947.

Cristina Zaga. 2012. Twitter: un'analisi dell'italiano nel micro blogging. *Italiano LinguaDue*, 4(1):167–210.

Yue Zhang and Joakim Nivre. 2011. Transition-based dependency parsing with rich non-local features. In *Proceedings of the 49th Annual Meeting of the Association for Computational Linguistics: Human Language Technologies*, pages 188–193, Portland, Oregon, USA. Association for Computational Linguistics.

Yuan Zhang, Tao Lei, Regina Barzilay, and Tommi Jaakkola. 2014a. Greed is good if randomized: New inference for dependency parsing. In *Proceedings of the 2014 Conference on Empirical Methods in Natural Language Processing (EMNLP)*, pages 1013–1024, Doha, Qatar. Association for Computational Linguistics.

Yuan Zhang, Tao Lei, Regina Barzilay, Tommi Jaakkola, and Amir Globerson. 2014b. Steps to excellence: Simple inference with refined scoring of dependency trees. In *Proceedings of the 52nd Annual Meeting of the Association for Computational Linguistics (Volume 1: Long Papers)*, pages 197–207, Baltimore, Maryland. Association for Computational Linguistics.

Hungarian copula constructions in dependency syntax and parsing

Katalin Ilona Simkó
University of Szeged
Institute of Informatics
Department of General Linguistics
Hungary
simko@hung.u-szeged.hu

Veronika Vincze
University of Szeged
Institute of Informatics
MTA-SZTE
Research Group on Artificial Intelligence
Hungary
vinczev@inf.u-szeged.hu

Abstract

Copula constructions are problematic in the syntax of most languages. The paper describes three different dependency syntactic methods for handling copula constructions: function head, content head and complex label analysis. Furthermore, we also propose a POS-based approach to copula detection. We evaluate the impact of these approaches in computational parsing, in two parsing experiments for Hungarian.

1 Introduction

Copula constructions show some special behaviour in most human languages. In sentences with copula constructions, the sentence's predicate is not simply the main verb of the clause, but the copula verb plus a nominal predicate (in "Peter sleeps" the sentence's predicate is the verb, "sleeps", while in "Peter is tired", it is the copula verb and the nominal predicate, "is tired") . This is further complicated by the fact that the copula verb shows non-conventional behaviour in many languages: it is often not present in the surface structure for one or more slots of the verbal paradigm.

These constructions are widely studied: many approaches are available in many different syntactic frameworks, like in Den Dikken (2006), Partee (1998) and É. Kiss (2002) in constituency grammar; or Dalrymple et al. (2004) and Laczkó (2012) in LFG.

In this paper, we focus on dependency syntactic approaches. In dependency syntax, the syntactic structure's nodes are the words themselves and the tree is made up of their hierarchical relations, making both two-word predicates and the missing verbal forms cause difficulties. Should the copula, the verbal part of the predicate, be the head of the structure, parallel to most other types of constructions? And if so, how can we deal with cases where the copula is not present in the surface structure?

In this paper, three different answers to these questions are discussed: the function head analysis, where function words, such as the copula, remain the heads of the structures; the content head analysis, where the content words, in this case, the nominal part of the predicate, are the heads; and the complex label analysis, where the copula remains the head also, but the approach offers a different solution to zero copulas.

First, we give a short description of Hungarian copula constructions. Second, the three dependency syntactic frameworks are discussed in more detail. Then, we describe two experiments aiming to evaluate these frameworks in computational linguistics, specifically in dependency parsing for Hungarian, similar to Nivre et al. (2007). The first experiment compares the three previously mentioned frameworks, while the second introduces our new approach, based on differentiating the copula and existential "be" verbs on the level of POS-tagging, which can improve the performance of the content head analysis.

2 Copula constructions in Hungarian

The Hungarian verb *van* "be" behaves similarly to "be" verbs in other languages: it has two distinct uses: as an existential and as a copular verb. In the existential use, *van* behaves just as any other main, content verb: it is the only predicative element in the clause and it is always present in the surface structure. On the other hand, in the copular use *van* requires a nominal predicate, a noun or an adjective in the nominative case; copular *van* is never present in the surface structure for 3rd person, present tense, declarative clauses, but its other forms are the same as for the existential.

Below we illustrate Hungarian copula constructions with several examples, see Table 1 and Ex-

Proceedings of the Fourth International Conference on Dependency Linguistics (Depling 2017), pages 240-247,
Pisa, Italy, September 18-20 2017

	Existential *van*	Copular *van*
1st Sg PR	vagyok	vagyok
2nd Sg PR	vagy	vagy
3rd Sg PR	van	-
1st Pl PR	vagyunk	vagyunk
2nd Pl PR	vagytok	vagytok
3rd Pl PR	vannak	-
1st Sg PAST	voltam	voltam
2nd Sg PAST	voltál	voltál
3rd Sg PAST	volt	volt
1st Pl PAST	voltunk	voltunk
2nd Pl PAST	voltatok	voltatok
3rd Pl PAST	voltak	voltak

Table 1: Present and past tense paradigm for existential and copular *van* in Hungarian.

amples (1-4), where (1) and (2) are present and past tense existential *van* sentences, while (3) and (4) are copular. In Examples (1) and (2), *van* and *volt* are the only predicative elements of the sentence respectively. In the copular *van* sentences (3) and (4), the first, present tense sentence has the zero copula, in the surface structure only *orvos* "doctor", the nominal predicate makes up the predicative part of the sentence, while in Example (4), where the copula is overt, the nominal predicate and the copula, *orvos* "doctor" and *volt* "was" jointly make up the predicative part of the sentence.

(1) Péter a szobában van.
    Peter.NOM the room.INE is.PR.3rdSG
    Peter is in the room.

(2) Péter a szobában volt.
    Peter.NOM the room.INE is.PAST.3rdSG
    Peter was in the room.

(3) Péter orvos.
    Peter.NOM doctor.NOM
    Peter is a doctor.

(4) Péter orvos volt.
    Peter.NOM doctor.NOM is.PAST.3rdSG
    Peter was a doctor.

The copula's behaviour in Hungarian is by no means unique: for most languages, the copula shows some difference from verbs in general and zero copulas in the verbal paradigm are also relatively common (Curnow, 2000).

3 Copula constructions in dependency syntax

Copula constructions in languages like Hungarian cause two problems for dependency syntax. First, with the dual predicate (nominal + copula) it is not obvious which one should be the head of the construction: should the verbal element be the head parallel to non-copular sentences or should the nominal be the head as that element is always overt? Second, how to handle the zero copula in the syntactic structures?

In this section, three approaches are described giving different answers to the questions above: the function head approach, the content head approach and the complex label approach.

3.1 Function head approach

The function head approach to dependency syntax goes back to the foundations of Mel'čuk's (2009) framework. He proposed that the function words of the sentence should be the heads over content words; function words should be the ones setting up the basic syntactic structure of the sentence.

Mel'čuk also writes about copular constructions and the above-mentioned issues in his work and stands by the function head analysis: he proposes that in languages where the copula is only zero in certain slots of the paradigm, but overt in others, a virtual, zero verb form should be inserted into the syntactic structure. This zero copula is the head of the structure, the nominal predicate is a dependent of it. This way, we preserve a common structure for all sentences in which the inflected verb is always the head of the clause, but we violate one of the core principles of dependency syntax: surface structure words are no longer the only nodes in the tree.

The function head approach is the annotation of the Szeged Dependency Treebank (Vincze et al., 2010), the large Hungarian dependency treebank used for the experiments described in the paper. The first column of Table (2) shows the Szeged Dependency Treebank's annotation for the existential sentence (Example (1)), and the copular sentences with overt and zero copula, Examples (3) and (4). The capitalized *VAN* is the inserted virtual node in zero copula sentences that was added manually to all sentences of this type in a preprocessing step.

3.2 Content head approach

The content head approach recently gained popularity in computational dependency syntax due to the Universal Dependencies project (Nivre, 2015).

This analysis considers content words the frame of the syntactic structure: content words are the heads and function words are their dependents. This separates the copula from all other verbs, even the existential verb. As all other verbs carry content, they are heads in this analysis also, while the copula, as a function word, becomes a dependent in this analysis. This way we no longer have a common structure for all clauses, but we have an analysis that has no issues with the zero copula.

A section of the Szeged Dependency Treebank has been converted to the Universal Dependencies annotation (Vincze et al., 2015; Vincze et al., 2017). In the experiments, this treebank is used as the content head analysis. The second column of Table (2) shows the sentences in Examples (1), (3) and (4) again, this time with the content head analysis in the Szeged Universal Dependencies Treebank.

3.3 Complex label approach

The complex label approach is a computational linguistic variation of the function head analysis detailed in Seeker et al. (2012).

They keep the function words as the heads, therefore keeping the copula as the head of the copular clause, but they deal with the zero copula in a different way. The analysis does not use virtual nodes, but instead "shows" the missing copula in the dependency labels originating from where it would be inserted. As in the zero copula example for complex label in Table 2.

, the root node of the structure in the function head analysis would be a virtual *VAN* node, the subject, *Peter* would be a dependent of *VAN*. Therefore the Complex label dependency label of the subject is **ROOT-VAN-SUBJ**: the original "route" to it would be **ROOT** label to *VAN*, **SUBJ** label to *Peter*, the virtual node is removed, but the "route" is still shown. This approach gives a similar structure for all clauses with overt verbs, only distinguishing the zero copula. Due to combinations of the complex labels, the approach also uses a lot more (potentially infinite) different dependency labels in the analysis.

The Szeged Dependency Treebank has also been converted to this analysis, which will be used in the experiments. Dependency trees for Examples (1), (3) and (4) are shown again in the third column of Table (2); in Figure (1) a sentence with two coordinated clauses with zero copula to show how the labels can combine.

Table 3 summarizes in which conditions the different approaches give syntactic structures different from regular content verbs analysis for copular sentences. The content head approach gives the most linguistically based distinction by drawing the line between copula and non-copula main verbs.

4 Experiments

We evaluated the three approaches in two parsing experiments. We used the same corpus with three different dependency annotations and the Bohnet parser (Bohnet, 2010) for both.

4.1 The corpus

We used a section of the Szeged Dependency Treebank that is available with all three analyses: the original annotation is function head based, there is an automatically converted complex label version, and the converted, manually corrected Universal Dependencies treebank for the content head version.

The section contains about 1300 sentences, 27000 tokens in total. The data contains 300 instances of virtual *V*, 230 overt copulas and 150 existential *van*s.

4.2 Experiment 1: Function head, content head or complex label

In the first experiment, the Bohnet parser was trained using the ten fold cross validation method on the same corpora of texts for the function head, the content head and the complex label representation separately, using gold POS tags and morphological features. In the evaluation of each model, we used UAS and LAS scores for the whole corpus as well as error analysis for the structures in question. Table 4 shows the UAS and LAS scores for each approach. We were interested in the parsing performances regarding different types of *van* sentences, so we created filtered subcorpora that contain only the sentences with existential *van*, only with overt copula and only with zero copula. We report results calculated for these datasets too.

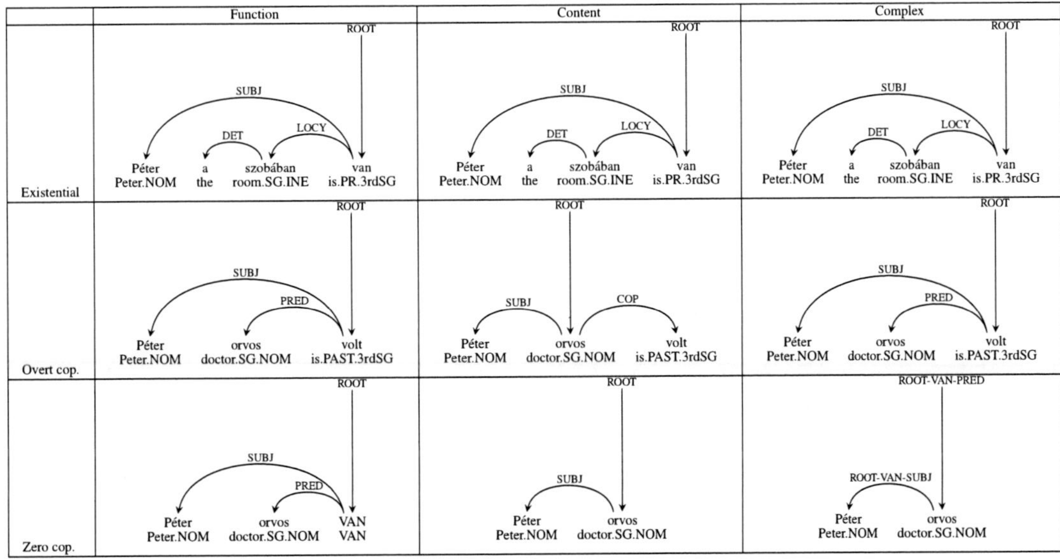

Table 2: Syntactic structures for existential, overt and zero copula sentences in function head, content head and complex label approaches. Note how all three trees for the existential sentence are the same, but the copular ones show differences in the analysis.

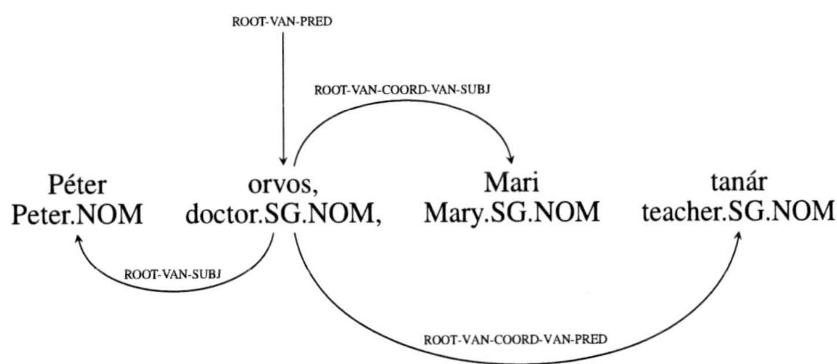

Figure 1: Complex label analysis of the coordinated copular clauses in *Péter orvos, Mari tanár* "Peter is a doctor, Mary is a teacher".

	Function	Complex	Content
Verb			
Exist.			
Overt cop.			
Zero cop.			

Table 3: Different analysis from conventional syntactic structure in the different approaches.

Based on these UAS and LAS scores, the function head analysis gives the best results with the complex label analysis as a close second, but we were interested in the specific relations of *van* and not the full sentences' parsing output. We did manual error analysis of the *van* verb's closest relations to investigate which dependency syntactic theory describes these relations best for computational parsing. We considered the following four errors in our analysis: incorrect head in the clause with *van*; incorrectly labeled or attached subject of *van*; incorrectly labeled or attached nominal predicate; subject and nominal predicate mixed up. Sentences showing none of the above errors were considered correct in the results shown below, regardless of other errors in the sentence. Table 5 shows the percentage of correct sentences for each analysis in the three above mentioned subcorpora and the overall results in the bottom row.

4.3 Experiment 2: POS-based approach to the copula

In the second experiment, we investigated a way to improve the content head analysis with a POS-based approach. Our hypothesis is that the existential *van* and the overt copula *van* are better disambiguated on the level of POS tagging: as the copular *van* has a syntactic structure (in the content head analysis), which is very different from the one of all other verbs, not treating it as a normal verb makes sense from a syntactic parsing point of view. For this reason, the level of POS tagging is a better fit to disambiguate existential and copular *van* than the actual parsing. We used the previously introduced Hungarian Universal Dependencies treebank with the content head annotation and created a new, POS-based copula version, where the copula *van* has a new POS tag, **COP** distinguishing it from all other verbs including the existential *van*, as shown in examples (5) and (6).

(5) Péter a szobában volt.
    NOUN DET NOUN **VERB**
    Peter.NOM the room.INE is.PAST.3rdSG
    Peter is in the room.

(6) Péter orvos volt.
    NOUN NOUN **COP**
    Peter.NOM doctor.NOM is.PAST.3rdSG
    Peter was a doctor.

In the experiment, we applied the Bohnet parser this time for POS tagger, morphology tagger, and dependency parser training and evaluation, using ten fold cross validation on the original content head treebank and the new version with the **COP** POS tag. Table 6 gives the UAS and LAS results for the two analyses on a subcorpus with only the sentences with existential, overt or zero *van* and on the full corpus.

The results in Table 6 show very little change on the full corpus and marginally better results on the *van* sentences for the POS-based approach. Again, we focus on manual error analysis of the affected structures.

In the new POS-based content head approach, the new **COP** POS tag for the copula *van* is assigned with 0.699 F-score over the whole corpus and the **COP** POS tag triggers the dependency parser to assign the content head copula structure as expected.

To evaluate the approach, we created a subcorpus of the sentences with existential and overt *van*s, as those are the ones we aim to better disambiguate. On these sentences, we evaluated the accuracy of dependency label prediction of *van*. In both versions in the gold analysis the overt copula *van* has the dependency label **cop**, while the existential *van* has the appropriate verbal dependency label. In our results, for the original content head analysis, the correct label is assigned with 58.14% accuracy, while our POS tag based content head approach assigns the correct label with 60.35% accuracy. Although this not a statistically significant improvement, we believe that the tendencies reported on this relatively small corpus are of importance for parsing sentences with copulas.

5 Discussion

The most common error for all three linguistically plausible analyses is incorrectly labeling or attaching the subject of *van* and mixing it up with the

	Function	Content	Complex
Existential - UAS	86.18	80.48	86.84
Existential - LAS	91.04	77.21	82.46
Overt copula - UAS	82.8	75.05	83.62
Overt copula - LAS	77.31	71.67	77.82
Zero copula - UAS	84.42	78.39	77.5
Zero copula - LAS	79.17	75.15	69.59
Full corpus - UAS	85.75	84.41	84.76
Full corpus - LAS	81.24	81.2	79.89

Table 4: UAS and LAS scores with the three analyses on different subcorpora.

	Function	Content	Complex
Existential	78	80	80
Overt copula	62	42	52
Zero copula	70	68	30
Overall	70	63	54

Table 5: Percentage of correct sentences in the manual error analysis.

nominal predicate. Correctly identifying the subject and the nominal predicate is very hard: both are nominative case nominal phrases and while with first or second person subjects, the agreement with the verb makes them easier to tell apart, when both subject and predicate are third person noun phrases, even native speakers of Hungarian find it difficult to assign the correct structure to the sentence (which can be further complicated by the free word order). With the free word order in Hungarian, both sentences in Figures (2) and (3) can express the same meaning (without having any additional contextual information or information about stress patterns in spoken language), but the subject and predicate relations are not straightforward to assign. In the gold annotation, the annotator must decide on one of the options, but in some cases, both options are plausible, causing issues for the parser.

The manual error analysis shows that the complex label approach gives the worst results for copula constructions: it gives fewer correct copula structures and wrongly assigns the complex labels to parts of the sentence without zero copulas. The training time is also an issue as the complex label model trains almost twice as long as the other two because of the huge number of different labels - the function head approach uses 26 different labels, the content head 50, while the complex label analysis in our case used over 200 distinct labels – theoretically, an infinite number of labels are possible for it. The huge number of distinct dependency labels used in this approach probably influences the lower scores achieved by the system as

well, as statistically the system has a much lower chance of assigning the correct label out of a set of 200, than that of 26 or 50 labels.

The function and content head approaches achieved similar results in most cases. Both show the lowest scores for the overt copula cases that are very hard to disambiguate between existential and copular *van*. The two approaches score very similarly on the different error types as well. In interpreting the results, it is important to note that the function head analysis requires a preprocessing step to add the virtual *VAN*s to the corpus in order for them to be analyzed parallel to all other types of verbs; these virtual nodes were already present in both training and test data in the experiment.

Our two experiments were done on the relatively small (approximately 1800 sentences) section of the Szeged Corpus available with function head, content head and complex label gold syntactic analysis, therefore our results are preliminary, but we think the tendencies shown would hold using bigger corpora.

Based on the results of our two experiments, we propose using content head dependency syntactic structures for the analysis of Hungarian copula constructions with our addition of treating the distinction of existential and copular *van* on the level of POS tagging.

6 Conclusions

Our paper discussed Hungarian copula *van* and different possible analyses of copula constructions in dependency syntax, evaluating them in com-

	Original	POS-based
Only *van* sentences- UAS	71.67	72.08
Only *van* sentences- LAS	65.87	66.3
Full corpus - UAS	77.8	77.77
Full corpus - LAS	72.02	72.05

Table 6: UAS and LAS scores for the original and POS-based content head analyses.

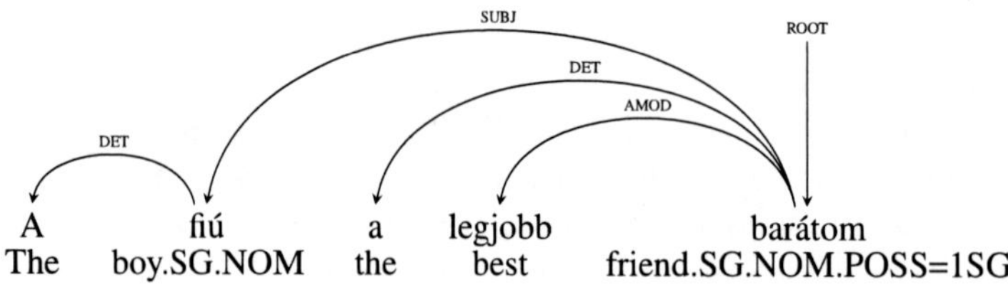

Figure 2: Content head analysis of the copular sentence, *A fiú a legjobb barátom* "The boy is my best friend".

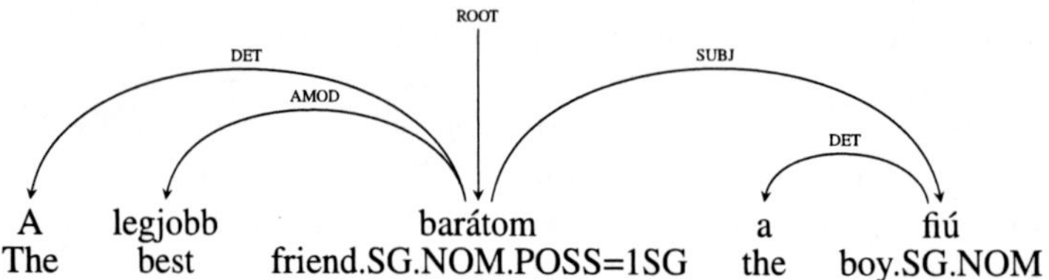

Figure 3: Content head analysis of the copular sentence, *A legjobb barátom a fiú* "My best friend is the boy.".

putational linguistics. We introduced the Hungarian verb *van* and its main linguistic properties, described the function head, content head and complex label approaches to represent copula constructions and showed the results of two parsing experiments focusing on the Hungarian copula. Based on the outcome of our experiments, we support the use of the content head approach with the POS tagging based additions proposed in this paper for the treatment of Hungarian copula constructions.

Our goals in this paper were to show how syntactic analysis can be influenced by not just the syntactic framework, but the specific approach within it and to highlight the importance of manual error analysis alongside the UAS and LAS values. Manual error analysis often shows nuances in the analysis of specific phenomena hidden in overall precision scores and offers more informative results from both computational and linguistics points of view.

In the future, we plan to repeat our experiments on bigger corpora and also for other languages, as well as to investigate other challenging syntactic constructions in a similar fashion.

Acknowledgements

This research was supported by the EU-funded Hungarian grant EFOP-3.6.1- 16-2016- 00008.

References

Bernd Bohnet. 2010. Top accuracy and fast dependency parsing is not a contradiction. In *Proceedings of the 23rd International Conference on Computational Linguistics (Coling 2010)*, pages 89–97.

Timothy Jowan Curnow. 2000. Towards a Cross-Linguistic Typology of Copula Constructions. In John Henderson, editor, *Proceedings of the 1999 Conference of the Australian Linguistic Society*, pages 1–9.

Mary Dalrymple, Helge Dyvik, and Tracy H. King. 2004. Copular Complements: Closed or Open? In *Proceedings of the LFG '04 Conference*, pages 188–198, New Zealand. University of Canterbury.

Marcel Den Dikken. 2006. *Relators and Linkers: The Syntax of Predication, Predicate Inversion, and Copulas*. MIT Press.

Katalin É. Kiss. 2002. *The Syntax of Hungarian*. Cambridge Syntax Guides. Cambridge University Press, Cambridge.

Tibor Laczkó. 2012. On the (Un)Bearable Lightness of Being an LFG Style Copula in Hungarian. In *The Proceedings of the LFG12 Conference*, pages 341–361, Stanford. CSLI Publications.

Joakim Nivre, Johan Hall, Sandra Kübler, Ryan McDonald, Jens Nilsson, Sebastian Riedel, and Deniz Yuret. 2007. The CoNLL 2007 Shared Task on Dependency Parsing. In *Proceedings of the CoNLL Shared Task Session of EMNLP-CoNLL 2007*, pages 915–932.

Joakim Nivre, 2015. *Towards a Universal Grammar for Natural Language Processing*, pages 3–16. Springer International Publishing, Cham.

Barbara Partee. 1998. Copular Inversion Puzzles in English and Russian. In Katarzyna Dziwirek, Herbert Coats, and Cynthia Vakareliyska, editors, *Formal Approaches to Slavic Linguistics*, pages 361–395.

Alain Polguère and Igor Aleksandrovič Mel'čuk, editors. 2009. *Dependency in Linguistic Description*. Studies in language companion series. Amsterdam Philadelphia, Pa. J. Benjamins.

Wolfgang Seeker, Richárd Farkas, Bernd Bohnet, Helmut Schmid, and Jonas Kuhn. 2012. Data-driven dependency parsing with empty heads. In *Proceedings of COLING 2012: Posters*, pages 1081–1090, Mumbai, India, December. The COLING 2012 Organizing Committee.

Veronika Vincze, Dóra Szauter, Attila Almási, György Móra, Zoltán Alexin, and János Csirik. 2010. Hungarian Dependency Treebank. In *Proceedings of LREC 2010*, Valletta, Malta, May. ELRA.

Veronika Vincze, Richárd Farkas, Katalin Ilona Simkó, Zsolt Szántó, and Viktor Varga. 2015. Univerzális dependencia és morfológia magyar nyelvre. In *XII. Magyar Számítógépes Nyelvészeti Konferencia*, pages 322–329, Szeged.

Veronika Vincze, Katalin Simkó, Zsolt Szántó, and Richárd Farkas. 2017. Universal Dependencies and Morphology for Hungarian - and on the Price of Universality. In *Proceedings of the 15th Conference of the European Chapter of the Association for Computational Linguistics: Volume 1, Long Papers*, pages 356–365, Valencia, Spain, April. Association for Computational Linguistics.

Semgrex-Plus: a tool for automatic dependency-graph rewriting

Fabio Tamburini
University of Bologna
FICLIT
Bologna, Italy
`fabio.tamburini@unibo.it`

Abstract

This paper describes an automatic procedure, the Semgrex-Plus tool, we developed to convert dependency treebanks into different formats. It allows for the definition of formal rules for rewriting dependencies and token tags as well as an algorithm for treebank rewriting able to avoid rule interference during the conversion process. This tool is publicly available[1].

1 Introduction

Creating a treebank, annotating each sentence with its syntactic structure, is certainly a time-consuming and error prone task. For these reasons, treebanks often require maintenance and revisions to correct mistakes or to adapt it to different needs.

In big projects, such as the Universal Dependencies (UD) project (Nivre et al., 2016), guidelines updates due to new language addition, change in theoretical approaches of a specific phenomenon management, mistakes or other changes often require specific tools to automate, at the maximum possible level, the process of treebank substructures rewriting. Moreover, the treebanks developed for a specific language need often to be completely converted to adhere to other standards, for example to comply to the UD specifications and conventions.

For phrase-structure treebanks there are various tools able to perform trees rewriting, such as *Tregex/Tsurgeon* pair (Levy and Andrew, 2006), but for dependency treebanks, largely dominant in these years, no specific rewriting tool seems to be available to the community. There are some generic, though very powerful, graph rewriting tools (Guillaume et al., 2012; Ribeyre, 2013) that

can be adapted to this task, but with some issues discussed in the last Section.

The StanfordNLP group developed a very interesting tool to perform treebank search by using a specialised query language. Using the *Semgrex* package[2] (Chambers et al., 2007) the user is able to specify search patterns and retrieve all the matching subgraphs inside a specific dependency treebank. This tool is very flexible and rich of operators, allowing the user to design powerful search patterns.

We extended the behaviour of this package adding some new functionalities for automatic dependency-graph rewriting useful for treebank maintenance, revision and conversion, producing a new tool, called *Semgrex-Plus*, that we made publicly available[1].

Semgrex-Plus can be used, in principle, to convert any dependency treebank represented using the CoNLL format into a different format that does not require re-tokenisation steps, or to rewrite some parts of the treebank using different dependency structures, labels and/or word tags.

This paper is organized as follows: we provide the description of the original Semgrex tool in Section 2; we then introduce the Semgrex-Plus tool describing the addition to the original tool in Section 3; in Section 4 the rule checking procedures and in Section 5 we present a treebank-conversion experiment using Semgrex-Plus; in the last Section we draw some provisional conclusion.

2 The Stanford Semgrex Search Language

Semgrex represents nodes in a dependency graph as a (non-recursive) attribute-value matrix. It then uses regular expressions for subsets of attribute values. For example,

---

[1] `https://github.com/ftamburin/Semgrex-Plus.git`

[2] `http://nlp.stanford.edu/software/tregex.shtml`

Proceedings of the Fourth International Conference on Dependency Linguistics (Depling 2017), pages 248-254,
Pisa, Italy, September 18-20 2017

{word:record;tag:/N.*/} refers to any node that has a value 'record' for the attribute 'word' and a 'tag' starting with the letter 'N', while '{}' refers to any node in the graph. The most important part of Semgrex regards the possibility to specify relations between nodes or group of nodes. See Table 1 for a reference taken from the original documentation and Table 2 for some examples of Semgrex search patterns together with the retrieved subgraphs.

For example, '{}=1 <subj=A {}=2' finds all the pairs of nodes connected by a directed 'subj' relation in which the first node ({}=1) is the dependent and the other the head. Logical connectives can be used to form more complex patterns and node/relation naming (the '=' assignments) can help to retrieve matched nodes/relations from the patterns. Please refer to (Chambers et al., 2007) or to the online manual[3] for a more complete description of the Semgrex query language.

3 Semgrex-Plus

Unfortunately Semgrex is only a query language and, in its original form, cannot be used to rewrite dependency (sub)graphs. In order to extend the possibility of Semgrex, we then modified the original application to manage pairs of patterns: the first is used to search into the treebank for the required subgraphs, and the second is used to specify how the retrieved subsgraphs have to be rewritten. For example the pattern pair "{tag:det}=1 >arg=A {tag:noun}=2" → "{tag:ART}=1 <DET=A {tag:NN}=2", what we called a 'Semgrex-Plus rule', changes the direction of the dependency between the head and the dependent and, at the same time, changes the words tags and relation label. The starting 'search' pattern and final 'rewrite' pattern have to contain the same number of nodes and dependency edges. Node and relation naming has been the fundamental trick to introduce such extension, allowing for nodes and relations matching between the search pattern and rewrite pattern.

3.1 Rule Application Procedure

For converting a treebank into a different format or to adjust some specific subgraphs, by applying a

complex set of Semgrex-Plus rules, it is necessary to define a specific procedure in order to avoid rule application interference: the application of a rule to the treebank changes the treebank structure potentially blocking the application of the remaining rules.

The solution we adopted decouples the search and rewrite operations for the rule application. We defined a set of new rewriting operations on a general dependency treebank:

- DEL_REL(graphID, depID, headID): deletes a dependency edge between two graph nodes;

- INS_REL(graphID, depID, headID, label): inserts a new labelled dependency edge between two graph nodes;

- REN_TAG(graphID, nodeID, tag): replace the tag of a specific graph node.

The conversion task has been implemented as a three-steps process:

- first of all, each Semgrex-Plus rule is always applied to the original treebank producing a set of matching subgraphs that have to be rewritten;

- for each match, a set of specific operations for rewriting the subgraph corresponding to the processed matching are generated and stored;

- lastly, the whole set of rewriting operations produced processing the entire set of Semgrex-Plus rules, each applied to the original treebank, is sorted by graphID, duplicates are removed and every operation is applied graph by graph respecting the following order: first dependency deletions, second dependency insertions and lastly tag renaming.

This way of processing the original treebank and transforming it into the new format should guarantee that we do not experience rule interference due to the conversion procedure, because the generation of the rewriting operations due to the Semgrex-Plus rules application is decoupled from the real treebank rewriting.

Figure 1 shows the results of the application of three Semgrex-Plus rules to two simple dependency graphs.

---

[3] https://nlp.stanford.edu/nlp/javadoc/ javanlp/edu/stanford/nlp/semgraph/ semgrex/SemgrexPattern.html

Symbol	Meaning
{}=1	Generic node without any attribute with ID='1'
{tag:W}=2	Generic node with attribute tag='W' and with ID='2'
A <reln=X B	A is the dep. of a rel. reln (with ID='X') with B
A >reln=X B	A is the gov. of a rel. reln (with ID='X') with B
A <<reln B	A is the dep. of a rel. reln in a chain to B following dep.->gov. paths
A >>reln B	A is the gov. of a rel. reln in a chain to B following gov.->dep. paths
A x,y<<reln B	A is the dep. of a rel. reln in a chain to B following dep.->gov. paths btw. dist. of x and y
A x,y>>reln B	A is the gov. of a rel. reln in a chain to B following gov.->dep. paths btw. dist. of x and y
A == B	A and B are the same nodes in the same graph
A . B	A is immediately precedes B, i.e. A.index() == B.index() - 1
A $+ B	B is a right immediate sibling of A
A $- B	B is a left immediate sibling of A
A $++ B	B is a right sibling of A
A $-- B	B is a left sibling of A
A @ B	A is aligned to B

Table 1: Supported node specification and relations and their symbols by the original Stanford Semgrex tool. Semgrex-Plus currently supports only the first four operators in rewriting rules.

Semgrex search pattern	Retrieved subgraphs
$\{A\} > X \left(\{B\} > Y\ \{C\}\right)$	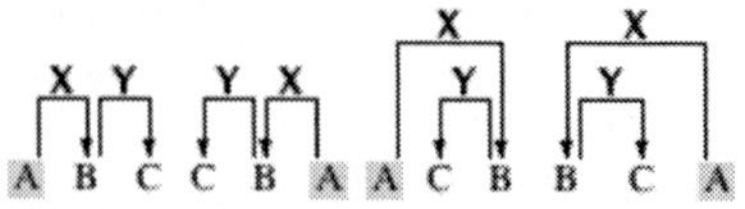
$\{A\} > X\ \{B\} > Y\ \{C\}$	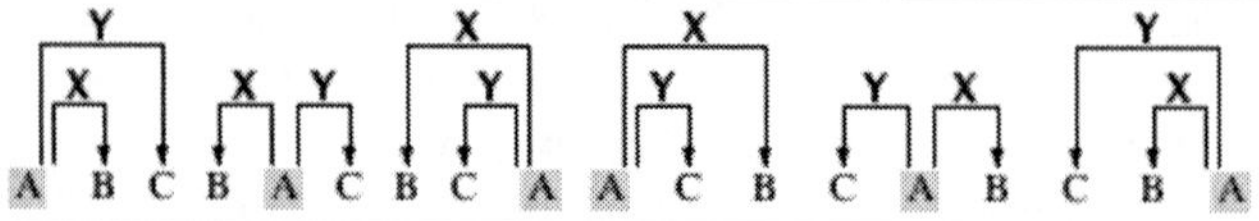
$\{D\} > Z \left(\{A\} > X\ \{B\} > Y\ \{C\}\right)$	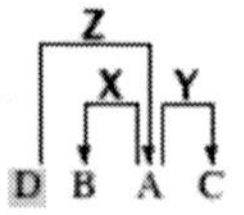 ... See previous example to build all retrieved subgraphs.

Table 2: Some examples of Semgrex search patterns and the corresponding retrieved subgraphs.

4 Rule Overlap/Interference Checking

Decoupling the 'search' from 'rewrite' operations should avoid any interference artificially introduced by the conversion procedure, but do not guarantee that errors in rules definition could generate problems due to rules interference.

We designed a specific tool that compare each rule in the ruleset with all the other rules and try to find potential interference between them. In order to find this potential problems (without applying the rules to a specific treebank we do not know in advance if a problem effectively will arise or not, thus we prefer to call them 'potential') we have to check if two rules exhibit specific kinds of overlaps, but only in the subgraphs that will be actually modified by the rewrite pattern.

The first step identify which edges in the search pattern are modified by the rewrite pattern of each rule. An edge is modified by a specific rule application if:

- the relation will be modified (the relation will connect different nodes, one or both, or it will have a different label);
- one of its nodes will be modified by an attribute change.

In the second step each rule is compared to all the others by considering the intersection between the two subgraphs formed by modified edges. If the intersection is not empty and

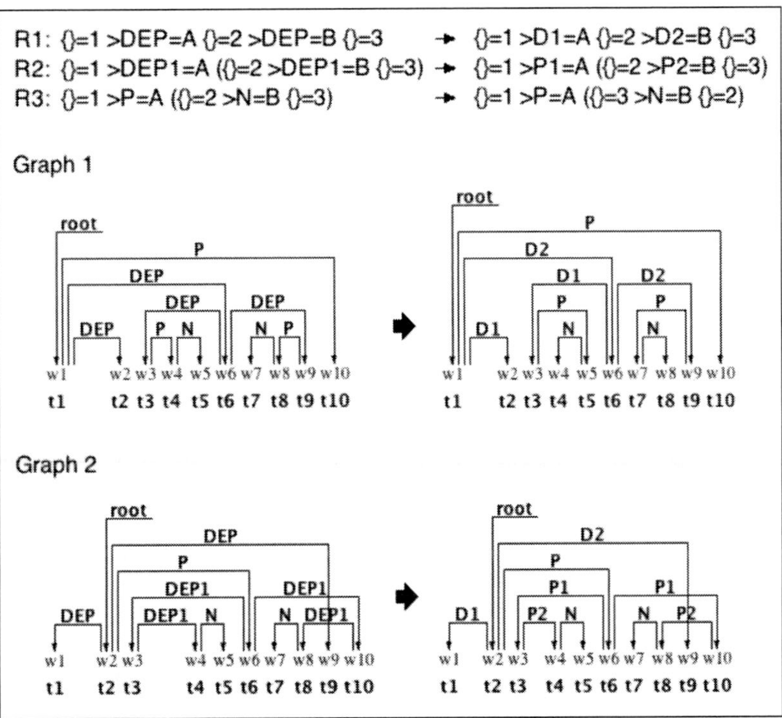

Figure 1: An example of graph conversion: the results of the application of three Semgrex-Plus rules to two simple dependency graphs.

Figure 2: Rules added to the first three (R1-R3 in Figure 1) to demonstrate rule overlap checking.

a) the two search patterns completely match, then we have a *full overlap* between rules and this mark a problem. The rule matching is similar to a unification process thus an empty node (e.g. {}=1) will match with any other node.

b) the two search patterns do not completely match, then we got a *partial overlap* between rules and this is only a potential problem because, in principle, the two rules should apply to different subgraph without creating real issues.

An empty intersection between rules modified subgraphs do not create any problem.

If we add the rules in Figure 2 to the ones presented in Figure 1 and apply the described algorithm to check for rule overlapping, we will obtain two full overlaps for rule pairs R3-R4 and R5-R6 and three partial overlaps for rule pairs R3-R5, R3-R6 and R4-R5.

5 Some Linguistic Examples

We used an early version of the Semgrex-Plus package to automate the conversion of the Venice Italian Treebank (Delmonte et al., 2007) into a different format, namely the MIDT+ format (Bosco et al., 2012), in order to start the merging of this treebank into the Italian Universal-Dependency treebank (Alfieri and Tamburini, 2016).

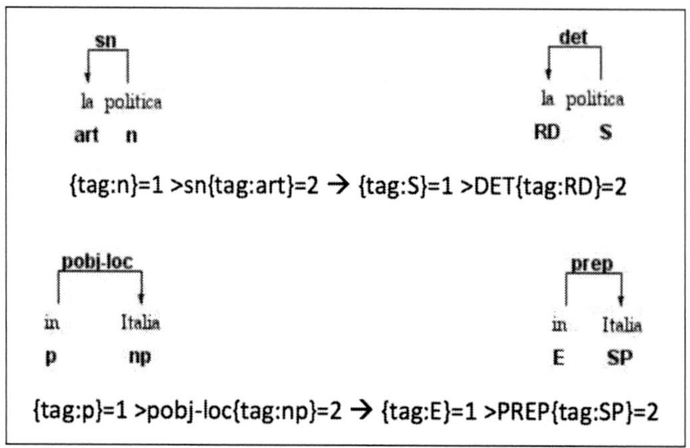

Figure 3: Some simple examples of rules that do not modify the dependency structures.

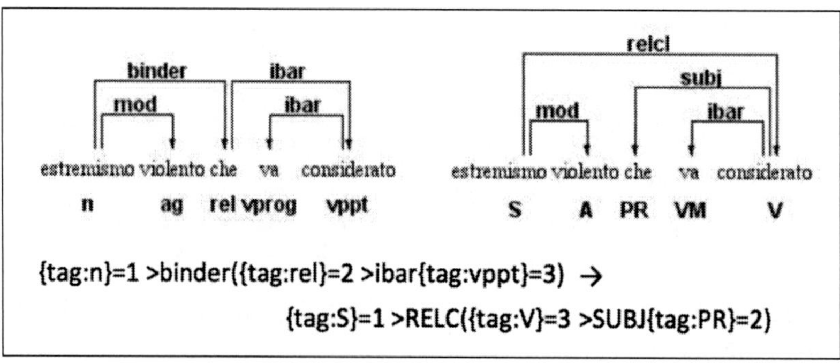

Figure 4: An example of rule that rewrite the dependency structure.

The set of rules manually written for converting VIT dependency structures can be subdivided into two macro-classes: (a) rules that do not modify the structures and (b) rules that need to modify the dependencies, both in term of edge direction and in term of different structuring between the involved nodes.

Regarding the rules that do not modify the dependency structures, they simply rename the dependency label using a 1:1 or an N:1 look-up table, as VIT, with respect to MIDT+, typically involves more specific dependency types. Figure 3 outlines some simple examples of such kind of conversions.

There are, of course, other kind of operations on subgraphs that require also the rewriting of the dependency structure. A good example concerns relative clauses in which the role of the relative pronoun and, as a consequence, the connections of the edge expressing the noun modification are completely different in the two formalisms. Figure

4 shows one example of this kind of rewriting.

Cases of coordination presented several problems for treebank conversions: in VIT the head of the coordinated structure is linked to the connective and then the two (or possibly more) coordinated structures can be linked with a wide range of different dependency types (e.g. between phrases - *sn*, *sa*, *savv*, *sq*, *sp*, predicative complements - *acomp*, *ncomp*, adjuncts - *adj*, *adjt*, *adjm*, *adjv*, subjects - *subj*, objects - *obj*, etc.) leading to a large number of different combinations. Moreover, each dependency combination has to be further specified by the different token tags. MIDT+ represents coordinate structures in a different way: the connective and the second conjunct are both linked to the first conjunct that is connected to the head of the coordinated structure.

Figure 5 shows one example: the first formal rule represents an abstract rule pattern that has to be filled with all the real tag combinations found in VIT, generating a huge number of different

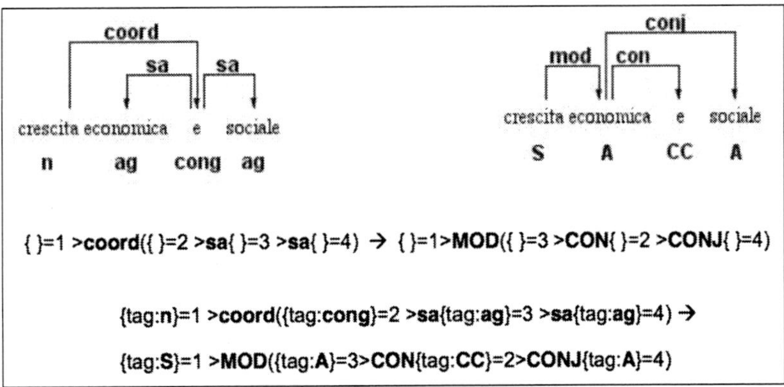

Figure 5: An example of coordination structures in VIT and MIDT+ and the conversion rule.

rules, one of them outlined by the second complete Semgrex-Plus rule. This process generated more than 2,800 different rules for handling all the coordinated structures in VIT.

There is also a need for a third kind of rules for rewriting single PoS-tags that might have remained unchanged during the main conversion process.

Applying all the 4,250 Semgrex-Plus rules we wrote, we obtained a converted treebank in which 228,534 out of 280,641 dependency relation were automatically converted, giving a global coverage of 81.4%.

To test the effectiveness of the conversion procedure and the conversion rules we randomly selected 100 sentences (2582 dependency relations to be converted) from the treebank and manually checked every newly created dependency relation, both in term of the connected nodes and the assigned label. We obtained the following results: among the 2008 relations that have been automatically converted we found 125 wrongly converted dependency relations. So, on this sample, we obtained a coverage of 2008/2582 = 77.8%, slightly less than on the whole treebank, with a conversion error rate = 125/2008 = 6.2%.

6 Conclusions

This paper presents the tool Semgrex-Plus, derived from the StanfordNLP Semgrex tool, we developed to allow for dependency structure rewriting inside a specific treebank.

This procedure can be, in principle, adaptable to any conversion between different dependency treebank formats or to modify the specific dependency structures, labels and/or word tags connected with a particular phenomenon.

Beside some simple examples of dependency structure rewriting using Semgrex-Plus we gave in this paper, we briefly reported on the use of this tool for automating the conversion of an Italian dependency treebank into a different format, in order to show the effectiveness of this tool when used in big and complex conversion projects.

To the best of our knowledge, there are only general-graph rewriting tools (Guillaume et al., 2012; Ribeyre, 2013) available to automatise this task for dependency graphs. Though this packages are very powerful and quite flexible, it is not clear, however, if they apply the rewriting operations when a rule pattern is found, modifying the treebank immediately, or not, and if there are some rule-checking procedures for raising potential problems in rules application, because, as we have seen in Section 4, a sequential application of the various rewriting rules could complicate the process of treebanks conversion. On the other hand, decoupling the pattern recognition from the rewriting operations, as done by the Semgrex-Plus tool, guarantee that we can write rules having in mind the original tagset without any modification, but we should still check and avoid interference among the conversion rules.

We can also find some powerful treebank converters in literature but they are usually tied to specific pair of tagsets (often tailored to the Penn treebank) (Johansson and Nugues, 2007; Choi and Palmer, 2010), and cannot be easily adapted to general needs, or are devoted to tree manipulation, for example the tool 'Tregex' (Levy and Andrew,

2006).

In any case, the formal rules for converting a treebank have to be manually written by using the proposed tool syntax and the final result has to be carefully tested to check the effectiveness of the conversion rules. The tool do not guarantee that, writing incomplete or wrong rules, the final result will be fine. For example, if we need to invert the direction of a dependency, we must include in the rule conversion also the node governing such dependency, in order to properly manage the graph and avoid the generation of illegal graphs (e.g. non-rooted trees/graphs).

References

Linda Alfieri and Fabio Tamburini. 2016. (Almost) Automatic Conversion of the Venice Italian Treebank into the Merged Italian Dependency Treebank Format. In *Proc. 3rd Italian Conference on Computational Linguistics - CLiC-IT 2016*, pages 19–23, Napoli, Italy.

Cristina Bosco, Simonetta Montemagni, and Maria Simi. 2012. Harmonization and Merging of two Italian Dependency Treebanks. In *Proc. of LREC 2012, Workshop on Language Resource Merging*, pages 23–30, Istanbul.

Nathanael Chambers, Daniel Cer, Trond Grenager, David Hall, Chloe Kiddon, Bill MacCartney, Marie-Catherine de Marneffe, Daniel Ramage, Eric Yeh, and Christopher Manning. 2007. Learning Alignments and Leveraging Natural Logic. In *Proc. of the Workshop on Textual Entailment and Paraphrasing*, pages 165–170.

Jinho Choi and Martha Palmer. 2010. Robust Constituent-to-Dependency Conversion for English. In *Proc. of 9th International Workshop on Treebanks and Linguistic Theories - TLT9*, Tartu, Estonia.

Rodolfo Delmonte, Antonella Bristot, and Sara Tonelli. 2007. VIT - Venice Italian Treebank: Syntactic and Quantitative Features. In *Proc. Sixth International Workshop on Treebanks and Linguistic Theories*.

Bruno Guillaume, Guillaume Bonfante, Paul Masson, Mathieu Morey, and Guy Perrier. 2012. Grew: un outil de réécriture de graphes pour le TAL. In Gilles Sérasset Georges Antoniadis, Hervé Blan-chon, editor, *12ième Conférence annuelle sur le Traitement Automatique des Langues (TALN'12)*, Grenoble, France. ATALA.

Richard Johansson and Pierre Nugues. 2007. Extended Constituent-to-dependency Conversion for English. In *Proc. of NODALIDA 2007*, Tartu, Estonia.

Roger Levy and Galen Andrew. 2006. Tregex and Tsurgeon: tools for querying and manipulating tree data structures. In *Proc. of 5th International Conference on Language Resources and Evaluation - LREC 2006*, Genoa, Italy.

Joakim Nivre, Marie-Catherine de Marneffe, Filip Ginter, Yoav Goldberg, Jan Hajic, Christopher D. Manning, Ryan McDonald, Slav Petrov, Sampo Pyysalo, Natalia Silveira, Reut Tsarfaty, and Daniel Zeman. 2016. Universal dependencies v1: A multilingual treebank collection. In *Proceedings of the Tenth International Conference on Language Resources and Evaluation (LREC 2016)*, pages 1659–1666, Portorož, Slovenia.

Corentin Ribeyre. 2013. Vers un système générique de réécriture de graphes pour l'enrichissement de structures syntaxiques. In *RECITAL 2013 - 15ème Rencontre des Etudiants Chercheurs en Informatique pour le Traitement Automatique des Langues*, pages 178–191, Les Sables d'Olonne, France.

Unity in Diversity: A unified parsing strategy for major Indian languages

Juhi Tandon and **Dipti Misra Sharma**
Kohli Center on Intelligent Systems (KCIS)
International Institute of Information Technology, Hyderabad (IIIT-H)
Gachibowli, Hyderabad, India
juhi.tandon@research.iiit.ac.in
dipti@iiit.ac.in

Abstract

This paper presents our work to apply non linear neural network for parsing five r esource p oor I ndian L anguages belonging to two major language families - Indo-Aryan and Dravidian. Bengali and Marathi are Indo-Aryan languages whereas Kannada, Telugu and Malayalam belong to the Dravidian family. While little work has been done previously on Bengali and Telugu linear transition-based parsing, we present one of the first parsers for Marathi, Kannada and Malayalam. All the Indian languages are free word order and range from being moderate to very rich in morphology. Therefore in this work we propose the usage of linguistically motivated morphological features (suffix and postposition) in the non linear framework, to capture the intricacies of both the language families. We also capture chunk and gender, number, person information elegantly in this model. We put forward ways to represent these features cost effectively using monolingual distributed embeddings. Instead of relying on expensive morphological analyzers to extract the information, these embeddings are used effectively to increase parsing accuracies for resource poor languages. Our experiments provide a comparison between the two language families on the importance of varying morphological features. Part of speech taggers and chunkers for all languages are also built in the process.

1 Introduction

Over the years there have been several successful attempts in building data driven dependency parsers using rich feature templates (Kübler et al., 2009) requiring a lot of feature engineering expertise. Though these indicative features brought enormously high parsing accuracies, they were computationally expensive to extract and also posed the problem of data sparsity. To address the problem of discrete representations of words, distributional representations became a critical component of NLP tasks such as POS tagging (Collobert et al., 2011), constituency parsing (Socher et al., 2013) and machine translation (Devlin et al., 2014). The distributed representations are shown to be more effective in non-linear architectures compared to the traditional linear classifier (Wang and Manning, 2013). Keeping in line with this trend, Chen and Manning (Chen and Manning, 2014) introduced a compact neural network based classifier for use in a greedy, transition-based dependency parser that learns using dense vector representations not only of words, but also of part-of-speech (POS) tags, dependency labels, etc. In our task of parsing Indian languages, a similar transition-based parser based on their model has been used. This model handles the problem of `sparsity, incompleteness and expensive feature computation` (Chen and Manning, 2014).

The last decade has seen quite a few attempts at parsing Indian languages Hindi, Telugu and Bengali (Bharati et al., 2008a; Nivre, 2009; Mannem, 2009; Kolachina et al., 2010; Ambati et al., 2010a). The research in this direction majorly focused on data driven transition-based parsing using MALT (Nivre et al., 2007), MST parser (McDonald et al., 2005) or constraint based method (Bharati et al., 2008b; Kesidi, 2013). Only recently Bhat et al. (2016a) have used neural network based non-linear parser to learn syntactic representations of Hindi and Urdu. Following their efforts, we present a similar parser for parsing five Indian Languages namely Bengali,

Proceedings of the Fourth International Conference on Dependency Linguistics (Depling 2017), pages 255-265,
Pisa, Italy, September 18-20 2017

Marathi, Telugu, Kannada, Malayalam. These languages belong to two major language families, Indo-Aryan and Dravidian. The Dravidian languages - Telugu, Kannada and Malayalam are highly agglutinative. The rich morphological nature of a language can prove challenging for a statistical parser as is noted by (Tsarfaty et al., 2010). For morphologically rich, free word order languages high performance can be achieved using vibhakti[1] and information related to tense, aspect, modality (TAM). Syntactic features related to case and TAM marking have been found to be very useful in previous works on dependency parsing of Hindi (Ambati et al., 2010b; Hohensee, 2012; Hohensee and Bender, 2012; Bhat et al., 2016b). We decided to experiment with these features for other Indian languages too as they follow more or less the same typology, all being free order and ranging from being moderate to very morphologically rich. We propose an efficient way to incorporate this information in the aforementioned neural network based parser. In our model, these features are included as suffix (last 4 characters) embeddings for all nodes. Lexical embeddings of case and TAM markers occurring in all the chunk are also included.

We also include chunk tags and gender, number, person information as features in our model. Taking cue from previous works where the addition of chunk tags[2] (Ambati et al., 2010a) and grammatical agreement (Bharati et al., 2008a; Bhat, 2017) has been proven to help Hindi and Urdu, our experiments test their effectiveness for other 5 languages in concern. Computationally, obtaining chunk tags can be done with ease. However, acquiring information related to gender, number, person for new sentences remains a challenge if we aim to parse resource poor languages for which sophisticated tools do not exist. We show that adding both these features definitely increases accuracy but we are able to gain major advantage by just using the lexical features, suffix features and POS tags which can be readily made available for low resource languages.

The rest of the paper is organised as follows. In Section 2 we talk about the data and the dependency scheme followed. Section 3 provides the

rationale behind using each feature taking into account language diversity. Section 4 details about feature representations, models used and the experiments conducted. In Section 5 we observe the effects of inclusion of rich morpho-syntactic features on different languages and back the results with linguistic reasoning. In Section 6 we conclude and talk about future directions of research our work paves the way for.

2 Data and Background

2.1 Dependency Treebanks

There have been several efforts towards developing robust data driven dependency parsing techniques in the last decade (Kübler et al., 2009). The efforts, in turn, initiated a parallel drive for building dependency annotated treebanks (Tsarfaty et al., 2013). Development of Hindi and Urdu multi-layered and multi-representational (Bhatt et al., 2009; Xia et al., 2009; Palmer et al., 2009) treebanks was a concerted effort in this direction. In line with these efforts, treebanks for Kannada, Malayalam, Telugu, Marathi and Bengali are being developed as a part of the Indian Languages - Treebanking Project. The process of treebank annotation for various languages took place at different institutes[3]. These treebanks are manually annotated and span over various domains, like that of newswire articles, conversational data, agriculture, entertainment, tourism and education, thus making our models trained on them robust. The treebanks are annotated systematically with part of speech (POS) tags, morphological features (such as root, lexical category, gender, number, person, case, vibhakti, TAM (tense, aspect and modality) label in case of verbs, or postposition in case of nouns), chunking information and syntactico-semantic dependency relations. There has been a shift from the Anncorra POS tags (Bharati et al., 2006) that were initially used for Indian Languages to the new common tagset for all Indian languages which we would refer to as the Bureau of Indian Standards (BIS) tagset (Choudhary and Jha, 2011). This new POS tagging scheme is finer than the previous scheme. The dependency relations are marked following the Computational Paninian Grammar (Bharati et al., 1995; Begum

---

[1] vibhakti is a generic term for postposition and suffix that represent case marking

[2] a chunk is a set of adjacent words which are in dependency relation with each other, and are connected to the rest of the words by a single incoming arc to the chunk

[3] The organizations involved in this project are Jadavpur University-Kolkata (Bengali), MIT-Manipal (Kannada), C-DIT,Trivandrum (Malayalam), IIT-Bombay (Marathi), IIIT-Hyderabad (Hindi)

	Types	Tokens	Chunks	Sentences	Avg. tokens / per sentence
Kannada	36778	188040	143400	16551	11.36
Malayalam	20107	65996	54818	5824	11.33
Telugu BIS	4079	11338	8203	2173	5.21
Telugu Ann.	4582	13477	8363	2322	5.80
Bengali	18172	87321	69458	8209	10.64
Marathi	24792	94844	69214	7983	11.88

Table 1: Treebank statistics for the 5 languages used in the experiments

et al., 2008). Partial corpus of all the languages containing 25,000 tokens has been released publicly in ICON 2017 [4], the rest is still being annotated with multi layered information and sanity-checked. The Telugu treebank data corresponding to BIS tagset is still being built so we used the data from ICON10 parsing contest (Husain et al., 2010). It was cleaned and appended with some more sentences. We automatically converted this data from Anncorra tagset to BIS tagset against some word lists and rules. Since 149 sentences are lost in automatic conversion we report results on both the datasets. The statistics of the treebank data in this work can be found in the Table 1. Previous work has been done to convert the Hindi Treebank to Universal Dependencies (UD) (Tandon et al., 2016). These new treebanks which are built on the same underlying principle, could also be converted to UD by the same process as a future work.

2.2 Computational Paninian Grammar

Computational Paninian Grammar (CPG) formalism lies at the heart of Indian language treebanking. Dependency Structure—the first layer in these treebanks—involves syntactico-semantic dependency analysis based on this framework(Bharati et al., 1995; Begum et al., 2008). The grammar treats a sentence as a series of modified-modifier relations where one of the elements (usually a verb) is the primary modified. This brings it close to a dependency analysis model as propounded in Tesnière's Dependency Grammar (Tesnière, 1959). The syntactico-semantic relations between lexical items provided by the Pāṇinian grammatical model can be split into two types.

1. **Kāraka**: These are semantically related to a verb as the direct participants in the action denoted by a verb root. The grammatical model has six 'kārakas', namely **'kartā'** (the doer), **'karma'** (the locus of action's result), **'karaṇa'** (instrument), **'sampradāna'** (recipient), **'apādāna'** (source), and **'adhikaraṇa'** (location). These relations provide crucial information about the main action stated in a sentence.

2. **Non-kāraka**: These relations include reason, purpose, possession, adjectival or adverbial modifications etc.

Both the **Kāraka** and **Non-kāraka** relations in the scheme are given in Table 2. The * in the gloss name signifies that the relation can be more granular in function and branches to different types. [5]

Relation	Meaning
k1	Agent / Subject / Doer
k2*	Theme / Patient / Goal
k3	Instrument
k4*	Recipient / Experiencer
k5	Source
k7*	Spatio-temporal
rt	Purpose
rh	Cause
ras	Associative
k*u	Comparative
k*s	(Predicative) Noun / Adjective Complements
r6	Genitives
relc	Modification by Relative Clause
rs	Noun Complements (Appositive)
adv	Verb modifier
adj	Noun modifier

Table 2: Some major dependency relations belonging to Computational Paninian Grammar

3 Getting the best Features

We first describe the rationale behind choosing each feature, why it is important for each language and report a series of experiments by adding them one by one to observe their effects. It is a known fact that language specific features play a crucial role in robust dependency parsing, but their generation may require expensive tools.

3.1 Part of Speech Tags

POS tags are very important for dependency parsing, as a purely lexical parser may lead to sparseness but adding POS tags provides a coarser grammatical category. This generalization of words

---

[4] (http://kcis.iiit.ac.in/LT)

[5]The complete set of dependency relation types can be found in (Bharati et al., 2009)

help as words belonging to the same part-of-speech are expected to have the same syntactic behavior. McDonald et al. (2011) have shown in their delexicalised parser that most of the information is captured in POS tags and just using them as features provides high unlabeled attachment score (UAS). However, for labeled dependency parsing, especially for semantic-oriented dependencies like Paninian dependencies these non-lexical features are not predictive enough.

3.2 Word

It is an indispensable unit for labeled dependency parsing. It is important for resolving ambiguous relationships for dependency parsing. But lexical units are sparse and difficult to learn given a limited training data set. This sparsity is observed more in morphologically rich languages.

3.3 Vibhakti (Suffix and Postpositions)

In a relatively fixed word order language like English the position of a word or phrase relative to the verbal head, gives cues for grammatical relations. On the other hand free word order and morphologically rich languages change the morphological form of the dependent word, the head word, or both in order to represent grammatical relations. This information about grammatical relations thus remains available irrespective of the position of words. The morphemes (suffixes) in Dravidian languages explicitly represent grammatical and semantic relations in a sentence. This is in contrast to Indo-Aryan languages where case marking can also be expressed lexically as postpositions to establish relations between nominals and verbal predicates, the degree of which depends on their varying morphological richness. Hindi and Urdu are relatively sparse in morphology when compared to Bengali, which in turn is less rich than Marathi. These units called vibhakti that exhibit case marking are important surface cues that help identify various dependency relations. Also are important the units that mark Tense, Aspect, Modality (TAM) of a verb. There exists a direct mapping between many TAM labels and the nominal case markers because TAMs control the case markers of some nominals. Different languages tend to encode syntactically relevant information in different ways. It has been shown in previous works for Hindi(Ambati et al., 2010b) that the integration of morphological and syntactic information boosts the accuracy for treebanks that are

syntacto-semantic in nature. We experiment to see the extent to which it helps the other Indian languages.

3.4 Chunk Tag

Previous work on Hindi (Ambati et al., 2010a) has shown that considerable improvement in parsing could be achieved using the local morphosyntactic features like chunk tags. In analytical languages, where information about finiteness or non finiteness of verbs is not captured in the chunk head alone but is also indicated by postpositions and auxiliaries following the head, the different chunk level tags[6]can help the parser identify different syntactic behavior of these verbs. For example a finite verb can become the root of the sentence, whereas a non-finite or infinitival verb cannot. Ambati et al. (2010a) used a coarser POS tag scheme so the improvement observed on addition of chunk was major. But in the new tagset that we are using, the finiteness information for verbs is marked at the POS level too. Therefore we experiment to see how far the chunk information helps us in this setting.

3.5 Gender, Number, Person

We want to capture the agreement between verb and its arguments in all languages by the addition of other morphological features such as gender, number and person (GNP) for each node. The verb agrees in GNP with the highest available karaka k1 usually. But agreement rules can be complex, it may sometimes take default feature or agree with karaka k2 in some cases. The problem worsens when there is a complex verb. Similar problems with agreement features have also been noted by (Goldberg and Elhadad, 2009). So we experiment to see if the parser can learn selective agreement pattern for different languages.

Kannada and Malayalam have a three gender system - gender marking is based on semantics. Human males and females are masculine and feminine gender respectively, whereas all things and animals are neuter gender. Telugu also has a three-gender system but human females are grouped with neuter nouns in singular, and human males in plural. The verb in Malayalam is not marked for number, gender person. Similarly in Bengali, the verb changes according to the person information

---

[6]finite, non-finite, infinitival and gerundial (Bharati et al., 2006)

only, it exhibits no grammatical gender phenomena at all. Marathi also has a three gender system - masculine, feminine and neuter.

4 Experimental Setup

In our experiments, we focus on establishing dependency relations between the chunk heads which we henceforth denote as inter-chunk parsing. The relations between the tokens of a chunk (intra-chunk dependencies) are not considered for experimentation as they can easily be predicted automatically using a finite set of rules (Kosaraju et al., 2012). Moreover we also observed the high learnability of intra-chunk relations from an initial experiment. We found the accuracies of intra-chunk dependencies to be more than 99.00% for both Labeled Attachment and Unlabeled Attachment. The treebanks available to us are in the SSF format (Bharati et al., 2007). We use in house built tool to convert from SSF to CoNLL format. This tool uses head and vibhakti computation tools as its dependencies. The head computation tool finds the head of a chunk based on certain rules written using POS tag information of nodes. The vibhakti computation module is again a simple, rule based tool that uses POS tag information to decide whether a lexical unit qualifies as a postposition or not. It then augments the head of the chunk with its postpositional features in the SSF format. Our parser uses data in the converted CoNLL format.

We use the arc-eager parsing model for parsing sentences containing projective arcs only, discarding the non-projective sentences. The data set is split in the ratio of 80-10-10 for training, testing and tuning the parsing model. Baseline for parsing is set using a delexicalised model having only POS tags as features . We explore with different feature sets by adding features like words, suffix, chunk tags and GNP information one by one. These features are represented as described below. In order to parse in more realistic settings, we also show parsing results using predicted POS and chunk tags obtained from the models discussed below. We report auto accuracy of the parsing model on the same training, development and testing sets that are used for parsing with gold tags.

4.1 Parsing Model

We have used a non-linear neural network greedy transition-based parser, similar in structure to (Chen and Manning, 2014). A few new features have been introduced in the input layer of the model as described below. Our parsing model is based on transition-based dependency parsing paradigm (Nivre, 2008). Particularly, we use an arc-eager transition system (Nivre, 2003). The arc-eager system defines a set of configurations for a sentence w_1 ,...,w_n where each configuration C = (S, B, A) consists of a stack S, a buffer B, and a set of dependency arcs A. For each sentence, the parser starts with an initial configuration where S = [ROOT], B = [w_1 ,...,w_n] and A = ϕ and terminates with a configuration C if the buffer is empty and the stack contains the ROOT. The parse trees derived from transition sequences are given by A. To derive the parse tree, the arc-eager system defines four types of transitions (t): 1) Shift, 2) Left-Arc, 3) Right-Arc, and 4) Reduce. We use a non-linear neural network to predict the transitions for the parser configurations. The neural network model is the standard feed-forward neural network with a single layer of hidden units. We use 200 hidden units and RelU activation function. The output layer uses softmax function for probabilistic multi-class classification. The model is trained by minimizing cross entropy loss with an l2-regularization over the entire training data. We also use mini-batch Adagrad for optimization (Duchi et al., 2011) and apply dropout (Hinton et al., 2012). The parameters like number of iterations, learning rate, embedding size were tuned on the development set.

From each parser configuration, we extract features related to the top four nodes in the stack, top four nodes in the buffer and leftmost and rightmost children of the top two nodes in the stack and the leftmost child of the top node in the buffer.

4.2 Part of Speech Tagging and Chunking Model

We trained POS taggers and Chunkers for all the five languages using a similar neural network architecture like parsing, discussed above. Second order structural features in the form of lexical and non-lexical units were used. The input layer consisted of the current word, words in the context size of 2 surrounding the current word and the last four characters of all these words. Intra-word information is extremely useful when dealing with morphologically rich languages as word internal features contribute more context than word external features while predicting POS and chunk tags.

Using POS tags as feature has obvious benefits for chunking. At least chunk tags can be deterministically predicted if the POS tags are known. But a chunking model using auto POS tags gives less accuracy than a sans POS model. For example in Kannada, using gold POS tags in chunker gave an accuracy of 99.46%, sans POS model gave 95.25% but model having auto POS tags reduced it to 95%. So we stuck to using only lexical and suffix features while chunking.

4.3 Representation of Lexical Units

In our non-linear parsing model, we use distributed representation of lexical features. Using distributed representation, units of words are projected to a low dimensional continuous vector space. Unlike sparse representation in linear models, these word embeddings allow words that are closer in the embedding space to share the model parameters, thus providing an efficient solution to the problem of data sparsity. Moreover since word embeddings are assumed to capture semantic and syntactic aspects of a word, they can also improve the correlation between words and dependency labels. The same representations are also used in the POS tagger.

The monolingual corpora of all the languages are used to learn their respective word embeddings. The data is collected from various sources such as Wikipedia dump[7], ILCI - health, tourism agriculture and entertainment data (Jha, 2010), raw corpus from EMILLE / CIIL (Xiao et al., 2004), LCC (Goldhahn et al., 2012), part of Opensubtitles corpus (Tiedemann, 2009), to train rich domain independent word-embeddings so that our parsing model is not biased. We use the Skipgram model with negative sampling implemented in the open-source `word2vec` toolkit (Mikolov et al., 2013) to learn word representations. The context window size was kept to 1, as shorter context captures more syntactic relatedness compared to longer contexts that capture semantic and topical similarity. The word embedding size was experimented with and embeddings of dimension 64 gave the best results.

4.4 Representation of POS, Chunk and GNP Tags

POS tags are small in number, but show semantic similarity like words. We use distributed represen-

tations for POS tags also by projecting them to a continuous low dimensional vector space. Similar settings as the above word embedding mode were used, while keeping the embeddings' dimension to be 20. The model for each language was trained on ILCI POS tagged data and treebank data that we were already using. The words were replaced by their corresponding tags to form a sequence. To represent chunk tags and GNP information, we use randomly initialized embeddings in the range of -0.25 to +0.25. The dimension of input vectors are taken to be 5.

In a real time setting, GNP information cannot be learnt from unlabeled monolingual data but require the presence of a morphological analyzer. It is an expensive tool to build. Due to the unavailability of a decently accurate tool for these resource poor languages, we have used gold tags in all our experiments just to observe their influence on parsing.

4.5 Representation of Vibhakti (Suffix and Postpositions)

Morphologically rich languages like Dravidian Languages, are highly agglutinative. The same root words inflect to have many word forms with different suffixes and prefixes. These morphemes denote the grammatical relation between a word and its arguments and may also represent TAM. This poses a problem to efficiently learn word embeddings for them. Most word embedding models consider word as a basic independent entity without considering its internal structure and shape. No explicit relationship among morphologically related words are captured too. While some work has been done to learn character based embeddings using deep neural networks for specific tasks like POS tagging, learning language models, learning word similarity etc, they are a different end to end architecture in themselves and cannot be used in integration with our parsing model. Therefore we thought it might be a good idea to treat suffixes - the last 4 characters of a word as separate units and learn embedding for them using `word2vec` to capture the linguistic regularity. This provides a potential solution for estimating rare and complex words rather than representing them in a crude way using only one or a few vectors. Instead of using the last few characters we could have used the case and TAM information present in the treebank in the form of

---

linguistic morphemes for each word, but due to the absence of a decent or no morphological analyzer for these languages, these features would not have been available for real time parsing of development and test set. Moreover since there are more than one morpheme in a word, methods to jointly learn word and character embeddings and composing them to yield a single representation (Bojanowski et al., 2016), need to be explored for these languages.

For Indo-Aryan langauges the degree of case and TAM marking being a part of word morphology varies according to the morphological richness of the language. This information can also be expressed lexically as postpositions or as auxiliaries in contrast to the Dravidian languages. Since we experiment on inter-chunk parsing and establish relations between heads of chunks, this information is lost. So we compose a vector by averaging the representations (that are looked up from the `word2vec` embedding model described above) of these postpositions and auxiliaries present in a chunk, and use it as a feature.

5 Results

The results of experimenting with the features described in Section 4 for all the 5 languages are presented in the Table 4. The metrics used for evaluation are Unlabeled and labeled attachment score (UAS and LAS) and label accuracy (LA). The performance corresponding to the highest performing feature set has been highlighted. The tags in our treebanks are syntactico-semantic and it has been observed with other treebanks that learning such tags is difficult (Nivre et al., 2007a). Despite that we achieve decent LAS for all 5 languages. We also experiment with a coarser scheme of POS tags for Telugu to see the effect of the granularity of POS tag on dependency parsing. Since some 149 sentences are lost in automatic conversion from coarser to finer treebank representation for Telugu, we cannot directly compare their parsing performance but can still get an idea that the coarser scheme is better in predicting LAS. This was not so intuitive as the richer information encoded in finer POS tagset should have helped the parser disambiguate dependency relations. We leave the label wise dependency relation analysis, taking into account the granularity of the POS tags for future work. Our delexicalised parser using only POS tags (f1) achieves good results for unla-

beled parsing for all languages and serves as a good baseline. However it gives poor results for LA and in turn for LAS as was expected, lowest LAS and UAS being for Marathi. On addition of suffix features to POS tags (f2) LAS shows a substantial increase for all languages, for an example +21.37% for Kannada gold test set. Though the highest increase is for Marathi as its baseline is very poor and even the partial lexical information gives the parser a major boost. The lowest increase of +9.1% is in Telugu gold test set. Different Dravidian languages show different levels of sophistication in case marking encoded in their suffixes. While in Kannada adding full lexical information (f3) to the baseline delexicalised parser does not increase accuracy a lot in comparison to f2, in Malayalam f2 that is partial lexical information (suffix and POS tags) perform better than f3.

We see that addition of suffix embeddings to word and POS tags (f4), acts as a complementary feature and shows substantial increase for Kannada and Malayalam, whereas quite less for Telugu. Bengali parser however does not show much increase as it is an Indo-Aryan language. Marathi shows a considerable increase despite being an Indo-Aryan language as it is morphologically richer and behaves likes pseudo Dravidian. Geographically it is also the southernmost Indo-Aryan language and shows syntactic convergence with the neighboring Dravidian language family. Similarly adding postposition information (f5) benefits Bengali parser considerably as compared to other Dravidian languages and Marathi.

It is noticed that adding chunk tag information (f6) helps across all languages, specially in LA as was conjectured. However the increase is slightly more for Indo-Aryan compared to Dravidian as in the latter the the average number of words in a chunk is less owing to the agglutinative nature of the languages. The head word and its morphemes encode most of the information for finite or non finiteness of verbs and case markers and is available to us in inter-chunk parsing. While in Bengali and Marathi the information marked by verb auxiliaries and postpositions supporting the head word in a chunk are lost, so the additional chunk information helps to disambiguate between the root and non root verb in complex constructions.

Next we see the effect of GNP information (f7) on parsing accuracies. There is an increase in all languages except Malayalam. It is reasonable as there is no agreement between Malayalam verbs and their arguments. However it increases for Malayalam in the auto development and auto test set. It could be due to inconsistencies within the data. GNP marking is also very noisy for Marathi data, may be it could be looked into for validation. We could not report results for Bengali for this feature as the data is not marked for morphological information.

We have also reported the performance of our POS tagger and chunker for all 5 languages in Table 3. With very simple features it gives better or comparable results for all languages compared to Bengali (Ghosh, 2013; Alam et al., 2016), Malayalam (V V and Sharma, 2016). Our results on Telugu and Bengali parsing or POS tagging cannot be compared directly to the previous works as we used a different dataset with a finer POS tagging scheme. Numerically it is still better than their results, it could be owed to the increase in size of the dataset, the architecture of our neural network models and dense representation of features.

Thus we show empirically that the presented feature set is useful for a range of morphologically rich languages across different language families, however some features are more important to certain languages than others.

6 Conclusion and Future work

We have presented our work to adapt an existing neural network parser to suit the particularities for 5 Indian languages Kannada, Malayalam, Telugu, Bengali and Marathi belonging to two major language families Dravidian and Indo-Aryan. We proposed a unified strategy for all languages for the inclusion of rich-morphosyntactic cues in the existing parsing framework. The cost effective representation of the linguistically motivated features such as suffix, postposition, chunk and GNP aim to capture the linguistic intricacies of all languages. A detailed discussion of the rationale behind each feature and their effect on parsing accuracy was presented. Our results provided the comparison that suffix information is more useful for parsing Dravidian languages while postposition is for Indo-Aryan languages, with the exception of Marathi. We showed the performance of our parser in real time settings by using auto POS and chunk tag. In turn we also built POS taggers and chunkers for these resource poor languages. Through our work we aimed to open av-

		Kan	Mal	Tel Bis	Tel Ann.	Ben	Mar
chunk	D	95.23	96.59	93.73	91.89	94.26	94.42
	T	95.25	96.74	91.28	93.17	94.25	94.93
pos	D	92.85	93.06	83.76	90.29	89.74	91.49
	T	92.31	92.78	83.31	88.81	89.34	91.83

Table 3: Accuracy of Chunker and POS Model for Kannada (Kan), Malayalam (Mal), Bengali (Ben), Marathi (Mar), Telugu (Tel) Bis and Anncorra (Ann.) tagset. D=Development Set, T=Test Set.

enues for further research in dependency parsing for these underrepresented languages. As a future work we propose to build cross-lingual parsers for these languages by exploiting the topological and genetic similarities among them. Since Indian languages are morphologically very rich, ways of learning character-aware POS tagging and dependency parsing models could also be explored.

Acknowledgement

We would like to thank the reviewers for their valuable and insightful comments that helped to improve the quality of this paper. We also extend our thanks to Irshad Ahmad Bhat for making his code from previous works available and giving relevant inputs.

References

Firoj Alam, Shammur Absar Chowdhury, and Sheak Rashed Haider Noori. 2016. Bidirectional lstmscrfs networks for bangla pos tagging. In *Computer and Information Technology (ICCIT), 2016 19th International Conference on*, pages 377–382. IEEE.

Bharat Ram Ambati, Samar Husain, Sambhav Jain, Dipti Misra Sharma, and Rajeev Sangal. 2010a. Two methods to incorporate local morphosyntactic features in hindi dependency parsing. In *Proceedings of the NAACL HLT 2010 First Workshop on Statistical Parsing of Morphologically-Rich Languages*, pages 22–30. Association for Computational Linguistics.

Bharat Ram Ambati, Samar Husain, Joakim Nivre, and Rajeev Sangal. 2010b. On the role of morphosyntactic features in hindi dependency parsing. In *Proceedings of the NAACL HLT 2010 First Workshop on Statistical Parsing of Morphologically-Rich Languages*, pages 94–102. Association for Computational Linguistics.

Rafiya Begum, Samar Husain, Arun Dhwaj, Dipti Misra Sharma, Lakshmi Bai, and Rajeev Sangal. 2008. Dependency annotation scheme

Feat.	Gold						Auto					
	Development			Test			Development			Test		
	LAS	UAS	LA	LAS	UAS	LA	LAS	UAS	LA	LAS	UAS	LA
Kannada												
f1	54.95	79.04	56.92	55.62	80.61	57.28	52.94	77.4	55.31	53.6	78.9	55.67
f2	75.82	90.8	78.58	76.99	92.29	79.18	73.15	88.71	76.76	73.89	89.88	76.99
f3	76.01	90.06	78.63	77.16	91.32	79.41	73.36	88.02	76.87	74.27	89.2	77.26
f4	79.46	91.54	82.37	80.74	92.94	83.03	76.63	89.36	80.42	77.53	90.76	80.71
f5	79.5	91.76	82.46	80.89	92.99	83.39	76.88	89.68	80.73	77.67	90.74	81.21
f6	**79.61**	**91.48**	**82.64**	80.68	93.07	83.27	76.92	89.95	80.79	77.59	90.98	81.02
f7	79.52	91.62	82.5	**80.99**	**93.26**	**83.47**	**77.01**	**89.83**	**80.82**	**78.07**	**91.03**	**81.45**
Malayalam												
f1	50.36	77.35	54.66	49.08	76.17	53.79	48.43	75.63	53.12	47.29	74.42	52.11
f2	65.15	84.29	70.57	66.69	85.94	71.34	62.06	82.29	68.21	64.18	83.8	69.66
f3	61.95	82.93	66.43	61.52	82.92	66.08	59.46	81.19	64.24	59.67	81.58	64.44
f4	67.88	85.41	72.88	68.5	85.99	73.47	64.66	83.35	70.5	65.91	84.37	71.12
f5	68.17	84.58	73.39	**70.76**	**86.29**	**75.64**	65.21	82.68	71.2	**68.12**	**84.58**	**73.36**
f6	**68.94**	**85.31**	**73.83**	70.02	86.5	74.79	65.28	83.03	70.88	67.44	84.65	72.81
f7	68.38	84.76	73.59	69.89	86.09	74.96	**65.78**	**83.32**	**71.42**	67.57	84.94	73.3
Telugu (Anncorra)												
f1	57.37	87.84	58.85	54.53	85.16	56.54	55.28	86.24	57.13	52.89	83.51	55.24
f2	69.04	92.63	70.02	66.67	93.17	67.49	68.3	91.65	69.16	65.72	92.46	67.02
f3	74.2	94.1	75.43	70.67	92.93	71.85	72.73	93.37	74.32	69.85	92.11	71.26
f4	74.69	93.98	75.92	**73.14**	**94.11**	**74.32**	74.03	93.73	75.68	**71.61**	**93.29**	**73.14**
f5	74.82	93.61	76.29	72.44	94.11	73.5	74.2	93.73	75.92	70.44	92.58	72.08
f6	**75.43**	**94.84**	**76.78**	71.73	93.05	72.91	**74.45**	93.37	**76.17**	70.55	93.05	71.97
f7	75.31	94.59	76.29	72.79	93.76	73.97	72.97	92.75	74.57	70.91	92.82	72.2
Telugu (BIS)												
f1	54.73	90.03	55.63	56.26	87.61	57.65	53.45	89.0	55.12	55.37	87.23	57.14
f2	66.11	93.09	67.65	65.36	92.04	66.88	63.55	91.82	65.86	65.23	91.66	66.75
f3	69.95	93.48	71.61	69.15	91.91	70.54	69.31	93.09	70.97	67.64	91.28	69.28
f4	70.72	93.09	72.76	69.28	91.4	71.3	70.72	92.97	72.89	68.72	91.15	70.54
f5	72.25	93.99	73.66	69.28	91.66	71.3	71.1	93.73	72.63	69.15	91.66	71.18
f6	**73.53**	**94.63**	**74.81**	71.55	93.17	72.95	**72.38**	**93.99**	**73.91**	**69.91**	**92.16**	**71.93**
f7	72.89	94.88	74.17	**71.93**	**92.92**	**73.58**	71.61	93.86	73.53	68.35	90.39	70.67
Marathi												
f1	34.81	59.92	39.29	34.06	59.11	38.5	34.83	60.24	39.1	33.45	58.63	38.24
f2	64.25	83.52	68.79	62.57	81.15	67.38	63.96	83.38	68.44	61.98	80.74	66.94
f3	66.27	84.6	69.67	65.22	83.66	69.2	66.08	84.58	69.45	65.11	83.41	69.14
f4	70.33	86.99	74.1	68.12	84.33	72.69	70.39	87.04	74.04	68.07	84.48	72.61
f5	70.47	87.32	74.26	68.42	85.18	72.44	70.25	87.19	74.15	68.0	84.92	72.07
f6	71.01	87.72	74.75	69.56	86.28	73.42	70.46	87.5	74.18	68.45	86.06	72.3
f7	**71.56**	**88.05**	**74.95**	**69.75**	**86.41**	**73.52**	**70.97**	**87.69**	**74.47**	**69.01**	**85.98**	**72.82**
Bengali												
f1	52.71	78.08	55.22	52.52	78.7	54.93	49.33	74.65	52.82	48.34	74.89	51.63
f2	68.19	85.37	70.82	67.6	84.86	70.68	64.42	82.1	68.26	63.61	81.75	67.38
f3	71.54	85.43	74.51	70.45	85.23	73.29	68.76	83.09	72.48	66.96	82.22	70.8
f4	72.86	85.81	76.07	71.66	86.26	74.55	69.55	83.22	73.55	68.5	83.62	72.69
f5	75.82	87.6	79.05	74.66	87.27	78.22	73.26	85.72	77.21	**72.65**	**85.86**	**76.55**
f6	**76.43**	**88.41**	**79.67**	**75.64**	**88.41**	**78.63**	**73.28**	**86.08**	**77.29**	72.24	85.99	75.92
f7	-	-	-	-	-	-	-	-	-	-	-	-

Table 4: Parsing accuracies of our neural network based parser for all 5 languages. Auto development and test set contain predicted POS and chunk tags. Gloss of the features are f1 = POS only, f2 = f1+ suffix, f3 = POS + word, f4 = f3 + suffix , f5 = f4+ PSP, f6 = f5 + chunk, f7 = f6 + GNP

for indian languages. In *IJCNLP*, pages 721–726. Citeseer.

A. Bharati, V. Chaitanya, R. Sangal, and KV Ramakrishnamacharyulu. 1995. *Natural Language Processing: A Paninian Perspective*. Prentice-Hall of India.

Akshar Bharati, Rajeev Sangal, Dipti Misra Sharma, and Lakshmi Bai. 2006. Anncorra: Annotating corpora guidelines for pos and chunk annotation for indian languages. *LTRC-TR31*.

Akshar Bharati, Rajeev Sangal, and Dipti M Sharma. 2007. Ssf: Shakti standard format guide.

Akshar Bharati, Samar Husain, Bharat Ambati, Sambhav Jain, Dipti Sharma, and Rajeev Sangal. 2008a. Two semantic features make all the difference in parsing accuracy. *Proc. of ICON*, 8.

Akshar Bharati, Samar Husain, Dipti Misra Sharma, and Rajeev Sangal. 2008b. A two-stage constraint based dependency parser for free word order languages. In *Proceedings of the COLIPS International Conference on Asian Language Processing 2008 (IALP)*.

Akshar Bharati, DM Sharma S Husain, L Bai, R Begam, and R Sangal. 2009. Anncorra: Treebanks for indian languages, guidelines for annotating hindi treebank (version–2.0).

Riyaz Ahmad Bhat, Irshad Ahmad Bhat, Naman Jain, and Dipti Misra Sharma. 2016a. A house united: Bridging the script and lexical barrier between hindi and urdu. In *International Conference on Computational Linguistics (COLING 2016)*.

Riyaz Ahmad Bhat, Irshad Ahmad Bhat, and Dipti Misra Sharma. 2016b. Improving transition-based dependency parsing of hindi and urdu by modeling syntactically relevant phenomena. *ACM Transactions on Asian and Low-Resource Language Information Processing (TALIP)*.

Riyaz Ahmad Bhat. 2017. Exploiting linguistic knowledge to address representation and sparsity issues in dependency parsing of indian languages.

Rajesh Bhatt, Bhuvana Narasimhan, Martha Palmer, Owen Rambow, Dipti Misra Sharma, and Fei Xia. 2009. A multi-representational and multi-layered treebank for hindi/urdu. In *Proceedings of the Third Linguistic Annotation Workshop*, pages 186–189. Association for Computational Linguistics.

Piotr Bojanowski, Edouard Grave, Armand Joulin, and Tomas Mikolov. 2016. Enriching word vectors with subword information. *arXiv preprint arXiv:1607.04606*.

Danqi Chen and Christopher D Manning. 2014. A fast and accurate dependency parser using neural networks. In *EMNLP*, pages 740–750.

Narayan Choudhary and Girish Nath Jha. 2011. Creating multilingual parallel corpora in indian languages. In *Language and Technology Conference*, pages 527–537. Springer.

Ronan Collobert, Jason Weston, Léon Bottou, Michael Karlen, Koray Kavukcuoglu, and Pavel Kuksa. 2011. Natural language processing (almost) from scratch. *Journal of Machine Learning Research*, 12(Aug):2493–2537.

Jacob Devlin, Rabih Zbib, Zhongqiang Huang, Thomas Lamar, Richard M Schwartz, and John Makhoul. 2014. Fast and robust neural network joint models for statistical machine translation. In *ACL (1)*, pages 1370–1380. Citeseer.

John Duchi, Elad Hazan, and Yoram Singer. 2011. Adaptive subgradient methods for online learning and stochastic optimization. *Journal of Machine Learning Research*, 12(Jul):2121–2159.

Arup Ratan Ghosh. 2013. *Memory Based Learner for Bengali POS Tagging*. Ph.D. thesis, JADAVPUR UNIVERSITY.

Yoav Goldberg and Michael Elhadad. 2009. Hebrew dependency parsing: Initial results. In *Proceedings of the 11th International Conference on Parsing Technologies*, pages 129–133. Association for Computational Linguistics.

Dirk Goldhahn, Thomas Eckart, and Uwe Quasthoff. 2012. Building large monolingual dictionaries at the leipzig corpora collection: From 100 to 200 languages. In *LREC*, pages 759–765.

Geoffrey E Hinton, Nitish Srivastava, Alex Krizhevsky, Ilya Sutskever, and Ruslan R Salakhutdinov. 2012. Improving neural networks by preventing co-adaptation of feature detectors. *arXiv preprint arXiv:1207.0580*.

Matt Hohensee and Emily M Bender. 2012. Getting more from morphology in multilingual dependency parsing. In *Proceedings of the 2012 Conference of the North American Chapter of the Association for Computational Linguistics: Human Language Technologies*, pages 315–326. Association for Computational Linguistics.

Matthew Hohensee. 2012. *It's only morpho-logical: Modeling agreement in cross-linguistic dependency parsing*. Ph.D. thesis.

Samar Husain, Prashanth Mannem, Bharat Ambati, and Phani Gadde. 2010. The icon-2010 tools contest on indian language dependency parsing. *Proceedings of ICON-2010 Tools Contest on Indian Language Dependency Parsing, ICON*, 10:1–8.

Girish Nath Jha. 2010. The tdil program and the indian langauge corpora intitiative (ilci). In *LREC*.

Sruthilaya Reddy Kesidi. 2013. *CONSTRAINT-BASED HYBRID DEPENDENCY PARSER FOR TELUGU*. Ph.D. thesis, International Institute of Information Technology Hyderabad, India.

Sudheer Kolachina, Prasanth Kolachina, Manish Agarwal, and Samar Husain. 2010. Experiments with malt parser for parsing indian languages. *Proc of ICON-2010 tools contest on Indian language dependency parsing. Kharagpur, India.*

Prudhvi Kosaraju, Samar Husain, Bharat Ram Ambati, Dipti Misra Sharma, and Rajeev Sangal. 2012. Intra-chunk dependency annotation: expanding hindi inter-chunk annotated treebank. In *Proceedings of the Sixth Linguistic Annotation Workshop*, pages 49–56. Association for Computational Linguistics.

Sandra Kübler, Ryan McDonald, and Joakim Nivre. 2009. Dependency parsing. *Synthesis Lectures on Human Language Technologies*, 1(1):1–127.

Prashanth Mannem. 2009. Bidirectional dependency parser for hindi, telugu and bangla. *Proceedings of ICON09 NLP Tools Contest: Indian Language Dependency Parsing, India.*

Ryan McDonald, Koby Crammer, and Fernando Pereira. 2005. Online large-margin training of dependency parsers. In *Proceedings of the 43rd annual meeting on association for computational linguistics*, pages 91–98. Association for Computational Linguistics.

Ryan McDonald, Slav Petrov, and Keith Hall. 2011. Multi-source transfer of delexicalized dependency parsers. In *Proceedings of the conference on empirical methods in natural language processing*, pages 62–72. Association for Computational Linguistics.

Tomas Mikolov, Kai Chen, Greg Corrado, and Jeffrey Dean. 2013. Efficient estimation of word representations in vector space. *arXiv preprint arXiv:1301.3781.*

Joakim Nivre, Johan Hall, Jens Nilsson, Atanas Chanev, Gülsen Eryigit, Sandra Kübler, Svetoslav Marinov, and Erwin Marsi. 2007. Maltparser: A language-independent system for data-driven dependency parsing. *Natural Language Engineering*, 13(02):95–135.

Joakim Nivre. 2003. An efficient algorithm for projective dependency parsing. In *Proceedings of the 8th International Workshop on Parsing Technologies (IWPT*. Citeseer.

Joakim Nivre. 2008. Algorithms for deterministic incremental dependency parsing. *Computational Linguistics*, 34(4):513–553.

Joakim Nivre. 2009. Parsing indian languages with maltparser. *Proceedings of the ICON09 NLP Tools Contest: Indian Language Dependency Parsing*, pages 12–18.

Martha Palmer, Rajesh Bhatt, Bhuvana Narasimhan, Owen Rambow, Dipti Misra Sharma, and Fei Xia. 2009. Hindi syntax: Annotating dependency, lexical predicate-argument structure, and phrase structure. In *The 7th International Conference on Natural Language Processing*, pages 14–17.

Richard Socher, John Bauer, Christopher D Manning, and Andrew Y Ng. 2013. Parsing with compositional vector grammars. In *ACL (1)*, pages 455–465.

Juhi Tandon, Himani Chaudhary, Riyaz Ahmad Bhat, and Dipti Misra Sharma. 2016. Conversion from pāninian kārakas to universal dependencies for hindi dependency treebank. *LAW X*, page 141.

Lucien Tesnière. 1959. *Eléments de syntaxe structurale*. Librairie C. Klincksieck.

Jörg Tiedemann. 2009. News from OPUS - A collection of multilingual parallel corpora with tools and interfaces. In N. Nicolov, K. Bontcheva, G. Angelova, and R. Mitkov, editors, *Recent Advances in Natural Language Processing*, volume V, pages 237–248. John Benjamins, Amsterdam/Philadelphia, Borovets, Bulgaria.

Reut Tsarfaty, Djamé Seddah, Yoav Goldberg, Sandra Kübler, Marie Candito, Jennifer Foster, Yannick Versley, Ines Rehbein, and Lamia Tounsi. 2010. Statistical parsing of morphologically rich languages (spmrl): what, how and whither. In *Proceedings of the NAACL HLT 2010 First Workshop on Statistical Parsing of Morphologically-Rich Languages*, pages 1–12. Association for Computational Linguistics.

Reut Tsarfaty, Djamé Seddah, Sandra Kübler, and Joakim Nivre. 2013. Parsing morphologically rich languages: Introduction to the special issue. *Computational Linguistics*, 39(1):15–22.

Devadath V V and Dipti Misra Sharma. 2016. Significance of an accurate sandhi-splitter in shallow parsing of dravidian languages. In *Proceedings of the ACL 2016 Student Research Workshop*, pages 37–42, Berlin, Germany, August. Association for Computational Linguistics.

Mengqiu Wang and Christopher D Manning. 2013. Effect of non-linear deep architecture in sequence labeling. In *IJCNLP*, pages 1285–1291.

Fei Xia, Owen Rambow, Rajesh Bhatt, Martha Palmer, and Dipti Misra Sharma. 2009. Towards a multi-representational treebank. In *The 7th International Workshop on Treebanks and Linguistic Theories. Groningen, Netherlands*, pages 159–170.

RZ Xiao, AM McEnery, JP Baker, and Andrew Hardie. 2004. Developing asian language corpora: standards and practice. In *The 4th Workshop on Asian Language Resources*.

Quantitative Comparative Syntax on the Cantonese-Mandarin Parallel Dependency Treebank

Tak-sum Wong
City University of Hong Kong
tswong-c@my.cityu.edu.hk

Herman Leung
City University of Hong Kong
leung.hm@gmail.com

Kim Gerdes
Sorbonne Nouvelle, LPP (CNRS)
Paris, France
kim@gerdes.fr

John Lee
City University of Hong Kong
jsylee@cityu.edu.hk

Abstract

This paper describes a new Cantonese-Mandarin parallel dependency treebank. We discuss the extent to which the treebank allows for comparative measures with the goal of quantifying structural differences between the two languages. After presenting syntactic differences between the two languages, we computed various frequency measures on the treebank. We present the results and discuss whether they reflect differences in text genre, differences in annotation scheme design, or actual structural differences. Finally, we compare the structural differences to previous accounts of the observed construction.

1 Introduction

Cantonese is part of the Yue dialect group which is spoken by more than 55 million people mostly in Canton, Hong Kong, Macao, the rest of the Pearl River Delta, and overseas Chinese communities. It is the "most widely known and influential variety of Chinese other than Mandarin" (Matthews & Yip 1994), and the early contact of Cantonese speakers with European explorers has given rise to the Western "Cantonese" pronunciations of some Chinese cities (e.g. *Canton*). Cantonese is not only used orally or in informal conversation, but also in the legislative councils in Hong Kong and Macao.

The special status of Hong Kong and Macao and the economic and educational importance of the region has made Cantonese a relatively well-studied and well-resourced language. A number of Cantonese corpora have already been tagged with part-of-speech (POS), including the Early Cantonese Tagged Database (Yiu 2012), the Hong Kong Cantonese Child Language Corpus (CANCORP, Lee et al. 1996), the Hong Kong

Bilingual Child Language Corpus (Yip and Matthews 2007), the Hong Kong Cantonese Corpus (HKCanCor, Luke & Wong 2015), the Cantonese Chinese Corpus of Oral Narratives (CANON, Law et al. 2012), and the Hong Kong Mid-1990s Newspaper Column Corpus (Li et al. 2016). However, to our best knowledge, no syntactic treebank has been published prior to our work, neither phrase structure nor dependency based.

This paper presents the first parallel dependency treebank for Cantonese and Mandarin and analyzes statistical differences between the treebanks. The rest of the paper is organized as follows. The next section summarizes syntactic differences between Cantonese and Mandarin. Section 3 discusses the construction process of the treebanks. Section 4 presents statistical analyses on the treebank. Finally, Section 5 concludes.

2 Linguistic background

Cantonese and Mandarin are similar languages in most major respects, leaving aside pronunciation and grammatical particles. Some significant linguistic differences between the two languages are well-established (Ouyang 1993), including phonology, vocabulary, and in particular the rich Cantonese system of utterance particles. Some differences of grammatical structure have been described as well but, due to the absence of a Cantonese treebank and, even less so, of a parallel treebank, descriptions of structural differences could not be put on empirical grounds so far. We will show that some of these differences reflect measures that we can take on our treebank; for other phenomena our treebank does not yet provide enough data to assess significant differences.

Proceedings of the Fourth International Conference on Dependency Linguistics (Depling 2017), pages 266-275,
Pisa, Italy, September 18-20 2017

2.1 Double objects

Among the commonly known syntactic differences we have to cite is the canonical word order of monotransitive and ditransitive verb constructions, which is reversed compared to Mandarin: For a ditransitive verb, in Cantonese we have the following word order:

verb + direct object + indirect object.

畀　　　一枝花　　　我
Péi　　yātjīfā　　　ngóh
give　　a flower　　1SG
'Give me a flower.'

In Mandarin it is

verb + indirect object + direct object.

給　　　我　　　一枝花ㄦ
Gěi　　wǒ　　　yīzhīhuār
give　　1SG　　a flower
'Give me a flower.'

These two alternative constructions recall the English dative shift alternation.

2.2 Use of the object marker

For monotransitive verbs, the object marker (OM) being more prominent in Mandarin, the SOV order is more frequent in Cantonese. The same word order exists in Cantonese but is marked. It is used when the speaker wants to put stress on the object. The two competing Cantonese constructions are:

閂　　　咗　　　度　　　**門**　　　啦！
*Sāan　　jó　　　douh　　**mùhn**　　lā!*
close　　PERF　　CLF　　**door**　　SFP
'Close the door!'
PERF=perfective particle
CLF=classifier
SFP=sentence final particle

vs.

將　　度　　**門**　　閂　　咗　　（佢）　　啦！
*Jēung　douh　**mùhn**　sāan　jó　（kéuih）　lā!*
OM　　CLF　　**door**　close　PERF　（3SG）　SFP
'the Door, close (it)!'

2.3 Post-verbal modifiers

Another notable difference of the two languages is the structure of post-verbal modifiers: Compare the following Cantonese sentence (Nr 0_189 of the parallel treebank) with its Mandarin counterpart.

Cantonese:

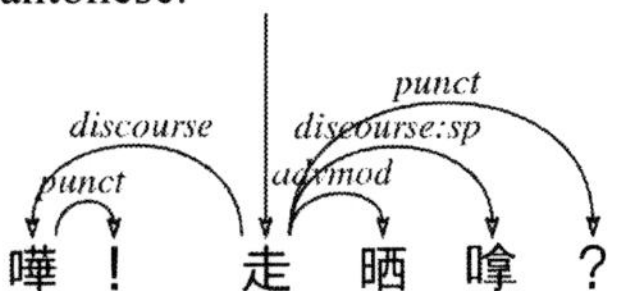

嘩　！　走　晒　嚹　？
INTJ　PUNCT　VERB　PART　PART　PUNCT
Wa!　Jáu　saai　làh?
Wow　go　**all**　　SFP
'Wow! All of them have gone already' / 'They have all gone?' / 'They have all been released from duty?'

Mandarin:

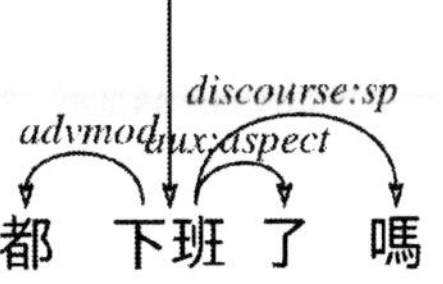

都　下班　了　嗎
ADV　VERB　AUX　PART
***Dōu*　xiàbān　le　ma**
all　off-duty　ASP　SFP

The Cantonese post-verbal modifier 晒 *saai* 'all' is often considered as a quantifying verb-compound with the verb grammaticalizing to a quantifying particle that can translate as "additionally, also". The Mandarin counterpart is an adverb in the standard preverbal position.

2.4 Coverb constructions

As pointed out by Francis and Matthews (2006), Cantonese coverbs are actually verbs, *e.g.* they can be used with aspect markers and verbal particles, In contrast, the Mandarin counterpart is rather a preposition – a preposition of verbal origin that has lost all of its verbal properties, except that it can still take a (prepositional) object.

Mandarin (0_28):

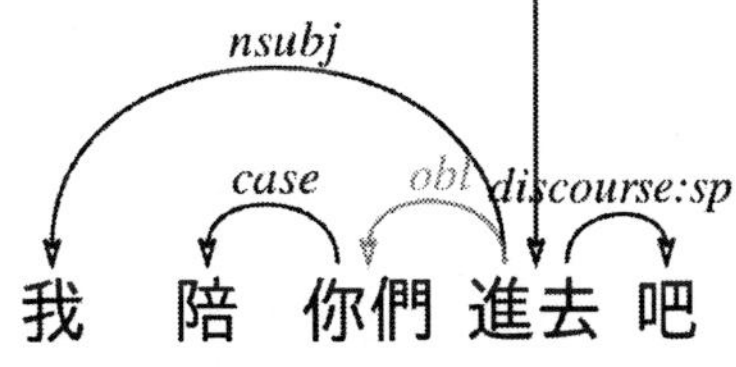

我　陪　你們　進去　吧
PRON　ADP　PRON　VERB　PART
Wǒ　péi　　　　　nǐmen　jìnqù　　ba
1SG　**accompany/with**　2PL　　go.inside　SFP

Cantonese:

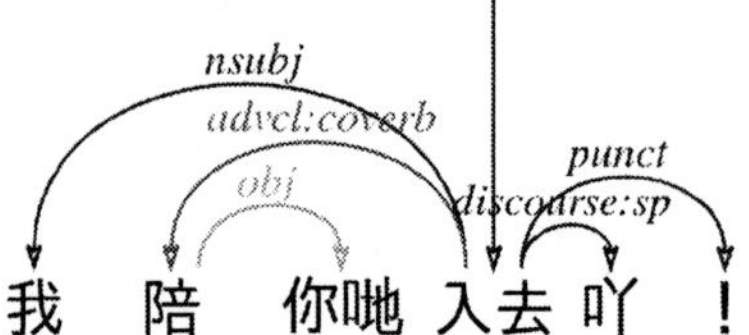

Similarly, in beneficial constructions, the English preposition *for* is translated by the polysemous character for *give*. Its usage in Mandarin is quite grammaticalized and it is usually considered a preposition, Cantonese remaining more analytical. In our Mandarin UD guidelines, we introduce a specific sub-relation of advcl, *advcl:coverb*, to account for these constructions.

2.5 Expletives

A last well-known difference between Cantonese and Mandarin is the existence of expletives in Cantonese (annotated with the relation name *expl*), which are completely absent from Mandarin. An example is 佢 *kéuih* '3SG'. The pronoun is part of a grammatical construction and actually does not refer to anything or anyone, the condition for qualifying as expletive.[1]

大家 飲勝 佢 ！
Daaihgā jámsing **kéuih**
everyone cheers **KEUHI**
'Everyone! Cheers (to it)!'
我 不如 死 咗 佢 好過 啦!
Ngóh bātyùh séi jó **kéuih** *hóugwo lā*
1SG had.better die PERF **KEUHI** better SFP
'It would be better for me to die.'

3 Treebank construction

Our corpus is based on television programs broadcast in Hong Kong (Lee, 2011). The Cantonese text is thus semi-planned spoken text. Cantonese TV dramas are widely distributed in southern China and beyond and mostly have Mandarin subtitles. The annotation is still ongoing and the texts that still await annotation are taken from movies that are distributed on Youtube, which will ultimately allow transforming this part of the treebank into a completely free language resource since the creators agreed to the distribution of the language data. The spo-

---

[1] For further details and examples see http://universaldependencies.org/yue/dep/expl.html

ken Cantonese was transcribed with traditional Chinese characters by a native speaker of the language.

Although the subtitles were in traditional Chinese, we added a transcription in simplified Chinese as a separate feature. The reason being that we need both character sets: The simplified characters are necessary in order to apply parsing and segmentation tools. And we kept the traditional characters because the ongoing alignment is more straightforward with identical character sets and also because the Hong Kong residents who are working on the project are more used to traditional characters. Moreover, the projection from traditional to simplified characters is mostly one-to-one but for some characters many to one, and thus easier in the direction *traditional → simplified*.

The Cantonese transcription was done independently of the Mandarin subtitles. This has important consequences on the measures that we are able to take, because, as we will see, the treebank is not as strictly parallel as we had hoped because the subtitles are condensed and simplified versions of the Cantonese original.

The currently annotated part of the corpus consists of 569 parallel sentences. The treebank is sentence-aligned. As shown in Table 1, the spoken Cantonese sentences are longer than their counterpart of Mandarin subtitles.

Language	Number of tokens	Average sentence length
Mandarin	4149	7.29
Cantonese	5428	9.54

Table 1: Corpus data

3.1 The UD annotation scheme

For the annotation of the parallel treebank, we decided to follow the Universal Dependency (UD, de Marneffe et al., 2014; Nivre et al., 2016) annotation scheme, as this allows the comparison of our resource also with external treebanks. However, even for Mandarin, no annotation guide existed, and the first UD v1 Mandarin treebank does not come with any explanation of the annotation choices and its annotation is, unsurprisingly, quite heterogeneous.

The Mandarin UD v1 annotation guide was explicitly developed for the UD dependency annotation of the Mandarin side of our corpus. Leung et al. (2016) describe the underlying discussions and choices, in particular for Chinese idiosyncrasies like classifiers, aspectual and sentence final particles, and light verb as well as serial verb constructions. In accordance with discussions around the development of this Mandarin annotation guide, UD v2 explicitly takes into account a specific *clf* 'classifier' relation, which is a unique type of syntactic relations that only exists for languages that have classifiers – Mandarin being the first language with this feature that is described in UD.

The UD v1 guide has been completed during the ongoing annotation experience and then adapted to v2. The Mandarin-specific part of the UD documentation is currently one of the most complete language specific annotation descriptions[2]

The similarity of Cantonese and Mandarin makes it reasonable to conceive the Cantonese annotation guide on the basis of the Mandarin guide, with modifications wherever necessary. The development of this guide is work in progress.

The whole semi-automatic annotation process is done in the Arborator annotation tool (Gerdes 2013), which allows blind and open annotation by multiple users as well as integrated parser bootstrapping possibilities

3.2 Outline

UD has been conceived with a double objective: The parallel construction of the treebanks facilitates the developments of parsers and other NLP tools. And, more importantly for the present study, it allows studies in empirical comparative syntax. There are some caveats to this claim, some of which we will discuss later. But any comparative measure on the current UD treebanks will always measure either structural differences, genre differences of the underlying corpus, differences in the design of the annotation scheme, or annotation errors and incoherences of course. Our corpus is, at least partly different in this aspect: Being a parallel treebank, the content of both treebanks is identical and any ascertained difference should be attributed to a structural difference. Alas, as we have mentioned before, this is not completely true, as the Mandarin subtitles are not precise translations of the original Cantonese words. Therefore, the measured differences can always either be an actual syntactic difference, or rather a difference of genre: The genre of spoken texts in TV dramas vs. the genre of subtitles in "Translationese" – although the pure informational content is mostly identical.

The measured differences between the two sides of the parallel treebank that cannot easily be attributed to the genre variation may either be new to us or corroborate known syntactic differences between the two languages.

4 Statistical measures

This section first presents the statistical measures that will be used to assure the validity of the significance of the observations (Section 4.1). Further, various difference measures based on the POS distribution will be presented and discussed (Section 4.2). Then we move on to differences in the functional distribution (Section 4.3) and finally we mix categorical and functional information (Section 4.4). After a short presentation of dependency directional measures (Section 4.5), we will conclude with an outlook on the ongoing annotation and alignment process.

4.1 Fisher Test and Specificity

In order to distinguish significant from insignificant over- and under-representation of features of our parallel treebank, we systematically apply the exact Fisher test which is based on the cumulative hypergeometric distribution. The null hypothesis is that the size of the two corpora as well as the number of total words having a specific category (or syntactic function) being fixed, the actually observed number of occurrences is due to chance. The p-value measures the probability that the observed frequency (or more occurrences if the number is already over-represented or less if already under-represented) actually occurred. To make the probabilities more readable, we transform them in *specificity* values (Lebart et al. 1991): specificity$=-\log_{10}(p)$ if the observed frequency is higher than the expected value and $\log_{10}(1-p)$ if the frequency is lower than expected. The expected value is the equi-distribution of categories and functions into the two corpora depending on the size of the corpora and the frequency of the categories and functions. This is a well-established method in textual statistics, but still quite rarely used in syntactic comparisons.

4.2 Categorical differences

Concerning the POS distribution we observe the following variation between Cantonese and Mandarin. The first line of Table 2 can be read as follows: Cantonese contains 999 of the total 1344 PUNCT(uation) tokens in our two treebanks. The positive Specificity value indicates

---

2   The annotation guidelines that we have developed can be accessed at: http://universaldependencies.org/zh/overview/introduction.html

that PUNCT is over-represented in Cantonese. The probability that this is due to chance is very low: $1/10^{31}$.

Type	Specificity	Cantonese	Total
PUNCT	31	999	1344
INTJ	23	97	97
PART	10	619	898
X	5	20	20
AUX	0	246	428
CCONJ	0	18	33
SCONJ	0	23	41
ADJ	-1	97	186
NOUN	-1	801	1449
NUM	-1	54	104
PROPN	-1	84	155
DET	-4	60	144
VERB	-4	347	688
PRON	-5	462	915
ADP	-8	93	239
ADV	-11	511	1080

Table 2: POS frequencies by specificity

Inversely, the last row of Table 2 indicates the following observation: Cantonese has only 511 of the total of 1080 ADV(erbial) tokens. This is less than statistically expected if the POS were distributed evenly, given that the Cantonese part of the corpus is larger. The probability that the observed frequency difference is due to chance is $1/10^{11}$. The upper shaded (green) rows of the table thus show significant over-representation of categories in Cantonese, the lower shaded (red) rows show significant under-representation. The unshaded rows have over- or under-representation of order 0 or 1 (p~1/10) and thus non-significant differences. The significantly lower frequency of adverbs in Cantonese is likely due to the prominence of Cantonese post-verbal particles where in Mandarin adverbs are often used to express the same meaning. For instance, for the progressive aspect, in Mandarin the adverb *zhèngzài* 正在 is used (*zhèngzài* + *V*) where the Cantonese counterpart is V-*gán* in which *gán* 緊 is a post-verbal aspect particle. (Also cf. section 2.3)

We see that the Cantonese treebank was not only punctuated very differently than the Mandarin subtitles. The Cantonese side contains all the observed interjections of the whole parallel treebank as well as a much higher frequency of particles. This underlines again that the subtitle translation is actually a condensed, not to say impoverished, version that lacks many of the oral features of the spoken original. The fact that the POS tag X (words where annotators cannot determine a POS, like the prefix *a* 阿) only appear in Cantonese can be attributed to possible disagreements between the annotators which may be due to the oral character of the transcription as well as to the underdeveloped formal grammars of Cantonese – making the annotation task harder.

Further, we observe the expected under-representation of ADP(ositions) in Cantonese due to the verbal character of many Cantonese equivalents of Mandarin prepositions, as discussed in section 2.4. It remains to explain why verbs are nonetheless also under-represented in Cantonese.

The under-representation of PRON(ouns) in Cantonese is unexpected. This may be an actual linguistic difference between the two languages or it may be due to the less oral character of the Mandarin translation compared to the Cantonese transcriptions, leading to less pronoun dropping. This will have to be examined further.

4.3 Functional differences

Table 3 shows the significant differences in the distribution of syntactic functions, partly corresponds to what has been observed for the POS (e.g. the high frequency of *punct*, *discourse*, and *discourse:sp* = "sentence final particle" relations), but also shows a few more interesting variations: The current Mandarin annotation does not contain any *advcl:coverb* relations, which is due to differences in annotation, but which nonetheless reveals a significant structural difference between the languages: The Mandarin prepositions are of verbal origin but have lost all verbal properties whereas their Cantonese counterparts can still be modified by verbal articles and have thus to be tagged and annotated differently (see section 2.4). The UD annotation scheme handles prepositions as case-markers, and thus as depen-

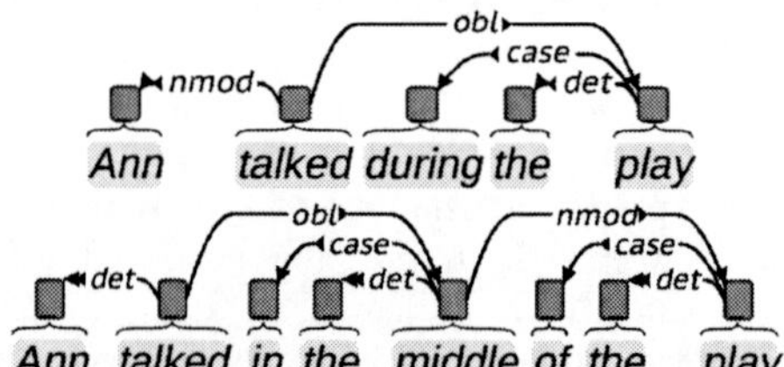

Figure 1: Analyses of two (semantically full) prepositions in UD 2.0 English, the first being a simple and the second a complex preposition

dent from their argument, i.e. what is commonly called a prepositional object. This results in UD's

infamous "Turkish" analysis of English prepositions (Chris Manning, 2016, personal communication). Figure 1 shows the situation for English
(example taken from Gerdes & Kahane 2016, updated to UD 2.0).

The following pair of sentence segments illustrates this point for Chinese. The 1st person singular pronoun in the Mandarin tree 我 *'wǒ'* is an
obl:dobj that has a case-marker. In the Cantonese
equivalent, what has been analyzed as a (verbal)
preposition in Mandarin is now a coverb, which
takes its argument as a regular direct object.

Mandarin (sentence 0-7):

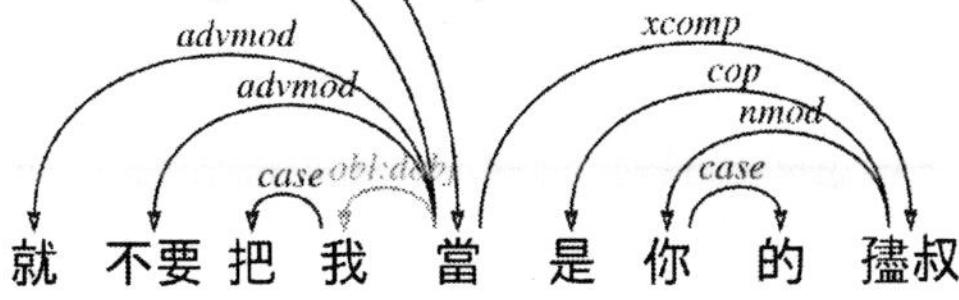

就	不要	把	我	當	是	你	的	孲叔
ADV	ADV	ADP	PRON	VERB	AUX	PRON	PART	NOUN

Jiù	*bùyào*	*bǎ*	*wǒ*	*dàng*	*shì*
then	do.not	OM	1SG	treat	COP

nǐ	*de*	*nāishū*
2SG	REL	youngest.uncle.on.paternal.side

'Don't treat me as your uncle.'

Cantonese:

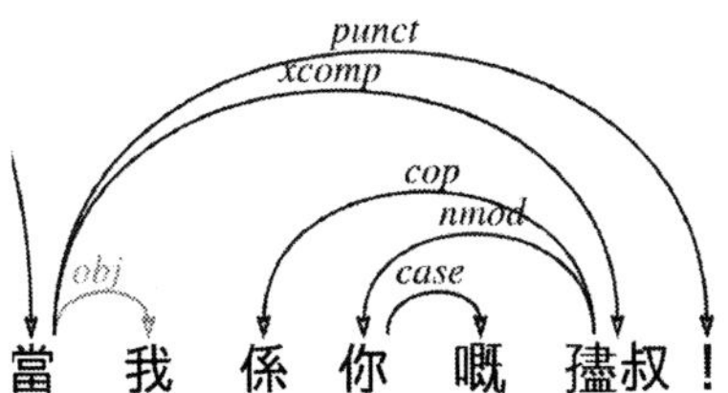

當	我	係	你	嘅	孲叔	！
VERB	PRON	AUX	PRON	PART	NOUN	PUNCT

Dong	*ngóh*	*haih*
treat	1SG	COP

léih	*ge*	*lāaisuk*
2SG	REL	youngest.uncle.on.paternal.side

'Treat me as your uncle.'

We end up with structurally very different
trees for a simple categorical choice. Note that
the proximity between verbs and preposition is
not reserved to Chinese. The English *during* or
the French equivalent *pendant* are similar cases
where the verbal character of the preposition is
still visible.

Alternatively, we could have decided to treat
all Cantonese coverbs as prepositions, so that the
Cantonese trees would be in line with the Mandarin ones. This is a difficult choice as UD seeks

"to maximize parallelism by allowing the same
grammatical relation to be annotated in the same
way across languages, while making enough crucial distinctions to differentiate constructions that
are not the same." (Nivre 2015 and UD home-

Type	Spec	Cantonese	Total
punct	31	1002	1345
discourse	26	204	226
discourse:sp	11	443	619
advcl:coverb	9	40	40
det	3	193	286
goeswith	2	25	33
advmod:df	1	12	17
aux:aspect	1	80	125
cop	1	76	125
appos	0	27	45
csubj	0	15	24
iobj	0	1	3
mark:dev	0	1	1
obl:agent	0	1	3
obl:clf	0	2	3
obl:poss	0	2	4
acl	-1	34	73
amod	-1	40	75
aux	-1	90	171
aux:pass	-1	0	2
case:loc	-1	26	52
cc	-1	17	33
clf	-1	47	88
mark	-1	38	76
nsubj:pass	-1	0	3
nummod	-1	53	99
obl:tmod	-1	83	154
parataxis	-1	84	161
vocative	-1	69	128
advcl	-2	91	184
nmod	-2	99	204
obj	-2	393	726
mark:rel	-3	20	56
nsubj	-3	362	707
xcomp	-3	64	140
dislocated	-4	62	148
obl	-5	58	147
ccomp	-6	56	145
advmod	-7	541	1087
obl:dobj	-7	0	18
case	-14	80	245

Table 3: complete dependency relation frequencies ordered by specificity

271

page. And although prepositions in English are considered by any syntactic analysis that we are aware of to be "crucially" different from case markers (Osborne 2015), UD decided to treat them just like Turkish case markers, leading to greater similarity between Turkish and English and at the same time to the structurally very different trees for simple and complex prepositions (Figure 1)

A good syntactic annotation scheme would allow for slight structural differences to be reflected by slight differences in the annotation, for example in the case of Cantonese coverbs by a different categorization of the coverb, once as a verb and once as a preposition, but with identical dependency structures in both treebanks. The "Turkish" analysis of prepositions, on the contrary, triggers a structural upheaval, for a small real difference: A "catastrophe" in a strictly mathematical sense of Thom's catastrophe theory (Saunders 1980, Gerdes & Kahane 2016), i.e. a brutal structural change in a continuum. This results in measures of important differences where there are few (between Mandarin and Cantonese for example), and in the absence of annotation differences where syntactic differences actually occur (e.g. English prepositions vs. Turkish case markers).

The UD annotation scheme obliges all dependency relations to be taken from a fixed set of 37 functions but it allows for the creation of idiosyncratic sub-relations when needed by a given language. The sub-relations are separated by a colon from the main relation: *relation:subrelation*. When grouping together subrelations, we obtain Table 4, a simpler table with similar significant variations between Cantonese and Mandarin. Concerning the adverbial clause (*advcl*) relation, we see that its distribution is no longer significantly different between the two languages: Mandarin had more simple *advcl*, Cantonese more coverb constructions which adds up to an equal distribution.

Type	Spec	Cantonese	Total
punct	31	1002	1345
discourse	27	647	845
det	3	193	286
goeswith	2	25	33
cop	1	76	125
advcl	0	131	224
appos	0	27	45
aux	0	170	298
csubj	0	15	24

iobj	0	1	3
acl	-1	34	73
amod	-1	40	75
cc	-1	17	33
clf	-1	47	88
nummod	-1	53	99
parataxis	-1	84	161
vocative	-1	69	128
nmod	-2	99	204
obj	-2	393	726
mark	-3	59	133
xcomp	-3	64	140
dislocated	-4	62	148
nsubj	-4	362	710
advmod	-6	553	1104
ccomp	-6	56	145
obl	-6	146	329
case	-14	106	297

Table 4: simple dependency relation frequencies ordered by specificity (simple meaning that sub-relations are grouped under the main relation)

4.4 Mixed measures

When grouping together the syntactic function and the POS of the dependent token, we obtain 128 classes of function-POS pairs. Although the small size of our current parallel corpus makes most differences fall under the significance threshold, some couples are significantly over- and under-represented. See Table 5 for details.

We observe for example that Cantonese particles are mostly in discourse or advmod relations whereas Mandarin particles are mark (~verbal complementizers) and case markers (~prepositions).

Since UD v2.0, the *dislocated* relation is used for objects in a non-canonical position "that do not fulfill the usual core grammatical relations of a sentence" (UD page for the *dislocated* relation[3]), so all the *obj* and *obl* relations in the above list are actually post-verbal. Since the Cantonese data is more oral, the over-representation of objects could also partially be due to this distinction and not to an actual difference in the valency structures of the observed verbal objects.

---

[3] It is not completely clear what is actually meant by "fulfilling the core grammatical relation" because a dislocated object usually fills the valency slot of the verbal governor. Mimicking what has been done for English and French, we decided to annotate preverbal objects with the *dislocated* relation.

Type	Spec	Can-tonese	Total
punct→PUNCT	31	998	1341
discourse→INTJ	23	97	97
det→NOUN	19	126	135
discourse→PART	18	516	692
advmod→PART	10	44	44
det→PRON	2	7	7
goeswith→NOUN	2	15	18
vocative→X	2	7	7
...			
acl→VERB	-2	32	70
dislocated→NOUN	-2	43	92
nmod→PRON	-2	71	146
nsubj→NOUN	-2	87	178
obj→NOUN	-2	266	505
obl→PROPN	-2	2	10
xcomp→VERB	-2	49	110
mark→PART	-3	25	68
nsubj→PRON	-3	252	490
obl→NOUN	-3	120	247
det→DET	-4	60	144
case→PART	-5	30	89
ccomp→VERB	-5	44	119
dislocated→ADV	-5	0	13
obl→PRON	-6	18	63
advmod→ADV	-10	472	1004
case→ADP	-10	73	204

Table 5: selection of dependency-POS couples, ordered by specificity

If we go one step further, we can measure triples *POS–func→ POS*. The two treebanks contain more than 300 of these triples, the two most frequent ones, with more than 700 occurrences being *VERB–punct→PUNCT* and *VERB–advmod→ADV*.

The most significantly over-represented Cantonese triples are shown in Table 6.

The significant over-representation of *NOUN–det→NOUN* relations in Cantonese may seem surprising and does not seem to follow directly from the POS distribution. Note first that the fixed UD POS tag-set does not include a specific category for classifiers which are therefore tagged as nouns. What we are actually observing here is that bare classifier noun phrases [CLF NOUN] is a common Cantonese strategy for definite NP constructions. In Cantonese only [CLF NOUN] and [DET CLF NOUN] are possible for

Type	Spec	Can-tonese	Total
VERB-punct→PUNCT	24	595	781
INTJ-punct→PUNCT	22	93	93
NOUN-det→NOUN	19	126	135
VERB-discourse→INTJ	15	64	64
VERB-discourse→PART	12	369	503

Table 6: The most over-represented triples POS – dependency – POS on the Cantonese side of the parallel treebank, ordered by specificity

definite NPs. In Mandarin we have [NOUN], [DET NOUN], or [DET CLF NOUN].[4]

Cantonese (sentence 0_2):

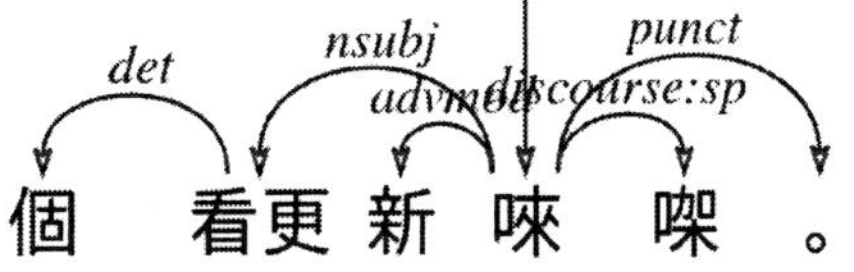

Mandarin:

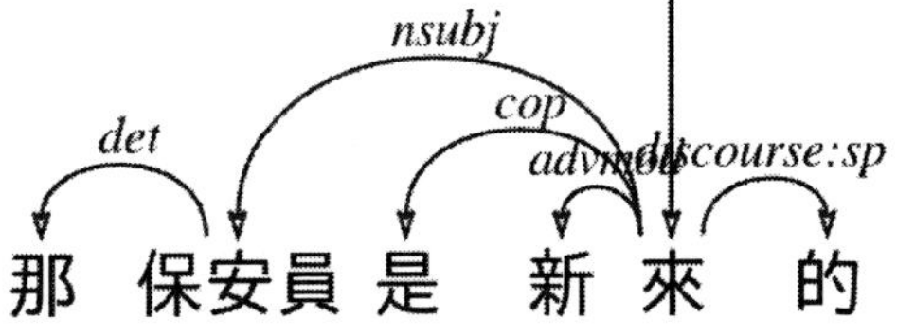

On the lower edge of the table, the most typically Mandarin triples are these:

	Spec	Can-tonese	Total
VERB-advmod→ADV	-10	332	729
AUX-ccomp→VERB	-14	0	38

Table 7: The most significantly over-represented triples POS – dependency – POS on the Mandarin side of the parallel treebank

In common copula constructions, UD imposes the analysis of the copula verb as the de-

---

[4] Note that [CLF NOUN] is also possible in Mandarin, but only in post-verbal position, and it can only have an indefinite interpretation, hence it occurs much less frequently than in Cantonese. In Cantonese, [CLF NOUN] can occur in both preverbal and postverbal position, but in preverbal position it must be definite; in postverbal position, it can be ambiguous between definite and indefinite.

pendent of the semantically full element, which is commonly a noun or an adjective. In the new UD v2 annotation scheme however, the auxiliary is considered the head of the construction if the semantically full argument is a verb itself, the copula verb becomes the head of the construction, a decision which attempts to avoid cases of embedded multiple auxiliary constructions where the subject can no longer be unequivocally attributed to its governor. This explains the existence of the *AUX–ccomp→VERB* triple, but it does not explain why this construction is over-represented in Mandarin. This will have to be explained by returning on the actual parallel data where the *AUX–ccomp→VERB* triple must have a structurally different translation in Cantonese.

4.5 Directional measures

A final set of measures on the treebank is based on the direction of the dependency link:

name	advmod	aux	obj	obl
Cantonese	13,74	48,82	100	28,08
Mandarin	3,81	35,16	100	19,67

Table 8: Percentage of right-pointing relations by syntactic function: A selection of functions

This kind of measures has been used in various treebank analysis methods, in particular in typological research, where the direction of the head-daughter relations has been shown to correlate with many important language features (Liu 2010, Chen & Gerdes 2017).

Here we just briefly want to point to a few aspects that have been mentioned above: We see that our annotation scheme only has objects to the right of its verbal governor – other positions would be annotated as *dislocated*. For the oblique verbal argument, however, we observe an important difference between Cantonese and Mandarin: Mandarin has around 20% of its oblique arguments to the right of their governor – Cantonese has 10% more, corresponding to the aforementioned structural preferences.

The higher number of right-branching *advmod* and *aux* relations in Cantonese, however, does not follow directly from the known language differences and should be explored further, preferably on more, and if possible, less genre dependent parallel data.

5 Conclusion

This article presents a method of empirical comparative syntax using statistical measures on a comparatively small sentence-aligned parallel dependency treebank. The specificity measurements, based on the exact Fisher test, are well-adapted to small corpora because the alternative test for categorical data, the approximating χ^2 test, gives incorrect results for very small (and very frequent) occurrences (compared to the size of the corpus) – and the frequencies of most words in a corpus are very low.

The significant observations can often be explained by actual differences in the language structure or at least in the language annotation scheme. Since the corpus is parallel, the differences are not due to different vocabulary etc., but the subtle genre differences on the two sides of our treebank (transcription vs subtitle) remain very visible in the resulting measures.

We can see that Cantonese has significant structural differences with its Mandarin counterpart, although some of these differences are reinforced by the UD annotation scheme while other actual structural differences may have remained hidden from our statistical analysis. Inversely, however, not all well-known structural differences between the languages can be put under scrutiny by means of the parallel treebank. The expletive, for example, is absent from our corpus – pointing to the fact that frequently discussed phenomena are not necessarily frequent syntactic phenomena. The specificity measure allows ordering the observed differences by statistical importance, the degree of astonishment, thus empirically guiding the research to actual hotspots of syntactic variation.

The annotation choices we face with different stages of prepositional grammaticalization in a parallel or comparable treebanks can be seen as part of a more general question about the goal of the syntactic annotation: The UD choice to favor similar structures whenever possible leads to skewed typological similarity measures. Future UD schemes should be evaluated as to the extent that they allow avoiding catastrophes and capturing similarities between closely related structures.

The ongoing word alignment of the parallel treebank will soon allow for more precise queries concerning the differences or similarity between the two languages. But just like for the annotation, the word alignment, too, is already a structural choice (one-to-many alignments?, one-to-zero alignments?) that determines which results can finally be extracted. Ideally the word-alignment would allow for complementary measurements that cannot be obtained on the sole sentence aligned parallel treebank. Work in progress on a parallel treebank online query tool could also benefit from the integration of these types of statistical measures. It would allow to not only search for and count pre-discovered structural discrepancy, but rather permit exploring interesting facts hidden in the raw data.

Acknowledgments

This work was supported by a grant from the PROCORE-France/Hong Kong Joint Research Scheme sponsored by the Research Grants Council and the Consulate General of France in Hong Kong (Reference No.: F-CityU107/15 and N° 35322RG); and by two Strategic Research Grants (Project No. 7004494 and No. 7004736) from City University of Hong Kong.

References

Chen, Xinying, and Kim Gerdes. "Classifying Languages by Dependency Structure: Typologies of Delexicalized Universal Dependency Treebanks", *Depling*, 2017

David C. S. LI, Cathy S. P. WONG, Wai Mun LEUNG and Sam T. S. WONG. "Facilitation of Transference: The Case of Monosyllabic Salience in Hong Kong Cantonese" Linguistics, Vol. 54(1), pp. 1–58, January 2016.

Francis, Elaine J., and Stephen Matthews. "Categoriality and object extraction in Cantonese serial verb constructions." *Natural Language & Linguistic Theory* 24.3 (2006): 751-801.

Gerdes, Kim. "Collaborative Dependency Annotation." *Depling*, 2013.

Gerdes, Kim, and Sylvain Kahane. "Dependency Annotation Choices: Assessing Theoretical and Practical Issues of Universal Dependencies." *LAW X (2016) The 10th Linguistic Annotation Workshop*: 131. 2016.

Law SP, Kong APH, Lee A, Lai CT, Lam VVV. 2012. "Cantonese Chinese corpus of oral narratives (CANON) with morphological tagging: a preliminary report." Presented in the *Workshop on Innovations in Cantonese Linguistics (WICL)*, Columbus, OH., 16-17 March 2012.

Lebart, Ludovic, André Salem, and Lisette Berry. "Recent developments in the statistical processing of textual data." *Applied Stochastic Models and Data Analysis* 7.1 (1991): 47-62.

Leung, Herman, Rafaël Poiret, Tak sum Wong, Xinying Chen, Kim Gerdes, and John Lee "Developing Universal Dependencies for Mandarin Chinese." *The 12th Workshop on Asian Language Resources*. 2016.

Lee, John. Toward a Parallel Corpus of Spoken Cantonese and Written Chinese. In *Proc. 5th International Joint Conference on Natural Language Processing* (IJCNLP), 2011.

Lee, Thomas H. T. and Colleen Wong. 1998. CANCORP: the Hong Kong Cantonese Child Language Corpus. *Cahiers de Linguistique Asie Orientale* vol. 27, no. 2, pp. 211-228.

Liu, Haitao. "Dependency direction as a means of word-order typology: A method based on dependency treebanks." *Lingua*, 120.6 (2010): 1567-1578.

Luke, Kang-Kwong, & Wong, May L-Y. 2015. The Hong Kong Cantonese Corpus: design and uses. *Journal of Chinese Linguistics* 25 (2015): 309-330

Matthews, Stephen and Virginia Yip. (2011) *Cantonese: A comprehensive grammar*. New York: Routledge.

de Marneffe, Marie-Catherine, Timothy Dozat, Natalia Silveira, Katri Haverinen, Filip Ginter, Joakim Nivre, and Christopher D. Manning. 2014. Universal Stanford Dependencies: A cross-linguistic typology. *Proceedings of the Ninth International Conference on Language Resources and Evaluation (LREC 2014)*: 4584-4592.

Nivre, Joakim. "Towards a Universal Grammar for Natural Language Processing." *CICLing (1)* 2015 (2015): 3-16.

Nivre, Joakim, Marie-Catherine de Marneffe, Filip Ginter, Yoav Goldberg, Jan Hajič, Christopher D. Manning, Ryan McDonald, Slav Petrov, Sampo Pyysalo, Natalia Silveira, Reut Tsarfaty, and Daniel Zeman. 2016a. Universal Dependencies v1: A Multilingual Treebank Collection. *Proceedings of the Tenth International Conference on Language Resources and Evaluation (LREC 2016)*: 1659-1666.

Osborne, Timothy. "Diagnostics for Constituents: Dependency, Constituency, and the Status of Function Words." *Depling*, 2015.

Ōuyáng, Juéyà. (1993) 普通話廣州話的比較與學習 *Pǔtōnghuà Guǎngzhōuhuà de bǐjiào yǔ xuéxí* (The comparison and learning of Mandarin and Cantonese). Peking: China Social Science Press.

Saunders, Peter T. *An introduction to catastrophe theory*. Cambridge University Press, 1980.

Yip, Virginia and Stephen Matthews. (2000) Syntactic transfer in a bilingual child. Bilingualism: Language and Cognition 3.3, 193-208

Yiu Yuk Man. Early Cantonese Tagged Database, presented at the *Workshop on Early Cantonese Grammar*, Dec 14 2014, Hong Kong: HKUST.

Understanding constraints on non-projectivity using novel measures

Himanshu Yadav
Jawaharlal Nehru University
Center for Linguistics
New Delhi
India
himans53_llh@jnu.ac.in

Ashwini Vaidya
IIT Delhi
Department of
Electrical Engineering
India
ird11278@ee.iitd.ac.in

Samar Husain
IIT Delhi
Department of Humanities
and Social Sciences
India
samar@hss.iitd.ac.in

Abstract

In this work we propose certain novel measures to understand non-projectivity in various syntactic phenomena in Hindi. This is an attempt to go beyond the analysis of non-projectivity in terms of certain graphical measures such as edge degree, planarity etc. Our measures are motivated by the findings in the processing literature that have investigated the interaction between working-memory constraints and syntactic complexity. Our analysis shows that the measures pattern differently for distinct phenomena and therefore could prove to be beneficial in understanding non-projectivity in a language. We also find some interesting differences in non-projectivity between conversation and news genre.

1 Introduction

One of the main aims of the modern linguistic theories has been to understand the formal properties of the grammar and its interaction with human linguistic competence (Frazier, 1985; Chomsky and Miller, 1963). In order to represent the syntactic structure of a linguistic utterance, most current theories posit some kind of a hierarchical structure (Steedman, 2000; Chomsky, 1995; Hudson, 2010). This hierarchical structure could either be represented via the notion of constituents or through dependency relations (Rambow, 2010). It is also known that languages allow for configurations that lead to discontiguous constituents. Such configurations are known to pose a challenge to grammar formalization and, not surprisingly, they are more difficult to parse computationally (Nivre, 2009; Joshi, 1990). They are also difficult to process by native speakers (Levy et al., 2012; Husain and Vasishth, 2015).

The discontiguous constituents are termed as non-projectivity in the dependency grammar literature. Non-projectivity is characterized by a non-canonical linear order of words in a sentence.[1] Formally, an arc $i{\rightarrow}j$ is non-projective if and only if there is at least one word k between i and j that i does not dominate (see Figure 1).

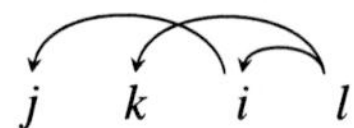

Figure 1: The dependency arc between i and its dependent j is non-projective. All other arcs are projective.

While non-projective dependencies (called discontiguous constituents in phrase structure grammar) are common in many languages that allow free word order, it is also known that not all such configurations are permitted, i.e. not all non-projective dependencies can be deemed grammatical (Joshi, 1985; Shieber, 1985). In order to describe the grammar of a language, it is therefore critical to understand the constraints on non-projectivity in that language. Understanding these constraints will throw light on the cognitive constraints that influence language comprehension and production. Needless to say, a better understanding of non-projectivity will also benefit computational parsers.

Non-projectivity occurs due to discontiguity in the yield of a node, specifically discontiguity in the head-dependent projection chain. This discontiguity in the head-dependent linear order is caused by the intervention of a constituent or sub-tree that is dependent on a head outside the current yield. The properties of this intervening element as well as the properties of the non-projective dependency (comprising a head and its dependent) can describe the constraining environ-

---

[1] This is of course a simplification. As we will discuss later, there are some constructions that are inherently non-projective.

Proceedings of the Fourth International Conference on Dependency Linguistics (Depling 2017), pages 276-286,
Pisa, Italy, September 18-20 2017

ment for a non-projective dependency. In this work, we will use such properties to identify constraints on non-projectivity in Hindi. In order to do this we use the Hindi-Urdu Dependency Treebank (HUTB) (Bhatt et al., 2009).

There has been some work on studying non-projectivity in Hindi. Mannem et al. (2009) carried out a preliminary study of non-projectivity in HUTB based on some widely used measures, e.g., gap degree, edge degree and planarity (Bodirsky et al., 2005; Kuhlmann and Nivre, 2006; Kuhlmann, 2007). In a similar and more elaborate work, Bhat and Sharma (2012) carried out a formal and linguistic characterization of non-projectivity for Hindi, Bengali, Telugu and Urdu. They characterized non-projectivity based on the nature of the linguistic phenomena (e.g., relativization, genitive constructions etc.) and the cause of non-canonicity (e.g., extraposition, scrambling, etc.). Similar to Mannem et al. (2009), they also used edge degree etc. to characterize non-projectivity.

In this paper, we go beyond this type of analysis to attempt a deeper linguistic understanding of non-projectivity in Hindi. In particular, we ask, what are the limiting conditions for a non-projective dependency? In other words, we attempt to uncover the kinds of non-projective configurations that are *disallowed* for a phenomenon. For example, while studying non-projectivity in genitive constructions, we attempt to identify which type of non-projectivity is not possible in such constructions. We examine the limiting conditions for a non-projective dependency with respect to hierarchical and linear distance and the nature of the intervening constituents and subtrees. A deeper understanding of non-projectivity in a language is critical for positing constraints on the generative power of a dependency grammar and understanding the interaction of working memory constraints and linguistic complexity.

Our paper is organized as follows, in Section 2 we motivate new measures for analyzing non-projectivity based on linear and hierarchical distance. In Section 3, we discuss these measures using a Hindi treebank. We conclude the paper in section 4.

2 A proposal for novel non-projectivity measures

Previous analyses of non-projectivity in Hindi (Mannem et al., 2009; Bhat and Sharma, 2012) and in other languages have characterized sentences that are non-projective using graph-based measures such as gap degree, edge degree, planarity and well-nestedness. While these measures have proven to be very useful, they do not explicitly capture certain information that could be used in positing constraints on non-projectivity for a particular linguistic construction. We propose three novel measures for non-projectivity in this section, based on linear word order as well as hierarchy.

2.1 Linear measures

We look at the examples in figures 3–6 to motivate the first type of linear measure. These figures show non-projective dependencies involving a genitive relation. The noun phrase (NP) *raam-kaa* 'Ram-GEN' is the dependent of *chashmaa* 'spectacles' in all these examples. Figure 2 shows the projective dependency for this phenomenon. The edge degree[2] in each of the non-projective structure is 1 (they also have same planarity), however, while 3 and 4 are grammatical, the sentences in figures 5 & 6 are completely ungrammatical. Critically, the type of intervening material that causes non-projectivity differs in these examples. In 3, the intervening element is an adverbial modifying the main verb; in 4, it is a non-finite clause modifying the main verb, and in 5, it is a relative clause modifying a noun outside the span of the genitive dependency arc. The example in figure 6 is ungrammatical because a negation intervenes. Note that the dependencies shown here are between chunks rather than individual words, which is in keeping with the HUTB representation.

These examples show that in order to understand the nature of non-projectivity for a phenomenon like genitive, it is important to study the *type of intervening material*. A metric like edge degree captures the number of intervening constituents spanned by a single edge (Kuhlmann and Nivre, 2006), but it is unable to capture certain linguistic nuances discussed above. Additionally, the type of intervening constituents also capture the complexity of these constituents. While both 3 and 4 are grammatical constructions, the intervening material in 3 is less complex than the one in 4. Capturing the complexity of the intervening

---

[2]Let e=(i, j) be a dependency arc with 'j' as the head and 'i' as the dependent. Edge degree of an arc e is the number of connected components c in the span of arc e such that c is not dominated by 'j' (Nivre, 2006).

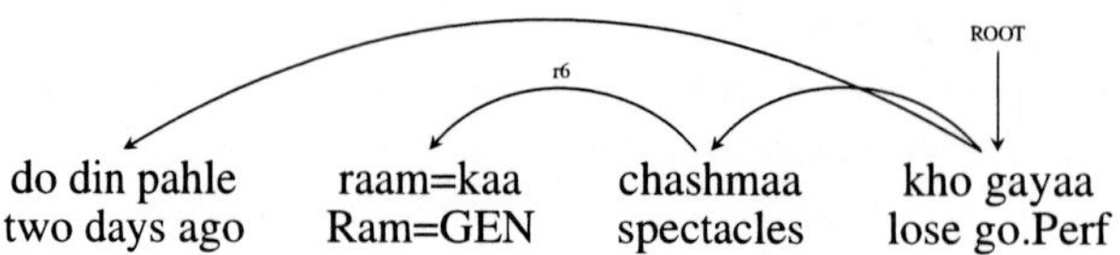

Figure 2: *'Two days ago Ram's spectacles were lost'*. Projective Genitive Construction.

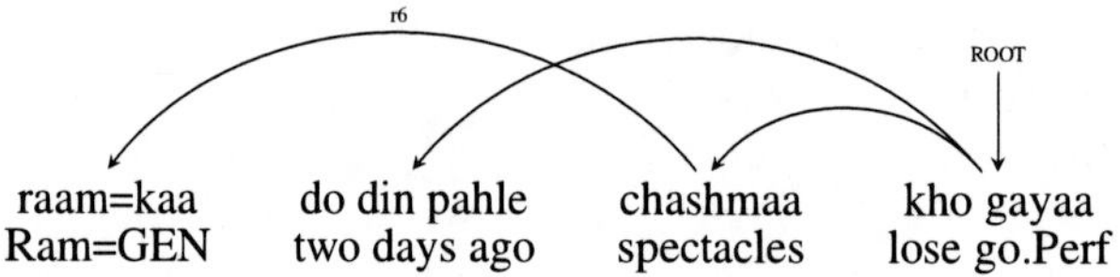

Figure 3: *'Ram's spectacles were lost two days ago'*. Non-projectivity with edge degree=1, Type of intervening constituent=NP. NP: Noun chunk.

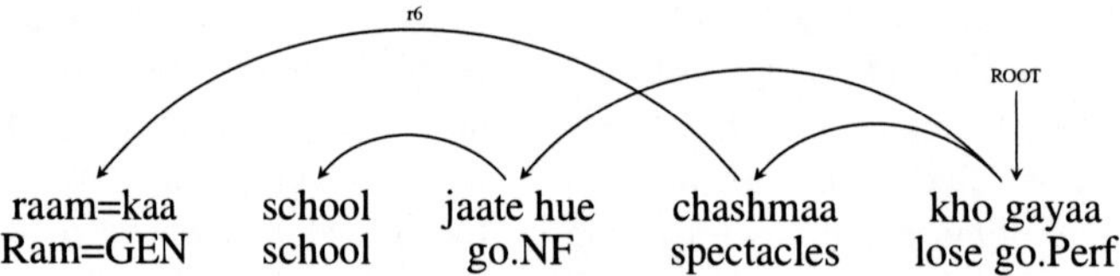

Figure 4: *'Ram's spectacles were lost while going to school'*. Non-projectivity with edge degree=1, Type of intervening constituent=VGNF, Length of intervening constituent (in words)=3. VGNF: Non-finite verb chunk.

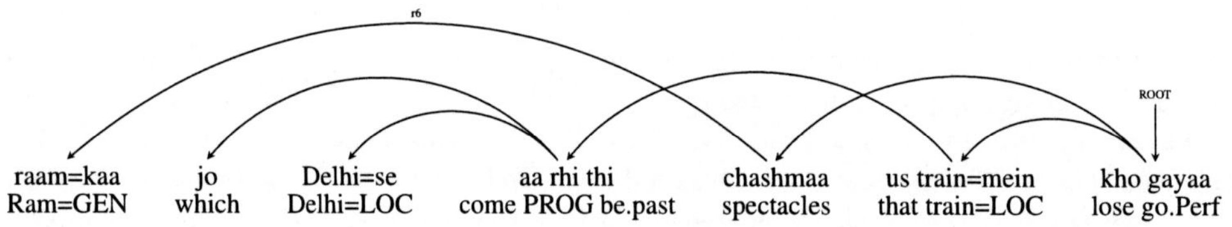

Figure 5: *'Ram's spectacles were lost in the train which was coming from Delhi'*. Non-projectivity with edge degree=1, Type of intervening constituent=VGF. VGF: Finite verb chunk.

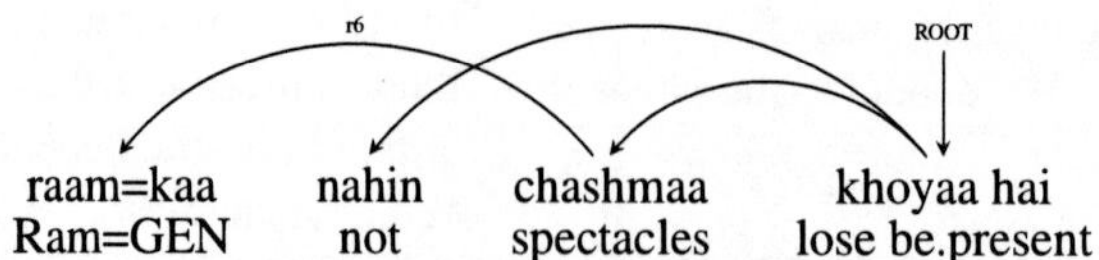

Figure 6: *'Ram's spectacles are not lost'*. Non-projectivity with edge degree=1, Type of intervening constituent=NEG. NEG: Negation.

constituents becomes important when we focus on comprehension or production of non-projective structures. It is known that non-projective structures are difficult to process (Levy et al., 2012; Husain and Vasishth, 2015). In addition we also know that the type of the intervening material between a head and its dependent matters during integration stages (Levy and Keller, 2013; Safavi et al., 2016).

As mentioned in the previous section, edge degree captures the number of intervening constituents spanned by a single edge. Intervening constituents are the independent projection chains or subtrees which modify neither the dependent nor the head of a non-projective arc, rather they modify something outside the scope of the non-projective arc. The number of these intervening constituents capture the degree to which a dependent has moved from its canonical linear position.

Again, examples 4, 7, 8 have the same edge degree (1). Intuitively, we would assume 4 to be more frequent and thereby more representative of the non-projective genitive constructions. Indeed, the average length of the intervening constituents in a genitive construction is 4. We therefore expect that *the length (in words) of the intervening constituents* will be highly constrained by the type of linguistic construction in which non-projectivity occurs. Therefore, it might be beneficial to use this as a constraint in our understanding of non-projective constructions. The larger the size of intervening constituents, the more difficult it will be to process the non-projective structure for the native speaker. Indeed, this short-dependency intuition is backed by research in psycholinguistics where it has been shown that cross-linguistically dependent-head distance tends to be short (Futrell et al., 2015). More recently, Liu et al. (2017) have argued for dependency minimization as a universal cognitive constraint. This idea has also been extended to explain the occurrence of non-projectivity across multiple languages (Gómez-Rodríguez, 2017).

2.2 Hierarchical measure

The two measures discussed in the previous section, viz., the type of intervening constituent and the length (in words) of the intervening constituents do not capture an important feature of a dependency tree, i.e., the hierarchical distance. In particular we are interested in measuring the hierarchical distance between the head of the intervening material (in a non-projective arc) and the head of the non-projective arc.

We illustrate this using examples 9–12. Examples 9 and 10 have the same type of intervening constituents and the same number of intervening constituents. But they differ with respect to the difference between the hierarchical position (or depth) of the head node of the non-projective arc (*yah* 'this') and the depth of the head of the intervening material (matrix verb). In 9, this depth difference is 1, while in 10, the difference is 2. In Figures 11 and 12 the depth difference is even higher. Interestingly, the sentences in figures 11 and 12 are less acceptable for Hindi native speakers.[3]

We propose a measure to capture the constraints on non-projectivity in terms of the *hierarchical depth difference* between the head of the non-projective arc and the head of the intervening constituent. It is evident from the examples in figures 9–12 that this measure captures the level of embedding of the non-projective arc. If the non-projective subtree is deeply embedded in the tree and the intervening constituent has a head that is higher up in the tree, we posit that the acceptability or grammaticality of the non-projective configurations will be determined by the notion of depth difference. Indeed, it has been previously shown that more embeddings in a sentence leads to processing difficulty (Gibson and Thomas, 1999).

Figure 13 shows a schematic of the environment of a non-projective dependency; X_d represents the dependent, X_h represents the head, X_i represents the intervening constituent whose head X_j is outside the span of the subtree headed by X_h. Based on the discussion in the previous sections, the constraining environment of a non-projective dependency will therefore contain the following:

(a) Type of intervening constituent X_i
(b) The length (in words) of the intervening constituents

---

[3] We note that the acceptability of 11 in comparison with 12 might be explained via the increased head-dependent distance in 12. However, a construction with the same head-dependent distance as 12 but with a lower depth difference (of 1) may be perfectly acceptable. An example of such a sentence would be *nalin yah do dinon se [logon ko kahte [chale jaa rahaa hai]] ki jaggu chor hai* 'Nalin is continuously saying this to people for last two days that Jaggu is a thief'. This shows that in these cases, depth and not the linear distance is leading to lower acceptability.

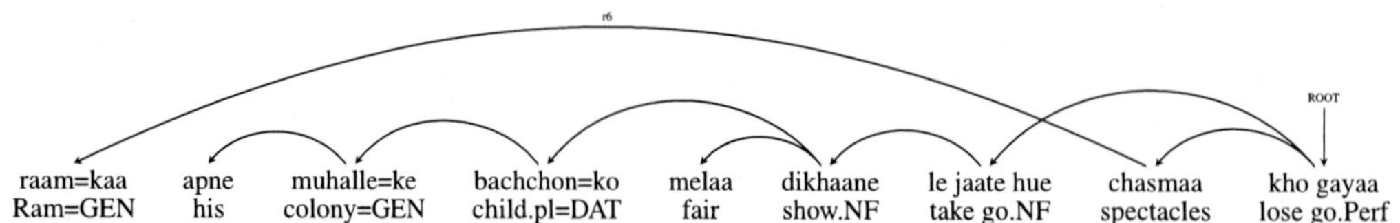

Figure 7: *'Ram's spectacles were lost while taking the children of his colony to see the fair'.* Non-projectivity with edge degree=1, Length of intervening constituents (in words)=10

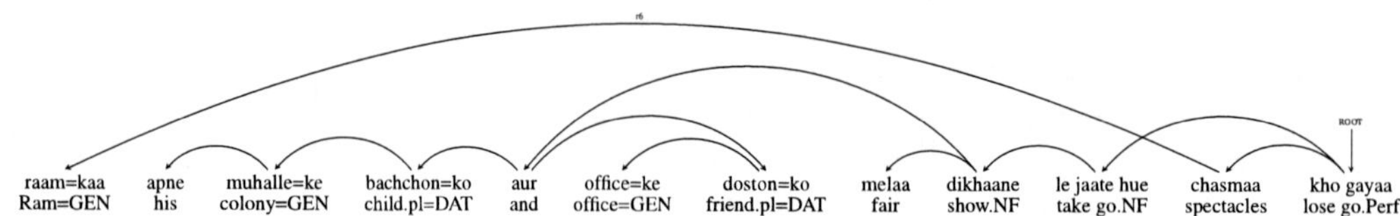

Figure 8: *'Ram's spectacles were lost while taking the children of his colony and (his) office friends to see the fair'.* Non-projectivity with edge degree=1, Length of intervening constituents (in words)=15

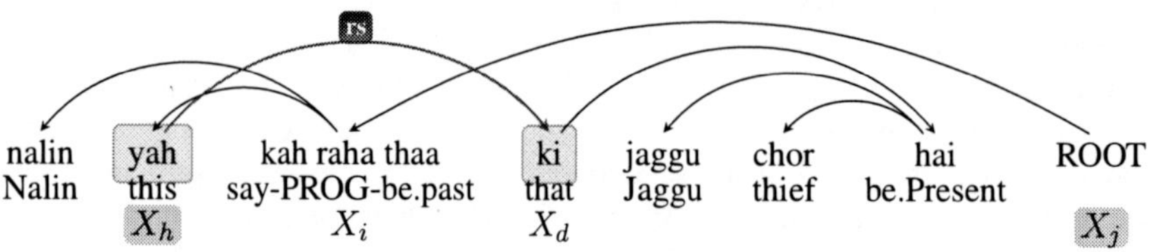

Figure 9: *'Nalin was saying that Jaagu is a thief'.* Clausal complement with nominal head. Length of intervening constituents=3, Hierarchical depth difference=1

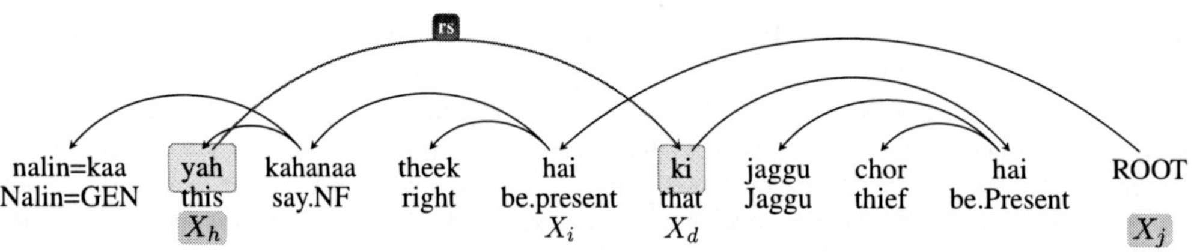

Figure 10: 'Nalin's saying that Jaggu is a thief is right'. Clausal complement with nominal head embedded in non-finite clause. Length of intervening constituents=3, Hierarchical depth difference=2

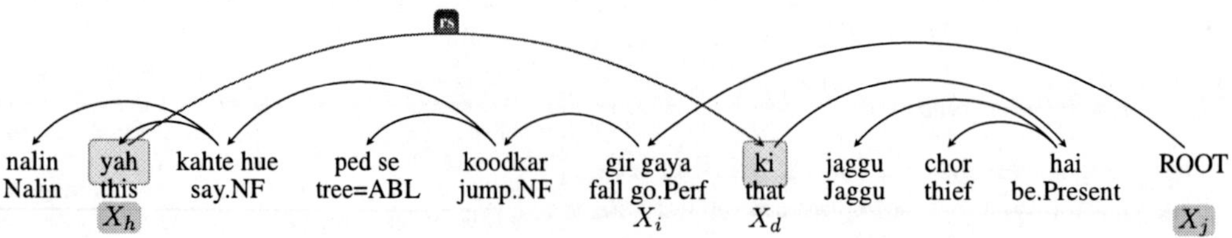

Figure 11: *'While saying that Jaggu is a thief Nalin jumped and fell from the tree'.* Hierarchical depth difference=3

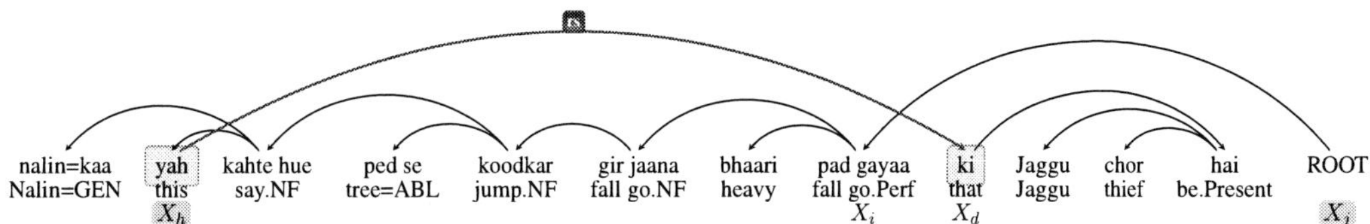

Figure 12: *'Nalin's jump and fall from the tree while saying that Jaggu is thief was a loss for him'.* Hierarchical depth difference=4

(c) The hierarchical depth difference between X_h and X_j.

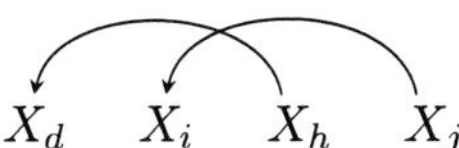

Figure 13: A non-projective configuration.

To summarize, the three measures of non-projectivity discussed above try to incorporate insights from the processing literature. Specifically, they try to reflect the notion of structural complexity and its interaction with working memory constraints. Assuming that a treebank is representative of the grammar of a language and its usage and that the proposed measures indeed reflect certain cognitive constraints, one hopes to observe some evidence for these measures while characterizing non-projectivity found in the treebank.

The measure in (a) is operationalized by using the syntactic constituent label (NP, CCP, VGNN or RBP etc.) of the intervening constituent. In order to define the property of these constituents we also see whether they are arguments or adjuncts (this information can be derived from the dependency labels).

The Hindi-Urdu Dependency Treebank (HUTB ver-0.05) was used to compute these constraints. We use the inter-chunk dependency information to extract dependency relations for a sentence. The treebank consists of 20931 sentences (Average word count per sentence: 20). The text in the treebank belongs to two genres: News (18857 sentences) and Conversation (2074 sentences). The news genre contains articles from a Hindi newspaper while the conversation has literary pieces containing dialogues.

3 Non-projectivity measures for the Hindi Treebank

In this section we try to uncover the constraining environment in which a phenomenon can occur in a non-projective configuration. In order to posit such constraints, we will use the three measures discussed in section 2: the nature of the intervening constituent, the linear distance between the head and the dependent, and the hierarchical depth difference. A constraining environment should help us in a deeper understanding of non-projectivity in a phenomenon independent of the annotation scheme. Out of the total non-projective sentences in HUTB, there are 15.4% cases that are non-projective due to annotation choices. We do not consider these cases in our analysis.

Many constructions become non-projective because of variation in word order. The word order variation could have discourse functions (Butt and King, 1996; Kidwai, 2000; Kothari, 2010). It is implied that one can projectivize these constructions by rearranging the words in their 'canonical' position. In our analysis we examine such non-projective constructions using the constraints shown in Table 1. As mentioned above, our analysis disregards the cases that are non-projective because of certain annotation choices in the treebank.

3.1 Type of the intervening constituent

Among GENITIVES, the most common type of intervening constituent is a nominal adjunct (67.7%). However, the intervening element in genitives can occasionally be non-nominal (like a conjunction, finite verb, non-finite verb etc.). Similarly, in NON-FINITE CLAUSE CONSTRUCTIONS, the intervening elements are nominal adjuncts (83%). The non-projective COORDINATION CONSTRUCTIONS and FINITE CLAUSE CONSTRUCTIONS are quite constrained with respect to the nature of intervening element. A coordination

Linguistic Phenomenon	Properties of the Intervening Constituents X_i			% non-proj	
	Category(X_i)	Avg-length(X_i)	Arg-Adj(X_i)	within	across
Genitive	NP(67.7%) CCP(9.3%) RBP(8.9%) VGF(7.2%) VGNN(3%) VGNF(2.4%)	4	Argument(25.7%) Adjunct(74.3%)	1.13%	7.2%
Non-finite Clause	NP(83%) RBP(6.6%) CCP(2.8%) VGF(2.2%)	4	Argument(31.5%) Adjunct(68.5%)	1.2%	4.6%
Coordination	NP(66.7%) CCP(33.3%)	3	Argument(38.5%) Adjunct(61.5%)	0.2%	0.5%
Finite Clause	CCP(84.5%) VGF(7.7%) NP(7.7%)	2	Argument(1.9%) Adjunct(98.1%)	0.3%	2.8%
Relative Clause	VGF(94.5%) NP(4.3%) CCP(0.5%) VGNF(0.3%) VGNN(0.1%)	3	Argument(2.9%) Adjunct(97.1%)	59.4%	23.7%

Table 1: Constraining environment for non-projectivity due to non-canonical word order. The data is taken from the News genre. Here Category(X_i) represents the phrasal category of the intervening constituents, Arg-Adj(X_i) represents whether an intervening element is either an argument or an adjunct and Avg-length(X_i) is the average length of intervening constituent(s). The *% non-proj within* construction means the percentage of non-projective constructions out of total constructions of a specific type say Genitive. The *% non-proj across* all constructions means the percentage of non-projective cases of a specific construction type out of total non-projective cases in the treebank. NP: Noun chunk, CCP: Conjunction chunk, VGNF: Non-finite verb chunk, VGNN: Verbal noun chunk, VGF: Finite verb chunk.

subtree becomes discontiguous because of a noun (66.7%) or noun-noun conjunction (33.3%). A finite clause becomes non-projective due to a paired connective (84.5%). This happens when the connective *agar* 'if' moves from its canonical sentence-initial position and intervenes between the finite verb and its modifiers. RELATIVE CLAUSE CONSTRUCTIONS have finite verbs as the intervening element due to right extraposition of the relative clause (94.5%), other types of intervening elements like noun, conjunctions, non-finite verb are rarely found. The dominant pattern that emerges from this is that when something intervenes within a dependency span to make it non-projective, it is more likely for it to be simple (e.g. noun phrase) than complex (e.g. clause).

3.2 Length of the intervening constituents

The head-dependent distance i.e. the length of the intervening constituents (in words) will vary across linguistic phenomena. The head-dependent distance is contingent on 'the size of the projection chain of an intervener'. The GENITIVE and NON-FINITE CLAUSE CONSTRUCTIONS have an average head-dependent distance of 4 words. However, in cases where a genitive construction allows an embedded non-finite clause and coordinated non-finite clause as intervening elements, the distance between the head and dependent can get quite large (up to 15 intervening words) as compared to the average of 4 words. The FINITE CLAUSE CONSTRUCTION has the average head-dependent distance of 2 words as they become non-projective due to a paired connective (which is just a single word).

3.3 Rightward scrambling & extraposition

Although the leftward scrambling of genitive noun (i.e. the genitive noun still remains to the left of its head) is more common among genitive constructions, rightward scrambling of dependent genitive noun is also observed in the treebank. Example (a) in Figure 14 shows the genitive marked noun *raam=kaa* 'Ram GEN' appearing after the copula *hai* 'is'. A similar kind of rightward scrambling causing non-projectivity is observed in case of NON-FINITE CLAUSES, where a modifier of non-finite verb is scrambled to the right of the main verb (see example (b) of Figure 14). In both cases, the scrambling could happen because the subtree headed by this noun is 'heavy' due to a relative clause modification. Such a heavy NP shift should be seen whenever the noun subtree becomes large. Non-projectivity due to right extraposition is very common in relative clause constructions in the treebank (see example (c) of Figure 14). Recent work in processing suggests that extraposition of Hindi relative clauses is highly constrained (Kothari, 2010). Together, these rightward scrambling and right-extraposition support the influence of working memory constraints during processing (Wasow, 1997; Gibson, 2000; Lewis and Vasishth, 2005).

For the construction types discussed above, we assumed that their projective counterparts had the canonical word order; the non-canonical word order in such constructions led to non-projectivity. There are some clausal complement constructions that are 'inherently' non-projective, i.e., there are no projective counterparts to these constructions. The complementizer is headed not by a finite verb, but a noun or a pronoun; an example – *mohan ne yah bataayaa ki aaj masterji school nahin aayenge* 'Mohan said that the teacher will not come to school today', where *yah* 'this' is the head of the clausal complement headed by *ki* 'that'. Out of all the clausal complements in the treebank 67.3% are of this type.

A few linguistic phenomena in the treebank are non-projective due to certain annotation choices. One such construction is the conditional or paired connective. Certain types of argument structure alternations with respect to complex predicates also become non-projective due to annotation choices. We do not include these cases in our analysis or in the computation of the non-projectivity measures. Such cases make up 15.4% of the total non-projective sentences in the treebank.

So far, we have been discussing non-projectivity using two of the three constraints that were introduced in Section 2. We will now discuss non-projectivity with respect to our third constraint, hierarchical depth difference.

3.4 Hierarchical depth difference

Linguistic	Depth Difference (no. of heads)			
Phenomenon	n=1	n=2	n=3	n>3
Genitive	88.6%	9.7%	1.7%	-
Non-finite clause	53.5%	38.2%	8.3%	-
Coordination	61.1%	38.9%	-	-
Finite Clause	18.4%	75.5%	5.1%	1%
Relative Clause	55.9%	42.2%	0.1%	1.6%
Clausal Complement	64.7%	34.9%	-	0.3%

Table 2: The depth difference constraint on non-projectivity across constructions (in the news genre)

As shown in table 2, as the depth difference increases, the no. of non-projective constructions decreases. Recall that this measure captures the level of embedding of the non-projective arc in the dependency tree. If the non-projective subtree is deeply embedded in the tree and the intervening constituent has a head that is higher up in the tree, we posit that the acceptability or grammaticality of the non-projective configurations will be determined by the notion of depth difference. This seems to be validated by the data and is consistent with previous work that has shown the cost of embedding during processing (Gibson and Thomas, 1999), also see Yngve (1960). In fact, since non-projectivity is costly, we could predict that non-projectivity at a larger depth difference will be extremely difficult to process.

It is interesting to note that the difference in percentage of non-projectivity across various depths (cf. table 2) is not the same. While the no. of non-projective constructions reduce dramatically as depth difference increases in the case of genitives, this is not true for relative clauses. Non-finite clause constructions frequently have depth differ-

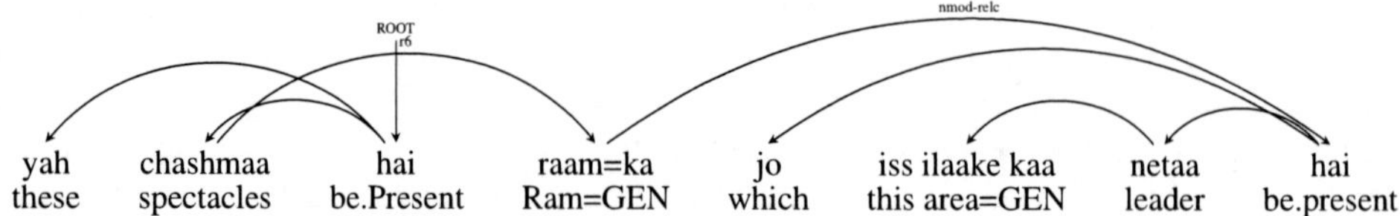

Example (a): *'These spectacles are Ram's, who is the leader of this area'*

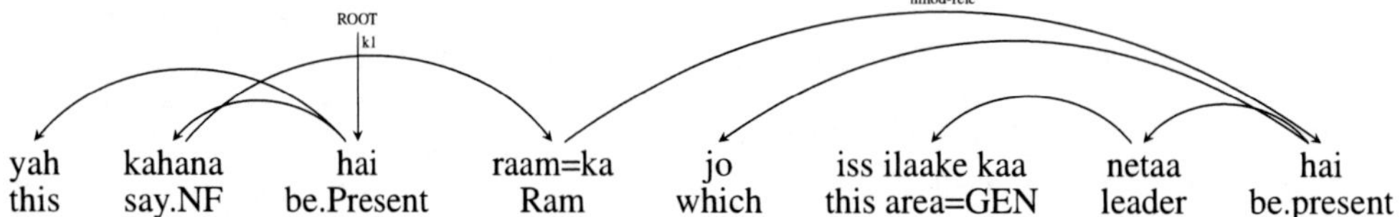

Example (b): *'This is Ram's saying, (the one) who is the leader of this area'*

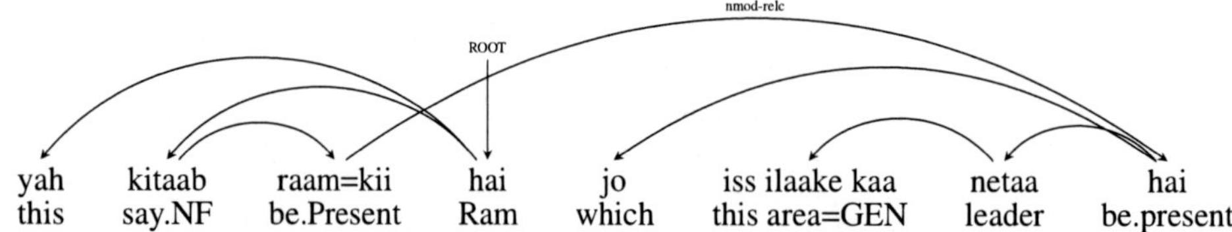

Example (c): *'This is Ram's book, (the one) who is the leader of this area'*

Figure 14: Non-projectivity due to extraposition/scrambling of a dependent to the right of the verb in (a) Genitive, (b) Non-finite clause, (c) Relative clause construction.

ence of 2. Such constructions allow shared arguments to be embedded inside a non-finite clause, which is in turn within another non-finite clause. Interestingly, there is a considerable number of non-projective cases at n=3 for the non-finite and finite clause constructions. It is very rare to have non-projectivity for depth >3. Finally, clausal complements allow a depth difference of up to 5. They allow a chain of embedded non-finite clauses inside the main clause, which increases the depth of embedded head of non-projective subtree.

3.5 Differences across genre

The news data has 18.36% non-projective sentences (3457 sentences) while conversation data has 11.14% cases of non-projectivity (231 sentences). This is surprising since one would assume conversation data to allow for more word order variation. While this requires further research, we found a considerable difference between the two genres (News vs Conversation) with respect to non-projectivity for some of the linguistic phenomena. In case of NON-FINITE CLAUSE CONSTRUCTIONS, it is more common for the intervening constituent to be an argument in the conversation data (71%) compared to the news data

(31.5%). The rightward scrambling of a genitive noun is highly productive in the conversation section of the treebank, making up 33% of all non-projective genitive constructions. This implies that speaker tends to move large phrases rightward (heavy NP shift) to minimize the dependency length in a sentence (Wasow, 1997).

Also, the maximum depth difference for genitives in the conversation data was 1, while in the news data this was 3 (cf. table 2). This points to a possibility that non-projectivity of this kind is simpler in conversation data.

Interestingly, the total number of non-projective RELATIVE CLAUSE CONSTRUCTIONS is half the amount in conversation (26.6%) as compared to news (59.4%). This is due to the frequent occurrence of relative-correlative constructions in the conversation data which are projective. E.g. (i) *ye dost jinse tumhe nafrat hai, vahi ek din tumhare kaam aayenge* 'These friends whom you hate, they will help you one day' (ii) *jisko kal tumne kitaab di thi, vah ladkaa aaj skool nahin aayaa* 'To whom you gave the book yesterday, that boy did not come to school today'. Also, embedded relative clauses, which are projective, are frequent in the conversation data. Together, these patterns support a well known claim in the production literature that syntactic choices are predominantly determined by production ease (MacDonald, 2013, amongst others), also see Arnold (2011).

4 Summary and Conclusion

This paper was an attempt to use certain novel measures to understand non-projectivity in Hindi. These measures were informed by the processing literature that has tried to formalize the notion of linguistic complexity using working memory constraints. The three measures, namely, the type of intervening constituent, its length, and the hierarchical depth, tried to capture and characterize the nature and complexity of non-projectivity in various phenomena. One would assume that overall non-projective structures will be less complex. These measures show that this is indeed true; on average the nature of intervening phrase is simple, the length of this phrase is not very large and the depth difference is small. In addition we also find support for the role of production ease in the data of the conversational genre compared to that of the news genre. It would be interesting to see the efficacy of the proposed measures across multiple languages. We intend to do this in the near future. We also hope to investigate if the proposed measures have any relevance for computational parsing.

References

JE Arnold. 2011. Ordering choices in production: For the speaker or for the listener. *Language from a cognitive perspective: Grammar, usage, and processing*, pages 199–222.

Riyaz Ahmad Bhat and Dipti Misra Sharma. 2012. Non-projective structures in indian language treebanks. In *Proceedings of TLT11*, pages 25–30.

Rajesh Bhatt, Bhuvana Narasimhan, Martha Palmer, Owen Rambow, Dipti Misra Sharma, and Fei Xia. 2009. A multi-representational and multi-layered treebank for hindi/urdu. In *Proceedings of the Third LAW*, pages 186–189.

Manuel Bodirsky, Marco Kuhlmann, and Mathias Möhl. 2005. Well-nested drawings as models of syntactic structure. In *In Tenth Conference on Formal Grammar and Ninth Meeting on Mathematics of Language*, pages 88–1. University Press.

M. Butt and T. C. King. 1996. Structural topic and focus without movement. In *M. Butt and T. H. King, eds., The First LFG Conference. CSLI Publications.*

N. Chomsky and G. A. Miller. 1963. Introduction to the formal analysis of natural languages. In *R. D. Luce, R. R. Bush, E. Galanter (Eds.), Handbook of Mathematical Psychology*, volume 2, pages 269–321. Wiley, New York.

N. Chomsky. 1995. *The Minimalist Program*. Cambridge, MA: MIT Press.

L. Frazier. 1985. Syntactic complexity. In *D. Dowty, L. Karttunen, A. Zwicky (Eds.), Natural Language Processing: Psychological, Computational and Theoretical Perspectives*, volume 37, pages 129–189. Cambridge University Press, Cambridge, UKWiley Online Library.

R. Futrell, K. Mahowald, and E. Gibson. 2015. Large-scale evidence of dependency length minimization in 37 languages. *Proceedings of the National Academy of Sciences*, 112(33):10336–10341.

Edward Gibson and James Thomas. 1999. Memory limitations and structural forgetting: The perception of complex ungrammatical sentences as grammatical. *Language and Cognitive Processes*, 14(3):225–248.

Edward Gibson. 2000. Dependency locality theory: A distance-based theory of linguistic complexity. In Alec Marantz, Yasushi Miyashita, and Wayne O'Neil, editors, *Image, Language, brain: Papers from the First Mind Articulation Project Symposium*. MIT Press, Cambridge, MA.

Carlos Gómez-Rodríguez. 2017. On the relation between dependency distance, crossing dependencies, and parsing: Comment on dependency distance: a new perspective on syntactic patterns in natural languages by haitao liu et al. *Physics of Life Reviews*.

R. Hudson. 2010. *An introduction to Word Grammar*. Cambridge University Press.

S. Husain and S. Vasishth. 2015. Non-projectivity and processing constraints: Insights from hindi. In *Proceedings of the Third Depling*, pages 141–150.

Aravind K. Joshi. 1985. Tree adjoining grammars: how much context-sensitivity is required to provide reasonable structural descriptions? In David R. Dowty, Lauri Karttunen, and Arnold Zwicky, editors, *Natural Language Parsing*, pages 206–250. Cambridge University Press, Cambridge.

Aravind K. Joshi. 1990. Processing crossed and nested dependencies: An automaton perspective on the psycholinguistic results. *Language and Cognitive Processes*, 5:1–27.

A. Kidwai. 2000. *XP-Adjunction in universal grammar: Scrambling and binding in Hindi- Urdu*. Oxford University Press, New York.

A. Kothari. 2010. *Processing Constraints And Word Order Variation In Hindi Relative Clauses*. Ph.D. thesis, Stanford University.

Marco Kuhlmann and Joakim Nivre. 2006. Mildly non-projective dependency structures. In *Proceedings of COLING-ACL*, pages 507–514.

Marco Kuhlmann. 2007. *Dependency Structures and Lexicalized Grammars*. Ph.D. thesis, Saarland University.

Roger Levy and Frank Keller. 2013. Expectation and Locality Effects in German Verb-final Structures. *Journal of Memory and Language*, 68(2):199–222.

R. Levy, E. Fedorenko, M. Breen, and E. Gibson. 2012. The processing of extraposed structures in English. *Cognition*, 122(1):12–36.

R. L. Lewis and S. Vasishth. 2005. An activation-based model of sentence processing as skilled memory retrieval. *Cognitive Science*, 29:1–45.

Haitao Liu, Chunshan Xu, and Junying Liang. 2017. Dependency distance: a new perspective on syntactic patterns in natural languages. *Physics of Life Reviews*.

Maryellen MacDonald. 2013. How language production shapes language form and comprehension. *Frontiers in Psychology*, 4:226.

P. Mannem, H. Chaudhry, and A. Bharati. 2009. Insights into non-projectivity in hindi. In *Proceedings of ACL-IJCNLP 2009 SRW*, pages 10–17.

Joakim Nivre. 2006. Constraints on non-projective dependency parsing. In *EACL*.

Joakim Nivre. 2009. Non-projective dependency parsing in expected linear time. In *Proceedings of ACL and IJCNLP*, ACL '09, pages 351–359.

O. Rambow. 2010. The simple truth about dependency and phrase structure representations: An opinion piece. In *Proceedings of ACL*, pages 337–340.

Molood S. Safavi, Samar Husain, and Shravan Vasishth. 2016. Dependency resolution difficulty increases with distance in persian separable complex predicates: Evidence for expectation and memory-based accounts. *Frontiers in Psychology*, 7:403.

S.M. Shieber. 1985. Evidence against the context-freeness of natural language. *Linguistics and Philosophy*, 8:333–343.

M. Steedman. 2000. *The Syntactic Process*. Cambridge, MA: MIT Press.

T. Wasow. 1997. Remarks on grammtical weight. *Language Variation and Change*, 9:81–105.

Victor H Yngve. 1960. A model and an hypothesis for language structure. *Proceedings of the American philosophical society*, 104(5):444–466.

Core Arguments in Universal Dependencies

Daniel Zeman
Charles University
Faculty of Mathematics and Physics
Institute of Formal and Applied Linguistics
Prague, Czechia
`zeman@ufal.mff.cuni.cz`

Abstract

We investigate how core arguments are coded in case-marking Indo-European languages. Core arguments are a central concept in Universal Dependencies, yet it is sometimes difficult to match against terminologies traditionally used for individual languages. We review the methodology described in (Andrews, 2007), and include brief definitions of some basic terms. Statistics from 26 UD treebanks show that not all treebank providers define the core-oblique boundary the same way. Therefore we propose some refinement and particularization of the guidelines that would improve cross-treebank consistency on the one hand, and be more sensitive to the traditional grammar on the other.

1 Introduction

The opposition of core vs. oblique dependents is one of the central concepts in Universal Dependencies (Nivre et al., 2016); this distinction is intentionally preferred to the argument/adjunct distinction. However, difficulties in recognizing core arguments in individual languages, combined with often incompatible traditional terminology, have led to confusion and data inconsistency. UD documentation has greatly improved since its version 1 and provides now a list of potential criteria that may help to draw the core vs. oblique borderline; however, it is still just a set of hints, not a definition. The English UD uses a relatively simple rule: as soon as a preposition is involved, the noun phrase cannot be analyzed as a core argument. Unfortunately, there are many languages where the situation is more complex. In the present work we are particularly interested in languages that use both case morphology and prepositions to mark arguments.

We review one possible universal methodology to identify coding of core arguments, and show how it applies to these languages. Terms like argument, transitive verb or indirect object are often taken for known and granted (both in the UD guidelines and in the literature) but the problem is that their definition may differ by language or by author, and it is not easy to see how they work across languages. Therefore we briefly define the necessary terms as well.

2 Core Arguments in Language Typology

In this section we provide a brief definition of core arguments; for a much more detailed discussion see (Andrews, 2007), which is our primary source.

2.1 Arguments and Adjuncts

Arguments are noun phrases that fulfill semantic roles determined by verbs, or more generally by predicates. Depending on language, the verb may also specify requirements on the position of the individual arguments and on their form, such as morphological case marking or preposition.

In contrast, adjuncts are noun phrases that specify additional circumstances such as location, time and manner. Neither their form nor their meaning is determined by the verb. They can accompany any predicate; some collocations may be difficult to interpret semantically but they are not ungrammatical. Likewise, the form of the adjuncts is determined by their meaning rather than by the verb.

Hence, the phrase marked by the preposition *on* is an argument in *I rely on him* or in *I will act on the matter*, but it is an adjunct in *I will work on Saturday* or *I live on an island*. These examples are relatively easy to understand; however, in general the argument-adjunct distinction is not always trivial, and UD avoids it (from the guidelines: "We take the distinction to be sufficiently subtle (and its existence as a categorical distinction sufficiently questionable) that the best practical solution is to

Proceedings of the Fourth International Conference on Dependency Linguistics (Depling 2017), pages 287-296,
Pisa, Italy, September 18-20 2017

eliminate it.") Nevertheless, we will see that even for the distinction between core and oblique arguments, it is sometimes necessary to make sure that the noun phrase is actually an argument and not an adjunct. Whenever we say 'argument' in the rest of the paper, we think of it as defined in the beginning of this section.

2.2 Transitive Verbs

The most reliable means of distinguishing between core and oblique arguments are the encoding strategies such as word order, adpositions and morphological case. However, the strategies are always specific to a language and cannot be used in a cross-linguistically applicable definition. Therefore we start with semantic roles to identify *prototypical core arguments*, then we observe the strategies that the language uses to mark them, and finally generalize to other arguments using the same strategy, despite their semantic roles being different from the prototypical core arguments.

The prototypical core can be observed with *primary transitive verbs,* i.e. verbs that take two arguments whose semantic roles are *agent* and *patient,* respectively. The agent, typically an animate entity, is responsible for an action, and the patient is directly affected by the action. *To kill* is an example of a primary transitive verb: in *George killed the dragon,* George is the agent who did the killing (note that it is not necessary for an agent to act willingly; it could also be an accident). Without any doubt, the dragon is the entity most affected by the killing, and the killing caused a change of the dragon's state. Hence the dragon qualifies as the patient.

Languages differ in how they make clear who killed whom. In English, it is the position of the arguments relative to the verb. In Czech, the agent would be in its nominative form, and the patient in the accusative.[1] However, in good many languages the same coding strategy is also used with verbs whose two arguments have other semantic roles. For instance, *to love* takes two arguments but it is not a *primary* transitive verb because the roles of the arguments are better described as "experiencer" and "goal" rather than "agent" and "patient". Nevertheless, the verb is transitive in both English and Czech because the two arguments are marked in these languages in exactly the same way as the arguments of *to kill.*

Following (Andrews, 2007), if a noun phrase is serving as an argument of a two-argument verb, and receiving a morphological and syntactic treatment normally accorded to an agent of a primary transitive verb, it has the **grammatical function A;** analogically, an argument receiving treatment normally accorded to a patient of a primary transitive verb has the grammatical function **P**.[2]

2.3 Intransitive Verbs

If a verb takes just a single argument, the verb is called *intransitive* and its argument has the grammatical function **S.** Depending on language (and in some languages depending on individual verbs), the S argument of intransitive verbs may conform to the same grammatical rules as the A argument of transitive verbs, or as the P argument, or it can be different from both A and P.

2.4 Core and Oblique Arguments in UD

S, A and P are considered core grammatical functions (Andrews, 2007, p. 164). As UD refers to Andrews,[3] we can project to UD: Arguments that have one of the **S/A/P functions are core arguments.** Nominals whose grammatical function is A or S are called *subjects* and their dependency relation to the verb is nsubj. Nominals whose grammatical function is P are called (direct) *objects* and their dependency relation to the verb is obj. Both subject and object are considered *core arguments.* In addition, UD uses a special relation iobj for what it calls *indirect objects;* we will investigate them in Section 4.

Using the concepts defined so far, it is now possible to lay down rules for core arguments in individual languages. For instance, in English, if a bare noun phrase (i.e. without a preposition) is an argument of a verb, it is a core argument; if it occurs in a simple declarative clause and precedes the verb, it is its subject; if it follows the verb, it is an object. Note the important condition *if it is an argument, not adjunct.* While adjuncts usually take prepositions in English, they occasionally appear as bare noun phrases too; as an example, consider

---

[1] Unless the verb is in its passive form.

[2] Note that some authors use the terms *agent* and *patient* to refer to what we call A and P here, rather than to the semantic roles; cf. the functors on the t-layer of the Prague Dependency Treebank (Hajič et al., 2006). It is important not to confuse that terminology with ours: for example, the two arguments of *to love* would then be agent and patient, while we argue that they are not.

[3] http://universaldependencies.org/u/overview/syntax.html, retrieved 2017-07-23

the temporal adjunct *this week* in *I am not working this week.*

On the other hand, verbs in many languages have arguments that are marked by coding strategies that are also used by adjuncts, but that are different from strategies used by core arguments. Such arguments are called *oblique*. For instance, the second argument of *act* in *I will act on the matter* is marked by the preposition *on*. Since core arguments in English do not take prepositions, this is an oblique argument. In UD, both oblique arguments and adjuncts are attached to the verb via an `obl` relation (if they are noun phrases).

Note that the methodology described in this section is not the only possible. (Dixon, 2012, vol. 1 sec. 3.2 and vol. 2 sec. 13) defines core arguments as those that "must be either stated or understood from the context;" the opposite of core are *peripheral arguments*. Dixon's core arguments are in spirit similar to those of Andrews, but his definition does not guarantee that no verbs have their core arguments marked by "oblique" strategies.

3 Languages with Case-Marking Morphology

A number of Indo-European languages have the morphological category of case. In these languages, the most typical coding of core arguments is the nominative case (subject) and the accusative case (object). However, there are usually more cases than these two, and the question arises whether arguments in other morphological cases count as core arguments. (Andrews, 2007) gives an example from German: the verb *helfen* ("to help") takes two arguments, one in nominative and the other in dative. We can say that *helfen* is a primary transitive verb because the roles of the two arguments are agent and patient. It can also be passivized, which is a typical property of transitive verbs; however, unlike verbs with accusative objects, the dative argument of *helfen* stays in the dative and does not become subject when the verb appears in the passive voice. We thus have an argument whose grammatical behavior is not identical with the more typical accusative object, yet it is sufficiently similar to qualify as a core argument. In consequence, all arguments that are bare nominals in dative are core arguments in German.[4]

A similar observation can be made in Slavic languages. In fact everything that we just said about the German verb *helfen* also applies to the Czech verb *pomoci* ("to help"). However, Czech has more cases than German, and there are two-argument verbs whose second argument is neither accusative nor dative. Bare genitives and instrumentals may act as arguments too; moreover, there are prepositional arguments in genitive, dative, accusative, locative or instrumental. Many of these verbs can be passivized in the same way as *pomoci*. For example, the verb *hýbat* ("to move") takes an instrumental patient-object: in *Martin hýbá nábytkem* "Martin moves the furniture", the noun *nábytek* ("furniture") takes its instrumental form. When passivized, the agent disappears and the patient stays in instrumental: *Nábytkem bylo hýbáno* "The furniture has been moved."

A somewhat different example is the verb *dotknout se* ("to touch"). This verb is inherently reflexive, i.e. obligatorily accompanied by the reflexive pronoun *se*.[5] It takes two arguments: the agent is in nominative as usual, and the patient is in genitive. According to the semantic roles we could argue that it is a primary transitive verb. However, reflexive verbs cannot be passivized in Czech: **Bylo se ho dotknuto* ("He has been touched") is not grammatical. Thus we have a two-argument verb whose arguments pass the tests on coreness laid out in Section 2, yet it does not permit passivization, an operation usually associated with transitive verbs (note however that passivization is not universal and cannot be added as a requirement for transitive verbs).

So we have three types of transitive verbs w.r.t. passivization (1. accusative; 2. non-accusative non-reflexive; 3. reflexive). We can also observe varying degree of coreness. The largest proportion of *primary* transitive verbs will indisputably be found among verbs with accusative objects. Verbs taking objects in genitive, dative and instrumental often select roles quite different from the (proto-) patient; only a handful can be regarded as primary transitive verbs. Even harder to find are patients among prepositional arguments, but some of them would deserve to be at least considered as candi-

---

[4]Note that this finding is not without controversy. Some authors classify the German dative as an oblique case, although they do not specify what are the properties their classification is based on (Foley, 2007, p. 377).

[5]With inherently reflexive verbs, the reflexive pronoun (sometimes termed particle), although syntactically autonomous, is part of the verbal lexeme, not an argument. However, transitive verbs can take reflexive pronouns as their objects.

dates. At the same time, bare accusative is very rarely used for adjuncts, which are slightly more common among other bare noun phrases, and the majority of them are prepositional phrases.

Strictly following the tests from Section 2 and from (Andrews, 2007), all Czech arguments would be core and none of them would be oblique. While this "classification" aligns with the notion of objects in the Czech grammar (see Section 5), it is of no benefit. It does not make sense to delimit the core of a set if it comprises the entire set; furthermore, the identification of core arguments would now be reduced to the argument-adjunct distinction, which UD wanted to eliminate.

So, is there a way to interpret Section 2 with less extreme results? There is one word that may provide the remedy. In 2.2 we say that the P function is recognized by treatment *normally* accorded to a patient of a primary transitive verb. Now we showed that bare accusative is the "most normal" coding strategy and prepositional phrases are still possible, but arguably "least normal" for patients. Out of the three possible coding strategies (bare accusatives, bare non-accusatives and prepositional phrases), we could decide that one or two are not normal enough. Our cross-linguistic detection of core arguments will become a bit less deterministic but more flexible; it may be the right compromise to use.

4 Ditransitive Verbs and Indirect Objects

Predicates may define more than two roles. In the Czech sentence *Firma mu zvýšila plat z dvaceti na třicet tisíc korun* lit. "Company him raised salary from twenty to thirty thousand crowns" (Lopatková et al., 2016) the verb *zvýšit* ("raise") has four or five arguments.[6] With an extreme interpretation of Section 2 we could even claim that all of them are core arguments. It is usually not assumed that languages have that many core arguments; nevertheless, it is accepted that some verbs in some languages have three. Such verbs are called *ditransitive*.

Verbs of giving, taking and related concepts (e.g. teaching = giving knowledge) are prototypical examples in many languages. Their arguments correspond to the semantic roles of agent, theme (or patient) and recipient (Dryer, 2007). In terms of grammatical relations they correspond to sub-

ject, direct and indirect object. There is a confusion potential though. Some grammars will define indirect object as the argument with the recipient role. However, this argument is not necessarily a core argument by our definition: in English in *John gave Mary a flower*, the recipient *(Mary)* is a core argument; but in *John gave a flower to Mary*, the recipient is oblique. When we restrict ourselves to core arguments, there are clearly languages and verbs with two objects but it is less clear whether (and why) one of them deserves a special term. (Andrews, 2007) notes that "the status of the notion of 'indirect object' is problematic and difficult to sort out. The top priority is to work out what properties recipients and themes do and do not share with P arguments of primary transitive verbs."

In Universal Dependencies, the v2 guidelines say that "The indirect object of a verb is any nominal phrase that is a core argument of the verb but is not its subject or (direct) object." Such a definition is not sufficient for us—any core argument that is not a subject is an object. The UD guidelines "define" the (direct) object as the second most core argument after subject. They do not provide means to quantify coreness, though. For our group of languages, we could use the observation from Section 3 that there are three coding strategies ordered by decreasing convincingness of their core status. However, UD also assumes that the relation `iobj` is only used with predicates that have more than one object, i.e., the indirect object cannot exist without a direct one. This rule would have to be changed, otherwise we cannot say that all bare dative arguments are `iobj`. For example, the German verb *helfen* does not have any accusative object that could be labeled `obj`.

5 Traditional Terminology

Traditional grammars in good many languages use less restrictive definitions of object than UD. It is not unusual to encounter non-accusative and even prepositional objects, no matter of their status as core or oblique arguments.

The school grammar of Czech (Havránek and Jedlička, 1966) is a concise but respected piece of work, which does not diverge from the mainstream terminology used by linguists. It provides a definition of object that is identical to our definition of argument in Section 2.1. Indirect object is mentioned only briefly as a possible name

---

[6] Depending on whether the beneficiary *him* is accepted as argument rather than adjunct.

	Nom	Acc	Dat	Gen	Abl	Loc	Ins	Voc	None
be	36/0	20/8	2/1	7/8		0/12	3/3		
bg	9/1	14/1	3/0						46/27
cs	29/0	29/5	5/2	3/7		0/12	3/3		2/1
cs$_2$	27/0	31/6	4/2	3/7		0/12	4/3		1/0
cs$_3$	32/0	27/4	1/3	2/10		0/12	5/2		1/0
cu	26/0	21/9	15/4	7/4		0/7	2/2	2/0	
de	35/0	19/6	3/20	0/1					6/11
el	35/0	29/29		1/2				1/0	2/1
got	28/0	26/6	15/20	2/1				1/0	
grc	26/0	34/7	14/5	6/6				2/0	
grc$_2$	23/0	31/11	14/6	5/8				1/0	1/0
hr	32/0	30/7	3/0	4/7		0/10	2/2		
la	24/0	33/8	8/0		16/9			1/0	
la$_2$	36/0	19/15	5/0		5/19	1/0			0/1
la$_3$	24/0	31/11	9/0	1/0	9/13			1/0	1/0
lt	33/0	22/6	5/0	11/5		7/0	7/1		2/1
lv	37/0	21/6	8/5	2/4		15/0			1/0
pl	29/0	20/7	4/0	5/8		0/10	3/3		10/0
pt	1/0	6/0	1/0						57/35
ru	29/0	15/8	3/4	5/8		0/19	6/3		
ru$_2$	34/0	20/7	3/3	5/7		0/11	6/3		
sa	43/0	30/0	1/0	4/0	3/0	6/0	9/0	3/0	1/0
sk	27/0	24/6	6/2	1/6		0/9	2/3		14/0
sl	22/0	24/8	6/1	6/4		0/14	0/6		10/0
sl$_2$	25/1	25/7	6/0	6/3		0/10	0/4		14/0
uk	33/0	22/9	4/0	4/10		0/10	4/3		

Table 1: Distribution (percentage) of morphological cases found at nominal dependents of verbs. Both occurrences with / without adposition are counted. Only Indo-European languages with three or more cases in UD 2.0 are shown. Languages are identified by their ISO 639 codes; when there are multiple treebanks per language, numerical indices are used instead of identifiers for brevity. Highlight red = mostly core relations (including `expl`). **Highlight blue** = mostly oblique, but significant (10% or more) amount of core also present.

for the dative argument of ditransitives. Textbooks use a question test to distinguish objects from non-objects. If a dependent of the verb can be queried by an interrogative adverb *(where, when, how)*, or by one of a few additional expressions such as *for what purpose*, it is an adverbial modifier—even if realized as a noun phrase! If we must use an interrogative pronoun *(who, what)* it is either a subject (if the pronoun is in nominative) or an object (otherwise). Thus in *spoléhám na kamarády* ("I rely on friends"), the prepositional phrase is object because the only plausible question is with a pronoun: *Na koho spoléhám?* ("Who do I rely on?"). In contrast, the prepositional phrase in *pojedu na Slovensko* ("I will go to Slovakia") is not normally queried by **Na co pojedu?* "What will I go to?"

Instead, we use an adverb and ask *Kam pojedu?* "Where will I go?" Thus this phrase is not an object. If objects are defined this way, then most objects are arguments and most adverbials are adjuncts; the notion of core arguments does not play a role.

According to (Karlík et al., 2016), some more detailed grammar descriptions do distinguish indirect objects but they still do not restrict objects to core arguments. Bare accusative objects are direct (even in the rare cases when a verb has two accusative objects). Objects in other cases, including prepositional objects, are indirect (even with verbs like *pomoci* "to help" where no direct object is possible). A verb is transitive if it takes a direct object. Looking back at Section 3, we see that these direct objects are always core arguments and they belong to the most core-like subset. Indirect objects may or may not be core arguments depending on how strictly we follow the principles from Section 2.

Such a perspective is not specific to Czech; it is rather dominant in European linguistics.

In their comparative grammar of Slavic languages, (Sussex and Cubberley, 2006, p. 339, 351–352) use the term *transitive verb* for verbs whose object is a bare noun phrase in any case; verbs with prepositional objects are neither transitive nor intransitive. *Direct object* is a synonym for bare accusative; other objects are referred to as *non-accusative objects* and *prepositional objects*. *Indirect object* seems to be used just for the semantic role of recipient (expressed by bare dative), probably assuming that the English readership will find the term familiar.

Another example, this time outside the Slavic group, is the cannonical grammar of German. (Helbig and Buscha, 1998, p. 53 and 545) distinguish accusative object, dative object, genitive object and prepositional object. Adjunct-like noun phrases are considered adverbial modifiers. Transitive verbs are those that take an accusative object and this object can become subject in a passive clause. Verbs that take an accusative object but cannot be passivized (*enthalten* "contain," *bekommen* "get" etc.) are called *medial verbs (Mittelverben)*. Intransitive verbs are those that do not take an accusative object, regardless whether they take a non-accusative object, prepositional object, obligatory adverbial or nothing at all.

It is neither prohibited nor unusual that the UD terminology diverges from the "traditional" one. Partly because there are many traditions, inconsistent with each other. However, it would be nice to at least preserve the distinctions expected in traditional grammar, and to be able to map the UD data to whatever annotation is expected by various communities. Even if UD does not aim at distinguishing arguments from adjuncts universally, the distinction is obviously important in grammars of many languages and there should be standardized means to capture it on the language-particular level.

6   Current UD Annotation

Let us now examine how the core-oblique distinction is dealt with in the current release (2.0) of Universal Dependencies. In order to stay focused on the issues discussed in the previous sections, we limit ourselves to Indo-European languages with case morphology. Table 1 gives an overview. In total, there are 26 UD treebanks (19 languages). Verb-dependent nominals in the data take from 3 to 8 different case forms (including the vocative, which marks a special type of dependent); some nominals are "caseless" (meaning that their annotation does not include the case feature, i.e. either the word does not inflect, or the annotation is incomplete).

Bulgarian and Portuguese represent a larger group of languages where the case system has been reduced to personal pronouns; but only in these two languages the actual numbers for each case surpassed 0.5% of examined nodes. Otherwise, there are all Balto-Slavic languages, all classical Indo-European languages (Ancient Greek, Latin, Gothic, Sanskrit), Modern Greek and German. Some languages have two or three treebanks provided by different groups. Case distribution differs across these treebank sets, but the difference is usually not dramatic. The largest gap can be observed between la_2 and the other two Latin treebanks; besides domain differences, the likely reason is that la and la_3 contain classical Latin while la_2 is from the 13th century.

The differences are more significant when we investigate for each case form whether and how often it occurs with a core dependency relation. Bare nominatives and accusatives are almost always core arguments. Bare datives and genitives also appear as core arguments in convincing numbers. Then the coding seems to be more and more oblique across the ablative, instrumental and locative down to prepositions. Most treebank providers seem to have simply adopted the English rule that oblique are those arguments with prepositions. Occurrences of the `obl` relation among bare noun phrases might as well just mean that these phrases are adjuncts; however, since UD does not distinguish oblique arguments from adjuncts, we cannot verify this hypothesis.

Table 2 is a zoom-in view of cases vs. relations in UD Czech 2.0. The annotation is ported from the Prague Dependency Treebank, which uses the traditional definition where object = argument; that is why the core relations appear in all nominal forms including those with prepositions.

Tables 3 and 4 demonstrate that while the current UD Russian SynTagRus incorporates the English rule for obliqueness, the first release (1.3), directly converted from the original SynTagRus annotation, was much closer to what we see in Czech. In the 1.3 release, nmod under verbs (now labeled obl), marked only nominals that are not traditional objects, i.e. adjuncts. In 2.0, these can be no longer distinguished from prepositional objects. Even if it is correct to assume that prepositional arguments are oblique in Russian, there is arguably a substantial amount of information that is important in Russian grammar and was available in the original data, but it is lost in the current UD release.

7 Refined Definition of Objects

Let us now summarize the issues identified in the preceding sections and propose refined guidelines that will hopefully address the issues better (at least in the studied subset of Indo-European languages).

There are three groups of arguments that are traditionally called objects and could be considered as object candidates in UD, ordered by decreasing strength of evidence of their coreness: bare accusatives, bare non-accusatives and prepositional phrases. UD assumes the core-oblique boundary to be clear-cut but it isn't, because identification of primary transitive verbs is not always trivial, and their distribution among the above groups is unbalanced. Nevertheless, drawing the line between bare nominals and prepositional phrases (which is what the majority of treebanks already adopts) seems a reasonable compromise.

In order to preserve the important distinction between prepositional objects and adjuncts, we propose to annotate prepositional objects by the language-specific relation obl:arg (except for demoted subjects in passive constructions, which should use obl:agent, a practice already established in several UD treebanks).

Bare non-accusatives can be considered core arguments in languages where there are reasonable examples of primary transitive verbs using these cases. (We have shown examples from German and Czech but we have not proved that all cases in all languages from Table 1 meet the criteria. We do believe though that the criteria are met for dative, genitive and instrumental in Slavic languages.) It might be useful to mark them by a language-specific label obj:nacc, although it would be just a shortcut: one can obtain the case information from the morphological features.

As for indirect objects, their current UD definition is problematic. It seems appealing to define them as core arguments that are mostly object-like, but grammatical rules applying to them are somewhat different from those used with the *prevailing* type of objects (i.e. the type that covers the largest group of primary transitive verbs). That is, instead of obj:nacc proposed above, we would use iobj for non-accusative objects (cf. (Karlík et al., 2016)). However, it would also wipe out indirect objects from English, which is a bit unfortunate, given that English seems to be responsible for introducing the very concept of iobj in UD. Hence the new guideline should perhaps provide more freedom for language-specific rules, saying that it is possible to mark a subclass of objects as secondary/indirect on language-specific grounds. In the long term, the relation should probably become a language-specific subtype of obj.

8 A Note on Subjects

In comparison to the various types of objects, identifying nominal subjects is relatively straightforward in our group of languages. They can be easily recognized by the nominative case and by cross-referencing on the verb (person, number and gender); they can hardly ever be confused with adjuncts. Occasional confusion with objects may stem from morphological ambiguity: in the Czech sentence *Krávy štípou mouchy*, both the nouns *krávy* "cows" and *mouchy* "flies" are in a form shared by nominative and accusative; the (probable) English meaning is "Flies sting cows" but since word order is flexible in Czech, it could also mean "Cows sting flies."

Tables 2 to 4 reveal that a significant subset of subjects in Slavic languages have a genitive form. However, these genitives are caused by numerals in quantified phrases, not by the verb. Under certain conditions, Slavic numerals and quantifiers require that the counted noun takes the genitive form.[7] The numeral itself has its nominative/accusative form, and the entire phrase (numeral + noun) behaves like nominative/accusative singular neuter (gender and number are cross-referenced on the verb). Hence in *Přišlo jen pět dětí* "Only five children came," the verb *přišlo* "came" has a singular neuter form, the numeral

---

[7]In addition, the genitive can be used partitively without an overt quantifier. In this case it no longer looks like a quantified phrase but it could be understood as one with an elided quantifier.

	nsubj	nsubj:pass	obj	iobj	expl:pv	expl:pass	obl	discourse
Nom (29%)	95	4						
Acc (29%)			69		21	7	2	
Dat (5%)	1		36	33	15		14	1
Gen (3%)	23	1	60	2			14	
Ins (3%)			26	4			69	
Acc+ADP (5%)			37	9			54	
Dat+ADP (2%)			31	3			66	
Gen+ADP (7%)	1		7	2			89	
Loc+ADP (12%)			10	2			88	
Ins+ADP (3%)			28	5			66	
None (2%)	58	1	19	6			12	
None+ADP (1%)	1		13	3			83	

Table 2: UD Czech. Distribution of core and oblique relations for individual case forms. Numbers indicate how many % of the nominals in the given case got the given relation. ADP indicates a preposition.

	nsubj	nsubjpass	dobj	iobj	nmod	nmod:agent
Nom (27%)	85	13	1			
Acc (17%)			97		2	
Dat (2%)			36		64	
Gen (4%)	30	4	51	2	13	
Ins (5%)			32		51	16
Acc+ADP (7%)			31		69	
Dat+ADP (3%)			29		70	
Gen+ADP (7%)	1		24	17	57	
Loc+ADP (11%)					98	
Ins+ADP (3%)			27		73	
None (12%)	60	3	26		10	1
None+ADP (2%)			30	7	63	

Table 3: UD Russian SynTagRus 1.3. Distribution of core and oblique relations for individual case forms. Numbers indicate how many % of the nominals in the given case got the given relation. ADP indicates a preposition.

	nsubj	nsubj:pass	obj	iobj	obl	obl:agent
Nom (34%)	90	8			1	
Acc (20%)			97		2	
Dat (3%)				5	95	
Gen (5%)	27	2		1	70	
Ins (6%)					79	17
Acc+ADP (7%)					99	
Dat+ADP (3%)					99	
Gen+ADP (7%)	1			6	93	
Loc+ADP (11%)					99	
Ins+ADP (3%)					100	

Table 4: UD Russian SynTagRus 2.0. Distribution of core and oblique relations for individual case forms. Numbers indicate how many % of the nominals in the given case got the given relation. ADP indicates a preposition.

pět "five" is in nominative and the noun *dětí* "children" is in genitive. Counted phrases are headed by nouns in UD, thus the genitive noun is attached directly to the verb; but a language-specific relation between the noun and the numeral preserves the information about who governs the case.

It has also been discussed[8] whether certain constructions in Slavic languages sanction subjects in the dative. An example (Russian) is *Мне было холодно* / *Mne bylo holodno* lit. "To-me it-was cold," meaning "I was cold." The dative argument *мне* is called *logical subject* by some grammarians. However, under the UD guidelines it will be subject only if it receives the treatment normally accorded to the single argument of a one-argument predicate in Russian. This "normal treatment" includes nominative case marking, but not only that. Its gender and number should be cross-referenced on the predicate, but *было холодно* is neuter singular regardless of the referent of *мне*. And finally, if the clause is converted to infinitive and complements another predicate, the infinitive should inherit the subject from the matrix clause. However, the dative pronoun cannot be removed and make room for an inherited subject. We still have it in "he will stop to be cold": *ему перестанет быть холодно* / *emu perestanet byt' holodno*. The verb "to stop" takes a normal nominative subject but if we provide it, the sentence becomes ungrammatical: **он перестанет быть холодно*. Thus the dative argument failed on all three accounts; on the other hand, the treatment it receives is not unlike the dative objects in Russian. Note that we are not saying that all subjects in all Indo-European languages must be nominative.[9] The point is that there usually is some typical treatment of subjects in the given language; the said dative argument does not receive the treatment typical in Russian, thus it is not subject.

9 Conclusion

We have reviewed the methodology proposed by (Andrews, 2007) for distinguishing core/oblique arguments; in particular, we have shown how it applies to the case morphology observed in a number of Indo-European languages. While UD focuses on core arguments in order to avoid distinguishing arguments from adjuncts, we observe that the distinction is needed (to some extent) to recognize core arguments. Similarly, UD does not label semantic roles but we still must consider them in order to recognize primary transitive verbs. Overall we found the method very useful (actually the only practically usable approach that has been proposed so far in the context of UD) but it has to be applied carefully and it does not provide absolute criteria (probably nothing does). If the properties of core arguments in all UD languages are defined following the principles we showed for German, Czech and Russian, the UD annotation will become much more consistent cross-linguistically than it is now.

We have also shown that defining objects in terms of core arguments conflicts with the traditional view in some languages, where all arguments are objects. We do not want to reject the core-oblique perspective; nevertheless, we propose to use the `obl:arg` relation and preserve the argument-adjunct distinction in UD if it is available.

Acknowledgments

The work was supported by the grant 15-10472S of the Czech Science Foundation.

References

Avery D. Andrews. 2007. The major functions of the noun phrase. In Timothy Shopen, editor, Language Typology and Syntactic Description. Volume I: Clause Structure. Second edition, pages 132–223. Cambridge University Press, Cambridge, UK.

Robert M. W. Dixon. 2012. Basic Linguistic Theory. Oxford University Press, Oxford, UK.

Matthew S. Dryer. 2007. Clause types. In Timothy Shopen, editor, Language Typology and Syntactic Description. Volume I: Clause Structure, pages 224–275. Cambridge University Press, Cambridge, UK.

William A. Foley. 2007. A typology of information packaging in the clause. In Timothy Shopen, editor, Language Typology and Syntactic Description. Volume I: Clause Structure, pages 362–446. Cambridge University Press, Cambridge, UK.

Jan Hajič, Jarmila Panevová, Eva Hajičová, Petr Sgall, Petr Pajas, Jan Štěpánek, Jiří Havelka, Marie Mikulová, Zdeněk Žabokrtský, and Magda Ševčíková-Razímová. 2006. Prague Dependency Treebank 2.0. CD-ROM, Linguistic Data Consortium, LDC Catalog No.: LDC2006T01, Philadelphia.

Bohuslav Havránek and Alois Jedlička. 1966. Stručná mluvnice česká. Fortuna, Praha, Czechia.

---

[8] http://github.com/UniversalDependencies/docs/issues/248

[9] In fact, (Andrews, 2007) gives an example of a dative subject in Icelandic.

Gerhard Helbig and Joachim Buscha. 1998. Deutsche Grammatik. Ein Handbuch für den Ausländerunterricht (18. Auflage). Langenscheidt, Leipzig, Germany.

Petr Karlík, Marek Nekula, Jana Pleskalová, et al. 2016. Nový encyklopedický slovník češtiny. Nakladatelství Lidové noviny, Praha, Czechia.

Markéta Lopatková, Václava Kettnerová, Eduard Bejček, Anna Vernerová, and Zdeněk Žabokrtský. 2016. Valenční slovník českých sloves VALLEX. Karolinum, Praha, Czechia.

Joakim Nivre, Marie-Catherine de Marneffe, Filip Ginter, Yoav Goldberg, Jan Hajič, Christopher Manning, Ryan McDonald, Slav Petrov, Sampo Pyysalo, Natalia Silveira, Reut Tsarfaty, and Daniel Zeman. 2016. Universal Dependencies v1: A multilingual treebank collection. In Proceedings of the 10th International Conference on Language Resources and Evaluation (LREC 2016), pages 1659–1666, Portorož, Slovenia. European Language Resources Association.

Roland Sussex and Paul Cubberley. 2006. The Slavic Languages. Cambridge University Press, Cambridge, UK.

Appendix A. Czech Examples

(1)

Jiří zabil draka
Nom   Acc
George killed dragon

(2)

Drak byl zabit Jiřím
Nom   Ins
Dragon was killed by-George

(3)

Karel pomohl Jiřímu
Nom   Dat
Charles helped George

(4)

Jiřímu bylo pomoženo
Dat
George was helped

(5)

Karel se dotkl draka mečem
Nom   Gen   Ins
Charles touched dragon with-sword

(6)

Jiří se obešel bez meče
Nom   Gen
George got-along without sword

(7)

Karel zabránil drakovi v útěku
Nom   Dat   Loc
Charles prevented dragon from escape

(8)

Drak pohnul skálou
Nom   Ins
Dragon moved rock

(9)

Drak se vrací každý rok
Nom   Acc Acc
Dragon returns every year

(10)

Král dal Jiřímu zlato
Nom   Dat Acc
King gave George gold

(11)

Zlato bylo Jiřímu dáno králem
Nom   Dat   Ins
Gold was George given by-king

(12)

Král odměnil Jiřího zlatem
Nom   Acc   Ins
King rewarded George with-gold

(13)

Karel učil Jiřího etiketu
Nom   Acc   Acc
Charles taught George etiquette